THE NATURE OF WOMAN
An Encyclopedia &
Guide to the Literature

THE

NATURE

OF

WOMAN

AN ENCYCLOPEDIA &
GUIDE TO THE LITERATURE

MARY ANNE WARREN

EDGEPRESS   INVERNESS   CALIFORNIA

Library of Congress Cataloging in Progress
Card Number 79-55299

International Standard Book Number ISBN 0-918528-07-0

© 1980 by Edgepress, Box 69, Pt. Reyes, CA 94956, U.S.A.

Manufactured in the United States of America

*To the women
who have fought
for all women*

THE AIMS OF THE BOOK

This book attempts to bring together in one volume an overview of the considerable literature, particularly from philosophy and the social sciences, on the nature of woman. It provides introductions to the arguments and conclusions about this topic of a wide range of Western thinkers, from Plato, Aristotle, and the authors of Genesis to the feminists and antifeminists of the 1970s. Each has presented original or influential theories on some or all of the following issues: (1) moral, psychological, theological and other "intrinsic" differences between women and men (apart from the obvious biological ones); (2) causal explanations of sex dominance, where it occurs; (3) the moral implications of sex roles, and the moral aspects of other issues of special relevance to women, e.g. abortion; and (4) possible means of engineering social change with respect to sex roles. The main body of the text addresses these issues with several hundred author and topic entries, the latter involving substantial cross-reference to the former. In its role as a guide to the literature as well as to the ideas, the book also includes a long separate section reporting briefly on approximately one hundred and fifty worthwhile anthologies and sourcebooks now available, a short section on the periodicals in this loosely circumscribed field, a glossary of special terms and an extensive bibliography.

It must be stressed immediately that this book does *not* deal primarily or substantially with fictional, historical, or biographical material which happens to be by or about women, unless it includes *explicitly formulated theories* about sex roles or the sexual dichotomy. (But many of the current anthologies and other sourcebooks referenced include some fictional and historical material, though the books themselves are chosen for their relevance to the main topic.) Nor is this book, nor could it be, entirely comprehensive within the defined ara. Although the net was cast fairly wide, some selection was necessary, and was done on the basis of the interest, influence, and merit of the authors considered.

The level of difficulty should present no serious obstacles to the undergraduate or reasonably well-read high school student; the academic reader is asked to forgive occasional parenthetic translations of terms that might prove a stumbling block for ordinary students.

THE AIMS OF THE BOOK

It is hoped that this work will contribute to a widespread societal recognition of the importance of that intellectual discipline which might be called the philosophy of woman, or more accurately described as the philosophical and social scientific aspects of male and female characteristics and roles. It is a field which has received far less attention than it deserves, given its importance for understanding the lives of individuals of both sexes, and for formulating the policies and opinions which control those lives. The remarkable surge of both public and academic interest in this area which has occurred in recent years is one measure of what all of us, whether we work in this field or not, owe to the contemporary women's movement.

HOW TO USE THE BOOK

For general reading. Look over the list of topics in the table of contents and follow a "reading trail" from any that interest you into the articles which it cross-references (the definitions of most puzzling terms are given in the glossary)—or do the same with any author whose name catches your eye. Or just open the book at random and browse; surprising and interesting things are buried in most articles.

Searching for discussion of a known author. The table of contents (or a quick look at the main body of the work, which is alphabetized) will show whether a full article is devoted to the individual: an asterisk in the index entry marks the page reference for such an article. If not, the index may uncover other references, possibly to work published in anthologies or source-books and treated in the Anthologies & Sourcebooks section. Even if there is an article on the individual, other references to her (or him) are likely to be found in the index.

Searching for discussion of a known book. If the author is known and covered in the main section, the book will be listed immediately after the author's name if it is specifically discussed in the main section article on that author. The actual places in that article where it is mentioned are easily located because book titles are in bold italics. If the author is unknown, or if incidental references are of interest, go to the index first.

Articles, and authors of articles only are—with one or two exceptions of unusual importance—covered in the Anthologies & Sourcebooks section. Page references can be obtained from the index.

Use as a course text. An "issues" approach would be to pick ten or twelve topics and read all the cross-referenced articles. An historical approach would use the articles on a group of leading figures (plus the trail of cross-references), and some primary sources (perhaps an anthology listed in the Anthologies & Sourcebooks listings). Use of this book as a text does encourage intellectual browsing (albeit amongst summaries), which is otherwise hard for students without ready access to a specialized library.

TABLE OF CONTENTS

AUTHORS

Abbott and Love, 1; Adler, 9; Amundsen, 14; Andelin, 15; Aquinas, 29; Ardrey, 33;Aristotle, 34; Astell, 39; Atkinson, 43; Saint Augustine, 46; Bachofen, 51; Barber, 54; Bardwick, 56; Beard, 58; Bebel, 60; Bednarik, 61; Bem, 62; Bernard, 65; Bird, 73; Bonaparte, 77; Borgese, 78; Boulding, 79; Briffault, 81; Brown, 84; Brownmiller, 86; Buck, 88; Bullough, 89; Buytendijk, 90; Chafe, 93; Chesler, 96; Daly, 99; Darwin, 103; Davis, 106; de Beauvoir, 107; de Castillejo, 113; Decter, 114; Delaney, Lupton and Toth, 116; Deutsch, 116; Diner, 120; Dinnerstein, 122; Dualism, 124; Dworkin, 127; Ehrhardt, 335; Ellis, 131; Ellman, 135; Engels, 137; Epstein, 143; Erikson, 145; Fast, 150; Figes, 153; Filene, 154; Firestone, 155; Foreman, 157; Fourier, 159; Fox, David, 44; Fox and Tiger, 164; Francoeur, 165; Freud, 166; Friday, 173; Friedan, 174; Friedl, 177; Fuller, 178; Giele, 181; Gilder, 182; Gilman, 184; Goldberg, 189; Goldman, 192; Greer, 194; Griffin, 195; Grimke, 196; Guettel, 198; Hamilton, 201; Hammer, 202; Harding, 203; Hays, 204; Hegel, 206; Heilbrun, 209; Herschberger, 211; Holliday, 214; Horner, 218; Horney, 220; Hume, 221; Hutt, 226; Jacklin, 289; Janeway, 231; Jewitt, 232; Johnson, 306; Johnston, 233; Jung, 235; Kant, 243; Key, Ellen, 246; Key, Mary Ritchie, 248; Kierkegaard, 250; Kinsey, 255; Klein, 259, 350; Komarovsky, 260; Lakoff, 263; Lang, 264; Lederer, 268; Le Guin, 268; Levi-Strauss, 273; Lewis, 277; Locke, 282; Lorenz, 284; Love, 1; Lundberg, 286; Mac-

TOPICS

ANTHOLOGIES & SOURCEBOOKS   511

INTRODUCTION

There are probably no issues in the history of human thought which have been debated or considered more intensely or for a longer span of centuries than those of the nature of woman and the proper relationship between the sexes. In 1792 Mary Wollstonecraft fired the opening round of the modern feminist/antifeminist debate with her *Vindication of the Rights of Woman.* Wollstonecraft attacked the male supremacist views of the popular Romantic philosopher, Jean Jacques Rousseau. Rousseau held that women lack the power for abstract reasoning, and that they should be educated solely to please and obey men. Wollstonecraft replied that women are (at least potentially) just as rational as men, and that they must be taught to think and act for themselves if they are to perform well even in their traditional role as wives and mothers. She held that the virtues of the sexes must be the same in kind, even if not in degree, and not, as Rousseau would have it, wholly opposite to one another so that what is a virtue for one sex is irrelevant, or a vice, for the other.

It is startling to reflect on the similarity between this philosophical debate and the one which occurred some two thousand years earlier, between Plato and Aristotle. Plato thought that women can and should do anything that men do, in the intellectual, social, and even military fields—although he also thought that they generally cannot do it as *well*. Aristotle rejected these more-or-less sexually egalitarian views of Plato's *Republic*, arguing that women's inferior powers of reason and self-control make it both natural and necessary that they should be strictly subject to man, and just as strictly confined to the domestic role.

But what is perhaps even more startling is the extent to which the detailed subject matter of our own contemporary debate between feminists (i.e., advocates of sex equality) and antifeminists (i.e., defenders of male supremacy) still turns around the same age-old questions. Are women, by nature, intellectually inferior to men? Are they naturally submissive? Is motherhood their (only) natural calling? Do they exercise the greatest and most beneficial influence on society when they confine themselves to "feminine" occupations, and refrain from competing with men in any of the fields which the latter claim as their own? Antifeminists answer such questions affirmatively, arguing that the male supremacist sex roles which we have inherited from the past are properly based on such permanent aspects of male and female nature.

If, on the other hand, the answer to all of these questions is negative, it becomes extremely difficult to justify the traditional sex roles or to view male domination as anything other than an archaic survival of the rule of the (physically) stronger party. Thus we find antifeminists appealing to a wide range of scientific (and pseudo-scientific) traditions to "prove" that something like the Aristotelian view of female nature is correct. There is usually some dispute about both the proper scientific conclusions and their moral or social implications. Recently, for instance, attention has been called to the considerable body of evidence that human males, like the males of many other animal species, are inherently more inclined towards aggressive behavior than females, a fact which antifeminists seek to associate with the supposed superiority of male leadership, dominance or intellect. (See Goldberg, Tiger, Hutt.) Feminists reply that a great deal of male aggressive behavior is socially learned and that if perchance males are also naturally more inclined to learn such behavior, this is by no means evidence that they should be taught it, supported in it, or receive superior social status from it.

We find, in short, that both the academic and the popular writers of today are debating many of the same issues with respect to the differences between women and men as Plato and Aristotle. The scientific theories and modes of investigation of our time are much more sophisticated; but it is impossible to say the same for the general level of the moral and philosophical debate in which such theories are used to support feminist or antifeminist conclusions. It has not benefited from the lessons of the earlier debates. Given the social importance of these issues and their intrinsic intellectual challenge, this lack of progress itself tells us something about the status of women and of serious thought about them. Significant discussion of this topic has never been part of the standard curriculum and only lately—with great difficulty and to a limited extent—has it secured a still precarious toehold at the college level. "Keep them ignorant" has never been far behind "Keep them pregnant" as a repressive measure. So it is important to be able to place the contemporary clash between sex–role traditionalists and women's liberationists into a context larger than our particular time or our own individual political, personal or academic perspective. If we understand the fallacies in Aristotle's theory of female nature, and if we can see the analogous fallacies in the misogynist philosophy of Augustine or Nietzsche or Weininger, then we will more quickly spot them and more thoroughly understand them when they appear in new and seemingly more scientific guise.

This encyclopedia is an effort to contribute to this wider understanding by making available in summary form the views and findings of a variety of Western thinkers and researchers who have contributed to the philosophy of the nature of woman. The core of the book consists of a set of articles on individuals whose views on the nature of the difference between the sexes and related issues are original, important, enlightening, or currently influential. These are presented in alphabetical, rather than chronological or taxonomic order. Where apropriate, the historical context is indicated, and references are provided to related topics and authors.

To choose from the entire sweep of Western intellectual history something under two hundred authors whose theories on the nature of woman seem particularly worthy of notice is a not inconsiderable task. It is unlkely that any two philosophers—let alone two researchers from quite different fields—would agree entirely on whom to include, or on what is most important in the work of those who are included. The task is in some ways comparable to that of selecting the brightest stars in the galaxy by looking at the sky visible from a particular place on the surface of the Earth. The results will necessarily be highly relative to the time and place of the observer. Some stars will be among the most visible simply because of their relative remoteness from others, or their closeness to Earth rather than because of their intrinsic size, color and brightness.

The selection was thus guided by a number of criteria, including the originality, clarity, coherence, historical importance, and present influence of the theories presented. However, the result that a majority of writers included are contemporary, and most of the others belong to the nineteenth or early twentieth century, is largely because by far the largest body of work on psychological differences between the sexes, sociological aspects of sex roles, and the moral problems which they raise, has in fact been done in the past two centuries. It is only partly because quite a few contemporary popular authors, individuals who may have little claim to scientific or philosophical immortality, are nevertheless well-known figures in the current debate.

The writers I have selected include philosophers, theologians, anthropologists, classicists, sociologists, psychologists, psychiatrists, psychoanalysts, biologists, sociobiologists, legal scholars, educators, historians, economists, political scientists, and journalists. There are very few whose work consists entirely of poetry, fiction, drama, biography or autobiography. This is simply because original, explicitly formulated and rationally supported theories of the nature of women or of sex roles are not usually presented first, best, or most influentially by means of these particular literary forms. A novelist like George Sand may have quite pronounced views on these subjects, views which may be more or less reliably inferred from her work—but to have detectable convictions on a subject is not the same as having a well-developed theory; and it is only the latter which falls within the scope of this book.

I do not by any means wish to imply by this that the student of sex roles can afford to be ignorant of the great works of fiction, poetry and drama. Any complete analysis of the development of Western views on the nature of woman would obviously need to take account of such works. The point is rather that works of art and literature are part of the enormous data base upon which theories of male and female nature must be built; but they do not, as a rule, themselves constitute or include such theories. Where they do include such theories, clearly presented and defended as the author's own, then the work crosses the boundary between (mere) fiction or poetry, and philosophy. (See, for instance, Griffin, Kierkegaard, Nietzsche, Le Guin.) A similar situation applies to political figures in the suffragette and liberation movements. The mere facts of their political importance and gender does not mean they made a contribution to the philosophy of woman. Good political histories of feminism exist (e.g. Chafe, Flexner); a good comprehensive compendium of its philosophy does not.

One of the dangers in speaking of the topic of this work as the *philosophy* of woman—a convenient shorthand—is that this may seem to imply that whatever any well-known philosopher has said about women will be dealt with. In fact, however, I have not attempted to include all of the important philosophers who have taken some position or said something of relevance to this subject, but only those who have made important contributions to it. There is of course room for disagreement as to who these philosophers are, and I have no doubt that some will find it strange that a philosopher like Hobbes—who has been criticized by contemporary feminists for his patriarchal views—was not treated. Perhaps in later enlarged editions of this encyclopedia it will be possible to include him, and other philosophers whose omission may be regretted. My judgment, however, is that their contributions *in this particular area* are not as great as that of the others whom I have included.

As for secondary sources on the authors dealt with, although I have consulted a great many, and although I have made reference to those which have seemed particularly important in the interpretation of a particular author, I have not tried to list or refer to most of those which are available. To do even minimal justice to secondary sources—most of which spend little time on discussing our topic—would have doubled or tripled the total number of references, thus increasing the size of the work beyond what seemed feasible. There are, however, a great many critical commentaries and other secondary sources included in the books which are cited in the section on anthologies and other sourcebooks, and, in addition, many others include bibliographies and secondary sources on their particular subtopics. References to these are provided in the index, under the name of the primary author.

In addition to these articles on individuals, there is a smaller number of topic articles (Marriage, Matriarchy, etc.) These are intended primarily to provide focal points for references to the individuals and schools of thought which are dealt with elsewhere. Where necessary, a definition of the term is provided, and the way in which the topic fits with others in the philosophy of woman is explained. In a few cases, where the topic is very important and in need of philosophical clarification, I set out a fairly substantial philosophical discussion. (See, for instance, Abortion and Androgyny.)

The section of (mostly) brief reviews of current anthologies and other sourcebooks again does not include every book of this sort which has been published in recent years, but certainly the majority of them, the ones which seemed particularly useful or important. In this section I could afford to and have cast the net somewhat more widely, including not only (collections of) materials which deal directly and in a theoretical way with the issues of concern to the philosophy of woman, but also, for instance, some collections of fiction by and about women (or men, as such) that seem to illustrate important issues in the philosophy of woman; studies of the social and economic roles and status of women in other cultures; theories about the etiology of male and female homosexuality; historical studies of women's contributions to art, science, or literature; philosophical analyses of sex and sexuality; psychological studies of sexual behavior; philosophical discussions of sexual and reproductive morality; studies of women's legal status in this country and elsewhere, and of past and present struggles to improve it; and so on. While material of this sort does not deal directly with the nature of woman, it does contribute to that vast range of empirical data with which any theory of woman's nature must at least be consistent; and for which it may at best help to account.

Next, there is a listing of current journals and periodicals which have frequently published high quality work in the philosophy of woman. And, finally, there is a bibliography which lists every-thing refered to in the text and some other works. References in the middle of an article are therefore abbreviated to author and title; full details will be found in the bibliography. Where more is said about a book at some other place in the encyclopedia, that place will be given, e.g. John Noonan, ed., **The Morality of Abortion** (See Anthologies V). If only a name is mentioned, then an article will be found about that person: if only a number is given (in parentheses) a correspondingly numbered "footnote" will be found at the end of that article.

So much for the ground plan of the book. A few words of explanation are also called for with respect to the subject.

In the first place, there is the question why it is that so many books and articles are being written about the nature of *woman*, rather than about the nature of the male sex, or—more neutral-ly—about the nature of the social and psychological differences between the sexes and their roles. Granted, a number of books *have* been written about the special problems and psychological traits of men (see Masculinity); but these are largely a conscious reaction to the far greater amount of attention which has been given to the nature and problems of women. At this time it still seems more natural, that is, more readily comprehensible, to speak of our subject as the philosophy of *woman*, rather than the philosophy of sexual differences, or the philosophy of sex and gender roles, even though these latter descriptions are really more accurate since every theory of the nature of woman is also, implicitly or explicitly, a theory of the nature of the male sex as well. When we speak of the "nature of woman," men are under-stood as the implicit contrast class; and yet when we speak of "the nature of man" we are still understood to refer to humanity in general.

This peculiar conceptual asymmetry is described by Simone de Beauvoir in the following words:

> In actuality, the relation of the two sexes is not quite like that of two electrical poles, for man represents both the positive and the neutral, as indicated by the common use of *man* to designate human beings in general; whereas woman represents only the negative, defined by limited criteria, without reciprocity. (**The Second Sex**, p. xv)

What this means is that most Western thinkers have dealt with the human sexual dichotomy via an examination of the nature of woman as distinct from that of man, rather than vice versa. In virtually every case it is *woman's* nature which is considered different, mysterious, inferior—or, occasionally, superior—and in need of special explanation. Male nature is the norm, the standard case, and hence in need of no explanations other than those which are valid for humanity in general. This fact is itself something of which any comprehensive theory of the human sexual dichotomy must give an account. Of course, the simplest and most obvious explanation for the asymmetry in the ways in which the two sexes have been conceptualized is that it is men who have done the conceptualizing. It is men who, at least since the beginnings of recorded history, have held a monopoly of power in the religious, political, scientific and academic establishments, and it is they who have produced the seemingly endless parade of androcentric (male-centered) theories of woman's nature and woman's "place." But one must also ask *why* men have had such a monopoly of power and status. This question, together with the related question of what, if anything, can be done to alter the situation, is a major focus of this book.

There are, indeed, some theorists who deny that men have always been the dominant sex. Some argue that patriarchy is a reaction against an earlier matriarchal, or at least sexually egalitarian, form of social organization. (See Matriarchy Theory.) Others deny that men actually are dominant now, claiming that women exercise so much covert social power, through their influence over men or their economic holdings, that the appearance of male supremacy is an illusion. (See, e.g., Rousseau, Kant, Vilar.) But no one denies that men have had overt control of all of the extra-familial power-wielding institutions of all the major civilizations known to history, with the possible exception of ancient Egypt. It is this fact which needs explanation, though it is not male dominance but female nature which has generally been *perceived* as mysterious by Western "man."

Another issue on which comment is necessary concerns the distinction between objectivity and neutrality. In presenting the views and theories of each writer, whether feminist, antifeminist or not clearly categorizable in those terms, I have tried to be as accurate and as fair as possible. I have not hesitated, however, to point out what I see as the more serious errors of fact or reasoning, particularly those which may not be evident to the reader. Nor have I concealed the fact that my own perspective is a feminist one. That is, I believe not only that women and men (and hermaphrodites, for that matter) are morally entitled to the same rights, freedoms and opportunities; and that whatever is found to impede the achievement of this moral goal must be opposed as an obstacle to human progress; but also I believe that we are still a long way from that goal and the acceptance of that equality.

It is important to stress that the above is by no means a confession of "bias." For to be a feminist is to believe that feminism is *true*, and certainly a feminist philosopher believes that its truth is objectively demonstrable. A bias is not just *any* debated or debatable commitment, but rather one which is reached or presupposed *without adequate reason and deliberation*. Since there appear to be more than adequate reasons to believe in the truth of feminism, to do so is not, *ipso facto*, to adopt a bias. Neither, on the other hand, is it automatically a sign of bias to hold an anti-feminist position, but only if such a position is adopted for other than plausible reasons. Philosophy, religion, and science have cooperated to produce such a plethora of doctrines, dogmas and theories "demonstrating" the essential or practical inferiority of female nature or "proper duties" that until quite recently very few of even the greatest (male) moral and social thinkers have doubted it, or have had to ignore good reasons in order not to doubt it.

To call all of these patriarchy-defending philosophers, scientists and theologians *biased* is therefore somewhat uninteresting, even though it may in many cases be true because their position is in the end unsound and proper diligence should have led them to suspect it. What is more interesting is to examine their arguments for male supremacy in the context of their overall philosophical or scientific perspective. In doing so, one learns to see many of the great philosophical, scientific and religious traditions in a new light—as weapons in the longest war of all, the war between the sexes. That war will continue to be waged just as long as unjustified social inequalities between the sexes persist.

It is necessary, finally, to apologize to all those persons who are specialists in the individual schools, topics and authors with whom I have dealt in this encyclopedia. As Bertrand Russell admits in the preface to his **History of Western Philosophy**, "every philosopher of whom I treat is better known to some others than to me." (1946, p.5) But as Russell also says, this is a situation which cannot be avoided if books covering a wide field are to be written at all, at least by a single author. Furthermore, there are advantages in single authorship; for, in Russell's words,

> If there is any unity in the movement of history, if there is any intimate relation between what goes before and what comes later,

it is necessary, for setting this forth, that earlier and later periods must be synthesized in a single mind. (*loc. cit.*)

Such a task of synthesis may seem formidable or even foolhardy, especially in an age which honors and requires specialization more than competence across a broad range of interests. But it is not an impossible task; and it is one which is demanded of any individual who seeks to understand how women and sex roles have been conceptualized in our own intellectual tradition, and why these conceptualizations have so often demeaned and degraded the female sex. To the extent that the attempted general picture has led to particular errors, I most earnestly request the assistance of the specialists, for I hope to improve this work in subsequent editions beyond merely keeping up with the burgeoning and increasingly sophisticated literature. Eventually, perhaps, it will be possible, and indeed at some point essential, for someone to attempt a wider synthesis, one which includes the traditions of the East and of the Third World. But *this* attempt on *this* subject is overdue. Movements without a history are seen as fads, and without philosophy they *are* fads.

AUTHORS & TOPICS

A

ABBOTT, Sidney, and **LOVE**, Barbara. *Sappho Was a Right-On Woman: A Liberated View of Lesbianism* (Stein and Day, New York, 1973; first published 1972.)

The new feminism of the 60s and 70s is the first woman's movement, at least in modern times, to recognize the link between the oppression of homosexuals of both sexes and that of women. *Sappho* is a defense of what might be called lesbian feminism, i.e. the position that being a lesbian—not just accepting lesbians and defending their rights—is or at least can be a feminist act. The open and unapologetic lesbian, the authors argue, is a walking refutation of many patriarchal myths about women, proof that although most women may *want* men they do not *need* them for love, sex, protection or economic support. It is an interesting question why in our culture male homosexuals have attracted so much more public attention and overt oppression than lesbians. Abbott and Love offer the explanation that female homosexuality is more threatening to patriarchy than male homosexuality, so threatening that even the recognition of its existence tends to be avoided (p.20).

Of course lesbians are also severely oppressed, even those who successfully conceal their sexual orientation. Covert lesbians are made to carry a heavy burden of guilt, and they typically try to compensate for their supposed fault by conforming particularly well to the patriarchal stereotypes of femininity, by being good wives, mothers, or perhaps workers. Overt lesbians suffer from a different set of stereotypes, some of them enforced by their own subculture, such as the expectation that they must be either "butch" ("dyke") or "fem," that is, play either a masculine or feminine role in all their sexual relationships. It seems obvious that the feminist and gay liberation movements are natural allies in that both are faced with the necessity of destroying the traditional sex-role stereotypes. Yet until quite recently most feminists have tried to dissociate themselves from lesbianism lest the movement's reputation be besmirched by what Betty Friedan called a "lavender herring." This book relates, rather polemically, the struggle of gay women in the National Organization of Women to obtain that organization's support for lesbian issues.

In a way, the authors note, those enemies of feminism who have long sought to denigrate the feminist philosophy by associating it with lesbianism are right; there is such an association, and there always has been, whether or not feminists have been willing to recognize it. Feminist arguments and analyses, although generally directed towards changing heterosexuality rather than eliminating it, also demonstrate (they suggest) the personal and political advantages of lesbianism. "Under present conditions, a feminist may well ask: Is heterosexuality a valid life style?" (p.152)

ABORTION The moral status of abortion (i.e., the deliberate termination of pregnancy before the fetus is able to survive outside the uterus) has been debated by theologians and philosophers for at least two thousand years. For women, the right to abort often seems a necessary condition for the free exercise of all other human rights, since there is not and never has been a fully reliable method of contraception (other than celibacy), and since bearing an unwanted child can be disastrous for a woman's health, happiness, personal life and career aspirations, and may even be fatal. No woman who must constantly face this threat can be fully free or equal. For this reason, contemporary American and European feminists have defended women's right to choose whether or not to bear children, in defiance of the pronatalist (antiabortion) attitude of the Christian churches and other traditionalist forces.

Prior to the 1960s few feminists of the modern era dared or considered it expedient to defend the right to abortion, so fiercely has it been condemned by the Judeo-Christian tradition, and, often, by the force of law. (See *Abortion in America*, by James G. Mohr, [Oxford] for an account of how antiabortion laws developed in this country.) The women of Greece and Rome—and, in all probability those of the earlier, goddess-worshiping cultures of the Mediterranean and Near East regions—practiced abortion freely and without threat of sanction. But, although the Bible does not specifically forbid abortion, the fathers of the Christian church (e.g. Augustine, Tertullian, Jerome and Chrysostom) condemned it both as a sinful and unnatural interference in the process of generation, and as the wrongful taking of human life. They considered sexual intercourse inherently sinful, partially redeemable only because of its procreative function; hence they viewed any interference with this function as rendering the sexual act equivalent to one of adultery or prostitution. The motive for sex must be duty, not pleasure, else it is a mortal sin—or at the very least a venal one.

Fortunately, this antihedonistic and pronatalist argument against abortion has lost much (though by no means all) of its force in this age of overpopulation and relative sexual enlightenment. Today, most proponents of the "right to life" of the fetus argue that the human conceptus (embryo) is a human being from the time of conception—or from some other point later in the pregnancy—and that killing it is therefore an act of murder. Often they "argue" for this point by exhibiting enlarged photographs of aborted fetuses, thereby prompting some pro-abortionists (fortunately only a few) to retaliate by exhibiting photographs of the bodies of women who died as a result of illegal "back-alley" abortions.

In 1973, in the case of *Roe* v. *Wade,* the United States Supreme Court rejected the claim that fetuses, at least those within the first or second trimester, are persons within the meaning of the law. The Court ruled that for a state to prohibit abortion during the first trimester of pregnancy violates the constitutional right to privacy; abortion during the second trimester may be legally regulated to protect the health of the woman; but it may be forbidden altogether during the third trimester, except when necessary to save the woman's life.

Since 1973, therefore, most American women have had access within the U.S. to safe and legal abortions—provided that they could afford to pay the often very high price for them. Congress and the state legislatures have recently cut off most tax funding for abortions, thus effectively leaving poor women in the same bind which most women who were not wealthy faced before the Supreme Court decision: either risk their lives at the hands of the illegal abortionist or bear the unwanted child. (Though New York and California had passed abortion reform laws before 1973.) This recent backing off from the position that society has a responsibility to provide all women with access to abortion is largely the result of the increasing political power of the conservative "pro-life" forces; but it can also be traced in part to the failure of the "pro-choice" forces to present their case as clearly and persistently as have their opponents.

The feminist case for retaining—and perhaps extending—the legal right to abortion, and for providing state-funded abortions for poor women is generally phrased in terms of the right of all persons to control their own bodies. This right may be construed

3

as a property right, or, more plausibly, as an inherent part of the rights to freedom and self-determination. For, clearly, when a woman is forced to complete an unwanted pregnancy, her freedom is seriously curtailed and her future mortgaged—unless she gives the baby away—to the care of the child. Her personal and/or career aspirations are all too frequently quashed; her health is threatened (since even a completely normal pregnancy is physically dangerous and demanding); and she faces some risk of death in childbirth, even in cases where no difficulty is foreseen. Thus, in the absence of either fully reliable contraceptives without serious side effects (which do not exist) or ready access to abortion, the possibility of an unwanted pregnancy hangs as a constant and severe threat over the head of every woman of childbearing capacity: our fertility can be seen as a curse rather than a blessing.

There are other proabortion arguments besides these feminist ones. Some argue for abortion on utilitarian grounds, e.g. that it is necessary to curb overpopulation, or to prevent the birth of children who, being unwanted and hence perhaps neglected, will be apt to become social misfits. Some point out that it costs the taxpayers less to fund an abortion than to support the woman and child on welfare indefinitely. Some argue that abortion is actually often in the best interest of the potential child, i.e. when it can be predicted that its quality of life will be very low, due to social deprivation and/or serious defects in the developing fetus. (See, for instance, Garrett Hardin's *Mandatory Motherhood*, in Anthologies III.)

Like the feminist arguments, these pragmatic points are relevant and important. Yet they cannot constitute a complete or adequate defense of the right to abortion; for they do not speak to the basic concern of the antiabortionists, i.e. that abortion is a form of murder. If abortion is murder, then it cannot be justified on any of the above grounds. The antiabortionist points out that the right to protect one's property or even one's freedom does not normally justify the killing of innocent human beings—e.g. children—who, through no fault of their own, place limitations on one's freedom or the use of one's property. Nor can we justify killing children in order to limit population growth, to save the state money, or to prevent them from having unhappy lives. None of these proabortion arguments is persuasive so long as the argument that a fetus is a human being, and that aborting it is murder, remains unchallenged.

Consequently, contemporary feminist philosophers have sought to refute this argument, either by showing that its premise

4

is false or by arguing that even if a fetus is human it does not follow that abortion is murder. Judith Jarvis Thomson, in her now classic article, "In Defense of Abortion" (See *The Problem of Abortion*, edited by Joel Feinberg, Anthologies, III), takes the latter tack. She argues that however human the fetus may be, the unwillingly pregnant woman has no moral obligation to make the huge personal sacrifices necessary to preserve its life, and neither does anyone else have the right to force her to do so. Her argument depends, however, on the assumption that the pregnant woman is in no way *responsible* for her condition, and for the existence of an entity whose survival depends on her willingness to make sacrifices for it. This is often true, but it is not true in every case in which abortion is requested; thus this line of argument, which admits the humanity and the right to life of the fetus but denies the woman's duty to preserve it, can justify abortion only in a limited set of cases, such as where the pregnancy is due to rape or unavoidable contraceptive failure.

Other philosophers have attacked the premise that a fetus is a human being with a full-fledged right to life. Granted, it is difficult to argue that a fetus is not human *in the biological sense of the term*. It has a complete human genetic code, and thus qualifies as a member of the human species. But it does not follow, as is presumed by such antiabortionist philosophers as John Noonan (*The Morality of Abortion*, Anthologies X) that all beings which are *genetically* human are also *morally* human, i.e. possessed of full and equal moral rights. It can be argued that what qualifies an entity for full moral status is not mere genetic humanity, but rather *personhood*. On this view, not all genetic humans are persons, and indeed it might not be true that all persons are genetically human (e.g. alien races).

Personhood is a complex concept, and there is little agreement among philosophers as to how it should be analyzed. Nevertheless, it is clear that any adequate analysis must have the result that normal adult humans are persons, while, say, normal adult cats are not. Moreover, it is not easy to give an analysis which has this result, and which does not beg the question by making genetic humanity a sufficient condition for personhood, without yielding the conclusion that fetuses are *not* persons. Probably the best hope is via the claim that potential persons are persons, but this runs into grave logical problems; potential leaders aren't (yet) leaders, potential wars aren't wars. It is further discussed below.

Thus Michael Tooley (in *The Problem of Abortion*, Anthologies III) argues that a person is a self-aware subject of conscious states; and while it is possible that some fetuses have conscious states, it seems quite unlikely that any fetus is self-aware. I have argued on the other hand, that a person is essentially an entity with a (present, and not merely potential) capacity for consciousness, rationality, self-motivation, self-awareness and—usually, but not always—linguistic communication (1). The ability to use language is clearly not a *necessary* condition for personhood, since children are people before (and adults after) they can speak; yet speech or some other form of symbolic communication is essential to the full development of most if not all the capacities constitutive of personhood.

The claim, then, is that it is all and only persons who have full moral rights. This is said to be so because it is all and only persons who have desires, fears, plans for the future, and personal goals, which are sufficiently clear, conscious and important—to the person itself if not to others—to demand recognition on a par with those of all other persons. One could argue that in some sense, nonhuman animals have some moral "rights," including the right not to be tortured, or killed for no good reason. (It might be better just to say that *we* have no right to torture *them*.) Nevertheless, we normally do not consider it murder, or any other kind of moral wrong, to kill a living being which is not a person, if doing so is necessary to protect one's own life, liberty or welfare or that of other persons.

Thus fetuses, especially those which have already acquired some degree of sentience, might possibly be said to have *some* moral rights; but their rights cannot override the full-blown and key rights of the woman who is unwillingly pregnant. Abortion, like the killing of nonhuman animals for food (at least at some stages of human existence) is at most a sad but often necessary and justified expedient.

One objection to this position which many philosophers consider crucial is that it appears to justify not only abortion but also infanticide, which most people intuitively feel is very wrong. For, since newborn infants (often called neonates in the literature) are not appreciably more personlike than are well-developed fetuses, it would seem that if it is permissible to kill fetuses then it must also be permissible to kill newborn infants. It must, however, be remembered that infanticide cannot be justified unless there are reasons for it which are as compelling as those which exist in the case of abortion. In an advanced and prosperous society like our own, there are usually no such reasons for infanticide. The infant's continued existence does not threaten the life, health or freedom of the mother, since she usually has the option of having the child adopted. The fact that there is a demand for babies to be adopted means that killing an unwanted infant is not only unnecessary, but morally reprehensible.

Unfortunately, a woman cannot simply walk away from an unwanted fetus. Perhaps someday she will be able to; but in the meantime a woman who finds herself pregnant must either abort the fetus, thus destroying it, or else resign herself to devoting a large share of her physical and other resources, expectations and capacities to its nurturance. If a fetus were a person, then perhaps she would be morally obligated to so resign herself—unless perhaps she were pregnant due to rape, or unless the pregnancy seriously threatened her life. But it isn't, and she isn't, hence on this view abortion is permissible even though infanticide normally is not. (See *Infanticide and the Value of Life*, Marvin Kohl, Anthologies III.)

Another frequent objection is that the argument for the non-personhood of the fetus takes no account of the fact that a fetus is a *potential* person, and thus different from any (known) non-human animal. Richard Hare, for example, argues that there is a *prima facie* obligation to permit potential people (not just fetuses but even ova and spermatazoa) to become actual people. For, he points out, most of us are glad that we were conceived and born, and we ought to treat other potential people as we are glad that we were treated (2).

Such a view is unattractive from both a feminist and a humanitarian point of view. For it would require that the Earth's human population be steadily increased, up to that point (which may have already been reached in some, but not all, parts of the world) at which the quality of life is so dismal that any additional persons will wish that they had never been born; whereas it seems more sensible to suppose that a world with fewer people enjoying a much higher quality of life is a better world than one with only a barely-better-than-death existence for all. Furthermore, Hare's view makes childbearing a moral obligation for women, rather than an option which they are free to reject without apology.

The briefest reply to Hare's argument is that it is real persons, not merely potential ones, who have full moral rights. Merely potential people lack the morally relevant properties—consciousness, self-awareness, and the rest—from which moral rights arise. *Future* people, those who will in fact exist, will *then* have full moral rights, and we are indeed obligated to respect their interests. But these rights do not include the right to be brought into existence. Everyone who has children is obligated to respect their interests; but *not* to have children is no violation of the rights of one's (indefinitely many) possible children, since these children never become actual and thus have no interests, and no rights to be violated (3). Indeed, the rights of the existing children may require that the others never materialize.

Still another objection to the proabortion line of argument is that abortion undermines the respect for all human life. For, it is argued, if we exclude one class of human beings from full moral consideration, what will prevent the progressive disenfranchisement of other groups of human beings as well—for instance the old, the poor, the feeble-minded, or those of other races or religions? What this objection overlooks, however, is that most of these other classes of human beings are undeniably persons and thus, on the present theory, absolutely entitled to full moral rights. Even the terminally ill or those in long-term comas remain persons, at least as long as the neural machinery remains intact in which resides the relevant personal capacities. Conversely, where these capacities are irretrievably lost, then personhood is also lost, and many of the rights of persons cease to be applicable. Far from being an absurd or objectionable conclusion, this is one which many physicians and medical ethicists have already arrived at independently.

Given the considerable difficulty of the philosophical issues involved in the abortion problem, not to mention the depth of the emotional responses which this problem evokes, it may be a long time before any consensus is reached, either among philosophers or in the public arena. Consequently, the ongoing attempt to educate public opinion on these issues must remain a priority of feminists for some time to come. The recent Islamic revolution in Iran has made us all too aware that progress towards sexual equality can be reversed; and abortion is one issue on which at present the forces of reaction appear to be gaining ground. (Also see Callahan, Beauchamp and Walters, Feinberg, and Cohen, Nagel and Scanlon, in Anthologies III.)

1. See Mary Anne Warren, "On the Moral and Legal Status of Abortion" (See Anthologies X, those edited by Beauchamp and Walters, Mappes and Zembaty, and Wassertrom).
2. Richard Hare, "Abortion and the Golden Rule," *Philosophy and Public Affairs*, Vol.4, No.3, Spring 1975.
3. See Warren, "Do Potential People Have Moral Rights?" in *Obligations to Future Generations*, edited by R.I. Sikora and Brian Barry (Temple University Press, Philadelphia, 1978), for a fuller presentation of this argument.

ADLER, Alfred (1870–1937). *Understanding Human Nature* (translated by W. Bean Wolfe. Greenberg, New York, 1927)

Adler was an early member of the Freudian circle, in the first decade of this century, but was forced to resign from the Vienna Psychoanalytic Society because of his basic theoretical disagreements with Freud. His views are of exceptional interest for the historian of feminist thought.

He rejected the most fundamental presupposition of Freud's work, that human behavior is motivated by unconscious, biologically-determined instinctual urges, primarily sexual in nature. He did not deny the existence of the subconscious mind, but he insisted that conscious thought processes were more important; most people, most of the time know why they do what they do. Each person, through social interaction with others, develops a style of life, that is, a particular goal and a particular set of strategies for approaching it. Since all infants are helpless and dependent on others, all suffer to some degree from feelings of inferiority, and all children strive to overcome those feelings through compensatory power over others. In a healthy child, these strivings will become channeled into socially responsible goals. But if a child is either neglected and not encouraged towards compensatory striving, or spoiled and allowed to become willful, then "erroneous solutions" to the problems of life may arise, and the child may adopt a life strategy which is self-destructive or antisocial, or both.

These ideas naturally lead to a view of so-called "feminine psychology" which is socially but not biologically deterministic, and is radically feminist when compared to Freud's view. Adler considered the psychology of the female to be essentially the same as that of the male, the observable difference between the life strategies of men and women being solely due to the different social attitudes and expectations which they encounter. Thus, "the story of the lesser capability of woman is a palpable fable." (p.130) If women tend to achieve less, it is because they lose their confidence as a result of the continual experience of social prejudices against them. "It is," Adler says,

> a frequently overlooked fact that a girl comes into the world with a prejudice sounding in her ears which is designed only to rob her of her belief in her own value, to shatter her self-confidence and destroy her hope of ever doing anything worthwhile. (p.131)

Thus, the observable character traits which may seem to demonstrate women's natural inferiority are only the predictable result of the exaggerated *feelings* of inferiority which women must suffer in a male-dominated society:

The psychic life of woman moves in much the same channels, and under much the same rules, as that of any human beings who find themselves the possessors of a strong feeling of inferiority because of their situation in the scheme of things. (p.131)

Because the advantages of the male's dominant role compared to the unhappy lot of women are so apparent, most women rebel against the female role in one of two ways. Some rebel through the so-called "masculine protest"; they develop as active, competitive and ambitious individuals, and generally scorn doing domestic work, whether or not they choose to marry. Adler points out that it is a mistake to think of such women as "mannish," since their rebellion is inevitable, and takes the form it does, "not as a result of some mysterious secretion, but because in a given time and place, there is no other possibility." (p.135) That is, since there are only two sex roles, to reject "femininity" is inevitably to appear "masculine," even though such sex-stereotyping of character has no biological basis.

Other women rebel more indirectly. The humble, obedient woman who seems to fully accept the feminine role may actually use her weakness and helplessness as a means of dominating others. Or, she may develop nervous diseases of a sort which serve to proclaim that her role has made her sick. Thus,

Her submission, her humility, her self-repression, is founded on the same revolt as that of her sister of the first type, a result which says clearly enough: "This is no happy life!" (p.136)

There is, finally, a third type of woman who does not rebel against the feminine role; she accepts the world's judgment of her sex as inferior, and "carries in herself the tormenting consciousness that she is condemned to be an inferior being." (p.136) Such a woman may prepare a subtle revenge, by using her helplessness and inferiority as an excuse for shifting all responsibilities onto men. All three types are deviations from a healthy personality, and Adler barely seems to recognize the existence, in this culture, of women who are not damaged in one of these ways.

Of course, males are also damaged by their social conditioning for dominance, but they suffer less because they are not made to feel doubly inferior, first as children and second as the subordinate sex. Rather, they are encouraged to develop delusions of grandeur, to overvalue themselves in accordance with the pernicious notion of masculinity which the culture endorses.

Masculinity is conceived as something purely egoistic, something which satisfies self-love, gives a feeling of superiority and domination over others ... (and requires) the winning of all manner of victories, especially those over women. (p.128)

This all-consuming male drive for dominance, together with the twin fallacies of male superiority and female inferiority, ensures that the relationships between the sexes will be one of hostility rather than companionship; for "the subordination of one individual to another in sexual relationships is just as unbearable as in the life of nations." (p.146) "Feminine" as well as "masculine" behaviors may be used to achieve dominance in this struggle (as in the second type of woman described above), but in either case personality distortions result which interfere with the development of social feeling. In this way the fallacious attitude of our culture towards women "negates the logic of our whole social life." (p.144) As for the origin of male domination, Adler says only that it probably arose during warlike eras of (pre)history, as a result of men's prominence as warriors, together with the institution of private property and inheritance rights; he refers to Bebel and the Vaertings' account of the matriarchate (p.125).

AFFIRMATIVE ACTION "Affirmative action" referred originally to the policy adopted by the federal government on the basis of Executive Order 11246 (as amended by Executive Order 11375), by President Johnson. This order requires that all companies, universities and other institutions which do business with the government, or receive federal funding, shall not only refrain from racial, sexual, or religious discrimination in hiring, promotion and admissions, but also "take affirmative action to ensure that applicants are employed, and that employees are treated during their employment, without regard to their race, color, religion, sex, or national origin." (*Reverse Discrimination*, Barry Gross, Anthologies XII) The term has since come to refer to any such institutional policy designed to open up white-male-dominated fields to larger numbers of women, blacks, Chicanos and other minority persons.

The moral and legal issues surrounding affirmative action are relevant to the nature of woman, because they illustrate the difficult problems of practical interpretation of the concept of equal opportunity. Some of the means employed under the heading of affirmative action are relatively noncontroversial— e.g., the national advertising of university and other job openings, with special efforts being made to attract women and minority candidates, and the use of nonsexist and nonracist criteria in evaluating candidates. But affirmative action has generally been interpreted to require more than this; it has often required that numerical goals and timetables be used to bring about defined increases in the numbers of women and minority persons hired or admitted, in areas in which they are strikingly underrepresented in proportion to their numbers in the candidate pool.

It is these numerical goals and timetables which have occasioned the extended and often acrimonious debate over affirmative action. Numerical goals have come to be referred to as *quotas*, thus calling to mind the infamous anti-Jewish quotas which were employed by some American universities earlier in this century. Critics have argued that the requirement to admit, hire or promote larger numbers of women and minorities can only be met by "reverse discrimination" against white males, and that this is the very type of injustice which affirmative action is supposedly designed to remedy. The specter has also been raised of large numbers of wholly unqualified women and blacks teaching in universities, doing brain surgery, and designing suspension bridges.

The defenders of affirmative action have responded to these charges in various ways. Some have admitted that reverse discrimination might sometimes occur, but argued that it is justified as a form of compensation to groups and/or individuals who have suffered from unjust discrimination in the past, or as a way of raising the status of downtrodden groups and providing role models for young women and minority people. Others have insisted that reverse discrimination is neither required nor permitted by federal regulations (the wording of which is unclear on this issue), and have rightly noted that no company or university has been penalized for failing to meet its affirmative action goals so long as it can demonstrate good faith efforts to do so, short of using reverse discrimination.

The second line of defense seems the more cogent one. This is especially true in the case of women; for given that the educational achievements and demonstrated abilities of working women are far in advance of their representation in high status jobs, it is both absurd and objectionable to argue that it is impossible to hire and promote more women without lowering the standards of merit and discriminating against men. In the universities, for example, the average rank and salary of women faculty still lags behind that of *comparably qualified* male faculty members. Thus increasing the number of women employed at the higher ranks can be expected to increase rather than decrease the degree to which merit is recognized and rewarded.

But, it is replied, why should quotas be necessary if there is such an abundance of qualified women? Indeed, doesn't the use of quotas tend to imply that women and minorities are *not* as well qualified, that they are unable to compete on their merits? (1) The answer is that women are still rarely judged on their merits alone, even when these are fully recognized. This is not only because old-fashioned sexism still exists—though perhaps it is less often openly admitted than in the past—but also because there are a great many practices and attitudes which de facto discriminate against women. A woman may be passed over because it is assumed that she doesn't "need" a job as much as a man; or that she will be absent more often or leave the job sooner than a man would; or that her sex will prevent her from obtaining the respect of her subordinates. These are de facto sexist *attitudes*; there are also de facto sexist institutionalized rules and practices, such as aspects of the seniority system, antinepotism rules, unfavorable conditions of employment for part-time workers, and rigid time limits on the earning of degrees, promotion or tenure. All of these practices tend to place women at a disadvantage, but in a relatively subtle way, which does not appear on the surface to be sexist—indeed, may be justified by entirely nonsexist arguments.

The point, then, is that women are still discriminated against in the job market, and that consequently a *true* merit system is not possible without specific pressures, of one sort or another, to increase the actual number of women hired and promoted. Numerical hiring and admissions quotas have proved a less-than-ideal means of applying such pressure, if only because of the intensity of the backlash they have generated. Properly understood, however, they are not unjust; and, now that they have survived two crucial tests of their constitutionality in the Supreme Court, they may yet become an effective means of fighting institutionalized sexism and racism. (See Warren article in Philosophy and Women, Anthologies XII.)

1. See, for instance, Alan H. Goldman, "Affirmative Action," *Philosophy and Public Affairs* Vol.5, No.2 (Winter, 1976), pp.185–186.

AMAZON Amazons are legendary women warriors, who, according to the ancient Greek legend, revolted against their husbands, killing them or driving them out, and thenceforth lived under the rule of no man. They mated with men only when they wished to conceive, and they either raised only their female children, or maimed the males so as to render them harmless. "Amazon" means "without a breast," an allusion to the fact that they were said to make a practice of amputating one of their breasts to facilitate the use of the bow. (See Bachofen and Diner, both of whom consider Amazons to be a historical reality.)

Many contemporary feminist groups have found inspiration in the image of the Amazon, without necessarily taking it for a historical reality. Women are certainly capable of being warriors, but there is no definitive proof that entire tribes of bronze-age women escaped from male rule through violent revolution, and defended their independence for generations, as the Amazons are supposed to have done. On the other hand, neither can the story be discounted as certainly mythical; the Greeks, after all, were in a better position than we are to know whether or not *they* had encountered Amazons.

AMUNDSEN, Kirsten. *The Silenced Majority: Women and American Democracy* (Prentice Hall, Englewood Cliffs, N.J., 1971)

As a political scientist, Amundsen effectively contrasts the actual power and status of women in America with the myth of the American matriarchy, and with the democratic ideals we have inherited. She presents extensive documentation of the economic exploitation of women, which she shows to be even more severe than that of black men, and demolishes the notion that women don't "need" economic equality because they share their husbands' economic status and work only for "extra" money. The exploitation of women workers benefits only their employers, she says, not male workers and not "society as a whole." And their virtual exclusion from political power leads to an apathy that undermines all the institutions of the democracy. Indeed, the traditional stereotype of femininity is itself in conflict with the democratic ideal: "Habitual compliance, passivity and dependence are the very qualities we do not want in our citizens, according to classic democratic theories." (p.138) Consequently, the feminist cause "rests firmly on the body of principle long accepted as democratic and wholly American." (p.173)

Amundsen sees the prospects for improvement in women's social, economic and political status in the United States as largely dependent upon their success in using the public media to alter traditional attitudes and force the implementation of progressive reforms. Revolution is not necessary, since our system provides the means for bringing about the necessary changes if only the previously apathetic and uninformed people, especially the non-voting women, can be persuaded of their importance. She proposes as key feminist goals for the near future, housewives' pensions, free abortions, free child care, free job training and "reeducation" for women reentering the job market, and the rewriting of all public textbooks to remove the sexual stereotyping.

ANDELIN, Helen B. *Fascinating Womanhood: A Guide to a Happy Marriage* (Pacific Press, Santa Barbara, 1974)

This is a practical guide to improving your marriage through principles which are the direct opposite of feminism. The way to a man's heart suggested here is through strict conformity to the "feminine ideal," i.e., through the cultivation of "girlishness, tenderness, sweetness of character, vivacity, and the . . . ability to understand men." (p.17) A wife must accept her husband as he is, never attempt to change him, never argue with him or hold fixed opinions which are different from his, never compete with him in his role as leader, protector and provider. "It was God who placed the man at the head of the family and commanded him to earn the bread." (p.119) A woman who seeks independence or equality undermines her man's pride and loses his love. Regardless of his failings she must remain subservient and obedient: "Serious consequences occur when the wife refuses to obey her husband . . . she sets a pattern of rebellion in the family." (p.125)

Andelin claims that most married women who work outside the home do so only out of boredom or to earn unnecessary luxuries. (A claim which is true only if one considers anything beyond the barest subsistence to be unnecessary luxury.) It is acceptable only because it is necessary, for unmarried women, widows or divorcees to work—though it would be better if they did not, since competition from *any* women on the job undermines men's masculinity—but married women ought not to work except in dire family emergencies or to further their husbands' education; raising the family's living standard, seeking personal fulfillment or easing the burden on the man are *not* acceptable reasons. Housewives should never feel like second-class citizens, because the work they do in the home is far more important than anything they could do in the outside world. "To be a successful mother is greater than to be a successful opera singer, or writer, or artist." (All married women presumably will become mothers.)

In spite of this appeal to the sacredness of motherhood, it would appear that motherhood must play a relatively small role in the life of the Fascinating Woman. Andelin cautions mothers against allowing their children to occupy more of their time and attention than their men do. To retain a man's love a woman must retain the "femininity" of her appearance, manner and personality. She must cultivate a "bewitching langour," avoiding activity, competence, and seriousness. She must project "an attitude of frail dependency upon men," be yielding and childlike. She should be fearful of mice, snakes and the like, in order to give her man the chance to protect her. Such a constellation of traits, as Mary Wollstonecraft pointed out in 1792, unfortunately bodes ill even for the possibility of competent motherhood.

Be that as it may, Andelin produces a remarkably boldfaced endorsement of the traditional feminine stereotype, as it has existed in the West at least throughout the Christian era. Her position is essentially the same as that of Rousseau, which Wollstonecraft so effectively demolished. The feminist arguments against such a view of women's "place," which have been reiterated throughout the past two centuries, are not countered but serenely ignored. Such a work would be merely an amusing anachronism if it were not so typical of the position of a large segment of the population, male and female, as witnessed by the success of the Fascinating Womanhood seminars for which it serves as a text.

ANDROGYNY During the past several years, many feminists have been attracted by androgyny as an ideal of human development: the view that it is both possible and desirable, if not morally mandatory, for *both* males and females to possess *both* what are traditionally known as masculine virtues and feminine virtues. This is a difficult issue and is approached here by means of a more formal (and longer) presentation than in any other article. The reason for this special treatment is simply that this may be both the most difficult and important topic concerning the nature of woman. The view that virtues are sexless, that there are no *feminine* virtues is a difficult one to accept—but also hard to avoid.

A case can be made that, properly understood, this thesis is not only true but demonstrable merely by virtue of the definition of the terms employed. Nevertheless, it will be suggested that the very concept of androgyny involves misleading presuppositions.

In the first part of this article androgynism is presented in what appears to be its strongest form, and defended against some of the objections orginating from the antifeminist camp. The second part takes on some of the recent objections to androgynism which certain feminists have raised, and argues that these too fail to

16

refute the thesis. In the third part it is argued that however true the intended content of androgynism may be, to express that content in terms of the combination of masculine and feminine traits is self-defeating.

The Ideal of Androgyny   Contemporary feminists use the term "androgyny" to refer to the state of a single individual, male or female, who possesses both traditionally masculine and traditionally feminine virtues (1). By *virtues* they mean morally—and generally also personally—desirable character traits, such as honesty, loyalty and compassion. Androgyny is thus a *psychological* condition or characteristic, not to be confused with *physical hermaphroditism*—the anomalous biological condition in which an individual has primary and secondary sexual characteristics of both the masculine or feminine sort (or lacks them to an equal extent). (*Webster's Third*, for example, confuses the two.)

Our patriarchal culture, like most (but not all) patriarchal cultures around the world and throughout history, has consistently labeled certain virtues masculine, meaning that they are more important, desirable and natural for males than for females. Other virtues have been labeled feminine. Everyone knows roughly what these so-called masculine and feminine virtues are. The usual list of "masculine" virtues include strength of will; ambition; courage; independence; assertiveness; aggressiveness (in some nonpejorative sense); hardiness; rationality or the ability to think logically, abstractly and analytically; and the ability to control emotion. The "feminine " virtues include gentleness; modesty; humility; supportiveness; empathy; compassionateness; tenderness; nurturance; intuitiveness; sensitivity and unselfishness.

Now, one must conclude that all of the above traits are genuine virtues, character traits which are indeed desirable. The essential point made by the feminists, however, is that to the extent that these are genuine virtues, they are *human* virtues, no more or less desirable in the one sex than in the other. Mary Wollstonecraft demonstrated nearly two centuries ago that even if one accepts the presumption that women and men are destined by nature for different roles in life—men for the dominant provider and defender role, women for the subordinate wife and mother role—one still cannot plausibly maintain that it is unnecessary or undesirable for the one sex to cultivate the virtues commonly associated with the other. A woman will be a better mother, for instance, if she is not only gentle and supportive but also rational and capable of firmness. And, just as clearly, a man will be a better husband and father if his strength, courage and ambition are tempered by humility, compassion and the other "feminine" virtues.

The point is significant—sexual stereotyping of human virtues is still common. For instance, it is still widely assumed that a person who possesses the "masculine" virtue of rationality will automatically be to that degree less capable of the "feminine" virtue of intuitiveness. But this is clearly false: *to the extent that intuitiveness is a virtue* (and not *defined* as irrationality), there is no such incompatibility.

Indeed, it is easy to show that all virtues are at least *logically* compatible. For a virtue is never simply a particular behavior pattern out of context. Every virtue involves not only a certain capacity, but the ability and disposition to exercise that capacity *when and only when it is morally appropriate.* Since morality never demands that one do both of two incompatible things, there can be no inconsistency between, say, the virtue of aggressiveness and that of compassion; some situations call for aggressive action, others for compassionate action, and some for action that is to some degree both.

On the prevailing feminist definition, then, an androgyne is a person who combines both "masculine" and "feminine" virtues, someone capable of both rationality and intuitiveness, humility and self-assertion, depending upon the demands of the situation. Unisex styles of dress or manner are not entirely irrelevant to androgyny in this sense—which we may call *psychological androgyny*—but they are at most a sign or symbol of it and not its substance. An androgynous appearance *may* be a sign of psychological androgyny, but it may also, as in the case of some rock stars, be a shallow veneer laid over a highly *macho* or male supremacist character structure.

Conversely, the psychological androgyne may, for reasons of his or her own, cultivate a strongly masculine or feminine appearance, though it might be argued that in such a case the incongruity between the outer appearance and the inner reality will lead to intrapersonal disharmonies. Simone de Beauvoir has pointed out that "feminine" styles of clothing are often designed to cut the feminine body off from any possible transcendence, to make a woman look and feel like an art object (feminine) rather than an agent (masculine); it is difficult, though not impossible, to be an active, efficient androgyne while hobbling about in hoop skirts or on spike heels or platform shoes (2).

Notice that psychological androgyny by definition involves only *genuine* virtues of the traditionally masculine and feminine kind, not masculine and feminine vices or pseudo-virtues. There are a great many character flaws which are traditionally associated with one sex or the other; e.g., unreasoning belligerence, pointless recklessness, drunkenness, and pigheaded insensitivity are "masculine" vices, traditionally considered to be not only more common, but much less blameworthy in men; while irrationality, excessive timidity, helplessness and petty vanity about one's appearance are "feminine" vices, to be forgiven or even deliberately cultivated in women. If androgyny meant combining "masculine" and "feminine" vices as well as virtues, then it might indeed be an inconsistent notion, since some of the "masculine" vices (e.g. excessive belligerence) may indeed be incompatible with some of the "feminine" vices (e.g. excessive timidity).

With these points in mind, it should be apparent that psychological androgyny can hardly be faulted on moral grounds as a goal for both women and men. Indeed, it is moral by definition, since by definition all virtues are desirable, and (theoretically at least) compatible. The more virtues one has the better. Of course some might argue that however desirable in theory, androgyny is impossible or impractical in reality, that although all virtues are logically compatible, some are incompatible in practice, psychologically at war with each other. Those who deny that masculine virtues are proper in women, or vice versa, often maintain that a woman who aspires to think in the rational mode will inevitably lose touch with her emotions and intuitions. (See, for instance, Rousseau, Kant, Jung, Deutsch, and Andelin.)

But this is nonsense. Not only are all virtues logically compatible, but a little reflection shows that those which the defenders of the patriarchal stereotypes take to be psychologically incompatible are in reality complementary. A person who knows how and when to employ formal or linear reasoning skills (e.g. in balancing a checkbook) and when to respond primarily on an intuitive and emotional level (e.g. in comforting a frightened child) is clearly more rational, and more fortunate, than a person who operates in only the first of these modes. Aggressiveness needs to be tempered by empathy and compassion, modesty and humility by self-respect, and so on. Indeed, it seems that in individuals whose character is predominantly of the so-called masculine or feminine kind, the "masculine" or "feminine" virtues tend to degenerate into the "masculine" or "feminine" vices. Aggressiveness, ambition, self-confidence and the like, in the absence of sensitivity to the rights of others, are ugly phenomena which lead directly to selfish, chauvinistic or even criminal behavior. The purely "masculine" character type is one which society can no longer afford to encourage, if indeed it ever could.

The purely "feminine" character type, on the other hand, while perhaps somewhat less dangerous to society, renders a person ill-equipped to defend her own rights or to secure her own happiness, at least by straightforward means. The "feminine" person appears on the surface to be the ideal victim of oppression, and it is not surprising that common stereotypes of blacks, lower class and other oppressed peoples bear a striking resemblance to the stereotype of femininity. Yet, as feminists have consistently pointed out, deprivation of the opportunity to develop and exercise "masculine" character traits has always had the effect of forcing women, like slaves, to resort to more subtle and underhanded ways of gaining their ends, e.g. manipulation, deceit, blackmail, and bribery.

The ideal of androgyny will clearly receive little support from those biological determinists who believe that the contrasting character structure which patriarchy prescribes for women and men are the inevitable results of male and female hormones, or some other presumably inalterable biological difference between the sexes. (See Biological Determinism.) But the facts do not support such an extreme view. It is as yet an open question to what extent the current masculine and feminine stereotypes represent exaggerations or overemphases of biologically based psychological differences between the sexes. Indeed, it seems false that males will develop predominantly "masculine," and females predominantly "feminine" characters *no matter how they are conditioned*. Money and Ehrhardt have shown that the sex to which an individual is assigned, and according to which she or he is reared, is a much more powerful determinant of so-called masculinity or femininity than either chromosomal sex or hormonal environment, even more important than the presence or absence of the appropriate physical secondary sexual characteristics. A genetic male who, for one reason or another, is classified and raised as a female will generally develop a personality within the normal "feminine" range, and vice versa for a genetic female raised as a male (3).

Thus, the androgynist (i.e. someone who favors androgyny) has no need to insist that biological differences between the sexes have no significant effect on personality and behavior. We are still in a poor position to say just what effects they do have, and the androgynist should keep an open mind on this issue, merely pointing out that if it should turn out to be true that certain virtues are naturally more difficult for individuals of one sex or the other to develop, this will only demonstrate the need for more education and other cultural forces to counteract that deficiency. If, for instance, it should turn out that the hormone testosterone tends to predispose men to violent, aggressive or domineering behavior, this will only underscore the necessity that males be encouraged to develop the so-called feminine virtues by applying an educational corrective to this unfortunate natural tendency.

One more point needs to made before we turn to some of the more serious objections to the ideal of androgyny. There are two importantly distinct versions of the androgynist ideal. Some androgynists argue that *everyone* should strive to become androgynous; they view androgyny as a state of being which is clearly superior to all others, as a norm to which all should aspire. Others see androgyny as merely one of a wide range of equally valid options, and argue for complete freedom of choice, for a tolerant attitude which permits each person to develop whatever so-called masculine or feminine traits she or he may happen to value or to be naturally predisposed towards. For instance, when Carolyn Heilbrun says that androgyny "suggests a spectrum upon which human beings choose their place without regard to propriety or custom, " (4) she seems to be endorsing this weaker or more libertarian version of the androgynist thesis. Joyce Treblicot compares the merits of the two alternatives in her paper "Two Forms of Androgynism," (5) opting for the weaker version on the grounds that it allows individuals a greater degree of freedom.

For the reasons given earlier, it seems clear that androgyny must be a universal ideal, though not one to which people could or should be *forced* to comply. As Wollstonecraft pointed out, virtues can develop only through the exercise of the individual's reason and will, and thus people can be encouraged but never forced to develop virtues.

The objections to the ideal of androgyny which next require consideration are equally relevant to either version of the ideal. They are not objections to its actual stated content, but rather to its supposed implications or connotations, or to its historical associations. These objections are without force, but they require some comment before turning to what seems to be the most serious problem with androgyny as an ideal.

Some Feminist Objections to the Ideal of Androgyny A number of feminists have objected to the ideal of androgyny because of its rather one-sided history. Barbara Charlesworth Gelpi (6) points out that in the long history of the androgynist ideal, it has generally been presumed to apply primarily to men. Men are to be complete or fulfilled by "getting in touch" with the so-called feminine aspects of their nature, but the idea that women can be similarly completed by the development of their so-called masculine capacities is not similarly stressed or accepted. Jung, for instance, in spite of the apparent sexual symmetry of his theory of the feminine *anima* in men and the masculine *animus* in women, is much more enthusiastic about the integration of "feminine" traits into the masculine psyche than he is about the integration of the "masculine" into the feminine. Jung even suggests that an excess of masculinity in women is a threat to the creative abilities of men; apparently femininity in men poses no similar threat to women. As Daniel Harris recently pointed out, "men have rarely had imaginations sufficiently capacious to envisage a female androgyne, i.e., a woman entitled to the same self-completion that men require for themselves." (7)

But while this is undoubtedly true as a historical point, it does not constitute an objection to the ideal of androgyny as proposed by contemporary feminists, who have made it quite clear that they intend to recommend androgyny as a goal for both sexes alike. They are increasingly aware that society cannot bring about equality between the sexes by liberating only *one* sex from the confines of the traditional sexual stereotypes. If women become androgynous while men remain as *macho* as before, or become more so in an effort to compensate for the change in women, we will not find ourselves much better off than before. It might be argued that the historical one-sidedness of the ideal of androgyny, though explicitly repudiated by contemporary androgynists, will inevitably linger on, insidiously corrupting the contemporary notion. But even if this is true to some extent, it is not a particularly telling objection; for the same objection would apply to any philosophical theory which has behind it a history of progress towards a more accurate vision.

Another feminist objection to the ideal of androgyny is that it takes no account of social context. Cynthia Secor says that androgyny is useless as a feminist ideal because it provides no clues as to how we can actually bring about a society in which androgynous men and women are valued as highly as masculine men. It is, she says, "a goal without any road map for getting there; a moral imperative without strategic direction." (8) But moral goals (equality of rights) typically do not come from preformulated recipes for their implementation. In fact the ideal of androgyny may be more suggestive than most of the specific strategies for bringing about greater sexual equality. It suggests a determined attack on sexual stereotyping via the enlightened reform of all the cultural media that perpetuate it, from television and children's textbooks to the English language itself. We need have no illusions that this by itself will suffice to bring about the millennium of perfect equality between the sexes, but it is surely progress in the right direction.

Catharine Stimpson has presented another interesting but ultimately unconvincing objection to androgynism. She argues that by idealizing the union of "masculine" and "feminine" traits, the ideal of androgyny implicitly endorses heterosexuality (9). This inference seems spurious. Far from implying that heterosexuality is the only valid form of sexual expression, androgynism undermines one of the most common rationales for heterosexuality, i.e. the notion that we must find our personal as well as physical complement in an individual of the opposite sex whose masculine strength will balance our feminine sensitivity (or vice versa). By locating the complementary virtues *within* each individual, androgyny obviates this reason for seeking sexual union (only) with persons of the opposite sex. It is reasonable to predict that insofar as the traditional sexual stereotypes are replaced by an androgynous ideal, homosexuality and lesbianism will lose their stigma, since they will cease to be associated with "womanishness" in men and "mannishness" in women.

These are only a small sampling of the objections which various feminists have recently raised against the ideal of androgyny. While none of the objections seem particularly persuasive as formulated, their proliferation is symptomatic of a deep uneasiness, an ambiguity about the notion which reflects a correct intuition. In the next section we consider what may be the underlying source of this uneasiness.

The Real Trouble with Androgynism　There is a paradox inherent in the ideal of androgyny, namely that, while it calls for the elimination of the sexual stereotyping of human virtues, it is itself formulated in terms of the discredited conceptions of masculinity and femininity which it ultimately rejects. Thus androgynism at least appears to undermine its own conceptual foundations. Carefully stated, the thesis of the androgynists is true, or even true by definition, and yet to express this thesis in terms of the need to unite so-called feminine and masculine qualities is to risk appearing to endorse the very stereotypes which we are trying to combat. Of course the androgynist needn't be involved in any *logical* contradiction. There are various linguistic devices for avoiding the logical implication that, for instance, rationality is *really* a masculine virtue or intuitiveness a feminine one, such as enclosing the terms "masculine" and "feminine" in quotes, or being careful to speak only of *so-called* or *traditionally* masculine or feminine traits. By using such devices, as in this article, we can dissociate ourselves from the usual implications of these terms, while retaining the terms as convenient referring devices. Nevertheless, for a number of reasons this does not entirely solve the problem.

In the first place, androgynists too often fail to avoid the presupposition that the traditional patriarchal stereotyping of human values has some validity. Indeed some androgynists, for example Jung and many of his followers (see, e.g., de Castillejo, Harding, Neumann, Scott-Maxwell, and Stern), believe that traits like rationality and creativity really *are* masculine, i.e. naturally and inevitably better developed in men than in women (10). June Singer is a contemporary androgynist who has drawn a good deal of her inspiration from Jung. In *Androgyny*, Singer describes the masculine and the feminine as conflicting natural forces, cosmic rivals which generate a duality which is inherent in all being. These rival forces, she argues, must be brought into balance within each human individual, if that individual is to achieve psychic harmony.

It should be apparent even from this very brief description that Singer's version of androgynism is very different from the feminist version. Rather than attacking the masculine and feminine stereotypes, Singer projects them into the universe, establishes them as basic ontological categories, and merely advocates peaceful coexistence and cooperation between these opposing forces. While (unlike Jung) she does not explicitly claim that men are naturally and inevitably more inclined than women towards those human traits which she labels masculine—the very traits which the patriachal tradition so labels—one cannot avoid the conclusion that her theory both presupposes and reinforces the presumption that they are. For if she is *not* making this assumption, then why does she continue to call such traits *masculine*? If, as feminists maintain, there is no reason to believe that men would be more rational, aggressive, or creative than women if culture and conditioning did not differentially encourage these traits in men, then it is surely a mistake to go on calling such traits *masculine*. After all, we don't call poverty a *negroid* trait just because a higher proportion of blacks than whites are impoverished; under the circumstances, to do so would be highly offensive.

One might suppose that it is somewhat unfair to condemn the ideal of androgyny just because *some* androgynists make the mistake of reifying masculinity and femininity. The *careful* androgynists, those who retain the quotation marks, make it clear that their ultimate goal is the total elimination of the sexual stereotyping of human virtues. Once we have ceased to think of rationality as more appropriate for males than for females, once we have recognized it as a human virtue which is equally desirable in either sex, then we will no longer need the ideal of androgyny, and will abandon it like Wittgenstein's ladder (11). This is an attractive strategy, and yet I fear that the ideal of androgyny may prove to be a ladder which cannot be thrown away after it has been climbed. For a pair of quotation marks is a frail and inconspicuous way of distinguishing between two theories which in substance are as different as night and day. So long as one has to introduce the concept of androgyny via reference to sexual stereotyped virtues, the impression will be fostered that androgyny is something which flies in the face of nature, requiring women and men to behave in ways which are contrary to their natural dispositions. This, of course, is the very opposite of what the careful and coherent androgynists are to be claiming.

In short, the feminist ideal of androgyny is self-defeating in a most interesting and frustrating way. It arises as a reaction against the sexual stereotyping of human character traits, but ends by reinforcing some of the very assumptions which it was designed to counteract. Nor is the problem entirely one of guilt by association, the confusion of the feminist form of androgynism and the Jungian version. What we are doing when we use the terms "masculine" and "feminine" in the statement of our own position, even with the quotes in place, is still uncomfortably close to what we are doing when we use these terms in their original, naive sense. We are still taking the two constellations of human traits and establishing them as polar opposites. This cannot help but encourage the further presumption that there is some inherent cohesiveness between traits within the same set. The notion that, for instance, rationality and aggressiveness are naturally related can be as insidious as the assumption that they are naturally opposed to intuitiveness and sensitivity. We can't, of course, entirely avoid using these terms in our analyses and attacks on patriarchal ideology; but we can try to avoid using them in the statement of our own theories, and it would seem to be a good idea to do so.

Which brings us to what may be the most telling objection to androgyny as a feminist ideal. To understand this objection we will need to take another look at the concepts of masculinity and femininity. What is left of these overblown, artificially extended concepts if we strip away the various illegitimate moral and psychological connotations which they have acquired during millennia of male domination? What if anything is *really* masculine or *really* feminine, that is *naturally* characteristic of most men or women, simply by virtue of their sex? The only answer which we can safely give at this stage of our ignorance is, primary and secondary sexual characteristics of a physiological kind. It is masculine to have a penis, testicles, relatively undeveloped breasts, and relatively broad shoulders and narrow hips. It is feminine to have a clitoris, a vagina, relatively larger breasts and a relatively wider pelvis. There are no other human traits, intellectual, psychological or behavioral, which we can confidently assert to be the natural, i.e. genetically determined, monopoly of one sex or the other.

Androgynism, however, perpetuates the assumption that there are innate and nearly universal differences between the sexes above and beyond the physiological ones. For even if there are in fact statistical differences in the innate behavioral dispositions of the sexes, it is clear that the extent of the overlap between the male and female ranges, plus the susceptibility of these dispositions to cultural modification, makes it wholly inappropriate to refer to any particular psychological trait as either masculine or feminine. There is only one strictly correct use of these terms, only one use which ought to survive the hoped-for demise of the patriarchal sexual stereotypes, and that is to describe the observable physical characteristics which typically distinguish women from men.

With this point in mind, we can state what seems to be the most damaging objection to androgynism. It is that with respect to this most basic and most clearly legitimate use of the terms "masculine" and "feminine," the notion that everyone ought to be both masculine and feminine makes no sense at all. Few of us would care to become physical hermaphrodites, and there is no reason why we *should* care for it. Of course, the feminist proponents of androgyny are not advocating anything of the sort; but the fact remains that this is the only coherent and empirically respectable meaning of the term "androgyny." Thus the androgynist is defeated by the logic of the terms she uses to express her thesis. It is indeed vital to attack the sexual stereotyping of human character traits. But to conduct that attack by arguing for the desirability of *combining* "masculine" and "feminine" traits is to misuse or invite the misuse of these terms; it is to play into the hands of the sexual fundamentalists who think that to reject the sexual stereotypes is to defy nature and to risk turning women and men into sexless, identical and mutually uninteresting neuters. One should not attempt to handle discrimination by race through advocacy of combining racial characteristics by decrying them. The ideal is not mulattos or characterological mulattos, but color-blindness.

It would thus seem to be a better strategy, as well as an improvement in conceptual clarity, for feminists to repudiate androgyny as a feminist ideal. Rather than advocating the combination of (even in quotes) "masculine" and "feminine" traits, we should insist that rationality, intuitiveness and all the other sexually stereotyped psychological traits have, so far as we know, *nothing whatsoever* to do with masculinity or femininity. The feminist goal, therefore, is not an androgynous society, one in which women and men are artificially homogenized to resemble one another, but one in which sexual character stereotypes have simply been forgotten, in which no one will think of aggressiveness as a sign of masculinity or of passivity as a feminine charm. For only in such a world, and surely *not* in a world devoted to the ideal of androgyny, will individuals be free to pursue their own goals without fear of the spurious accusation that their behavior is too "masculine," too "feminine," or not "masculine" or "feminine" enough. (See also Emotion, Intellect, and the Sexual Dichotomy.)

1. See, for instance, Bem, Heilbrun, and Singer; also see Kaplan and Bean, in Anthologies XIII.
2. Simone de Beauvoir, *The Second Sex*, pp.146–148.
3. At the same time, however, a fetally androgenated female (one who has been exposed to excessive amounts of male hormones while still in the womb) or a genetic male mistakenly raised as a female, often seems to be somewhat "tomboyish" in his or her behavior. (Money and Ehrhardt, pp.101–108).
4. Carolyn Heilbrun, 1973. p. xi.
5. Joyce Treblicot, "Two Forms of Androgynism," in *Feminism and Philosophy*, edited by Mary Vetterling-Braggin, Frederick A. Elliston, and Jane English, in Anthologies XII.
6. Barbara Charlesworth Gelpi, "The Politics of Androgyny," *Women's Studies*, Vol. 2, No. 2, 1974; pp.151–160.
7. Daniel Harris, "Androgyny, the Sexist Myth in Disguise," *ibid.* p.172.
8. Cynthia Secor, "Androgyny: An Early Reappraisal," *ibid.* p.164.
9. Catherine Simpson, "The Androgyne and the Homosexual," *ibid.* pp.237–248.
10. See, for instance, Jung's "Woman in Europe."
11. Ludwig Wittgenstein, *Tractatus Logico-Philosophicus*, translated by D.F. Pears and B.F. McGuinness, (Routledge

and Kegan Paul, New York, 1963; first published 1921):

> My propositions serve as elucidations in the following way:
> anyone who understands me eventually recognizes them as
> nonsensical, when he has used them—as steps—to climb up
> beyond them. (He must, so to speak, throw away the ladder
> after he has climbed up it.) (6.54)

ANTHROPOLOGY OF WOMEN   Many of the founders of the
science of anthropology, in the latter part of the nineteenth century, were deeply interested in the origin and evolution of sex
roles, and in the relation between sex-role patterns and levels of
cultural development. Bachofen, Morgan, McLennan, Engels,
and later Briffault and others, defended theories of social evolution which linked primitive cultural and economic conditions
with matrilineal and matriarchal forms of social organization, and
patriarchy with civilization and higher levels of social and economic development. On the other hand, patriarchy theorists like
Maine and Westermarck argued that human society has *always*
been organized along patriarchal lines, and that civilization tends
to *improve* the lot of women.

Such evolutionary theories have been discounted by most
twentieth-century anthropologists, who have tended to focus
their efforts on studying individual cultures, rather than theo-
rizing about such general issues as the etiology of patriarchy. At
the same time, however, the gradual accumulation of data about
cultures whose sex roles are radically different from those of our
own culture has made it increasingly clear that sex roles are at
least largely shaped by culture—even if not in so simple a way as
the early matriarchy theorists imagined. (See Malinowski, Mead;
also Strathern, and Schneider and Gough, in Anthologies I.)
Consequently, some contemporary anthropologists, many of
them feminists, are turning again to the question of which particular aspects of culture, environment, mode of production and
the like serve to determine whether a society develops along
patriarchal or relatively egalitarian lines. (See Martin and
Voorhies, Reiter, and Rosaldo and Lamphere, in Anthologies I.
For surveys of current research in the anthropology of women,
see the review essays by Louise Lamphere and Rayna Rapp, in
Signs.)

ANTIFEMINISM   If feminism is the conviction that women are
entitled to the same moral and legal rights as men, and essentially

the same social status and opportunities, then antifeminism is the denial of this claim. All antifeminist thinkers hold in common the thesis that there are innate and unalterable psychological differences between women and men, differences which make it in the interests of both sexes for women to play a subordinate, private role, destined for wife-and-motherhood. Aristotle is one of the earliest antifeminists, and one whose influence has permeated much of later Western thought. The Christian tradition, as represented by Paul, Augustine, and Aquinas, has been almost uniformly antifeminist, if not misogynous.

Antifeminists of the modern era do not usually consider women to be simply *inferior* to men, across the board. The great moral philosophers of the Enlightenment, including Rousseau and Kant, often defended women's subordinate status precisely on the basis of their moral and emotional superiority; this paradoxical line of reasoning became even more popular in the nineteenth century. On the other hand, the antifeminism of Schopenhauer, Nietzsche and (to a lesser extent) Kierkegaard, the primary forerunners of the contemporary existentialist movement, was distinctly misogynist in nature. During the same period, Darwin and Spencer developed the evolutionary explanation and rationale for male supremacy.

The twentieth century has produced a wide variety of antifeminist theories, from the transcendental sexual dualism of Weininger to the psychobiological determinism of Freud and many of his followers. (See, e.g., Deutsch, Malinowski, Bonaparte, Lundberg and Farnham, and Erikson.) There are straightforward misogynists, like Reyburne, Wylie, and Vilar. There are those who argue that male domination is mandated by our sexual hormones (Goldberg) or built in behavioral patterns which evolved during the era of Man the Hunter. (See Ardrey, Fox, Lorenz, Morris, Storr, Tiger, and Wilson.) Popular writers like Andelin, Decter, Gilder, and Vilar glorify feminine subordination as a source of greater power for women than could be gained through the abolition of sex roles. And Mailer, who is in a class by himself, argues that female subordination is necessary for the sexual satisfaction of both parties.

AQUINAS, Saint Thomas (1225–1274). *Summa Theologica,* in three volumes (translated by fathers of the English Dominican Province; Benziger Brothers, New York, 1947)

Thomas Aquinas is the most important Catholic philosopher since Saint Augustine. His work has had an enormous influence on Church doctrines, including those concerning the nature and social role of women. Aquinas was an Italian of royal blood, cousin to the Holy Roman Emperor; but he scandalized his family by joining the Dominican order and becoming a simple monk. He wrote voluminously, and while some of his work—e.g. the hundreds of pages in the *Summa Theologia* concerned with the nature of angels—is of historical interest only, his philosophy of mind and of law, his epistemology and ethics and of course his theology remain a powerful influence to this day. The *Summa* is a collection of treatises on theology and moral philosophy which, while massive, is so well organized and lucidly written as to be quite accessible to the modern reader.

Aquinas' primary philosophical inspiration, apart from the Bible, was Aristotle. In this respect, he was something of a revolutionary. Augustine and the other fathers of the Church had for the most part been Platonists, as had most of the scholastic theologians prior to Saint Thomas. These earlier Christian thinkers tended to take from Plato a radical asceticism which included a contempt for the body, for sensual pleasures, and for the things which can be learned through the sense organs. Aristotelianism represented a more naturalistic outlook. Although Aquinas treats the Scriptures as unquestionably true in every detail, his is a *relatively* empiricist philosophy, which holds that most, though not all, knowledge is ultimately based on sense perception. He sees a human being not as an immaterial substance, a soul or mind, which is tragically confined within a corrupt material body, but as a union of mind and body. Mind is form and body is matter, and the relation between the two is so close and essential that immortality requires the resurrection of the body as well as the soul.

Unfortunately, Aquinas' relatively empiricist attitude did not extend to the nature of women; his views on the subject are basically a combination of those of Aristotle and Saint Paul. Like Aristotle, he describes woman as a misbegotten male, formed as a result of some defect in the process of generation. "As regards the individual nature," he says,

> woman is defective and misbegotten; for the active force in the male seed tends to the production of a perfect likeness of the masculine sex; while the production of a woman comes from defect in the active force or some material disposition ... (Volume I, p.466: Part I, Question 92, Article 1).

However, Aquinas continues, woman is defective only as an individual human being. She is not a defect in human nature in general, "but is included in nature's intention as directed to the process of generation." (*Loc. cit.*) Woman was created in order to help man in the work of generation—and *only* in this work, "since man can be more efficiently helped by another man in other works."(*Loc.cit.*) But although reproduction is the purpose or end of woman's existence, she possesses only the *passive* power of generation, the active power belonging to the male alone. She contributes, in other words, nothing of the form of the offspring, but only the matter. In all of this, Aquinas follows "The Philosopher," Aristotle.

Like Aristotle too, Aquinas associates the absence of the active power of generation in the female with the lack of rationality and intellect. Lacking this active power, woman is weak in both body and mind when compared to man. She exists only for the purpose of generation, while man was not made for this alone, but is "ordered to a still nobler vital action, and that is intellectual operation." (*Loc. cit.*) This natural difference between the sexes, Aquinas holds, is the reason why a man is said to be effeminate (and blamed for it), when "by natural disposition . . . his mind is less persevering through the frailty of his temperament." (Vol. II, p.1575: Q.138, Art. 1) Women's lesser powers of reason are the natural result of their physical frailty: "since woman, as regards the body, has a weak temperament, the result is that for the most part, whatever she holds to, she holds to it weakly." (Vol. II, p.1831: Pt. II, Q. 155, Art. 1) Aquinas admits that *some* women may be able to reason, but he considers these to be rare exceptions. (*Loc. cit.*)

Woman's lesser rationality is one of the reasons why she must always be subject to man within the family.

> For good order would have been wanting in the human family if some were not governed by others wiser than themselves. So . . . woman is naturally subject to man, because in man the discretion of reason predominates. (Vol. I, pp.466–467, Pt. I, Q. 92, Art. 1)

This natural lack of reason makes women incapable of the virtue of continence. Aquinas follows Aristotle in holding that it is impossible to describe women as continent, "because they are vacillating through being unstable of reason, and are easily led so that they follow their passions readily." (Vol. II, p.1831: Pt. II, Q. 155, Art. 1) Their lack of self-control makes it all the more essential that women be under the control of men, especially since sexual misbehavior on the part of a (married) woman is a much greater sin *against marriage and the family* than it is on the part of the man. (See Vol. II, p. 2766: Pt. III, Q. 62, Art. 4.) Aquinas says that although adultery on the part of the man is less a sin against marriage, it is more serious in that the man "has more of the good of reason" and should therefore be better able to control himself; these two factors counterbalance one another, making adultery equally sinful for either party (*op. cit.* p.2796).

It is also because of women's lack of rationality, together with their subordination to men, that, as Saint Paul maintains, they must not be permitted to speak, lecture or preach in public. (They may, however, speak privately, "to one or a few, in familiar conversation.") (Vol. II, p.1923: Pt. II, Q. 176, Art. 2). Neither may they take orders—that is, become members of the clergy—or administer sacraments such as baptism except in emergency situations, "since it is not possible in the female sex to signify eminence of degree, for a woman is in the state of subjection." (Vol. III, p.2698: Pt. III, Q. 39, Art. 1)

In his attitudes towards sexual intercourse and the pleasures thereof, Aquinas' Aristotelian naturalism is overshadowed by his Christian asceticism. For him, as for Augustine, the sole purpose of intercourse is reproduction, and the "lust" which accompanies it is a mark of shame, a divine penalty inflicted on mankind as a consequence of the sin of Adam and Eve. Like Augustine and Paul, he considers lifelong virginity (for either sex) morally preferable to even the most virtuous and fruitful marriage. Nevertheless he holds that sexual intercourse can be performed without sin *if* (and only if) it occurs between husband and wife, not too frequently, and for the sole purpose of begetting children. If, however, one has intercourse with one's spouse out of lust, then it is a sin, and a mortal sin if lust is the *predominant* motive. Furthermore, even if the "marriage act" is performed sinlessly, it is still shameful. Its shame is the shame "of punishment inflicted for the first sin, inasmuch as the lower powers and the members do not obey reason." (Vol. III, p.2713: Pt. III, Q. 41, Art. 3)

Although marriage is morally inferior to virginity, Aquinas considers it natural, and says that it must have existed, together with the supremacy of the male, as soon as woman was created, since the natural purpose of both woman and marriage is the production and rearing of children under the guidance of the male. Successful childrearing requires both parents, and thus divorce is forbidden, even for the childless; the one exception is when the woman has been adulterous, in which case it is up to the man to decide whether to "put her away"; or to correct her instead by "words and blows." (Vol. III, p.2794: Pt. III, Q. 41, Art. 4) Adultery on the part of the man, though on the whole equally sinful, is not a ground for divorce.

In sum, perhaps the kindest thing which can be said regarding Saint Thomas' views on women and sexuality is that they are about as moderate and reasonable as they could be given his *a priori* commitment to the androcentric doctrines of the Old and New Testaments and the Church fathers. A non-Christian, however (or a Christian who is also a feminist), could scarcely help but marvel—not that male priesthoods and male philosophers have been capable of promulgating such self-serving, female-denigrating doctrines, but rather that men of such towering intellect as Aquinas could unblinkingly accept these doctrines.

Truly, in the words of Adrienne Rich, "power seems to engender a kind of willed ignorance, a moral stupidity," (*Of Woman Born*, p.65) to which even the greatest of philosophers are subject.

ARDREY, Robert. *African Genesis: A Personal Investigation into the Animal Origin and Nature of Man* (Atheneum, New York, 1963; first published 1961)
The Territorial Imperative: A Personal Inquiry into the Animal Origins of Property and Nations (Atheneum, New York, 1966)

Ardrey is an American playwright and student of ethology, who maintains that the fact that the human race apparently evolved from a strain of carnivorous, weapon-wielding primates on the dry Pliocene plains of Africa proves that human males today possess powerful instincts of a sort which rather closely resemble those of baboons, another species of carnivorous terrestrial primate. These include a territorial instinct, a dominance instinct (aimed primarily at other human males), and an instinct for "social order," that is for the formation of status hierarchies. Men, like the males of a great many other species, compete with one another for status and territory, not for females. In such species it is the female who chooses a mate; in the higher species the female is a "sexual specialist," in whom the procreative and mothering intincts take the place of the territorial and status instincts of the male.

While it is by no means Ardrey's stated purpose to refute feminism or to demonstrate the inalterability of the traditional patriarchal sex roles, it is quite clear that his thesis has the implication that the struggle for sexual equality and androgyny of roles and character goes deeply against the grain of human nature. The woman of today, he says,

> is the product of seventy million years of evolution within the primate channel in which status, territory and society are invariably masculine instincts, in which the care of children has been a female preserve, and in which social complexity has demanded of

> the female the role of the sexual specialist. Yet . . . society . . .
> idealizes her behavior in every masculine expression for which she
> possesses no instinctual equipment, [and] downgrades the care of
> children as insufficient focus for her activity . . . she lives in an
> upside down world." (*African Genesis*, p.165)

As an argument for the existence of innate and probably immutable psychological (instinctual) differences between the sexes,
this may be seductive, but it is hardly compelling. Whatever
instincts may have directed the behavior of *Australopithecus afri-
canus*, Ardrey's armed carnivorous ancestor, it requires much
more than a dramatic appeal to the continuity of the evolutionary
process to prove either that the same instincts continue to exist in
Homo sapiens, or if they do, that they are more potent than the
forces of culture, individual deliberation, and choice.

ARISTOTLE (384 B.C.–322 B.C.). *The Nichomachean Ethics*
(with an English translation by H. Rackham, Harvard University
Press, Cambridge, Massachusetts, 1947)
The Politics (with an English translation by H. Rackham, William
Heinemann, London, 1932)
Generation of Animals (with an English translation by A.L. Peck,
Harvard University Press, Cambridge, Massachusetts, 1943)

Unlike Plato, his teacher for twenty years, Aristotle is unlikely
ever to be accused of having been a feminist. He defends the
male-dominated nuclear family and the traditional divisions of
labor between the sexes as natural and therefore good, and firmly
rejects Plato's proposal that women—at least those of the ruling
class—be assigned social and political roles as nearly as possible
like those of the men. Furthermore, he consistently defines the
female as a defective male, distinguished only by her inability to
do what males can do (1). This is the first (known) scientific and
philosophical defense, in the Western tradition, of patriarchy and
male supremacy.

The Nichomachean Ethics, though it deals mainly with the
vices and virtues of men, and with relationships *between* men,
contains several brief but revealing passages about the husband-
wife relationship. Aristotle says that friendship *is* possible between husband and wife—as it generally is not between master
and slave—since unlike the latter case, there is a community of
interest between the married pair. It is, however, a friendship
between unequals, similar to that between a father and son, or
between older and younger persons generally. In such unequal
relationships, he maintains,

> The affection rendered should also be proportionate: the better of the two parties ... should receive more affection than he bestows; since when the affection rendered is proportionate to dessert, this produces equality in a sense between the two parties ... (p.479; Book VIII, vii, 2)

Furthermore, Aristotle has no doubt that the superiority of the husband is not merely a matter of strength and power, but of superior ability:

> The relation of husband to wife seems to be in the nature of an aristocracy: the husband rules in virtue of fitness, and in matters that belong to a man's sphere; matters suited to a woman he hands over to his wife. (p.493; Book VIII, x, 5)

In *The Politics*, which extends the discussion of the *Ethics* into the realm of government and the state, Aristotle further develops his theory of the proper relation between man and woman. The patriarchal family—i.e. a man, his wife, children (and grandchildren, etc.), and slaves—is the unit of which the state is composed. Aristotle holds that both the family and the state are the result of the operation of the principle of rule and subordination in nature, that inferior and superior elements naturally unite for the benefit and preservation of both, with the superior element naturally ruling the inferior. He cites as examples of the operation of this principle the facts that the mind rules the body, reason rules the affective part of the soul, masters rule over slaves, and humans rule over domestic animals. "Again," he says,

> as between the sexes, the male is by nature superior and the female inferior, the male ruler and the female subject. (p.21; Book I, II, 12; 1254b, 13–15)

Aristotle considers it important, however, to distinguish between the three types of rule which exist within the family; the relationships between husband and wife is not to be identified with either that between master and slave or that between parent and child.

> For the free rules the slave, the male the female, and the man the child (each) in a different way. (p.63; I. v. 12; 1260a 11–12)

The rule of a master over slaves, he explains, is like the rule of a tyrant over his subjects, i.e. based primarily on the interests of the master, while the male's rule over the female is like that of a statesman over his fellow citizens; and the rule of a parent over a child is like that of a benevolent monarch. This threefold distinction is explained and justified in terms of the different types of degrees of rationality which are to be expected from inferiors of the three sorts:

> ... all possess the various parts of the soul, but possess them in different ways; for the slave has not yet got the deliberative part at all, and the female has it, but without full authority [2], while the child has it, but in an undeveloped form. (p.63; I. v. 6–7; 1260a 12–16)

As a result of their different natures and social positions, the moral virtues of these four classes (rulers, slaves, women and children) must be somewhat different from one another. They have many virtues in common, but they possess them in different ways:

> The ruler ... must possess intellectual virtue in completeness ... while each of the other parties have that share of this virtue which is appropriate to them ... Hence ... the temperance of a woman and that of a man are not the same, nor their courage and justice, but the one is the courage of command, and the other that of subordination, and the case is similar with the other virtues. (p.63; I. v. 7; 1260a, 16–24)

Furthermore, there are some traits which are virtuous in women but not in men:

> ... as the poet said of women,
> Silence gives grace to woman—though that is not the case likewise with a man. (p.65; I. v. 8; 1260a, 30–32)

All of these differences between the virtues of men and women are, Aristotle holds, necessary and desirable, "since even the household functions of a man and of a woman are different—his business is to get and hers to keep." (p.195; II. ii. 10; 1277b, 24–25)

In brief, then, Aristotle takes a traditonal and conservative view of masculine and feminine roles, in sharp opposition to Plato's position that women can and should perform all the tasks, hold all the offices, and cultivate all the virtues that men do (although, Plato thought, most women can never be as good as men at *any* of these pursuits). As for Plato's theory that the wives and children of the ruling class should be held in common, Aristotle finds that this would be undesirable for a number of reasons. It would destroy the self-sufficiency of each family unit, which he considers necessary for a strong state, and create disharmony and neglect of duty, since rather than extending family feeling and affection throughout the community, as Plato predicted, it would attenuate it to the vanishing point. Furthermore, Aristotle thinks, it would mean that necessary domestic work would be neglected; for he seems not to have conceived of the possiblity of its being done in any way other than by women who have no other occupations available to them. In the *Republic*,

Socrates had argued that the rulers, or Guardian class, should be like watchdogs guarding a flock, and that we do not expect female watchdogs to do no work besides bearing and rearing puppies. (Book V, 451D–452A) Aristotle replies,

> It is . . . strange that Socrates employs the comparison of the lower animals to show that the women are to have the same occupations as the men, considering that animals have no households to manage. (p.97; II. ii. 15; 1264b, 4–9)

In Aristotle's own ideal state, then, the patriarchal household will remain the basic social unit for all classes. Men will marrry at about 37, women at about 18, in order that their reproductive years should terminate at roughly the same time (p.621; VII. xiv. 6; 1335a, 28–30).Women should not be married too young, since very young women are more apt to die in childbirth; and they should receive exercise and plenty of food—but not much mental stimulation—while pregnant. Infanticide will be mandatory for infants which are deformed, but it shall be illegal to expose infants simply because they are unwanted; consequently, abortion will have to be practiced in order to limit the size of the families:

> . . . there must be a limit fixed to the procreation of offspring, and if any people have a child as a result of intercourse in contravention of these regulations, abortion must be practiced on it before it has sensation and life; for the line between lawful and unlawful abortion will be marked by the fact of having sensation and being alive. (pp.623–4; VII. xiv. 10; 1335b, 23–27)

And, finally, adultery is to be treated as a disgrace for either husband or wife; in this one respect Aristotle did reject the double standard.

The ideas about male and female biology presented in the *Generation of Animals* are considerably quainter in light of today's knowledge than is *The Politics* (biology having progressed much further than social and political philosophy), but they remain interesting as an example of the way in which empirical observation combined with inappropriate value assumptions, can lead to false and pernicious theory. Aristotle's theory about the generation of animals is that the male contributes, through his semen, the form, or soul, or "principle of movement," while the female provides the body, the matter, from which the new creature develops. Insofar as form is superior to matter and mind to body, this means that the female is intrinsically an inferior type of being, is, in fact, essentially a defective male.

> . . . a woman is as it were an infertile male; the female . . . is female on account of inability of a sort, viz., it lacks the power to

> concoct semen . . . because of the coldness of its nature. (p.103, I. xx; 728, 17–20)

Semen, Aristotle thinks, is concocted from blood, a process which requires heat, and females are colder than males. Menstrual blood is the material from which semen would have been produced, if there were enough *pneuma* (literally, "hot air") in the female's body. *Pneuma* is a sort of fifth element, in addition to earth, air, fire, and water, a

> "hot" substance, which is not fire nor any similar substance . . . this substance is analogous to the element which belongs to the stars.

Elsewhere, Aristotle says that *pneuma* is divine, eternal and ungenerated (***De Caelo***, Bk. I). *Pneuma* is what the male contributes to the process of generation; conception occurs when the *pneuma* in the male's semen, which is active, takes control over the material within the woman, which is passive, and shapes it— acting upon it, he says, much as rennet acts upon milk. (p.191; 739b, 23–24) Because she is lacking in this divine element,

> the female is as it were a deformed male . . . the menstrual charge is semen, though in an impure condition, i.e., it lacks one constituent, and one only, the principle of Soul. (p.175, II. iii. 739a, 28–30)

The female, then, is a defective male, which is produced when the process of generation is imperfect, that is, when the male's semen fails to adequately shape and inform the material provided by the female. Thus,

> we should look upon the female state as being as it were a deformity, though one which occurs in the ordinary course of nature. (p.461; I. vi. 775a, 14–17)

The defectiveness of the female is said to explain women's shorter lifespans (3), as well as their earlier maturity:

> on account of its weakness it quickly approaches its maturity and old age, since inferior things all reach their end more quickly. (p.461; IV. vi. 775a, 21–23)

This absolute inferiority of the female even explains why male and female animals exist as separate types of organism. Since the male represents soul or form—that which is eternal in all organisms—while the female represents matter or body—that which is not eternal, which admits of being and not being; and since

> the proximate motive cause, to which belong the logos and the Form, is better and more divine in its nature than the Matter, it is

better also that the superior one should be separate from the inferior. That is why whenever possible and so far as possible the male is separate from the female, since it is something better and more divine . . . (p.137; II. i. 732a, 4–9)

1.   It is interesting that, although Aristotle's metaphysics and epistemology were considerably less dualistic than Plato's in that he rejected Plato's concept of "forms" or "ideas" which exist and can be perceived independently of matter and particular objects, nevertheless his treatment of the sexual dichotomy is far more dualistic than Plato's. This would seem to constitute a counterexample to those who suggest that extremes of sexual dualism are naturally or logically associated with a strongly dualistic philosophy in other areas. (See Dualism; also see Marcia Keller's unpublished paper, "Political-Philosophical Analysis of the U.S. Women's Liberation Movement.")
2.   Ernest Barker translates this, "the female indeed possesses it, but in a form which remains inconclusive." (*The Politics of Aristotle*, Clarendon Press, Oxford, 1948; p.43)
3.   See *Goddesses, Whores, Wives and Slaves*, ed. Sarah B. Pomeroy; in Anthologies VII.

ASTELL, Mary (1666-1731). *A Serious Proposal to the Ladies for the Advancement of their True and Greatest Interest* (Source Book Press, New York, 1970; first published by J.R. Wilkin, London, 1701)
Some Reflections Upon Marriage (Source Book Press, New York, 1970; first published by William Parker, London, 1730)
   Mary Astell is perhaps best described as an early proto-feminist—a defender of women's rights and capacities, who wished to improve the condition of her sex, but whose religious orthodoxy and political conservatism prevented her from thoroughly rejecting the basic institution of male supremacy. Because most of her work was originally published anonymously, the true authorship of some of the essays that have been attributed to her is debatable. In particular, *An Essay in Defense of the Female Sex*, a witty piece which bore her name unchallenged for almost two centuries, is now thought not to be hers, but that of some unknown and more liberal writer (1).
   Both Astell's literary style and her philosophy are apt to be somewhat opaque to modern readers. Politically, she was a royalist, a believer in the divinely ordained right of the monarch to

absolute sovereignty, and in the propriety and essential immutability of class distinctions. Religiously, she was a defender of the Church of England, and a bitter opponent of Deists and "freethinkers" who presumed to doubt the literal veracity of (parts of) the Bible. Yet she was also a thoroughgoing rationalist and a follower of Locke and Descartes. She held that not only can all true religious and political doctrines be fully justified on rational grounds, but it is the right and duty of each individual, man or woman, to learn to comprehend these rational foundations of religion and law, in order to better understand and appreciate his or her duties to God and country.

It was with this goal in mind that Astell made her *Serious Proposal to the Ladies*. She proposed the foundation of a college or seminary for women students, whence they could temporarily withdraw from the world to study (only) those academic subjects necessary to enable them to better understand their Christian and domestic duties.

> A Seminary to stock the Kingdom with pious and prudent Ladies, whose good Example it is to be hoped will so influence the rest of their sex, that Women may no longer pass for those little useless and impertinent Animals, which the ill conduct of many has caus'd 'em to be mistaken for. (p.17)

The idea of a college for women was a radical one in the opening years of the eighteenth century, and though it attracted a great deal of attention—and made its author famous, if not infamous—it was not to be realized for another one hundred and fifty years. With the closing of monasteries (actually, monasteries and convents), women had lost the opportunity to receive any kind of formal academic training outside the home. Astell's seminary was to be secular, in that no religious vows would be taken, but its curriculum would include a good deal of theology, as well as philosophy. (It most certainly would *not* include any "Plays and Romances," which Astell blamed for contributing to the corruption of women's moral standards.)

Furthermore, it is from religion that Astell draws her major arguments for the establishment of such a seminary, and her responses to those who claim that women are incapable of learning, or that learning would remove them from their proper sphere. Why, she asks, "since GOD has given Women as well as Men intelligent Souls . . . should they be forbidden to improve them?" (p.18) If women are destined for eternal life, and if life on earth is a preparation for life in the hereafter, then surely women ought to study and improve their minds; for how "can Ignorance be a fit preparation for Heaven?" (p.19) And if it is not, then

> Let such . . . as deny us the improvement of our Intellectuals
> [sic] either take up *his* Paradox, who said that *Women have no
> Souls* . . . or else let them permit us to cultivate and improve
> them [2] (p.19)

Though she insists on women's intellectual capacities, Astell is
careful to deny that education will make women wish to leave
their proper sphere, i.e. the home and family. "We pretend not,"
she says "that Women should teach in the Church, or usurp
Authority where it is not allow'd them; permit us only to understand our *own* duty, and not to be forced to take it upon trust from
others." (p.20) At the same time, she maintains that women's
domestic duties must not supersede their duties to God; and in
this she betrays more than a trace of rebelliousness against (the
excesses of) patriarchal rule. There is a dawning feminist awareness in her rebuke to

> those who think so Contemptibly of such a considerable part of
> God's Creation, as to suppose that we are made for nothing else
> but to Admire and do them Service, and to make provision for the
> low concerns of an Animal Life . . . (p.158)

This rebellious spirit is even more apparent in Astell's **Reflections Upon Marriage**, written many years later and from the
perspective of a woman who had herself avoided marriage. On
the surface, she recommends complete obedience to one's husband, "exhorting Women, not to expect to have their own Will in
any thing, but to be entirely Submissive, when once they have
made Choice of a Lord and Master . . . " (p.96) A wife should
be chaste and discreet, no matter how flagrant her husband's
indiscretions. She should take comfort in religious contemplation
and charitable deeds, not in light reading or frivolous companionship. Yet in making such statements, Astell's tone is invariably ironic; she satirizes the views she purports to endorse.
Though refusing to claim that the husband's power has just limits
and that rebellion against it is sometimes justified, she strongly
implies that a rational person cannot avoid this conclusion, as
when she notes that,

> whatever may be said against Passive Obedience in another Case, I
> suppose there's no Man but likes it very well in this; how much
> soever Arbitrary Power may be dislik'd on the Throne, not . . .
> any of the Advocates of Resistance would cry up Liberty to poor
> *Female Slaves*, or plead for the Lawfulness of Resisting a Private
> Tyranny. (pp.34–55)

Astell's considered position seems to be that the rule of the
husband in marriage may be unjustified, but that to resist it is

futile. Given that the husband's "Prerogative is settled by un-doubted Right and the Prescription of Many Ages," (p.48) and since he has all the force of law and (usually) superior physical strength on his side, it is pointless for a woman to oppose his authority. "Thus it is in Matter of Fact, I will not answer for the Right of it." (p.43) This means that there is only one thing which a woman can do to protect herself from a lifetime of tyranny (di-vorce being against the law of God, except in the most extreme cases), and that is to educate herself in order that she may choose her husband with extreme care and foresight. For,

> She who elects a Monarch for Life, who gives him an Authority she cannot recall, however he misapply it . . . had better need to be very sure that she does not make a Fool her Head, nor a Vicious Man her Guide and Pattern. (p.38)

Yet, while claiming that resistance to male rule is *useless*, Astell points out that where that rule is harsh and unreasonable, female rebellion is *inevitable*: "I don't say that Tyranny *ought*, but we find in *Fact*, that it provokes the oppress'd to throw off even a lawful Yoke that fits too heavy." (p.89) She therefore cautions men to remember that even though women may be their lawful subor-dinants, they are deserving of respect; and that the less a man "requires, the more he will merit that Esteem and Deference, which those who are so forward to exact, seem conscious they don't deserve." (p.91)

Also of interest is Astell's ironic admission that she is "ignorant of the *Natural Inferiority* of our sex, which our Masters lay down as a Self-evident and Fundamental Truth." (p.97) She boldly uses the supposed divine sanction of the monarchy to deny that same sanction to the universal rule and superiority of men:

> For if by the Natural Superiority of their Sex, they mean, that *every* Man is by Nature superior to *every* Woman, which is the obvious meaning, and that which must be stuck to if they would speak Sense, it would be a Sin in *any* Woman, to have Dominion over any Man, and the greatest Queen ought not to command, but to obey, her Footman . . . (*loc. cit.*)

In other words, man's dominion over woman is a matter of civilly delegated authority, not of the natural superiority of the male. As such it is at least potentially subject to challenge, as it could not be if it were a law of nature (3). Thus, though herself declining to advocate rebellion against the rule of the husband, or against male supremacy in general, Astell quite deliberately reveals the vulnerability of these institutions to attacks much more radical than her own.

42

1. See Florence M. Smiths's *Mary Astell* (Columbia University Press, New York, 1916) pp.173–182.
2. It is interesting that this argument is also used by Mary Wollstonecraft, nearly a century later, though Wollstonecraft makes no reference to Astell's work.
3. There are many contemporary scientists, e.g. (most of) the sociobiologists, who continue to argue that indeed male domination, if not male superiority, *is* a law of nature. (See Ardrey, Morris, Tiger, Fox.)

ATKINSON, Ti-Grace. *Amazon Odyssey* (Links Books, New York, 1974).

This is a collection of papers and speeches written by Ti-Grace Atkinson between 1967 and 1972. During these years, the women's movement was reborn in this country, and radical feminism emerged as a distinct theoretical analysis and a separate wing of the movement. Atkinson is one of the primary theorists of radical feminism. She was the leader—though she would reject that term—of the group which broke away from NOW (the National Organization of Women) and became the Feminists—though she eventually left that group also because of the ideological split between herself and less radical members. Atkinson's analysis of the causes of male domination and the means of overthrowing it is closely related to that of Shulamith Firestone, but also owes a great deal to Simone de Beauvoir.

The oppression of women, Atkinson stresses, is a class oppression. Women are a political class—the oldest, largest and most historically stable and geographically general of all political classes. She defines a political class as a group of persons (the Oppressed) who are grouped together by other individuals (the Oppressors), and who are socially defined by the latter in such a way as to deprive them of their humanity. The Oppressors, in this case men, define the Oppressed in terms advantageous to the former; the *capacities* of women, particularly the childbearing capacity, are appropriated as a *function* of society: Women, she says,

> have been *murdered* by their so-called *function* of childbearing . . .
> The *truth* is that childbearing *isn't* the function of women. The
> *function* of childbearing is the function of *men* oppressing women.
> (p.5)

Marriage and the (patriarchal) family are the primary institutions through which the oppression of women is maintained. There is no possibility of making these institutions egalitarian, for their very raison d'etre is to reinforce inequality. The vaginal orgasm is a myth designed to make marriage and (hetero) sexual intercourse seem to be in the interests of women. In fact, sexual intercourse is also a political institution, invented by males for the oppression of females. That is, the physical act of intercourse is institutionalized as the only natural and desirable form of sexuality, and the presumption of male dominance and female submission is built into the social definition of the act.

For these reasons, Atkinson is critical of feminists who are married or otherwise associated with men who have not publicly dissociated themselves from the role of Oppressor. Her own position is never to appear publicly with such men, in any context in which it might be taken that they were friends. She points out, however, that it is not men *as such* who are the enemy, but rather the *behavior* of men. Men's behavior is not determined by their genital structure; hence she rejects Valerie Solanis' claim that men must be physically eliminated if women are to be free (p.55).

Like Firestone and de Beauvoir, Atkinson sees the phenomenon of "love" (i.e., heterosexual love, in the context of patriarchy) as "the psychological pivot point in the persecution of women." (p.43) Love is a pathological mental state which results from overwhelming oppression, "a euphoric state of fantasy in which the victim transforms her oppressor into her redeemer." (p.62) It is also the internalization of coercion, an internalization which is necessary because of the size of the oppressed class, women, and because of "the striking grotesqueness of the one-to-one political units 'pairing' the Oppressor and the Oppressed." (p.43)

Atkinson's analysis of *why* women have been oppressed in this way is existentialist in spirit. The pathology of oppression begins with the nature of human rationality, and in particular its quality of constructive imagination, i.e., the capacity to conceive of nonexistent states of affairs. As a rational animal, man is frustrated by his inability to do all that he can imagine doing: "The powers of His body and the powers of His mind are in conflict within the organism; they are mockeries of each other." (p.58) He is also insecure in his encounter with others of his kind, unsure of his own individual identity and autonomy.

For these reasons, Atkinson argues, all humans look for potency, that is for power over others, which will both provide a measure of security, and enable them to partially close the gap between their physical and mental powers. In order to take power over another, one must catch the other at a disadvantage, a moment of physical weakness and mental depression. At such a time, it is possible for an aggressor to simultaneously "devour the mind" of the victim, and to "appropriate their substance to one-self." (p.59) Atkinson maintains that it was largely because of the temporary weakness of pregnancy and childbirth that men were able to reduce women to a state of subjugation:

> . . . it was because one half the human race bears the *burden* of the reproductive process and because man, the "rational" animal, had the wit to take advantage of that that the child bearers . . . were corralled into a political class. (p.54)

This process, whereby one party seizes control of the mind and body of another, is what Atkinson calls "metaphysical cannibalism." It has enabled members of the male sex to meet, at least in part, their needs for potency and for the venting of frustration through aggression. Through this process, "Some psychic relief was achieved by one half the human race at the expense of the other." (p.54) Nevertheless, metaphysical cannibalism is not a satisfactory solution to the existential problems of either the Oppressor or the Oppressed.

> The Oppressor can only whet his appetite for power . . . and thus increase his disease and symptoms. The Oppressed floats in a limbo of un-Consciousness . . . rejecting life but not quite dead, sensible enough to still feel the pain (p.62)

Thus, the male need for power is only magnified by the subjugation of women. Indeed the latter is the underlying cause of all other systems of political repression. It is unclear, Atkinson says, whether the oppression of women is merely the model for other forms of oppression, or whether the latter are created primarily in order to maintain the former (p.103). Either way, she holds, women cannot be free until all oppressed classes are free, and neither can there be any real revolution without the elimination of the sexual class system. The liberation of women will require the elimination of the patriarchal institutions, the family, love, and sexual intercourse. The institution of sexual intercourse will be replaced by an unrepressed sexuality, which will no longer be focused primarily in the genitals; nor will it be constrained to heterosexual genital contacts.

As for lesbianism, Atkinson does not consider that it is *in itself* a political or liberated activity; she notes that the very concept of lesbianism is a result of male supremacy. Nevertheless, she holds that lesbians play an important role in the conflict between the sexes. Lesbians constitute a "buffer zone" between the Oppressed and Oppressor classes. Like the "criminal" element in society, lesbians function as the "fall guy for the Oppressor, when it is necessary to obscure especially oppressive measures."

(p.139) The members of the buffer zone are in the most danger if revolution begins; consequently, they may become either revolutionaries or reactionaries, but they do not have the option of remaining neutral. It is for this reason, Atkinson concludes, that feminists must defend lesbians and identify with them; for it is necessary to "absorb" the buffer zone and make it strong if it is to work for rather than against the revolution.

SAINT AUGUSTINE (Augustinus Aurelius: 354–430 A.D.). *The Confessions* (*A Select Library of the Niocene and Post-Niocene Fathers of the Christian Church*, edited by Philip Schaff, Vol. I, pp.33–208; translated by J.G. Pilkington. William B. Eerdmans Publishing Company, Grand Rapids, Michigan, 1956)
The City of God (Vol. II in same series, pp.1–511; translated by Marcus Dodds)
On the Good of Marriage (Vol. III in same series, pp.397–413; translated by C.L. Cornish)
Of Holy Virginity (Vol. II in same series, pp.417–438; translated by C.L. Cornish)
Of the Work of Monks (Vol. III in same series, pp.503–525; translated by H. Brown)
Sermons on Selected Lessons of the New Testament (Vol. VI in same series, pp.237–545; translated by R.G. MacMullen)

Augustine was a citizen of Roman North Africa during the period when Rome fell to the barbarians; *The City of God* was inspired in part by the need to persuade his contemporaries that the disaster overtaking civilization was not due to the anger of the old gods over the victory of Christianity. Catholic Christianity was endorsed by the Roman state, but various "heretical" sects, notably the Manicheans and the Pelagians, still flourished. Augustine himself began as a Manichee, but after his conversion to Catholicism and his appointment to the post of Bishop of the town of Hippo (near Carthage), he spent much of his energy combating these rival sects. He wrote voluminously—mostly on theology and Biblical interpretation—and for nearly a millennium his works retained an authority second only to that of the Bible.

Augustine's views on women and sexuality are strictly Pauline, that is, ascetic, puritanical, and male supremacist. Yet, unlike Tertullian and other Church fathers, he avoided the extremes of misogyny and insisted upon the *spiritual* equality of male and female. In the City of God, male and female will stand as equals; on earth, however, woman must be strictly subject to

46

man. The man is the head of the woman, as Paul held, and she must call him her lord and master. Thus Augustine praises his saintly mother Monica for her humility and obedience toward her ill-tempered husband, and for admonishing other married women,

> that from the hour they heard what are called the matrimonial tablets read to them as instruments whereby they were made servants; so being always mindful of their condition, they ought not to set themselves in opposition to their lords. (*The Confessions*, Book IX; 19)

One strand of the Augustinian rationale for woman's earthly subjection to man is the appeal to the sin of Eve. "The poison to deceive man," he says, "was presented him by woman . . . so let the woman make amends for the sin by which she deceived the man." (*Sermons*, I: 3) The question of why Eve's female descendants should be held any more responsible for her mistake than her male descendants, or why either should be reponsible for it at all, is one Augustine could not have asked without casting doubt on the wisdom of the deity. Women bear the curse of Eve, and can redeem themselves from it only by being the humble servants of men and by bearing sons (*loc. cit.*).

Augustine's other primary justification of male domination reflects the Greek, especially the Platonic, philosophical tradition. In each human being, there is a higher and a lower part, the higher being the rational, willing part and the lower the lustful, desiring, animal nature. Augustine holds that woman, in her physical being, represents the lower animal nature, while man represents the rational mind. This, he thinks, is why Paul instructed women to cover their heads but said that a man should not do so, "forsomuch as he is the image and glory of God." Spiritually, both sexes can reflect the image of God.

> But in the sex of their body they (i.e. women) do not signify this; therefore they are bidden to be veiled. The part . . . which they signify in the very fact of their being women, is that which may be called the concupiscential, over which the mind bears rule . . . when life is most rightly and orderly constructed. (*Of the Work of Monks*, 40)

Thus it is not woman as such that Augustine considers sinful and degraded, but rather sexual lust—which woman's body "signifies." It does not occur to him to ask whether men's bodies might not seem equally significant of sexuality, from a female point of view. Nor, perhaps, *could* it have occurred to him, since in the very act of assuming that there is one and only one god, and that it is male, he had already established the viewpoint of the male as the only objective and eternally valid one.

Augustine, in fact, views the process of sexual arousal as a divinely ordained punishment for the original sin of Adam and Eve. Before the Fall, he claims, Eve and Adam could have propagated lustlessly; their sexual members would have obeyed the will, just as do other parts of the body now. It is the involuntary nature of sexual arousal which seems to disturb Augustine most. "Lust" represents the triumph of the lower animal nature over the rational mind, and is therefore always shameful: "by the just retribution of the sovereign God whom we refused to be subject to and to serve, our flesh, which was subjected to us, now torments us by insubordination." (*The City of God*, XIV: 15)

Consequently, in spite of the facts, as related in *The Confessions*, that he had himself enjoyed an active sex life and even kept two mistresses (though not at the same time) prior to his conversion, Augustine became a champion of the virtues of chastity and virginity. The virgin state, he maintains, is morally superior to even the most dutiful married existence. Indeed, he held that if *everyone* were to abstain from sexual intercourse, such that the entire human race disappeared, this would be all to the good, since it would bring about the Judgment Day that much sooner. (See *On the Good of Marriage*, 10) Virginity does not, however, absolve women of the duty to serve and obey men; "for who knows not that an obedient woman is to be set before a disobedient virgin?" (*Of Holy Virginity*, 45)

Although, like Paul, he considers virginity the highest achievement, Augustine also follows Paul in holding that marriage is a not-necessarily-sinful alternative for those who are incapable of "containing"—and thus would otherwise be guilty of—fornication. Marital sex is sinless only when it is engaged in for the sole purpose of begetting offspring; but even when it is motivated by lust it is less sinful than adultery or fornication. Indeed, a married person has the duty to yield to his or her partner's desire for intercourse even when the purpose is not procreation, in order to avoid driving the latter into the commission of adultery.

Needless to say, the bond of marrriage is held to be an unbreakable one, even in cases where one partner proves to be infertile, though a widow or widower is permitted to remarry. Contraception and abortion represent the very worst sort of sin and perversion. In *Marriage and Desire*, Augustine speaks of the "sadistic licentiousness" of those who "procure poison to produce infertility . . . (or) destroy the unborn and tear it from its mother's womb." (1) Also forbidden are all "unnatural" forms of sexual intercourse, whether homo- or heterosexual.

Some of Augustine's interpreters have suggested that his—to our eyes—scarcely rational views about sexuality are the result of "an unmastered fear complex with regard to women." (2) But such an explanation is unnecessary given the more obvious sources of Augustine's particular blend of asceticism and male supremacism, i.e. in the Judeo-Christian tradition, on the one hand, and the Platonic tradition on the other. Augustine was generous in praising the virtues of particular women; he feared women only insofar as they represented a temptation and a reminder of sinful lust.

From a feminist point of view, one of the few virtues of this otherwise pernicious intellectual merger is that it makes impossible the double standard of sexual morality which is so evident in the Old Testament. Augustine urges married women to insist on strict fidelity from their husbands.

> Do not suffer it if your husbands make themselves guilty of unchastity . . . In all other things be subject to your husbands, but where this matter is concerned, defend your cause. (3)

For the rest, perhaps the best that can be said for Augustine is that his conviction that the soul of woman, unlike her body, is able to remain free of sexual taint, prevents him from depicting women as inferior to men in what he considers the most essential respects. "The woman," he says, "is a creature of God, even as the man." (*The City of God*, XXII: 17) The notion that she must nevertheless be the absolute slave of man throughout her life is a strange, if not contradictory one, which could only have seemed plausible in the light of some equally implausible doctrine, such as that of the original sin of Eve plus the inheritance of Eve's guilt by all women. If it is distressing that a thinker of the caliber of St. Augustine could accept such a view, it is even more unfortunate that the leadership of the Catholic Church, for the most part, accepts it to this very day.

1. Quoted by F. Van der Meer, in *Augustine the Bishop*; translated by Brian Battershaw and G.R. Lamb (Sheed and Ward, London and New York, 1961); p.189.
2. *Op. cit.*, p.185.
3. Quoted by Van der Veer, p.182.

B

BACHOFEN, Johan Jakob (1815–1887). *Das Mutterrecht* (Krais and Hoffman, Stuttgart, 1861; portions available in English in *Myth, Religion, and Mother Right: Selected Writings of J.J. Bachofen*, translated by Ralph Manheim, Princeton University Press, Princeton, New Jersey, 1967)

J.J. Bachofen, a Swiss jurist and student of ancient law and mythology, was the first modern scholar to call attention to the existence of ancient matriarchies, i.e. preclassical Mediterranean and Near Eastern cultures which were matrilineal, goddess-worshiping, and—so Bachofen held—politically controlled by women as well. He maintained that matriarchy is a universal phase of human cultural development, the second of three; it is preceded by a primordial period of sexual promiscuity in which lineage is traced on neither side, and gives way to the patriarchal era, in which lineage is traced on the male side only.

This general theory gained very wide acceptance in the latter part of the nineteenth century. It was supported by the American anthropologist Lewis Henry Morgan and apparently confirmed by Morgan's studies of the matrilineal Iroquois tribes. Through Morgan's work, it came to the attention of Marx and Engels and was incorporated into the dialectical materialist theory of social evolution. Its popularity declined, however, after Westermarck's attack on the hypothesis of primitive promiscuity, and also as a result of rejection by twentieth-century anthropologists of the belief in a single universal pattern of human cultural development. But some version of the ancient matriarchy theory is still supported by such feminist researchers as Evelyn Reed and Merlin Stone; and indeed many of Bachofen's inferences about the early evolution of our own civilization have since been amply confirmed (1).

Before Bachofen's thesis became known, it was generally assumed that patriarchy—patriliny and the rule of the (eldest or strongest) male—was a cultural universal which had existd from the earliest beginnings of human society. The *patria potestas* of Roman laws was considered to be a direct outgrowth of the primordial system of isolated patriarchal family units (2). Bachofen began to doubt this received view while still a student; for not only parts of Roman law but much of the artistic and religious symbolism of the Romans and Greeks seemed to him incomprehensible as products of a patriarchal culture. He found a crucial clue in Herodotus' report that the Lycians inherited their names, property and social status from their mothers rather than their fathers.

It is primarily in mythology that Bachofen finds evidence that this Lycian custom was not an isolated instance, but a remnant of a system of mother right which had preceded the system of father right throughout the ancient world. Mythology, he held, is in one respect an accurate historical record. For myths are expressions of the religious conceptions of earlier ages, and enable us to discover the meaning of religious symbols.

> Myth is the exegesis of the symbol. It unfolds in a series of outwardly connected actions what the symbol embodies in a unity.
> (*Myth, Religion and Mother Right*, p.48)

Religious symbols and ideas, he held, are not only accurate reflections of the cultures in which they appear, but are themselves "a profound influence on the life of nations ... first among the creative forces which mold men's whole existence." (p.84) Furthermore, by surviving (even in altered form) into later cultural eras, they preserve, like the various levels of an archeological site, a record of the otherwise unrecorded past. In *Mother Right* he explores mythological evidence for the three-stage pattern of cultural development in Lycia, Athens, Lemnos, Egypt and India; in the later *Myth of Tanaquil* (1870), he does the same for Rome.

Bachofen named the earliest cultural stage the *hetaeric*, or *tellurian*. It corresponds to what he took to be the very beginnings of human existence (since he accepted the Biblically derived estimate that the Creation occurred about 4000 B.C.). At this stage he holds,

> man's sexual life is promiscuous and public. Like the animals, he satisfies the urge of nature before the eyes of all, and forms no lasting bond with any particular woman. (p.134)

Tellurian life is preagricultural, nomadic and communistic with respect to women and (other) property. Each tribe is controlled by an individual (male) tyrant; for

> The holding of women in common necessarily implies the tyranny of an individual ... since no selection occurs in sexual relations and there is consequently no such thing as individual paternity, the

whole tribe has only one father, the tyrant; all are his sons and daughters, and all belong to him. (p.141)

Yet this first stage is also a first stage of mother right—which does not mean matriarchy or female rule, but only matriliny. Since the only known line of descent is the maternal one, political power is transmitted "by way of the womb." That is, a man's heir is his sister's son, rather than his own. Mother right comes into its own, however, in the second stage, the Demetrian matriarchy. Both marriage and matriarchy grew out of women's revolt against the chaotic and exploitative state of hetaerism. Often the revolt took the form of Amazonism, in which women took up arms against their own husbands and fathers. Defeated by the male hero (represented in Lycian myth by Bellerophon), the Amazons willingly agree to marriage, in which they submit to sexual possession by a single man in return for support and protection. Since mother right persists, women then gain in power and influence, in the family, the state and the religion; they lead the way in the development of a settled agricultural life style, a more just morality, and a more spiritual religion.

Matriarchy thus represents a cultural advance over hetaerism; but Bachofen considers its religious and spiritual level inferior to the stage of father right. For in both periods of mother right, the leading divine figure is the mother goddess, who represents life and death as equal and mutually dependent forces. The crude earth goddess of the tellurian period becomes the lunar goddess of the matriarchal era; in the lunar goddess man is recognized as having a higher spiritual nature, but as still being in bondage to matter and the maternal forces of life and death. Father right, on the other hand, represents the "higher" religious conception of spirit as transcending matter, as immortal. As the male escapes from mother right, so too the spirit escapes from the maternal principle of subjection to the cycle of life and death. Furthermore, Bachofen seems to believe that the patriarchal revolution, the replacement of mother with father right, occurred primarily *because* it was entailed by a higher level of spiritual development.

As for why women and mother right should have been so closely associated with the "lower," chthonic and lunar religious ideas, and men and father right with the "higher," solar religions, Bachofen considers this a natural result of the difference between the maternal and paternal functions.

The mother's connection with the child is based on a material relationship ... and remains always a natural truth. But the father as a begetter presents an entirely different aspect ... he always appears as the remoter potency ... [Hence] the triumph of paternity brings with it the liberation of the spirit from the manifestations of nature . . . Maternity pertains to the physical side of man, the only thing he shares with the animals: the paternal-spiritual principle belongs to him alone. (p.109)

Most of the later matriarchy theorists, however, have considered this religious-developmental explanation of the rise of patriarchy inadequate, and have looked for causes in the changing material conditions of life. Thus, Marx and Engels blamed the fall of the matriarchies on improved technology, e.g. in the implements of war, which increased the economic power of men in relation to that of women.

Later matriarchists have also generally—though not in all cases —de-emphasized Bachofen's poorly supported assumption that matriliny and the worship of the mother goddess must, once marriage was instituted, have led to the actual supremacy of women in the family and the state. It is possible, of course, that it did, and that (as the Vaertings held) later patriarchal historians have eliminated or ignored most evidence of women's one-time political supremacy. But it is equally possible that power and wealth may have remained primarily under the contol of men, though inherited through the female line (3). That women's position in the goddess-worshiping cultures was considerably better than in most of the patriarchal societies of the historical era is certain; that they achieved widespread political supremacy, however, is not.

1. It is now clear, for instance, that in most of the Middle East at least, matrilineal, goddess-worshiping cultures did indeed precede the patriarchal cultures of the historical era. See Briffault, Reed, Stone.
2. The thesis is set out in Henry Maine's classic defense of the patriarchal theory, *Ancient Law*, which was published in the same year as Bachofen's *Mother Right* (1861).
3. See, for instance, Malinowski's description of the Trobriand Island culture.

BARBER, Benjamin R. *Liberating Feminism* (Dell Publishing Company, New York, 1975)

Barber seeks to find a middle ground between what he considers complementary fallacies and exaggerations of the radical feminists (e.g., Greer, Millet, Firestone, and Mitchell) and the antifeminist "naturalists" (e.g., Goldberg, Gilder and Mailer). Both camps see natural sexual differentiations, and the current institutions of marriage and the nuclear family, as inimmical to equality between the sexes. Radical feminists respond to this perceived barrier by demanding that what has been considered natural be changed; to be free, women must avoid marriage and even motherhood and seek to become androgynous, no longer identifying themselves primarily as women or as feminine. Naturalists respond by vehemently defending what they consider natural from such feminist attacks, insisting that men are by nature dominant providers and women submissive childbearers, and that any significant change in this situation is either impossible (Goldberg) or dangerous and undesirable (Gilder).

Barber criticizes feminists for claiming that women are *oppressed* by men; "oppression," he thinks, refers only to the literal and deliberate enslavement of one class of people by another, a description which supposedly does not apply to the relationship between the sexes. Viewing men as the enemy, radical feminists attack heterosexual relationships, marriage and motherhood, and present a romanticized notion of self-fulfillment through work, which in fact can serve as a satisfactory substitute for the maternal role only for a few fortunate middle-class women. Motherhood and the family are not themselves the enemies of freedom; indeed they are among the few forces acting to humanize people in our capitalist culture. Androgyny is the logical but absurd consequence of the notion that sexual differentiation is incompatible with equality. Masculinity and femininity cannot be rejected in the name of individual freedom, because they are not mere social overlays upon individuals who are essentially neuter; take them away and there is very little of the human identity left.

The naturalists, on the other hand, are criticized for overlooking the difference between our natural condition, as animals, and our human condition, as historical, political and moral beings. They fail to realize that women's servitude to the reproductive function, far from being inevitable, has already been greatly ameliorated. Furthermore, they commit a version of the naturalistic fallacy by presuming that facts about the sort of behavior that comes *naturally* to human beings have normative significance. In fact, of course, even the clearest proof that it is natural for men to strive to kill one another and to dominate women would not provide the slightest moral argument against using the forces of law and society to prevent them from doing so.

What both sides need is to realize that we cannot entirely escape our sex-differentiated animal nature, but neither need we submit to it passively; that done they could both get on to the more serious business of finding particular social and political means of making life more humanly fulfilling for both sexes. (He suggests, for instance, more part-time jobs to enable parents to both work and care for children, and special childbearing licenses, to prevent people from having children without the necessary maturity and commitment.)

Barber's criticisms of both the radical feminist and naturalist positions have some plausibility, but fail to be decisive, since the brevity and generality of the book preclude the kind of careful analysis and criticism which is necessary for the satisfactory refutation of either position. He does not, for example, refute Firestone's argument that biological motherhood itself places women in a subordinate position *vis a vis* men, or Goldberg's claim that male hormones make male domination not just natural but socially inevitable, the truth of either of which would render his own program for equality through sexual complementarity infeasible. Nor does he pay enough attention to the proandrogyny argument (presented e.g. by Heilbrun) that femininity without masculine strengths is impotent, masculinity without feminine sensitivity dangerous. Androgynists would argue that the complementarity Barber speaks of works only when the masculine and feminine traits coexist in each person, and that when one set of people is predominantly masculine and the other predominantly feminine the former will invariably tend to dominate the latter (See Androgyny, and Heilbrun; also Kaplan, in Anthologies XIII.)

BARDWICK, Judith M. *Psychology of Women: A Study of Bio-Cultural Conflicts* (Harper and Row, New York, 1971)

Bardwick presents a powerful case for what she calls an *interactive* theory of the origin of the observable psychological differences between the sexes. She suggests

> that the origin of the sex difference lies in cultural molding of a constitutional-psychological disposition, and that the overwhelmingly vast majority of cultures have defined the roles of the sexes in terms of the given disposition. (p.166)

There are, she argues, certain innate differences in the perceptual and behavioral patterns of boys and girls, differences which arise from physiological factors—genital, constitutional, hormonal and, probably, differences in their central nervous systems. These differences affect the behavior of parents in ways which tend to accentuate the original differences.

Thus, from an early age girls are less muscularly active, more attendant to social stimuli, and, because of their smaller and more concealed genitals, less apt to have strong sexual urges or to masturbate. They are less apt to come into conflict with parental authority and more apt to be permitted and encouraged to remain in the close, dependent, and affectionate relationship with their parents which is normal for all very young children. Boys, on the other hand, are constitutionally more likely to behave in ways their parents find offensive, and thus receive less parental approval and more discipline. They are also conditioned towards exclusively "masculine" behavior earlier and more severely than are girls towards exclusively feminine behavior. These processes force boys to develop internal controls and an independent sense of self-worth, while girls remain much more dependent upon social approval for a sense of their own value. Thus, boys tend to value achievement above social affiliations and girls to value it less. Hence most girls have little difficulty in accepting the traditional feminine role, which forces them to sacrifice personal achievement to the role of wife and mother. Only after they have achieved a stable marriage and raised their children do large numbers of women begin to think seriously about the pursuit of a career, thus demonstrating that they do have a need for achievement but that it is subordinate to their need to succeed in the traditional role.

The theory is more complex than can be indicated here, and it is open to debate on a great many points. For instance, Bardwick rejects aggressiveness as a trait toward which males have an inherently greater disposition, although this position is increasingly difficult to justify in the light of the preponderance of apparent evidence that males do naturally tend to be not just more active but more actively aggressive. (See Maccoby and Jacklin, 1974, pp.242–249.) Nevertheless, it is likely that an interactive theory of this general type represents the closest approach thus far to the truth about the origins of psychological differences between the sexes. It is no longer feasible to insist that there are not, or cannot be, any biologically conditioned differences in the behavioral propensities of the sexes; and if there are such differences then it is reasonable to suppose that they are part of the explanation of why culturally elaborated sex roles have taken the form they have and why they prove so difficult to alter. This general position is entirely consistent with a feminist stance, so long as it is remembered that the fact that the traditional sex roles are in some way the result of (the exaggeration of) natural differences between the sexes in no way justifies their continuation in unaltered form. And Bardwick does recognize that:

> The formalization of adult sex-roles not only enhances differences between the sexes, it also goes, in stereotyped form, beyond what is necessary or desirable. (p.217)

She is not, however, convinced that any major change in women's roles is taking place, or even that a major change is called for. She considers that relatively few women are seriously discontent with their role and that feminist objectors are a small minority. Herself a mother, she is furthermore convinced that to be "normal," at least under the existing social circumstances, a woman must not only desire and enjoy motherhood and a lasting heterosexual relationship, but must make it her primary goal. She says that:

> In the reality of current socialization and expectations, I regard women who are not motivated to achieve the affiliative role with husband and children as not normal. (p.162)

and

> if a woman has a feminine and normal core identity, failure in the feminine role will preclude feelings of self-esteem. (p.158)

It is distressing that one still finds universal claims to this effect in serious works of psychology, in the face of the existence of large numbers of unmarried and/or nonmaternal women who are as content with themselves as anyone can reasonably expect to be in today's society. (See *Pronatalism*, edited by Ellen Peck and Judith Senderowitz, in Anthologies VIII.)

BEARD, Mary (1876–1958). *On Understanding Women* (New York, London, Toronto, 1931)
Woman as Force in History: A Study in Traditions and Realities (Collier, New York and Toronto, 1973; first published 1946)
A noted historian, Mary Beard wrote a majority of her works—though not these two—in partnership with her husband Charles Beard, also a historian. In both of these books she is concerned to rescue women's history, on the one hand from male historians who have ignored women's contributions almost altogether, and on the other hand from the feminists whom she accuses of falsely depicting the entire history of women as one of subjection and exclusion from the male world of power and achievement. Beard accepts Robert Briffault's thesis that primordial human society was centered around women, who invented agriculture, cook-

ing, spinning, weaving, pottery, sculpture and most other arts and industries, and who were in no way subordinate to men. But she rejects the claim, accepted by both feminists and Marxists, that this early period of mother right was succeeded by unbroken millennia of male supremacy, arguing that (some) women have always held power and been actively involved in the shaping of history.

On Understanding Women ranges over the whole sweep of recorded history, speaking of women's actual situation as opposed to their legal situation, which was generally worse. There is special emphasis on women such as Aspasia (the teacher of Socrates and consort of Pericles, who probably wrote Pericles' funeral oration), Sappho (the sixth century B.C. lyric poet who celebrated love), Aggripina (Empress to Claudius and mother of Nero, who made the latter emperor and was murdered by him), Cornelia (the mother and teacher of the Gracchi), Hypatia (the fifth century A.D. neoplatonist philosopher of Alexandria, murdered by a mob for her paganism), Khadija (the wife and patron of Mohammed, who helped in the launching of his new religion), and the powerful women of the royal families of Europe. The French Revolution, she holds, was largely spawned in the intellectual salons of upper-class Parisian women, who provided virtually the only havens for free thought and open political discussion. Unfortunately, the French Revolution led to a decrease in the power and status of women, for it shifted political control from the aristocratic families, in which women were influential and often dominant, to parliaments and political offices filled and elected entirely by men. So too, the Industrial Revolution led to a diminution of women's economic base, by removing from the home many of women's economically productive tasks.

In *Woman as Force in History*, Beard presents the case that it was William Blackstone who was primarily responsible for the still-current myth that women have always been totally subject to men. In his *Commentary on the Laws of England* (1765), Blackstone placed great emphasis on the common law doctrine of coverture, according to which, "By marriage, the husband and wife are one person in law; that is, the very being or legal existence of the woman is suspended during the marriage. . . . " Under this doctrine, married women had no contractual or property rights whatever; all that they owned prior to the marriage or that accrued to them during it was the property of the husband alone, who could dispose of it entirely as he saw fit. Blackstone, she points out, was accepted throughout most of the nineteenth century, especially in the United States, as the foremost and indeed almost the only authority on English law. Feminists like Mary Wollstonecraft and John Stuart Mill accepted Blackstone's account as not only an accurate picture of the "rights" of married woman at the time, but as typical of the legal status accorded women throughout history.

What Blackstone failed to emphasize was that common law was never the whole of English law regarding the property rights of married women. Equity, a separate judicial system administered by courts of chancery, permitted married women to be the recipients of trust funds, properties held in their name but administered by trustees, by which means many married women were able to secure independent incomes. While this is a necessary correction to the historical picture, however, Beard perhaps overemphasizes the degree of economic equality which women could achieve by the trust device. It is somewhat puzzling that in spite of her insistence that women's historical role has not only been important but on the whole a beneficial, civilizing one, Beard is entirely inhospitable to feminist philosophy, which after all only demands for women the equal status that, according to her, they lost only in the past few centuries. She does not, however, clarify the underlying reasons for her rejection of feminism as a whole, rather than of some feminists' faulty views of history.

BEBEL, August (1840–1913). *Women Under Socialism* (translated by Daniel de Leon, Schocken Books, New York, 1971; first published 1883)

A highly successful popularization of the feminist ideas of the nineteenth-century German Social Democratic Party. Although the arguments are largely derivative, Bebel's nonacademic style, his fierce concern for the problems of working-class people and women in particular, and his great faith in the sweeping benefits to be brought about by the coming socialist revolution made *Women Under Socialism* a source of inspiration for generations of activists.

Bebel holds, after Marx and Engels, that women in the orginal state of primitive communism were the equals if not the superiors of men. It was private property which brought about the demise of matriarchy, matriliny, and matrilocality, etc., the subsequent disenfranchisement of women, and their confinement to the home. Thus, with the social ownership of the means of production and the communal organization of domestic work and child-rearing, women will be restored to a status of complete equality with men. Like Engels, he charges capitalism with making marriage into an economic proposition for the bourgeois and an intolerable burden for the poor, resulting in miserable marriages, rampant prostitution and promiscuity, unwanted and mistreated children, and unhappy spinsterhood for many women. Socialism will cure all these ills by making women and men free to marry on the basis of love and desire, without fear of being unable to support their children.

Bebel is distinctly anti-Victorian in his insistence that sexual gratification is necessary for the mental and physical well-being of both men and women; yet he also retains some unfortunate prejudices. The only acceptable form of sexuality, in his view, is heterosexual intercourse engaged in for the purpose of procreation. He deplores both contraception and abortion and dismisses the threat of overpopulation as a scare tactic, insisting that rapid population growth is essential for the full exploitation of the earth's resources. He endorses numerous bits of pseudo-scientific nonsense (e.g. that women's blood is thinner than men's, that women are naturally unstable, etc.), while placing an inordinate faith in the capacity of technology to work miracles.

In spite of these shortcomings, Bebel presented a courageous defense of women's rights to equal pay, equal opportunity, equal legal status and equal freedom and self-determination, even in sexual matters. To him belongs considerable credit for the relatively high level of feminist awareness present in most socialist movements today.

BEDNARIK, Karl. *The Male in Crisis* (translated from the German by Helen Stebba; Alfred A. Knopf, New York, 1970; first published by Fritz Molden Verlag, Vienna, 1968)

Bednarik argues that throughout the world, in capitalist and communist, democratic and dictatorial nations alike, men are suffering from a loss of authority and autonomy, and a shortage of socially approved outlets for aggression. Power is steadily being concentrated into the hands of fewer and fewer men, leaving most men unable to live up to the traditional image of the male as an independent, powerful and rebellious individual. There are no more heroes. Consequently men are forced to find alternative ways to express their aggression; for they are, he thinks, naturally far more aggressive than women, due to "the phallic nature of . . . (their) sex." (p.14) Male aggression has been displaced into sex, sports, vandalism and crime, the latter often directed against women. Women have become shock absorbers for male ferocity, which was originally directed into the struggle for existence and intermale competition. Homosexuality, sadism, child molesting, rape and rape-murder are some of the results.

Men, he suggests, need to create more socially useful channels for their aggressive and expansive urges by organizing into smaller groups, at work and elsewhere, and thus creating new authority structures which will begin to disperse power from the bottom up, i.e. democratically. When men regain their individual autonomy and authority they will have less need to prove their masculinity by dominating women, then, perhaps, the proper "complementary" (i.e. different but equal) relationship between the sexes will be regained. This position is nonfeminist, if not antifeminist, not so much because Bednarik denies that women have the same innate need for authority and other outlets for their aggression as men—for this may indeed be true—as because he establishes the ministration to this male need as the highest social priority. He does not oppose patriarchy as such, but only the "superpatriarchy" which gives power to too *few* men.

BEM, Sandra L. "Probing the Promise of Androgyny" (*Beyond Sex-Role Stereotypes*, edited by Alexandra G. Kaplan and Joan P. Bean, Little, Brown and Company, Boston, 1976: pp.48–61)

Sandra Bem is a research psychologist whose studies have provided concrete evidence of the ill effects of the sex stereotyping on human personality, and the value of psychological androgyny—i.e., freedom from sex stereotyping. This article summarizes the data on androgyny collected by Bem and her associates between 1971 and 1976 (1).

To measure the masculinity, femininity, or androgyny of subjects, a test was developed, called the Bem Sex-Role Inventory (BSRI). The BSRI is a personality scale on which subjects rate the degree to which each of sixty adjectives or descriptions are applicable to themselves. Twenty of these are stereotypically feminine (e.g. "affectionate," "cheerful," "childlike"), twenty are stereotypically masculine (e.g. "aggressive," "ambitious," "analytical," "assertive"), and twenty are sexually neutral. The BSRI differs from previous psychological tests designed to measure masculinity and femininity, in that masculinity and femininity are treated as two separate dimensions rather than as the opposite ends of a single scale. Consequently, it is possible for a person to score high in *both* masculinity and femininity; such persons are said to be psychologically androgynous. In one sample of 2,000 undergraduates of both sexes, a third turned out to be androgynous, while another third were strongly sex-typed (i.e. masculine if male, feminine if female); only about ten percent were "sex-reversed" (i.e. masculine if female, feminine if male), and a very few scored low on *both* masculinity and femininity. (These latter were not considered androgynous.)

Using the BSRI to classify male and female subjects as masculine, feminine, or androgynous, Bem studied what she calls cross-sex behavior, in each of the six groups. The subjects were told that they were to be photographed performing a variety of activities, not competitively, but simply to procure materials for another experiment. They were allowed to choose between pairs of activities, one of which was congruent with the stereotype of their sex, while the other was not; the cross-sex activity was more highly rewarded (4¢ vs. 2¢). As had been predicted, masculine men and feminine women tended to avoid cross-sex activities even though doing so cost them money, while androgynous and sex-reversed individuals were less stereotyped in their responses. In addition, sex-stereotyped subjects reported a much greater discomfort when they had no choice but to perform cross-sex activities.

Next, Bem did a pair of studies designed to test sex-typed and androgynous persons for independence and nurturance. In the first experiment, subjects were asked to judge whether certain cartoons, flashed onto a screen, were funny or unfunny. Very unfunny cartoons were accompanied by taped laughter, suggesting that the other subjects found them very funny. As predicted, the masculine and androgynous individuals did not differ significantly from one another, and both were much more independent in their judgments than were the feminine individuals. In the second experiment, subjects were allowed to play with a kitten or a human baby, or to listen to a fellow student talking about his or her personal problems. The feminine and androgynous men, and androgynous women, proved much more responsive to the kitten and the baby than did masculine men. Surprisingly, however, the feminine women were *less* responsive to the kitten and the baby than the androgynous or masculine women; on the other hand they were superior to all the other groups in listening sympathetically to a fellow student. (Bem suggests that the feminine women's lack of responsiveness to kittens and babies may be due to their inhibition, in a situation where the correct behavior was unclear, rather than to a lack of "nurturance.")

All of these studies, Bem argues, demonstrate that androgynous persons are capable of both "masculine" and "feminine" behavior, and perform well in both domains. Feminine men and feminine women, however, perform well only in the feminine, or expressive area, and masculine men only in the masculine, or instrumental area. Interestingly, masculine women, like androgynes, seem to do well in both areas. Bem suggests that the experience of "growing up female in our society may be sufficient to give virtually all women at least an adequate threshold of emotional responsiveness." (p.54) The lack of emotional responsiveness observed in masculine males, on the other hand, is a cause for concern.

Bem concludes that androgyny should be viewed as a necessary condition for mental health or ideal human personality. A stereotypical sex-role identity is not only unnecessary for mental health but conducive to its opposite. Hence, "the best sex-role identity is no sex-role identity." (p.60) *Gender* idenity, on the other hand, i.e. "a secure sense of one's maleness or femaleness," is something which even a healthy androgyne needs to have. But gender identity, in the minimal sense, is in no way bound up with the traditional concepts of masculine and feminine personality; it involves "little more than being able to look into the mirror and be perfectly comfortable with the body that one sees there." (*Loc. cit.*)

The work of Bem and her associates has undoubtedly provided valuable scientific support for the ideal of psychological androgyny, and for the classical feminist claim that the sexual stereotyping of human character is psychologically pernicious. The BSRI may be open to criticism however, for treating masculinity and femininity as unidimensional (though separate and distinct) constructs. Masculinity and femininity are complex concepts, in which some of the different dimensions (e.g. analytic intelligence and physical aggression, both traditionally considered masculine), may *not* be at all closely correlated with one another. To the extent that this is true, masculinity and femininity, as unitary psychological concepts, are suspect from the beginning and not merely, as Bem points out, notions which can be expected to gradually fade away as the message of psychological androgyny gains more general acceptance. (See Androgyny.)

1.   See also Sandra Bem, "The Measurement of Psychological Androgyny," *Journal of Consulting and Clinical Psychology*, 42 (1972) pp.155–162; "Sex-Role Adaptability: One Consequence of Psychological Androgyny," *Journal of Personality and Social Psychology*. 31 (1975), pp.634–643; Sandra Bem and E. Lenny, "Sex-Typing and the Avoidance of Cross-Sex

Behavior," *Journal of Personality and Social Psychology*, 33 (1976), pp.48–54; Sandra Bem, W. Martyna, and C. Watson, "Sex-Typing and Androgyny: Further Explorations of the Expressive Domain," *Journal of Personality and Social Psychology*, 34 (1976), pp.1016–1023; and Sandra Bem and Daryl J. Bem, "Case Study of a Nonconscious Ideology: Training the Woman to Know Her Place," *Female Psychology*, edited by Sue Cox, Science Research Associates, Chicago, 1976.

BERNARD, Jessie Shirley. *American Family Behavior* (Harper and Brothers, New York and London, 1942)
Academic Women (Meridian, New York, 1974; first published 1964)
The Sex Game (Prentice-Hall, Englewood Cliffs, New Jersey, 1968)
Women and the Public Interest: An Essay on Policy and Protest (Aldine-Atherton, Chicago and New York, 1971)
The Future of Marriage (Bantam Books, Toronto, London and New York, 1972)
The Future of Motherhood (Penguin Books, New York and Baltimore, 1975; first published 1974)
Women, Wives, Mothers: Values and Options (Aldine Publishing Company, Chicago, 1975)

Jessie Bernard has been a prominent figure in American sociology for over three decades. Her method stresses *sociometrics*, i.e. the concentration on precisely measurable social variables. Her earliest book, *American Family Behavior*, is dedicated to the value-free approach, to describing what is rather than what ought to be. Nevertheless, she agrees with Margaret Mead that male dominance is a cultural rather than a natural phenomenon and points out that the confinement of women to domestic work lowers their social status relative to men, although it is compatible with the possession of a great deal of *personal* power by many women. Conversely, the assignment of the earning and supporting role to men tends to give them higher status at home, but only so long as their earning power lasts; they are very vulnerable to status loss due to unemployment, as was amply illustrated during the economic depression of the 1930s.

In her important study of *Academic Women*, Bernard argues that the small and (proportionally) declining number of women in academic post is not due to discrimination but to women's unwillingness to enter and compete within the academic world.

Those that do become professional academics tend to be associated with low-status institutions and to remain in the lower ranks, even though they earn their doctorates from equally good universities and, indeed, tend to be intellectually superiro to male Ph.D's. She suggests that this is largely because women tend to prefer teaching to research, and the role of "instrument of communication" to that of "man [sic] of knowledge." The Budner-Meyer study showed that academic women are as productive as men in comparable ranks and institutions and with the same amount of experience, making position a much better prediction of productivity than sex (pp.148–150). Yet if women gravitate to less productive positions, it is because they prefer them; they have more options and less at stake and so are less involved and less apt to fall into the "driven, high-producing category." (p.156) To be sure, the reasons for this fact are cultural rather than biological. Women have less desire to be innovative because the "innovative role is an instrumental one and not consonant with the emotional-expressive role assigned to women. . . . " (p.174) Furthermore, most people still find it difficult to accept women in instrumental roles: "identical ideas presented by women seem to have less power to trigger acceptance than when presented by men." (p.176) These are only cultural facts, but culture can be as difficult to alter as biology.

The Sex Game is a less scholarly work, dealing with practical communication problems between the sexes. Here Bernard argues that not all mental and behavioral differences between women and men are purely cultural, though most are. Because of their anatomical differences the two sexes are exposed to different internal stimulations and also to different reactions on the part of other people. Women have a greater capacity for sexual abstinence, probably for biological reasons. Whether for biological reasons or not, our society demands that men prove their masculinity by dominating women, a phenomenon which has been dubbed the "cichlid effect." (See Konrad Lorenz.) Supposedly, men's sexuality, like that of the male cichlid, "is vulnerable to female aggressiveness, or even to lack of subservience or awe." (p.60) It is this expectation that women should subordinate themselves to men in order to preserve male sexuality which explains their exclusion from most high-status jobs. Bernard comments that

> If millions of women are willing to do this, no one can deny them their right. But the question raised by the women who do not make this choice is also understandable: are the people they work with fish or are they men? (p.287)

Women and the Public Interest is an avowedly feminist ("albeit disciplined") statement, reflecting the ideas of the Movement women of the 1960s who invented the concept of sexism. Bernard argues that sexism, the culturally imposed sexual specialization of functions, is "the most serious threat to the public interest today." (p.41) The only function which is biologically assisigned to women is the reproductive one; all the other functions which our society assigns to women—homemaking, childrearing, glamour and emotional support—are susceptible to alteration by public policy. Women are above all assigned the "stroking" function, the role of boosting the egos of others. This assignment tends to undermine their own self-confidence, and is probably "incompatible with the kind of aggression called for by creativity." (p.94) It disqualifies women, therefore, from a wide range of jobs, thus interfering with the optimum utilization of the labor force. For, from "the point of view of the public interest . . . the best job for any worker is the highest, most valuable one he [sic] is capable of performing." (p.120)

The Future of Marriage is perhaps the best known of Bernard's popular books, and provides considerable ammunition for the feminist critique of marriage. Each marriage, she argues, is really two marriages, the husband's and the wife's, and of the two his is better. Married men live longer and are mentally and physically healthier than unmarried men. Married women, however, have a much higher incidence of mental illness than unmarried women, particularly those who are fulltime housewives; the housewife role literally makes women sick. What we need are new life styles which will relieve women of the unequal burdens of housework and child care which our system of isolated nuclear families has imposed. One possiblity is Shulamith Firestone's dream of a "stable reproductive structure," a living unit of up to a dozen people who will agree to live together long enough to communally rear a number of children. But the most practical alternative is the shared-role pattern, in which the nuclear family remains but the wife and husband share both the breadwinning and the homemaking roles, for instance by each working half time and looking after the children the other half. This pattern will, of course, require changes in the organization of work and the expansion of opportunities for part-time work.

The Future of Motherhood develops a similiar theme. Like work and marriage, work and motherhood must be reintegrated. The still-prevailing pattern in which a mother of young children cares for them full time and does little else is good for neither of them. Working mothers are happier, whether they work for survival or for self-fulfillment, and in spite of the fact that their paid jobs are generally added onto their domestic responsibilities, with no reduction of the latter. Child-care centers, more flexible work hours and other institutional reforms are needed to ease the strain on working mothers, but the most necessary change is the expansion of fatherhood, the sharing by men of parental responsibilities.

Women, Wives, Mothers, finally, is a collection of papers documenting changing attitudes towards sex roles and continuing to urge that the traditional roles be transcended through role sharing.

THE BIBLE *The Modern Reader's Bible* (edited by Richard G. Moulton, The MacMillan Company, New York, 1950; this translation first published 1895)

The Bible is one of the greatest anthologies of all time, spanning over a thousand years of Hebrew writings, both religious and political. The earliest parts of the Old Testament were written or composed before 1000 B.C., the latest parts of the New Testament, after 100 A.D. Certain passages from the Bible—particularly from Genesis and the Pauline espistles—have been quoted *ad nauseam* for (more or less) two thousand years as evidence that God intended women to be subordinate to men. For the most part the authors of the Bible *presume*, rather than *defend*, the propriety of male domination. There is some, but relatively little, overt misogyny, and almost no explicit moral or other argument for the severely patriarchal institutions and attitudes of the ancient Hebrews.

In the Old Testament the closest approach to an explicit rationale for male supremacy is found in the story of Adam and Eve. Genesis reverses the natural order of creation, in which females give birth to males but not vice versa; God is said to have created Adam first and Eve only later, and only as a gift for Adam—a gift which proves troublesome. Eve allows the serpent to persuade her to eat of the fruit of the forbidden tree of knowledge and then persuades Adam to do the same. For this sin, God expels Eve and Adam from the Garden of Eden, and curses Eve in the following terms.

> I will greatly multiply thy sorrow and thy conception; in sorrow thou shalt bring forth children; and thy desire shall be to thy husband, and he shall rule over thee. (Genesis 3:16)

Adam is also cursed, condemned to poverty, labor, suffering and death. But Adam's curse would seem to describe the condition of the majority of men and women alike, not of men in particular. Eve's curse falls on women alone. Motherhood and love for but submission to men are to be viewed as penalties righteously inflicted upon women—all women, forever—because of the sinfulness of Eve (1).

Such, at least, has been the usual understanding of the Adam and Eve myth. As early as the seventeenth century, feminist and proto-feminist thinkers have made efforts to reinterpret the story so as to minimize its implication of female sinfulness and male superiority (2). Yet in spite of some of the interesting details of the account (e.g. that Eve ate the apple in pursuit of the—to our minds—laudable goal of gaining knowledge), it is difficult to perceive it as anything other than a more or less deliberate rationalization of the patriarchal order. It may also have been inspired in part by a reaction against the older creation myths which gave to female deities an at least equal and often predominant role in the creation process. Certainly the Jewish priesthood regarded the worship of female deities like the Phoenician Astoreth as abominable, and therefore had a pragmatic motive for degrading females and female sexuality.

Throughout the Old Testament patriarchal attitudes are present as a rarely mentioned but never absent undercurrent which occasionally breaks through in particularly dramatic form—as in the wording of the tenth commandment, which reads,

> Thou shalt not covet thy neighbor's house, thou shalt not covet thy neighbor's wife, nor his manservant, nor his maidservant, nor his ox, nor his ass, nor anything that is thy neighbor's. (Exodus 20:17)

Unless this is a gross mistranslation, it is hard to avoid the conclusion that not only were the commandments addressed only to men (presumably since women owe obedience to men and not to God), but furthermore, women's status was defined as, if not identical, at least closely analogous to that of slaves, domestic animals, and other personal property of men.

Nor is this an isolated instance; numerous passages lead to the same conclusion. Perhaps the most distasteful piece of evidence is the propensity of (otherwise) upright and God-fearing men to offer their wives or daughters to be raped and killed by their enemies in order to save themselves or their (male) guests. (See, for instance, Genesis 19:5–8 and Judges 19:28.) Also striking is the tone of the Proverbial advice against the commission of adultery, which is both androcentric and misogynist. The primary cause of adultery, it would seem, is the wickedness of certain women:

> For the lips of a Strange Woman drop honey, and her mouth is

> smoother than oil: But her latter end is as bitter as wormwood
> . . . Her feet go down to death . . . (Proverbs 5:3–4)

No comparable degree of wickedness is ascribed to the adulterous man; he is merely "void of understanding," in that he allows himself to be lured, and thereby brings upon himself both monetary expense and danger from the woman's husband. (See Proverbs 6:32 and 7:7.) The prescribed penalty for the adulterous woman is death; for the adulterous man there seems to be no official penalty other than the risk of vengeance on the part of the man whose property rights he has violated.

Thus there is in the Bible an extremely sharp distinction between masculine and feminine virtues. It is not the rationality/emotionality distinction which we find dominant in the modern era but is, as we have seen, based on wholly undisguised male supremacy and a particularly vicious double standard for sexual behavior. A virtuous woman is one who obeys her husband at all times, who works night and day to feed and clothe her family, and who is both chaste and fertile. (See Proverbs 31:1–9) The virtuous man, on the other hand, is one who obeys the divine commandments, shuns "idolatry," and avoids intercourse with his neighbor's wife or female slave—though he is free to indulge with his own female slaves or with women who belong to no other (Hebrew) man in particular.

The only noteworthy exception to the prevailing misogyny and male supremacism among the thinkers of the Bible is found in the dominant New Testament figure of Jesus Christ. On the assumption that the Gospels provide a reasonably accurate account of Christ's teaching, it is fairly clear that his overall doctrine of tolerance and forgiveness included a relatively humane attitude towards women and women's sexuality. While previous prophets had endorsed the notion that even to come near to a menstruating woman would defile a man (see Ezekiel 18:6), Christ healed a woman with an abnormal discharge, and did not rebuke her for touching him (Mark 5:24–34). There is also the case of the adulterous woman whom he refuses to condemn to death by stoning, although this was the legally prescribed penalty; and there is the case of Mary, the woman who won more approval for listening to Jesus' teachings, and thus neglecting her domestic chores, than her sister Martha, who kept to her domestic duties (Luke 10:38–41). It may also be significant that Christ's first postresurrection appearance is said to have been made to two women.

Jesus did not, however, explicitly state any doctrine of sexual equality—on earth at least. He would not have advised either wives or slaves to rebel against their earthly masters. Furthermore, any tendency towards sexual egalitarianism which may have existed in the early Christian churches was apparently soon crushed by the severely male supremacist doctrines of the Apostle Paul. In the first letter to Timothy, Paul (or, as is generally thought now, some pseudo-Paul who nevertheless followed the teachings of the real Paul) writes:

> Let a woman learn in quietness with all subjection. But I permit not a woman to teach, nor to have dominion over a man, but to be in quietness. For Adam was first formed, then Eve; and Adam was not beguiled, but the woman being beguiled hath fallen into transgression; but she shall be saved through childbearing, if they continue in faith and love and sanctification with sobriety. (I Timothy 2:12–13)

It makes little difference whether these words were written by Paul or by some impostor, since they agree with the general tenor of Paul's remarks elsewhere. This doctrine of St. Paul has probably done more to retard the progress of sexual equality than any other single influence in Western history. Even today there are a surprising number of male supremacists—not all of them male— who are not above quoting the words of Paul as evidence that God himself endorses male domination and female subjugation. Such unreasoning appeal to dubious and self-interested authority has no part in serious discussion.

1. Merlin Stone has suggested, quite plausibly, that the forbidden fruit is a metaphor for certain contemporary "pagan" religions which involved goddess worship and the ritual use of serpents. (See *When God Was a Woman*, Dial Press, New York, 1976.)
2. See, for instance, Judith Sargent Murray, "On the Equality of the Sexes," first published in the *Massachusetts Magazine* in 1790 and reprinted in *The Feminist Papers* (edited by Alice S. Rossi, Bantam Books, New York, London and Toronto, 1973) pp.18–24.

BIOLOGICAL DETERMINISM   For our purposes, *hard* biological determinism may be taken to be the thesis that certain (real or alleged) social and psychological differences between the sexes— e.g. the greater aggressiveness of males—are the result of biology and not (just) culture, and that these differences make male supremacy and the patriarchal social system inevitable. In other words, not only do the biological differences between the sexes play a key role in *causing* male domination, but they also make all attempts to achieve sexual equality futile if not dangerous.

Aristotle is one of the earliest of these biological determinists on record. He held that it is natural for women to be ruled by men, because women are less rational and less able to control their emotions and desires; and he was followed in this opinion by Augustine, Aquinas, Kant, Rousseau, and, indeed, the great majority of Western (male) thinkers who have addressed the subject at all. Darwin provided new ammunition for the determinists with his account of the way in which competition between males for access to females shapes the physical and psychological traits of the former.

Among the hard biological determinists of the twentieth century, we must count Freud and many of his followers (e.g. Deutsch and Bonaparte), as well as Jung and many of the Jungians (e.g. Harding, Scott-Maxwell, de Castillejo). Then there are those who argue from the data of sociobiology, the study of the social behavior of animals, e.g., Lorenz, Wilson, Morris, Ardrey, Tiger, and Storr.

And, finally, there are those like Steven Goldberg, who argue that the hormone testosterone so predisposes men towards aggressiveness that they will never yield equal social status to women.

All hard biological determinists are *ipso facto* antifeminists, or at least nonfeminists. But it is not the case (as is often alleged by antifeminists) that most feminists deny that the biological differences between the sexes are in part *responsible* for male supremacy. Wollstonecraft and Mill emphasize the role of men's superior strength in the subjugation of women; Firestone emphasizes the economic disadvantages consequent upon female reproductive biology; and Holliday argues that males are dominant because of psychobiological predisposition towards violence and aggression. The difference, of course, is that feminists see no reason to believe that the influence of sexual biology on human social relations is, any longer, something which we are powerless to alter.

Soft biological determinism may be a useful term to describe the view that biological factors cause but do not (necessarily) justify sex-role differences. It is neutral with respect to feminism and, on present evidence, probably correct.

BIOLOGICAL DIFFERENCES BETWEEN THE SEXES Most antifeminists and some feminists as well (see Wollstonecraft,

Mill, Firestone, Holliday) have held that the obvious biological differences between the sexes—particularly the greater muscular strength of the male and the heavier reproductive burden of the female—play a prominent role in bringing about male domination. (See also Antifeminism, and Biological Determinism.) The more subtle biological differences were extensively explored by Ellis in the early part of this century. Ellis' theory that males are "katabolic" (energy-expending) and females "anabolic" (energy conserving) has implications for male and female psychology—implications which might seem to be confirmed by more recent studies which indicate a greater male tendency towards aggression, perhaps as a result of the effects of the male hormone on the brain. (See Bardwick, Goldberg, Hutt, and Maccoby and Jacklin.)

On the other hand, Money and Ehrhardt, Stoller, and other researchers, have utilized studies of hermaphroditic and transsexual individuals to demonstrate how slight—although perhaps not negligible—is the direct influence of male or female physiology in the formation of gender identity. Kinsey, Masters and Johnson, and others, have studied the sexual behavior and responses of male and female subjects, and found that the physiology of the sexual response is remarkably similar in the two sexes. (Indeed, Sherfey interprets the Masters and Johnson data to show that women have a much *greater* sexual capacity than men, and suggests that this was the primary reason why men found it necessary to subjugate them.)

BIRD, Carolyn (with Sara Welles Briller). ***Born Female: The High Cost of Keeping Women Down*** (Pocket Books, New York, 1968)

This is a useful sociological survey of discrimination against women in the American work place and the forces acting to change it. Bird gives a good account of how the word "sex" got into Title VII of the Civil Rights Act, resulting in the legal prohibition of sexist discrimination in hiring. She argues that we are moving inexorably toward an androgynous society, one in which jobs will no longer be sex typed, and one's sex will no longer be the single most important fact in one's life. There remains, however, an "invisible bar" against women who seek responsible and well-paid jobs, especially if those jobs involve authority, technology or machinery, or work out of doors. The bar is the false but stubborn presumption that women are not serious about their work because what they really care about is marriage and motherhood, and that therefore men deserve preference. Interestingly, men seem to be more aware of this prevailing bias against women than women themselves are. "Loophole women," those few who make it to the top in the work world, tend to believe that there are no barriers which any talented woman cannot overcome. In fact, their success tends to be due to exceptional circumstances such as a dynastic or sexual relationship with a successful man, tokenism, or the use of a woman as a gimmick, a ratebuster, or a "woman's woman" (i.e. someone to interpret the business world to women or vice versa). They rarely succeed simply on the basis of merit and hard work, and must still prove that they are twice as good as a man in order to advance half as far.

Bird makes a useful distinction between the old and the new masculinism. Old masculinists insist that woman's place is in the home because biology is destiny. (Freud falls into this category.) New maculinists hold instead that women should be allowed into the larger world, not because simple justice demands that they be given the same opportunities as men, but because their special feminine qualities equip them to play certain roles, e.g. muse, teacher, social worker, or even in government, where their feminine virtues are badly needed. The new masculinist, in other words, accepts the traditional stereotype of masculinity and femininity and the traditional division of labor, but transplants these into the job world. What we need, says Bird, is not more feminine jobs, more "opportunities" for women as such, but an end to the sex-typing of all jobs. The enforcement of the Civil Rights Act will be a major step towards this end, but it will also be necessary to end sexual discrimination in every aspect of law, e.g. in draft, alimony, inheritance, child support and child custody and worker protection laws, as well as in life insurance and retirement plans. This will make laws more rational, forcing their statement in terms of situations rather than sexual stereotypes, and will undermine the presumption that men are entitled to higher paying jobs than women because they may have families to support.

BIRTH CONTROL Women in many, perhaps most, periods of history have had at least some knowledge of means of contraception or abortion, and many of them must have been fully aware of how vital such knowledge is if they—and, for that matter, men—are to have even a small measure of freedom to plan their own lives. But the Christian tradition, from Paul, Augustine, and Aquinas to the contemporary Catholic Church, has generally viewed any method of birth prevention other than total abstinence (or, now, the "rhythm" method) as an abominable crime against nature. Consequently, most feminists prior to our own century failed to claim the right to contraception—let alone abortion—either because they shared the Christian view of these practices, or because they did not wish to endanger the other rights which women were seeking by associating them with so dangerous an issue.

There were, however, many feminists in the latter eighteenth and nineteenth centuries whose apparently prudish advocacy of celibacy before and for long periods during marriage (which was often coupled with the belief that women have little or no sexual desire) was more or less explicitly linked to the avoidance of illegitimate or too numerous births. (See Wollstonecraft, Fuller, Mill and Taylor.) Only a few extreme radicals, such as Goldman and Woodhull, dared to suggest that women should be able to enjoy sex apart from mandatory marriage and motherhood.

It was Margaret Sanger who almost single-handedly led the struggle for legal, effective and available contraceptive methods in this country. Now that an almost complete victory has been won in this campaign, contemporary feminists—radical and liberal alike—have moved on to the defense of the right to abortion, a right which the absence of contraceptives that are both fully safe and fully effective makes a nearly absolute necessity for women's personal autonomy.

BISEXUALITY A bisexual is a person of either sex who enjoys and willingly engages in both heterosexual and homosexual eroticism. As a category, bisexuals have received less attention than have homosexuals (male and female), even though there may in fact be many more bisexuals than exclusive homosexuals. (See Kinsey.) The tendency to overlook the bisexual is no doubt largely due to the fact that persons who are at all inclined towards homosexuality tend to be regarded as (active or latent) homosexuals, even if they happen to also enjoy heterosexual lovemaking. This in turn is probably a result of the powerful taboo against homosexuality which has existed in most Christian societies; if homosexuality, like stealing, is assumed to be wrong, then it is natural to regard anyone who commits homosexual acts as a homosexual, just as anyone who steals is a thief—even if they also sometimes purchase goods legally.

It is not surprising then, that bisexuals, unlike male homosexuals and lesbians, have not organized any large-scale movement for their own liberation. Although some radical feminists have announced their own bisexuality (e.g. Kate Millett), few have argued that a woman must be bisexual to be liberated. There are, on the other hand, radical lesbians who consider that all heterosexual intercourse is humiliating to women, and therefore reject the bisexual as well as the heterosexual lifestyle. (See Abbot and Love, Johnston; also Lesbianism.) Less radical feminists, (in this respect) argue that sexual equality requires the elimination of *all* such taboos on sexual interaction between consenting adults (or consenting children, for that matter), leaving each individual free to choose whatever form of sexual expression they may happen to prefer. (See Firestone, Dworkin, Millett; also Radical Feminism.)

There is probably no direct relationship between bisexuality and the nature of woman—that is, no more and no less than in the case of men. It is probable that there are more male bisexuals in America than female bisexuals; Kinsey found that some 40 percent of adult males had had both homosexual and heterosexual experiences, and though the estimates vary, no one supposes that an equally high proportion of women have had lesbian experiences in addition to heterosexual ones. But this difference is almost certainly due at least in part to the repression of female sexuality of *all* sorts, rather than to an inherently lesser bisexual inclination in women. Of course, there may also be a biological factor which helps to account for the difference. Havelock Ellis ascribed the greater male tendency towards "deviant" sexual behavior of all kinds to the greater genetic variability of the male; but this hypothesis remains unproven.

Freud, on the other hand, held that although both sexes are inherently bisexual, women are more so. This, he says, is because

A man, after all, has only one leading sexual zone, one sexual organ, whereas a woman has two: the vagina—the female organ proper—and the clitoris, which is analogous to the male organ [1].

It is clear that Freud is speaking not so much of bisexuality of sexual orientation, as of biological bisexuality—i.e., the possession of physiological parts more characteristic of the other sex. Nevertheless, this argument is based on a confusion. The clitoris is not a masculine organ, or one which is merely a female analogue of an essentially male structure. It is, rather, a structure which is present in the female fetus, as in the male fetus, as soon as there is any recognizable genital structure at all. And since it is the male hormone which triggers the development of this structure into the male penis, whereas without hormonal intervention it will retain the female form, it might be more accurate to say that the penis is an enlarged version of the clitoris, rather than that the clitoris is a small (analogue of the) penis. (See Seaman, Sherfey.)

All things considered, however, it is probably better to say neither of these things. Human females and males are variations upon a single biological pattern; their biological similarities greatly outnumber their biological differences, but there are in each sex biological structures which are larger or more highly developed in the other. This being the case, it makes little sense to say that either sex is biologically more "bisexual" than the other. The notion of biological bisexuality should be reserved for persons whose physiology is sexually indeterminate, i.e., hermaphrodites and pseudo-hermaphrodites. (Also see Androgyny, Lesbianism, Sexuality.)

1. Sigmund Freud, "Female Sexuality," 1931; in *Women and Analysis*, edited by Jean Strouse (Grossman, New York, 1974), p.41. Also see Wolff.

BONAPARTE, Marie (1882–1962). *Female Sexuality* (International Universities Press, New York, 1953; first published 1949, as *"De La Sexualite de la Femme,"* in *Revue Francaise de Psychoanalyse*, XIII; translated by John Rodken.)

A disciple of Freud, Bonaparte takes a strictly Freudian approach to the subject of female nature. She holds, in opposition to Karen Horney, that females never experience vaginal sensitivity prior to puberty; the "labidinal cathexis" is originally "masculine," that is, phallic/clitoral in focus. In the process of maturation, however, the "normal" female accepts the "loss" of the phallus and rejects the active, convexly-conceived orgasmic sensations of the clitoris for the purely passive and receptive (concave) function of the vagina. Phallic sexuality is not only active, but sadistic; the small boy is a would-be Jack the Ripper, who yearns "not just to penetrate his mother with his penis, but (to) disembowel her." (p.78) The young girl in the phallic phase has traces of this attitude, but her sadism must be turned inward and converted into masochism.

The switch from clitoral to vaginal sensitivity is not automatic, however; it is achieved, Bonaparte maintains, only through the occurrence and subconscious acceptance of masochistic fantasies, especially of beating. Because of the female's natural, and not irrational, fear of penetration and childbirth, "a degree of erotogenic masochism" is necessary to enable her "to accept the vital dangers inherent in the feminine function." (p.51) The prognosis for sexual normality is better for a woman with no sexual sensitivity whatever than for one who remains "clitoroidal." (So pernicious did Bonaparte consider clitoral sensitivity that she favored, and experimented with, surgical intervention, not to remove the clitoris—which her research led her to consider ineffective—but to place it closer to the opening of the vagina.) The clitoroidal woman is not only sexually but socially abnormal. Because she has never accepted her "castration," she is driven to compete with men. The truly feminine woman, of a vaginal orientation, is "acceptive," passive, and seeks autoplastic rather than alloplastic adaptation; that is, she tries to change herself to fit her environment rather than attempting to modify the latter.

From the work of Masters and Johnson, and other researchers, we now know that the Freudian distinction between clitoral and vaginal orgasms is a false one. All orgasms are clitoral, in that they are tiggered by direct or indirect stimulation of the clitoris, whether or not the vagina is also stimulated. But the issue between the orthodox Freudians and the anti-Freudian feminists (and not *all* feminists are anti-Freudian) is not primarily an empirical one. The Freudian position rests on the evaluative judgment that a passive and even masochistic acceptance of their "feminine" fate is *desirable* in women. The core of the feminist position, on the other hand, is the rejection of such an attitude as inconsistent with human dignity and self-respect.

BORGESE, Elizabeth Mann. *Ascent of Woman* (George Braziller, New York, 1963)

This is a socialist utopian vision, reminiscent in many ways of the (later) work of Shulamith Firestone. The central claim is that all evolution, whether in the natural, animal world or in the cultural, human world, proceeds by means of two processes: competition between individuals and cooperation between individuals; and that where evolution proceeds through competition, males are dominant, whereas women are dominant where it proceeds through cooperation. The greater the individualism of a society the greater the power of males; and conversely where the individual is totally subordinate to the collective, as in insect societies, females are dominant. Another key claim is that operative in all human societies is a "group force," an impersonal, amoral influence the strength of which is proportional to density of population, and which conduces to femininity and collectivization.

Thus, as in the Marxist analysis, history is interpreted in the light of a single dialectical process, though Borgese chides Engels for seeing only the economic aspects of the dialectic. Contrary to Bachofen, Morgan, Briffault and the Marxists, Borgese holds that primordial human society was not matriarchal, that is dominated by women. Men, being larger, stronger and more aggressive, were always dominant to some degree. Yet the primitive state of mind was dominated by the group force. The individual and the group, mind and world, man and nature, are still not sharply differentiated; the mother goddess is the primary object of worship. The fall of the mother goddess was the result of the rise of individualism, civilization, reason and law, all of which, Borgese thinks, implied patriarchy. Now, however, having passed through the age of individualism and male supremacy, human society is entering the post-individualist phase, in which a balance will be struck between competition and cooperation and between the power of men and women.

Borgese's utopia features a worldwide socialist state, the minimization and strictly equal distribution of labor, and the collective rearing of children. Its most striking aspect, however, is the alteration of the nature of the sexual dichotomy. Through a gradual process of evolution it will eventually come about that everyone is born female but becomes male after about the age of forty-four. Women will do most of the labor and fill most positions in the executive branch of government; men will fill the legislative and judicial positions. Children will be gestated artificially, as was foreseen by Aldous Huxley in *Brave New World*. This is an interesting fantasy, no doubt, but one must question whether—quite apart from the obvious empirical improbability of the biological evolution involved—it is not a profound form of pessimism, almost of antifeminism, to presume that true equality between the sexes is impossible without such radical changes in the nature of the sexual biological dichotomy itself. (And it's not clear that Borgese's roles *are* equal.) If, on the other hand, biologically induced psychological differences between the sexes exist, and if they prove extremely resistant to change through nonsexist education and other social reforms, then it is possible that more and more feminists will begin to consider the possibility of genetic engineering, to alter the physiological aspects of the sexual dichotomy.

BOULDING, Elise. *The Underside of History: A View of Woman through Time* (Westview Press, Boulder, Colorado, 1976) *Women in the Twentieth Century World* (John Wiley and Sons, New York, 1977)

Elise Boulding is a contemporary American sociologist, married to sociologist Kenneth Boulding. *The Underside of History* is a huge and extremely interesting study of women's changing fortunes throughout history. The chapters on human prehistory are especially valuable. Boulding suggests that sexual differentiation and male dominance may have been enhanced in the human species by the development, probably sometime during the Paleolithic era, of right-handedness and the corresponding specialization of the left side of the brain. "As a result, the capacities of the right hemisphere, governing the left hand, began to be underexercised, and consequently undervalued. . . . " (p.59) A dualistic classification system arose, which associated the female with weakness and the left hand and the male with strength and the right side. This dualistic system

> has in effect powerfully reinforced small adaptive behavioral differences that probably go back to the beginning of hunting, and has acted to amplify these differences. [p.59]

Boulding does not accept the notion of a matriarchal "stage" of cultural development, but she does hold that women must have reached their highest level of social power and participation in the agricultural villages of the Neolithic period. These were generally matrilineal and matrilocal; women controlled the home bases and had at least an equal share in economic, religious and political life. With the growth of cities and civilized technologies (c.6000–2000 B.C.), and of the enclosed courtyard pattern of architecture, women were increasingly pushed out of public life. Yet their loss of power and freedom was not total; "the shadow of the old equalitarian society did not totally disappear." (p.183) Women in the great urban cultures of the second and first millennia B.C. maintained a vigorous counterculture, largely religious in nature, and retained many freedoms which they were later to lose.

Boulding's theme throughout is that women have always played an active part in the life of society, even when legally disenfranchised and historically invisible, indeed even from *purdah*. (See also Beard.) They are the submerged part of the historical iceberg: "steadily and creatively they have built century after century from the underside." (p.791) Furthermore, she argues, prior to the Industrial Revolution—and especially in agricultural or nomadic societies—women have always had economically productive roles and economically viable alternatives to marriage. In the Middle Ages, for instance, women could find considerable freedom in the religious orders or secular communes, or in the life of a traveling entertainer. Their status in the guilds was never completely equal, but they were at least permitted to and did practice most of the trades and professions. Not until the eighteenth century were they wholly excluded from all but the most menial and underpaid employment.

Women in the Twentieth Century World is a collection of papers on the themes of the United Nation's International Women's Year: equality, development, and peace. Boulding analyzes data from developing nations which shed light on the relation between economic progress, industrialization, and the status of women. There is, she shows, a mutually enhancing relationship in the developing nations of the twentieth century between marked sex-role and economic dualism, i.e. extreme differences between economic classes. Where women's productive labor is recognized and adequate resources allotted them, especially in agriculture, poor families are smaller and more able to escape from poverty.

Boulding suggests that (only) women have the capacity to solve the world food problem, to develop more humane food distribution systems, and, eventually, nonhierarchial alternatives to current national governments. Up to the present, the "underlife situation" of women has held human potential in check. "The basic organizational principles on which the entire set of civilizational enterprises of the past eight thousand years, at least, have been founded, that of hierarchical organization, has played itself out." (*The Underside of History*, p.783) Women, precisely because of their "underside skills," are now the sector of society "best equipped to replace hierarchy with decentralized structure based on nonhierarchical communication." (p.784)

BRIFFAULT, Robert (1873–1948). *The Mothers: A Study of the Origins of Sentiments and Institutions*, Volumes I, II and III. (The MacMillan Company, New York, 1927. Abridged edition, edited by Gordon Rattray Taylor, Grosset and Dunlap, New York, 1963; first published 1959)

This is a massive work (some one and a half million words in the orginal edition), which continues to influence many feminists, even though it has long been out of favor with mainstream anthropologists. Briffault, the son of a Scotswoman and a French diplomat, was a medical doctor, a successful novelist, and a man with an almost encyclopedic knowledge of languages, customs and cultures. In *The Mothers* he marshals anthropological, historical, and mythological data in support of the matriarchy theory of cultural evolution. According to his version of this theory, all human societies began as matriarchies, patriarchy being a relatively late development generally coinciding with the rise of private property and civilization.

By "matriarchy" Briffault did not mean the political rule of women (as did Bachofen), since he saw the matriarchal era as prior to the emergence of political power structures. Nor did he define it primarily in terms of matriliny, the accounting of descent through the female line (as did Morgan), since he realized that matriliny is consistent with a low social status for women. Matriarchy generally involves matriliny and matrilocality, but it is essentially "a state of society in which the interests and sentiments which are directly connected with the instincts of women play a more important part than is the rule in the civilized societies with which we are most familiar." (Vol. I, p.84; Taylor edition, p.28) Briffault's claim is that it is the mother-child relationship, not the sexual relationship between females and males or the cooperative/competitive relationship among males, which was the first and most powerful social bond amongst our primate ancestors, and the basis of primitive human society.

This thesis stands in opposition to the patriarchal theory of Maine and Westermarck, who held that the monogamous patriarchal family was the original social unit. Briffault points out that permanent monogamous relationships are a relatively rare phenomenon, among animals and humans alike. Most male animals and primitive human males do not exhibit sexual jealousy of the sort that leads to monogamy; they are attracted to sexually ready females in general, not to a particular female as such. Consequently, the earliest human families must have been matrifocal, i.e. centered around a woman and her offspring. The family is the result of the female's maternal instinct, not the male's sexual instinct, which produces only the herd. Even the herd is not truly patriarchal, since the male's control is purely sexual; but the herd could not have been the form of the first human groupings, for it is inconsistent with the prolonged period of human infancy, which demands an extensive period of maternal care.

The first social units, then, were matrilocal, matrilineal and exogamous families, in which the daughters remained in the mother's group, taking husbands from outside it, and the sons left the maternal family to find wives elsewhere. Exogamy, Briffault argues, cannot be explained by any innate fear of incest, or by the (scientifically unproven) ill effects of inbreeding. There is no reason to suppose, as Westermarck does, that children raised together will naturally avoid sexual contact with one another. Exogamy arose because it was necessary for the preservation of the maternal family. Had women's sons and brothers also been their mates, the increased authority and rivalry between the latter would have brought about patriarchal dominance; hence the mothers imposed the incest taboo. Like Morgan, Briffault considers marriage to have originally been an arrangement between whole families rather than between individuals; group marriage, in which a whole set of brothers is married to a whole set of sisters, is the earliest form of marriage.

Like Morgan too, Briffault holds that the shift from matriarchy to patriarchy is usually brought about primarily by economic progress. The primitive division of labor is entirely voluntary; the sexes enjoy independence and equality, each doing the work it prefers to do. Men are not originally the only hunters and warriors. Primitive women are much less different from men with respect to size and strength, and often show considerable skill in hunting and fighting. In general, however, women specialized in home-based industries, inventing and monopolizing such crafts as pottery making, leatherwork, basketry, weaving, the building of shelters, medicine and surgery, and trade between groups. While there may be male "chiefs" under matriarchy, their power is small and they usually function primarily as war leaders. Patriarchy tends to emerge after the development of agriculture and/or the domestication of animals, which place economic power in the hands of men, enabling them to purchase their wives, thus severing their connection to the maternal clan and establishing themselves as the heads of families. This pattern is not a universal one. Where women did agricultural work and men did not own the fields or herds, women sometimes retained their influence. Sometimes, too, men are able to establish patriarchy at a much more primitive cultural level, as among many of the aboriginal Australian tribes; in such cases the men's weapon and motivation is the monopoly of magical powers. Yet the most common pattern is that as men are freed from hunting they gradually take over the plow, the herding of animals, and most of the productive crafts that had previously belonged to women. As a result women lose their economic independence, their personal freedom, and much of their social influence.

Like most of the matriarchy theorists, Briffault draws heavily upon mythology and primitive religions for evidence of a matriarchal era. He claims that moon worship always precedes sun worship, the latter being in most cases a late product of patriarchal priesthoods and not a spontaneous cultural development. Whether the moon deity is conceived as male or female, it is always associated with female fertility, with the activities associated with women's part of the sexual division of labor, and with the magical powers of women. Hence, "the supremacy and importance of the [moon] deity as the primitive cosmic power and first object of nature worship is the counterpart of the magical faculties and functions of primitive woman," and a proof of women's original preeminence. (Vol. II, p.640; Taylor edition, p.305) Women were probably the first priests, and the major creators of the earliest religions; for the great mother goddess, who is everywhere the first deity to be worshiped with any feeling other than dread, could not have been the creation of men.

Except with a few feminist scholars, Briffault's work has not received the attention it deserves. This is in large part due to the general, and appropriate, rejection of the idea that all human cultures must develop according to some single evolutionary schema. But this objection is not as telling against Briffault as it is against the earlier matriarchy theorists (e.g. Bachofen, McLennan, Morgan), since his theory, based as it is on a much richer accumulation of anthropological data, allows for more diversity in patterns of cultural development. While all theories as to the family structure of prehistoric humans remain highly speculative, Briffault's theory—at least in its major outlines—remains a fairly plausible one. Its truth or falsity makes little difference to the ultimate validity of feminist goals, but it makes a good deal of difference to the way in which those goals are conceptualized. If the matriarchy theory is even partially correct, then the struggle for sexual equality is not a revolt against human (or primate) nature itself—as has been claimed not only by anti-feminists but by radical feminists such as Shulamith Firestone—but rather a long delayed return to what is really a *more* "natural" state of affairs.

BROWN, Rita Mae. *A Plain Brown Rapper* (Diana Press, Oakland, California, 1976)

This is a collection of speeches and essays on the women's movement, written between 1969 and 1975. Brown is a radical lesbian feminist who argues that a strong feminist movement can only be built by women who love and identify with other women. Lesbianism is not simply a matter of preferring women as sexual partners. It means, Brown says, "that you forget the male power system, and that you give women primacy in your life—emotionally, personally, politically." (p.90)

As a radical feminist, Brown holds that sexism, or male supremacy, is the root of all other forms of class oppression:

Imperialism, racism and the attendant disregard for human life (change that to all forms of life) spring from sexism. Way back down in the dim mists of prehistory when man beat down, degraded and enslaved women, he clearly showed his career preferences. (p.65)

Lesbianism, she maintains, "politically organized, is the greatest threat that exists to male supremacy." (p.109) Lesbians threaten supremacist males simply by ignoring them; for the character structure of the latter demands that he feed on the energy of women. Heterosexual women, she holds, cannot avoid catering to this male need; thus heterosexual women necessarily lend some support to the continuation of male supremacy, however radical they may be otherwise.

In the early years of the rebirth of the feminist movement in this country (i.e., the late sixties and early seventies), there were few feminist leaders who were willing to recognize any connection between lesbianism and feminism, or to view lesbianism as a feminist issue, for fear that this association would discredit the movement. A number of the articles in this book deal with Brown's efforts to persuade the National Organization of Women and other feminist organizations to take a public stand in solidarity with lesbian women. (Also see Friedan.)

Brown associates this overly cautious approach to the lesbian issue with the larger failure of many white middle-class feminists to come to grips with the real diversity of movement women, e.g. in class and ethnic background. Having herself grown up in poverty, she criticizes middle-class women for paying too little attention to the needs of working-class and nonwhite women.

Lesbian love, Brown argues, is the key to the basic "emotional/spiritual change" which women must undergo on the way to liberation. Material change—e.g. the elimination of restrictive abortion laws, and equal pay for equal work—is essential, but so is (individual and collective) self-discovery. Lesbianism, i.e. the whole-hearted identification and involvement of women with women, helps women to rediscover their own power, and creates a sense of purpose that is undistorted by sexist and heterosexist values (1).

> By identifying with other women, with ourselves, we gain a definite goal: Freedom. Our self is linked with other selves. The ultimate act of humanness, identifying with others, guides us. (p.200)

1. See Robin Morgan, *Going Too Far*, for a critique, from the radical feminist point of view, of the claim that the women's

movement must be led (at least spiritually) by lesbian women.

BROWNMILLER, Susan. *Against Our Will: Men, Women and Rape* (Simon and Schuster, New York, 1975)

This is the most comprehensive of the many recent feminist studies of rape. It is interesting, Brownmiller notes, that Freud, who built a psychology of women around the notion of penis envy, had nothing to say about rape, the use of the penis as a weapon of aggression. (She defines rape somewhat more broadly, as any act of sex forced upon an unwilling victim; the rapist is not necessarily male, nor is the victim necessarily female, and penetration need not occur. This, of course, is not the usual legal definition.) The central claim is that rape is the primary means for the enforcement of male domination, "a conscious process of intimidation by which *all men* keep *all women* in a state of fear." (p.5) She thinks that rape is also the original cause of women's subordination to men via marriage, which is a classical protection racket in which a woman purchases protection from rape at the cost of her freedom.

As women were the earliest and most valued form of private property, rape entered the law as a property crime of man against man, a genesis which is still apparent in the legal treatment of the crime in this country. Rape has always been a part of war, women being among the spoils that go to the victor, and Brownmiller provides massive and depressing documentation of the prevalence of rape on all sides in World Wars One and Two; of the rape of the women of Bangladesh (1971); the rape of Vietnamese women by American and ARVN troops (the Viet Cong apparently did little raping, but it was standard practice among the Americans); of rape during the American Revolution (on both sides), the Ukrainian pogroms, and the Mormon persecutions; of rape as part of mob violence against blacks in the South, the systematic rape of black women by white men, and (less frequently) of white women by black men, of Indian women by white men and white women by Indians.

Brownmiller argues that recent sociological research has refuted a number of traditional beliefs about rape. The typical "police-blotter" rapist is *not* psychologically abnormal, does not act in the grip of an "uncontrollable urge," and is not "incited" by provocative dress or behavior on the victim's part. Rape is most often planned in advance, very often by groups of men (or boys), and is motivated by contempt for women and a desire to demonstrate masculinity by exercising power over a woman. In short, rapists are perfectly ordinary men who nevertheless carry "an age-old burden that amounts to an historic mission: the perpetuation of male domination of women by force." (p.228)

Men are encouraged to rape by the myth of the heroic rapist, the "real man" who takes what he wants in the name of revolution, social protest or simply his own manhood. The New Left's adulation of the rapist Eldridge Cleaver (who "practiced" on black women, so he says, before commencing to rape white women as a protest against racism) and the tabloid press' sensationalist treatment of rape and rape-murder show how prevalent this myth remains. The Freudian school has contributed to the rape ideology by maintaining that women, being naturally masochistic, subconsciously *want* to be raped; even Helene Deutsch and Karen Horney, Freud's most important women disciples, accepted this presumption, thinking it proved by the prevalence of rape and rape metaphors in the fantasy life of their women patients. Rape fantasies, Brownmiller argues, do occur in women, perhaps more frequently than fantasies of any other sort, but they are the result of patriarchal ideology rather than the natural psychology of women, and will be eliminated by feminism.

Along with the supermale rapist-hero, Brownmiller says, tradition has long glorified the beautiful and passive victim (the Virgin Mary, Mary Queen of Scots, Snow White, the Sleeping Beauty, Marilyn Monroe, Jean Harlow). Police still urge women not to resist an attacker lest they "provoke" him to further violence, though they may also judge a rape complaint as unfounded if the woman did not struggle. But though no formal studies have been done of why some rape attempts fail, it seems extremely likely that active resistance improves one's chances of escape.

Perhaps the most controversial of Brownmiller's claims—at least among feminist thinkers—is that total opposition to pornography and prostitution is necessary for the fight against rape. Prostitution and pornography, she argues, are intolerable, not so much because they are direct causes of rape (though she thinks that pornography may indeed incite acts of rape) as because they embody and perpetuate the "philosophy of rape," the attitude that women's bodies are a commodity to which men have a right of access. This is an important argument, although it contains a crucial *non sequitur*. It is undoubtedly true that prostitution and pornography, in most of their current forms, do encourage the rape mentality; it must be questioned whether this is inevitably so. Liberated pornography may be a contradiction in terms, but liberated erotic art is not, and even after the revolution there may be a legitimate demand for professional sexual services (available to both sexes of course). Furthermore, even if prostitution and pornography *are* inherently sexist, it is doubtful that this constitutes a sufficient reason for the encroachment on civil liberties entailed by their prohibition. Of course, it is possible to oppose pornography vigorously without advocating legal censorship, and without overlooking the difference between sadistic, sexist material and erotic art which is not sexist (1). However, the failure to make these distinctions clearly invites misunderstanding.

Another troublesome point is Brownmiller's assertion that rape is used by *all* men to keep *all* women in a state of fear. As a universal generalization this is surely false, under any literal interpretation. But this is little more than a semantic quibble; for as a *general* claim, as a claim about the objective or symbolic social function of rape, it is in all probability true.

1. See Ann Garry, "Pornography and Respect for Women," in *Philosophy and Women*, Anthologies X.

BUCK, Pearl S. (1892–1973). *Of Men and Women* (John Day Company, New York, 1971; first published 1941)
This little-noticed essay deserves attention for its simple and persuasive statements of time-honored feminist perceptions. Buck was the child of missionary parents and spent a large part of her life in China, where she experienced traditional Chinese family life almost from the inside. Her judgment is that American women, though freer and better educated than Chinese women under the old system, are not only unhappier but less influential. Women who are strictly confined to the home and educated only for this role can usually gain a good deal of manipulative power over their husbands and children; and they tend to be content with this power. But American women are educated for freedom and a role in the men's world outside the home, then denied the opportunity to exercise their freedom. They are confined within homes that have lost their former functions and importance. To be sure, many have denied *themselves* the opportunity to be free, and few women seem to *want* freedom. They cling to their greatest handicap, the privilege of being supported by men. Their only hope is to abandon this privilege, "to go the way that men have gone—the way of work or starve, work or be disgraced." (p.91)

Buck argues that we needn't fear that women who play active roles in what has been men's world will lose their genuine femininity, since a woman who is genuinely feminine will remain so regardless of what role she plays. We needn't fear—nor should we hope—that social institutions will be "feminized" by the entry of women; for what is *called* femininity (gentleness, goodness, weakness, etc.) has nothing to do with women as such, but is a result of women's place. She explains this place by the notion that men dreamed of being watched over by angels, lovely, pure, gentle, good, feminine beings, and they persuaded women to pretend to be such beings in return for protection and material support. In reality of course, women are just as pragmatic, corruptible, selfish and perverse as men. They must repudiate every vestige of the "angel myth," and take their place alongside men in running the affairs of the world, not because they are better than men but because they are equally human.

The alternative, Buck argues, is facism and a retreat of women into domestic slavery and ignorance. When women go back to medievalism, they take men with them. Where women are confined to the home, men are permanently damaged by the ignorance and domination of their mothers. They grow to dislike all women, and to insist on the very thing, confinement to the home, which makes women tyrants there. To break this pattern, men and women ought to be educated for one another. They should be taught together at all ages and learn exactly the same things. The aim of their whole education should be to remove the present antagonism between women and men and to open the world to women and the home to men. Men should do an equal share of domestic work, women of all else. In the Epilogue, written thirty years later, Buck makes it clear that she considers communism, communal child care and the fragmentation of the family a disaster for China, and fears that it could also happen here. She wants to see children raised by both parents equally, but within the family unit rather than communally. Whether this is a feasible goal under either capitalism or socialism remains to be seen.

BULLOUGH, Vern L. *The Subordinate Sex: A History of Attitudes Toward Women* (Penguin Books, Baltimore, 1974)

A study of misogynous attitudes in Western history, beginning with classical Greece and Rome, and with chapters on Byzantium, the Islamic cultures, the Middle Ages, the period of the Industrial Revolution, the colonial and frontier periods in America, and brief comments on India and China. Bullough's major theme is that women have always been treated as inferiors, throughout Western and also Eastern history, and that this is equally true of "sex-negative" cultures (i.e. cultures which treat sexual pleasure as sinful and unclean) like those of Western Christianity, and of "sex-positive" cultures like the Islamic ones, the Hindu culture in Indian and Confucianism in China. This conclusion is contrary to that of G. Rattray Taylor, who argues in *Sex and History* that women's status tends to be much higher in cultures which take a positive attitude towards sex and sensuality.

Bullough offers no causal explanation of why women have been so universally subjugated and denigrated, but the final chapter by his wife, Bonnie Bullough, emphasizes women's lesser size and strength and their childbearing function, which placed them in need of protection from and by men. In effect, women have been forced to trade their freedom for security. The development of effective contraceptive methods must therefore be seen as perhaps the most important single factor in accelerating the process of liberation. The Industrial Revolution forced large numbers of women to seek outside employment (which may also be a necessary condition for liberation), but so long as women had no way to avoid frequent pregnancies except by remaining "old maids" there was no way in which they could effectively demand equal pay for equal work or promotion to more responsible and better paid jobs.

BUYTENDIJK, Frederick Jacobus Johannes. *Woman: A Contemporary View* (translated from the Dutch by Dennis J. J. Barrett; Newman Press and Association Press, New York, 1968)

A rich and impressive phenomenological study which attempts "to grasp the connection between woman's *nature*, . . . the *ways she manifests herself,* and her *existence*." (p.50) The thesis is that woman's world, her mode of existence, is essentially characterized by *care*, men's by *labor*. In labor, one acts on the world to alter it to one's own end; objects are "projected" as either resistances or means to that end. In care, one discovers or elicits the "real" or "intrinsic" value of an object and seeks not to alter it but to dwell with it, to preserve it, and to facilitate its growth and development. Other people are the paradigm objects of care, and "mothering," i.e. caring for a human child, is its highest expression.

Buytendijk takes a middle road between the biological determinism of Freud, who considered passivity, masochism and narcissism to be built into the nature of (normal) women, regardless of their conscious choices, and the radical libertarianism of Simone de Beauvoir, who insists that to the extent that women

and men conform to traditional feminine and masculine stereotypes their conformity is a result of free individual choice, guided
by norms which are merely cultural and historical in origin.
Buytendijk agrees that the choice between the feminine and
masculine modes of being is not causally predetermined by female and male biology, or anything else, yet denies that the
choice is as radically free as Sartre and de Beauvoir hold, in that
the norms by which we judge and regulate our own behavior are
in part conditioned by the physical characteristics of our bodies.
In his view, the lesser size and strength and the greater softness
and youthfulness of a woman's body incline—not cause—her to
choose the mode of care. De Beauvoir herself admits that wom-
en's lesser physical strength means that she has a less firm and
confident "grasp" on the world, and so is less suited to the
expansive, aggressive, energy-expending behavior typical of the
male. Yet, Buytendijk chides, she permits woman to be fully
human "only to the extent that she attains to that mode of
existence which, on good grounds, is called masculine." (p.47)
He holds that the feminine mode of existence is an equally human
relationship to the world, one which is necessary for the highest
moral development, for unselfish love and "being-together-
with" other people.

Predictably, Buytendijk holds that this feminine mode of existence also involves a specifically feminine mode of knowledge.
Women's greater "vegetative lability," that is the supposedly
greater reactivity of their autonomic nervous systems, makes
them naturally more emotional; but, contrary to Sartre's view,
emotions are not mere breakdowns of rational consciousness, but
have positive value for the understanding of the human world.
Thus women understand much that is "hidden from the man
whose existence is more rationally directed toward objective
fact." (p.139) The choice of the feminine mode of being, he
argues, springs in large part from an early preference for the
feminine type of pleasure, the pleasure of escape, of overcoming,
of transcendence. Both the physical differences between girls and
boys and the culturally determined differences in the ways in
which they are treated by others incline them to prefer these
distinct types of pleasure and the distinct modes of being which
go with them.

On this analysis, women's eroticism is fundamentally different
from men's, but not in the way in which Freud and some of his
followers (e.g. Helene Deutsch) have held. The feminine mode of
pleasure cannot be equated with passive masochism; most wom-
en do not enjoy pain, humiliation or submission for their own

sake, but rather seek a type of pleasure and security which, for both cultural and biological conditions, can often be attained only through the toleration of pain or submission. Women's pleasure preferences and their corresponding mode of being explain their "mysterious interiority," which is something Buytendijk finds entirely lacking in men. Pure femininity is pure immanence, a plant-like, Buddha-like return to a state in which the need for active striving is transcended. Men are not mysterious for they are always active, engaged in purposeful projects which are therefore clearly comprehensible.

Although more than a trace of biological determinism survives the passage through Buytendijk's existentialist filter, Buytendijk emphasizes that the masculine and feminine modes are both *human* modes of being and therefore fully accessible to *all* human beings, regardless of sex. Not only are all of us bisexual in our modes of being, but it is crucial that there be a balance within each person between the two modes. In effect, pure masculinity is soulless, pure femininity impotent. The balance, however, needn't be an even one. Like Jung, he recommends at best a partial androgyny of human character. He assumes that the differences between the male and female physique will continue to lead men towards the masculine mode and women towards the feminine, and merely urges men to moderate their masculine outlook by an infusion of feminine sensibility, and women to do the same in reverse.

C

CAPITALISM   See Socialism and Feminism

CHAFE, William H. *The American Woman: Her Changing Social, Economic and Political Roles, 1920–1970* (Oxford University Press; London, Oxford, New York; 1972)
Women and Equality: Changing Patterns in American Culture (Oxford University Press, New York, 1977)

These are two excellent historical studies of the American women's movement, the economic status of American women, and the effects of each on the other. *The American Woman* deals with the "dark age" of American feminism, the period between the winning of the vote in 1920 and the revival of radical feminism in the late 1960s; *Women and Equality* ranges across the whole of U.S. history. In *The American Woman*, Chafe argues that the early feminist movement in America (1848–1900) was radical from the beginning, not concentrating on single issues or reforms but advocating a complete transformation of women's role. After 1900, however, both the philosophy and the strategy of the movement became more moderate. Instead of boldly attacking the sexual stereotypes, new leaders like Carrie Chapman Catt began to exploit those very stereotypes in order to make an effective case for the franchise; Jane Addams, for instance, argued that the vote would enable women to become housekeepers for the nation, exercising their special feminine talents in the public arena.

This strategy proved effective, but the loss of the radical perspective helped ensure that the vote made little difference to women's overall situation. The female labor force continued to grow during the 1920s, but there was little or no progress towards economic equality. During the economic depression of the 1930s women lost ground as they were increasingly denied work on the grounds that jobs should go to men who have families to support. During World War Two more women were hired than ever before, often to jobs previously reserved for men (though at much

93

lower rates); but when the war ended many were again driven out of their jobs, while debate raged between the Freudians and other advocates of the "eternal feminine," who urged women to go back to the home, and social scientists like Mirra Komarovsky, who argued that it is good for women to work outside the home and good for their families if they do.

Chafe sees the new wave of feminism which emerged in the 1960s as ideologically very similar to the first wave, but as having a much greater depth and breadth of support than the old feminism ever enjoyed. Though World War Two did not move women toward real equality, it did act as a catalyst, enlarging women's economic role, altering previously fixed attitudes, and generally providing the preconditions for a powerful renewal of the drive for equality.

In **Women and Equality**, Chafe examines the interaction between sexual stereotypes and economic realities during the last three centuries. He argues that there has been very little change during that period in the prevailing stereotypes of masculinity and femininity, but that prior to industrialization the feminine stereotype did not prevent women from being both economically productive and relatively active in public life: " . . . a strangely distant relationship appears to have existed between the received cultural norms about woman's "place" and the actual content of most women's lives" (p.20) in the colonial period and the early decades of the nineteenth century. Only in the latter nineteenth and the twentieth centuries did the reality of most women's lives move closer to the stereotype, as the isolation of middle-class women from the work place enabled and/or forced them to devote most of their time to housework and childrearing.

This book also contains an especially useful chapter, "Sex and Race," in which Chafe considers the much used and much a-bused analogy between sexist and racist oppression in America. He admits that the analogy is a bad one in terms of the material conditions of (for example) blacks vs. those of white women; clearly, blacks in America have suffered more than women and have been more keenly aware of their oppressed status. Nevertheless, the analogy is useful as a way of revealing "the modes of control emanating from the dominant culture." (p.58) Both blacks and women, he argues, have been kept in their "place" by (1) physical intimidation; (2) white male control over their economic status; (3) the psychological power of white males to persuade the culture of certain definitions and limitations on the capacities of blacks and women; and finally (4) by the control exercised in self-defense by blacks and women over their own kind.

CHASTITY AND THE DOUBLE STANDARD "Chastity" refers either to complete sexual abstinence, or to virginity before marriage plus sexual fidelity thereafter. Often, the avoidance of masturbation or any other form of sexual self-stimulation is also implied. However it is defined, chastity is a virtue which has usually been demanded of women more than men. The Old Testament mandated death by stoning for a female adulteress, but recommended no particular penalty for the man involved. Plato, on the other hand, proposed (hetero) sexual abstinence for both men and women of the guardian class (except on special state-planned occasions), both for eugenic reasons and because he viewed physical eroticism as an inferior form of love; and Aristotle also rejected the double standard, at least within marriage.

St. Paul and the fathers of the Church (e.g. Jerome, Tertullian, and Augustine) considered all intercourse to be contaminated by original sin, and thus held that lifelong virginity was morally preferable to even the most proper marriage. Thomas Aquinas held the same views. The apparent sexual symmetry of these views is belied by the fact that these thinkers also considered women to be morally weaker and more vulnerable to sexual temptation than men, and hence held that they should be kept strictly under the control of their husbands if they are married, or of their parents or other guardians if unmarried.

The secular (male) philosophers of the Enlightenment, on the other hand, tended to defend the sexual double standard on pragmatic grounds, such as that it provides men an assurance of the paternity of their heirs (Hume), and enables women to influence and manipulate men to their own advantage (Rousseau). Indeed, in the period before there were effective contraceptive methods, it was neither uncommon nor unreasonable for feminists to advocate chastity as the way in which unmarried women must protect their health and freedom, and married women limit the frequency of their pregnancies. These recommendations were often accompanied by the assurance that women feel much less sexual desire than men, and thus find it easier to practice continence. (See Wollstonecraft, Fuller, Mill, Taylor, Gilman.)

The overriding value of chastity was questioned in the nineteenth century by a few radical feminists. (See Goldman, Fourier.) The view that chastity is a natural feminine virtue was challenged by the matriarchy theorists, who held that in the primordial state of human society general promiscuity or "group marriage" was the rule, and that men later instituted monogamous marriage and the sexual double standard, in order to secure male heirs of their own begetting to whom to leave their names and property. (See Bachofen, Morgan, Engels, Briffault; also Matriarchy Theory.)

In the present century, Christian and other religious arguments for chastity continue to be made. A more influential point of view, however, has been that of the Freudian school. Freud considered the repression of sexual impulses in early childhood to be the cause of a variety of types of neurosis in later life; at the same time, sexual sublimation is necessary for the formation of the ego and hence for civilization itself. Since Freud also thought that the sexual impulse of the female was weaker than that of the male, it followed that females have less well-developed egos and must play a lesser role in civilization. (Also see Bonaparte, Deutsch, Reich, Unwin.)

Recent scientific research has tended to discredit these Freudian views. The findings of Kinsey, Masters and Johnson, and others have exploded the myth of the lesser sexual capacity of the female, while failing to find any evidence that the repression or sublimation of the sex drive enhances either moral development or intellectual creativity. Many of the radical feminists of today reject the notion that chastity is a virtue for anyone, and hold that sexual freedom for all, and the elimination of all sexual taboos, is a necessary condition for the liberation of women. (See Firestone, Greer, Sherfey.)

CHESLER, Phyllis. *Women and Madness* (Avon, New York, 1972)

An important feminist critique of psychiatry and its contribution to women's enslavement. Patriarchal culture, Chesler argues, conditions women to be self-destructive, to sacrifice their individual identities to motherhood and the service of man. Demeter and Persephone are symbols of this sacrifice of self which culture and their own biology demand of women. Most of the women whom psychiatrists label mentally ill are not mad; they are either acting out this feminine role too well, or departing from it too markedly. Female psychiatric patients are punished—shocked, drugged, exploited as cheap labor and as sex objects—for their self-destructive i.e. hyper-"feminine" behavior. They are "sick" because they have accepted the "sick" role, which is a feminine prerogative in our culture. In becoming "sick" they are accepting their sex-role stereotype "in too deadly a manner."

Much of the book consists of interviews with women psychiatric patients, and with lesbians, Third World women and feminist women, many but not all of whom have been patients. Chesler views lesbianism as a healthy and superior alternative to submission to men and motherhood in the patriarchal family. Women will not be free of the self-destructive behaviors that lead to "madness" until their ties to biological reproduction and the family are severed. Science must be used either to release women from biological motherhood, or to enable men to experience the process also. The image of the Amazon, the woman warrior, is presented as an inspiring (and, Chesler thinks, historically real) instance not of female equality but of female domination. Equality she believes to be impossible, either in the family or in society, between women and men who have been raised and conditioned within a male surpemacist culture. What is necessary for women's freedom is that women gradually come to dominate all public social institutions, to gain control of the means of production and reproduction, and then to ensure that these will no longer be used against women. When women are warriors, they will achieve the radical psychological reorientation which will enable them to strive for various powers directly, and not through a man or a family.

CHRISTIANITY Christianity emerged from the patriarchal Greek and Hebrew traditions, is devoted to a divinity conceptualized as masculine, and has for the most part lent its support to patriarchal ideas and institutions. Christ himself, as reported in the New Testament, seems to have little or nothing to say about the equality or inequality of the sexes, although he also seems to have behaved as if he considered women at least the spiritual equals of men. (See The Bible.) Unfortunately, it was not the founder's example, but the patriarchal pronouncements of Paul of Tarsus which became established as Christian dogma. The church fathers (e.g. Clement, Jerome, Tertullian, Augustine) not only defended male rule in the Church and the family, but considered women morally weaker and more sinful than men. The great scholastic theologian Aquinas made use of Aristotle's dictum that a woman is a misbegotten man, to support similar conclusions.

Even in the modern era, few (male) Christian theologians have seriously challenged the patriarchal aspects of the tradition.

Since the eighteenth century and even earlier, there have, however, been feminists who have sought to reinterpret both the spirit and the letter of the Scriptures in a more sexually egalitarian manner. (See Astell, Wollstonecraft, Grimke, Stanton, Daly, Jewett, and Letty Russell.) Others, especially in this century, have rejected the entire Judeo-Christian tradition as antiwoman, and have sought religious inspiration elsewhere (See Gilman, Daly [in her later work], Ruether, Stone.) Still other feminists, perhaps the majority in our own time, find no need either to reconcile feminism and Christianity, or to develop alternative religious perspectives, simply because their own moral philosophy is firmly grounded in secular concepts. (See also Goddesses, and Spiritual Feminism.)

D

DALY, Mary. *The Church and the Second Sex* (Harper and Row, New York, 1975; first published 1968)
Beyond God the Father: Toward a Philosophy of Women's Liberation (Beacon Press, Boston, 1974)
Gyn/Ecology: The Metaethics of Radical Feminism (Beacon Press, Boston, 1978)

Mary Daly is one of the most important contemporary theorists of what has been termed spiritual feminism. She has represented, at earlier and later stages in the development of her thought, both the reformist wing of spiritual feminism, which seeks to eliminate the elements of male supremacy with the established (Christian) churches; and the revolutionary wing, which rejects Christianity and the Judeo-Christian God as inherently male supremacist, and seeks inspiration in prepatriarchal Goddess-centered religions, and in the tradition of Wicce (so-called witchcraft).

In *The Church and the Second Sex*, Daly attempts to dissociate the basic core of Catholic Christian doctrine from the sexist uses and interpretations to which it has been subjected throughout the ages. She agrees with Simone de Beauvoir's criticism of the Church, that it has repressed sexuality, condemned women to passivity and subordination, and equated the male sex with the divine; but she rejects Sartre's position (which de Beauvoir also accepts), that belief in God is inseparable from belief in an immutable human nature. She also denies that the Genesis story of the creation of Eve was intended to teach the subordination of woman to man, pointing out that woman's subordination and the sexual division of labor are not mentioned in connection with the creation, but as consequences of the fall. She even defends the Pauline texts, with their notorious injunctions to women to be silent in church and obedient to their husbands, as primarily concerned with the maintenance of social order and respectability, rather than with the defense of patriarchy as such.

The fact remains, she says, that for two millennia these Judeo-Christian doctrines and stories have been used to justify the exclusion of women from most positions of responsibility and respect in the Church as in society. The Virgin Mary has been held up as a model for all women, the image of the Eternal Feminine. This image is flattering to men but it is static, hardly an inspiration for change. Catholic theology, Daly contends, must be "exorcized" of such elements of androcentrism. There has always been a circular relationship between the misogynism of Christian societies and that of the Church; but Daly sees hope in some of the statements of Pope John XXIII, and in the widespread demand for reforms within the Church. The most important reform will be the admission of women to all offices in the Church, including the priesthood. Also necessary is the rejection of the notion that God is male, and of the sin-haunted view of life that has distorted Christian doctrines. Given such changes, Daly claims, we can still look to Catholic theology for a useful philosophy of growth and liberation, which is equally applicable to both sexes.

By the time she wrote *Beyond God the Father*, however (as she explains in her "post Christian Introduction" to the 1975 edition of *The Church and the Second Sex*), Daly was no longer a Catholic or a Christian. She criticizes her earlier self for failing to see that sexism is inherent to the symbol system of Christianity and that there is no hope for equality for women in the church (a word she no longer capitalizes). She now thinks that scholarly reintegration of the Biblical texts cannot possibly change the overwhelmingly patriarchal and misogynous character of the Biblical tradition. The church is sexually hierarchical to its core. The new perspective is (more clearly) that of radical feminism. Sexism is seen as society's deepest problem, a disease which is at the heart of racism and of dogmatic doctrines like Christianity.

Daly now makes a major point of the use of liberated language, a process she speaks of as the "castration" of older linguistic forms which are reflections of a sexist world. Women are learning to live in "a new space and time," located on the boundary of patriarchal institutions but shaped by their own comprehension of reality. She speaks of this as women's "second coming," and as the Antichrist, which will bring about the end of "phallic morality." It is a *second* coming by reference to the ancient age of matriarchy described by Elizabeth Gould Davis. It is antichrist because Christianity has almost always lowered the status of women, and because the very concept of Christ as God-man is oppressive to women. Phallic morality is the major ethical tradition of our culture, in which certain of the qualities imposed on the oppressed (meekness, servility, etc.) have been hypocritically idealized, a process which conceals the actual values and motivations which are operative in patriarchal society (competitiveness, domination, expediency, etc.). Phallic morality leads to the glorification of motherhood and the prohibition of abortion or contraception, and to rape, genocide and war. Because phallic morality is built into the church, the new feminist movement is antichurch. It is nevertheless identifiable, according to Daly, as God, or the "final cause," because it is the only social movement that points the way to a nonaggressive and nonhierarchial society.

In her most recent book **Gyn/Ecology**, Daly places still more distance between herself and Christian theology. She no longer uses the term *God*, for, she says, its androcentric and life-denying implications are part of the core of its meaning.

> *God* represents the necrophilia of patriarchy, whereas *Goddess* affirms the life loving be-ing of women and nature. (p.xi)

Gyn/Ecology deals with the process of escaping from patriarchal ideology in all its forms, and with the rediscovery of what Daly calls "the radical be-ing of women." (p.1) This be-ing of women is the Goddess within; it is a verb rather than a noun (see **Beyond God the Father**, p.33). Its rediscovery requires a journey into the "Background," i.e. toward a comprehension of reality which is free of the reifications and mystifications of patriarchal thought.

Patriarchal mind control, Daly argues, operates in a variety of ways, including the outright erasure of women and women's history—as illustrated by the burning of some nine million witches, most of them women, during the so-called Renaissance in Europe. It also operates by reversing reality; the more blatant the lie, it seems, the more effective the tactic. Thus, the myth of Adam's giving birth to Eve is a reversal of biological reality; and the subordinate Virgin Mary is a reversal of the original image of the Goddess and her subordinate son. Similarly, under patriarchy,

> The Tree of Life (one of the symbols of the Goddess) has been replaced by the necrophilic symbol of a dead body hanging on dead wood. (p.18)

The purpose of patriarchal mind control, Daly holds, is gynocide, i.e. the murder of women and/or of the free selves within them. Gynocide is necessary for the appropriation by males of women's creative energy, which is perhaps the most fundamental motivation of patriarchy. The patriarchal attitude towards abortion is instructive. Patriarchal males, she says, identify with fetuses, because like fetuses they feed on the energy of women.

But it is not only women's biological power of reproduction which men envy and seek to control, as Karen Horney maintains. It is "female creative energy in *all* of its dimensions." (p.60)

The patriarchal act of gynocide is accomplished in part by mind-bending myths and other conceptual traps, such as false polarization (e.g. masculinity/femininity). It is also accomplished through sadistic violence, ritually directed against women (sado-rituals). Sado-rituals are reenactments of Goddess-murder; they include the Indian *suttee* (the traditional "suicide" of a widow, by leaping or being thrown into her husband's funeral pyre); Chinese footbinding; the genital mutilations still practiced on women in many parts of Africa; the European witch burnings; and, finally, the American institution of gynecology (i.e. the medical treatment of women, as such, whether physiological or psychological). Gynecology belongs on this list of gynocidal atrocities by virtue of its history of abusive "treatments," from the clitoridectomies and female castrations of the nineteenth and even the first half of the twentieth century to the current epidemic of unnecessary breast surgery and hysterectomy.

Daly argues that each of these sado-ritual practices follows a similar pattern. The atrocities are performed in the name of the "purity" of women (or to purify society of impure women). Always there is an erasure of male responsibility, either through the cloak of divine sanction or scientific objectivity, or through the use of women to inflict torture on other women. There is an obsession with orderliness and with the repetition of minute acts which serves to obscure the horror of the act. Through these processes gynocidal behavior becomes socially acceptable and indeed normative; and male scholarship completes the process by legitimating and/or minimizing the significance of these ritual atrocities.

Unlike many radical feminists (e.g. Mitchell, Firestone, Dinnerstein), who consider that a modified Freudian theory can help explain the internalization of oppression within the patriarchal family, Daly rejects all psychoanalytic theories as mind-bending myths. The *seemingly* egalitarian Jungian notions of animus and anima are in reality "pernicious traps which often stop women in the initial stages of journeying." (p.253) Freud she describes as,

> an Earthly Representative of the Divine Spirit-Eraser and as model for the procession of therapeutic erasers who have succeeded him, erasing as deeply as possible the pre-possessed patient's Self. (p.267)

Indeed, Daly argues, all forms of psychological "therapy" are inherently oppressive. Hence, "the very concept of 'feminist therapy' is . . . a contradiction." (p.282)

Because patriarchy is the ruling force in all parts of the world, liberation will require a global revolution. This revolution will spring from the affirmation of freedom which is fostered by radical friendship among women. The friendship of Sisters (and of Hags, Crones, Amazons and other free women) is unlike male comradeship in that it accentuates the freedom and individuality of each woman. This is the significance of Lesbian love, which threatens patriarchy by defying the sadomasochistic pattern of institutionalized heterosexuality. Love and friendship between women (which are not sharply distinct) span the "split consciousness" which is the source of male sadism. They are the antitheses of

> the normal mode of existence of the patriarchal male, who is unable to relate to the inner mystery, integrity, Self of the Other, unable to connect with the originally moving be-ing. (p.387)

The feminist, or gyn/ecological revolution will be the work of Spinsters, i.e. free, self-defined women who will create new worlds—conceptual, artistic, social and political—in Daly's words, new time/spaces. Their task is to break the grip of patriarchal myth and ritual upon the human consciousness. The intensity of their individual creative energy makes success possible, in spite of the relatively small numbers of such Spinsters.

DARWIN, Charles (1809–1882). *The Descent of Man and Selection in Relation to Sex* (D. Appleton, New York and London, 1874; first published 1871)

Darwin's epoch-making defense of the theory of natural selection or the "survival of the fittest" was presented in *The Origin of Species* (1859). Natural selection is the motive force behind the evolution of all living organisms, the process whereby maladaptive variations are eliminated through the tendency of such individuals to perish early, while those exhibiting more adaptive variations survive to pass these traits to their progeny. Darwin distinguished between *natural* selection, which results from environmental pressures acting on the species as a whole, and *sexual* selection, which results when certain individuals of one sex gain an advantage over others of that sex with respect to reproductive success. *The Descent of Man and Selection in Relation to Sex* (a later work) presents a wealth of evidence and examples of the effects of sexual selection on the secondary sexual characteristics of creatures ranging from crabs, fish and reptiles to birds, mammals and finally "man."

Darwin observed that it is usually (though not always) the males of a species who compete with one another for sexual access to the females, either by fighting to establish dominance or by increasing their attractiveness to females, through improvements of appearance or courtship and display. Consequently it is almost always the males of a species who develop the more marked secondary sexual characteristics, e.g. special colors, markings or courting behaviors designed (as it were) to attract the favor of females; or special weapons such as spurs or antlers, designed to defeat other males of the species rather than to capture prey or defend against predators. Depending on the "mode of inheritance," these male-acquired traits may or may not also be acquired by the female (1). Hence the males of a species are usually more specialized, less like the ancestral stock than the females.

As for why it is generally the males of a species who compete for access to the females, rather than the other way around, Darwin has no answer except that males usually have "stronger passions" than females, i.e. are more eager for sex, while females are usually more "coy." (As an explanation this verges on circularity.) But whatever the cause of this greater male competitiveness, its result is that males are subjected to a much more intense process of sexual selection; and Darwin thought that this is as true of humankind as of other species. In general, male mammals tend to compete for females by doing battle with one another, rather than by displaying their charms before the females in order to influence their choice, as with male birds. Men, like the males of other primate species, have in this way been sexually selected for size, strength and combativeness—and also, Darwin thought, for intelligence. "Man," he says, "is more courageous, pugnacious and energetic than woman, and has a more inventive genius." (pp.568–569)

Needless to say, it does not follow from the fact (and it probably is a fact) that men tend to be more "pugnacious" than women, that they also are more intelligent; fighting requires a limited range of mental capacities. But Darwin takes the mental superiority of the male as evident (2), and holds that "higher powers of imagination and reason" were developed in men, "partly through sexual selection—that is, through the contest of rival males, and partly through natural selection—that is, from success in the general struggle for life." (p.577) This line of reasoning overlooks the fact that women must also have been selected for intelligence, since mental acuteness would not only have improved their own chances of surviving but—perhaps to a much greater degree than in the case of men—those of their offspring.

Although Darwin rejected the Lamarckian hypothesis, that traits acquired through habit can be inherited by offspring, as the *sole* or *primary* mechanism of evolution, he did not reject it outright. Some acquired traits he thought, can be inherited, and furthermore those which are acquired late in an animal's development are more apt to be passed on to members of the same sex than those which are acquired early. Thus men's powers of reason have been "transmitted more fully to the male than the female offspring" (p.577) in part because they tended to be acquired late, through the struggles that occur during maturity. On the other hand, he suggests that the same principle might be exploited to improve women's intellectual abilities:

> In order that woman should reach the same standard as man, she ought, when nearly adult, to be trained to energy and persever-ance, and to have her reason and imagination exercised to the highest point; and then she would probably transmit these quali-ties chiefly to her adult daughters. (p.578)

This suggestion illustrates the extent of Darwin's confusion about the inheritance of acquired traits; but it also shows that in spite of the unreflective ease with which he presumed the inherent mental superiority of the male (3), he does not make the mistake, so common among contemporary popularizers of evolutionary and sociobiological theories, of supposing that if some aspect of male supremacy is "natural," that is explicable in terms of general biological laws, then it must also be inevitable, and not worth trying to change.

1. Darwin had originally thought that the male-acquired traits would at first be transmitted to both sexes, but that they would gradually disappear in the female sex because of the greater dangers to which females are exposed in bearing and rearing the young. Later observations, however, led him to conclude that the mode of inheritance of sexually selected traits cannot easily be altered. That is, traits which are acquired by males through sexual selection and which are originally passed only to males will continue to be passed only to males, even if potentially beneficial to females, while those originally passed to both sexes will continue to be passed to both sexes even if actually detrimental to females.

2. "The chief distinction in the intellectual powers of the sexes," Darwin says, "is shown by man's attaining to a higher excellence in whatever he takes up, than can woman—whether

requiring deep thought, reason, or imagination, or merely the use of the senses and hands." (p.576)
3. The white male, in fact; for Darwin also assumed that "the ancient races stand somewhat nearer in the long line of descent to their remote animal-like progenitors." (p.26)

DAVIS, Elizabeth Gould (1910–1974). *The First Sex* (Penguin Books, Baltimore, Maryland, 1973; first published 1971 by G.P. Putnam's Sons)

One of the boldest of the "early matriarchy" theories, this work combines extensive scholarship with unfettered speculation. The result is probably closer to myth than to history—a fact which would not dismay Davis, who believed, after Bachofen and Briffault, that mythology contains clues to otherwise long forgotten periods of human history. Society, she holds, was matriarchal from its beginnings; that is, culturally, politically and economically dominated by women, and goddess-worshiping. Contemporary civilizations are descended from a single great Mediterranean culture which flourished and fell some ten thousand years ago, and whose "ancient mariners" sailed the globe, mapping it and establishing outposts as far away as Polynesia.

This great matriarchal civilization was destroyed by a worldwide cataclysm, the nature of which is unknown (though Davis favors Velikovsky's theory of shifting poles and/or worldwide drought). A dark age ensued, but some remnants of the old culture survived and flowered again in Anatolia (Asia Minor), Crete, Sumer, Egypt, Athens, Carthage, Etruria and Rome, all of which were matriarchal within recorded history. But, for reasons which Davis does not clarify, a patriarchal revolution occurred. It involved the switch, sometimes sudden and violent and sometimes by gradual stages, from the worship of the mother goddess to harsher male deities, and from matrilineality to patrilineality in the inheritance of names, power and property. Although these changes began before the Christian era, women retained a position of relative freedom and respect throughout the Classical period of Greece and Rome. The radically misogynist attitudes characteristic of the Christian era were inherited from the Hebrews. Not until Constantine's conversion and the spread of Christianity throughout Europe did women's status sink to that of a despised slave, subject to the vilest abuses and outside the protection of the law. The Church deprived women of human status and throughout the Middle Ages they were murdered, tortured and executed in vast numbers for heresies that often consisted soley in stepping outside the lowly place to which they were assigned.

The age of patriarchy, however, is now drawing to a close. The new Aquarian age will see a revival of women's powers, including their supernatural and extrasensory powers, which Davis thinks were highly developed in the ancient matriarchies, and which she predicts will again be central to the science and technology of the next civilization. Matriarchy and the worship of the great goddess will return, and with them reason, humanity, and a new golden age.

A visionary work such as this should, perhaps, be forgiven for failing to separate fact from fantasy. What is harder to forgive is the failure to ask difficult questions from a feminist point of view. For instance, what reason is there to think that goddess worship is a sign of female domination, rather than just an earlier stage in man's depiction of woman as Other? (See Simone de Beauvoir) Are women really much better off in matrilineal societies? And must we assume that the only alternative to patriarchy is matriarchy? (Also see Matriarchy Theory.)

de BEAUVOIR, Simone. *The Second Sex* (translated and edited by H.M. Parshley, Bantam Books, New York, 1952; originally published in France by Librairie Gallimand, in two volumes, as *Le Deuxieme Sexe: I. Les Faits et les Mythes; II. L'Experience Vecue*, 1949)

This is perhaps the most profound analysis of the situation of women which has yet appeared, and certainly one of the most influential. Simone de Beauvoir is well known for her lifelong association with her fellow existentialist Jean Paul Sartre, but she has won independent recognition as a philosopher, novelist and autobiographer (1). In *The Second Sex*, she uses the concepts of (nontheistic) existentialism to illuminate the origin, nature and phenomenology of male domination. The thesis is that woman has always been defined by man as the Other, the inessential, while man himself is defined as the One, the Subject, the being capable of trandscendence—of free, independent, and creative activity. The paradigm human, in other words, is conceived as male, and the female as a deviation from this norm:

> man represents both the positive and the neutral, as is indicated by the common use of *man* to designate human being in general; whereas woman represents only the negative, defined by limiting criteria, without reciprocity. (p.xv)

The concept of the Other is a Hegelian one, and it is central to the existential philosophy of Sartre and de Beauvoir. It is, in de Beauvoir's words, "a fundamental category of human thought" (p.xvii), "as primordial as consciousness itself" (p.xvi). To be conscious is to be aware of oneself as a subject, as the One, which in turn is necessarily to be aware of *other* subjects, though not necessarily *as* subjects. Fear of others leads the existent to (tend to) see them as Others, as inferiors, and as objects rather than subjects. Hence, there is a fundamental imperialism in human consciousness, which, for de Beauvoir, is the key to understanding man's domination of woman.

> following Hegel we find in consciousness itself a fundamental hostility toward every other consciousness; the subject can be posed only in being opposed—he sets himself up as the essential, as opposed to the other, the inessential, the object. (p.xvii)

This tendency to objectify others, other individuals and other groups, can be overcome; reciprocity, the mutual recognition of one another as free beings, is possible and to some extent present among *men* (of the same nation, race, village, etc.). But when men say "we," when they think of themselves as peers who are in some sense equal, they do not include women in this "we"; woman remains "the absolute Other, without reciprocity." The situation is in no way symmetrical, since women do not say "we" in the same way. They do not pose themselves as the One and men as the Other, thus setting up a world view competitive with that of men. Instead, they generally accept the male viewpoint as their own and conceive of themselves as men conceive of them— as inessential, unfree and passive.

Why, de Beauvoir asks, has this asymmetrical situation come about? "It is easy to see that the duality of the sexes, like any duality, gives rise to conflict. But why should men have won from the start?" (p.xxi) The answer is to be found not in women's biology or their psychology *per se*, but in their life situation. Women have, nearly always, *chosen* to accept the male definition of themselves and their role, and, since they are free beings whether or not they conceive of themselves as such, nothing could ever really force them to make that choice—they could always, in the extreme case, die rather than submit. Yet the choice must be made within a life situation in which numerous biological and cultural factors conspire to present women with a powerful *temptation* to make the inauthentic choice—accepting the traditional, passive, secondary and purely immanent (non-transcendent) role of woman.

Of the factors contributing to the asymmetry of the life situations of women and men, the biological ones are by no means the least important. De Beauvoir maintains that, for a variety of reasons, the biological and sexual nature of the male is much more easily integrated into his individual human identity than in the case of the female. In the sex act itself, for instance, the male animal is more active, the female more acted upon:

> Even when she is willing, or provocative, it is unquestionably the male who *takes* the female—she is taken . . . Her body becomes a resistance to be broken through, whereas in penetrating it the male finds self-fulfillment in activity. (pp.18–19)

Furthermore, in the changes undergone by her body—in puberty, menstruation, pregnancy, childbirth, lactation and finally menopause, "The female is the victim of the species." (p.18) For these are essentially processes which are undergone, not actions which are performed, and yet they absorb a great deal of a woman's energy and attention. Thus, a woman's sexual nature competes with her individual freedom and identity, while "the male on the contrary integrates the specific vital forces into his individual life." (p.21) His biological role in reproduction takes relatively little of his time and strength, and it can more readily be experienced as action, as an expression of the individual will, rather than a process passively undergone. And, finally, the greater size and strength of the male is significant because it means that women are less able "to learn the lesson of violence," to feel secure in the knowledge that if necessary they can defend themselves with blows, to "feel their transcendence in their fists." Because of woman's relative physical weakness, "Her grasp on the world is . . . more restricted." (p.31)

But, as de Beauvoir emphasizes again and again, none of these biological factors actually *force* women to make the inauthentic choice. A woman today who is committed to an active and independent existence need not be unduly hampered by her biology. It is rather that woman's biology has invariably led men to see her as the Other, while hampering her enough to enable this male point of view to prevail. There has never been a true matriarchy. Engels is right to hold that the rise of private property facilitated the oppression of women; but woman has always been the Other. Had this not been the case, the institutions of private property could not have led to her downfall.

> If the human consciousness had not included the original category of the Other and an original aspiration to dominate the Other, the invention of the bronze tool could not have caused the oppression of woman. (p.52)

Engel's theory therefore presupposes male supremacy rather than explaining it. The same is true of Freud's theory that penis envy is the key to feminine nature; the (symbolic) significance of the male organ is a result of the superior social status and power of the male, not vice versa.

The imperialism of consciousness, plus the biological handicaps of women, have always and everywhere led to male domination; even when woman was worshiped in the abstract as the giver of life, she was still the Other, and political power was still in male hands. The coming of private property did mean that women became economically dependent on men, thus increasing the oppressiveness of marriage and the family. As economic dependents women can achieve social status, security and political efficacy only indirectly, through men. To choose independence may mean poverty and social stigma. Hence marriage, in spite of the inevitable loss of independence, of authentic existence, which it means for a woman, is a terrible temptation to a woman, and "she will need to make a greater moral effort than would a man in choosing the road of independence" (p.127).

If women's submission to the male definition of woman is due to bad faith, so too is men's desire to make them submit. All existents need other existents around them to enable them to experience their own transcendence. But men experience the freedom of other men as continually threatening, while at the same time they feel in their own free existence a disquieting nothingness, a painful alienation from nature and mere immanent existence. Hence man dreams of finding, in woman, on the one hand a conscious being who is at the same time passive and nonthreatening, and on the other hand a bridge between himself and nature, through the possession of which he will regain his wholeness. Seen as the Other, woman

> opposes him with neither the hostile silence of nature nor the hard requirement of a reciprocal relation; through a unique privilege she is a conscious being and yet it seems possible to possess her in the flesh. (p.130)

God created Eve for the benefit of Adam and therefore she appeared to him "in the guise of privileged prey . . . She was nature elevated to the transparency of consciousness; she was a conscious being, but naturally submissive." (p.131)

Because the concept of the Other is itself inconsistent (since no conscious being is naturally passive), woman is inevitably seen as radically ambiguous and indeed contradictory in nature. She is virgin or whore, guardian angel or evil witch, but never simply a fellow human creature with a human mixture of good and bad qualities. Paradoxically, by seeking to encounter nature through her, man dooms her to artifice; for unless she is youthful, and beautiful in a conventionalized way, she will represent to him not the good and bountiful aspects of nature, but its fearful, death-dealing aspects. This is why "The old woman, the homely woman, are not merely objects without allure—they arouse hatred mingled with fear." (p.149) It is also why women are seen as treacherous and fickle. As the Other woman is essentially evil, capable of achieving goodness and worth only through total submission; any independence on her part must therefore seem ominous and threatening.

There is, however, a factor in this dialectic which facilitates woman's gradual emancipation. Man's project with respect to woman is ultimately self-defeating, since by subjugating her he deprives her of what originally made her valuable to him:

> With woman integrated into the family and in society, her magic is dissipated rather than transformed; reduced to the condition of a servant, she is no longer that unconquered prey incarnating all the treasures of nature. (p.175)

For this reason, love and marriage can rarely coexist. Deprived of her own freedom, a woman will inevitably wish to restrict the man's freedom in return. She will seek both to share in his transcendence, to live in the world through him, and to limit it by keeping him at her side or under her influence as much as possible. Her submission therefore becomes a heavy burden, which can be relieved only by ending the relationship or increasing its reciprocity. The more civilized man, therefore, will want a woman who is not merely a slave.

> Such a recognition is necessary if genuine love between the sexes is to exist. What passes for love is generally an inauthentic, idolatrous relation in which each makes impossible demands on the other. Insofar as love is the most important thing in a woman's life, and the source of her sense of worth, while it is only one part of a man's life, she will inevitably demand more devotion than he can provide, and be disappointed as a result. Because he must idealize her as better than all other women, in order to justify joining himself to a member of an inferior class, he will inevitably be embittered by the discovery of her actual human characteristics. Real love is possible only when the woman, like the man, is personally and economically independent. It must be founded on the mutual recognition of two liberties; the lovers would then experience themselves both as self and as other: neither would give up transcendence, neither would be mutilated; together they would manifest values and aims in the world. (p.628)

This, de Beauvoir points out, is one reason why some rebellious women choose lesbianism; for it is very often difficult or impossible for the independent woman to find a man "whom she can regard as an equal without his considering himself superior." (p.652)

Whether lesbian or heterosexual, the free woman must be economically independent, and she must avoid not only marriage but motherhood—the latter being a function which de Beauvoir (herself a principled nonmother) says is almost impossible, under the present circumstances, for a woman to perform in freedom. What is most important is that she fully assumes her own liberty, that like an artist she "passionately lose herself in her projects," in order to find herself in action and transcendence, rather than in what she appears to others to be.

The Second Sex is arguably the greatest work of feminist theory in existence. As Shulamith Firestone remarks, de Beauvoir comes close to presenting the definitive analysis of male domination. Its weaknesses are primarily those of the existentialist metaphysics and psychology in which it is couched. One may wonder, for instance, whether the Hegelian doctrine of the imperialism of consciousness—the claim that every human consciousness is originally and fundamentally hostile to every other—is not simply empirically false. At any rate its truth or falsity can only be decided by empirical investigation; it is surely not a logical truth, or deducible from (the concept of) consciousness itself, since a fundamentally empathic, nonhostile (yet free) consciousness is at least conceivable. Perhaps, as Firestone suggests, the general tendency of men to view women as the Other is a *result* of the practical significance of her biological nature, rather than vice versa, as de Beauvoir would have it. It is, however, extremely difficult to say just what evidence would bear on the solution of this chicken-and-egg problem.

More seriously, perhaps, de Beauvoir is often charged with placing too much emphasis and value on the so-called "masculine" virtues of transcendence, independence, creativity, intellect and achievement, and too little on such "feminine" virtues as nurturance, empathy and intuition, on the capacity to *enjoy* merely immanent existence. (See Buytendijk.) Many women resist and resent the suggestion that women's liberation requires the emulation of the male, in any respect whatever. But, while the criticism is not entirely without point, de Beauvoir *could* reply—though she does not use just these terms—that her position is not that women, or men, should avoid nurturance, empathy, and so on through the list of "feminine" virtues—those which are real virtues and not manifestations of slavishness or incapacity—but rather that to confine oneself to these virtues alone is to be false to one's nature as a free being; and this claim is relatively difficult to dispute.

1. The novels include *She Came to Stay* (1943), *The Blood of Others* (1945), *All Men are Mortal* (1947), *The Mandarins* (1954), and *Les Belles Images* (1968). De Beauvoir's autobiography has been published in four volumes—*Memoirs of a Dutiful Daughter, The Prime of Life, Force of Circumstance*, and *All Said and Done*—from 1958 to 1972. *A Very Easy Death* (1967) is an account of her mother's death by cancer, in a sterile hospital setting. *The Ethics of Ambiguity* (1947) deals with the atheist-existentialist view of moral values. *The Coming of Age* (1970) is an exploration and indictment of society's attitudes towards old people.

de CASTILLEJO, Irene Claremont. *Knowing Woman: A Feminine Psychology* (Harper and Row, New York, 1974; first published 1973, by G.P. Putnam's Sons, New York)

This is a explication of certain Jungian ideas. The author advises women to "get in touch" with their masculine side, or animus, but only in order to better realize their essential femininity. Femininity is defined (after Neumann) in terms of "diffuse awareness," masculinity in terms of "focused consciousness." Feminine consciousness involves a passive taking-in, rather than an active effort to understand or analyze, which is a masculine characteristic. Thus,

> the feminine, in a far greater degree than the nothing-but masculine, is subjected to numinous elements in nature . . . [and] its relation to nature and to God is more familiar and intimate. (p.62)

Women today, say the Jungians, are in danger of losing their femininity, both because Western culture stresses the masculine at the expense of the feminine, and because they are competing with men in formerly all-male professions. De Castillejo warns women that they cannot compete successfully with men, since, with very rare exceptions, a woman's intellect "is inferior to that of a man. It is apt to be less original and less creative." (p.110) Women's most important role in life is to help inspire *men* to creative achievement, by "mediating" between men and their own unconscious psyches. Woman is "to be a mediator to man of his own creative inspirations, a channel whereby the riches of the unconscious can flow to him more easily." (pp.54–55)

To perform this role, a woman must have a working relationship with her own animus, or rather with the several distinct masculine personalities through which the animus manifests itself. The helpful animus can give her "focus," enabling her to express her feminine insights. But the menacing animus, who tells her she is worthless, and the authoritarian animus, who represents unreflective adherence to traditional opinions, must be confronted and deprived of their power. Thus, a woman's task is

> a peculiarly difficult one. She needs the focused consciousness her animus alone can give her, yet she must not forsake her woman's role of mediator to the man. Through a woman, man finds his soul . . .Through a woman, not through a pseudo-man . . . (p.86)

As is noted elsewhere in this book (see C.G. Jung), the essential and insurmountable difficulty with this type of theory is the complete absence of empirical support for the Jungian conception of the nature of masculine and feminine consciousness. This conception is a variation on the notion that men are rational and women emotional, a notion which Simone de Beauvoir has analyzed as the result of men's viewing woman as the Other, an inferior, not-quite-human being. Whatever its origin, the belief that men (of their nature) reason more, or better, while women are more emotional, intuitive and the like, is, on the best available evidence, false. There may perhaps be differences in the specific types of intellectual excellence characteristic of the sexes (e.g. males may "naturally" excel in mathematics, females in linguistic skills (1)), or in the specific types of emotion to which they are prone (e.g. males may tend to be more aggressive, for largely physiological reasons). But such specific differences in no way support the claim that "masculine consciousness" is naturally more "focused" and "feminine consciousness" more "diffuse" and emotional.

1. See, for instance, Eleanor Maccoby and Carol Jacklin, *The Psychology of Sex Differences*.

DECTER, Midge. *The Liberated Woman and Other Americans* (Coward, McCann and Geoghegan, New York, 1971)
The New Chastity and Other Arguments Against Women's Liberation (Capricorn Books, New York, 1972)
  The Liberated Woman and Other Americans is a collection of

essays, most of which were originally written for **Harper's Maga-zine** or **Commentary**, and most of which have little to do with feminism. The title essay, ''The Liberated Woman,'' depicts that person as a pampered middle-class ''girl'' who is bewildered by too much freedom and too little responsibility. The ideology of women's liberation appeals to her because it helps her to escape the freedom she does not know what to do with, by denying that women are now entirely free to decide whether or not to be wives, mothers or sex objects.

The New Chastity develops the same line of thought. Women can't really be as oppressed by marriage and motherhood as the liberationists maintain, since if they were they would not be so eager to marry and become mothers. Everyone knows that it is women who have to trap men into marriage rather than vice versa; ergo marriage must be a better deal for women than for men. The liberationists give women too little credit when they claim that women have had to be coerced and brainwashed into accepting the traditional roles. And, whatever may have been the case in the past, women today are entirely free to decide whom to sleep with, whom or whether to marry, and whether to pursue a career in addition to or instead of motherhood. What the femi-nists are really objecting to (whatever they may *say* they are objecting to) is this *surplus* of freedom. And the freedom they are most eager to reject is the freedom to engage in sexual relation-ships with men; they fear this freedom and therefore advocate a return to ''chastity,'' via lesbianism and the clitoral orgasm.

As for the feminists' claim that women must be freed from the responsibility for housework and child care, this is nothing but a self-indulgent and rather childish refusal to accept a reasonable share of responsibility. Women's connection to outside, paid labor is entirely voluntary, unlike men's. Women who work do so (at least if they are married) only because they want to, whereas men *have* to work (1); consequently women cannot complain if the housework continues to be their obligation. Decter does not consider the obvious alternative—by now incipient—of women undertaking more responsibility for financial support of the fam-ily at the same time that men undertake more responsibility for child care and housekeeping.

1.   See Kirsten Amundsen, **The Silenced Majority** for an exten-sive rebuttal of this claim.

DELANEY, Janice, and **LUPTON**, Mary Jane, and **TOTH**, Emily. *The Curse: A Cultural History of Menstruation* (New American Library, New York, 1977)

A feminist study of cultural attitudes towards menstruation, from primitive men's nearly universal fear of contamination by menstrual blood, which led to the seclusion of menstruating women in isolated huts, to the recent pronouncement by a member of the national Democratic leadership that women's raging hormones render them unfit to hold high office. Throughout history, and no doubt in prehistoric times as well, men have played "menstrual politics"; that is, they have invented and exploited a multitude of myths about the dangerousness, uncleanliness, madness, viciousness and so on of the menstruating women, in order to justify the exclusion of women from any role or status which they preferred to reserve for their own sex. "Menstrual politics," the authors conclude, "has dominated social and political relations between the sexes since the beginning of time." (p.55)

Although men continue to seize on women's menstrual cycle as proof of their inferiority and unsuitability for various occupations, there is no evidence that all or even most women suffer significant physical or mental impairment during the menses. Of course, the authors admit, there are various mental and physical symptoms connected with menstruation; this is especially true of the premenstrual phase, when some degree of bloatedness, lethargy, irritability or depression is frequent enough to be considered normal. But such symptoms can be reduced and their negative significance lessened as women develop a more affirmative and informed attitude towards the menstrual process, and as science develops ways of making menstruation less of a nuisance, or of eliminating it entirely. They consider the process of menstrual extraction (in which the entire flow is painlessly removed in a few seconds, thus eliminating the bleeding) a promising technique, though one the dangers of which are still unknown. They think that, if it were not for the fact that most scientists are men, with a stake in maintaining the apparent superiority of men, they would probably have long since developed more effective ways of dealing with menstruation.

DEUTSCH, Helene. *The Psychology of Women: Volume I - Girlhood* (Bantam, New York, 1973; first published by Greene and Stratton, New York, 1944)
Volume II - Motherhood (Bantam, New York, 1973; first pub-

lished by Green and Stratton, New York, 1945)

Deutsch is a disciple of Freud who worked with him in Vienna from 1918 to 1933. Her *Psychology of Women*, which was published in this country during the Second World War, greatly expands and in some ways modifies Freud's theory of female psychology. Her position is in some respects more "Freudian" than that of Freud himself, for instance in her insistence that the essence of femininity is passivity, while activity is essentially masculine. Freud had expressed doubts about the identification of femininity with passivity, pointing out that motherhood is an acitve role (1). Deutsch, however, maintains that

> the fundamental identities "feminine-passive" and "masculine-active" assert themselves in all known cultures and races . . . and we can assume that this principle will continue to assert itself until we succeed in influencing the internal, hormonal constellation of the human body. (Vol. I, p.230.)

This fundamental female passivity, Deutsch holds, is the inevitable result of female reproductive anatomy: "the female's passivity . . . came to the fore at the very moment when external fecundation was replaced by internal fecundation." (p.225) The girl first turns towards passivity not, as Freud thought, as a result of the envy and self-depreciation which follows upon the discovery that boys have penises and girls do not, but much earlier, and as a result of the anatomical difference itself. The girl, like the boy, has active sexual impulses from the earliest age, although these are always weaker in the girl. But since the vagina remains inactive until it is awakened by the male penis, and since the clitoris is "inadequate" for the expression of these active sexual impulses, the girl's activity—sexual and otherwise—is inhibited and transformed into passivity. "Her genital trauma . . . lies between the scylla of having no penis and the charybdis of lacking the responsiveness of the vagina." Penis envy comes later, and is a secondary phenomenon of passing significance.

The passivity of the female does not imply that she is entirely inactive—which is obviously false—but rather that the bulk of her interest and activity is confined within herself, rather than directed towards the outside world.

> The boy's more active sexuality leads to a stronger turn toward reality and toward conquering the outside world than is the case with the young girl. Hence an important psychologic difference between the sexes: man's attention is principally directed outward, and woman's inward. (p.133)

This turning inward of feminine activity makes females more

subjective, more engrossed in their own fantasy life, and more prone to identify with others. It also gives rise to narcissism and masochism, the two traits which Deutsch, here following Freud, considers to be equally definitive of femininity. In the normal feminine woman, the narcissism (self-love) and the masochism (desire to suffer) serve to balance one another. The narcissism enables her to retain her self-respect even while passively subordinating herself to others, and thus protects her from the *pathological* forms of masochism. True feminine masochism does not mean the actual desire to be beaten, raped and humiliated, but rather the selfless desire to give without receiving. Masochism is necessary for normal femininity, because it enables a woman to accept and perhaps even welcome the pain and self-sacrifice which are an inevitable part of her experience of sex, childbirth and motherhood.

Feminine passivity also accounts, in Deutsch's view, for "the most striking feminine characteristic, intuition." (p.138) Deutsch defines feminine intuition as an "irrational" tendency, yet one which women must fully accept for the sake of their psychic health. Rationality and objectivity are masculine qualities, difficult or impossible for women to achieve, and inconsistent with true femininty. Thus,

> Only exceptionally talented girls can carry a surplus of intellect without injuring their affective lives, for woman's intellect, her capacity for objectively understanding life, thrives at the expense of her subjective, emotional qualities. (p.146)

This sharp contrast between femininity and intellect has been the target of feminist attacks at least since 1701, when Mary Astell made her *Serious Proposal to the Ladies*. Yet Deutsch suggests that her formulation ought not to be unacceptable to feminists, since there is a certain parallelism between male and female psychology which suggests equality in spite of difference. Thus,

> Woman's activity directed inward is parallel to man's intensified activity directed outward, and her masochism is parallel to the masculine aggression that accompanies his activity. (p.195)

Nevertheless, she is aware that the social superiority—if not the moral superiority—of the male is an inevitable consequence of such a psychological dichotomy. Feminine women have no interest in personal status or achievement, but rather "fulfill their destinies when silent and in the background they inspire their husbands, always stimulating, encouraging and understanding them." (p.222)

It is also significant that Deutsch labels the two major phases of female life *girlhood* and *motherhood*. Deutsch views motherhood as not only woman's biological destiny, but her natural vocation and primary source of happiness. Some women may find happiness without motherhood, but only within those activities which give full scope for the development of "motherliness," i.e. the purely altruistic attitude of self-sacrifice and identification with others. She therefore regrets the fact that the war made it necessary for many women to work in masculine fields.

Indeed, Deutsch considers motherliness even more important in feminine psychology than eroticism. Feminine women are essentialy monogamous, not so much from love of a single man as from the need to experience their motherhood within a triangular situation which includes the father. They are erotically passive, capable of sexual receptivity but also able to tolerate sexual inhibition. Deutsch considers it the women's obligation to adjust herself to the man's sexual needs rather than vice versa, and she ridicules sex manuals which advise the man to increase the woman's enjoyment by extensive foreplay. Women do not need or desire sex or orgasm for its own sake, but only as a prelude to childbirth and motherhood, with which in their unconscious minds it is inseparably linked.

It is obvious that Deutsch's psychology of woman is hostile to the possibility of any fundamental change in women's social role, probably even more so than that of Freud. For her shift of emphasis from "penis envy" as the cause of female passivity to the "organlessness" of the female results in an even more solidly biologically determinist position. Freud's theory is susceptible to sympathetic reinterpretation from a feminist point of view, as Mitchell and Firestone have shown. The girl's envy of the penis, it may be held, is only a symbolic expression of her more basic desire to share in the superior status and privileges that accompany biological maleness in our culture. This being the case, penis envy, female passivity, and all the other "feminine" traits may be expected to fade with progress towards sexual equality.

If, however, the female's passivity is determined by her own genital structure, i.e. by the lack of either a penis or a spontaneously sensitive vagina, then there is little hope that social change can have much effect on her psychology: she will be passive, narcissistic and masochistic in *any* society. Some women may develop an almost masculine level of activity, but only at the expense of their own happiness and that of those around them:

> . . . when woman's activity goes beyond a definite degree of intensity, it is accompanied by forces that inhibit the activity of the

persons in her entourage and thus becomes dangerous especially for the male members of the family. (p.292)

Active women, in Deutsch's terminology, suffer from the masculinity complex, a neurotic condition which creates "conflicts with the woman's environment and . . . with the remaining feminine inner world." (p.296) Intellectual women are also "masculinized"; in them, "warm intuitive knowledge has yielded to cold unproductive thinking." (p.298) If one asks why thought should be any "colder" or less productive in women than in men, or why intuition should be more desirable in women than in men, the response is simply, anatomy. The supposed inadequacy of the clitoris as an organ for the expression of active sexual impulses dooms the female to passivity or to being, at best, a poor imitation of the active male.

It is this thesis of clitoral inadequacy which is the keystone of Deutsch's version of biological determinism. With it, the rest of the theory may still be challenged; but without it the theory collapses. Given that no one can experience sexual orgasm *both* as a man and as a women (2) for purposes of comparison, it is impossible to say with certainty which sex, if either, experiences more pleasure. However, the behavioral evidence—in particular the work of Masters and Johnson—certainly tends to refute the claim that the clitoris is inferior as an organ of sexual expression. Women's orgastic capacity, while possibly somewhat slower to reach its peak, is anything but inferior. Clitoral inadequacy seems, therefore, to be a myth, and singularly unpromising as an explanation of the (perhaps equally mythical) passivity of the female. (See also Sherfey.)

1. Sigmund Freud, "Femininity" (1933), in *Woman and Analysis*, edited by Jean Strouse (Grossman, New York, 1974) pp.75–76.
2. Notwithstanding the occurrence of so-called sex change operations, which cannot be assumed to result in a duplication of the normal sexual sensations of the other sex.

DINER, Helen. *Mothers and Amazons; The First Feminist History of Culture* (Edited and translated by John Philip Lundin, Anchor Press, Garden City, N.Y., 1973)

This is a bold defense of the early matriarchy theory, written and first published by Bertha Ekstein-Diener under one of her several pseudonyms. It is a work of considerable scholarship, but unfortunately includes almost no proper references, forcing the nonomniscient reader to take scores of highly debatable historical claims entirely on the author's word. Diner's claim is that innumerable matriarchal societies have existed in the past and exist still among primitive peoples. Her evidence and argumentation draw heavily from Bachofen—whom she credits with the discovery of matriarchy—and Briffault, though she does not agree with either on all points. She argues, as they do, that Egypt, Sparta, Lydia, Babylonia, Carthage, Etruria and other Mediterranean cultures were all matriarchal within strictly historical memory, while Rome and Athens preserved evidence of their matriarchal prehistory in their myths and legends.

As usual, there is considerable unclarity surrounding the term *matriarchy*, which Diner distinguishes from gynocracy, the intensification of matriarchy into political dominance. Matriarchy does not mean for her the same as matrilineality (the inheritance of names and property through the maternal side) or matrilocality (in which men leave their mother's clan to reside with their wives, but not vice versa), but she does consider either to be a strong *indication* of matriarchy. Also generally characteristic of matriarchal cultures is the worship of a mother goddess as the prime deity; the freedom of women to take lovers before and after marriage; the absence of (the concept of) illegitimate children; extensive knowledge and use by women of contraceptive and/or abortive techniques; close (sometimes sexual) relationships between brothers and sisters with the same mother; and total ignorance of the biological fact of paternity. Matriarchy is everywhere the primordial state of humanity, since motherhood was the strongest natural bond, and the object of worship and veneration. Contrary to the historical materialists, economic factors are not the key to matriarchy, which can exist not only during the agricultural phase, when women dominate the primary means of production, but at any economic stage from the Stone Age Seris of Lower California to the highly civilized Egyptians.

Diner describes Amazonism as an extreme form of matriarchy, a militaristic, horse-worshiping society of women who either shun men except for procreation (killing or sending away their infant sons) or keep them only as slaves. She thinks that numerous Amazon societies existed east of the Mediterranean, into historical times. Amazon tribes were the historical enemies of the Athenians, whose victories over them helped turn the tide of history against matriarchy. And although matriarchy does not *necessarily* perish with economic and cultural progress, once a society evolves into patriarchy it never (contrary to the Vaertings' pendulum hypothesis) swings back again.

Diner also endorses the notion that the female is the older and more basic human form, not only because each male is born of a female, but because parthenogenesis (reproduction by females without males) is the earlier method of animal reproduction, the male being a later development. (The translator finds it necessary to regret Diner's support of this notion, but the latter might be pleased by the recent discovery that every human fetus begins its development as an apparent female and will remain morphologically feminine unless altered by the action of male hormones. See Mary Jane Sherfey.) It is even more revealing that Diner holds America to be a true matriarchy, in which the men work for the benefit of the women, a condition she believes to be in part at least due to a mystical power inherent in "the American soil, with its ancient, matriarchal soul." Ignoring the oddness of this causal hypothesis, a skeptic might still wonder whether the concept of matriarchy which has the result that the United States is highly matriarchal isn't rather too broad to be of much use as an analytic tool.

DINNERSTEIN, Dorothy. *The Mermaid and the Minotaur* (Harper and Row, New York, Hagerstown, San Francisco, London, 1976)

This book is representative of a growing trend among radical feminists toward using Freudian insights into the etiology of personality to help explain the continuing predominance of patriarchy and the traditional sexual stereotypes, rather than rejecting Freud's work *in toto* because of his antifeminist biases. Dinnerstein's thesis is that the key factor which has brought about male domination and which continues to perpetuate it today is the rearing of infants and small children primarily by their mothers. People who are raised by women, she argues, retain throughout their lives powerfully ambivalent feelings toward the female sex. To the infant the mother seems to be a magical and omnipotent source of life and love; as such she is also the target of the child's first rage and resentment when the child experiences discomfort or frustration.

This fact, Dinnerstein thinks, explains the emergence of "masculine" attitudes in males and "feminine" attitudes in females; "Early rage at the first parent . . . is typically used by the "masculine" boy during the Oedipal period to *consolidate* his tie with his own sex by establishing a principled independence, a more or less derogatory distance from women. And it is typically used by the "feminine" girl in this same period to *loosen* her tie with her own sex by establishing a worshipful, dependent stance toward men." (p.53) It also explains the sexual double standard, the greater jealousy and possessiveness of men; men identify their female lovers with the original goddess of the nursery, whose failure to instantly gratify their every need caused them such intense rage and grief when they were infants. Consequently, they feel that they must have total possession of the woman, who is still experienced as the magical life source and whose every hint of infidelity reawakens that unreasoning infantile fear and rage. Women, on the other hand, subconsciously feel that they contain the magical life source within themselves, and are less apt to require total possession of a man to feel secure, at least so long as they feel that he continues to desire possession of them.

Mother-raised people are also very apt to be suspicious and resentful of females in positions of power in the larger world outside the nursery. For the mother is not only the first source of pleasure and frustration, but also, at a later state of development, a smothering presence from which a child must escape in order to emerge into full personhood. She is the siren song that lures us back towards comfortable nonbeing. As children, boys and girls alike, we gladly escape from her confining authority, and throughout our lives we remain profoundly uncomfortable about feminine authority in any guise.

The predominance of the mother in the early life of the child also explains why woman has always been regarded, in the language of Simone de Beauvoir, as the Other, a half-human being who is closer to nature but farther from personhood than man, the true human. The reason, Dinnerstein argues, is that we encounter a woman, our mother, before we learn to distinguish between persons and impersonal natural forces. As a result, males, who must define themselves as males and as human individuals by the contrast with the mother, the female, have difficulty seeing women as persons; the original ambiguity of the feelings and ideas projected onto the mother is never resolved, but reprojected onto women as a class and onto nature as well. Woman is underpersonified and nature overpersonified, and both are approached with a "greedy and murderous infantilism."

It will be possible, therefore, to end male domination, and to turn the world back from the suicidal course on which it is embarked under male leadership, only when men become as active in the rearing of small children as women. Once "father-hood, like motherhood, means early physical intimacy, man's procreativity will seem in its own way as concretely miraculous as woman's." (p.150) Hence both sexes will be forced, or at least enabled, to face and resolve the fundamental ambiguities about what we are as human beings—rational or emotional, active or passive, etc.—rather than perpetuating them in the form of the traditional sexual stereotypes.

DOUBLE STANDARD: see Chastity, Christianity, Rousseau, Hume, Hegel.

DUALISM In metaphysics and the philosophy of mind, dualism is the view that mind and body are separate and distinct existences—i.e., either different substances, or in some other way ontologically dichotomous. There are many forms of metaphysical dualism, but all in some way affirm the ultimate reality of the mind/body distinction. The major philosophical alternatives to dualism are idealism (the view that only the mental is ultimately real) and materialism (which accords basic ontological status only to the physical). Today idealism is not a major philosophical contender, at least not among Western philosophers. The debate is primarily between dualists (usually interactionists) and the so-called "identity theorists"—who hold that mental states are *identical* to physical states of the brain.

Now it is important to realize that there is absolutely no *logical* connection between these various philosophical positions with respect to the mind/body problem and the issues which divide feminists and antifeminists. A feminist can be a dualist, or an antifeminist, a monist, without any overt inconsistency. Nevertheless, as feminists have often pointed out, there is a longstanding historical connection between mind/body dualism and misogynist or antifeminist views, in that women have traditionally been associated with the material side of the dichotomy—with the earth, the body, the sexual and other passions, and mortality—while men have been associated with the "higher," mental side—with the sky, the soul, reason, and transcendence. In this way, the mind/body dichotomy and the male/female dichotomy have become conflated in much of Western thought.

This basic set of associations, between the female and the material, and the male and the mental, appears in innumerable variations in the work of virtually all antifeminist writers, and even (in somewhat disguised form) in that of some who must on the whole be considered feminists, such as John Stuart Mill. Aristotle, for instance, held that in the process of generation the

124

male contributes the form or soul of the offspring, while the female contributes only the matter. The male, he maintained, possesses the full power of reason, while the female possesses this power only in a defective form.

The Judeo-Christian notion that man was created before woman, and more in the image of the (male) deity (see St. Paul), and that it was through woman that suffering and death entered the world, exhibits the same associations between maleness and the higher human powers and between femaleness and our material, animal nature. So does Kant's notion that the male intellect is sublime while the female intellect is beautiful (i.e. oriented towards the sensual and aesthetic rather than the abstract and universal); and so does Darwin's and Spencer's assertion that the male has been more highly selected for intelligence and aggressiveness than the female; so does Weininger's equation of femininity with unconscious sexuality and the male with conscious intellect; and Freud's claim that the superego, intellect and sense of justice are less well developed in women than in men; and Jung's definition of femininity as Eros, and masculinity as Logos.

Simone de Beauvoir's philosophical analysis is probably the best, and certainly the most extensive critique of the traditional association between the female and nature, matter, and the absence of higher mental powers. She argues that men have always claimed the realm of transcendence, of freedom, creativity and intellect, for themselves, and sought to confine women within the realm of the immanent, i.e. mere biological existence. She suggests that both sexes must learn to assume their fundamental ambiguity, as beings who are both immanent and transcendent.

Some of the feminists of today, however, argue that we must do more than simply reject the patriarchal conflation of the mind/body and male/female dichotomies. It is also necessary, they hold, to reject the dualistic mode of thought, which stresses polar oppositions and hierarchical orderings between the opposite poles.

> Male dominance, it is claimed, rests on the splitting, the disintegration of reality which should be understood as one, one human reality, one mindbody, one spirit-matter, one art-science continuum, etc. (1)

As Marcia Keller explains, this feminist opposition to philosophical dualism is not a new metaphysical monism which denies altogether the validity of such distinctions as mind and body, male and female, art and science. What is demanded is rather a recognition that it is not these oppositions which are ontologically fundamental, but rather their "ultimate, ambiguous unity." (2) In other words, reality itself is holistic, though the mind/body distinction and other dualistic concepts may be valid enough within a particular context and relative to a particular purpose.

Thus, some feminist philosphers with whom I have conversed would go so far as to deny that (it is a basic or ultimate truth that) humanity is divided into two sexes, males and females. Human beings, they argue, are creatures whose similarities outweigh their differences, even though the latter provide a basis for distinguishing between indefinitely many types of human being. Our language and culture have established the male/female dichotomy as more important than any other dimension of human difference; but this is only a contingent fact, one which might have been otherwise and which may cease to be true in the future.

Such a line of argument is attractive in many ways, but it also has its pitfalls. We must avoid prejudging the truth of metaphysical doctrines like mind/body dualism on the basis of theorized historical or psychological connections between such doctrines and the oppression of women and other subordinate groups. It is, after all, conceivable that the mind/body distinction (or the male/female distinction, for that matter) *is* in some sense ultimate, and not merely an artifact of language, even though of course the difference between mind and body ought never have been used to define the difference between men and women.

We must also be extremely wary of the tendency to lump all philosophical dualisms together, as though a refutation of one dualistic theory amounted to a refutation of them all. It may well be that all of the sharp dichotomies so characteristic of Western thought (e.g. mind/body, male/female, time/space, matter/energy, science/art, reason/emotion, subject/object, essence/existence, etc.) will ultimately be shown to be invalid, or of relative validity only. But each of these problem areas is to a degree both logically and empirically separate from each other, and thus they cannot all be simultaneously dispensed with under the heading "patriarchal dualist thought."

If these points are kept in mind, then the current feminist attack upon particular artificial dualities in Western thought may prove philosophically fruitful. If not, then the overly broad assault upon dualism in general may generate more confusion than clarity.

1. Marcia Keller (Department of Philosophy, San Francisco State University), from an unpublished manuscript, "Politi-

cal-Philosophical Analysis of the U.S. Women's Liberation
Movement"; also see Firestone, Ruether.
2. *Ibid.*

DWORKIN, Andrea. *Our Blood: Prophecies and Discourses on
Sexual Politics* (Harper and Row, New York, 1970)
Woman Hating (E.P. Dutton and Co., New York, 1974)

Dworkin is a radical feminist who dates the emergence of the
women's movement as a revolutionary force from the publication
of Millett's *Sexual Politics* (1969). The position is that sexism is
the root cause of virtually all other social evils, from fascism and
slavery to war, capitalism, and the rape of the environment.
Civilized men have always held, as a central part of their view of
reality, a distorted view of woman as the opposite of man, his
negation. Women have been presumed not only to be a separate
and distinct type of being, but the polar opposite of men. Furthermore, the male (with a very few exceptions, e.g. in the Hindu
Tantric tradition) is always the positive pole, endowed with all
the active human capacities (strength, will, intellect, morality),
while the female is the negative pole, defined only by her emptiness, her lack of masculine qualities. This sharp and utterly
arbitrary division between the sexes has been the core of men's
identity, the *sine qua non* of their experience of themselves as men.

Women have paid an appalling price for men's propensity to so
define themselves. Seen as pure negativity, woman becomes a
threatening evil force if she is in the least degree active or self-
sufficient. Grimm's fairy tales (for instance, "Snow White" and
"Cinderella") illustrate the patriarchal moral that the only good
woman is a dead one, or one who is as close to dead—as passive
and helpless—as possible; active women are wicked witches and
tend to come to bad ends. The thousand-year-long Chinese custom of mutilating women's feet is a stunning example of the
lengths to which men have gone to transform women into passive objects of men's enjoyment. What is remarkable is that to the
Chinese the crippled feet were the very essence of femininity and
eroticism; yet this, or something like it, is what femininity has
always meant. Witches, Dworkin thinks, were for the most part
women who were followers of the "Old Religion," an anti-Christian cult which worshiped a deity which Christians mistook for
the Devil, and which celebrated nature, sexuality and women's
fertility with ritual orgies. To eradicate this cult and preserve its
antinature, antisexual and antiwoman world view, the Christian

Church burned perhaps nine million people, most of them women.

The revolution which Dworkin proclaims will take as its model the ancient myth of the primal androgyne—the original human being (or race) which was (were) neither male nor female. Androgyny means the end of masculinity and femininity. Dworkin rightly points out that what Jung and his followers have advocated—that men get "in touch with" their feminine side, women with their masculine side—is *not* androgyny in the revolutionary sense. For Jung assumed that masculinity and femininity were natural onotological categories, eternal archetypes; and like the Chinese foot-binders he identified femininity with Eros (carnality) and masculinity with intellect. There can be no escape from misogyny and male domination within such a conceptual framework. Dworkin does not recommend somehow *combining* masculine and feminine elements into an androgynous whole, but rather recognizes that the very notions of masculinity and femininity are lies, fictions, cultural constructs which are inimical to human becoming. "We are," she says, "a multi-sexed species which has its sexuality spread along a vast fluid continuum where the elements called male and female are not discrete." (*Woman Hating*, p.183)

The feminist revolution, Dworkin argues, will mean the end of heterosexuality as we know it. It has become almost impossible, she notes, for feminist women to engage in sexual intercourse with men. Lesbians do not necessarily achieve liberated, androgynous sex, but they are one step closer to it insofar as neither has a male, phallic identity. Postrevolutionary sex will be free of taboos on homosexuality, incest or even bestiality; it will be pansexual. There will, however, be no more fucking—which is not to say that there will be no sexual intercourse between men and women. "Fucking is entirely a male act designed to affirm the reality and power of the phallus, of masculinity." (*Our Blood*, p.108) The revolution will consist in the destruction of this paradigm of masculine sadism and feminine masochism; there will be no more masculinity or femininity, hence, in this sense, no more men or women.

E

ECOLOGY AND FEMINISM   Ecology is the systemic relationship between organisms and their environment, or the study thereof. In recent years the term has become identified with the movement to conserve natural resources and free the environment from chemical and other man-made pollutants, and with the realization that the human race has a moral obligation to coexist with the planet's other inhabitants. Ecology is also often taken to imply the need for a more equitable balance between rich nations and poor, with respect to access to the planet's resources.

From the beginning there has been a close association between feminism and the ecology movement. Both tend to reject the competitive, dominance-oriented capitalist ethic, which rationalizes the exploitation of nature, women and other "inferior" people as the inalienable right of the stronger party. Both wish to substitute for it a more "feminine" morality, one stressing cooperation and a nurturant concern for all (human and other) life. The philosopher Peter Singer points to the analogy between the rights of animals and those of women and oppressed minority groups (1). Among the feminists who have recently explored the relationship between feminism and ecology are Boulding, Firestone, Giele, Griffin, Holliday, and J.B. Miller.

1.   Peter Singer, "All Animals Are Equal," in *Animal Rights and Human Obligations*, edited by Tom Regan and Peter Singer, Prentice-Hall, Englewood Cliffs, New Jersey, 1976; pages 148–162.

ECONOMIC ROLE OF WOMEN   In most cultures and periods, women have been important economic producers—a fact which has often been obscured in recent centuries by the standard sex-role patterns of our present culture. (See Briffault, Beard, Boulding, Hamiliton, Reed.) The naturalness and inevitability of the male-breadwinner/female-homemaker dichotomy was rarely challenged by the first generations of feminist thinkers. (See

129

Astell, Wollstonecraft, Grimke, Mill; Harriet Taylor was one exception.) Nor was it recognized as an artifact of industrial capitalism, until Marx and Engels analyzed sexual oppression as a
function of class oppression. (See Matriarchy Theory, Marx,
Engels, and Socialism and Feminism.)

Even before Marx, however, socialist feminists argued that
sexual equality requires more than the opening of previously all
male professions to women; it requires the wholesale elimination
of the sexual division of labor, into domestic work (which women
do, without pay) and public work (which men and some women
do, with pay). (See Fourier, William Thompson, Gilman.) Liberal
feminists, on the other hand, have argued that women must
work in both the public and private spheres, though not necessarily during the same periods of their lives. (See Taylor,
Schreiner, Myrdal and Klein, Friedan.)

More recently, the economic function of women's domestic-
labor capitalist system has been explored (See Hamilton, Oakley,
Zaretsky.), while the cross-cultural relationship between gender
dichotomies and the sexual division of labor has been investigated by Friedl, Boserup, and other contemporary feminist anthropologists. (See Martin and Voorhies, and Reiter in Anthologies I.) For analyses of women's current economic status in this
country, and of their difficulties in combining domestic and public work, see Bird, Epstein, Horner; and Kreps, Dahlstrom,
Theodore, in Anthologies XIV.

EDUCATION OF WOMEN The question whether women
should be educated for anything other than domestic work has
been debated at least as early as Plato; he argued that women
(i.e., those of the ruling class) should receive the same education
as men, to prepare them for the same occupations. But few men
shared Plato's view, and public education for females was a
relative rarity in most Western nations prior to the nineteenth
century. (The Italian universities are one outstanding exception
to this rule; see Mozans, Anthologies VII.) The earliest feminists
were ardent advocates of wider if not necessarily identical educational opportunities for women. (See Astell, Wollstonecraft,
Fuller, Mill, Taylor.) Antifeminists have replied that the only
things women need to learn are how to be charming, how to
please men and keep house for them; and that the development
of their intellectual capacities would destroy their feminine
charm and intuition, and hence their special influence over men.
(See Rousseau, Kant, Nietzsche, Kierkegaard, Jung, Harding,

Deutsch, Goldberg.)

Now that women have gained entry to most educational institutions (in our part of the world), the issues have shifted to their relative status and educational opportunities within those institutions. Some have argued that the preponderance of women teachers in the elementary schools creates an atmospere inimical to males—a situation which is reversed at the secondary and college levels, where the instructors are predominantly male. (See Sexton.) Feminists have presented overwhelming evidence of sexism in public-school texts, and in institutionalized practices at every level. (See Stacey, Nilsen, B.H. Harrison, in Anthologies V.) The universities—particularly the most prestigious ones—are still largely a male preserve; but affirmative action requirements, federal antidiscrimination statutes, women's studies programs, and the increasing awareness of women faculty and students have created the means whereby this hegemony can now be challenged. (See Rossi, Howe, Furniss, *loc. cit.*)

ELLIS, Havelock (1859-1939). *Man and Woman: A Study of Human Secondary Sexual Characteristics* (Walter Scott Publishing Company, London and New York, 1904; first published 1894)
Studies in the Psychology of Sex, Volumes I and II (Random House, New York, 1942; first published in seven volumes, from 1898 to 1928)
Little Essays of Love and Virtue (George H. Doran Company, New York, 1921)
More Essays of Love and Virtue (Doubleday, Doran and Company, Garden City, New York, 1931)
Psychology of Sex (Emerson Books, New York, 1944; first published 1933)
Sex and Marriage: Eros in Contemporary Life (Edited by John Gawsworth; Random House, New York, 1952)

Havelock Ellis devoted most of his long life to the elucidation of the problems of sexuality, primarily from a biological point of view. His first book on the topic, *Man and Woman*, is also the most significant with respect to the feminist controversy. Ellis sorts through the maze of often contradictory data concerning sexual differences, using an evolutionary criterion to attempt to separate innate differences from those which are environmentally conditioned. Women, he argues, are physiologically and indeed psychologically more infantile than men; their smaller size, shorter legs, finer bone structures and proportionately larger heads are all evidence of infantilism. This is not to say, however, that women are underdeveloped men. On the contrary, women and children are the vanguard of human evolution. "The progress of our race has been a progress in youthfulness." (p.446) The infant ape is more human-like than the adult, male or female. Women and children bear "the special characteristics of humanity in a higher degree than men." (p.447)

At the same time, Ellis maintains that women are biologically and psychologically more conservative than men; that is, they exhibit a lesser variational tendency. Men show a wider range of mental and physical traits, as a result of which there are more male idiots and defectives of all sorts. Consequently males are more apt to die at birth and tend to be shorter lived. Women's smaller stature and their mental and physical precocity are symptoms of their evolutionary conservatism, since our prehuman ancestors were presumably smaller and faster maturing than are contemporary humans. Women, he thinks, are also more conservative of energy, or anabolic, while men are more catabolic or energy-consuming. The usual division of labor among primitive peoples seems to reflect this fact: women work steadily and at tasks which do not generally require either sudden bursts of intense energy or long periods of recuperation, while men do little besides hunt and wage war, activities which are highly catabolic, and which require that they rest a great deal in order to regain their strength.

Ellis also thinks that women are considerably more "affectable" than men, that is more readily responsive to physical or psychic stimuli; they laugh, cry and blush more easily and are more prone to functional (as opposed to congenital) mental disorders such as neurosis. All of these sexual differences, he holds, are at least to a large extent innate and inalterable. Women's affectability, for instance, is a result of their sexual periodicity (which, he thinks, is absent or far less pronounced in men), their tendency to be "anaemic" (that is, to have a lower blood haemoglobin level), and their relatively greater mass of nervous tissue; for although men's brains are on the average both absolutely larger and larger relative to height, they are smaller relative to body weight, especially if a correction is made for the fact that a larger proportion of women's weight tends to consist of fat, which does not require as much nervous regulation as muscle.

Most antifeminists would probably welcome such conclusions as these, as clear evidence that male domination, or at least the traditional division of labor which conduces to it, is biologically determined. Ellis, however, refuses to draw any such conclusions. He rejects the tradition of male supremacy as immoral and disastrous to marital happiness, and insists that there is nothing in his findings which shows either that one sex is superior to the other, or that women's sphere should be limited or defined in any particular way. "The facts," he says, "are much too complex to enable us to rush hastily to a conclusion as to their significance." (p.441) (Unfortunately he does not remain entirely faithful to this position, and is not above remarking that "nature has made women more like children in order that they may better understand and care for children." (p.450)) He is sympathetic to the feminist movement, but sees no possibility of liberating women from the preponderance of childrearing responsibility, maintaining instead that the social status and independence of mothers ought to be increased. He follows Morgan in ascribing the fall of the classical ancient civilizations to their failure to develop the capacities of women. "The hope of our future civilization lies in the development in equal freedom of both the masculine and the feminine elements in life." (p.451) Men and women are not alike or equal, but they are equivalent and entitled to equal liberty; how this is possible when women but not men are tied to the responsibilities of parenthood he does not explain.

Ellis's monumental *Studies in the Psychology of Sex* defy summary, but an idea of their range can be obtained from the list of titles (here presented in the order in which they appear in the Random House edition, rather than in which they were originally published): *The Evolution of Modesty; The Phenomenon of Sexual Periodicity; Auto-Eroticism; Analysis of the Sexual Impulse; Love and Pain; The Sexual Impulse in Women; Sexual Selection in Man; Sexual Inversion; Erotic Symbolism; The Mechanism of Detumescence; The Psychic State in Pregnancy; Eonism and Other Supplementary Studies;* and *Sex in Relation to Society.* These works represent a major milestone in the understanding of sexual phenomena. His approach to a great many hitherto taboo topics is thoroughly modern and enlightened. He argues, for instance, that masturbation, a practice severely condemned by the Victorians, is not only virtually universal (among women as well as men) and an almost inevitable consequence of sexual deprivation, but also harmless when not practiced to great excess.

On the other hand, Ellis sides with Freud (whose work he admired but did not entirely accept) in holding that it is both normal and biologically inevitable for women to enjoy and desire the experience of physical pain when inflicted by a male lover, and to be eager to accept subjection to his will. (Vol. II, Part 1, p.89) He does point out that this masochism operates only within certain limits: women enjoy being forced to do only those things which they find pleasurable. Yet this qualification does not prevent him from lending his support to the pernicious notion that most women would enjoy being raped. (p.90) (Unbelievably, this is almost the sole reference to rape in the *Studies!*) He explains that he arrives at these conclusions not out of a desire to support the subjection of women, but because of overwhelming evidence in this direction, and also because they are consistent with what he sees as the sexual role of the female throughout nature, i.e. the role of the hunted animal who lures her pursuer on until she is finally caught and overpowered.

Of the *Studies* the most relevant to femininism is *Sex in Relation to Society*. Here Ellis argues for improved working conditions and adequate pregnancy leave for employed women, more honest and earlier sexual education, and an end to the double standard which represses women's sexuality. He views female frigidity on the one hand and prostitution on the other as the inevitable results of a system of marriage which divides women into two equally oppressed classes—those who are to be only minimally exposed to sexual pleasure (and then only within marriage and for the purpose of procreation), and those who are to be sacrificed to the sexual desires of men in general. He attacks those who defend prostitution as necessary for the purity of married women and notes that marriage itself is very often a form of prostitution, in which sexual favors are traded for material support.

Psychology of Sex is an introductory text on sexual phenomena, which in spite of Ellis's denial that it is a summary of the *Studies*, does recapitulate in briefer form much of the material presented there. *Little Essays of Love and Virtue* is a moral and philosophical primer for adolescents of both sexes, *More Essays on Love and Virtue* a similar collection intended for older readers. *Sex and Marriage* is a posthumous collection of essays on similar topics, i.e. love, motherhood, the family and sexual morality. In these last works Ellis continues to defend the traditional division of labor in marriage, maintaining that, "since the mother must necessarily devote a larger share of time and care to the child, the father may be called upon to take a larger financial share, without the economic equality of the two parents being thereby injured." (*More Essays*, p.32) This is a tempting but ultimately rather implausible viewpoint, since it is impossible to avoid the fact that the provision of financial support constitutes a far greater potential source of power than does the provision of child care and other domestic services. (See H. Taylor, Bernard, de Beauvoir.)

ELLMAN, Mary. *Thinking About Women* (Harcourt Brace Jovanovich, New York, 1968)

An insightful and humorous examination of sexual stereotyping in modern American literature and literary criticism. Both
amply illustrate what Ellman calls "the sexual analogy," the
ubiquitous tendency to interpret human and even natural phenomena on the model of the traditional conceptions of male and
female temperaments. The old stereotypes are increasingly
(known to be) inaccurate; the only significant differences between the sexes are that only women bear children and that men
tend to be stronger, and both strength and reproductive capacity
have lost most of their former importance. Yet the sexual traditionalists (Norman Mailer *et al.*) insist all the more vehemently
upon interpreting the minds of women and men through a ridiculous analogy with their genitals: the male mind is supposed to
function aggressively, like a penis; the female mind is supposed
to be passive and receptive, like a womb. And while "men may
congratulate themselves upon the productivity of their own mental wombs . . . they are displeased to come across women who
have mental penises." (p.21) Women and women writers can be
criticized either for their femininity or their lack of femininity;
contradictory opinions about women proliferate and generate
endless controversy about women's nature. It is always presupposed that women cannot simply be normal human beings, but
must be inferior or superior, always different, from the (male)
norm. It is men's social superiority that produces these stereotypes of femininity, and not vice versa: "By whatever accident
control is placed in one human group, another will assume the
characteristics of contradiction." (p.209)

EMOTION, INTELLECT, AND THE SEXUAL DICHOTOMY

It is difficult to say just when the idea arose that men naturally
have more intellectual capacity than women but less emotional
sensitivity; and that the reverse is true of women. The Biblical
idea that women are prone to sexual incontinence is at best
remotely related to this notion. One might suppose that there is
an early echo of it in Aristotle's view that in women the rational
part of the soul is weaker than it is in men and thus less able to
control the appetitive or emotional part; but Aristotle simply saw
women as intellectually inferior to men, not as possessing special
emotional capacities which men lack.

Whenever it began, the notion of special feminine emotional
capacities was fully developed by the time of the Enlightenment.

Both Rousseau and Kant claim that women's lesser intellectual abilities are compensated for not only by their own more sensitive emotions and aesthetic sensibilities, but by their greater responsiveness to the moods and emotions of others: women's celebrated "intution." Wollstonecraft and a few other early feminists condemned this artificial division of human capacities into "masculine" intellect and "feminine" emotion. (See also William Thompson.) Other feminists, including John Stuart Mill, were inclined to believe in feminine intuition, which Mill described as a superior capacity for grasping the immediate situation. This, and the related claim that women are morally superior to men, was often used to support women's demands for a larger share in public life. (See Chafe; also Marlow and Harrison, and Kraditor, Anthologies VI.)

The psychoanalytic movement has tended to support this supposed dichotomy between masculine and feminine talents. Boys, Freud thought, emerge from the Oedipal conflict with better developed egos than girls, and hence greater intellectual creativity. Girls, on the other hand, experience (if they are normal) two separate waves of passivity, one at the Oedipal stage and another at puberty; as a result, they are more inward-oriented and presumably—although Freud does not say this—more attentive to (at least their own) emotional states. Deutsch held that intellectual development in women tends to damage their feminine emotional capacities. Jung held that reason (Nous) is masculine and emotion (Eros) feminine, and that although each person should be in communication with his or her "contrasexual" element it is a mistake to become identified with it; women, in particular, must not become too intellectual. (See also Stern, Harding, Scott-Maxwell, de Castillejo, Singer.)

Today, many feminists support some version of the ideal of androgyny; that is, they argue that a person must possess both "masculine" and "feminine" traits, e.g. both emotion and intellect, in order to be a fully functional human being. (See Bem, Heilbrun; also Kaplan and Bean, Anthologies XIII.) Others have attacked the concept of androgyny as itself contaminated by patriarchal presumptions. What is necessary, they argue, is to *break* the association between masculinity and intellect, femininity and emotion—and not merely to give each sex a limited permission to display traits "belonging" to the other. (See Androgyny.)

ENGELS, Friedrich (1820-1895). *The Condition of the Working Class in England in 1844* (George Allen and Unwin Ltd., London, 1950; first published 1845)
The Origin of the Family, Private Property and the State (International Publishers, New York, 1970; first published 1884)

Engels' theoretical analysis of the oppression of women is to a large extent the product of his long intellectual partnership with Karl Marx. Here as elsewhere it was undoubtedly Marx who was the more active theorist; but it was Engels who wrote—or at least put into final form—the definitive Marxist account of the prehistoric origin and future abolition of male domination. Marx intended to write on the origin of the family and the state, and made extensive notes on the subject before he died in 1882. Engels wrote *The Origin of the Family* on the basis of these notes. It contains by far the most extensive treatment of the historical role of women in the work of either Marx or Engels and is still the primary Marxist text on the subject.

Marx and Engels had long been sympathetic to the particular plight of women workers under industrial capitalism. In *The Condition of the Working Class in England in 1844* Engels documented the harsh treatment of women (and children) workers in the British mills, mines and factories, and commented on the damage which the employment of married women does to working families, especially when the husbands are not able to find work. Such a reversal of roles, he says, "unsexes the man and takes from the woman all her womanliness." (p.146) It would have been easy to conclude from this, and from the way that the employment of women and children was used to drive down the wages of all workers, that women belong at home; indeed so great a liberal as John Stuart Mill, twenty years later, was still prepared to argue in this way. But instead, Engels pointed out that

> so total a reversal of the sexes can have come to pass only because the sexes have been placed in a false position from the beginning. If the reign of the wife over the husband, so inevitably brought about by the factory system, is inhuman, the pristine rule of the husband over the wife must have been inhuman too. (*Loc. cit.*)

In one of their earliest collaborative works, Marx and Engels wrote that the first division of labor was that between man and woman for the propagation of the species (1). Furthermore, the first inequality of property and the first exploitation occur "in the family, where the wife and children are the slaves of the husband." (*Loc. cit.*) Thus, from the beginning they perceived woman's economic dependence within the individual family as the basic source of their oppression. But it was not until much later that they came to see the patriarchal family as itself the result of prior economic developments, rather than as a simple and natural extension of the original division of labor between the sexes.

Marx was greatly impressed with the American anthropologist Lewis Henry Morgan's work in reconstructing the prehistoric stages of human cultural evolution. On the basis of his research among the Iroquois and other native American tribes, Morgan argued that primitive matrilineal and communistic cultures, which practice group marriage, evolve under the influence of private property into monogamous, patrilineal and patriarchal cultures. He thereby provided a materialistic explanation of the transition from mother right to father right, which Bachofen had discovered, but could only explain as due to the emergence of new religious ideas. Marx found Morgan's theory entirely consistent with his own dialectical materialist analysis of history, and Engels incorporated it into *The Origin of the Family*.

Following Morgan, then, Engels divides human cultural evolution into three major periods or stages, i.e. savagery, barbarism, and civilization, the first two being further subdivided into lower, middle and upper stages. Each cultural stage is defined by the mode of production, i.e. the means of obtaining the necessities of life. For instance, in the lowest stage of savagery (of which there are no surviving representatives) our ancestors were vegetarian forest dwellers, subsisting on fruit, nuts and roots. Each cultural stage also corresponds to a particular form of marriage and family structure, and it is always changes in the mode of production which prompt changes in marriage and family.

In the middle and upper stages of savagery (essentially hunting and gathering cultures), so the theory goes, group marriage and the matrilineal, matrilocal and communistic clan prevail. At first, all the men of the clan are "married," that is, in Engel's words, "have sexual access to," all of the women. Since paternity cannot be known under these conditions, lineage is necessarily traced through the maternal side only. Gradually, the scope of group marriage is narrowed by the imposition of incest taboos, first on marriage between generations, then between brothers and sisters of the same mother. Finally, all marriage within the maternal clan is forbidden, and exogamous pairing marriage appears.

Pairing marriage appears at about the time of the transition to lower barbarism, when hunting and gathering as a mode of subsistence is replaced by agriculture and/or the herding of domestic animals. It does not, at first, upset the communistic maternal clan, which gives women social status at least equal to that of men. Thus,

> Among all savages and all barbarians of the lower and middle stages, and to a certain extent of the upper stage also, the position of women is not only free, but honorable . . . The communistic household, in which most or all of the women belong to one and the same gens, while the men come from various gentes, is the material foundation of that supremacy of the woman which was general in primitive times. (p.113)

Indeed, Engels follows Morgan and Bachofen in holding that the emergence of pairing marriage was almost entirely women's doing. In what might be seen as a Victorian ignorance of the sexual capacities of women, Engels argued that women must have found group marriage increasingly distasteful.

> The more the traditional sexual relations lost the naive character of forest life . . . the more oppressive and humiliating must the women have felt them to be, and the greater their longing for the right of chastity, of temporary or permanent marriage with one man only. (p.117)

Nevertheless, pairing marriage, together with the growth of private wealth which occurs during the barbaric period, forms the basis for the overthrow of mother right and the establishment of the patriarchal family. In the cultures of the Near East, wealth accumulated in the form of herds and slaves, and slavery became profitable for the first time. Rather than remaining the communal property of the clan, Engels argues, this new wealth was appropriated from the beginning by the man. For,

> According to the division of labor within the family at that time, it was the man's part to obtain food and the instruments of labor necessary for the purpose. He therefore also owned the instruments of labor . . . Therefore . . . the man was also the owner of the new source of subsistence, the cattle, and later of the new instruments of labor, the slaves. (p.119)

Thus men's economic power grew, while the value of women's domestic labor, once equal to that of men, shrunk to relative insignificance. Possessing private wealth, men began to desire to leave it to their own children—whom, because of pairing marriage, they could now identify. Under the system of mother right, however, a man's property reverted to the maternal clan. Hence mother right was overthrown, and the clan became patrilineal and patrilocal: "A simple decree sufficed that in the future the offspring of the male members should remain within the gens, but that of the female should be excluded by being transferred to the gens of the father." (p.120) This event was the turning point in women's history.

> The overthrow of the mother right was *the world historical defeat of the female sex*. The man took command in the house also; the woman was degraded and reduced to servitude; she became the slave of his lust and a mere instrument for the propagation of children. (pp.120–121)

Because father right requires that the paternity of children be undisputed, it brings with it so-called monogamous marriage, which from the beginning means monogamy for the woman only. Unlike pairing marriage, monogamous marriage places the woman under the dominion of the man; it "comes on the scene as the subordination of the one sex by the other; [and] it announces a struggle between the sexes unknown throughout the whole previous prehistoric period." (p.128) Monogamy appears at the same time as slavery, and for the same reasons. Hence,

> The first class oppression that appears in history coincides with the development of the antagonism between man and woman in monogamous marriage, and the first class oppression coincides with that of the female sex by the male. (p.129)

Indeed, the patriarchal family is the microcosm of the class divisions which exist in the society as a whole. "It is the cellular form of civilized society in which the nature of the oppositions and contradictions fully active in that society can already be studied." (*Loc. cit*) Thus, in the bourgeois family the husband is, as it were, the capitalist, and the wife is the proletariat, whose labor and reproductive power are exploited. This is why, Engels argues, the legal reforms which liberal feminists demand will, in themselves, do little to liberate women; they will only make it all the more clear that the real source of women's oppression is their role in the family, which excludes them from the public process of production. So long as the family is the economic unit of society, in which the woman runs the household as a private service while the man alone earns money, a wife is little more than a prostitute. She "only differs from the ordinary courtesan in that she does not let out her body on piecework as a wage worker, but sells it once and for all into slavery." (p.134)

For this reason, Engels holds, the proletarian family—however badly it may have suffered in the process of industrialization—has become more egalitarian than the bourgeois family. For the proletariat do not as a rule marry for economic reasons.

> And now that large-scale industry has taken the wife out of the

home onto the labor market and into the factory, and made her often the breadwinner of the family, no basis for any kind of male supremacy is left in the proletarian household, except, perhaps, for something of the brutality toward women that has spread since the introduction of monogamy. (p.135)

Among the proletariat, therefore, the family has already largely ceased to be the economic unit, and in this sense proletarian marriage is no longer monogamous. For the liberation of all women, it will be necessary "to bring the whole female sex back into public industry," (p.138) and to free women of private housekeeping tasks by converting domestic work into social industry. The traditional division of labor in the family will thereby be abolished—except of course for its strictly reproductive aspects.

Engels does not, however, expect the family itself to disappear under socialism. Some socialist thinkers—e.g. the early utopian socialist Charles Fourier and the contemporary radical feminist Shulamith Firestone—have argued that monogamous (one man/ one woman) marriage, once deprived of its economic foundations, will tend to die out, and that a return to something more like group marriage will occur. But Engels predicts instead— though cautiously—that under socialism monogamous love will come into its own, and that, "the equality of women . . . will tend infinitely more to make men really monogamous than to make women polyandrous." (p.145)

Given the advantage of nearly a century of anthropological research and historical experience, it is possible to make some telling criticisms of Engels' theory of the origin and imminent end of male domination. The Bachofen-Morgan group marriage hypothesis, and the theory of the stages through which group marriage must pass on the way to pairing marriage, has been wholly discredited. But this is a relatively unimportant part of Engels' theory, which can be modified without much damage to the basic contention that male domination is economically determined. Furthermore, the common objection that Engels falsely assumes that there is a single pattern of cultural evolution for all human societies, is largely an attack on a straw man, since Engels clearly intends his specific (pre)historical reconstructions to apply primarily to the societies to which he actually refers, e.g. the Iroquois and the ancient Athenians, Romans, and Germans.

Nevertheless, Engels' thesis that patriarchy is essentially the result of the accumulation of private wealth in the postsavage era does make it somewhat difficult to explain the various primitive, communistic and prebarbaric, but distinctly patriarchal cultures which are now known to exist (or to have existed), e.g. in Australia. It would seem that private wealth is not a necessary condition for male supremacy, however much it may tend to intensify its effects. Nor is it a *sufficient* explanation of the rise of male domination, even in those cultures which did follow something like the historical pattern Engels describes. Engels explains men's appropriation of wealth in the form of land, herds or slaves as a natural result of men's role as food providers in the original division of labor between the sexes. But if, as now seems certain, women's food gathering was from the beginning as important as a food source as men's hunting, then it is not clear why any new means of subsistence should automatically have belonged to men. Obviously some other causal factor was at work besides the growth of private property, though critics of Engels disagree as to what the key additional cause was—women's biological disadvantages, men's hormonally induced drive for power, the dualistic ideology which denigrated the female, or all three.

But although a purely economic explanation of male domination will not suffice, it is clear that Marx and Engels are right about the overall effects of the institution of private property on the relation between the sexes. As contemporary matrilineal cultures have come into contact with Western civilization and begun to acquire individual wealth, they have almost invariably undergone a conversion to patriliny, with a concomitant loss of status for women. Civilization is undeniably a process which tends to aggravate whatever original tendency towards male domination may exist in the human race, and largely for the reasons Engels points out. That is, it places in male hands the economic power which enables them to subordinate women as they cannot be subordinated so long as their labor remains as valuable and productive as that of men.

It does not, of course, follow—and indeed Engels does not claim—that the elimination of private property and of the family as an economic unit will *automatically* restore women to full social equality with men. But neither would Engels, with his somewhat over-simplified view of ideologies (such as sexism) as products of economic circumstances, have predicted the actual length and difficulty of the postcapitalist struggle for sexual equality. The situation of women in most if not all of the socialist states of the twentieth century demonstrates that women can be integrated into the public production process without either being relieved of their traditional domestic responsibilities or accorded equal standing with men in their work and political role. Efforts to eliminate women's domestic workload by socializing housework, as Engels prescribes, have generally been unsuccessful or insufficient. As long as there are individual family residences there is some private domestic labor to be done; and even when there are not, socialized domestic labor may still be underpaid and done by women. It is perhaps not unfair to point out that the necessity that domestic labor be *shared* by men and women is unlikely to have occurred to either Engels or Marx, who never questioned their own personal right to the housekeeping services of women.

1. Marx and Engels, *The German Ideology* (International Publishers, New York, 1967; written 1845–46, first published 1932), p.21.

EPSTEIN, Cynthia Fuchs. *Woman's Place: Options and Limits in Professional Careers* (University of California Press, Berkeley, 1970)

Epstein, a sociologist whose dissertation dealt with women in the legal profession, here deals with American women's participation in the whole range of prestige professions—academic, political, clergical, medical and scientific. Surprisingly, the proportion of women in these fields remained roughly constant over the first seventy years of this century, in spite of advances in women's legal and political status. Epstein seeks to explain both why this is so and how those relatively few women who survive in professional occupations manage it. She identifies no single primary cause of this waste of women's potential, but presents evidence for a number of circular processes that contribute to this result. A major factor is that our culture still conceives of the maternal and professional role-configurations as mutually exclusive, so that most women feel they must choose one or the other. Thus women with talent often decide against a career—or continuation of a career—because they anticipate failures and difficulties which are in fact no longer inevitable. The uncertainty as to whether or not they will be able to make use of professional training makes it difficult for women to formulate and retain ambitious career goals.

But it is not only their own (socially conditioned) choices that hold women back. Those who do enter the professions find that their social status as women is in conflict with their professional status. While men are encouraged or at least readily forgiven for giving higher priority to their occupational obligations than to their families, married women are invariably expected to put their families first. Thus the man's status set is complementary, while the woman's is contradictory. Women who succeed in reconciling the two statuses do so by such *ad hoc* and often unsatisfactory devices as limiting their number of friends, outside interests and offspring, pursuing a career which can be defined as an adjunct to their family role (e.g. as the husband's partner or assistant), by activating the conflicting statuses intermittently and one at a time, or by hiring other women to help with the housework and child care. It also helps to have a job that is visibly important and that has fixed and observable demands (rather than one like writing or painting which is self-paced), to have friends in the same field, and to have a supportive husband. Yet even with all of these advantages married career women are frequently tempted to quit, especially since they are usually underpaid and usually make little net financial gain from working, after subtracting all their work-related expenses.

Finally, Epstein argues, the structure of American professions acts to ensure that men will continue to predominate in the well paid and prestigious areas. All occupations in America are heavily sex-typed (with a few recent exceptions such as computer programming), and furthermore, men do much better in terms of pay and advancement even in the female professions like nursing and library work. Women in the male professions on the other hand are generally concentrated at the bottom of the ladder, in part because they are excluded from the informal interactions, e.g. clubs, protege systems and man-to-man understandings, which may be necessary for success. Although it has been demonstrated that women with Ph.D.'s publish just as much or more on the average than men, women *seem* to contribute even less to the professions than their proportional numbers would lead one to expect. This is largely because women's contributions tend to be overlooked, credited to men, or taken less seriously than men's. The conflict between their sex status and their professional role may generate enough noise to drown out whatever they have to say.

Epstein concludes that women will not be able to compete in the professions on an equal basis with men until their numbers are significantly increased and until social presumptions about women's place are radically restructured. (Soviet women are well ahead of Americans in the former respect, but they have yet to equal men's achievements in the professions because they are still burdened with extensive domestic responsibilities.)

ERIKSON, Erik H. "Womanhood and the Inner Space," in *Women and Analysis: Dialogues on Psychoanalytic Views of Femininity*, edited by Jean Strouse (Grossman Publishers, New York, 1974, pp.291–319; first published 1968, in *Identity, Youth and Crisis*, edited by Erik Erikson.)
"Once More the Inner Space: Letter to a Former Student" (*op. cit.*,pp.320–340)

Erikson is a contemporary psychoanalyst who was born in Germany (of Danish parents) and studied in Vienna with Freud and his circle. His analysis of female psychology is not extensively developed, but it has attracted a great deal of attention. It is as biologically deterministic as that of Freud or Deutsch (with whom he also worked), but seemingly less androcentric, in that it assigns primary importance not to the little girl's (recognition of her) lack of a male genital organ, but to her awareness of her own genitalia, specifically the "inner space" of the vagina and uterus. Feminists like Millett (1) and Janeway (2) have objected to Erikson's conclusions as sexist, although he reverses the usual deterministic line of argument and claims that the biologically-conditioned uniqueness of the female psyche is a reason *for* women's taking a larger share in the running of the larger world.

Erikson's analysis arises from live observations of the play behavior of some 300 ten- to twelve-year-old boys and girls in Berkeley, the subjects of a longitudinal study on child development. Each was asked to construct, using blocks, dolls and other available toys, an "exciting scene" from an imaginary motion picture, and then to describe the scenes they had created. Erikson reports that in constructing these scenes, "girls and boys used space differently . . . the girls emphasized *inner* and the boys *outer* space." (p.298) The girls, that is, more often (in two out of three cases) depicted interior scenes, initially peaceful, which are intruded upon by boys, men or animals, while the boys more often depicted outdoor scenes, with high, projecting structures which collapse, or animals or machines moving along roadways, sometimes getting into accidents, sometimes being stopped or directed by police.

Erikson considers it significant that this observed behavioral difference is in some way parallel to

> the morphology of genital differentiation itself: in the male, an external organ, erectable and intrusive in character, serving the channelization of mobile sperm cells; in the female, internal organs, with vestibular access leading to statically expectant ova. (p.300)

He suggests that the explanation of the behavioral difference is

the "profound difference . . . between the sexes in the experience of the ground plan of the human body." (p.301) The differing genital experiences of the two sexes account not only for their
different way of organizing space, but also for certain differences
in their "identity functions." One such difference, Erikson suggests, is that women, unlike men, cannot achieve a mature, adult
identity until "they know whom they will marry and for whom
they will make a home." (p.309) In other words,

> womanhood arrives [only] when attractiveness and experience
> have succeeded in selecting what is to be admitted to the welcome
> of the inner space, "for keeps." (p.310)

Furthermore, *all* of a woman's goals and commitments will "naturally also reflect the ground plan of her body." For

> since a woman is never not-a-woman, she can see her long range
> goals only in those modes of activity which include and integrate
> her natural dispositions. (p.316)

One may well wonder whether the empirical foundations of
Erikson's theory (or sketch of a theory) are secure. There would
seem to be little need to refer to the psychological influence of
genital morphology in explaining the observations derived from
the Berkeley study, since there are several alternative explanations (not necessarily mutually exclusive) which are considerably
more plausible; e.g., that the differences only reflect what children of that age have long since learned about the style of play or
of fantasy which is culturally assigned to members of their sex,
and/or that the differing styles of play are influenced by hormonally induced differences in the organization of the central nervous
system, with, perhaps, females being more verbally inclined and
males more inclined towards vigorous motor activities (3).

More seriously perhaps, Erikson's theory, like Freud's, depends upon the confusion between an individual's awareness of
the shape, etc. of his or her genitals (and of their unlikeness to
those of the opposite sex) and the assignment of a particular
meaning or significance to the difference. There are indefinitely
many meanings which could have been assigned to the male/
female genital difference under different circumstances, including meanings precisely opposite to those Erikson proposes. Consider the popular science fiction fantasy in which the existing
social roles of the sexes are exactly reversed. In that world, female
psychoanalysts might explain the preference of females for active
outdoor scenes by reference to their possession of a dynamic
inner body space which enables them to be immediately at home
in the active outer spaces of the world; similarly, the preference of

males for quiet indoor activities might be seen as due to a certain natural modesty and introversion which results from their awareness of the vulnerability of their external genitals. That such a theory should arise in such a world would be understandable, though the nature of the fallacy is fairly clear.

In other words, the question with which Erikson begins is what some philosophers call an improper question. He asks,

> how does the identity formation of women differ by dint of the fact that their somatic design harbors an "inner space," destined to bear the offspring of chosen men and, with it, a biological, psychological, and ethical commitment to the care of human infancy? (p.295)

The question is unanswerable because its presumptions are false; women's wombs do *not* "destine" them to be mothers, with a primary commitment to child care. Or, at least, they no longer do in some societies. The choice is there (and to some extent it always has been), and it is an insult to both mothers and nonmothers to treat the commitment to motherhood as a necessary and inevitable part of mature womanhood.

1. See Kate Millett, *Sexual Politics*, pp.210–220.
2. See Elizabeth Janeway, *Man's World, Woman's Place*, pp.93–96.
3. See Barkwick, Maccoby and Jacklin, and Money and Ehrhardt.

ESTROGEN: See Hormones.

ETHOLOGY   Ethology is the scientific study of the social behavior of animals, and its roots e.g. in instinctive behavior. Patterns of dominance and submission have been a prime concern of ethologists like Lorenz, and of sociobiologists like Wilson, who attempt to systematize the results of ethology and genetics, and to devise theories which are applicable to human as well as animal societies. In recent years many popular writers have appealed to the discoveries of ethologists about the sex-role behavior of nonhuman primates (particularly certain species of baboon, which are highly "patriarchal" in their social structure) to support the claim that male dominance is an inherited and inalterable aspect of human behavior. (See Ardrey, Fast, Fox, Morris, Storr, Tiger.)

Herschberger, in 1948, produced a brilliant critique of this kind of rash extrapolation from primate to human behavior (or vice versa). Naomi Weisstein gives a concise summary of the reasons why such ethologically based arguments for the human sexual status quo are uniformly fallacious. Also see Evelyn Reed, and Elaine Morgan; and *Man and Aggression*, edited by Ashley Montagu, in Anthologies VIII.

EVOLUTIONARY THEORY The theory of the evolution of biological species through natural selection, or the survival of the fittest, may be helpful in explaining whatever innate psychological or other differences are found to exist between human males and females, but it cannot validly be used to argue that any particular psychological differences *must* exist, or that they must be innate. It is even less relevant to the question of whether any particular sex-role system is the most desirable one for humans. It has, nevertheless, often been used to argue that patriarchy is biologically inevitable. (See Darwin, Spencer, Westermarck; also see Antifeminism, and Biological Determinism.) There are, on the other hand, feminist thinkers who reject the usual assumption that it was the hunting activites of the males which provided the driving force behind human evolution (as argued, for instance, by Morris, Ardrey, Tiger, Fox), and who have found in their own interpretation of evolutionary theory an argument for fundamental changes in existing sex roles. (See Gilman, Sherfey, Elaine Morgan; also see Montagu's, *Man and Aggression*, in Anthologies VIII.)

EXISTENTIALIST FEMINISM: See Buytendijk, de Beauvoir.

F

THE FAMILY The "biological" or nuclear family—consisting of a man, usually one woman, and the latter's (and presumably also the former's) children—is certainly one of the oldest of human institutions. Whether it was originally matriarchal, patriarchal or neither, and whether it is the oldest human social organization or was generally preceded by a different kind of family (e.g. a matrifocal one to which adult males were only loosely attached) are questions which are still debated. Such questions are relevant, if only indirectly, to the debate over the existence or non-existence of innate psychological differences between the sexes. For if, as many have argued, the biological family is universal to the human species (or even an inheritance from our prehuman ancestors), and if it has always been male dominated, then this would seem to indicate—though not entirely to prove—that it is so firmly grounded in our biological and psychological nature as to be difficult or impossible to change in any fundamental way. If, on the other hand, it is a product of particular historical and socioeconomic conditions rather than of human nature itself, then changing conditions may alter or eliminate it; it may become more egalitarian, or it may be replaced by other kinds of personal living and childrearing arrangements. (See Matriarchy Theory, Patriarchy Theory, Socialism and Feminism.) This view incidentally, is perfectly compatible with the view that there are inherited biological *tendencies*("soft" biological determinism).

Whatever its origins, it is clear that the biological family has existed in all of the major civilizations of the world at least since the beginnings of recorded history, and that it has been almost uniformly patriarchal—that is, patrilineal and male dominated. It is also clear that the patriarchal family promotes a division of roles between the sexes which is far more conducive to the freedom and social status of the male than of the female. Her sexual freedom is usually limited as his is not, and most of the child care and other domestic responsibilities are generally also hers; whatever activites she pursues in the "outside world" must be arranged around and in whatever time may be spared from these domestic concerns. Why this should seemingly always have been so, and the moral arguments for and against its continuing to be so, are among the central concerns of most of the writers dealt with in this encyclopedia. (See also Marriage, Motherhood, Radical Feminism, and Sociology of Women.)

FAST, Julius. *The Incompatibility of Men and Women and How to Overcome It* (Avon Books, New York, 1971)

A lightweight popular book, the main thesis of which is largely derived from Konrad Lorenz's observations of animal behavior. Lorenz describes a species of cichlid (a fish), in which the four major instincts, sex, aggression, fear and submission, are differently related to one another in the otherwise identical male and female: male cichlids can mix sex with aggression but not with fear or submission, while females can mix sex with fear and submission but not with aggression. Consequently, the male cichlid is aggressive in the sexual act and the female submissive. Fast maintains that the same is true of humans, the only difference being that in humans these *instincts* are reduced to *drives*, that is behavioral tendencies whose expression is not inborn but must be learned. Evolution, he says, "has . . . selected sexual aggression as the man's role in sex and sexual submissiveness as the woman's role." (p.148) Supposedly, the key to overcoming the incompatibility of men and women is the fuller recognition of this evolutionary necessity, and towards this end Fast provides a set of encounter group games, played with male and female paper dolls.

Fast attempts to remove the sting of his conclusion (for feminists) by explaining that the necessary sexual aggressiveness of men and submissiveness of women does not mean that men cannot help *dominating* women. He distinguishes between aggressiveness and domination or exploitation and holds that men can learn to be aggressive towards women without being domineering or exploitative. Nor does the submissiveness of women mean that they must be *passive* in their sexual relationships with men. The woman may actively stimulate the man to aggressiveness; but if she herself is aggressive then neither she nor the male will be capable of sexual performance. From this he concludes that feminists are wrong to argue for the *equality* of men and women; men and women are *different*, and therefore not *equal*. This is, of course, a *non sequitur*, since the moral, legal and political equality demanded by feminists is in no way premised on the physical or psychological *identity*, i.e. exact similarity, of the parties.

Be that as it may, the legitimacy of the cichlid/human analogy remains to be determined. (See Bernard.) It is not *universally* true of humans—as it presumably is of cichlids—that males must combine sexuality with aggression, females with submission. (See Jessie Bernard.) *Some* men and women (the more enlightened ones, one might argue) prefer a more symmetrical and fully reciprocal sexual interaction. Some successfully reverse the traditional roles. Thus the way is open for the feminist to argue that insofar as it may prove to be true that men instinctively associate sex with aggression, violence or victory over a woman, or that women associate it with submission, these are unfortunate and anachronistic vestiges of the animal condition which civilized human beings can be expected to outgrow. The suggestion that men should be aggressive but not domineering, women submissive but not passive, is unhelpful since the relationship between the person who always aggresses and the person who always submits is hardly one of moral or personal equality, on *any* of the many slippery meanings of "aggress" and "submit."

FEMINISM   The term "feminism" refers to the moral or political commitment or movement to achieve equality for women. Very few feminists have seriously advocated or even wished for female supremacy, i.e., the simple reversal of the present power relationship between the sexes (but see Davis, Solanas). Most would regard a situation in which women monopolized social, economic and poltical power as objectionable for much the same reasons that patriarchy is objectionable. Feminism, then, is based on the active conviction that women and men are morally entitled to the same moral and legal rights, the same degree of personal autonomy, and the same educational and occupational opportunities: and the conviction that these goals are at present far from being realized. All the major feminist groups agree on these points, though they disagree as to the fundamental causes of male domination, and about the social changes necessary to eliminate it.

Thus, liberal feminists tend to blame the oppression of women on patriarchal laws, sexist content in the school curricula and public media, and the stereotyped beliefs about the nature of women which these reinforce. They do not, however, regard marriage, or women's role as primary childrearer and homemaker as necessarily oppressive or incompatible with sexual equality. (See, e.g., Astell, Wollstonecraft, John Stuart Mill,

Harriet Taylor, Bertrand Russell, Ellen Key, Friedan, Bird, Epstein.) Socialist feminists agree that the patriarchal elements of the legal and educational systems are oppressive, but hold that it is capitalism (and the older economic systems based on private property and surplus wealth) which is the underlying cause of male domination. They argue that only under socialism can women be liberated, through their reintegration into the public production process, and the socialization of child care and other domestic duties which under patriarchal capitalism are the private responsibility of women. (See William Thompson, Fourier, Engels, Bebel, Guettel, Marx, Reed; also see Anthologies X.)

Most of the radical feminists of today are also socialists; but they hold that it is not just capitalism, but the patriarchal family—which preceeds capitalism historically and can survive its demise—which accounts for the oppression and inferior social status of women. They therefore call not only for the end of capitalism and the legal, educational and occupational inequality of the sexes, but for the elimination of the biological family, at least as an economic and childrearing institution; they also demand the elimination of the sexual taboos which operate to preserve the biological family. (See Atkinson, Borgese, Firestone, Greer, Millett.) There are also lesbian separatist feminists, who add to these radical feminist demands the rejection of heterosexuality as a valid life style for any free woman. (See Abbot and Love, Dworkin, and Johnston.) (For some recent studies of the contemporary feminist movement and its subdivisions, see Yates, Ware, and Mitchell (1971); also Deckard, and Hale and Levine, in Anthologies IV.)

Although the various wings of the feminist or women's liberation movement are divided on many vital theoretical issues, it is important to remember that they are united on the most fundamental moral issues. All would agree that personhood transcends sex, i.e. that the biological sex to which a person belongs determines neither moral worth nor proper social role. All agree that the innumerable attempts to prove that women's intelligence is inferior to men's; or that women are "naturally" subservient, masochistic or service-oriented; or that men have a natural *need* (as opposed to an observable propensity) to dominate women and public life, are false and pernicious rationalizations of a manifestly unjust state of affairs.

This is not to say that all feminists reject outright the possibility that there may be *some* inherent psychological differences between the sexes. The case, for instance, for a greater readiness on the part of males to learn violent or aggressive behavior has become too powerful to ignore (see Bardwick, Goldberg, Hutt, Maccoby), and some feminists stress the importance of this factor as a cause of male domination (see Holliday, Johnston). The feminist point is rather that, whatever the (average or statistical) differences between the psychological traits and behavioral dispositons of women and men, they most certainly are *not* of such a kind as to justify the imposition of social, legal, educational and occupational disabilities upon women, or to justify confining women to those social roles which our culture traditionally defines as feminine. (Also see Antifeminism; Biological Determinism; Liberal Feminism: Lesbianism; Radical Feminism; Spiritual Feminism; and Socialism and Feminism.)

FEMININITY: See Androgyny; Emotion; and Psychology of Women.

FIGES, Eva. *Patriarchal Attitudes* (Fawcett Publications, Greenwich, Connecticut, 1971)

A concise and well-reasoned look at Western men's self-serving conceptions about the nature of women, particularly since the (so-called) Enlightenment. Since the discovery of paternity, she thinks, men have dominated women and limited their freedom in order to gain for themselves a kind of immortality in the form of children (especially sons) whom they know to be theirs, and to whom they can leave their name and property. (Prior to this discovery, human society was necessarily matrilineal, but it probably was not matriarchal, in the sense of female-dominated; it was simply non-male-dominated.) Perhaps the primary means whereby patriarchy is preserved is through men's image of women, to which women are conditioned to conform. Men have considered women their inferiors and as naturally opposite to men with respect to the properties men value most in themselves—rationality, independence and so on. Yet as Mill pointed out over a century ago, there are no scientific grounds whatever for holding these or any other mental traits to be inherently—that is by nature rather than nurture—more characteristic of one sex than the other. All that empirical studies of women as they are today can show is the extent to which patriarchal attitudes continue to affect us.

Figes does a good job of illustrating the consistency with which patriarchal attitudes towards women have appeared in the work of the greatest thinkers, from St. Augustine through Rousseau and the Romantics, the German idealists (Hegel, Fichte, Schopenhauer, Nietzsche and Weininger), and the Freudian school of psychoanalysis. She ends with an attack on marriage, which she considers the greatest barrier to equality, but one which will endure as long as it remains the best available economic haven for women and children. Women could more readily escape marriage and dependency if children were treated as a responsibility of the state, by the provision of substantial allowances for each child and of adequate nurseries. This would make economically motivated marriages unnecessary, and would benefit men as well as women, since they would no longer be required to support women and children.

FILENE, Peter. *Him/Her Self: Sex Roles in Modern America* (Harcourt Brace Jovanovich, New York, 1974)

A useful overview of shifts in American sex roles and prevailing attitudes toward them, especially among the middle class, from the end of the Victorian era to the early seventies. Radical feminists before and after the turn of the century had urged women to achieve economic independence and freedom by pursuing professional careers and refusing to be bound by the traditional duties of wife-and-motherhood. But the women who fought and won the vote did so by making concessions to Victorian presumptions about the feminine nature, which they argued would lead to a purification of politics and public life once women were enfranchised. By these concessions they won the battle but temporarily lost the war for serious changes in traditional sex roles. Relatively few women were willing or able to seek fulfillment through careers and though many continued to work, even during the great depression of the thirties when working women were bitterly attacked for stealing jobs from male breadwinners, they did so more to raise their families' standard of living than to find their true identities. In the seventies, however, the preconditions for fundamental change in sex roles and sex stereotypes have begun to exist in the awareness of the new feminists—some of them men—that men's roles as well as women's must change if women and men are to be able to combine work with marriage and parenthood, without unduly sacrificing one to the other.

FIRESTONE, Shulamith. *The Dialectic of Sex: The Case for Feminist Revolution* (Bantam Books, New York, 1972; first published by William Morrow and Company, New York, 1970)

Firestone's *Dialectic of Sex* has already become a classic of feminist thought. It is the clearest and boldest presentation thus far of the radical feminist position. Firestone holds that it is the biological sexual dichotomy itself, particularly the biological division of labor in reproduction, which is the root cause not only of male domination, but of economic class exploitation, racism, imperialism and ecological irresponsibility. Sexual inequality is "an oppression that goes back beyond recorded history to the animal kingdom itself." (p.2) It is, in this sense, natural, and until now it has been universal and inevitable; but now, at last, the cultural and technological preconditions exist which make its elimination possible, and perhaps necessary for human survival.

Firestone describes her approach as a dialectical materialism of a kind more radical than that of Marx and Engels, who in their preoccupation with economic processes failed to perceive "the sexual substratum of the historical dialectic." (p.4) Unlike Engels, she holds that male domination, being biologically based, existed long before the institution of private property and the monogamous patriarchal family which private property produced. Male domination is the result of the "biological family" (whether matrilineal or patrilineal) and the inevitable dependence of women and children within it upon men, for protection if not subsistence. There were no ancient matriarchies (woman-ruled societies), and the apparently superior status of women in matrilineal cultures is due only to the relative weakness of men. For whatever the lineage system, women's vulnerability during pregnancy and the long period of human infancy necessitate the protective and hence dominant role of the male.

This dependence of the female and the child on the male causes "specific psychosexual distortions in the human personality," distortions which Firestone says were accurately though androcentrically described by Freud. She describes Freudianism as a "misguided feminism"; for the only real difference between Freud's analysis and that of the radical feminists is that Freud and his followers accept the social context in which sexual repression develops as immutable. Freud demonstrated that the source of repression and sex-class distinction is the inherently unequal power relationship in the biological family; women and children are alike oppressed by the more powerful father. The young boy identifies first with the mother, whose oppression he shares, but soon switches his identification to the father, whose power he fears but will some day inherit. In the process he accedes to the incest taboo and the strict separation of sexuality and emotion which this requires, and which is the psychological foundation of political and ideological oppression. The girl, meanwhile, envies the father's power too but learns that she cannot inherit it and can only share in it indirectly, by currying favor with the dominant male.

Not only are both women and children inevitably oppressed in the biological family, they are doubly oppressed by the particular form of it which prevails in the industrialized nations, i.e. the patriarchal *nuclear* family, which isolates each couple and their offspring. Compulsory schooling and the romantic mythology of childhood are devices which serve to prolong the isolation of children and their economic dependence. The socialist-feminist revolution will free both women and children, leaving them with complete economic independence and sexual freedom, and integrating them fully into the larger social world.

The end of the sex-class system must mean the end of the biological family, that is, the end of women's biological reproductive role through artifical means of gestation. Love between the sexes will remain, for it is not necessarily oppressive—contrary to the view of the radical lesbian feminists (see e.g. Atkinson, Dworkin, Johnston)—but becomes oppressive when joined to the reproductive function. The biological family turns sexual love into a tool of oppression. Within it, women give their love to men, thus inspiring the latter to greater cultural creativity, and providing the former with an emotional identity of the sort denied them in the larger world. But men, as a result of the Oedipus complex and the incest taboo, are unable to love; they must degrade the women they make love to, in order to distinguish them from the mother, the first and forbidden love object. They can respect women or be sexually attracted to them, but not both. This is why the so-called "sexual revolution" is no liberation for women, who are still bound by the double standard and the need to combine love and sexuality. By eliminating the biological family and the incest taboo, the feminist revolution will enlarge the opportunity for real heterosexual love, as well as legitimating every other type of voluntary sexual relationship.

As for the way in which children will be raised once they are no longer born of women in the biological family, Firestone hesitates to make any exact predictions, but suggests that there will be a variety of childrearing social units, including couples "living together" and households of unrelated persons, up to a dozen or so, who contract to remain together long enough to provide a home for their children until the latter are ready to enter the world—which they will do at a much earlier age than is now considered possible.

The feminist revolution presupposes socialism, but goes beyond it. Existing socialist societies, Firestone notes, have tried to expand women's roles without fundamentally altering them, to integrate women into a male world, rather than eliminating sex class altogether. The feminist revolution will end the cultural split between the "Aesthetic Mode" (feminine, intuitive, artistic) and the "Technological Mode" (masculine, empirical, aimed at the control of nature through the comprehension of its mechanical laws). The end of sexual repression will free Eros to diffuse throughout and humanize the entire culture. Eventually it will lead to the end not only of alienated labor but of all labor as such, that is activity which is not performed for its own sake. Cybernation will eliminate domestic and other drudgery, leaving everyone free to do work which is intrinsically rewarding. There are many questions to be asked about Firestone's theory, but perhaps the most serious is the question whether it has been demonstrated that it is women's biological role in reproduction which is the source of their oppression. While there has probably never been a true matriarchy, there is considerable evidence that the matrilineal, goddess-worshiping cultures of the Near East, in the second and third millennia B.C. and earlier, were at least very nearly sexually egalitarian. If so, then the childbearing function does not sufficiently explain women's inferior social status in later civilizations, and there is less reason to stress the elimination of that function as an essential part of liberation.

FOREMAN, Ann. *Femininity as Alienation: Women and the Family in Marxism and Psychoanalysis* (Pluto Press, London, 1977)

Foreman is a radical feminist who seeks to explain the alienated concept of woman—our culture's view of woman as Other (see Simone de Beauvoir)—through combining the insights of Marx and Freud. To do this, she says, it is necessary to understand the relationship between the economic and the psychic realms. Liberal thought drove a wedge between these two realms by basing individual liberty on the distinction between the public arena (politics and economics) and the private realm of the family (to which women are confined). Even *feminist* liberals like John Stuart Mill did not advocate any basic change in women's domestic role; for they did not see the latter as political, or as conditioned by the prevailing economic system.

This dualism in liberal thought, Foreman argues, has been reproduced in both Marxist and psychoanalytic theory. Freud held that the Oedipus Complex (in which the child is sexually attracted to the parent of the opposite sex, but learns to repress that attraction) shapes the human psyche in every culture and in every historical period. In fact, however, the Oedipus Complex is not a cultural universal; in matrilineal cultures it is not parent/child incest but brother/sister incest which is most strictly tabooed, and the desire for which must be repressed. Thus the particular structuring of the psyche which results from the Oedipus Complex must be seen as the *result* of the patriarchal family, not its original cause.

Marx and Engels had an entirely different view of human nature, which they held to be the result of productive activity and the social relations conditioned by this activity. Patriarchy, they maintained, arose not because of any universal features of human psychology, but because of certain developments in the mode of production. It was private property and surplus wealth which provided men with the motive for the creation of patriarchal institutions; before there was any surplus product which could be accumulated by individual males and passed on to their sons, patriarchy would have been pointless.

But Engels combined this economic and historical explanation of patriarchy with a noneconomic and a historical one. Women, he suggested, naturally came to desire monogamy, whereas men did not. Women therefore "purchased" the right to be married to a single man, at the cost of many of their former freedoms. This second account, Foreman notes, is inconsistent with the first; it reflects, in fact, the liberal assumption that sexual relationships within the family are wholly separate from the economic and political institutions of the society.

This dualist tendency in Marxist thought, according to Foreman, was strengthened by the economic determinist interpretation of Marx's theory, which held that ideology was part of the "superstructure" of society, and that it was merely a reflection of the economic base. On this interpretation, women's domestic role is part of the ideological superstructure, and therefore can only be changed through changing the economic system. This led to the attitude among "scientific" Marxists that freedom for women would have to wait until after the revolution. Nor was there any understanding of the way in which the oppression of woman functions as an integral *part* of the capitalist economic system.

Foreman argues that in spite of the patriarchal bias of Freud, Freudian theory provides the key to understanding the shaping of sexuality and the human psyche under capitalism. Her thesis is that the liberal/bourgeois stereotypes of masculinity and femininity are fundamentally a result of the alienation of labor under the capitalist system of commodity production. Capitalism detached social production from the family, thus depriving the latter of its apparent economic significance, and the former of its personal meaning. The alienation of the work place under capitalism required that the family function as a haven for the personal, the subjective and the emotional. Women served as the guardians of these values, and consequently came to be defined in terms of the familiar alienated stereotype of femininity: as passive, subjective, and emotional. Contrary to the existentialist analysis of de Beauvoir, this particular stereotype of femininity is not universal:

> It was only with the onset of capitalist organization, where the split between the family and social production became generalized through all the classes and social relations of society that the conditions for women's alterity [otherness] were developed. (p.87)

Foreman argues that this alienated definition of femininity developed simultaneously with the modern concept of the human individual. Both developments were the results of the destruction of the kinship system as the basis of economic production. Under capitalism, marriage and male/female relations developed a peculiar sanctity, as the locus of human individuality. Through the process of reification, however, the historical specificity of the male/female relation under capitalism is hidden. Ideology is taken for eternal truth, and (the comprehension of) the process whereby this occurs is repressed. It is this process which explains the particular structuring of the human psyche into conscious and unconscious levels, and into masculine and feminine patterns, which Freud describes.

Foreman concludes that radical feminism is the one political movement which has the potential for breaking the grip of patriarchal ideology. For it is only radical feminists who have begun to understand and to expose the fundamental relationship between the prevailing sexual roles and stereotypes and the capitalist system of production. This is the real significance of the slogan that the personal is political, and the political personal.

FOURIER, Francois Marie Charles (1772-1837). *Design for Utopia: Selected Writings of Charles Fourier* (translated by Julia

Franklin, Schocken Books, New York, 1971; this selection and translation first published 1901)

The Utopian Vision of Charles Fourier: Selected Texts on Work, Love, and Passionate Attraction (translated and edited by Jonathan Brecker and Richard Bienvenu; Beacon Press, Boston, 1971)

Harmonian Man: Selected Writings of Charles Fourier (edited by Mark Poster, translated by Susan Hanson; Doubleday and Company, Garden City, New York, 1971)

Charles Fourier was a utopian thinker who, though not a socialist (1), produced a devastating critique of capitalism and bourgeois morality and thereby contributed to the thought of Marx and Engels. He made complete equality between men and women, plus complete sexual freedom and gratification, a central part of his utopia—though these features were de-emphasized in his later published work and that of his disciples. Fourier published about eight volumes in his lifetime and left as much in unpublished manuscripts. His complete works have been published in French (2), but unfortunately they have never been translated into English except in selected excerpts, as in the volumes listed above. Most of his sexual doctrines are contained in the *Theorie des Quatre Mouvements*, published in 1808, and the incomplete manuscript *Le Nouveau Monde Amoureux*, which was first published in 1967 (3).

Fourier is probably best known to feminists for his contention that the degree of freedom or subjugation of women is not only the best index of a society's progress towards civilization (and beyond), but the "pivot mechanism" which triggers cultural progress or regression. "As a general proposition," he says,

> Social advances and changes of periods are brought about by virtue of the progress of women towards liberty, and the decadences of the social order are brought about by virtue of the decrease of liberty of women." (*Design for Utopia*, p.77)

Thus, for instance,

> If a barbarous people adopted *exclusive marriage*, they would in a short time become civilized through this innovation alone; [and] if we adopted the *seclusion and sale of women*, we should in a short time become barbarous through this single innovation . . . (*Op. cit.* p.76)

Fourier posited eight periods of human cultural progress, beginning with the most primitive (Eden) and ending with Harmony, the state of perfect association in which all human needs are fulfilled. Of these, barbarism is the fourth, and is marked by the complete slavery of women, and civilization the fifth, marked by exclusive marriage and some civil liberties for women. Further progress will require the end of exclusive marriage and an increase in sexual freedom for both sexes; of this, more later.

The economic system which Fourier designed for the Harmonians (and which Marx labeled merely utopian) combines maximum freedom and happiness for all with maximum wealth and productivity, especially agricultural productivity. There will still be private ownership of wealth and distinct economic classes, but through the skilled collective management of resources, population control, and communal living, the "poor" will be wealthier in absolute terms than the rich are under "civilized" conditions. Work will be made attractive by its voluntariness, by the social interactions it will provide, and by frequent changes of occupation throughout the day. Harmonians may participate in as many kinds of work as they choose, and each work specialty will involve membership in a "passionate series," i.e. a group of individuals who cooperate and compete for recognition within this field. Manufacturing and commerce will be kept at a minimum, and the resources of the planet will be devoted to agriculture, each region producing only the finest produce of which it is capable. Cooking, cleaning, infant care and other domestic work will be done professionally, in the Phalansteries, living and dining units of 1,600 persons each which will operate rather like fine hotels. Thus freed of their domestic duties, women will be fully equal members of Harmonian society.

Fourier deplores the "civilized" system which requires that women be kept in a state of domestic servitude. He reproaches his fellow Frenchmen for their hostility toward women who have "a passion for study," asking,

> Are not women destined to exhibit in literature and the arts, the same capacity they have exhibited on the thrones, when, from the days of Semiramis to Catherine, there have been seven great queens to one of inferior capacity, while among kings, seven have been incapable to one that has been great? (*Harmonian Man*, p.210)

If women were equally educated with men, and not "smothered by a social system which engrosses . . . [them] in the complicated functions of our isolated households " (*loc. cit.*), they would surpass men in many executive fields. But, unlike Mary Wollstonecraft before him and the mainstream nineteenth and twentieth-century feminists afterwards, Fourier did not consider it desirable to improve women's educational opportunities without at the same time moving beyond capitalism, beyond civilization itself. For,

> Having, in civilization, as a general rule no higher function than

that of housekeeper, it is well that their education should stultify their intellects, and make them fit for such menial occupations. (*Loc. cit.*)

Even more unlike that of most early feminists was Fourier's attitude towards the pleasures of physical love. Fourier developed an elaborate psychology, based on the twelve basic human passions, of which love (both physical and spiritual) is one. He held that to deny any of these passions its full and proper gratification is to pervert it, to drive it into unnatural and undesirable channels. Hence in Harmonian society all of the "passional needs" will be richly and variously satisfied, including that of love. Marriage and marital fidelity will be forgotten, and no one, old or young, rich or poor, male or female, will be deprived of opportunities for sexual pleasure. There will be an enormous variety of life styles with respect to love and sex; some people will be serially monogamous, while others will enter more or less lasting sexual relationships with anywhere from two to eleven other persons. All will have the opportunity to be adventurers in the "courts of love" and to participate in elaborate and well-planned orgiastic festivities. In civilization, such practices would lead to debauchery and excess, but in Harmony they will not, since

> ... orgy is one of man's natural needs. What should be regulated is the exercise of this pleasure which is, like so many others, incompatible with civilization. (***Harmonian Man***, p. 278)

In Harmony, there will be no *merely* physical sexual encounters; all sex will be a meeting of the spirit as well as the body, and all but the most fleeting encounters will blossom into lifelong friendships, forming a kind of greatly extended family network.

Fourier's theory of the passions is in some ways an anticipation of Freud's theory of sexual repression, even though unlike Freud he considered children to be without specifically sexual urges. Both hold that civilization requires the suppression of most erotic urges, through the institution of monogamous marriage. The difference is that Fourier considers this suppression to be no longer necessary, and indeed henceforth a barrier to human progress. Monogamous marriage cannot *eliminate* polygamous love; Fourier estimated illicit sex acts to be five times as frequent in France as licit ones. Instead it makes love an outlaw, antisocial in its manifestations and results; whereas, on the other hand,

> An order of things which tolerated a triple or quadruple development of love, which legally elevated love to the degree that it has risen illegally, would . . . commute into social and useful diver-

tissement that pleasure whose prescription now becomes the leaven of disorder. (*Harmonian Man*, p.258)

Fourier also anticipates the contemporary radical feminists in calling for the abolition of marriage and the family, not just for women's sake but equally for men's. He points out that,

> The masculine sex, although stronger, has not made the law to its advantage in establishing isolated households and permanent marriage . . . What dupes men are that they have compelled themselves to wear a dreadful chain; what punishment they endure for having reduced women to bondage. (*Op. cit.*, pp.203–204)

He lists the major risks and disadvantages for men in permanent monagamous marriage as: (1) unhappiness due to a poor match; (2) expense; (3) the need to spend time supervising a household; (4) monotony; (5) sterility of one or both spouses; (6) widowerhood, with sole responsibility for the children; (7) unpleasant family alliances; and (8) "cuckoldom." (He even goes so far as to describe seventy-two distinct *types* of cuckoldry (4).) "What," he asks, "must one think of an institution so wearying to the strong sex who established it, and even more wearying to the female sex from whom no complaint is permitted." (*Op. cit.*, p.208)

Fourier, again like some of the contemporary radical feminists, links the liberation of women with that of children. In the Harmonian world, children will be reared communally from birth, and will by the age of three spontaneously do enough work to earn their keep and thus eliminate their economic dependence and the need for most child care activities by adults. Because children love dirt, the "little hordes" will be given some of the dirtiest jobs, thus freeing adults for work more suitable to their own tastes. But, unlike some contemporary radical feminists, e.g. Shulamith Firestone, he does not envision children beginning to engage in lovemaking at an early age. Instead, there will be considerable honor given to these young men and women who voluntarily preserve their virginity until the age of sixteen, eighteen, or even twenty.

In Harmonian society, even animals are entitled to happiness, and children take an active part in ensuring the well-being of animals, seeing to it, for instance, that those which are slaughtered do not suffer.

It is unfortunate that the part of Fourier's thought that, through Marx and Engels, became incorporated into the mainstream of socialist philosophy was primarily his critique of bourgeois society and the capitalist economic system rather than his positive visions. Attractive work, sexual and other freedoms, and the socialization of all domestic labor are still lacking in most existing socialist states, a fact which Fourier would have taken as proof that no portion of humanity has yet escaped from civilization into the next phase of development. It is true that Harmonian societies (such as the one set up at New Harmony, Indiana) did not prove stable social alternatives either, but they did not have as good a chance to prove themselves as socialism.

1.   That is, he did not advocate the end of private property or of class divisions by wealth, though his utopia might be called socialist in other respects.
2.   ***Oeuvres Completes de Charles Fourier***, 12 volumes, Editions Anthropos, Paris, 1966–1968.
3.   Volumes I and VII, respectively of the ***Oeuvres Completes***.
4.   See ***The Utopian Vision***, pp.183–188.

FOX, Robin and **TIGER**, Lionel. *The Imperial Animal* (Holt, Rinehart and Winston; New York, 1971)
   The theory here is substantially the same as that presented by Tiger in *Men and Groups* (1969), but more carefully worked out. Fox and Tiger are sociobiologists who maintain that human behavior is universally patterned—though not, of course, determined completely or in detail—by certain innate neural programs, or *biograms*, which evolved out of the survivial needs of our carnivorous ape ancestors. They see in the behavior of the savanna baboon, another carnivorous ape, the closest existing analogue to the human "biogrammar." Both species possess social systems based upon hierarchical orderings of males. Males compete for status in the hierarchy and for sexual access to fertile females; older, stronger males dominate younger, weaker ones. But to compete males must also cooperate, especially in the hunt and the defense of the group's territory, and towards this end they form "bonds" with other males, bonds which necessarily exclude females. The male initiation rites of primitive peoples illustrate this process.
   These male bonds, the authors claim, form the structural basis not only of prehistoric human and prehuman primate society, but of all the complex political systems men have since developed. Females have no place in the male hierarchy, although they do have (less structured and more fluid) rankings of their own, and can often influence which males rise in status. Unlike Tiger in his earlier work, they admit that females do form bonds; with their young, with males and with other females. But they hold

that these bonds form only the microstructure of society, for they are directed towards interpersonal ends, while the male bond is outward directed. There are matrilineal societies, but no matriarchal ones; even if the succession is through females it is predominantly males who exercise power. A matriarchy theorist might reply that nevertheless the widepread existence of primitive and even advanced societies with matrilineal descent and matrilocal marriage systems shows that it was the maternal bond, not the male-to-male bond which formed the political basis of prehistoric society. The male status hierarchy may have gained political ascendancy only relatively recently. (See, e.g., Bachofen, Briffault, Davis.)

Tiger and Fox, however, conclude that male dominance of politics, like the male propensity towards aggression and violence, is "built into our wiring." On the other hand, they do not draw the further conclusion that it is either inevitable or morally justifiable. "Equality and an equal participation of men and women in the political arena are things that must be energetically striven for. Ultimately, they must be imposed. In both cases we must say "no" to nature—our own human nature." (p.101) The biological explanation of male dominance is not one which precludes social change; it merely means that for social reform to be effective it will have to take account of human biogrammar. The reality of male drives and male-female interactions means that equal participation by women in government and other aspects of the national life cannot be expected to come about spontaneously or as a result of simply removing the legal barriers against them. "It may need something much more drastic like laws that compel boards of directors to have female members, or female quotas in the legislatures, before the greater particpation [by women] which would obviously be to everyone's benefit could be effected." (p.236)

FRANCOEUR, Robert T. *Utopian Motherhood: New Trends in Human Reproduction* (A.S. Barnes and Company, New York, 1973; first published 1970)
Eve's New Rib: Twenty Faces of Sex, Marriage, and Family (Dell Publishing Company, New York, 1972)

Francoeur is a biologist who is also a Catholic priest, and married. In *Utopian Motherhood* he explores the achievements and promise of various new reproductive technologies, and points out that these will inevitably lead to changes in the family and in male-female relationships. He describes the process of artificial insemination, extrauterine conception and/or gestation, the use of surrogate mothers (i.e. gestators), sex determination, the detection of fetal abnormalities and the medical treatment of the unborn fetus, and other new or soon-to-be feasible methods of altering and controlling the reproductive process.

Francoeur argues that as such technological interventions in the reproductive process become more common they will force us to revise some of our traditional assumptions about marriage, sex, parenthood and the family. His analysis is marred, however, by a persistent insensitivity to feminist issues. He invariably speaks of women's liberation not as an ongoing process but as a *fait accompli*; thus he is unable to ask the crucial question of how the new reproductive technologies can be made to serve the cause of sexual equality, rather than merely to increase the power of the (mostly male) medical establishment over women's lives.

In *Eve's New Rib*, Francoeur argues for a more open-minded approach on the part of the Church toward the inevitable current and upcoming changes in traditional sexual mores. The increasing separation of sex from procreation is leading to a greater toleration of all forms of nonprocreative sex. Open marriages (in which "adultery" is accepted for both spouses), nonmarital cohabitation, unisex marriages, polygamous and polyandrous marriages—all may be expected to become more common, and all should be accepted as potentially valid life styles. Again, however, although lip service is paid to the newly liberated condition of women there is little trace of a feminist perspective. The viewpoint remains androcentric, as, for instance, when Francoeur worries that a child who was artificially gestated might

> come to resent his [sic] mother who put him out to pasture while she played gourmet cook and cultured hostess, lover and intellectual companion to his father. (*Utopian Motherhood*, p.106)

The patriarchal biases in this passage are obvious and painful to observe. Why is it assumed that a woman liberated from gestation will have nothing better to do than cook and entertain (for) her husband? Why is parenting still presumed to be primarily the woman's responsibility? When even the self-proclaimed radicals among the clergy fail to ask such elementary questions there is reason to suspect that sexual equality still has an uphill battle to fight within the Church.

FREUD, Sigmund (1856–1939). *Three Essays on the Theory of Sexuality* (translated and edited by James Strachey, The Hogarth

Press, London, 1974; this translation first published 1949; original German edition published, 1905, Leipzig and Vienna)
"Some Psychical Consequences of the Anatomical Distinction Between the Sexes" (*Women and Analysis*, edited by Jean Strouse, Grossman Publishers, New York, 1974, pp.17–26; from *The Standard Edition of the Complete Psychological Works of Sigmund Freud*, edited by James Strachey, The Hogarth Press, London, 1953–1960, Vol. 19. Written 1925.)
"Female Sexuality" (*Women and Analysis*, pp.39–56; from the *The Standard Edition of the Complete Psychological Works of Sigmund Freud*, Vol. 21. Written 1931.)
"Femininity" (*Women and Analysis*, pp.73–94; from *New Introductory Lectures on Psychoanalysis*, translated and edited by James Strachey, W.W. Norton and Company, New York, 1974. Written 1933.)

Freud's statements on feminine psychology constitute only a small part of his work and as is often pointed out he did not write the first of his three rather short articles on the subject of female psychology as such until 1925, when he was already suffering from the cancer which eventually killed him. Nevertheless his theory of "penis envy" as the primary factor in the psychological development of women is one of his best known and most influential contributions. It has been widely invoked in defense of the inevitability of male domination and just as widely attacked by feminists as androcentric and blind to the role of culture and social expectations in the shaping of female psychology. Yet it has also been defended by a number of contemporary feminists as an invaluable tool for understanding the patriarchal mentality, both masculine and feminine, and the way in which it is transmitted within the family from one generation to the next.

Freud's theory of human psychosexual development is presented here for the first time in fairly complete form in the 1905 *Three Essays on the Theory of Sexuality*. The theory is presented as applying, at least in most respects, to children of both sexes, although Freud readily admits that it is based primarily on his observations of male patients, since the erotic life of women, "partly owing to the stunting effect of civilized conditions and partly owing to their conventional secretiveness and insincerity—is still veiled in an impenetrable obscurity." (p.17)

Contrary to the previously prevailing assumption that children are innocent of sexual desires, Freud holds that the *libido* or sexual instinct—the drive for sexual gratification—is present from birth, although it is not at first specifically centered in the genital organs. The earliest libidinal gratifications come orally, from nursing and spontaneous sucking; later the child takes pleasure in controlling its bowels. Hence Freud calls the first two stages of development the oral and the anal. The third stage begins when masturbation, which appears first in early infancy but soon subsides, reappears, usually before the fourth year. He calls this the phallic stage because he considers that in both sexes the libido now centers in the phallus, i.e. the penis or the clitoris, which he regards as a tiny penis; the vagina, he held, does not become an erotogenic zone until after puberty, when clitoral sensitivity is largely repressed in the normal course of feminine development.

Freud at first thought that the early stages of psychosexual development, prior to puberty, are the same in both sexes. Both sexes are inherently bisexual, though females are more so, since thay have *two* leading sexual zones (i.e. the clitoris and the vagina) instead of one, as males do. In both sexes the phallic phase is interrupted by the castration complex, and driven into a period of latency lasting until puberty. In the original *Three Essays* Freud writes that

> . . . it is not until puberty that the sharp distinction is established between the masculine and feminine characters . . . It is true that the masculine and feminine dispositions are already easily recognizable in childhood. The development of the inhibitions of sexuality (shame, disgust, pity, etc.) takes place in little girls earlier and in the face of less resistance than in boys; the tendency to sexual repression seems in general to be greater; and, where the component instincts of sexuality appear, they prefer the passive form. The auto-erotic activity of the erotogenic zone is, however, the same in both sexes, and owing to this uniformity there is no possibility of a distinction between the two sexes such as arises after puberty. (p.85)

But between 1905 and 1925 Freud came to believe that the castration complex, and the Oedipal complex which is associated with it, are very different in the two sexes. In the 1925 article "Some Psychical Consequences of the Anatomical Distinction Between the Sexes," he holds that for girls but not boys the Oedipal phase involves a traumatic change in the original love object. Infants of both sexes are sexually attracted to their mother; she is the first to provide oral satisfaction, and to awaken genital sensations through her ministrations, and thus it is normal for both sexes to experience their first sexual desire in connection with her. But the girl normally changes her libidinal object, switching her attachment from her mother to her father. This is the first of the two processes which girls must undergo on the road to normal femininity and which have no parallels in the case of boys.

The girl's change of objects comes about, Freud held, through her unhappy discovery that males have penises and she does not, and her subsequent envy of the male organ:

> They notice the penis of a brother or playmate, strikingly visible and of large proportions, at once recognize it as the superior counterpart of their own small and inconspicuous organ, and from that time forward fall a victim to envy for the penis. (1925, p.20)

The girl, so the story goes, blames her mother bitterly for sending her into the world without a penis, and when she learns that her mother has no penis either, she feels contempt for her and for all females. She then turns to her father in the hope that he will be able to provide her with the missing organ, or at least with a baby (preferably male), which she learns to accept as a substitute for the male organ. For her, the castration complex is not the fear that she *will* be castrated, but the realization that she *has* been castrated, and it *gives rise* to the Oedipal complex, the libidinal attachment to the opposite sex parent, rather than ending it.

For a boy, on the other hand, the castration complex begins the process that ends in the *destruction* of the Oedipal complex. The boy, on seeing female genitalia, at first refuses to believe that the penis is really missing. Once he admits that it is he becomes fearful that he too may lose his penis; for he imagines that women's penises have been cut off as a punishment, and he fears that his father may cut off his to punish him for his desire for the mother. In order to escape this fear, he suppresses his desire to marry his mother and kill his father, and internalizes the social prohibition of those acts, thus leading to the formation of the super-ego.

The girl, however, does not necessarily suppress her Oedipal attachment; it may linger into adulthood and never be entirely surmounted. Consequently, she does not develop, to the same degree, the powerful super-ego which makes possible the sublimation of sexual instincts into socially productive channels, which is the basis of all civilization. Thus, Freud says, one result of penis envy is that,

> . . . for women the level of what is ethically normal is different from what it is in men. Their super-ego is never so inexorable, so impersonal, so independent of its emotional origins as we require it to be in men. Character-traits which critics of every epoch have brought up against women—that they show less sense of justice than men, that they are less ready to submit to the great exigencies of life, that they are more often influenced in their judgments by feelings of affection or hostility—all these would be amply ac-

counted for by the modification in the formation of the super-ego
. . . (1925, p.2)

Another result of penis envy is that the girl develops, "like a scar, a sense of inferiority." (1925, p.21) She also shares men's contempt for women in general. Convinced of the inferiority of her clitoris, she generally gives up masturbation, and suppresses not only her active libidinal impulses, but often her passive ones as well. Freud speaks of this as the first wave of repression, which eliminates some of the girls' "masculinity," i.e. her active and phallic libido. The second wave of repression comes at puberty, when after a partial revival of clitoral sensitivity, it must again be repressed, in order to permit the vagina to become the primary erotogenic zone.

As Freud points out in the 1931 article, "Female Sexuality," the development of a girl into a "normal woman," with a "normal feminine attitude," is (by his account) much more complicated and difficult than is the development of a man. For although the girl "acknowledges the fact of her castration, and with it, too, the superiority of the male and and her own inferiority . . . she rebels against this unwelcome state of affairs." (p.43) In the "normal" case, this rebellion leads to the female Oedipus complex; but it may also produce a general revulsion from sexuality, or a defiant clinging to masturbation and masculinity in the hope of one day gaining a penis (the "masculinity complex"). Freud considered the latter two responses pathological; but he also recognized that the path of so-called normal femininity can also lead to mental disorders. In the *Three Essays*, he says that

> The fact that women change their leading erotic zone . . . together with the wave of repression at puberty, which, as it were, puts aside their childish masculinity, are the chief determinants of the greater proneness of women to neurosis and especially to hysteria. (p.87)

Freud was a lifelong defender of the sexual status quo, or at least of women's role within the family. He firmly rejected John Stuart Mill's arguments in *The Subjection of Women*, believing that if women earned their own incomes it would destroy their feminine charm. "Law and custom," he wrote, "have much to give to women that has been withheld from them, but the position of women will surely be what it is: in youth an adored darling and in mature years a loved wife." (1) Nevertheless, he recognized the harmful effect of the sexual double standard on women, and he was capable of describing women's condition within the traditional marriage in terms which, in the words of Elizabeth

Janeway, "make one's blood run cold." (2) He points out that women's limited powers of sublimation make it even more difficult to endure sexual deprivation;

> as a substitute for the sexual object the suckling child may suffice, but not the growing child, and under the disappointments of matrimony women succumb to severe, lifelong neurosis . . . Marriage under the present cultural standard has long ceased to be a panacea for the nervous sufferings of women; even if we physicians in such cases still advise matrimony, we are nevertheless aware that a girl must be very healthy to "stand" marriage. (3)

Nevertheless, Freud considered women's plight to be due *primarily* (though not entirely) to biology, rather than patriarchal institutions. The leading traits of femininity, he held, are passivity, narcissism, and masochism, all of which stem directly from penis envy. The narcissism is a defensive reaction of the ego to the discovery of the lack of a penis, the masochism a turning-inward of the girl's aggressive impulses, "which is prescribed for them constitutionally and imposed on them socially." (1933, p.76) As for passivity, Freud realized very well the problematic nature of the equation between this trait and femininity. "Women," he says, "can display great activity in various directions, [and] men are not able to live in company with their own kind unless they develop a large amount of passive adaptability." (*Loc. cit.*) Thus, for instance, nursing a child is an active as well as a passive activity, and the doll play of a girl child is distinctly active. Yet he continued to make this equation in spite of his doubts; and many of his followers, notably Deutsch and Bonaparte, have ignored his warnings and insisted on an entirely unqualified identification between passivity and femininity, activity and masculinity.

A key question in the interpretation of Freud's theory of feminine psychology is whether the notion of penis envy ought to be understood literally, or as a symbol for something more basic. Taken literally, the penis envy theory involves some presumptions which—as has been pointed out by critics like Karen Horney—are androcentric and implausible. Why, for example, should the small girl automatically suppose that having a penis (and no womb or vagina) is vastly preferable to having both a clitoris and a womb? Since she has experienced the phallic sensitivity of her clitoris, why should she not consider it quite adequate, and its compactness a virtue rather than a deprivation? As Horney and Mead have pointed out, Freud ignores motherhood except as "substitute" for the possession of a penis; but mightn't the truth be closer to the reverse, at least in societies where motherhood is highly valued? Besides, Freud's theory cannot possibly be applicable to *all* human cultures, since where naked-ness is not generally concealed there could not be any sudden *discovery*, by either sex, of the genital differences between the sexes.

On the other hand, feminists like Juliet Mitchell and Shulamith Firestone have pointed out that if we interpret the concept of penis envy symbolically, understanding it not as envy of the male organ *per se* but as envy of the superior power and freedom accorded the male under patriarchal society, then most of the surface absurdities of the theory seem to vanish, as does the overt contradiction between Freud and the feminist position. Janeway argues that when Freud insists that the girl accepts "the fact of her castration," he cannot intend the phrase to be taken literally, since, of course, the girl has *not* in fact been castrated, at least not physically (4). Rather, she is emasculated *psychologically*, by being relegated to a submissive and inferior social role; the penis, the most obvious physical emblem of the male/female distinction, therefore becomes a symbol of male social supremacy. It is this which the girl child passionately rebels against, and which shapes her psychology in the ways Freud sought to describe.

This symbolic interpretation of the penis envy theory seems incorrect if intended as a hypothesis about what Freud actually *meant*. For he gives no indication that he suspects that what the girl really envies is not the male's penis, but the social status which the penis comes to stand for. He does refer to the social demands made of women, but only as factors which reinforce their inherent biological tendencies. It is fair to say that he con-ceives of the lack of a male organ as an ontological defect, which necessarily, through the girl's inevitable psychological reaction to the knowledge of her defectiveness, tends to result in passivity and repression. Though he evidently has a good deal of compas-sion for women's plight, he has no sympathy at all for the femi-nist cause, and warns against heeding the protests of those "who are anxious to force us to regard the two sexes as completely equal in position and worth " (1925, p.25).

It is, however, possible to separate much of the descriptive and phenomenological content of Freud's work from the biologically deterministic interpretation which he himself placed upon it. It may make relatively little difference to the attitude and psycho-logical development of the female child whether the social infer-iority imposed upon women is or is not in some way biologically inevitable. Either way, it cannot help but have lasting effects on her psychological development, and one does not need to construe Freud as a closet feminist to concede that he was a remarkably astute observer of these effects.

1. Quoted by Juanita H. Williams, *Psychology of Women*, p.18.
2. Janeway, "On Female Sexuality"; in Strouse, p.66.
3. Freud, "Civilized Sexuality and Modern Nervousness," in *On War, Sex and Neurosis*, edited by Sander Katz (Arts and Science Press, New York, 1947), p.176.
4. *Op. cit.*, p.57.

FRIDAY, Nancy. *My Secret Garden: Women's Sexual Fantasies* (Pocket Books, New York, 1976; first published 1973, by Trident Press)
My Mother/My Self: The Daughter's Search for Identity (Delacourt Press, New York, 1977)

My Secret Garden is a collection of women's sexual fantasies, as told to the author, which proves beyond doubt that (at least some) women's private imaginings are as racy—and a good deal more imaginative—than anything produced by the (mostly-male) pornography industry. Such fantasies, she suggests, serve to produce or heighten sexual excitement, either as a substitute for sexual intercourse or a way of enhancing intercourse or masturbation.

Many of the fantasies involve rape or coercion, or at least complete passivity on the part of the woman fantasizing. This fact might appear to provide confirmation for the Freudian claim that women are essentially passive and masochistic. Friday points out, however, that rape fantasies function to enable the woman to enjoy sexual sensations in a context free from guilt or responsibility; they do not indicate that she has any actual desire to be raped, or that she would enjoy it if she were. Fantasies about having sex with an anonymous stranger are also popular, as are those involving an audience, animals, incest, a number of men and/or women, and domination or pain inflicted by or on the fantasizer. Fantasies involving young boys (or girls), fetishes or prostitution, on the other hand, proved rare.

Apart from their considerable entertainment value, the significance of such a collection of female sexual fantasies is to demonstrate that in all probability women fantasize at least as much as men, and that such fantasies serve a useful purpose. They are by no means always an indication of sexual frustration or mental pathology, as Wilhelm Reich, for example, held. Once women come to see their sexual fantasies in this light they may learn to employ them more consciously and with less guilt.

My Mother/My Self is a set of reflections on the mother-daughter relationship. The main theme is symbiosis versus separation. In its first year or two of life a child needs the closest possible symbiotic relationship with its mother. Thereafter, however, it needs an increasing degree of independence and separation in order to achieve a secure sense of itself as a distinct person. Since a girl is the same sex as the mother it is harder for her to achieve this separation than it is for the boy—especially since the mother is apt never to have achieved adequate separation from *her* mother either. Women who lack a separate sense of self tend to keep their children, especially their daughters, too close to them too long, and so the cycle is perpetuated.

The other primary theme of the book is that our culture's idealized and nonsexual conception of the mother role greatly aggravates the mother/daughter problem. Mothers are required to conceal their sexuality from their children, and to discourage the latter—especially the daughters—from discovering their own sexual capacities. The repression of masturbation is not only more severe in the case of girls, but more effective, since their sexual anatomy and its functions are less self-evident. For this reason most adult women still experience their own sexuality as a guilt-inducing rebellion against their mother. Conversely, " . . . the declaration of full sexual independence is the declaration of separation from my mother." (p.292)

These observations are plausible enough in the context of our own particular time and traditions. But like the Freudian analysts whom she frequently quotes, Friday has little apparent awareness that motherhood as we know it is not a biological given. It is merely one phase in the evolution of motherhood as an institution of patriarchy. To realize this is to realize the futility of attempting to produce universal generalizations about the psychological parameters of motherhood and daughterhood as such.

FRIEDAN, Betty. *The Feminine Mystique* (W.W.Norton and Co., New York, 1963)
It Changed My Life: Writings on the Women's Movement (Random House, New York, 1976)

The Feminine Mystique is the book which many have credited with starting the contemporary women's liberation movement. The thesis is that the promise held out by women's legal enfranchisement, the promise of full and equal participation in the social world, was blocked by an ideological backlash which took the form of a mystique of feminine fulfillment through wife and motherhood, which constricted women's sphere of interest and influence to the domestic circle. While Freudians and functionalists blame women's discontent on their loss of femininity, Friedan points out that it is the women who have dedicated their lives to the pursuit of femininity who suffer most from "the problem with no name," the malaise and lack of identity which afflicts so many housewives. The housewife's problem is not penis envy, but that stunting of her individual development inevitably produced by domestic confinement.

Instead of enabling women to understand and escape this confinement, modern sociology, psychology and anthropology have all tended to reinforce the feminine mystique via a circular process in which what is observed is treated as a necessary norm, and the status quo thereby preserved. Even Margaret Mead has been, Friedan thinks, guilty of reinforcing the feminine mystique. In spite of Mead's own demonstration of the extreme malleability of human sex roles (as illustrated by the three New Guinea tribes described in *Sex and Temperament*), popular culture has paid more attention to her apparent glorification of women's procreative role. Psychologists have tried to blame mental illnesses on maternal rejection and the absence of a full-time female parent; but in reality children are more apt to be psychologically damaged by maternal overprotection, which is almost inevitable when the mother has no nondomestic interests.

Furthermore, since the Second World War there has been a virtual conspiracy by American capitalists to return women to the home or persuade them to remain there, as compulsive and uncritical consumers. But in spite of all the propaganda, housewifery is not a route to individual fulfillment. To remain at home is to sacrifice individuality for sexuality and security. It is not feminism that makes housewives discontent; rather both feminism and that discontent are the result of the sheer emptiness of the housewife's role.

Women who have outside interest and employment, Friedan argues, actually make better wives and mothers because they do not have to live through their husbands and children and so are less apt to place excessive demands on them, to become domestic tyrants. Contrary to the claims of some feminists, women need not choose between family and career. With foresight and determination they can plan for both. Since housework expands (and hopefully contracts) to fit the time available, working women find they can do the housework which once took them all day in much less time. And work—not just any job but work that is challenging and useful—is a woman's only way to individual selfhood.

Left relatively unexplored in this bible of liberal feminist thought are such key problems as whether and how the economy can be altered so as to provide more high-paying jobs for women, and how mothers who are not superwomen can compete on the job market if parenthood is to remain a much larger part of their lives than in the case of men. She warns against "extreme" forms of feminism which alienate the majority of women by attacking marriage and motherhood as incompatible with liberation, at least under current conditions, but she does not present an entirely persuasive case that the two goals are at present compatible, for more than a few fortunate women.

It Changed My Life is a collection of articles and journal entries written by Friedan since the publication of *The Feminine Mystique*, describing her participation in the founding of NOW (National Organization for Women) in 1966, her reasons for leaving it later, and her various travels and efforts on behalf of the ERA, the right to abortion and other women's issues. A major focus of many of these essays is the development of an ideological conflict between Friedan's relatively conservative feminist stance and those more radical feminists who call for the abolition or socialist reorganization of the family, for bisexuality (e.g. Millett) or for lesbianism and female separatism to free women of the need to love and live with men.

Unfortunately, Friedan's attacks on these "extremist" positions are primarily *ad hominem* and/or pragmatic and political. She suggests that the radical feminists are women who once bought the feminine mystique so completely that they now feel they must repudiate men, marriage and motherhood entirely in order to escape it. And she fears that to talk of men as oppressors and the relationship between the sexes as one of class warfare is to alienate men (and women who love men) needlessly. The conditions which must be changed are not the result of a deliberate conspiracy by men. Women still need men and motherhood, and women and men of good will can still make marriage work. Friedan is opposed to the linking of feminism with lesbianism, and to making gay rights a major feminist issue. Here the arguments are entirely pragmatic: lesbianism scares straight women and references to it weaken the movement.

Also included are a (singularly nonprecognitive) article on Indira Ghandi; and a dialogue with Simone de Beauvoir, in which de Beauvoir insists that until social conditions change, free women must avoid marriage and motherhood. Friedan's answer is to say that this purist position is not helpful to real women who want both to be wives and mothers and to have a place in the public world.

FRIEDL, Ernestine. *Women and Men: An Anthropologist's View* (Holt, Rinehart and Winston, New York, 1975)

Friedl explores the relationship between the relative power and status of women and such factors as the mode of subsistence, residential patterns, the right to distribute valued goods, and myth and ritual, particularly within hunting and gathering, and primitive agricultural societies. She argues that it is above all "the right to distribute and exchange valued goods and services to those not in a person's own domestic unit . . . which confers power and prestige," (p.7) a hypothesis which helps to explain why, contrary to Marx, the economic importance of women's work in preagricultural societies does not necessarily guarantee their equality with men. The prevalence of male domination is a result of the fact that women tend to produce those goods and services which are consumed primarily within the domestic unit.

In hunting and gathering societies, for instance, women usually gather and prepare well over half of the food consumed by all. But it is the meat which the men bring back from the hunt which is the most valued food and which is most apt to be distributed to in-laws and others outside the immediate family. Hence the greater the dependence upon game, which only the men hunt, the lower the status of women. (An extreme case is that of the North Alaskan Eskimos, who subsist almost entirely upon game which the men hunt, and among whom women are allegedly treated as sex objects whose erotic services are the negotiable property of men.)

Another key claim Friedl makes is that women are much more apt to achieve positions of power and status when eligibility for such positions is hereditary rather than determined by egalitarian competition. Systems of lineage and residence are also important; women's status is lowest in patrilineal and patrilocal societies, and generally higher in matrilineal and/or matrilocal societies. An insight of potential importance for contemporary feminism is that women's childbearing patterns and child care obligations are invariably adapted to fit the other work they do, rather than vice versa. Friedl leaves largely unexplored the consequences of these findings for feminist theory; yet the work is a useful corrective to those idealistic theories of early matriarchy (see e.g. Davis, Diner, Reed) which presume that all societies must have been female-dominated or at least sexually egalitarian prior to the rise of private property and the worship of male gods. This may of course have been the case, but the attempt to prove it by reference to existing preagricultural societies no longer appears very promising.

FULLER, Margaret (1810–1850). *Woman in the Nineteenth Century* (W.W. Norton and Company, New York, 1971; first published 1845)

Margaret Fuller was a Romantic writer and literary critic of the Transcendentalist school; a close friend of Ralph Waldo Emerson; the editor for two years (1840–1842) of the Transcendentalist journal, *The Dial*; America's first female journalist (she worked for Horace Greeley's *New York Tribune* from 1844 to 1846); and the author of the first important American feminist work. She died in a shipwreck on the way back from a four-year stay in Europe, choosing to remain with her Italian husband, Giovanni Ossoli, and their small son, rather than be rescued alone.

Woman in the Nineteenth Century is an expansion of an essay Fuller published in *The Dial* in 1843 under the somewhat awkward title, "The Great Lawsuit: Man versus Men, Woman versus Women." (1) Fuller's theme is that the liberation of women is one with that of man: "that she, the other half of the same thought, the other chamber of the heart of life, needs now take her turn in the full pulsation." (p.24) Women must take part in business, government, and all of the affairs of society. Those who say that they are too delicate and weak to do this are hypocrites who make no objection to female slaves laboring in the fields or seamstresses working in the factories under brutal conditions. "We would," she proclaims,

> have every barrier thrown down. We would have every path laid open to Women as freely as to men. Were this done . . . the divine energy would pervade nature to a degree unknown in the history of ages, and . . . no discordant collision, but a ravishing harmony of the spheres, would ensue. (p.37)

Like Mary Wollstonecraft—of whose sexual behavior she felt it necessary to express disapproval—Fuller admits many of the charges made against women of her day, e.g. of intemperance, frivolity and superstition, but attributes these faults not to nature but to a lack of education and of a wide enough scope for the exercise of their capacities. Women need education and opportunities to use it, not that they may be better companions for men (an argument Fuller says she has heard all too often), but for the sake of their own intellectual and spiritual development; "a being of infinite scope must not be treated with an exclusive view to any one relation." (p.96) Unlike Wollstonecraft, however, she does not attack the traditional distinctions between masculine and feminine virtues but rather reifies them into cosmic principles. "The growth of Man is twofold, masculine and feminine." (p.169) The masculine side exhibits energy, power and intellect, the feminine, harmony, beauty and love.

This does not mean that women are incapable of intellect, however, since both aspects of human development can and should be nurtured in each human being. Geniuses like Shelley always have a higher degree of feminine development than most men, but, "There is no wholly masculine man, no purely feminine woman." (p.116) These ideas distinctly foreshadow those of Jung and his followers. They represent a version of the ideal of androgyny, though a weaker version than that defended by Wollstonecraft. Yet Fuller can still hold—as Wollstonecraft would certainly not have—that it is more "native" for a woman to be the model than to be the artist, "to inspire and receive the poem, than to create it." (p.115) Woman's special talent is "an instinctive seizure of cause, and a simple breathing out of what she receives, that has the singleness of life, rather than the selecting and energizing of art." (*Loc. cit.*)

Although she was less radical than either Wollstonecraft or her own contemporary George Sand (whom she was later to meet and with whom she got on famously), Fuller risked bringing upon herself the calumny which the names of these heroines universally invoked, in her day, by defending their spirit if not their sexual behavior. "Such beings as these," she says, " . . . ought not to find themselves, by birth, in a place so narrow that, in breaking bonds, they become outlaws." (p.75) She considers celibacy for the unmarried, and for some the permanent avoidance of marriage, the best route to freedom for women, and wishes to end the sexual double standard through increasing the chastity of men, rather than the reverse. A maiden should want to marry only "a man . . . in whom brute nature is entirely subject to the impulse of his better self." (p.135) She considers sexual continence important not just because of the unfortunate social results of a "bad reputation," but because she sees it as associated with self-reliance and independence from men. She cautions women against looking to men for advice or assistance in their search for freedom; for men are too much creatures of habit, too accustomed to viewing women with contempt to see the justice of their cause. Thus "women must leave off asking them and being influenced by them, but retire within themselves, and explore the ground-work of life till they find their particular secret." (p.121)

1. An abridged version of this earlier essay is reprinted in *The Feminist Papers*, edited by Alice P. Rossi, Bantam Books, New York, 1974, pp.158-182)

FUNCTIONALISM: See Malinowski, and Parsons and Bales; also Sociology of Women.

G

GENDER The term *gender* is often used as a synonym for *sex*, i.e. biological malenes or femaleness. However, it is also used, particularly by contemporary writers, to refer to the socially imposed dichotomy of masculine and feminine roles and character traits. Sex is physiological, while gender, in the latter usage, is cultural. The distinction is a crucial one, and one which is ignored by unreflective supporters of the status quo who assume that cultural norms of masculinity and femininity are "natural," i.e. directly and preponderantly determined by biology.

To insist on the distinction between sex and gender is not to assume, on the other hand, that biology has *no* causal influence on the cultural phenomena associated with gender, but only that whatever causal relationships there may be are much less direct, universal and resistant to change than in the case of genuinely natural human behaviors like sleeping, sneezing, and eating. Contemporary researchers have demonstrated that gender can develop in direct opposition to its usual, biologically indicated direction. There are biologically normal males who are "feminine" in both gender identity (the gender they perceive themselves to be) and gender role, and biologically normal females whose gender is "masculine." (See Money and Ehrhardt, Stoller.) Furthermore, there are cultures in which the traditional gender role and personal temperament of women are what we would typically describe as masculine, and cultures in which those of men are feminine. (See Mead.)

GIELE, Janet Zollinger. *Women and the Future: Changing Sex Roles in Modern America* (The Free Press, New York, 1978)

Giele presents a feminist vision of "what the world would be like if the values for which women have traditionally stood were given larger place"; (p. ix) a vision which, she holds, is not merely utopian, but "a projection of changes already in progress." (p. xi) We are witnessing a revolution in sex roles, which will eventually reshape the structure and value system of society. Giele uses an evolutionary model of social change, which combines features of both the Marxist and the functionalist approaches. Sex roles are shaped largely by economic pressures. During the early part of the Industrial Revolution, the status and activities of men and women were driven further apart by the removal of paid labor from the home and the consequent emergence of the male as, theoretically, the sole breadwinner. Now, however, a number of social and economic forces are converging to break down the sharp distinction between masculine and feminine roles, and to make crossover between them more frequent.

Sex-role crossover, Giele argues, is the wave of the future. It means an increasing similarity between the life styles of men and women. The family will become symmetrical, with both husband and wife doing paid labor outside the home while sharing the necessary domestic work. Crossover promotes, and is promoted by, two complementary forms of social change. The first is what Giele calls the redistribution of women between the core and the periphery of social institutions; that is, the movement of women into more important positions in, e.g., government, business and higher education. The second, an equally crucial process, is the redistribution of *rewards* between the core and periphery; through this process, the real value of the work that women do, as secretaries and housewives, will be more adequately recognized and rewarded. Ultimately, these changes will bring about a basic restructuring of the value system of the society, "a reconfiguration of transcendent values to express complementarity and interdependence rather than priority and social hierarchy." (p. x)

Such social change, Giele holds, occurs at four successive levels: in the personality and behavior of individuals; in the organizational features of social collectivities, such as the family; in the institutional principles of law and government; and, finally, on the level of social values. Thus, reform movements and scientific analyses of social institutions follow a parallel logic, which begins with a concentration upon the traits of individual persons, and on the modes of social organization, and ends by challenging traditional social values.

GILDER, George. *Sexual Suicide* (Bantam Books, New York, 1973)

A denunciation of feminist goals, the achievement of which, Gilder argues, could lead to the downfall of civilization. Civilization depends upon the "socialization" of men within the family, which in turn requires male domination, particularly in political, economic and professional areas. The sexuality of men makes them naturally antisocial and irresponsible, oriented towards short-term pleasures and conquests; women's reproductive function, on the other hand, makes them naturally more responsible and oriented toward the long-term project of raising children. Consequently, men are economically unproductive and socially disruptive until they are subordinated to the long-term sexual cycles of women. This "subordination" can occur only within the nuclear family, in which a man undertakes to cooperate with a woman in raising their joint offspring.

Such cooperation, however, requires that men have a source of identity, of status and achievement, outside the family, in a sphere from which women are excluded; otherwise, they will inevitably feel inferior to women and superfluous as a member of the family, because of their incapacity to bear and nurse babies. Far from being a liability (as, for instance, Firestone argues) women's childbearing function gives them a vast sexual superiority, for which men must compensate by achievements outside the family if they are to feel themselves the equals of women within the family. In particular, the modern husband needs to be the major financial provider for the family. Wives who work to make money, even when the family needs it badly, upset the "sexual constitution" of the family by depriving the male of this necessary role, and thus encourage men to desert the family and/or abdicate their social responsibilities entirely.

Social stability, then, requires male domination within a patriarchal family. It also requires that procreative heterosexual sex be recognized as the norm. Sex must remain tied to procreation if men are to be socialized. Hence Gilder attacks homosexuality, pornography, promiscuity, "open marriage," artificial insemination, the idea of the artificial womb, abortion, and even contraception, as factors which all tend to divorce sex from procreation. He deplores busing, welfare, day care, and affirmative action for women as further threats to society's sexual constitution. He sees the women's movement as the chief enemy of justice and social progress, especially for blacks and poor people, since it encourages women to compete for jobs which men need to support their families and maintain their male identities. It is also responsible for the current increase in crime and violence, since men whose sexual identities are undermined often turn to antisocial methods of establishing their masculinity. The feminist ideal of the androgynous, sex-role-free society is "behavioral gibberish," which violates our deepest nature as human beings and can only lead to social chaos.

A feminist might reply that economic equality between man and wife can hardly be a psychological impossibility, since it appears to have been the normal situation throughout most of human prehistory (and in many contemporary families). In hunting and gathering societies, women's contribution to the group's subsistence is generally at least as great as men's, yet the men somehow manage neither to collapse from inferiority complexes nor to desert their families *en masse*. One might also wonder whether, if Gilder is right that men's egos are so fragile that they must be constantly propitiated by the deference, submission and self-denial of other family members, the family might not be better off without them—at least in a reasonably egalitarian society in which women could earn incomes comparable to those of men.

GILMAN, Charlotte Perkins (Stetson) (1860–1935). *Women and Economics* (Harper and Row, New York, 1966, edited by Carl N. Degler; first published in 1898 by Small, Maynard and Company, Boston)
The Home: Its Work and Influence (University of Illinois Press, Urbana, 1972; first published in 1903 by McClure, Phillips and Company)
The Man-Made World, or Our Androcentive Culture (T. Fisher Unwin, London, 1911)
His Religion and Hers: A Study of the Faith of Our Fathers and the Work of Our Mothers (Hyperion Press, Westport, Connecticut, 1976; first published in 1923 by The Century Company, New York and London)
Charlotte Perkins Gilman was one of the best known feminist thinkers of the early decades of this century, and a forerunner of both the radical and socialist feminists and the spiritual feminist movements of our own time. She stood apart from the mainstream of the American feminist movement, which concentrated its efforts on the winning of the vote and other legal reforms, and argued that women must, above all, be liberated from economic dependence and domestic drudgery. Her first works were published under the name Charlotte Perkins Stetson, (Charles) Stetson being her first husband. The marriage would have been a happy one, except that she found confinement to wife-and-motherhood intolerable; she developed an acute mental depression which was relieved only when she left her husband's home. The divorce took place in 1890, and the rest of her life (though she remarried, in 1900, "and lived happily ever after" (1)) was spent

in exploring and explaining the implications of the traditional division of labor in marriage.

Women and Economics is her best known and perhaps her best work. It was an immediate success and was translated into over half a dozen languages. Here, most of the ideas developed or presupposed in the later work appear for the first time. Although Gilman spoke of herself as a socialist, her primary philosophical inspiration is not Marxist but Darwinian. From the theory of evolution, she derives a progressivist interpretation of human history and prehistory, an enviable optimism about the future, and a humanistic and teleological ethic, directed toward the achievement of human happiness and development through more rational forms of social organization. From the sociologist Lester F. Ward, she takes the idea that, in spite of all appearances, it is the human female, rather than the male, who is the "race type," that is, the clearest embodiment of "the distinctive qualities of the species." (See *His Religion and Hers*, p.82; and (2)).

The male, Gilman argues, is a modification of the basic human type, the female, for the sole purpose of sexual reproduction. The male is a sexual specialist, and his "catabolic" energy, his instinctive urge to fight and compete with other males, and his drive toward self-expression, are part of his sexual specialization. The human female, on the other hand, at least among our prehistoric ancestors, is specialized not for sex but for motherhood. As the period of human infancy lengthened, the female was increasingly selected for her ability to nurture and provide for her helpless offspring. Mother love was the first social bond, and the first source of productive industry; women invented all of the basic human arts and industries, including language, in the process of providing for their young. It was the maternal industry of women, not the crude hunting and fighting activities of men, which pulled us over the threshold of humanity.

But women's maternal industry was also their downfall, since it made them valuable to men as well as to children. Men first took possession of women, subordinated them and rendered them dependent, not because of their sexual attractiveness, but because of their productive value. (This event took place sometime before the dawn of history; Gilman does not speculate about just when or how it happened.) As the property and dependents of men, women were forced to become the sexual specialists. They were strictly confined to sexual and domestic functions, while men claimed the whole larger world of social activity and production as their own.

Gilman calls this arrangement, whereby women become the

domestic servants of men, the "sexuo-economic relation." The evolutionary usefulness of the sexuo-economic relation was that it brought about the "feminization" of men. Men were stimulated to rise to the level of humanity of women, and far beyond, by the labor, cooperation and inventiveness expended in providing support for women and children. Through the sexuo-economic relation, the sexual energy of the male was put to work in the development of culture and civilization:

> Without the economic dependence of the female, the male would still be merely the hunter and fighter, the killer, the destroyer; and she would continue to be the industrious mother, without change or progress. (***Women and Economics***, p.133)

The sexuo-economic relation, then, was necessary to bring about a certain level of human development. Now, however, it stands in the way of further progress, and is therefore changing. Women have been kept at a level of development and in a form of industry thousands of years behind that of men. This has weakened them, mentally and physically, and thereby weakened the race as a whole. Far from being necessary for the protection of motherhood and the home, women's dependence and domestic isolation makes them incompetent as mothers, unable to educate their children for the world, or even to feed them properly and protect them from disease. Meanwhile the male monopoly of most nondomestic and nonsexual human enterprises ensures that the belligerent, competitive values of the male, rather than the humanistic and cooperative values of the female, prevail in the world at large.

Consequently, we cannot reach a higher level of social development unless women take their place in the larger human world, earning their way independently and bringing the benefits of their feminine attitudes to all social institutions. Gilman saw that this will be possible only to the extent that women are liberated from domestic labor. Toward this end, she advocated that domestic industries be professionalized, that most cooking and cleaning, and some routine child care, and early education, be done outside the individual family home, by paid professionals who will do it more expertly and more economically than it can possibly be done by the individual housewife.

Gilman has often been misinterpreted as advocating collective or communal living and childrearing, and the end of the private home and the close nuclear family. In fact, she emphasizes that communal *housekeeping* would be disastrous. People require privacy and a private family relationship; in her scheme, she says, the home will be *more* private rather than less, since cooking and so on will be done outside it rather than inside it by servants. Family relationships will be improved, not undermined, since men and women will have more in common and will be more equal; parents will have more time to spend with their children, mothers because they have less domestic labor to interfere with child care, and fathers because they need not struggle to earn enough to support the entire family.

Women's entry into economic independence and human equality will improve the mental health, happiness and social awareness of both sexes. The dominant-subordinate relationship between men and women means that both are "checked in their social faculties." (**Women and Economics**, p.176) It produces "a domineering selfishness in man and a degrading abnegation in woman—or sometimes reverses this effect." (p.178) Free women will be strong and competent—no less feminine but much more human.

In all of this, Gilman is quite modern, quite close to some of the radical feminists of the 1970s. She is less modern in some other aspects of her thought, e.g. in her tendency to speak of the nonwhite races and their cultures as "lower" than our own, and in her attitude towards sex and sensuality. She endorses the virtue of chastity and considers the double standard wrong, not because it demands too much continence of women but that it demands too little of men. She rejects as unprovable, and a throwback to ancient phallus worship, Freud's view that all creative impulses are the result of sublimated (male) sexual energy. Men, like women, ought to practice strict monogamy, not to increase their creative energy, but to avoid the obvious and immediate results of their indulgence, especially prostitution and the spread of venereal diseases. Perhaps she ought not to be blamed for failing to predict that these evils could be eradicated without a decrease in nonmonogamous sexual activity, since there is as little sign in our own age as there was in hers of such an ideal solution emerging.

Gilman is a philosophical ancestor not only of radical feminism, but of the spiritual or religious feminists of the 1970s. (See, for instance, Mary Daly.) In **His Religion and Hers**, she attacks the androcentrism of the world's major religions. All of these, she says, are death-oriented, that is, primarily concerned about what happens to the human personality after death. This is because they were invented by men, who because they lived by killing, in war and in the hunt, naturally saw death as the most important event in life. Had religion come to us through the minds of women, it would have been concerned less with death and more with birth and growth. For the birth-based religion the main question is, "What must be done for the child who is born?" not, "What will happen to me after I am dead?" (p.46)

Because our religions have been excessively other-worldly, they have had little effect upon our behavior in this world, and have not increased our care for the future of the race. Rather than promising eternal rewards or punishments in the unknown world beyond death, a "birth-based religion would steadily hold before our eyes the vision of a splendid race, [and] the duty of upbuilding it." (p.50) It would encourage the hope of immortality through an improved and happier human race, not through personal survival. God, in the minds of women, would have been "the Life-Giver, the Teacher, the Provider—not the proud, angry, jealous, vengeful deity men have imagined." (p.51)

Not only have the patriarchal religions been other-worldly and vengeance-oriented, they have stunted our powers of moral reasoning and our general rationality by stressing unreasoning belief and obedience to authority in ethics and religion, rather than a scientific and empirical search for truth. They have taught that all the important truths were settled long ago, when in reality "truth is something never finished and always calling for further inquiry." (p.172) They have encouraged fatalism, rather than intelligent efforts to improve the human lot. And, needless to say, all the androcentric religions have accepted the subjection of women as right and good.

Gilman predicted, therefore, that with the emergence of women into full humanity, we will see a new kind of religion, a rationalistic, this-worldly religion, based on "the principle of growth, of culture, of applying service and nourishment in order to produce improvement," rather than the masculine ethos of struggle, conflict and competition. (p.271) The sexuo-economic relation will come to an end, and with it the unhealthful androcentrism of all our institutions. The androcentrism *must* end, can't help but end, because it is no longer conducive to human progress, and progress is the law of evolution. This is Gilman's real religion, the prime postulate of all her philosophy, and it gives her work an optimism which few thinkers in our more disillusioned era find it easy to share.

1.   *The Living of Charlotte Perkins Gilman*, p.281.

GODDESSES   The worship of goddesses and female fertility figures in the Neolithic period, in the early civilizations of the

Middle East, and in the classical ages of Greece and Rome, has been taken by some theorists to demonstrate that these cultures passed through an early matriarchal phase, prior to the rise of patriarchy. (See Bachofen, Morgan, Engels, Briffault, Diner, and Reed; also see Matriarchy Theory.) The existence of such goddess -worshiping cultures in the past probably does not, however, support the inference that women were once socially or politically dominant—as the word "matriarchy"implies. It *may* indicate that religion was not originally an exclusively male creation. On the other hand, as de Beauvoir, Ruether, and others have argued, the religious image of woman as the divine mother—a symbol of natural fertility—may have been a male invention, in which women were already dehumanized, i.e., associated with nature rather than with the higher creativity of man.

If further historical and archeological research does indicate that goddess worship was associated, at least in some instances, with a degree of female supremacy, this would constitute a powerful objection to all those theories which seek to show that patriarchy is biologically or psychologically inevitable. It may, however, be significant for quite different reasons. Some feminists, while not necessarily accepting the assumption that goddess worship is a sign of matriarchy, have found in these very ancient religious traditions an inspiration for a more humanistic and life-affirming form of spirituality than has been present in any of the patriarchal religions. (See Gilman, Reed, Stone. For an example of recently discovered evidence of goddess worship in the Neolithic period, see Mellaart, in Anthologies I.)

GOLDBERG, Steven. *The Inevitability of Patriarchy* (William Morrow and Company, New York, 1973)

This is one of the more carefully argued of the recent antifeminist reactions. Goldberg claims that the male hormone system renders male domination (i.e., the subjective feeling on the part of both sexes that the male's will predominates) and patriarchy (i.e., male monopolization of positions of status and power in society) not only universal phenomena, but inevitable ones. Not only has there never been a matriarchy (a society ruled by women), but there has never even been a sexually egalitarian society, and there never could be. Women's rights, and the respect shown them, may vary from culture to culture, but all power and status, other than that attached to roles which only women are biologically capable of playing, is invariably concentrated in male hands. Goldberg thinks that this is simply because the greater exposure of males to certain homones (androgens), during the fetal stage, at puberty, and thereafter, makes them more aggresive than females; which in turn makes their attainment of greater social power inevitable. Females may be as aggressive as males in *some* senses or respects, but male aggression is the sort specifically suited to the attainment of power and status, and female aggression is not.

The feminist goal of equality of power and status between the sexes is, then, an utterly hopeless one. There is no possible way of reducing the extent to which male aggression leads to male monopolization of power and status, Goldberg thinks, since any such reduction would mean the sacrifice of science, hierarchical social organization, industrialization and democracy. For, he thinks, all of these civilized institutions require that there be distinctions of power and status; and so long as such distinctions exist, male aggression will ensure that the high status positions remain in male hands. This being the case, it is important to retain the traditional sex roles and sexual stereotypes. Women must be socialized not to compete with men or to try to gain their ends by aggressive means, since if they try to do this they will be defeated by men and will suffer more than if they had been content to use "feminine" means.

Goldberg criticizes feminist thinkers for ignoring the role of male hormones in the etiology of male domination, but has relatively little to say about those other biological factors, such as the greater size and strength of males and the greater reproductive burden of women, which various feminists have seen as key causes of male domination. He considers size unimportant since he thinks that *among men* the attainment of high status positions is not closely correlated with size or strength. And he suggests that women's maternal duties cannot help explain their inferior status, since the extent of their maternal obligations varies from culture to culture, whereas their inferior status (he thinks) does not.

In a separate section, Goldberg argues the secondary thesis that in addition to being naturally more aggressive than women, men have a greater natural capacity for abstract thought. The primary evidence for this is that men excel far more often than women in such highly abstract intellectual pursuits as logic, mathematics, chess, music and philosophy. He attributes this male excellence to the fetal androgenization of the male brain, plus the presence in males (after puberty) of a higher androgen level than in females.

The Goldberg line of argument is attractive, at least, for its simplicity; but the feminist response to it cannot consist in an equally simple denial of the empirical premises. There remain a good many unanswered questions about the effects of androgens (and, for that matter, estrogens) on human psychology. On the one hand, it is impossible to ignore the evidence that exposure to male hormones, especially during the fetal stage, *can* have an effect upon later behavior. (See, for instance, Money and Ehrhardt's findings on the "tomboyism" of fetally androgenized girls (1).) On the other hand, in spite of Goldberg's claims to the contrary, there are human societies, e.g. the Arapesh of New Guinea, described by Margaret Mead, in which the temperament and social status of men and women is so nearly identical as to definitely refute the claim that male hormonal chemistry is *in itself* sufficient to produce aggressive and dominant men.

The truth, then, is somewhere between the dogmatic claim— which Goldberg wrongly ascribes to all feminists—that there are absolutely no innate differences between the psychological and behavioral propensities of the sexes, and the equally fallacious view that male hormones make male domination inevitable for all time. Even if males are, and remain, more aggressive in some sense, it need not follow that they will continue to monopolize high status, professional and leadership roles. Aggressiveness, after all, is hardly a sufficient qualification for leadership or re- sponsibility, and may even be negatively correlated with these qualities. (Hence the often-noted fact that there are a higher proportion of successful queens than successful kings in human history.)

With respect to Goldberg's secondary claim, that testosterone gives men a greater capacity for abstract thought, it should be pointed out that the mathematical superiority of the average male is balanced by the linguistic superiority of the average female (2). It would be hard to argue that natural language provides a lesser scope for the exercise of abstract thought than does mathematics. Moreover, it is still too soon to conclude that the mathematic superiority of males and the linguistic superiority of females are the result of hormonally-induced brain differences, since there remain innumerable cultural factors which would seem capable of producing the same result.

1. John Money and Anke Ehrhardt, *Man and LWoman, Boy and Girl* pp.99–103.
2. See Eleanor Maccoby and Carol Jacklin, *The Psychology of Sex Differences*.

GOLDMAN, Emma (1869–1940). *Anarchism and Other Essays* (Dover Publications, New York, 1969; first published by Mother Earth Publishing Association, New York, 1917)

Red Emma Speaks: Selected Writings and Speeches by Emma Goldman, compiled and edited by Alix Kate Shulman (Random House, New York, 1972)

Emma Goldman is a figure larger than life, a feminist anarchist who spent her life struggling for a revolution much more radical than that envisioned by Marx, or that which she saw betrayed by the Russian Bolsheviks. She was born in Czarist Russia, emigrated to the United States at the age of seventeen, worked in the dress factories of New York, and was precipitated into radical political activity by her outrage at the execution in Chicago of five anarchists in 1887, for supposed complicity in the Haymarket bombing. Goldman defended terrorist actions against the ruling class, not as morally right but as the inevitable results of gross social injustices. For this, the government persecutors tried unsuccessfully to implicate her as a conspirator in the assassination of McKinley—the assassin having once heard her speak. She was finally deported to Russia in 1919, after two years in prison for her oppostion to the military draft. After her disillusioning stay in what she later wrote was in no way whatever a *communist* society, she became a British citizen and continued to speak, write and organize; she died suddenly in the midst of a campaign to raise funds for the anti-Franco side in the Spanish Civil War.

Although her commentators find it necessary to point out that Goldman was "an activist and not a theoretician," (1) she was not only a potent evangelist but a lucid exponent of the union of anarchist, libertarian, and feminist ideas which was uniquely hers. As anarchist, she rejected all law and government as essentially tyrannical, as serving no possible purpose other than to protect private monopolies, and as inconsistent with the freedom which is needed above all else by the human individual. Anarchy means not chaos, but strictly voluntary association and organization, with all property belonging to all the people, not to private interests or to the state, as in Soviet Russia. Goldman's feminism follows naturally from her anarchism, and it is a feminism far removed from that of the liberal woman suffragists in the America of her day. It is in many respects a forerunner of the radical feminism of our own time.

Unlike those feminists who (in overreaction to the sexual freedom of George Sand or Mary Wollstonecraft) tried to outdo the traditionalists in their praise of exaggerated versions of chastity, monogamous marriage and (compulsory) motherhood, Goldman denounced these Puritan shibboleths as an essential part of the enslavement of women. The Puritan ideal condemns women either "to celibacy, or the indiscriminate breeding of a diseased race, or to prostitution." (***Anarchism and Other Essays***, p.171) Free love and the prevention of unwanted conception would provide far better protection for women, and children, than legal marriage. Marriage, she holds, is incompatible with both love and freedom; it

> makes a parasite of woman, an absolute dependent. It incapacitates her for life's struggle, annihilates her social consciousness, paralyzes her imagination, and then imposes its gracious protection. (p.235)

Furthermore, it is marriage, together with the sexual double standard and the insistence that respectable young women be kept in complete sexual ignorance, which creates prostitution—which indeed is not essentially different from marriage. For,

> Nowhere is woman treated according to the merit of her work, but rather as a sex. It is therefore almost inevitable that she should pay for her right to exist . . . with sex favors. Thus it is merely a question of degree whether she sells herself to one man, in or out of marriage, or to many. (p.179)

Women's liberation, then, requires freedom from marriage, freedom to love or not, to bear children or not, as they choose. Goldman has little use for the freedoms sought by liberal feminists, i.e. suffrage and the right to work at (under-) paid jobs as well as in the home. Votes for women she considers a fetish, like religion, with which she has even less patience. Suffrage is

> an evil, that . . . has only helped to enslave people, that . . . has but closed their eyes that they may not see how craftily they were made to submit. (p.197)

More important than the vote, more important than the entry of women into the labor market, is the self-liberation, mind and body, of the individual woman.

> Her development, her freedom, her independence, must come from and through herself. First, by asserting herself as a personality, and not a sex commodity. Second, by refusing the right to anyone over her body; by refusing to bear children, unless she wants them; by refusing to be a servant to God, the State, society, the husband, the family . . . (p.211)

1. Introduction, by Alix Kate Shulman, to ***Red Emma Speaks***, p.21.

GREER, Germaine. *The Female Eunuch* (Granada Publishing, London, 1970)

A highly literate statement of radical feminism which takes issue on key points with both liberal and leftist wings of the women's movement. Greer follows the tradition of Mary Wollstonecraft in that she directs her harshest criticism not towards men but towards women as they have been misshapen ("castrated," in her terminology) by the patriarchal image of femininity and the feminine role. Housewifery, as currently practiced in the Western world, makes women miserable, frustrated and resentful, and causes them to behave destructively towards themselves, their children and their spouses. Because housewives tend to resent women who have escaped the slavery of traditional wife-and-motherhood they form the core of the conservative backlash against feminism.

Greer accuses liberal feminists such as Betty Freidan of wanting nothing more than equality of opportunity within the status quo for middle-class women. To fail to reject marriage and enforced monogamy, or to defend them on the grounds that they are conducive to love or the best environment in which to raise children, is to succumb to patriarchal mythology; in reality both love and children tend to fare badly in the patriarchal nuclear family. She defends women's involvement in (extramarital and nonmonogamous) sexual relationships with men as the arena in which new values will be born. She rejects the interpretation of the significance of the Masters and Johnson research on clitoral orgasms put forward by Anne Koedt and others: while it is true that Freudians have been wrong to consider the vagina the only proper locus of sexual pleasure for mature women, it is a mistake to conclude from the fact that all orgasms involve the clitoris that the vagina is *irrelevant* to women's pleasure, or that it is only men who enjoy heterosexual intercourse. The avoidance of sexual intercourse with men, whether it is displaced by masturbation, lesbianism or chastity, is not in itself a revolutionary action.

Greer is also critical of socialist feminists who believe that the liberation of women can come only after the downfall of capitalism and therefore consider the struggle for socialism more important than bringing about a specifically feminist revolution. She considers the attempt to prove, by excursions into anthropology, that matriarchy was the primordial form of human society both dubious and unnecessary; the form of life feminists envisage might as well be completely new as extremely ancient. Her own program for feminist revolution stresses women's individual assumption of autonomoy. Marriage and monogamy must be avoided at all costs, even by women who wish to be mothers; children are better raised by single parents or in communal living groups than in patriarchal family units. Women must refuse to give men the right to know with certainty which children are theirs, since once this is denied, patriarchy will become impossible. Women are encouraged not to work for reforms within the capitalist system, which Greer considers worse than useless, but to undermine capitalism directly by refusing to function as its chief consumers. The rejection of expensive, fashionable clothing, of commercial cosmetics and household products and the cooperative wholesale purchase of food, eliminating the middleman, contribute to this end, and also make it more feasible to retain economic independence. When women independently insist on their own autonomy and reject the feminine role, men will be relieved of the burden of supporting them as dependents, which in rational terms is a better alternative for them as well. Gone too will be the basis for men's abiding hatred and contempt for women, so aptly illustrated in the abusive language which they apply to women.

GRIFFIN, Susan. *Woman and Nature: The Roaring Inside Her* (Harper and Row, New York, 1978)

This book is more poetic than expository; it manages to display rather to state its theses explicitly. The main point is simple (and clearly true): that men have achieved power over both women and nature by portraying both as passive, inert matter, and themselves as active, potent, rational and creative. Griffin traces the attitudes of Western patriarchal culture towards women and nature by juxtaposing quotations from male philosophers, poets and scientists, from Plato and Aristotle through the medieval witch burners to Freud and the contemporary capitalist/imperialist mentality. (She does not, unfortunately, give the source of the quoted passages and ideas; to do so might have marred the flow of the poetry but would have been a help to less erudite readers.)

In the second part of the book, Griffin shows how all of the artificial dualism of patriarchal thought will be eliminated, the false dichotomies overcome, by a feminist-ecological revolution in thought and feeling. Women's anger, so long denied, will burst forth and propel us into a new conceptual "space," in which we will be free.

As a literary work, *Woman and Nature* has been justly praised; but it is frustrating from a philosophical point of view because it suggests and dramatizes, rather than stating and clarifying, the new ideas and attitudes which may be expected to emerge from the union of feminism and ecology.

GRIMKE, Sarah (1792–1873). *Letters on the Equality of the Sexes and the Condition of Woman* (Burt Franklin, New York, 1970; first published 1838)

Sarah Grimke and her sister Angelina grew up in the slave-based culture of Charleston; in the early 1830s they moved to Boston where they began to speak and write against slavery and for women's rights, thereby breaking the taboo against public speaking and political activism on the part of women. The *Letters* were prompted by a denunciation of the Grimkes' abolitionist activities in a pastoral letter promulgated by the Massachusetts Congregationalist Clergy. In the Congregationalists' view woman's place is definitely not in the public arena; when a woman "assumes the place and tone of a man as a public performer . . . she yields the power which God has given her for her protection, and her character becomes unnatural."(1) In response, Sarah Gimke produced an aggressive and lucid defense of women's right to full equality with men, a work which was the first major feminist work by an American.

Grimke bases her argument on her own reading of the Bible, which she accuses male scholars and theologians of thoroughly misunderstanding, if not deliberately distorting, in its application to women. Nowhere in the Scriptures, she maintains, is woman said to be inferior to men or morally bound to submit to his will. God gave man dominion over the birds, the beasts, and the fishes, but not over woman. Eve was created to be Adam's companion, not his slave; women and men alike are consistently held to owe their allegiance to God alone, and not to any human intermediary. When, after the fall, God said to Eve that henceforth she would be subject to her husband, this was a prediction and not a commandment. Even if one admits (as she does not) that Eve was more to blame than Adam, still men's subsequent domination of women is sinful and a defiance of God's will, who designed men and women to occupy the same moral sphere. "I ask no favors for my sex," she says, in one of the most famous passages in feminist literature,

> I surrender not our claim to equality . . . All I ask of our brethren is, that they will take their feet from off our necks and permit us to stand upright on the ground which God designed us to occupy. (p.10)

Like Mary Wollstonecraft (whom she does not mention) Grimke attacks the invidious distinction, so much insisted upon by the Congregationalist clergy, between what are called masculine and feminine virtues. It is, she insists, not a Christian doctrine, but "one of the anti-Christian "traditions of men" which are taught instead of the "commandments of God" " (p.16) By such doctrines men have enslaved women, deprived them of their most basic human rights, and freed them to commit the sin of giving their obedience to man rather than to God and their own consciences. She blames complacent women who recognize the wrong of slavery but do nothing about it—out of deference to their husbands—for the continuation of that evil.

Like Wollstonecraft, too, Grimke stops well short of questioning woman's traditional role as mother and housekeeper. She protests the inequality in wages that makes it so difficult for a single woman or a woman with dependents to make a living, but she believes that the moral and legal equality of the sexes will strengthen rather than undermine woman's place in the home. Independent and well-educated women will be better mothers and more intellectually rewarding companions for men. But she is sensitive to the oppressive effects of traditional aesthetic standards which require women to be "beautiful" if they are to win the approbation of men. "To me, it appears beneath the dignity of a woman to bedeck herself in gewgaws and trinkets . . . to gratify the eye of man." (p.71) She boldly attacks the double standard in all its aspects, maintaining that anything which is right for a man to do must also be right for a woman to do, including preaching the Gospel and fighting against social evils.

One of the major Scriptural arguments for the supremacy of men and the exclusion of women from the ministry has long been Paul's letters to the Corinthians, in which he commands women to be silent in the church, and wives to obey their husbands. Grimke admits that Paul "may have been imbued with the prevalent prejudices against women" (p.91) but argues that properly tranlated and read in context these passages do not really imply the moral inferiority of women. The injunction to be silent is not meant to preclude women's teaching and serving as ministers or priests, but only to dissuade them from interrupting the services with impertinent questions and comments (a habit into which they may have fallen). And the command to obey their husbands should be read as an instance of the Christian principle, "Resist not evil," *not* as a confirmation of the husband's moral *right* to exact obedience.

Needless to say, such an interpretation glosses over Paul's

consistently expressed misogyny. Grimke's effort to strip the Scriptures of what she saw as later patriarchal overlays may really have been a case of peeling the onion, in that the patriarchal implications of Genesis and the Epistles are part of the very core of their meaning. (Whether Christ himself favored or opposed male supremacy is another and more difficult question.) All the same, Grimke's analysis is undeniably brilliant. This is a seminal (ovarian?) work, which still repays study.

1. Quoted by Sheila Rowbotham, *Women, Resistance and Revolution* (Random House, New York, 1974), p.107.

GUETTEL, Charnie. *Marxism and Feminism* (The Woman's Press, Toronto, 1974)

This is a brief but useful exposition of the "scientific Marxist" analysis of the oppression of women. Scientific Marxism is opposed to what Guettel calls the "feminist" position, in that it interprets women's oppression as a result of, rather than as independent of or prior to, the economic oppression of one class by another.

> Women are oppressed by men because of the forms their lives have had to take in class society, in which both men and women have been oppressed by the ruling class. (p.2)

Guettel rejects John Stuart Mill's explanation of male domination as due to women's physical weakness in comparison to men, on the grounds that prior to the rise of civilization (which corresponded to the appearance of exploited classes), "nothing like the exploitation of the last five thousand years existed." (p.6) She criticizes Simone de Beauvoir for her notion of the imperialism of consciousness, an innate tendency towards the pursuit of domination which is supposed to exist in all human beings independent of the economic system under which they live; and she criticizes Kate Millett for treating economic power as a *consequence* of psychological domination rather than its cause. It is, she thinks, a mistake to concentrate on the need to change *attitudes*, "rather than necessarily transforming the production relations which in the long run cause these attitudes." (p.25) Shulamith Firestone she sees not as enlarging upon the analysis of historical materialism, as Firestone claims to do, but as rejecting it in favor of a neo-Freudian analysis which wrongly treats the repression of sexuality, rather than economic exploitation, as the basis of all oppressive institutions.

For the scientific Marxist, class rather than sex is "the primary contradiction"; (p.49) "the mode of production is more important than the mode of reproduction," since "the oppression of man over woman would not exist for long if man were not in the first place a provider in a *class* society." (*Loc. cit.*) The failure of existing socialist systems thus far to eliminate sexist attitudes and practices is, Guettel thinks, no argument against this analysis, since the change will simply require a good deal more time. If socialist states have not yet made women fully equal, as well as a participant in the production process, it is because this will require "the socialization of maternity, which means that parenthood must be shared, in the sense that males and females participate equally in childrearing." (p.59) While the social and technological preconditions for this do not yet exist, they can and will come to exist (only) under socialism.

What is disappointing about this essay (and in this it is not unlike the Marxist approach in general) is its postulation of the primacy of exploitative production relations in the etiology of male domination, not as an hypothesis in need of examination, in the light of the evidence, but as an axiom which is treated as self-evident. In fact it is by no means evident that the existence of an exploitative class system is either necessary or sufficient for patriarchy or male domination. The fact that there are highly male-dominated societies — e.g. among the aboriginal Australians—which are not divided into economic classes seems to demonstrate that it is not necessary; and it is at least conceivable that a society could achieve virtual equality between the sexes (within a given class), without ceasing to exploit its poorer members. This is not to suggest that the political and philosophical link between socialism and feminism is not of the utmost importance. It is; but the attempt to reduce either socialism or feminism to a corollary of the other, or to prove that economic oppression is "more fundamental" than sexual oppression (or vice versa), seems futile.

H

HAMILTON, Roberta. *The Liberation of Women: A Study of Patriarchy and Capitalism* (George Allen and Unwin, London, 1978)

Roberta Hamilton is a Canadian sociologist who argues that to understand the oppression of women today it is necessary to make use of both the Marxist and the feminist analyses. Marxism explains the (very different) oppression of bourgeois and working-class women in terms of the capitalist economic system, in which the privileged class lives on the surplus value or unpaid labor of the exploited class. Feminism, on the other hand, views male supremacy as the result of women's biological disadvantages, and of the patriarchal institutions and ideologies which maintain and amplify these disadvantages.

Hamilton argues that a Marxist analysis enables us to understand the crucial changes in women's role and status which occurred during the seventeenth century, when the feudal system was replaced by capitalism and the home consequently ceased to be the center of economic productivity. When wage labor replaced domestic industry as the primary mode of production, the wife's role changed from that of an almost (though never entirely) equal economic partner to that of an economic dependent. Bourgeois and upper-class women became idle consumers, isolated from the economic and political life of society. Working-class women either had to depend on their husbands' wages (which were rarely adequate for the support of a family), or to suffer long hours and inhuman working conditions in order to earn wages which were often inadequate even for their own support. In the latter case they were, and remain, doubly exploited, since their childrearing and other domestic responsibilities are not usually lightened when they become wage laborers.

But while the Marxist analysis is valid as far as it goes, Hamilton points out that it does little to explain the universality of women's oppression, throughout history and in virtually all human cultures. Nor does it explain why this oppression shows little sign of disappearing under existing socialist economic systems. To explain these aspects of male supremacy a feminist analysis is required.

Hamilton illustrates the feminist mode of analysis by focusing on the shift, during the seventeenth and eighteenth centuries, from the Catholic view of woman's nature and role to that of the Protestants. Catholic teaching emphasized the inherent evilness of woman, and consequently viewed marriage as a morally debased condition—preferable to fornication but inferior to chastity. (See Paul, Augustine, Aquinas.) Protestant opinion, on the other hand, increasingly favored marriage over celibacy. Protestant preachers muted the doctrine of the evil nature of woman, while continuing to emphasize the necessity of her subordination in marriage. Furthermore, unlike the Catholics, they recognized no worthy role for women outside of marriage and motherhood. The home became a private refuge from the harsh amoral world of commerce and industry, and woman as homemaker was idealized in sentimental and romantic terms.

These two analyses, Hamilton concludes, are complementary rather than antagonistic. Both economic and ideological factors play a role in determining women's oppression, and thus neither Marxism nor feminism alone is adequate. Hamilton agrees with Firestone, Mitchell and certain other radical feminists, that Freudian psychoanalysis is a useful tool for investigating the psychological shaping of females and males which occurs within the patriarchal family. She argues, however, that in order to avoid the reactionary conclusions drawn by Freud and many of his followers (e.g., Bonaparte and Deutsch), we need the historical perspective which the Marxist analysis provides. Nevertheless, she believes that it is unrealistic to attempt a *merger* of the Marxist and feminist analyses. Both politically and conceptually the alliance between the two movements remains an uneasy one, for their methods and goals are not identical. Consequently,

> Different structures are developing for the overthrow of capitalism and the dismantling of patriarchy . . . More than one revolution is needed, but . . . each can succeed only with the realization of the other. (p. 105)

HAMMER, Signe. *Daughters and Mothers: Mothers and Daughters* (New American Library, New York, 1976)

This is a psychological study of some of the ways in which the mother-daughter relationship, within the patriarchal family, helps to perpetuate a defective sense of self in many women. According to the Freudian scenario, because the mother—the girl's first love object—is also of the same sex, the girl has a more difficult task than the boy in achieving "separation" from the other and developing a clear sense of her own individual identity. Women's social position as economically dependent childrearer creates "a vicious cycle . . . in which women who were not encouraged to grow up, raise daughters who are not encouraged to grow up either." (p.xv)

Hammer maintains that "the mother-daughter relationship endures as the bedrock of every other [relationship] in a woman's life, including those with her father, with other men, and with her own children." (p.1) Thus, if a woman does not achieve adequate psychic separation from her mother she will tend to develop the same type of self-negating symbiotic relationship with men and with her own children. If, on the other hand, the mother has enough sense of her own identity to encourage her daughter to be active and self-motivated, and does not harshly repress the child's masturbatory explorations (which repression, in Freudian theory, is a key cause of the feminine turn towards passivity), then she will be able to grow into a strong, independent woman and to raise daughters who are also strong.

HARDING, Esther M. *The Way of All Women* (Harper and Row, 1970; first published 1933)
Woman's Mysteries, Ancient and Modern (Putnam, New York, 1971)

A student and follower of C.G. Jung, Harding uses the Jungian notions of the masculine and feminine principles (animus and anima) to describe pitfalls women encounter in attempting to develop as human individuals. The masculine principle is Logos, the rational and egoistic pursuit of one's own desires. The feminine principle is Eros, which includes not just erotic relationships but all relationships which are interpersonal and involve the transcendence of egoistic goals. Femininity is natural for women and necessary for their psychological health, but an exclusive identification with femininity prevents a woman from becoming an individual in her own right, and from finding happiness in marriage and motherhood. She needs to become aware of her animus, her masculine tendencies, and incorporate them into her conscious psyche, just as a man needs to become aware of his anima.

This does not mean that women should become masculine or make work and career their main preoccupation, as men tend to do. Harding has harsh words for the feminist who attempts to

become just like or fully equal to a man, thus selling "her birth-
right, her feminine inheritance, her uniqueness . . . the difference arising from the fact that she is female." (*The Way of All
Women,* p.3) A woman's main goal is a good relationship with her
husband or lover and/or children, and it is towards this end that
she must become conscious of her animus. Otherwise she will
project it onto the man she loves, and love a false image rather
than an individual. The man in turn, if he has not integrated his
anima into his conscious personality, will project it onto the
woman, and each will love not the other but the image of him/
herself in the other. Only when each is aware of him/herself as a
person with both masculine and feminine tendencies (though
predominantly one or the other) can each relate to the other as an
individual rather than as his or her "other half." The position is
intermediate between that of the Freudians, who view any manifestations of so-called masculinity in women as a sign of pathology, and the androgynists, who maintain that each individual,
female or male, should strive to be neither predominantly masculine nor predominantly feminine but a well-rounded mixture of
the two. (See Heilbrun, Singer.)

   Woman's Mysteries is a search for archetypal representations
of the feminine principle in myths and religious symbols, which
are said to represent unconscious psychic processes common to
all people. The ancient mystery religions and the worship of the
Great Goddess are interpreted as means whereby women were
able to gain direct contact with the feminine principle, which
contact enabled them to transcend their egos and personal destinies and to love unselfishly. (See C.G. Jung, and Androgyny.)

HAYS, H.R. *The Dangerous Sex: The Myth of Feminine Evil*
(G.P. Putnam's Sons, New York, 1964)
   A study of misogynist attitudes and customs through the ages,
from the menstrual taboos and *vagina dentata* (toothed vagina)
myths of the primitive peoples to the castration-anxiety-laden
contemporary myth of the American matriarchy, propounded by
writers like Philip Wylie. Hays argues that men have always had
difficulty recognizing women as "female men," that is as fellow
human beings: men have always regarded women "at best with
condescension and suspicion, at worst with hatred and fear."
(p.12) Primitive men saw women as suffused with magical energy, both good and bad, but with the evil mana always seeming
to prevail. Savage initiation rites, in which young boys are often
sexually brutalized by older men, are part of a "phallic" phase in

the development of male attitudes, in which the rejection of women is closely associated with violence, homosexuality and sadomasochism.

In Greek and Judeo-Christian mythology, for instance in the stories of Eve and the apple and of Pandora's box, the magical, superstitious basis of misogyny is disguised by a layer of moral and religious ideology, yet remains fundamentally unaltered. As before, woman and woman's sexuality are associated with death, corruption and loss of potency; men project their deepest anxieties onto women and insist that women are intrinsically evil, dangerous, inferior, and worthless. Hays interprets the witch burnings of the fourteenth and fifteenth centuries as a massive outbreak of male sexual paranoia. He regards the theory that witches—or at least many of them—were members of an actual underground religion as unproven and implausible. "The whole affair," he says, "has the stamp of male fantasy," of the lurid imaginings of the celibate clergy, whose nocturnal emissions led them to believe that they were being attacked by *succubi*, i.e. female demons. He also examines the lives and work of a number of distinctly misogynous nineteenth-century writers, including Poe, Baudelaire, Swinburne, Schopenhauer, and Balzac, and suggests that all of them suffered from what Frederick Wertham called the Orestes complex—a syndrome characterized by both excessive attachment and intense hostility towards a mother image, a generalized hatred of women, and strong (though not necessarily overt) homosexual tendencies.

The explanation of male domination, then, is the fundamentally neurotic attitudes of men towards women. Why men have always projected their own fear of death and failure onto women is not entirely clear, but Hays seems to think that it is primarily because of men's sexual "fragility." Men are insecure about their sexuality because it is dependent upon the capricious functioning of their erectile tissues, which is often independent of conscious control. Women seem menacing because they make sexual demands, and because their own sexual role can be fulfilled "without effort, by mere acceptance." (p.283) In short, men blame women for their own fear of impotence. Hays ends with the suggestion that the contemporary male must alter his conception of masculinity, abandoning his magical and irrational attitudes towards women and realizing that "the menace of the female lies within himself." (p.295) But the prospects for such a change occurring would not seem to be particularly bright, given Hays' view that male attitudes towards women are subconsciously determined by "deep anxieties which are probably universal and basic as the young male grows up in the family relationship." (p.281) He does not consider the possibility that certain fundamental changes in the family relationship, e.g. greater male participation in the rearing of children, may be necessary if this subconscious process is to be altered; but as Dorothy Dinnerstein points out, this would seem to be a necessary conclusion from Hays' psychoanalytic premises (1).

1.   Dinnerstein, *The Mermaid and the Minotaur*.

HEGEL, Georg Wilhelm Friedrich (1770–1831) *The Phenomenology of Mind* (translated by J.B. Baillie, George Allen and Unwin, London, and Humanities Press, New York, 1966; first published 1807)
Philosophy of Right (translated by T. M. Knox, Oxford University Press, London, Oxford and New York; first published 1821)
   Next to Kant, Hegel is the most important philosopher of the German idealist school. His writing is difficult and obscure, yet many of his ideas remain current, especially among Marxists, existentialists and phenomenologists (1). Hegel held that human history as a whole is a reflection of the coming into existence of the Absolute Idea, or God. The Absolute Idea is pure self-awareness, existence become entirely translucent to itself. It is a spiritual being, and it is ultimately identical with the whole of reality. "Spirit," Hegel says,

> is alone Reality. It is the inner being of the world, that which essentially is . . . it is self-contained and self-complete, in itself and for itself [i.e., object and subject] at once. (*The Phenomenology of Mind*, p. 86)

Because he viewed reality as essentially constituted by spirit and ruled by reason, logic became for Hegel the objective science of reality. Hegel's logic is dialectical; he held that every thought or proposition (the thesis) leads to its contradictory (the antithesis), with which it is then reconciled through a third proposition (the synthesis). The synthesis then becomes a new thesis, and the process continues. Consequently, Hegel held that the laws of nature and history are also dialectical; they form an intimately interconnected unity, like the thoughts of a single mind—which is exactly what they are.
   Hegel's views on the nature of women and women's role are an integral part of his philosophical system. As a student, Hegel read both Kant and Rousseau, and his romantic patriarchal con-

ception of sex roles reflects their influence. Hegel holds that woman's place has always been and always will be within the family; her existence necessarily centers in the roles of wife and mother. The family he conceives as strictly patriarchal, and as isolated from civil and political society, which are the exclusive province of men.

The fact that women are destined for the family, men for the larger social world, justifies, among other things, the sexual double standard. Hegel says that,

> a girl in surrendering her body loses her honour. With a man
> . . . the case is otherwise, because he has a field for ethical activity
> outside the family. A girl is destined in essence for the marriage tie,
> and for that only; it is therefore demanded of her that her love shall
> take the form of marriage . . . (*The Philosophy of Right*, p.263)

Hegel's analysis of the ethical and intellectual nature of women must be understood in terms of the contrast he draws between human relationships within the family and those in civil and political society. The family, Hegel claims, is "a *natural* ethical community, held together by feelings of love, rather than by contracts or legal rights. There are no moral or legal rights within the family, only duties. Rights exist only within civil and political (i.e. male) society, or within the family when it is in the process of dissolution (e.g. through divorce). This is because in the larger society (or in the dissolving family) the ruling principle is not love but self-interest; consequently law and contractual relationships are essential in the larger world, whereas they are utterly incompatible with the spirit of family life.

Hegel holds that within the family persons are not related to one another as unique individuals, but through certain universalized relationships—i.e. husband/wife, parent/child, and brother/sister. These family relationships are originally purely natural. With the development of human consciousness they generate a kind of ethics. It is, however, a universalist, altruistic ethics in which human individuality plays no part.

Woman's nature, Hegel says, is revealed through her role in these three relationships. In neither the parent/child relationship nor the husband/wife relationship does she achieve any experience of herself as a unique individual. For, he argues,

> In a household of the ethical kind, a woman's relationships are not
> based on a reference to this particular husband, this particular
> child, but to *a* husband, to children in general. The distinction
> between her ethical life . . . and that of her husband consists in just
> this . . . (*Phenomenology of Mind*, pp.476–477)

Nevertheless, Hegel says, it is possible for a woman to gain some awareness of herself as an individual through the third major family relationship, i.e., that between brother and sister. Individuality is impossible in the spousal and parental relationships because of the difference in status and power in both cases, and because of the presence of sexual desire in the former. Between brother and sister, however, there is ideally neither sexual desire nor inequality of power; hence this relationship is the most important for a woman's discovery of her individual nature. Hegel does not consider the sister/sister relationship as a possible means of self-discovery for women, and would probably have denied that it could play such a role. For in his view the brother can provide a woman with an image of her own individuality only because he is destined to play a role in the larger world outside the family:

> He passes from the divine law . . . to the human law. The sister, however, becomes, or the wife remains, director of the home and the preserver of divine law. (*Op. cit.*, p. 478)

For Hegel, therefore, man represents "universal spirit conscious of itself"; woman, on the other hand, represents "*unconscious* spirit." (*Op. cit.*, p.481) Marriage, he says,

> unites into one process the twofold movement in opposite directions—one from reality to unreality, the downward movement of human law . . . to the danger and trial of death—the other, from unreality to reality, the upward movement of the law of the nether world to the daylight of conscious existence. Of these movements the former falls to man, the latter to woman. (*Op. cit.*, p.482)

Despite its obscurity, this formulation can be recognized as a version of the romantic division of human virtues and "spheres" into masculine and feminine, public and private, rational and emotional, active and passive. Hegel does not view this privatized, sentimentalized role of woman as the product of a particular historical situation, but as something eternal, and inherent in the nature of the female sex. It is, he says, "Nature, not the accident of circumstances or choice, which assigns one sex to one law, the other to the other law." (*Op cit.*, p. 485) It would, however, be a mistake to describe Hegel as a *biological* determinist. His claim is not that anatomy is destiny, but rather, that

> The difference in the physical characteristics of the two sexes has a rational basis and consequently acquires an intellectual and ethical significance. (**Philosophy of Right**, p.114)

The ethical significance of the difference (according to Hegel) we have already seen: women belong in the family, where they have no moral or legal rights, and no public role whatever. Intellectually, Hegel thinks, women are distinctly inferior. Echoing Kant and Rousseau, he says that

> Women are capable of education, but they are not made for activities which demand a universal [i.e. abstract intellectual] faculty such as the more advanced sciences, philosophy, and certain forms of artistic production. Women may have happy ideas, taste, and elegance, but they cannot attain to the ideal. (*Op. cit.*, p. 263)

Because of their moral and intellectual inferiority, Hegel says, women pose a threat to the higher moral order of the state. They "ridicule the grave widsom of maturity," and assert "that it is everywhere the force of youth that counts." (*The Phenomenology of Mind*, p.496) They are, from the viewpoint of the state, an "enemy . . . within its own gates" (*loc. cit.*). Furthermore,

> When women hold the helm of government, the state is at once in jeopardy, because women regulate their actions not by the demands of universality but by arbitrary inclinations and opinions. (*Philosophy of Right*, p.264)

These male supremacist doctrines are entirely consistent with the overall political conservatism of Hegel's philosophy. Hegel defends not only patriarchy and the isolation of women within the home, but the division of society into rich and poor, masters and servants, the assumption of absolute power by the state, and the periodic waging of war, as necessary phases in the self-development of the Absolute. (For a good feminist criticism of Hegel's views on women and the family, see Carol C. Gould, "The Woman Question," in *Women and Philosophy*, edited by Gould, Anthologies XII.)

HEILBRUN, Carolyn G. *Toward a Recognition of Androgyny* (Alfred A. Knopf, New York, 1973)

In this widely acclaimed work, Heilbrun traces the literary development of the ideal of androgyny, that is the rejection of rigid sexual stereotypes, and the recognition that full humanity requires the exercise of both "masculine" and "feminine" capacities. "Androgyny," for Heilbrun, means not that everyone should be equally masculine and feminine (which has been called the "strong" version of the ideal of androgyny (1)), but that everyone should be free to choose his or her place on the human spectrum, from masculine to feminine, "without regard to propriety or custom." (p. xi) The result will be a fuller range of experiences open to both sexes, and the amelioration of the disastrous results (war, exploitation, overpopulation) of the domination of the affairs of the world by masculine men. Femininity without masculinity is impotent; masculinity without femininity is malignant. Creative and humane men and women are always somewhat androgynous.

Heilbrun finds a recognition (conscious or unconscious) of the androgynous ideal in the plays of Aeschylus and Sophocles. She endorses the early matriarchy theory, and finds in Greek writers and in the Bible traces of an earlier and more respectful attitude towards women than already prevailed at the dawn of Western history. She sees the worship of the Virgin Mary throughout the Middle Ages (and especially in the twelfth and thirteenth centuries) as a survival of the androgynous ideal, and a threat to the patriarchal powers of the Trinity. Shakespeare, she argues, was a devotee of the androgynous ideal; his use of interchangeable boy-girl twins is symbolic of the lack of polarized sex roles which was an ideal of the Renaissance.

The primary interest of the author centers, however, on the novel; the greatest novels, she argues, have from the beginning been androgynous, in that they have depicted the waste and misery that resulted from the polarization of the sexes. (Dickens is a counterexample and a novelist whose female characters invariably lack human substance.) A useful distinction is drawn between feminist novels, in which we identify only with female heroes, and androgynous novels, in which we identify only with female heroes, and androgynous novels, in which we identify with characters of both sexes. *Jane Eyre* is a feminist novel; **Wuthering Heights** and **The Scarlet Letter** are androgynous novels.

In the twentieth century, the androgynous ideal has emerged most strongly from the work of the Bloomsbury Group, who were also an outstanding example of the androgynous ideal put into practice. Heilbrun interprets Virginia Woolf, e.g. in **The Lighthouse** and **Mrs. Dalloway**, as attacking the sterility of the totally feminine earth-mother role, and demonstrating the failure of marriages based on the traditional male/female stereotype. And Lytton Strachey's studies of Queen Victoria and Queen Elizabeth argue for the androgynous ideal by showing that Victoria abdicated her chance for greatness by her subordination of her own will to that of her husband, while Elizabeth was able to function as a great ruler by retaining her independence, without denying herself the love and companionship of men.

The controversy over the usefulness of androgyny as an ideal of human character still rages among feminists and no doubt will do so for some time. Some have argued that to try to develop a unified ideal from the union of masculine and feminine traits is like trying to derive such an ideal from combining the traits of slaves with those of slave owners; hardly a promising enterprise (2). But however this dispute may eventually be resolved, Heilbrun must be credited with a powerful and groundbreaking defense of the androgynous ideal. Its value lies above all in the evidence she compiles that this ideal has survived and resurfaced again and again, like a recurring dream of unity, during all the ages in which humanity has been polarized by sexual stereotypes and rigid sexual roles.

1. See Joyce Treblicot's "Two Forms of Androgynism,"in *Feminism and Philosophy*, edited by Mary Vetterling-Braggin, Frederick A. Elliston, and Jane English, Anthologies XII.
2. See, for instance, Janice Raymond, "The Illusion of Androgyny," *Quest*, 2:1 pp.57–66.

HERSCHBERGER, Ruth. *Adam's Rib* (Harper and Row, New York, 1970; first published 1948, by Harper and Row)

A lively protest against sexual stereotyping in the guise of scientific objectivity, which is highly contemporary in tone and written with considerable humor and wit. Herschberger points out that both physiologists and psychologists have tended not only to exaggerate the observable differences between the sexes, but to treat these exaggerated differences as norms, deviation from which is undesirable if not pathological. Scientific data is invariably interpreted so as to accord with the prevailing sexual stereotypes, however much distortion this may entail.

For example, Herschberger describes an experiment by R.M. Yerkes, in which a male and female chimpanzee were tested as to dominance. Jack, the male, dominated the food chute—keeping all the extra treats dispensed for himself—for sixteen of the thirty days of the experiment, while Josie, the female, dominated the food chute for the remaining fourteen days, which happened to be the period during which she was in estrus. The experimenters concluded that the male was "naturally" dominant over the female, merely "allowing" her access to the food in order to gain her sexual favors. Furthermore, they compared Josie's domination during her estrus period to human prostitution. Herschberger has Josie point out in her "own" words that (1) she was dominant nearly half the time, in spite of the fact that (2) Jack was the largest male in the colony; and (3) that she took charge of the food chute while she was in heat largely because she felt hungrier and "feistier" then. The experiment hardly amounts, therefore, to a demonstration of male supremacy in the chimpanzee world.

Herschberger is strikingly ahead of her time in her views on rape, and on female sexuality. She argues that rape is a custom which is encouraged by the patriarchal myth of the natural sexual aggressiveness of men and the passivity of women. She anticipates the findings of Masters and Johnson and their feminist significance by pointing out that the clitoris is actually much more sensitive than the vagina, being in fact more richly supplied with nerve endings than is the penis. Since this fact contradicts the male conceit that a woman's greatest pleasure is to be penetrated by a penis, the importance of the clitoris has been ignored. She also offers an interesting explanation of why "clitoris" is usually pronounced with a short *i* (clitt-or-iss), rather than a long *i* (clite-or-iss) as recommended by Webster, and as would be indicated by the word's Greek derivation; namely, that the short vowel gives the word a weaker and less aggressive sound. A "bird that *flits*," she says,

> has not nearly the emphasis of a bird in *flight*. A little *bit* does not shock like a *bite*. A *fit* is more passive than a *fight*. And therefore a clittoris is likely to be much less of a problem than a clietoris would be. (p.35)

Patriarchal biology, she notes, views the female as an infantilized, underdeveloped male, describing any female organ which resembles but is not identical to a male organ, *vestigial*. In reality it makes no more sense to speak of a clitoris as a vestigial penis than to speak of a penis as a vestigial clitoris. A biologist in a matriarchal society would probably assume that it is the penis which is an infantilized, underdeveloped version of the clitoris. Patriarchal biases are also evident in medicine's treatment of women's menstrual cycles as a type of illness, a female frailty. Men have always seen menstruation as something abnormal, unclean and dangerous, and used it as an excuse for isolating women and regarding them as the weaker sex. The fact, of course, is that menstruation is not an illness, but on the contrary a sign of the continued health of the woman's reproductive system.

Menopause is another aspect of feminine biology which has been treated by medicine and psychology in an extremely negative way: it is generally presumed to mark the end of a woman's womanhood—her femininity, physical beauty and sexual desire. Yet the objective fact, Herschberger argues, is that menopause is of great biological value, since it relieves older women of the bother of menstruation and the danger of pregnancy. Contrary to the general belief, the ovaries do not suddenly cease to produce estrogen, and sexual desire—which is not dependent on this hormone anyway—often increases rather than decreases. Scientists generally ignore the fact that men also undergo a diminution of sexual functioning in middle age (a male climacteric), preferring to think of the "change of life" as a purely feminine phenomenon.

HISTORY OF WOMEN   Although matriarchal and patriarchal theories of primitive social organization were debated in the nineteenth century, the history of women did not emerge as a distinct field of study until quite recently, when feminist historians began to realize the extent to which women have been simply omitted from most of the histories written by men. Mary Beard broke new ground in the field. She argued that (some) women have always held social power, and been an influence upon history. Simone de Beauvoir's portrayal of women's history, on the other hand, reveals an almost unrelieved oppression. Elise Boulding describes women as the submerged part of the historical iceberg—always important but usually invisible to the historian.

   In the past decade, scholars have considered and reconsidered a great many aspects of the history of women, including the history of Western attitudes towards women (See Bullough, Hayes and O'Faolain; the latter, like the following references, is in Anthologies VII.); the role of women in classical Greece and Rome (Pomeroy); the woman's suffrage movement (Chafe, O'Neill, Flexnor, Kraditor, Sinclair); the history of women in America (Douglas, George, Hogeland, A.F. Scott, Marlow and Harrison); the history of black women in this country (See Cade, Scott); women as revolutionaries (see Rowbotham; and Griffin); women's past contributions to the sciences (see Mozans), to the arts (Hess, Peterson and Wilson), and to literature (Moers, Spacks); and the (usually sexist) views about women held by the great philosophers and theologians of the Western tradition (see Osborne, Ruether, Agonisto, Mahowald, in Anthologies XII). There has also been a new interest in, and some new defenses of, the ancient matriarchy theory. (See Reed, Stone, Matriarchy Theory.) For an assortment of other recent academic studies of the history of women, see Hartman, and Carroll, in Anthologies VII.

HOLLIDAY, Laurel. *The Violent Sex: Male Psychobiology and the Evolution of Consciousness* (Bluestocking Books, Guerneyville, California, 1978)

This is an important recent contribution to the theory of radical feminism. Following Shulamith Firestone, Holliday explains male supremacy in terms of the biological differences between the sexes and consequent psychological differences, yet maintains that fundamental change is not only possible but absolutely necessary. However, while Firestone focuses on the fact that it is women who bear children, Holliday makes use of a wide range of contemporary discoveries about male and female psychobiology.

Of these, the most important involve the behavioral effects of the male hormone testosterone. There is quite persuasive evidence that in human males, as in most other male mammals, exposure to this hormone tends to produce a predisposition towards hostility and aggressiveness. In the eighth week of fetal development the testes of the male fetus normally begin to secrete testosterone, which not only causes the development of the male genitals, but alters the brain in ways which are as yet little understood. Apparently, the more testosterone the fetus is exposed to at this very early stage, the more aggressive and sexually driven the individual will tend to be in later life, and the more sensitive his system will be to subsequent exposure to testosterone.

Some of the evidence for these claims comes from extrapolation from the results of experiments with rats and other laboratory animals; but there is also evidence which is directly relevant to human males. It is known, for instance, that testosterone production in the fetus is triggered by genes on the Y chromosome, and that the larger this chromosome is the more male hormone will be produced; men with two Y chromosomes (the XYY configuration) theoretically get a double dose of testosterone. And it has also been claimed that men with a single large Y chromosome, and XYY males, tend to be more aggressive than the average male, and more predisposed towards unpredictable violent outbursts (1). Testosterone is also known to increase the production of the adrenal hormone norepinephrine, which is associated with the anger reaction, and seems to lower its threshold.

Females, of course, also produce testosterone, but in smaller amounts. The female hormone estrogen seems to neutralize the behavioral effects of testosterone, and unless they were exposed to unusually high amounts of the male hormone during the crucial fetal stage, females will be less sensitive than males to the male hormone. Consequently, females have, from the beginning and throughout their lives, a much greater propensity for peacefulness, social cooperation, and nurturance. Because of the absence of fetal exposure to testosterone, their left brain hemispheres, which control language and hence most interpersonal communication, are better developed and more dominant than those of the male. Women lack the male propensity for violence and aggression, and thus they have been dominated by men "from time immemorial"—with the possible exception of a relatively brief period of matriarchy in the Neolithic era. (p.131)

Like the populizers of sociobiological theory (e.g. Morris, Ardrey, Tiger, Fox), Holliday views the evolution of the aggressive human male as primarily a result of the hunting adaptation. At some time in the distant past—perhaps over fifteen million years ago—our hominid ancestors abandoned their primarily vegetarian diet and began to hunt and eat large animals. This turn toward predation was unlike the predation of "naturally" carnivorous animals in that it occurred through a development of male aggressiveness. Thenceforth men were selected for the traits which were adaptive for killing—and killing not just animals but other humans as well, since warfare and cannibalism increased along with the hunting of animals. Women could not follow men in this evolution towards violence, since the increasingly long-term helplessness of their infants made it necessary for them to stay nearer home base, and prevented their hunting along with the men. As a result, they became to some degree dependent upon men for their existence and that of their young.

Unlike some of the sociobiologists, however, Holliday does not confuse the evolutionary *explanation* of male aggressiveness with either a *justification* of this trait, or an indication that we can do nothing to reduce the male propensity for violence. Evolution, she points out,

> is not necessarily the reflection of "What is natural to the species" and . . . according to nature's grand design; at least in human evolution, we are experiencing the throes of an *unnatural* development, a *maladaptive selection* that we must consciously come to recognize as such and vigorously try to overcome. (p.141)

She also offers some practical suggestions for how this might be done. Women could begin by choosing nonviolent men to father their children, since aggressiveness is to a large degree hereditary; and they can have more girls and fewer boys. They can also take care to avoid exposing their offspring to brain damage, to which males are especially vulnerable, and which tends to increase their aggressiveness. Men can avoid hard liquor, which frequently increases their testosterone levels and therefore their aggressiveness. But, above all, we must stop *teaching* aggressive ways to males. At present, boys are conditioned to violence through harsher punishments than those used on girls, denigration of "sissy" behavior, and constant exposure to television violence. At the same time, we must surrender the "meateater's dominion" over other earthly life forms.

> the root of the problem is in our blithely *taking power over* the lives and deaths of other creatures whose suffering is in no way necessary for our survival . . . The crime of condoning violence against animals is part and parcel of all human violence.

The Violent Sex is on the whole well argued and sensible. An exception to this is Holliday's (possibly tongue-in-cheek) endorsement of Jerome Cobb's theory that the human race originally consisted entirely of parthenogenetic females, but was transformed into a two-sexed race by some cosmic disaster. "There are," she says, "strong indications that males are a genetic afterthought." (p.229) She points out that the Y chromosome looks like a damaged X, and that the male is a less constitutionally sound organism, as shown by the much higher rates of death and genetic abnormality among males. But however emotionally appealing it may be to view the human male as a recent and unfortunate mutation, the theory can hardly be said to enjoy much plausibility. The fact that the sexual dichotomy is present in most of the vertebrate species suggests that our ancestors were probably sexed many millions of years before they were human, or even mammalian. Fortunately, none of the rest of Holliday's arguments hinge on an acceptance of this hypothesis.

1. See John Money and Patricia Tucker, *Sexual Signatures*, p.52, for a summary of the evidence against this claim about the inherent aggressiveness of the XYY male.

HOMOSEXUALITY: See Lesbianism.

HORMONES   The discovery in this century of the difference between the "hormonal environments" (i.e. the different quantities of the various sex hormones produced) of men and women has stimulated a new round of theories about the biological determinants of (differences between) male and female behavior. Many people assume that the fact that women's primary sexual hormones (estrogen and progesterone) vary both in quantity and in ratio during the menstrual cycle means that women are subject to "raging hormonal influences." (1) Some psychologists routinely speak of the "premenstrual syndrome," a period of tension and irritability which is said to occur during the three to five days prior to menstruation (2). The evidence for the universality or severity of this syndrome may be questioned, however, particularly since much of it is derived from the self-observations of women, whose perceptions may well be influenced by their awareness of the calendar.

But even if the premenstrual syndrome is as significant as Bardwick and others claim, it cannot be said to have much direct bearing on the issues which divide feminists and antifeminists. The moods of (some) women may prove to vary cyclically, but without varying any more widely, more often or with more ill effect than do men's moods—which, indeed, may also prove to be affected by cyclical variations in hormone levels (3). Be that as it may, most women seem able to function adequately at all phases of the menstrual cycle, and few writers have seriously argued that it is *women's* particular hormonal environment which accounts for patriarchy and male domination.

The operation of the male hormone testosterone, on the other hand, has sometimes been held to be the central cause of these phenomena. (See Goldeg, Holliday, Hutt.) Testosterone, it is argued, causes males to behave more aggressively and thus to achieve dominance over females. It has long been known that the uncastrated males of domestic animal species are more aggressive than females or castrates; and experiments with laboratory animals also show a correlation between testosterone levels and aggressive behavior in male mammals. (See Money and Ehrhardt.) The difficulty, of course, is showing that such a correlation, let alone a direct causal relation, exists in the case of human males. Morality precludes such experimentation on human subjects, but studies of hermaphroditic individuals by Stoller, and Money and Ehrhardt, lend some support to this conclusion. For instance, Money and Ehrhardt found that fetally androgenized girls, who were exposed to medically administered hormones before their birth, tended to be more "tomboyish," that is more active and status seeking—though not necessarily more aggressive—than girls in the control groups.

At the same time, however, both Stoller's and Money and Ehrhardt's studies indicate that the sex to which a child is assigned and perceived to belong by those around him/her is almost always a more powerful determinant of gender identity than are homonal and other physiological factors. The fetally androgenized girls considered themselves fully female: the authors emphasize that they were not particularly aggressive. Nor is it entirely clear that higher levels of aggression are in fact associated with physiological maleness, or male gender identity; Bardwick finds no overall difference in aggressiveness in human males and females, only differences in the ways in which they customarily *express* their aggressive impulses. Furthermore, Mead's studies of Papuan cultures in which the sexes quite clearly do *not* differ with respect to aggressiveness (though the cultures differ widely from one another in this respect) show that whatever the influences of hormones on human behavior, those of culture prove far more powerful. If this is so, then while physiological factors of this sort may still prove useful in *explaining* the prevalence of patriarchy, they neither show that it is inevitable nor provide justification for its preservation. (See Lips and Colwill for a good survey of the currently available evidence on the psychological effects of sexual hormones.)

1. So said Dr. E.F. Berman, in a speech July 25, 1970, in which he worried about what might have happened if we had had a woman as President during the Bay of Pigs incident. Cited in Cox, 1976, p.27 (in Anthologies XIII).
2. See Bardwick, 1971, pp.20–40; and M.B. Parlee, "The Pre-Menstrual Syndrome," **Psychological Bulletin**, 80 (1973), pp.454–465.
3. See Lips and Colwill, 1978, pp. 93–95 (in Anthologies XIII).

HORNER, Matina. "The Motive to Avoid Success and Changing Aspirations of College Women" (**Readings on the Psychology of Women**, edited by Judith M. Bardwick, Harper and Row, New York, 1972, pp.62–67).

A research psychologist and president of Radcliffe College, Horner is famous for her thesis that talented American women suffer from a fear of success, which often causes them to lower their career aspirations. In this article, she summarizes her research on this topic.

To test subjects for fear of success, Horner had them write short stories in response to a hypothetical situation presented by the experimenter. For instance, college students were asked to react to the situation of Anne (or John, in the case of male subjects), a first-year medical student who finds herself at the top of the class. Women who are said to be high in the motive to avoid success tend to depict Anne's competitive success as leading to negative consequences, such as rejection by her peers or internal emotional conflicts; in one extreme case Anne is attacked by her fellow students and "maimed for life." Women who are relatively low in the motive to avoid success tend to write stories which are more optimistic in tone.

By using this type of test, Horner has found that white women fear success far more often than do white men. (Interestingly, black women fear success *less* often than do black men.) For white women, the occurrence of this fear varied from a low of 47%, in a sample of seventh grade girls, to a high of 86.6%, found both in a group of women law students and a group of secretaries. Achievement-oriented women seem to be the ones most apt to fear success, no doubt because for them competitive success is a real possibility.

Horner finds that during the period of years in which her studies were conducted, the fear of success among young women —both black and white—increased rather than decreased. The subjects, at an eastern women's college, tended to modify their career ambitions downward as they approached graduation. While she confirms Komarovsky's finding that as women finish college they are subjected to increasing pressure from their parents to marry instead of pursuing a career, Horner concludes that parental influence is usually much less important than that of the woman's male friends. Women with a high fear of success are usually either not dating at all, or are dating men who disapprove of "career women." Indeed, a subsequent study showed that the sex-role atitudes of male friends was "the most significant factor accounting for the presence or absence of fear of success." (p.66)

Horner believes that women's motivation to avoid success helps to explain why women are not making more rapid progress in the professions and other public arenas, now that the legal barriers have been largely removed. The interpretation of the data has, however, been challenged on several grounds. In the first place, it is not obvious that one can conclude, from the fact that many women exhibit a realistic awareness of the negative consequences which success may have in the case of a woman, that they fear success *per se*, or are motivated to avoid it. Other researchers have shown that when male subjects are asked to tell stories about Anne instead of John they also tend to picture her success as leading to negative consequences. (Conversely, women writing about John include fewer negative consequences.) (1) In writing of Anne, then, both sexes may be expressing not so much their own personal attitudes toward success, as the cultural belief that public success for women is (i.e. presently tends to be) linked with personal defeat.

In the second place, it has been objected that what Horner considers a generalized fear of success in competitive situations may be primarily a function of the particular situation, rather than a global disposition on the part of the subject. It is rational to be apprehensive about Anne's future in a male-dominated profession, in which there is still much hostility towards aspiring women; but even those who score high on Horner's test for the so-called fear of success might have no similar apprehensions about competitive success in a context in which they could be sure that achievement would be unequivocally appreciated and rewarded. If so, then the claim that (many) women fear success reduces to the much less interesting observation that they have mixed feelings about it *when it is apt to be accompanied by social sanctions, life-style complications, and other unpleasant consequences.* Thus it is at least potentially misleading to attempt to locate the cause of women's disappointingly slow progress in competitive fields within the attitudes of women themselves, rather than within the social context which shapes those attitudes.

1. Monahan, L., Kuhn, D., and Shaver, P. "Intrapsychic Versus Cultural Explanations for the "Fear of Success" Motive." *Journal of Personality and Social Psychology*, 29 (1974), pp.60–64. (Quoted in *The Psychology of Sex Differences*, by Hilary M. Lips and Nina Lee Colwill.)

HORNEY, Karen (1885–1952). *Feminine Psychology* (edited by Harold Kelman, W.W. Norton and Company, New York, 1967)

Karen Horney is one of the best known and most rebellious of the disciples of Sigmund Freud. Trained in Berlin, she practiced psychoanalysis there from 1815 to 1932, and in the United States thereafter. Beginning in 1923 she published a series of papers in which she took issue with such Freudian dogmas as the role of penis envy and masochism in feminine development; many of these are available in English translation in the Kelman collection. She repeatedly chided Freud and his followers for allowing their male point of view to shape their allegedly objective theories of feminine psychology, for exaggerating the determinative role of biology, and for failing to take account of the effects of the male supremacist culture and other aspects of the social situation in which women find themselves.

With respect to penis envy, for instance, Horney agrees that it is natural for girls in the so-called "phallic" stage of childhood to envy the genital structure of boys. But she argues that this infantile jealousy is a passing phase; once the girl realizes her own capacity for motherhood and sexual gratification she has little reason to envy male genitalia as such. If she develops a "castration complex," i.e. a conviction of guilt and inferiority because of her femaleness, it is more as a result of the general social subordination of women than of early penis envy.

Indeed, Horney argues, envy and jealousy of the genital functions of the opposite sex is by no means confined to females. She observes in her male patients an intense envy of women's capacity for pregnancy, childbirth, and suckling, in short of motherhood, and makes the suggestion that much of men's creative and competitive impulse is a result of their feeling biological inferiority due to their relatively small role in the reproduction process, which forces them to compensate by achievement of other sorts. She also questions Freud's presumption that early sexuality in both sexes is exclusively phallic (the clitoris being construed as a small phallus), with the vagina remaining undiscovered until the commencement of (heterosexual) intercourse. She believes, on the basis of psychoanalytic evidence, that vaginal sensations and vaginal masturbation are extremely common in young girls, and are only later repressed. If so, then little girls must have a lively awareness of their own sexuality *before* they become aware of the anatomical difference between the sexes; consequently, she reasons, they are not likely to develop a primary penis envy of the strength that Freud postulated.

While Horney generally does not pursue the feminist implications of her findings she does on occasion present explicitly feminist analyses. In "The Problems of Feminine Masochism" she argues that the Freudian dictum that masochism is a natural and inevitable psychic consequence of feminine anatomy is empirically unfounded, and the accepted account of its genesis in penis envy logically unpersuasive. It is one of the ideologies concerning the fixed and inferior nature of women which "function not only to reconcile women to their subordinate role by presenting it as an unalterable one, but also to plant the belief that it represents a fulfillment they crave, or an ideal for which it is commendable and desirable to strive." (p.231) (Also see Helene Deutsch.)

HUME, David (1711–1776). *A Treatise of Human Nature*, Book III, Part II, Chapter XII (edited by L.A. Selby-Bigge, Clarendon

Press, Oxford, 1967; first published 1739–40.)

Essays, Moral, Political and Literary, Volumes I and II; especially "Of the Rise and Progress of the Arts and Sciences"; "Of Polygamy and Divorces" (Vol. I); and "Of Love and Marriage" (Vol. II). (Longman, Green, and Company, London, 1875; first published 1742 and 1748; in Edinburgh.)

Hume won his place among the philosophical immortals through his radically empiricist epistemology and psychology. In the words of Bertrand Russell, Hume "developed to its logical conclusions the empirical philosophy of Locke and Berkeley, and by making it self-consistent made it incredible." (1) His views about the relation between the sexes are less well known and fairly briefly stated, yet extremely interesting; for he brought to this issue some of the same clear-headed analytic intelligence which distinguishes the rest of his philosophy.

There is a short chapter in the *Treatise*, entitled "Of Chastity and Modesty." It is located at the end of Hume's discussion of the artificial virtues (such as justice). Chastity and modesty, Hume maintains, are artificial feminine virtues, the result of social conventions which have arisen in response to social necessity. These conventional female virtues, Hume argues, are essential for the very existence of human society, since without them man would be unwilling to contribute to the support and rearing of children. For,

> in order to induce the men to impose on themselves the restraint, and undergo cheerfully all the fatigues and expenses to which it [i.e. supporting and rearing children] subjects them, they must believe, that the children are their own, and that their natural instinct is not directed to a wrong object, when they give a loose to love and tenderness. (p.570)

Thus, the basic reason why the artificial virtues of chastity and modesty must be cultivated in women to a much greater degree than in men is that reproductive biology makes paternity much more difficult to determine than maternity:

> . . . since, in the copulation of the sexes, the principle of generation goes from the man to the woman, an error may easily take place on the side of the former, tho' it be utterly impossible with regard to the latter. *From this trivial anatomical accident is deriv'd that vast difference betwixt the education and duties of the two sexes.* (p.571; emphasis added)

This trivial anatomical difference, Hume holds, not only *explains* the sexual double standard, but, given that men must work to support their children, *justifies* it as well.

Men are induc'd to labour for the maintenance and education of their children by the persuasion that they are really their own; and therefore 'tis reasonable, and even necessary, to give them some security in this particular. (p.571)

Thus, in order to give men such security, and "to impose a due restraint on the female sex," society "must attach a peculiar degree of shame to their infidelity, above what arises merely from its injustice, and must bestow proportionable praises on their chastity." (p.571) It is necessary too—or at least psychologically inevitable—that the demand for female chastity be extended far beyond what is strictly necessary to ensure knowledge of paternity. No exceptions are made for women who are above or below the childbearing age, or otherwise known to be infertile, since "the general rule carries us beyond the original principle, and makes us extend the notions of modesty [and chastity] over the whole sex, from their earliest infancy to their extremest old age . . . " (p.573)

Furthermore, Hume argues, if women are to be prevented from going astray, the social demand for female chastity must be supplemented by the sister virtue of modesty. For Hume is far from supposing that women's sexual desires are naturally weaker than those of men. "All human creatures," he says, "especially those of the female sex, are apt to over-look remote motives in favor of any present temptation: [and] The temptation is here the strongest imaginable." (p.571) Hence it is desirable that

besides the infamy attending such licenses, there shou'd be some preceding backwardness or dread, which may prevent their first approaches, and may give the female sex a repugnance to all expressions, and postures, and liberties, that have an immediate relation to such enjoyment. (p.572)

As for males, they are exempt from the demand for such backwardness or modesty; and while they have *some* moral obligation with respect to chastity, it is a far weaker one, and departures from the supposed ideal are always much more readily forgiven. For, Hume notes,

'Tis contrary to the interest of civil society, that men shou'd have an *entire* liberty of indulging their appetites in venereal enjoyment: But as this interest is weaker than in the case of the female sex, the moral obligation, arising from it, must be proportionately weaker. (p.573)

Hume does not point out, yet he could not have been unaware of the fact that social tolerance of a greater degree of sexual indulgence on the part of men necessarily results in the division of women into two classes, the "respectable" ones, and the prostitutes or "loose" women, who are available for the satisfaction of male desires. In such a system, both classes of women suffer, the former from sexual repression, the latter from sexual exploitation and social contempt; hence Hume's position requires the assumption that this double oppression of the female sex is a morally acceptable price to pay for the preservation of a disproportionate degree of sexual freedom in the male.

It is also easy to see, from a contemporary perspective, that Hume's argument for the social necessity of female chastity rests on several dubious sociological assumptions. One is that inheritance must be patrilineal. Matrilineal societies, we now know, have much less interest in guarantees of paternity and hence less need for the double standard. Another is that men will continue to have a monopoly of material wealth; for it is the male's *financial* support of the child that Hume thinks gives him the right to demand assurances that he is its father. And, finally, Hume must assume that the unwillingness of men to contribute to the support of children which are not "their own" is not only reasonable, but immune to social alteration, whereas we now know that in matrilineal cultures men typically help to support children other than (those we would consider) their own, and often consider biological fatherhood a thing of little significance. (See, for instance, Malinowski.)

Hume must, of course, be forgiven for not anticipating the late nineteenth century discovery of matrilineal cultures; and even if he had anticipated it he might have argued that conversion to a matrilineal system of inheritance is not a viable option for our own society. What is harder to understand is his failure to consider the effect of the double standard on the quality of the marital relation, which, he argues elsewhere, requires friendship and at least an   approximation of equality. In "of Polygamy and Divorces" (*Essays*, Vol. I), he rejects polygamy on the grounds that it vastly increases the power of the husband. For, he says,

> this sovereignty of the male is a real usurpation and destroys that nearness of rank, not to say equality, which nature has established between the sexes. We are, by nature, their lovers, their friends, their patrons: Would we willingly exchange such endearing appellations, for the barbarous title of master and tyrant? (p.234)

Similarly, Hume rejects divorce on the grounds that it prevents a total merger of the interests of the two parties, and may increase the power of the unscrupulous husband. (p.239) It is clear that this objection applies equally to the sexual double standard; but Hume's celebrated logical rigor fails at this point, and he overlooks the parallel.

It is true, on the other hand, that Hume never advocated *complete* equality in marriage. What he objected to was extreme inequality; for male tyranny destroys both love and friendship, and distorts the character of children as well. "Those who pass the early part of their lives among slaves," he says, "are only qualified to be, themselves, slaves and tyrants . . . " (p.234) He recognized, too, that male tyranny creates a countertyranny on the part of women. In "Of Love and Marriage," he criticizes women's "love of dominion," but traces its origin to male abuses of authority:

> Tyrants, we know, produce rebels; and all history informs us, that rebels, when they prevail, are apt to become tyrants in their turn. For this reason, I could wish that there were no pretension to authority on either side . . . (**Essays**, Vol. II, p.385)

Nevertheless, Hume apparently felt that such complete equality is not to be hoped for. He recommends, not that male authority be abolished, but that it be exercised in a generous and unselfish manner:

> As nature has given *man* the superiority above women, by endowing him with greater strength both of mind and body; it is his part to alleviate that superiority, as much as possible, by the generosity of his behavior . . . Barbarous nations display this superiority, by reducing their females to abject slavery . . . But the male sex, among a polite people, discover their authority in a less evident manner: by civility, by respect, by complaisance, and in a word, by gallantry. (**Essays**, Vol. I, p.193)

A cynic might describe Hume's position by saying that he favors only the *appearance* of sexual equality, and that only to the extent that men find it in accordance with their own best interest. Hume believes neither in equality of rights nor in equal consideration for the interests of the two sexes. But having said this, even the cynic must give Hume due credit for the honesty and clarity with which he states what might be called the secular rationale for the sexual double standard. As Annette Baier points out, his failure to protest against it in any way "may stem from pessimism, from a conviction that the best care for children cannot be combined with the best form of love between men and women." (2) If so, then he is guilty of no contradiction in recognizing equality in marriage as an ideal, but holding that in practice it must be compromised in order to induce men to participate in the raising of children.

1. Bertrand Russell, *A History of Western Philosophy* (George

Allen and Unwin, London, 1946) p.685.
2.   Annette Baier, "Good Men's Women: Hume on Chastity and
      Trust"; forthcoming in *Hume Studies*.

HUTT, Corinne. *Males and Females* (Penguin Books, Baltimore,
1972)

Corinne Hutt is a British psychologist who defends a primarily
biological explanation of the observable psychological differences
between the sexes. The book provides a concise summary of how
sex is genetically determined, the role of hormones in the process
of sexual differentiation, and the studies of animals and humans
which demonstrate that hormones can have behavioral as well as
physiological effects.

Hutt states that although there is probably no difference in the
average intelligence of men and women, women's IQ's tend to
cluster around the average, while men's are more widely spread.
This means that there are more men with low IQ scores but also
more with unusally high ones. Women tend to have better verbal
skills, but men tend to excel in mathematical and even verbal
reasoning. Indeed, she concludes that "men more often have a
capacity for divergent and imaginative thinking, as well as a
greater drive to bring their ideas to fruition." (p.101) This, and
not social limitation, she claims, is the reason why it is almost
always men who are the creative artists, musicians, and
philosophers.

Men are also more aggressive on the average than women, and
Hutt claims that the evidence suggests a strong link between
male aggressiveness, which "ostensibly may seem undesirable"
(p.118), and the greater creativity, ambition and achievement of
men: all of these male traits are the result of the action of testosterone on the brain of the fetal male, and on the fetally androgenized brain in later life.

The neurochemically based psychological propensities of the
female are very different. Hutt lists altruism, passivity, nurturance and a regard for intimacy and personal relationships as
inherent traits of women. She infers from these traits that "a
woman's primary role is that of motherhood." (p.136) Not surprisingly, she sees little need and little chance of any fundamental change in the social roles of the sexes. Women should
have equal pay for equal work, but most of them will continue to
be family oriented and to shun careers in highly competitive
fields.

Males and Females is a small book which provides only a

226

summary introduction to the contemporary scientific case for the biological determination of sex roles. It is, however, lucid, provocative, and a prime example of the kind of reasoning, ostensibly based on empirical fact, which feminists who advocate fundamental social change must continue to contend with if they are to make their case.

I

INTELLECT: See Emotion.

J

JANEWAY, Elizabeth. *Man's World, Woman's Place* (Dell Publishing Company, New York, 1971)
Between Myth and Morning: Women Awakening (William Morrow and Company, New York, 1975; first published 1972)

Man's World, Woman's Place is an examination of the history, function and phenomenology of the social myth that woman's place is in the home, man's in the world; the book also suggests certain general conclusions about the operation of social mythologies. Social myths like this one are not purely descriptive, but are also normative; that is, they imply that even if the world does not in fact fit the mythical account, it should. Furthermore, they are designed to *make* the world conform to the image they present. Being rooted in prerational experiences that may seem instinctive, they are largely immune to refutation by logic. Unlike hypotheses about the physical world, they are not readily abandoned in the face of contradictory evidence, but rather tend to obscure the facts that challenge them. (Kuhnians might say that in this respect they are no different at all from scientific theories, but that is another matter.)

Janeway traces the myth of woman's place to two older myths, those of female power and female inferiority. Though seemingly contradictory these myths are in fact complementary. Private power is the very real reward offered women in exchange for public inferiority. This explains why so many women cling to the traditional role: it has supplied them with the only form of power thay have had, that is power over their children and husbands. For each man, the myth of female power is rooted in early memories of an all-powerful mother. This myth underlies the assumption that a woman can never be exactly the equal of a man: she must either be his subordinate or his superior, an assumption which causes many to view the women's movement as a demand not for equality for women but for the submission of men. (See George Gilder, *Sexual Suicide*.)

The analysis of women's shrinking status as homemakers is a perceptive one. It is not so much private property or capitalism

231

that has reduced the status of women as homemakers in the modern era, as the fact that economically productive work—work with monetary value—has moved outside the home, leaving women with no objective standard by which to value their work as homemakers. Deprived of a place in the larger world and forced to live vicariously, such women make excessive demands on their children and husbands, which, ironically, adds fuel to the twin myths of female power and inferiority.

Social mythologies are inescapable, and necessary for the definition of roles. But if we cannot escape them we can understand them, and learn to distinguish them from rationally supported plans or hypotheses. Understanding how social mythologies operate will reduce anxiety about changes in them, and about alternative mythologies, and promote tolerance on both sides.

Between Myth and Morning is a collection of essays on women's liberation, including "Freud's View of Female Sexuality" in which Janeway argues that Freud was aware that the difference between masculinity and femininity, activity and passivity, is socially as well as biologically engendered, and indeed that he decried the effect of the double standard on women.

JEWITT, Paul K. *Man as Male and Female: A Study in Sexual Relationships from a Theological Point of View* (William P. Eerdmans, Grand Rapids, 1975)

This is an elucidation of certain fairly progressive conceptions of human sexuality in the Old and New Testaments. Jewitt believes that key passages in Genesis (e.g. Genesis 1:27: "And God created Man in his own image, in the image of God created he him; *male and female* created he them"), as well as the teachings and practice of Jesus, point to the notion that men and women are equally human, and that both masculinity and femininity are grounded in *Imago Dei*, that is, are aspects of man's resemblance to God. Such a conception of sexuality, he argues, requires that the relationship between men and women be one of equal partnership, not of dominance and submission. When St. Paul insisted, in his epistles, that women should fear and obey their husbands and cover their heads and keep silent in the church, he may have been reacting against an early "feminist" movement in the church, inspired perhaps by the attitude of Jesus himself, who conspicuously refused to treat women as inferiors.

Because he believes that masculinity and femininity are both somehow grounded in divine reality, Jewitt rejects the androgynous ideal of human nature. He criticizes theologicans who interpret human sexual polarity as part of man's fallen condition, and as something that must be transcended by the union of masculine and feminine traits within each individual; in his view, reducing or eliminating sexual polarity would mean dehumanizing man. Nevertheless, he rejects the traditional Christian stereotypes of femininity, such as the glorification of the Eternal Feminine in the cult of the Virgin, and the misogynous appeals to the sin of Eve as proof of the inferiority of women; regarding them as masculine obfuscations designed to rationalize men's refusal to recognize women as their equals. He considers the true nature of masculinity and femininity to be entirely mysterious, as mysterious as the difference is evident. He does not, unfortunately, explain how we can rationally act to preserve a difference the nature of which is wholly unknown.

JOHNSTON, Jill. *Lesbian Nation: The Feminist Solution* (Simon and Schuster, New York, 1973)

   This is one of the most militant and uncompromising presentations of the radical lesbian or lesbian feminist position, which surfaced in New York and elsewhere during the early 1970s. The format is autobiographical, the style a pun-laced stream of consciousness which defies standard spelling, punctuation and grammar. Johnston relates her own spiritual journey from the dark ages of the 50s, when lesbianism was something one didn't mention, and "there wasn't a dyke in the land who thought she should be a dyke or even that she was a dyke," (p.58) through the identity crises of the 60s—during which she had many women lovers, but also four years of straight marriage, two children, and several bouts with schizophrenia—to the eventual emergence of a feminist lesbian awareness in the present decade.

   Johnston's sociopolitical analysis is not so much argued for as illustrated by its development in her own life and the context of the times. Her position is that the root causes of the oppression and second-class status of women is heterosexual sex, "the heterosexual institution with its role-playing dualities which are defined as the domination of one sex over the other." (p.155) She sees no hope for equality within any heterosexual relationship, for both biological and cultural reasons. Heterosexual sex, she says, is always a defeat, "an invasion of the woman . . . and although a woman may be conditioned to believe that she enjoys this invasion and may in fact grow to like it if her male partner has rare qualities of consideration and technical know-how, she remains the passive receptive hopeful half of a situation that was unequal from the start." (p.166)

Johnston rejects the claim made by some lesbian feminists, that the vagina is wholly insensitive and the clitoris the only organ of female orgasm. She agrees with Freud that the vaginal orgasm "*is* more mature in the sense that the activation of the inner walls brings about a more profound intensification of orgasm." Yet she insists that sex with a man cannot help but be degrading for a woman.

> If radical feminism is addressing itself to the "total elimination of sex roles" while still talking sex in relation to the man who defines these in the sex act by a certain historical biological-cultural imperative, they are going in circles of unadulterated contradictory bullshit. (p.176)

Men, Johnston holds, and not just sexist cultural traditions, are the enemy, and sexual intercourse with them is treason to the feminist cause. So is the personal solution of an *apparently* egalitarian heterosexual relationship. Men cannot be educated, at least not in our time, to accept women as equals. Fundamental social and political change requires that women become lesbians and withdraw as far as possible from the source of their oppression, men. The hope of nonlesbian feminists for cultural changes which will enable women and men to live together without oppression are vain, for culture and biology are inseparable: "The cultural takeover of the male is biologically motivated. All systems of inequity are rooted in some biological imperative of the male." (p.187) What is necessary is a regression to the tribal matriarchal living pattern described by Engels and the matriarchy theorists, in which families are matrilineal, men are peripheral to the family structure, and women are completely free to pursue their own sexual gratification.

In such tribal structures—the lesbian nation—women will return to a parthenogenetic state of mind, independently creative and needing neither support nor inspiration from men. Indeed, this psychic parthenogenesis already exists, and needs only to be recognized. "All women are lesbians" (p.269), since for all women (as for all men) the prime parent and first love is a woman. But to be a lesbian consciously and openly is a politically revolutionary act. Radical lesbianism implies not just sexual relationships with women, but "activism and resistance and the envisioned goal of a woman committed state." (p.278)

One problem with this approach, which makes the mass conversion of women to homosexuality a necessary condition for feminist revolution, is that, given the enormous unlikelihood of any such mass conversion, it makes such a revolution a very remote possibility. Another is the persistent confusion between heterosexual relationships as they generally are now, and as they can be, in a nonsexist society. Johnston wants to have it both ways, to hold both that in a "matriarchal" society women will be free, though presumably only their minds and not their wombs will conceive parthenogenetically, and that the biological nature of the heterosexual act itself makes it inevitably a defeat and a humiliation for women. But why should *free* women be demeaned by (hetero) sex? And if women in past and future matriarchies were not and will not be so demeaned, then it will require a very powerful argument, which Johnston does not provide, to show that independent women of today must be, in every case.

JUNG, Carl Gustav (1875–1961). "Woman in Europe" (*The Collected Works of C.G. Jung*, translated by R.F.C. Hull, Volume 10, Random House, New York, 1964, pp.113–133; first published in *Europaische Revue*, Berlin, 1927)
"Mind and Earth" (*Collected Works*, Volume 10, Random House, New York, 1964, pp.29–49; first published in *Mensch und Erde*, edited by Hermann Keyserling, Darmstadt, 1927)
The Relations Between the Ego and the Unconscious (*Collected Works*, Volume 7, Princeton University Press, 1966, pp.123–244; first published by Rascher Verlag, Zurich, 1928)
"Concerning the Archetypes, with Special Reference to the Anima Concept" (*Collected Works*, Volume 9, Part I, Princeton University Press, 1959, p.54–74; first published in the *Zentralblatt fur Psychotherapie und ihre Grenzgebiete*, Leipzig, 1936)
Aion: Researches into the Phenomenology of the Self (*Collected Works*, Volume 9, Part II, Princeton University Press, 1968, first published by Rascher Verlag, Zurich, 1951)
Jung, together with Freud and Adler, is one of the trio of thinkers who founded the theory and practice of psychoanalysis, and who remain its guiding lights. His *Collected Works* fill over seventeen volumes, most of which are directly or indirectly relevant to feminine and masculine psychology; however his most important theses on the psychological differences between the sexes are found in the above works. As we will see, Jung's theory of the role of what he called contrasexual elements in feminine and masculine psychology has a political import which is somewhere between the feminist egalitarianism of Adler and the thoroughgoing male supremacism of Freud.

Like his predecessor and fellow countryman J.J. Bachofen, Jung pursued a lifelong interest in the various dualistic sybolisms through which the male/female polarity is expressed in ancient art and mythology. But while Bachofen saw in these ancient symbolisms clues to prehistoric eras and events (specifically, a matriarchal era followed by a patriarchal revolution), Jung saw them as reflections of certain timeless and universal patterns in the human psyche, which he called archetypes. Archetypes are the components of the collective unconscious, a level of psychic reality supposedly deeper and even less accessible to observation than the personal unconscious with which Freud dealt. They are inherited mental structures, but not innate *ideas*; rather they are "innate *possibilities* (empasis added) of ideas, *a priori* conditions for fantasy-production, which are somewhat similar to the Kantian categories." (1) That is, they are psychic forces which condition human experience and determine its significance, though the particular form in which their influence is manifested depends on an individual's own character and environment.

Among the most important of the archetypes are the *anima* and the *animus*. The anima is the feminine "soul" of the human male, a female figure who represents the feminine elements present in his (personal and collective) unconscious. Conversely, the animus is the masculine soul of the woman, the symbol and effective agent of her unconscious masculine traits.

Jung defines femininity in terms of Eros, the principle of subjective, emotional, interpersonal relatedness. Masculinity, on the other hand, is said to be characterized by Logos, the principle of reason, judgment and objectivity. Most women, he holds, are naturally predominantly feminine in this sense, and most men are predominantly masculine, at least on the conscious level:

> . . . woman's consciousness is characterized more by the connective quality of Eros than by the discrimination and cognition associated with Logos. In men, Eros, the function of relationship, is usually less developed than Logos. In women, on the other hand, Eros is an expression of their true nature, while their Logos is often only a regrettable accident. (*Aion*, p.14)

Nevertheless, the existence of the anima and the animus demonstrates that all human beings are to some degree bisexual in their psychological make-up. However strictly masculine or feminine a person's conscious personality may be, there will always be contrasexual elements in the unconscious. Indeed, because the unconscious acts to counteract and compensate for any one-sidedness in the conscious functions, the more outwardly masculine or feminine a man or woman, the more powerful will be the unconscious contrasexual soul.

From this view there arises an apparent paradox. For Jung

holds that with very rare exceptions the feminine element *ought* to prevail in a woman, and the masculine element in a man; the less the influence of the unconscious anima or animus, the better. Jung has only scorn for the emotional, "effeminate" man or the "animus-ridden" woman. He doubts that it is generaly desirable for either women or men to step too far outside their traditional roles; he is particularly dubious about career women. For, he says,

> . . . no one can get round the fact that by taking up a masculine profession, studying and working like a man, woman is doing something not wholly in accord with, if not directly injurious to her feminine nature. (Woman in Europe," p.117)

It is, Jung maintains, harmful—a betrayal of one's true personal identity—to allow oneself to be dominated by the opposite-sexed elements of one's psyche. For the Logos of the female and the Eros of the male are inferior (that is underdeveloped) functions, and remain so even where they are dominant in the individual's psychology.

> . . . since masculine and feminine elements are united in one human nature, a man can live in the feminine part of himself, and a woman in her masculine part. None the less the feminine element in the man is only something in the background, as is the masculine element in a woman. If one lives out the opposite sex in oneself, one is living in one's own background, and one's own individuality suffers. (*Op. cit.* p.118)

The apparent paradox which Jung propounds is that the masculine or feminine element cannot prevail in a man or woman, as it should, unless the contrasexual element is also accepted and made conscious. So long as the anima or animus is confined to the unconscious, rather than integrated into the conscious personality, it retains the power to influence behavior in irrational and annoying ways. In men, the unassimilated anima causes extreme moodiness and uncontrolled outbursts of emotion. This is because

> Feeling is a specifically feminine virtue, and because a man in trying to attain his ideal of manhood represses all feminine traits . . . In so doing, he piles up effeminacy or sentimentality in the unconscious, and this, when it breaks out, betrays him . . . ("Mind and Earth," p.42)

In women, on the other hand, repressed masculinity expresses itself in the form of banal, dogmatic and irrational opinions, and in a pseudo-intellectual argumentativeness.

> When the animus breaks out in a woman . . . she begins to argue

> and to rationalize. And just as his anima-feelings are arbitrary and
> capricious so these feminine arguments are illogical and irrational.
> (*Loc. cit.*)

In either sex, then, repressed contrasexual elements come together in the unconscious to form a *complex*, a constellation of
psychic forces which operates almost as an independent person
or splinter personality; this, in fact, is what the animus or the
anima is, unless it is made a part of the conscious personality.
Repressed, the animus or anima not only affects behavior ad-
versely but appears in dreams and waking fantasies. The anima
generally appears as a single female figure with clearly distin-
guishable features; the animus is more apt to appear as a plurality
of figures, or simply as a voice. This is by way of compensation,
Jung says, for the fact that consciously and biologically, women
are inclined towards monogamy, men towards sexual variety.
(*Op. cit.*, p.42) The repressed animus or anima is also apt to be
projected onto persons of the opposite sex; it may be projected in
a positive form, causing the subject to fall in love with the object
of the projection, or in a negative form, causing instant antipathy.
Hence most heterosexual relationships are in fact quadrilateral—
four persons, not two, are involved. This risks a falsification of
the relationship, which may occur more between the man's
anima and the woman's animus than between the man and
woman themselves. (See *Aion*, p.15)

Jung's solution to this apparent paradox—i.e. that the power of
the anima or animus increases the more it is repressed, is what he
calls *individuation*. This process, which is the goal of Jungian
psychotherapy, brings about the integration of the various splinter personalities (2) (or complexes) in the unconscious, with the
conscious self. The previously unconscious psychic contents are
brought into the light through dream analysis, drawing and
painting, and active fantasizing; and the psychic energy previously claimed by the complexes is made available to the conscious
personality. When individuation is complete, the anima or animus ceases to exist as a distinct personality, but continues to
function as a "bridge" between the conscious and the unconscious. Consequently, certain feminine capacities become available to the conscious man, or vice versa.

> Just as the anima becomes, through integration, the Eros of con-
> sciousness, so the animus becomes a Logos; and in the same way
> that the anima gives relationship and relatedness to a man's con-
> sciousness, the animus gives to woman's consciousness a capacity
> for reflection, deliberation, and self-knowledge. (*Aion*, p.16)

Thus through individuation the anima or animus is deprived of its power to cause irrational behavior, or to project itself: "the anima forfeits the daemonic power of an autonomous complex; she can no longer exercise the power of possession, since she is depotentated." (**The Relations Between the Ego and the Unconscious**, p.225) Hence the solution to the apparent paradox is itself somewhat paradoxical; the contrasexual elements in the personality are "depotentated" through integration and acceptance, rather than repression.

The result is a truer masculinity or femininity than before, since the contrasexual elements become subservient to the primary sexual principle. The integrated man will benefit from greater feminine intuitiveness, and the woman will be able to express herself more clearly because of the integration of her masculine elements, but he will still be guided above all by Logos, and she by Eros.

What should a feminist think of this rather intriguing theory of masculine and feminine psychology? While Freud has been the object of innumerable feminist critiques (and some defenses), Jung has received much less attention from the feminist camp (3). Many feminist students are attracted to Jung for his emphasis on the need to "get in touch with" the contrasexual elements of the psyche, and for his criticisms of Western civilization for its suppression and undervaluation of the feminine principle.

Nevertheless, the Jungian view is a long way from being a foundation for feminism, certainly not for that radical feminism which attacks the traditional stereotypes of (psychological) masculinity and femininity as oppressive and perverse. Jung and his followers (see Harding, Stern, de Castillejo, Scott-Maxwell and Singer) consistently caution women against "losing their feminine values," or allowing their "masculine" traits too large a role in their psychological economy. This in itself might not be wholly inconsistent with a feminist or egalitarian stance. What is worse is that if a woman is predominantly rational, a thinking rather than a feeling type (4), then in the Jungian view this automatically shows that she has failed to achieve integration and is under control of her unconscious animus. "In intellectual women," Jung says

> the animus encourages a critical disputatiousness and would-be highbrowism, which, however, consists essentially in harping on some weak point and nonsensically making it the main one . . .
> Without knowing it, such women are solely intent upon exasperating the man and are, in consequence, the more completely at the mercy of the animus. (*Op. cit.*, p.207)

It is true that Jung recognizes the existence of a few very rare women whose predominantly intellectual bent does not result in argumentative opinionatedness (5). But even in such cases he apparently presumes not that the woman is simply and naturally the intellectual type, but that she is suffering from animus-possession, and in need of psychiatric treatment. The very same behavior and personality traits, in a man, would be judged to be in themselves quite normal.

Jung, therefore, is an opponent of psychological androgynism, the thesis that both men and women ought to (be educated and encouraged to) have both masculine and feminine virtues, preferably with neither set of virtues in the dominant role. This is the thesis which has been defended by radical feminists from Mary Wollstonecraft to the present, and it is at the farthest remove from the Jungian thesis that one should integrate one's contrasexual elements primarily in order to subordinate them, and to avoid lapses into animus- or anima-controlled behavior.

The issue between Jung and feminist supporters of psychological androgyny is at base largely an empirical one. Jung's identification of masculinity with Logos or reason and of femininity with Eros or emotional relatedness rests upon his claim that the majority of "masculine genes"—or some other purely physiological factor (6)—normally suffices to make males predominantly rational and unemotional, at least on the conscious level, and vice versa for females. But there is little or no evidence that anything of the sort is true. Even the measurable psychological differences between boys and girls, women and men, who have been subjected to a lifelong exposure to the sexual stereotypes Jung employs—male/rational, female/emotional—do not conform to those stereotypes.

Thus, for instance, it is known that males in our culture—for whatever reason—tend to excel in certain mathematical and spatial abilities, while females tend to excel in linguistic abilities (7). But this is a distinction between *types* of rational or intellectual capacity, not between rationality and emotionalism. So too, it is argued that males are naturally more aggressive, because of their male hormones and their inherited hunting instincts (8), while females are more cooperative; but this, if true, is a distinction between the *types* of emotional and interpersonal behavior to which the sexes are prone, not (to say the least) an illustration of the greater rationality of the male or the greater emotionality of the female.

It would seem, then, that Jung's original equation of femininity with Eros and masculinity with Logos is a mistake. Granted these assimilations are amply illustrated in ancient and modern art, literature and mythology; but this shows only that these particular stereoytpes are both ancient and pervasive, not that they are accurate. To accept these stereotypes at face value, to elevate them into psychological axioms, as Jung does, is to be guilty of the same androcentric glorification of the masculine at the expense of the feminine that Jung criticizes in Western civilization.

One might suppose that this is true only if one neglects the Jungian insistence that both Logos and Eros must be given their due. But the assumption that the "masculine" mode of consciousness represents a *higher* level of human development than the "feminine" mode is, in fact, built into the Jungian system. For the feminine, matriarchal mode of consciousness is the primal state from which the rational, spiritual, male principle struggles to free itself, "the Logos . . . eternally struggles to extricate itself from the primal warmth and primal darkness of the maternal womb." (9) This is true of the female's Logos as well as the male's; but the male's conscious rationality, one might say, makes good its escape, while the female remains in the more primitive state. The male reaches for higher, more spiritual and more creative realms of human experience, while the female remains behind, serving, like the anima which is projected onto her, to link the male to his own emotional and prerational roots.

Thus, in Jung's view, it is woman who can inspire man to the highest levels of creativity, not vice versa:

> Woman, with her very dissimilar psychology, is and always has been a source of information about things for which a man has no eyes. She can be his inspiration; her intuitive capacity . . . can give him timely warning, and her feeling, always directed towards the personal, can show him ways which his own less personally accented feeling would never have discovered. (*The Relations Between the Ego and the Unconscious*, p.186)

If, on the other hand, a woman strives to develop her own rational capacities, if her thought is as objective and logical as a man's (is supposed to be), then she is "possessed by the animus . . . [and] . . . in danger of losing her femininity" (*Op. cit.*, pp.207–298). She becomes incapable of playing a mediating role between a man and his unconscious, and thus loses her greatest value—for men. That she may have gained a greater value for *herself* is a possibility which Jung and his followers do not consider.

1.   "The Role of the Unconscious," **Collected Works**, Volume 10 (Random House, New York, 1964), p.10.

2. There are, Jung holds, other complexes besides the anima and the animus, e.g. the Shadow (the side of the person's character which is neglected and denied) and the Persona (the public role one plays).

3. But see Andrea Dworkin, *Woman Hating*, for one excellent feminist critique of Jung.

4. See Jung's *Psychological Types* (translated by H. Godwin Baynes; Routledge and Kegan Paul Ltd., London, 1949; first published London, 1923).

5. See "A Study in the Process of Individuation," *Collected Works*, Volume 9, Part I (Princeton University Press, 1969), pp.290–291.

6. *Collected Works*, Volume 2 (Princeton University Press, 1962), p.30.

7. See Eleanor Maccoby and Carol Jacklin, *The Psychololgy of Sex Differences*.

8. See Goldberg, Ardrey, Fox, Tiger and Morris.

9. Jung, *Psychological Aspects of the Mother Archetype*, *Collected Works*, Volume 9, Part I (Princeton University Press, 1959), p.96.

K

KANT, Immanuel (1724–1804). *Observations on the Feeling of the Beautiful and the Sublime* (translated by John T. Goldthwait, University of California Press, Berkeley and Los Angeles, 1960; first published in Konigsberg, 1764)

Kant's *Observations on the Feeling of the Beautiful and the Sublime* belongs to the so-called precritical phase of his work, the period prior to his development of the transcendental idealist philosophy for which he is primarily known (1). Indeed, he prefaces this relatively brief essay with the remark that it is not really a work of philosophy at all, but only—as the title suggests—a collection of empirical observations about certain aspects of the human aesthetic response.

Kant was being somewhat too modest, however, since the *Observations* contains at least the germ of the brilliant and, many feel, definitive subjectivist analysis of aesthetic properties which appears over twenty years later in the *Critique of Judgment*. It also contains some noteworthy comments about the different aesthetic, moral and intellectual qualities of women and men. Noteworthy too is its easy and elegant style, which is in startling contrast to the dense and technical prose of the *Critiques*.

There are, Kant holds, two kinds of "finer feeling" or aesthetic experience: the beautiful and the sublime. The beautiful is that which is charming, attractive, pretty, natural, and gladdening; the sublime, on the other hand, arouses awe or admiration, and sometimes terror. Thus, the "sight of a mountain whose snow-covered peak rises above the clouds, [or] the description of a raging storm" are sublime; while "the sight of flower-strewn meadows, valleys with winding brooks and covered with grazing flocks" is beautiful. (p.47) The beautiful may be small and delicate, while the sublime is always impressively large.

Woman is the beautiful sex, Kant maintains, not only because "her figure is finer, her features more delicate and gentler, and her mien more engaging and more expressive of friendliness, pleasantry, and kindness than in the male . . . "but also because "certain specific traits lie especially in the personality of this sex which distinguish it clearly from ours . . . " (p.76) In other words women are beautiful both in appearance and in character. Man, on the other hand, is the noble or sublime sex.

The "beautiful" nature of women means, among other things, that women are, and furthermore ought to be, creatures of emotion and (aesthetic) judgment rather than reason and intellect. Kant, in an apparent effort to avoid seeming to disparage the "fair sex," makes the rather strained claim that

> The fair sex has just as much understanding; but it is a *beautiful understanding*, whereas ours should be a *deep understanding* . . . (p.78)

Nor does Kant hesitate to draw the logical conclusions of this claim with respect to women's education. Kant had read and greatly admired Rousseau's *Emile*, and the influence of Rousseau is very evident at this point. Women should receive only the scantiest intellectual education—no history, geography, mathematics or philosophy. Instead they should be trained in the appreciation of music and the other fine arts, and in domestic skills: "Never a cold and speculative instruction but always feelings, and those indeed which remain as close as possible to the situation of her sex." (p.81) For, Kant says,

> Deep meditation and long-sustained reflection are noble but difficult, and do not well befit a person in whom unconstrained charms should show nothing else than a beautiful nature. Laborious learning or painful pondering, even if a woman should greatly succeed in it, destroy the merits that are proper to her sex . . . at the same time they will weaken the charms with which she exercises her great power over the other sex. (p.78)

This last line of thought is also typical of Rousseau, who, on the assumption that women are and would remain hopelessly inferior at any task involving the application of intellect, concluded that the only means by which they can hope to gain any influence over men and hence over the affairs of the world is through the use of their feminine charms. Guilty, it would seem, of the same assumption, Kant holds that it is a mistake for women to attempt to compete with men on intellectual grounds.

> For, well aware of their weakness before her natural charms and of the fact that a single shy glance sets more in confusion than the most difficult problem of science, so soon as woman enters upon this taste they are themselves in a decided superiority and are at an advantage that otherwise they hardly would have . . . (p.79)

But whatever the supposed tactical advantages to women of abandoning the intellectual realm to men, such a sexual division of mental labor has some inevitable consequences for (one's view of) women's moral nature and for their role and status in marriage. Kant, moreover, is too good a philosopher to ignore those consequences. Women, he holds, are not moral or virtuous in the same way that men are, that is out of a sense of duty and an allegiance to moral principles. For women are constitutionally incapable of understanding or acting upon such concepts as duty and obligation. "They do something," Kant says, "only because it pleases them . . . I hardly believe that the fair sex is capable of principles"; though he adds that, "I hope by that not to offend, for these are also extremely rare in the male." (p.81)

Now if women are incapable of acting on principle, it would certainly seem to follow from Kant's (much later) formulations of the Categorical Imperative (2) that women are wholly amoral beings. But the theory of the Categorical Imperative was as yet unborn when Kant wrote the *Observations*, and he seems at this earlier time to have believed in a type of moral virtue which did not involve allegiance to universalizable principles. Women's aesthetic sensitivity, he holds, makes them capable of a moral virtue which is prerational—beautiful rather than sublime. Thus,

> The virtue of a woman is a *beautiful virtue*. That of the male sex should be a *noble virtue*. Women will avoid the wicked not because it is unright, but because it is ugly; and virtuous actions mean to them such as are morally beautiful. (p.81)

Kant's vision of the ideal marriage follows naturally from this notion of the distinct moral natures of men and women. He holds that in marriage, "the united pair should, as it were, constitute a single moral person, which is animated and governed by the understanding of the man and the taste of the woman." (p.95) Simply put, this would seem to mean that the man is to make all of the decisions except those which are merely aesthetic—such as, perhaps, how to decorate the house. Yet Kant denies that either partner is the superior. Neither has the right to command or the duty to obey. Indeed,

> If it comes to such a state that the question is of the right of the superior to command, then the case is already utterly corrupted; for where the whole union is in reality erected solely upon inclination, it is already half destroyed as soon as the "duty" begins to make itself heard. (p.96)

Thus Kant maintains that women are intellectually different, yet morally equal. He does not address the evident difficulty of maintaining equality of rights in a two-party relationship in which one party is (considered to be) necessarily the intellectual superior of the other. Nor does he consider the inequality of power which results from the confinement of women to unpaid domestic labor, while men act as the primary breadwinners. Marxist feminists have argued that the Romantic view of marriage exemplified by Kant, Rousseau, and Hegel, is really an idealized portrait of what marriage had become within the bourgeois class. It is an interesting question whether such mystifications of actual power relationships between the sexes represent any moral or philosophical advance over the straightforward insistence on male supremacy, such as is found, for example, in Aristotle or St. Paul.

1. Kant's better known critical works include the *Critique of Pure Reason* (1781); the *Prolegomena to All Future Metaphysics* (1783); the *Foundations of the Metaphysics of Ethics* (1785); the *Critique of Practical Reason* (1788); and the *Critique of Judgment* (1793).

2. The Categorical Imperative is, "So act that the maxim of your will could always hold at the same time as a principle establishing universal law." It is the ultimate foundation of all moral law, and the conformity with it the sole criterion of moral right. (*Critique of Practical Reason*; translated by Lewis White Beck, Bobbs-Merrill, New York, 1956, p.30).

KEY, Ellen (1849–1926). *The Century of the Child* (G.P. Putnam's Sons, New York and London, 1909)
The Morality of Woman and Other Essays (translated from the Swedish by Mamak Bouton Borthwick; The Ralph Fletcher Seymour Company, Chicago, 1911)
Love and Marriage (translated by Arthur G. Chater; G.P. Putnam's Sons, New York and London, 1911)
The Woman Movement (translated by Mamak Bouton Borthwick; G.P. Putnam's Sons, 1912)
The Renaissance of Motherhood (translated by Anna E.G. Fries; G.P. Putnam's Sons, New York and London, 1914)
The Younger Generation (translated by Arthur G. Chater; G.P. Putnam's Sons, New York and London, 1914)

Ellen Kay, well-known Swedish reformer, was a democratic socialist and a feminist who held that woman's place is in the home, at least during the childrearing years. She was the apostle of motherhood and motherliness in women, which she saw as the source of all social virtue, and as threated by the outside employment of married women. Yet as a feminist she insisted on absolute legal and economic equality between wife and husband, and argued that most women will not be financially able to remain at home with their children, nor will they receive the proper respect of society for doing so, until they are paid by the state for their motherly functions. Key was strongly influenced by certain philosophical interpretations of Darwin's theory of evolution and Nietzsche's vision of the superman—the creative, self-willed being who will emerge from humanity as it presently exists. Together, she maintained, these theories demonstrate the necessity of eugenics, of making the production of healthy and genetically sound future generations the highest duty of both the society and the individual. Capitalism, class inequality, and the economic dependence of women on men are diseugenic factors which prevent many biologically sound men and women from reproducing, or from taking the best care of their offspring. Poor mothers are forced to work long hours under unsanitary conditions, with the result that their health is ruined and their children neglected; while the pittance wages they earn not only fail to compensate for the loss of their presence in the home but inevitably undermine their husband's earning power and that of single women who have no choice but to work.

Under socialism, on the other hand, motherhood will be recognized as the socially invaluable work it is, and compensated accordingly. Women will not be forced to marry, or if married, to work for economic security; hence all healthy and normal women will be able to marry and have children (or to bear children outside of marriage), and fewer women who are *not* fit to become mothers will be forced to do so. The distinction between "legitimate" and "illegitimate" children will be eliminated, as will the social disapproval of extramarital sex—so long as it is motivated by love and results in the procreation of healthy children.

As an individualist, Key saw the loss of individual human uniqueness in favor of collective uniformity as the greatest danger posed by the coming of socialism, and the maintenance of the individual, mother-centered home as the greatest bulwark against that danger. She criticizes feminists such as Charlotte Perkins Gilman, who advocate the collectve rearing of children in order to free women for outside work, for failing to see that the individual family home is the primary source of originality and uniqueness in human personality. Hence although women require econmic equality, the traditional division of labor between the sexes must remain more or less unchanged.

The system Key advocates would be an improvement in many ways over that which prevails today in most of the developed world—capitalist and socialist alike—whereby most mothers must either struggle to do two full-time jobs at once or rely upon some man for economic subsidy. But Key ignores the obvious alternative to keeping women at home raising children and men away from home doing virtually everything else, namely a system which allows parents to share the domestic duties and does not require the one parent more than the other to sacrifice individual interests for the sake of future generations. She is undisturbed by the fact that "woman by her maternal functions, uses up so much physical and psychical energy, that in the sphere of intellectual production she must remain of less significance" (*The Century of the Child*, p.58); whereas it ought to be self-evident that this condition is one which must be altered before we can speak of equality. Of course the moral if not the pragmatic argument for expanding woman's role would be somewhat weakened if, as Key maintains, virtually all women were *happier* as full-time mothers than in any other capacity. But by now it has become obvious that this is false, and furthermore that the level of reproduction which results from making motherhood women's full-time function is something we can no longer afford.

KEY, Mary Ritchie. *Male/Female Language* (Scarecrow Press, Metuchen, New Jersey, 1975)

A first-rate sociolinguistic study, from a feminist point of view, of linguistic usages, e.g. grammatical forms and referring terms, inflections, intonations and the like, which are differently used by or of men and women in our culture; the book also includes a comprehensive bibliography on the subject. Key points out that the universality of role differences between the sexes means that in every language and every culture men and women to some extent speak differently and are differently spoken to—and about. In extreme cases such as the Carib tribes of the Caribbean area, men and women may speak almost entirely different languages. In our own culture, women (are supposed to) speak in softer and higher tones, with more inflection, while men speak louder, longer and in more of a monotone. Women use devices like the tag question ("It's raining, isn't it?"), and the rising pitch at the end of the sentence, to soften the impact of what they say and avoid the appearance of decisiveness. Interestingly, women also tend to speak more grammatically than males, avoiding such nonstandard forms as "ain't" and the double negative, which are associated with the lower classes. Key explains this as due to women's efforts to raise their status by one of the few means available, on the one hand, and on the other hand to males' deliberate use of nonstandard forms as an assertion of masculinity, which in our culture is seen as antithetical to culture and correctness.

There is a valuable discussion of the so-called generic use of masculine pronouns and nominals (e.g. "he" supposedly used to mean "he or she," "man" to mean "men and women" or "a man or a woman"). Key argues that such uses are not generic, whatever the stated rules of grammar may say; for instance if "he" were genuinely equivalent to "he or she," (or "she or he") then it would not be the case that "she" is used in speaking of (sexually unidentified) secretaries, nursery school teachers and the like. (As in "The secretary must know *her* job.") The use of pseudo-generic terms like "the average man" serves to exclude women from the field of discourse, perpetuating the presumption that they are not as important and indeed not as human as men. Sex-neutral third person singular pronouns are badly needed, but all efforts to introduce such substitutes for the so-called generic "he" and "his" have so far failed, pronouns being a part of language which is extremely resistant to change. Still, it is worth experimenting with forms like "he or she" (or "she or he"), in the hope that eventually stable alternative forms will be established.

There is also a very good chapter on "linguistic tyranny," the process whereby, through "put downs," interruption, and other devices, men have generally paralyzed women into a kind of silence. It is not that women do not speak, but that they have been discouraged from speaking publicly, authoritatively, argumentatively or at any length. As always, tyranny generates countertyranny, and women may respond to men's verbal domination by henpecking, by becoming "emotional," by demanding that men avoid crude language in their presence, and so on. Thus, the linguistic aspects of sex stereotyping are oppressive to both sexes. Key heralds the coming of an androgynous language, that is one which is not only used by males and females alike, with no sex-linked differences in vocabulary, etc., but one in which people are conceptualized as human first and male or female second. In the future, she hopes and expects, men will not need to use blustering, opinionated or obscene language, and women will not be expected to speak softly, modestly and sweetly, except to the extent and on the occasions that the same is expected of men.

KIERKEGAARD, Soren (1813–1855). *Either/Or* Volumes I and II (Volume I, translated by David F. Swenson and Lillian M. Swenson. Princeton University Press, Princeton, New Jersey, 1971; Volume II, translated by Walter Lowrie, Princeton University Press, 1974; both volumes first published 1843, in Copenhagen)
Stages on Life's Way (translated by Walter Lowrie, Schocken Books, New York, 1967; first published 1845, Copenhagen)
The Concept of Dread (translated by Walter Lowrie, Princeton University Press, 1957; first published 1844, Copenhagen)

Kierkegaard is one of the pioneers and leading figures of existentialist philosophy. He is a Christian existentialist whose primary interest is in the subjective nature of religious faith and the internal processes by which it may be reached. Kierkegaard's theory of the nature of women, like the rest of his philosophy, is difficult to interpret. This is particularly true of the earlier, so-called aesthetic works, which were published under a variety of pseudonyms, each of which represents a distinct point of view. Kierkegaard explicitly points out that these pseudonymous works do not directly represent his own views (1). Furthermore, it is precisely in these works that Kierkegaard has the most to say about women.

There is, nevertheless, a clear-cut pattern in Kierkegaard's pronouncements on the subject of women, both in the pseudonymous and the "direct" writings, a pattern consistent with the traditional Christian view of woman as expressed, for instance, by St. Paul. The view is essentially that while women are in some sense spiritually equal to men (and will be equal in the afterlife), nevertheless on earth they must be strictly subject to men, on account of their physical, intellectual and moral inferiority.

A crucial part of Kierkegaard's philosophy is the view that there are three main "spheres of existence," or modes of living and understanding one's life, namely the aesthetic, the ethical and the religious. The aesthetic is the realm of immediate experience and sensory enjoyment, while the ethical is the realm of the rational and the universal. An aesthetically oriented person lives in and for the present moment, rather than being guided by general rules or long-term goals. The ethical person, on the other hand, lives according to rationally universalizable principles. Religion subsumes the aesthetic and the ethical but goes beyond the latter through a "leap of faith." To make a leap of faith is to adopt a life-shaping belief, e.g. in Christ as the Savior, a belief which is subjectively certain but objectively unprovable and indeed paradoxical.

Although Kierkegaard's various pseudonymous voices are in general agreement about most of the aspects of woman's nature, they differ in their *attitudes* towards women depending in part upon their existential outlook. In *Either/Or*, indeed, the fundamental choice between the aesthetic and the ethical realms is expressed primarily in terms of the speakers' contrasting modes of relationship to women. Volume I is a collection of essays alleged to be by a young man who lives aesthetically. For him, women are attractive only at that fleeting moment when they are mature but sexually inexperienced; and his interest in them begins and ends with the act of seduction. Volume II, on the other hand, is said to be the work of a married man—one Judge William —who sings the praises of women and maintains that they only grow more beautiful with time.

The aesthetic man's attitudes towards women are best spelled out in the *Diary of a Seducer*, which forms the last section of Volume I, and which has also been published separately. The *Diary* represents a deliberately distorted account of Kierkegaard's own engagement, which he had felt compelled to end for the sake of his philosophical and religious calling. In this account, the young man becomes engaged solely as a means of seducing the young woman, and afterwards cleverly induces her to break the engagement herself.

Johannes the Seducer, as the young man is called, maintains that woman should be viewed "under the category of being for another." (p.424) Man, he says, is characterized by spirit, but woman is a part of nature, which is also being for another; she is like a plant, which "unfolds in all naivete its hidden charms and exists only for another." (p. 425) She is "the dream of man," as is shown by the fact that Eve was created from Adam while Adam slept. By this Johannes does not mean that man only *dreams* that woman is a part of nature or that she exists only for him; he presumes that here at least the dream is also the reality. Woman, he says,

> is a flower . . . and even the spiritual in her exists only in a vegetative manner. She is wholly subject to Nature, and hence only aesthetically free. (p.426)

Johannes is an admirer of women, if only those who are young and virginal. "Truly" he says, "a young girl is and remains the *Venerabile* of Nature and the whole of existence . . . the only pity is that this glory is so short-lived." (pp.405–406). Kierkegaard's other aesthetically oriented pseudonyms (all male) are much more cynical about women and about the possibility of establishing any satisfactory relationship with them, even a fleeting one. At the banquet recounted in **Stages on Life's Way** (2) each of the five aesthetes delivers a speech on the nature of woman and on how to cope with her. While the speakers differ in their degree of hostility towards the "fair sex," they agree that woman's lack of intellectual capacity and hence of ethical understanding makes any positive relationship with her impossible.

Thus, for example, the character called Constantive Constantius argues that woman can only be regarded as a jest. For, he maintains,

> It is man's part to be absolute, to act absolutely, to give expression to the absolute; women, on the other hand, has her being in relationships. Between two such different beings no genuine reciprocal action can take place. This incongruity is precisely what constitutes jest . . . (p.61)

And, in a similar vein, Victor Eremita makes the observation that

> To be a woman is something so strange, so mixed, so complex, that no predicate expresses it, and the many predicates one might use contradict one another so sharply that only a woman can endure it. (p.68)

Although there are many speakers for the aesthetic point of view in Kierkegaard's pseudonymous work, the ethical point of view, because it is a universalist one, has and requires only one defender—the Judge William mentioned above. The Judge's response to the aesthetic viewpoint is the "Or" of **Either/Or**, and takes the form of a series of letters from the Judge to his young friend Johannes the Seducer. The Judge maintains that the aesthetic life, the life of the moment, leads always to despair (p. 197). Salvation—at least for all but the exceptional few, the poets and creators—is found in marriage, which is central to the ethical sphere.

Marriage, the Judge holds, enables a man to unify what Kierkegaard calls the finite and the temporal—the experience of the moment—with the infinite and eternal; the married man lives in the present but in accordance with universal principles and a lifelong commitment. What makes it possible for marriage to perform this role for man is woman's distinctive nature. Woman is more sensual and more aesthetic than man, but she is *also* more religious (p.67). She cannot reflect (and if she did it would be unfeminine), and thus cannot reach the religious sphere through the ethical, as man does. She can, however, make a transition from the aesthetic directly to the religious, a feat impossible for man. Yet she can make this transition only through total love and surrender to a man. In *Stages on Life's Way*, the Judge gives this touching account of the process:

> . . . at the moment when on the border of her consciousness there passes by the thought which man's reflection ideally exhausts, she falls into a faint, her husband hastens to her aid, and although equally moved, but through reflection, he is not overwhelmed, he stands fast, the loved one supported upon his breast, until again she opens her eyes. In this swooning state she is translated from the immediacy of love into the religious sphere, and here again the two meet. (p.163)

On this point—that woman can reach the religious sphere directly from the ethical, but only through surrender to a man— the Judge and the Seducer agree. They differ, however, as to the feasibility of a lifelong commitment to a single woman, because Johannes believes that a woman can make this magic transition only once (i.e., when she is seduced for the first time), whereas the Judge thinks that within the commitment of marriage she can continue to make it indefinitely. She serves the man, in effect, as a permanent bridge between the two realms, even as the man is such a bridge for her.

Thus, the Judge holds that the aesthetic man is wrong to deride woman and to consider himself more perfect than she. (*Either/Or*, Volume II, pp.115, 311) There is a kind of equality in marriage, but an "equality" which depends upon difference, and upon the woman's submission. "For the other sex," he says, "it is rather natural to feel the preponderance of man and to submit to it . . . the woman feels joyful and happy in being nothing." (p.58) And he makes use of the venerable antifeminist argument that if women were emancipated they would lose even this (distinctly limited) degree of equality, while gaining nothing of comparable value (3). An emancipated woman "can be nothing for man except as prey to his whims, whereas as woman she can be everything to him." (p.317)

So much for the views about women presented in Kierkegaard's pseudonymous works. Those in the direct or nonpseudonymous works are essentially similar, a fact which confirms the hypothesis that the views of Johannes and the Judge on woman's nature—as opposed to the views on how a man should relate to her—are basically Kierkegaard's own as well. The concept of woman which emerges from the religious works, those in which Kierkegaard speaks in his own voice is, if anything, even more pejorative. This seems natural in light of the fact that, in his view, the religious man must eschew all serious relationships with women in order that his defining relationship, that which determines the content of his life, may be to Christ alone.

Although *The Concept of Dread* was published under a pseudonym, it was written and intended as a direct communication, and the views here are therefore presumably Kierkegaard's own. Virgilius Haufriensis, the pseudonymous author, describes woman as "the derived being," and holds that she is naturally weaker, less spiritual and more sensuous than man. "The fact that woman is more sensuous than man," he says, "is shown at once by her bodily organism." (p.58) Her very beauty shows her lack of spirituality, since, "Where beauty claims the right to rule it brings about a synthesis from which spirit is excluded." (*Loc. cit.*)

Virgilius argues that woman's greater sensuousness is demonstrated by the fact that it is she who bears children.

> Ethically regarded, woman culminates in procreation. Therefore the Scripture says that her desire shall be to her husband. It is true also that the husband's desire is to her, but his life does not culminate in this desire, unless it is either a sorry sort of life or a lost life. But the fact that in this woman reaches her culmination shows that she is more sensuous. (p.54)

Furthermore, in accordance with the Christian tradition Kierkegaard associates woman's allegedly greater sensuality with sinfulness. Sex and sensuality exist only as a result of Adam and Eve's original sin, the guilt of which is inherited by us all. Since sinfulness is accompanied by dread, and since woman is more sensual and hence more sinful, she is always more in dread than man, and her dread is a symptom of her sensuousness. By this line of reasoning, even woman's quite rational apprehensions with respect to sex and childbirth are evidence of her lack of spirituality. (See pp.60, 65)

To comment seriously on such notions as these, as though they were even moderately reasonable hypotheses, should not be necessary. The one possible saving grace of the Christian/Kierkegaardian concept of woman is that it promises her freedom from the taint of sexuality in the afterlife. In Virgilius' words,

> without sin there is no sexuality . . . A perfect spirit has neither the one nor the other, hence also the sexual difference is annulled in the resurrection. (p.44)

The meaningfulness of such a claim depends, of course, upon whether one believes in a Christian-style afterlife. If, as Kierkegaard believed (but admittedly without evidence) we can all look forward to an eternity of perfect happiness beyond the grave, then to deprive women—or any other group for that matter—of their rights on earth would be relatively insignificant. If, however, one does not choose to make the Christian leap of faith, then the Christian attitude towards women can most charitably be seen as a tragic series of errors. Childbearing in no way implies greater sensuality (in any plausible sense of that term), and even if women were more sensual (4) it would in no way follow that they are morally or intellectually deficient. Nor is the notion of inherited guilt a plausible one; hence the Adam and Eve story, even if true, would be irrelevant to the issue of women's rights.

1. See the note appended by Kierkegaard to the *Concluding Unscientific Postscript* (translated by David F. Swenson and Walter Lowrie, Princeton University Press, 1974, pp.551–554).
2. In *In Vino Veritas*, an essay supposedly written by one William Afram. The three essays in the *Stages* are presented by still another pseudonymous character, one Hilarius Bookbinder. His multiplicity of pseudonyms is a device Kierkegaard employed to distance himself from the views expressed—although he does not, in the later work, repudiate *all* of these views.
3. This same argument is found, for instance, in Rousseau, Kant, and the contemporary advocates of "fascinating womanhood."
4. Though it *is* probably true that women have a greater average orgastic capacity than men. (See Masters and Johnson.) Needless to say, a greater capacity for orgasm does not necessarily imply greater sensuality, since to have a capacity is one thing and to wish to use it to the fullest possible extent is quite another.

KINSEY, Alfred C. (1894–1956). With **POMEROY**, Wardell B., and **MARTIN**, Clyde E.: *Sexual Behavior in the Human Male* (W.B. Saunders Company, Philadelphia and London, 1948) With **POMEROY**, Wardell B., **MARTIN**, Clyde E. and **GEBHARD**, Paul H.: *Sexual Behavior in the Human Female* (W.B. Saunders and Company, Philadelphia and London, 1953)

Alfred Kinsey was an obscure midwestern biologist until the publication of the so-called "Kinsey Reports" made his name a household word—and gave Americans, for the first time, what appears to be a reasonably accurate portrait of the sexual activities of at least a portion of the population. For these volumes, Kinsey and his colleagues at Indiana University interviewed 5,300 males and 8,000 females, ranging from two to ninety years of age, all of them white (1), but from diverse educational and economic strata. Each was asked from two to three hundred questions about his or her sexual practices and experiences, and the enormous body of data obtained was subjected to extremely extensive statistical analysis. The results revolutionized Americans' conceptions of what is sexually normal and demolished a number of myths about the nature of and differences between male and female sexuality.

Kinsey takes the stance of a value-free scientist, one who merely reports what he or she observes and who refuses to pass moral judgments on the activities investigated. Yet the reports also embody a deep faith in the goodness and naturalness of (most forms of) sexuality, and a heartfelt plea for social change. In his view, human patterns of sexual behavior are a particularly indelible part of our mammalian inheritance, and as such subject only to limited modification by law, religion and social attitudes.

This position is argued with most force in the earlier volume, which deals only with males. The data show that in spite of the efforts of the Christian and Jewish religions and the laws of most American states to restrict sexual outlet to intercourse between married persons, most males begin to experience orgasm (often through nocturnal emissions and/or masturbation) soon after the beginning of adolescence, and reach their peak of sexual activity, in terms of orgasms per week, in their teen years—long before most of them are married. Furthermore,

> Nearly all males (about 95%), after they have been initiated into regular coital experience . . . repudiate the doctrine that intercourse should be restricted to marital relations. Nearly all ignore the legal limitations on intercourse outside of marriage. Only age finally reduces the coital activities of those individuals, and thus demonstrates that biological factors are, in the long run, more effective than man-made regulations in determining the patterns of human behavior. (p.295)

So unsuccessful are the restrictive sex laws that, according to the Kinsey data, nearly all males are involved at some time in their lives in illegal sexual activity: 85% in premarital sex; 59% in oral-genital contact; 70% in relations with prostitutes; 35% in extramarital affairs; and 37% in homosexual encounters (p.392). Yet social class makes a considerable difference to the type, if not the frequency, of sexual outlet. Males who do not go beyond grade school or high school in their education tend to have more premarital intercourse and more intercourse with prostitutes than do college-educated, upper-class males. The latter, however, compensate by masturbating more and having more nocturnal emissions. Religious orthodoxy has a more telling effect on the *quantity* of sexual outlet; the more devout males of all religions tend to have a somewhat lower average number of orgasms per week than the nondevout.

Kinsey also found, however, that age, not social class or religion, is the most important determinant of sexual frequency in the male. After the teen years, the male's frequency and responsiveness declines steadily, due to biological aging. Women, on the other hand, reach their peak of sexual responsiveness much later—often not till their thirties—and usually show no signs of decreased capacity due to aging until their fifties or sixties. This very marked difference in the rate of sexual aging in men and women is one of the most important of the Kinsey findings.

Another key finding was the unexpectedly high incidence of male homosexuality. Only half of the male population, Kinsey found, is 100% heterosexual (i.e. all their lives), while some 8% are exclusively homosexual, and the rest are to some degree "bisexual." (These figures are more than 30 years old, of course, and probably too low, partly because of the effect of their publication.) It is, Kinsey rightly insists, absurd to treat an activity which is engaged in by half the male population as either abnormal or unnatural, whatever one's view of its moral status. "The homosexual," he says,

> has been a significant part of human sexual activity ever since the dawn of history, primarily because it is an expression of capacities that are basic in the human animal. (p.666)

Kinsey firmly rejects the notion of sexual "perversion," as either an inherited defect or a psychological abnormality. He views not only homosexuality but all of the common forms of sexual outlet (except perhaps rape, which he unfortunately says almost nothing about) as "biologically and psychologically part of the normal mammalian picture." (p.677)

The volume on women is much more muted in its moral tone, and much less strongly committed to the conclusion that biology is a more important determinant of sexual behavior than are social codes and other environmental factors. Female sexual behavior proved to be more variable and seemingly more subject to social influence. While the researchers found no significant increase in the sexual activities of the (then) contemporary generation of males, they found that females born after 1900 were twice as apt to engage in premarital sex as women of the earlier generation, and much more apt to reach orgasm in marital sex. Yet some 36% of the women interviewed had never experienced orgasm prior to marriage, and 25% never experienced it after marriage either, while with men the corresponding percentages are close to zero.

In the earlier volume, Kinsey had expressed the opinion that these differences in female sexual behavior were biological in origin, the result of the female's slower sexual maturation and lesser sensitivity to sexual stimulation. His subsequent research, however, contradicted that hypothesis. The physiology of male and female sexual response appears to be basically similar. There is no evidence that females are less well supplied with the end organs of touch which trigger sexual response, that it takes them any longer to respond to effective stimulation of these end organs, or that their biological readiness to respond develops any more slowly than that of the male (p.593). Thus, the human female seems to be just as well equipped for orgastic response as the male; it is not biology that imposes the double standard, but the demands of the male (p.323).

Indeed, Kinsey anticipated most of the later findings of Masters and Johnson with respect to the potentially much *greater* female responsiveness to sexual stimulation. Laboratory observations—which were apparently more extensive than Kinsey admits—had shown that the clitoris and not the interior of the vagina (as Freud had held) was the locus of the female sexual response. Furthermore, it was found that with continued stimulation, many females can achieve multiple orgasm within a short space of time, a feat impossible for most males. While there are more females who are nonorgastic, there are also many who are capable of far higher levels of repeated response than any man.

These findings may help to explain why female sexual response has been the subject of so much more controversy and of so much wider a range of theoretical interpretation than has male sexuality. Since the female orgasm is unnecessary for procreation, it has been possible for cultures and institutions to subject it to a much greater degree of restriction. And, as feminists like Mary Jane Sherfey have pointed out, some of the vehemence of the repression of female sexuality in patriarchal societies may in fact stem from a realization that the sexual capacities of women are potentially much greater than those of men.

1.   Blacks were interviewed as well, but not in large enough numbers, the authors felt, to justify any generalization from the data, which was therefore omitted.

KLEIN, Viola. *The Feminine Character: History of an Ideology*
(University of Illinois Press, Chicago, 1971; first published 1946)
(with **MYRDAL**, Alva) *Women's Two Roles: Home and Work* (see
Myrdal, Alva)

The Feminine Character is a pathbreaking study of ways in
which femininity, i.e. feminine character and temperament, has
been conceptualized by experts in various academic fields. Klein
examines the work of Havelock Ellis, Otto Weininger, Sigmund
Freud, Helen B. Thomas, L.M. Terman and C.C. Miles, Mathias
and Mathilde Vaerting, Margaret Mead, and W.I. Thomas, as
representative of the biological, philosophical, psychoanalytic,
experimental psychological, psychometric, historical, anthropological and sociological approaches, respectively. Her perspective is that of the sociology of knowledge and her central theme is
that however objective each researcher may have tried to be, his
or her views were nevertheless heavily conditioned by personal
biases and preconceptions, and by the prevailing thought of their
times.

Amongst these radically different theories, Klein finds very
little common ground, and little that casts light on what femininity is, as opposed to what it has been presumed to be. The
Vaertings were probably the first to perceive a systematic relationship between the character traits ascribed to women and their
social status, but their pendulum theory, according to which
periods of matriarchy alternate with periods of patriarchy (with
the dominant sex being characterized in each case as what we
would consider masculine, and the subordinant sex as feminine)
is a gross oversimplification, which recognizes the effects of only
one variable, domination of one sex by the other. Mead has
demonstrated the virtual irrelevance of biological differences between the sexes in determining the social characters of women
and men, but her reification of culture as the single determining
factor seems to give too large a role to chance, and ignores the
functional relationship between social roles and the personal
characteristics demanded of those who fill them. She considers
Thomas' approach the most promising in that he recognizes the
influence of both the biological differences between the sexes
(males, he thinks, are more catabolic, or energy-expending; females are more anabolic, or energy-conserving), and the force of
habit and custom. Women's character is shaped in part by their
biology and in part by the social roles to which they are assigned,
but, she concludes, we are as yet in no position to draw any
specific conclusions about the respective effects or relative importance of these two influences.

KOMAROVSKY, Mirra. *Women in the Modern World: Their Education and Their Dilemmas* (Little, Brown and Company, Boston, 1953)

Komarovsky, a Barnard sociologist, deals here with the question of whether women's colleges ought to offer a special feminine curriculum, one less abstract and more "practical," i.e. designed to prepare women for marriage and motherhood. Not only was this a much-debated demand during the post-war period when women were returning home from their wartime jobs, but some women's colleges actually made steps in this direction. Komarovsky argues that this is no solution to the real problems facing women. Such a separate curriculum cannot possibly be justified on the basis of what we know of masculine and feminine psychology, since psychological tests show that there is a much greater variation in IQ, memory, mechanical aptitude and the like between members of the same sex than there is between the sexes. Although we do not know whether there are any innate psychological differences between the sexes, we do know that the *observable* differences are so small, and the social pressures reinforcing them so powerful, that any innate differences that do exist must be very slight.

Komarovsky uses a well-chosen set of case studies of middle-class American women to argue that women's problems are not due to a lack of special instruction in the feminine role, but to the radically inconsistent social demands made of women today. Women are still subject to the expectation that they will value marriage and motherhood above personal achievement; yet at the same time they absorb the "masculine" values of our culture, which emphasize financial success and a professional career as the measure of a person's worth. Consequently many women sacrifice their possible careers to marriage and motherhood resentfully, with an awareness of the injustice that such a curtailment of their development should be required. Without the discipline and self-respect provided by paid outside work, housewives tend to become bored and unhappy, and often damage their children by their excessive emotional demands. Contrary to the Freudian dogma that the pursuit of a career is a sign of neuroticism in a (married) woman, Komarovsky argues, it is generally only exceptionally healthy women who manage to combine marriage and a career, and where this is possible it is a benefit to both the woman and her family. It is usually not possible however, unless the woman has not only exceptional strength, but a willing husband and a high enough income to hire good domestic help. That her husband might take on his full half of the domestic work is a possibility which she does not consider.

Although Komarovsky rejects the "neo-antifeminist" demand that career women go back to full-time housewifery, she also criticizes what she calls the "old feminist" notion that full-time homemaking is a wholly unsatisfactory career for an intelligent and well-educated woman. She says that what is necessary is a change in social values such that full-time housekeeping will be seen—in reality and not just in the fictions of the antifeminists—as one of several equally valid options for the college woman. Yet she recognizes that women are not likely to believe that raising children is as important as building bridges and other "masculine" professions, so long as men themselves do not believe it. And it is obvious that men *don't* believe it, since if they did they would demand a larger share of child raising.

One might suppose that the next step in the argument would be the demand that men take over half the childrearing, thereby increasing their respect for or appreciation of it and freeing mothers to pursue careers without being superwomen. Komarovsky, however, does not consider such a demand, though she does think that it would be desirable for fathers to spend *somewhat* more time with their offspring. She considers no radical options and offers no real solutions, but does present a lucid rebuttal of the simplistic solutions offered by supporters of what Friedan called the feminine mystique. (Also see Komarovsky's 1976 *Dilemmas of Masculinity*, in Anthologies XI.)

L

LAKOFF, Robin. *Language and Woman's Place* (Harper and Row, New York, 1975)

Lakoff uses linguistic analysis, with a nice dash of humor, to explore evidences of sexism in ordinary language—particularly that dialect of English spoken by contemporary white middle-class Americans. She finds "that women experience linguistic discrimination in two ways: in the way they are taught to use the language, and in the way general language use treats them." (p.4) Women's speech is (supposed to be) less forceful, both in vocabulary and in syntax. Women make finer color discriminations ("mauve," "lavender," etc.), and use weaker expletives ("oh dear" rather than the sort of expletive that has to be deleted) and more trivializing terms of admiration (e.g. "adorable," "sweet," "charming" and "divine"). Such usages "suggest that the concepts to which they are applied are not relevant to the real world of (male) influence and power." (p.13) Women also tend to use the tag question construction (as in "It's cold, isn't it?") and the rising intonation pattern typical of questions more often than men; these too are devices for avoiding assertiveness or the appearance of assertiveness in one's utterances.

Lakoff points out that the lack of forcefulness and the exaggerated politeness expected of the speech of respectable women places women in a double bind, a no-win situation. Either they talk like ladies, which will be taken as evidence of frivolity, lack of intellect, indecisiveness and other "feminine" failings; or they don't, in which case they will be considered unfeminine and suffer social disapproval. Either way they lose, for they are denied acceptance as rational and competent (female) human beings. Men's language use is also constrained, but in reward for conformity they receive acceptance, influence and power, whereas women are punished whether they conform or not.

Speech *about* women also reveals sexist presumptions. As a euphemism for "woman," "lady" has the curious double function of diverting attention from what is embarrassing about women, i.e. their sexual nature, and of subtly denigrating women, of suggesting that women "are not to be taken seriously, are laughing stocks." (p.24) There are no comparable euphemisms for "man" (*gentleman* is not used in a parallel fashion) because none are felt to be needed, since the nature of men is not a source of confusion or embarrassment. The language used to refer to women continually reveals their status-dependency, the extent to which they are defined in relation to men, but not vice versa. The nonparallelism between originally or logically symmetrical pairs of terms like master/mistress, bachelor/spinster, widow/widower, the very distinct senses attached to the word "professional" when applied to a woman and to a man, and the use of "Miss" and "Mrs." to indicate women's marital status, are cases in point.

Because she views such linguistic evidences of sexism as symptoms rather than significant *causes* of sexist attitudes, Lakoff is fairly pessimistic about the possibility of bringing about social change through linguistic reform. True, there are some sexist usages which are more directly harmful than others, and we need to single out those which "by implication and innuendo, demean the members of one group or another, and . . . to make speakers of English aware of the psychological damage such forms do." (p.43) But she doubts the wisdom of attempting to change such basic and nearly subconscious usages as the supposedly generic "man" and the use of the male third person singular pronoun when the referent is not necessarily male since these usages are, she judges, neither extremely harmful nor at all easy to alter. And she points out that *some* of the linguistic "reforms" which have received feminist support, e.g. "herstory" for "history," are in fact the result of etymological howlers.

It is possible to question Lakoff's conclusion that it is "social change which creates linguistic change, not the reverse"; and that "at best language changes influences changes in attitudes slowly and indirectly." (p.47) Even though this *may* have been true throughout all previous history, it is possible that instant mass communication has greatly increased the attitude-shaping power of linguistic usages, making it possible for feminist-inspired reforms not only to become fairly standard in a relatively short period of time but to function as significant components of social change. (Also see Ellen Key, *Male/Female Language*.)

LANG, Theo. *The Difference between a Man and a Woman* (Bantam Books; Toronto, London and New York, 1973; first published 1971)

A distinctly misogynous defense of a number of traditional

notions about the nature of women. Lang draws much of his material from Havelock Ellis, but typically misunderstands its significance. He points out, after Ellis, that women are in some respects more infantile in their physical morphology, having relatively shorter legs, larger heads and less prominent bony ridges in their skulls. Lang concludes that women are therefore more primitive than men, that they lag behind men in their evolutionary progress, have "come down from the trees" more slowly; whereas Ellis himself interpreted this infantilism as proof that women are *leading* men in evolutionary development, the latter being a progress in the direction of physical infantilism. As Ellis notes, infant apes are more human-like in their appearance than adult apes, and human men are more ape-like in their hairiness and the structure of their skulls than are women. While the utility of such comparisons may be minimal, the perjorative implications certainly can cut both ways.

Lang also argues that women, while they may score somewhat better on IQ tests (which he thinks measure learned skills rather than creative intellectual ability) are intellectually far inferior to men—so much so that "conceptual thought" must be seen as *entirely* beyond the capacity of women. (p.22) The main line of argument for this is physiological: men's brains are on the average ten percent larger than women's, giving them hundreds of millions of additional possible neural connections. (p.265) Furthermore, he thinks that at least another ten percent must be subtracted from women's mental capacities by the demands of the female reproductive system. He fails to take note of Ellis' point that although the brains of men are *absolutely* larger, women's brains are larger relative to body weight, and *much* larger relative to quantity of muscle tissue, the sort which requires most nervous regulation.

Predictably, Lang arues that in spite of their intellectual inferiority, women have a special intuitive capacity to understand others and to size up situations quickly. He also follows Deutsch in maintaining that any "excessive" development of their rational capacity will damage this intuitive faculty. Rationality is not natural in women: "the essentially intellectual process of analysis is alien to her mind." (p.318) One wonders whether the same might not more truly be said of the minds of misogynists who argue as badly as Lang; yet it is perhaps a measure of how far we have come that Lang admits that "of course" women should have equal pay for equal work and legal equality inside and outside of marriage. Rather than denying women equal legal or moral rights he adopts the position that while they ought to have such rights, they must remember that if they insist on them too vehemently they will lose their "femininity" and hence their "erotic power" over men, which is in Lang's view, women's primary source of influence in the world.

LANGUAGE AND WOMEN   Linguistic usage reflects social attitudes towards women's nature, status, and proper role in two major ways: first, in the differences between the ways that men and women tend to speak, and, second, in the ways they are spoken about. In the past decade, feminists have focused attention on linguistic reflections of sexism, of both these sorts. Lakoff, in *Language and Woman's Place*, argues that women are in effect expected to speak a different language, one which is fussy, deferential, aesthetically rather than pragmatically oriented, and lacking in forcefulness (1). Mary Ritchie Key's *Male/Female Language* also explores these differences in female speech, as well as the implications of the so-called generic use of masculine pronouns and nouns e.g. "man." Casey Miller and Kate Swift's book covers these topics and others, such as the practice of calling women by their husbands' names. (Also see Una Stannard's *Mrs. Man*, which traces the history and social and psychological impact of this latter custom.)

A number of philosophers have also, in recent years, produced enlightening analyses of sexist language. Robert Baker, for instance, has demonstrated the sexist connotations of the common four-letter words for sexual intercourse (which generally take a male subject and a female object, and imply that harm is done to the latter), and of various slang terms for women (2). Elizabeth Beardsley examines the phenomenon of referential generalization, i.e. linguistic devices like pronouns, proper names and even adjectives, which require or imply the making of sexual distinctions (3). Janice Moulton argues that the generic or sexually neutral use of "man" and the masculine pronouns is a myth, and that such usages not only reflect but *cause* unfair discriminations (4). Carolyn Korsmeyer shows that such generic uses of masculine terms help to explain the sources and impact of sexist humor; for they tend to foster the impression that whenever a woman departs from a certain stereotype of feminine behavior, her action is incongruous and hence laughable (5). And Patrick Grim points out that the sexism in sexist utterances is very often not found in their explicit content, but in the more subtle implications of the terms used; thus, the statement, "If broads deserve what they get, then broads deserve what they get," while necessarily true, is also quite blatantly sexist (6).

There have also been a few philosophical attacks on the feminist view that certain usages are sexist and must be changed. Michael Levin, for instance, argues that language is *not* intrinsically sexist, and even if it were, attempts to change it would be misguided, in that they make us unduly self-conscious about the way we speak. He also holds that the Miss/Mrs. usages ought to be retained, because men, being the sexual aggressors, need to be informed as to which women are sexually available—an argument whose sexist presuppositions are quite striking (7). Fortunately, such insensitivity to the significance of language is unusual, at least among those philosophers who have published views on the subject. The traditions of ordinary language philosophy and Wittgensteinian analysis have given academic philosophers the basic conceptual tools necessary for elucidating the logic, implications, and presuppositions of sex- and gender-related linguistic usages. There is no longer any excuse for philosophers, or other educated people to fail to detect and correct at least the more obvious and easily alterable sexist usages—e.g. "man" in the mythical generic use—in their own speech and writing. Still unresolved, however, are the questions of how to alter such deeply engrained, and arguable sexist aspects of language as pronominal genderization, and whether it is in fact counterproductive to invest energy in a struggle against usages which are apt to resist all such efforts at reform. (See Lakoff.)

1. See also Virginia Valian, "Linguistics and Feminism, in *Feminism and Philosophy*, edited by Mary Vetterling-Braggin, Frederick A. Elliston, and Jane English, for a critique of this dual language theory.
2. Robert Baker, ""Pricks" and "Chicks": A Plea for "Persons,"" in *Philosophy and Women*, edited by Sharon Bishop and Marjorie Weinzweig (Anthologies XII), pp.21–25.
3. Elizabeth L. Beardsley, "Traits and Genderization," in *Feminism and Philosophy*, pp.117–123.
4. Janice Moulton, "The Myth of the Neutral 'Man'," *op.cit.*, pp.124–137.
5. Carolyn Korsmeyer, "The Hidden Joke: Generic Uses of Masculine Terminology," *op.cit.*, pp.138–153.
6. Patrick Grim, "Sexism and Semantics," *op.cit.*, pp.105–109.
7. Michael Levin, "Vs. Ms.," in *Sex Equality*, edited by Jane English, pp.216–219.

LEDERER, Wolfgang. *The Fear of Women* (Harcourt, Brace Jovanovich, New York, 1968)

In the spirit of Karen Horney, Lederer rejects Freud's notion of penis envy and argues that on the contrary it is men who have always stood in awe and fear of the reproductive functions of women. Versions of the Great Earth Mother have been worshiped in innumerable times and places; often she is a bloodthirsty goddess, representing death as well as life. Lederer views the primacy of the Great Goddess in prehistoric eras as evidence that precivilized cultures were matriarchal in the fullest sense— i.e. not only matrilineal and matrilocal, but ruled by women. Men, he claims, overcame the rule of women through violent rebellion, organization and political institutions.

But though the rule of women is gone, men retain the fear of women, and every step women make towards equality enhances that fear. As therapy for this male paranoia Lederer suggests that men learn to admit and overcome their fear of women, and that women help them by letting them know how badly they (men) are needed. Women, he remarks, don't need independence, but they need men to protect them and curb their destructive tendencies. Men, on the other hand, need women to nurture and inspire them, but they also need independence.

Had he paid more attention to feminist analyses, Lederer might have been less inclined to suppose that men's negative reactions to women can be ameliorated by reemphasizing the same sexual stereotypes which are responsible for those reactions in the first place. Women inspire fear in men only insofar as they are seen as alien, as the Other; and they cease to be fearful only insofar as they are recognized as fellow human creatures, no more and no less.

LE GUIN, Ursula. *The Left Hand of Darkness* (Ace Books, New York, 1972; first published 1969)

This is a science fiction novel, and strictly speaking it cannot be said to put forward a thesis about the consequences of the male/ female dichotomy, or anything else. Nevertheless, it déserves attention as a lucidly conceived and persuasive speculation about what human life might be like if humanity were not permanently divided into male and female sexes. The action in the novel occurs on Winter, a harsh planet whose population has been mutated by past genetic experimentation. Sexless four-fifths of the time, they experience a monthly phase caled *kemmer*, in which their bodies are either masculinized or feminized (the direction of metamorphosis being unpredictable), and they experience intense sexual desire. The same individual, at different times, experiences both sexual phases, with relatively equal frequency, and can both father children and give birth to them.

This, of course, is only one of indefinitely many logically possible forms of androgyny. But Ursula Le Guin's description of a society of *physiologically* genderless humans would pass for a utopian vision of a society of *psychological* androgynes.

> Consider: Anyone can turn his hand to anything. This sounds very simple but its psychological effects are incalculable. The fact that everyone between seventeen and thirty-five or so is liable to be . . . "tied down to childbearing," implies that no one is quite so thoroughly "tied down" here, as women, elsewhere, are likely to be—psychologically or physically . . . everybody has the same risk to run or choice to make. Therefore nobody here is quite so free as a free male anywhere else.
>
> Consider: a child has no psycho-sexual relationship to this mother and father. There is no myth of Oedipus on Winter.
>
> Consider: There is no unconsenting sex, no rape . . .
>
> Consider: There is no division of humanity into strong and weak halves, protection/protected, dominant/submissive, owner/chattel, active/passive. In fact the whole tendency to dualism that pervades human thinking may be found to be lessened, or changed, on Winter. (pp.93–94)

It should also be noted that there is no war on Winter. The androgynous inhabitants, "though highly competitive . . . seem not to be very aggressive . . . They kill one another readily by ones and twos; seldom by tens or twenties; never by hundreds or thousands." (pp.95–96) (Of course, the observer in whose mouth these words are placed remarks, this lack of organized aggression might be due to the extreme severity of the climate rather than to the sexual anomalousness of the inhabitants.)

Above all, Le Guin's androgynes are proud, independent, and individualistic. The very conceivability of such people challenges the deep-seated assumption—natural to a sexually dichotomized species like our own—that to be a person entails having either a masculine or feminine gender identity. Our language endorses this assumption: the only alternative to "he" or "she" is "it." So too, visionary speculations like this one can help to counter the claim that the erosion of gender stereotypes would necessarily lessen human diversity (1).

1. Margaret Mead, for instance, argues in this way in **Male and Female**.

LESBIANISM   Ever since the sixth century B.C., when the Ae-
olian poet Sappho operated a school for women on the island of
Lesbos and sang of the power of erotic love, "lesbianism" has
been a synonym for sexual interaction between women. Whether
Sappho was herself a physical lover of women (certainly she
wrote love poems to women, as well as to men) or whether this
was merely a comtemporary or later slander which was accepted
as fact, is unclear. (See Beard, 1946, p. 320. Also see Dolores
Klaich, **Woman and Woman: Atitudes Toward Lesbianism** (Simon and Schuster, New York, 1974).) But it is very likely that
lesbian love did exist in Sappho's time, and that indeed there
have always been female as well as male homosexuals. (See
Kinsey, 1953.)

One of the earliest theories about the origin and purpose of
both heterosexual and homosexual love is found in Plato's **Symposium** (1). Here, Aristophanes relates that there were once *three*
human sexes. Each individual had four legs, four arms, two
heads, and two genital organs; in some, the organs were both
male, in some both female, and in some of the two different
kinds. The first type, Aristophanes says, sprang from the sun,
the second from the earth, and the third from the moon, which
partakes of the nature of both sun and earth. Because these
compound human beings were strong enough and arrogant
enough to challenge the gods, Zeus caused each of them to be cut
in half. As a result, each human being is incomplete, and must
search for its other half—which may be of either the same or the
opposite sex.

Of the two sexual orientations, Aristophanes approves more
highly of the homosexual—particularly the male homosexual. It
is heterosexual men who become adulterous, and heterosexual
women who are apt to be promiscuous (p.62; 191d). Homosexual
men, on the other hand, are "the best of their generation, because
they are the most manly." (*Loc. cit.*) Whether, conversely, lesbian
women are the most womanly, he does not say; but it is clear that
neither he nor any of the other speakers is particularly interested
in either lesbian or heterosexual love.

But, while it is necessary to object to the androcentricity of the
Athenian view of homosexuality and lesbianism, there is little
doubt that it is a far saner attitude than that which has prevailed
in the Christian tradition, which has generally regarded all sex as
sinful and/or against nature, unless it takes place between married persons and solely for the purpose of procreation. (Obviously, homosexual love meets neither condition.) Plato's Aristophanes at least realizes that procreation is only one of the pur-

poses of sexuality. In his account, Zeus reasons that

> if male coupled with female, children might be begotten, and the race thus continued, but if male coupled with male, at any rate the desire for intercourse would be satisfied, and men set free . . . to attend to the rest of the business of life. (*Loc. cit.*)

Thus it would seem that a perfectly rational patriarchal culture could consider both male homosexuality and lesbianism to be valuable as alternatives to heterosexual fornication and adultery—even as St. Paul, Augustine, Aquinas, and other Christian thinkers have considered marriage preferable to fornication. Consequently, the fact that our own cultural tradition has been strongly antihomosexual cannot be explained solely by the fact that it is patriarchal.

Gregory Lehne has recently argued that the reason why so many American men (at least) are homophobic (i.e. hate and fear homosexuals, and/or indications of homosexuality in themselves) is that they tend—unlike Plato—to confuse the homosexual male with the effeminate male. Hence the suspicion of homosexuality becomes a threat to a man's sexual identity; and this threat is used by some males to force others to conform to the prevailing stereotype of masculinity(2). It is interesting that this analysis of the function of male homophobia (that is, male fear of male homosexuality) does not apply nearly as well (nor was it intended to apply) to social attitudes towards lesbianism. It is true that feminists have often been accused of being either old maids or lesbians; yet most women in our culture do not fear the accusation of homosexuality as deeply as men do. Although lesbianism may be severely censored, and although lesbians, like male homosexuals, have often been excluded from military service and teaching positions, it is still true that lesbianism is less often noticed or made into an issue.

This difference may be due in part to the survival of the Victorian/Freudian view that women are naturally deficient in sexuality as compared to men, or to the presumption that the act of sexual intercourse requires the participation of at least one male. (Some people still wonder what two lesbians could *do* together.) Or, it may be a result of the fact that homosexuality—like all forms of "deviant" sexual behavior—is in fact a less common phenomenon in females. (See Ellis, Kinsey.) Then again, it may be that there have always been enough *other* means of keeping women in line with the social stereotypes of femininity that the fear of female homosexuality has never had to play as central a role in this regard as it has in the case of men.

Be that as it may, the claim that there have always been some lesbians in the feminist movement is probably true. Prior to the upsurge of radical feminism in the sixties, however, they tended to keep their lesbianism as invisible as possible, for fear of discrediting the movement. At that time, however, certain feminists who happened also to be lesbians began drawing theoretical connections between their oppression as women and their oppression as homosexuals. (See Abbott and Love, Atkinson, Brown, Johnston, Millet (4).) If, in our society, a woman is almost inevitably placed in an inferior position in any heterosexual relationship, while at the same time she has been taught to *need* a lasting and intimate relationship, then the taboo on lesbianism is a crucial part of the social apparatus by which male domination is maintained, and lesbianism itself is a way of escaping, in part, from patriarchal oppression.

Some radical lesbian feminists have gone further than advocating lesbianism as an escape from male domination, and have held that it is also an intrinsically more satisfactory sexual experience for a woman. They have taken the finding of Masters and Johnson, that the female sexual response (contrary to Freud) is *always* to some extent clitoral, and not entirely vaginal, as proving that sexual intercourse with a man is less enjoyable than lesbian lovemaking, which generally focuses on the clitoris (4). They conclude that heterosexuality itself is a patriarchal institution, and one which must be eliminated if women are to be free. (See Johnston.)

One might suppose that there is support for this claim, e.g. in the work of Weininger, who holds that heterosexual intercourse is inherently humiliating for women, or of some of the followers of Freud (See Deutsch, Bonaparte.) who hold that a woman must be somewhat masochistic to enjoy copulating with men. But common sense, and—it would seem—the phenomenological observations of most heterosexual women, would indicate that it is not sexual intercourse *per se* which is humiliating to women, but the conditions under which it is too often performed—e.g., when it is rape-like, or when it is part of an economic bargain, as in prostitution or patriarchal marriage. (See Greer.)

But even if lesbian lovemaking cannot be shown to be essentially superior to heterosexual sex, it is still undoubtedly true that (as de Beauvoir pointed out long before the current lesbian feminist movement), for many women, women who have no prospects or no desire for an egalitarian heterosexual relationship, lesbianism is the only authentic mode of life. It is not, however, one which many women can opt for simply by making a conscious decision; women (like men) more often discover that they *are* homosexually oriented than decide to *become* so. Lesbianism is not, therefore, a solution easily generalizable to all women.

The etiology of both male and female homosexuality is extremely obscure. Both physiological and environmental factors have been suspected, and it may be that both are at least sometimes involved. (See Wolfe (5).) Freudians tend to view homosexuality and lesbianism as due to a failure or regression in personality development, which can be brought about by factors of either sort. Radical feminists, on the other hand, view lesbianism as a form of personal liberation, and one which also has political significance. Both may, indeed, be right; for exclusive heterosexuality is part of the personality development which our particular form of patriarchy still treats as both natural and desirable, but which some individuals—whether because of their physical constitution, their personal value system, or both—are compelled to reject. (See also Bisexuality.)

1. Plato, *The Symposium*, translated by Walter Hamilton, (Penguin Books, Middlesex, England, 1951), pp.58–68 (188–193).
2. Gregory K. Lehne, "Homophobia Among Men," in the *Forty-Nine Percent Majority*, edited by Deborah S. David and Robert Brannon (Anthologies XI), pp.66–85.
3. Also see the Radicalesbians, "The Woman Identified Woman," in *Radical Feminism*, edited by Anne Koedt, Ellen Levine, and Anita Rapone; and Friedan, 1976, for a liberal feminist critique of the radical lesbian movement.
4. Anne Koedt, "The Myth of the Vaginal Orgasm," in *Radical Feminism*. (*ibid.*)
5. Also see *Sexual Inversion: The Multiple Roots of Homosexuality*, edited by Judd Marmor (Anthologies XIII).

LESBIAN SEPARATISM: See Lesbianism

LEVI-STRAUSS, Claude. *The Elementary Structures of Kinship* (translated by James Harle Bell, John Richard von Sturmer, and Rodney Needham, Eyre and Spottiswoode, London, 1969; first published 1949)

The French anthropologist Levi-Strauss is the foremost exponent of the structuralist approach to social analysis. As a structuralist he rejects all attempts to discern a general pattern in human cultural evolution. Evolution and change occur, of course, within particular societies; but, contrary to the cultural evolutionist theories of the nineteenth century (see, e.g., L. H. Morgan, Bachofen, McLennan, Engels), there is no single series of stages through which all cultures pass on the way to civilization. Nevertheless, like the evolutionists, Levi-Strauss seeks to produce a theoretical framework adequate to explain the institution of marriage, in all its complex and varied forms.

The theory presented in *The Elementary Structures of Kinship* is that marriage is essentially a means whereby groups of men form social bonds with one another, through the exchange of women. Exchange, or reciprocal gift giving, is the first form of social organization above the level of the individual family or clan. Because women are "the most precious possession," they are the most important item of exchange. Levi-Strauss says that

> the likening of women to commodities, not only scarce, but essential to the life of the group, [has] to be acknowledged. (p.36)

Marriage, then, is the institutionalization of the reciprocal exchange of women between men. Invariably, Levi-Strauss claims, "it is men who exchange women and not vice versa" (p.115). In other words, women are in no way parties to the exchange, but are merely goods which are exchanged by men:

> The total relationship of exchange which constitutes marriage is not established between a man and a woman . . . but between two groups of men, and the woman figures only as one of the objects in the exchange, not as one of the partners between whom the exchange takes place. (*Loc. cit.*)

This is equally true, Levi-Strauss holds, regardless of whether the system of descent is matrilineal or patrilineal. Matriliny, he says, does not imply any greater power on the part of women; for kinship systems, like marriage, represent arrangements made between men only. Matriliny and matrilocality are merely expressions of

> the permanent conflict between the group giving the woman and the group acquiring her . . . The woman is never anything more than the symbol of her lineage. Matrilineal descent is the authority of the woman's father or brother extended to the brother-in-law's village. (p. 116)

Thus, matriliny is not to be seen as a survival of a golden age of matriarchy, as many evolutionary anthropologists have held. Nor is it in any sense a more primitive system than patriliny. Indeed, instead of precluding male supremacy, matrilineal descent presupposes it; it is only

274

because political authority, or simply social authority, always belongs to men, and because this masculine authority appears constant, that it adapts itself to a bilineal [i.e., neither exclusively
patrilineal nor exclusively matrilineal] or matrilineal form of
descent . . . (p. 117)

Systems of marital exchange, Levi-Strauss argues, are the basis
of the transition from nature to culture. The intergroup relationships forged by the exchange of women are stronger and more
lasting than those based solely on the exchange of other forms of
property, both because the marriage relationship is usually relatively permanent, and because women are the most valuable of
all commodities. The necessity for such interfamilial bonds between men, he holds, explains the universality of the taboo
against incest. For men would naturally retain possession of their
own sisters and daughters, were it not for the rules of exogamy,
which make these or other female relatives sexually off limits.
Exogamy represents a reciprocal renunciation on the part of men:

> As soon as I am forbidden a woman, she thereby becomes available
> to another man, and somewhere else a man renounces a woman
> who thereby becomes available to me. (p. 51)

Levi-Strauss explains all elementary systems of kinship and
marriage as elaborations of two basic types of exchange: restricted (in which just two groups are involved) and general (in which
more than two groups are involved). Either mode of exchange
can be combined with matrilineal, patrilineal or bilineal kinship
structures. Insofar as kinship structures are, in his view, largely
conscious human creations, they can be altered and elaborated in
innumerable ways. His survey of primitive kinship structures in
Asia, Africa, Australia and North and South America reveals an
enormous variety of systems, some of them fantastically complex. Yet the function and the underlying concept of all such
systems is the same; for, he says,

> the . . . elementary structures of exchange . . . are always
> present to the human mind, at least in an unconscious form, and
>   . . . it cannot evoke one of them without thinking of this struc-
> ture in opposition to . . . the . . . others. (p. 464)

Levi-Strauss does not explore the implications of his theory for
the explanation of the origins of male supremacy. But, since he
argues that it is through the incest taboo and the exchange of
women that culture becomes possible, and since in his view
women are never parties to the exchange, but only the objects
exchanged, it would seem to follow—as Gayle Rubin points
out—"that the world historical defeat of women occurred with

the origin of culture." (1) The exchange of women, as Levi-Strauss explains it, not only requires the institutionalization of male domination, but provides a rationale for the sexual double standard. For if women's sexual and reproductive capacities are the property of their male relatives then they cannot be permitted the same sexual freedom as men typically enjoy. (This is particularly true of married women, whose sexual freedom would endanger the social bond between the father's family and the husband's.)

The sexual division of labor is also a functional part of all social systems based on the exchange of women. Its function, in all primitive societies, is to make heterosexual marriage an economic necessity.

> Not only do man and wife have different technical specializations, one depending on the other for the manufacture of objects necessary for their daily tasks, but they are each employed in producing different foodstuffs. Accordingly, a complete, and above all regular, food supply depends on that "production cooperative," the household. (pp. 38–39)

On Levi-Strauss' theory, then, all human culture depends upon the subjection of women and the exaggeration of the sexual dichotomy. He does not, however, explain how this subjugation of women came about. Women, he says, become exchange objects because of their value and scarcity, which in turn are a result of men's "deep polygamous tendency, which . . . always makes the number of available women seem insufficient." (p. 38) But this does not explain how men gained the *power* to treat women as commodities, however great their incentive for doing so. He presumably thinks it was a simple matter of brute strength.

Marxist theorists, following Lewis Henry Morgan (to whom Levi-Strauss dedicates *The Elementary Structures of Kinship*), explain male domination as arising from the institution of private property—a relatively recent event as compared with the beginnings of culture and society. This theory fails to explain how male domination can exist in (some) primitive societies which lack private property. Levi-Strauss, on the other hand, presupposes that women are treated as private property by people who otherwise lack any such concept or institution. Obviously neither approach is entirely satisfactory. But the Marxist approach does take account of women's contributions to the development of culture. On Levi-Strauss' theory women have had no more direct or conscious role in this process than the money which changes hands in a poker game. One need not be a matriarchy theorist to recognize the androcentricity of such a view. (Also see Briffault, Davis, Reed, Stone.)

1.   Gayle Rubin, "The Traffic in Women," *Toward an Anthropology of Women*, edited by Rayna Reiter (Anthologies I), p.176.

LEWIS, Helen Block. *Psychic War in Men and Women* (New York University Press, 1976)

Lewis is a Freudian psychoanalyst who recognizes and rejects some of the androcentric aspects of Freud's thought—e.g. his belief in the inherent physical, intellectual and moral inferiority of women—but insists on the value of his other contributions. Her theses are that humans of both sexes are naturally affectionate, affection being more central to human nature than aggression or competition; and that the conflict between their natural affectionateness and the artifically differentiated patterns of self and superego imposed on women and men by an exploitative society drives both towards insanity, each in a different way.

To say both women and men are naturally social beings, demanding and wishing to give affection, is not to say that there are no genetically determined behavioral or temperamental differences between the sexes. Lewis is impressed with the evidence that not only do males tend to be more aggressive than females, possibly because of some gene(s) carried on the Y chromosome, but females naturally tend to be more social and more affectionate. Many feminists object to any such conclusion, because it seems to lend support to the system of male domination, and some would like to prevent further research into the genetic differences between the sexes. But Lewis draws an analogy between this attitude and the Lysenko case in the Soveit Union, in which Soviet science was severely set back by the official imposition of the "ideologically correct" view that acquired traits may be inherited. Whatever the differences between the sexes may be, we need to know about them, even though the knowledge may be used by some to argue for the inevitability of patriarchy.

Such arguments would, Lewis argues, be invalid. For if it is a fact that aggression comes more naturally to males and nurturance to females, as so many antifeminists have insisted, it does not follow that male domination is inevitable (1). Biological factors alone cannot explain the prevalence of male domination, since societies vary greatly in the degree to which women are subjugated, with some, e.g. the Zuni, being almost completely egalitarian. The key variable is not the biological differentiation between the sexes, but the degree of authoritarianism and exploitation in the society. The less exploitative and authoritarian the culture, the freer both women and men will be, and the more equal. "The subjection of women," Lewis says, "is a corollary of the development of the exploitative relation between the classes." (p.58)

As to why class exploitation and authoritarian social structures first arise, Lewis says that no one really knows. It can't be adequately explained along Marxist lines, as the result of the accumulation of private wealth, for this is itself usually a result of authoritarianism and exploitation, or at least of a shift away from the more natural cooperative modes of social interaction. Nor can it be explained, as Simone de Beauvoir maintains, as the result of the inherent imperialism of human consciousness, the supposed fear and hostility of each human consciousness for each other, out of which, according to the existentialists, the soul is born. For the self, Lewis claims, originates not (just) in the attempt to dominate other people, but in the "mutual delight" of mother and child in one another's being (p.119).

Male domination and authoritarianism is not an inevitable result of the biological family, either, as radical feminists like Shulamith Firestone have argued, because even a patriarchal family structure—e.g. in the case of the Arapesh culture (2)—is consistent with equal or nearly equal freedom and stature for women, provided that there is no economic exploitation and no authoritarian political system. And, finally, it can't be explained by the theory suggested by Karen Horney, that men react against the fearful power of the mother over their early lives by subjugating women (and one another). For in a nonexploitative, non-authoritarian society the early power of the mother is not experienced as fearful.

Whatever its origin, Lewis holds that an exploitative male-dominated culture like our own distorts the psychological development of both men and women, in different but equally harmful ways, which act to maximize anxiety in both sexes. Women are supposed to be loving and subordinate; their loving identification with others, together with the society's denigration of this central feminine trait, make them prone to shame and self-contempt. Hence women are vulnerable to depression and hysteria, mental dysfunctions which "originate in and reflect a profound inner contradiction between their natural affectionateness which has become an ego-ideal, and the internalized cultural scorn of it as weakness." (p.263)

Men, on the other hand, are more prone to the more active or bizarre mental abnormalities, particularly schizophrenia and sexual deviations, such as transvestism, fetishism, sadism, rape and homosexuality (sic). They suffer from the conflicting social and internal requirements that they be both tough and tender, a conflict they may try to solve by becoming sadistic, thereby combining aggression with sexuality, if not with love or tenderness. Or, they may solve the conflict by withdrawing from emotional involvements altogether and developing weird and obsessive notions, as in schizophrenia. Men's proneness to sexual abnormalities is probably due to the fact that not only is their first caretaker, the person with whom they first identify, a woman, but her personal traits are severely devalued and presumed to be inconsistent with masculinity. As a result, men's gender identity, their conviction of membership in their own sex, is much less secure than women's and more subject to distortion.

Psychiatrists, Lewis says, have failed to perceive the significance of these different patterns of madness in women and men or to recognize their origin in sexist and exploitative social attitudes. From Freud on, they have taken as their major model of ego development the typically male mode of identification with an aggressor or power figure, to the neglect of the typically female mode of loving identification with the parent figure. Their standards of mental health have stressed the "masculine" virtues, the virtues necessary for exploiters, e.g. aggressiveness, independence, objectivity and emotional control. Consequently, they fail to understand or to respect women's symptoms and their origin in dependency and shame, and their treatment of women is often counterproductive. Depression and hysteria are symtoms which, because of the androcentric bias of the culture, are apt to evoke scorn and contempt, even on the part of psychiatrists, whose attitudes towards their shame-ridden female patients often make them even more ashamed. If psychiatrists and others in the "helping professions" wish to be part of the solution rather than part of the problem, they will have to "shed their exploitation-dominated notions of individual development, and their implicit acceptance of aggressive values." (p.313)

1. See Steven Goldberg, who maintains that the behavioral effects of testosterone does make male domination inevitable.
2. See Margaret Mead, *Sex and Temperament*.

LIBERAL FEMINISM   The usual definition of a liberal feminist is, someone who believes in the goal of sexual equality and thinks that it can be achieved through reform rather than revolution. There are several problems with such a definition, however. One is that what is perceived as revolutionary change is highly relative to time and place. Thus, Mary Wollstonecraft's demand that higher education and the practice of law, medicine, and other professions be opened to women was very radical for her time, yet today we tend to think of these changes as reforms rather than revolutions. Does this make Wollstonecraft a liberal? It would hardly seem so. Another problem is that anyone who advocates complete equality between the sexes, almost of necessity contemplates changes in large areas of life, which seem much too fundamental to be thought of as mere reforms.

With these points in mind, one can at least say that a liberal feminist today, in our culture, is one who advocates such reforms as legal equality between the sexes, equal pay for equal work, and equal employment opportunities, but who denies that complete equality requires radical alterations in basic social institutions, e.g. the capitalist economic system, the biological family, monogamous marriage, biological motherhood (see Firestone), or in the presumption that most childrearing must be done by women. John Stuart Mill and Bertrand Russell remain the greatest philosophical proponents of liberal feminism, with Betty Friedan and (some of) the leadership of NOW representing the liberal wing of the woman's movement today. (See also Amundsen, and Bird.) There is a notable scarcity of liberal feminist *theorists* in our own time, however.

This may in part be due to the disappointing aftermath of the long struggle for women's suffrage. The vote had become almost the single reform in which feminists had invested their hope and their energies, but it proved to have very little practical effect on the overall social, political, and economic status of American women. (See Chafe.)

Another, perhaps more important reason for the decline of liberal feminist theory (as opposed to liberal feminism as a political force) is the increasing realization of the extent to which male domination is a cultural universal, which has up to now (or so the best anthropological data suggest) existed, to a greater or lesser degree, in virtually every known human society. This means that it cannot be simply the result of any particular system or law or ideology, since these vary between cultures. These institutions may greatly increase its severity and oppressiveness, and prevent its demise in our own time, but they do not suffice to explain its origin. Consequently, most theorists have turned to other cultural factors to explain male supremacy, such as modes of production and resulting systems of social class, reproductive and hormonal differences between the sexes, or differences between male and female psychology. (Also see Radical Feminism, Socialism and Feminism, and Biological Determinism.)

LITERATURE BY AND ABOUT WOMEN   Fictional representations of women, in drama, poetry, and novels of all historical periods, are a rich source of data on the ideas which the writers and those around them had about women's nature and social role. As a rule however, they do not constitute well-defined theories, supported by rational argument, on either topic. This is equally true of female fictionalists; they may be culturally or politically influential and they may provide inspirational models for feminists, but they generally do not contribute, through their fiction, to feminist (or antifeminist) *theory*. (Of course, there are writers of fiction who *also* contributed to the theory of the nature of woman, e.g. Wollstonecraft, Gilman, de Beauvoir and Millett; but that is another matter.)

There are, however, many feminists who have used analyses of literature to demonstrate the prevalence of male supremacist attitudes throughout Western history. (See Ellman, de Beauvoir, Figes, Janeway, Millet; also Rogers, Anthologies VII.) Students of misogyny find ample material in Western literature of all sorts. (See Bullough, Hayes, Lederer, Stern.) On the other hand, one can find surprising flashes of feminist insight in the literature of, for instance, classical Greece (see F.A. Wright) or Medieval Europe (see Goulianos, in Anthologies II).

In the modern era, powerful literary expressions of feminist sentiment have come from playwrights (e.g. Henrik Ibsen, George Bernard Shaw), novelists (e.g. George Sand, the Bronte sisters, George Elliot, Dorothy Richardson, Doris Lessing, Kate Chopin), and poets (e.g. Sylvia Plath, Erica Jong, Anne Sexton, Adrienne Rich). Once again, since none of these writers is an important contributor to scientific or philosophical theory, they are not dealt with here. (The one marginal case included is Ursula Le Guin.) Of somewhat more theoretical interest is the discussion amongst feminist literary critics of whether or not there are distinctively feminine styles or concerns in literature. (See Ellman; also Moers, and Spacks in Anthologies II.) For some recent collections of poetry and fiction by and about women, see Berg,

Goulianos, Solomon, Ferguson, Cooke, Murray, Parker, Segritz, Chester, Iverson and Miller, also in the same Anthology section.)

LOCKE, John (1632–1704). *Two Treatises of Government* (Hafner Publishing Company, New York, 1947; first published 1690)

Locke is known as the founder of the political philosophy of liberalism, though his work also had an important influence on Marx. His ideas have had a particularly lasting influence in the United States, many of them having been written into the American Constitution. The theory of majority rule; the separation of powers within the government and the system of checks and balances; and the belief that all "men" are created with the same God-given rights to life, liberty and the profits of their own labor—all are Lockean in origin. So is the liberal faith in the inherent rationality of human beings and their capacity to act according to enlightened self-interest.

Locke's philosophy also provided a vital part of the conceptual foundation of feminist thought. Locke himself, however, had relatively little to say about the rights of women as such. His constant use of masculine terms like *man* and *men* to refer to human beings makes it difficult to determine the extent to which his views about the "rights of men" were intended to apply to women as well. He certainly did not advocate extending all of the *political* rights of men to women; he does not believe, for instance, that women should vote, or retain control of their own property during marriage. He does not, however, deny (and the logic of his argument would seem to imply) that the basic *natural* rights of man—those which they enjoy in the state of nature and which they cannot rightly surrender to any master, state or commonwealth—belong to women too. These natural rights include life, liberty, and property. Locke holds that reason, which is the law of nature,

> teaches all mankind who will but consult it that, being all equal and independent, no one ought to harm another in his life, health, liberty, or possessions . . . [for,] being furnished with like faculties, sharing all in one community of nature, there cannot be supposed any such subordination among us that may authorize us to destroy another, as if we were made for one another's use as the inferior ranks of creatures are for us. (p. 123)

Locke's most extensive discussion of women's rights are found in Chapter 5 of the first of the *Two Treatises of Government*, and Chapter 7 of the second. The first *Treatise* is an extended attack upon Sir Robert Filmore's defense of the theory that the power of monarchs is absolute and divinely ordained. Filmore had argued that monarchial authority is derived from the authority which God gave to Adam, to rule over nature, Eve, *and all of his children* and his children's children (1). This authority, Filmore claimed, extends even to the power of life and death. It is inherited by the eldest male child in each generation, and it provides the basis for all political authority, both in the family and in the state. Locke points out that on this line of argument there could be only one legitimate heir of Adam in each generation; and since there is no possible way of determining who that one man is, any man would have as good a claim to be king as any other.

Locke does not challenge Filmore's assumption that it is appropriate to base political philosophy on the Scripture. he denies, however, that the Bible demonstrates that Adam was given any absolute power, either over Eve or over his (i.e., their) children. God's curse against Eve ("and thy desire shall be to thy husband, and he shall rule over thee"; Genesis 3:26) was meant, Locke says, as a punishment of Eve for being the first to eat the forbidden fruit, not as a grant of power to Adam. Because Adam sinned too, his superiority over Eve is accidental, not essential. God's words were directed only to Eve and her female descendants,

> and import no more but that subjection they should ordinarily be in to their husbands. But there is here no more law to oblige a woman to such subjection, if the circumstances either of her condition or contract with her husband should exempt her from it, than there is that she should bring forth her children in sorrow and pain, if there could be found a remedy for it . . . (pp. 36–37)

Locke holds, in other words, that the power of husbands over wives is the result of human rather than natural law. It is a voluntary contract between a man and a woman, for the protection of their common interests and those of their children. As such, it cannot give the husband the power of life and death over his wife. It is not improper, however, for the husband to be given the ultimate authority in decisions affecting the family's common interest, including the control of their joint property. For, Locke says,

> the husband and wife . . . having different understandings, will unavoidably sometimes have different wills too; it therefore being necessary that the last determination—i.e., the rule—should be placed somewhere, it naturally falls to the man's share as the abler and stronger. But this, reaching but to the things of their common interest and property . . . gives the husband no more power over her life than she has over his. (p. 161)

Because women's inferior status in marriage is the result of human law rather than natural law or divine command, women are under no obligation not to strive to avoid subjection, by altering the terms of the contract (p. 37). Although Locke does not mention in this context the political and other legal inequalities imposed upon women in addition to those of marriage, his argument would seem to imply that women have the right to struggle against these as well.

Locke's position is probably best described as protofeminist rather than feminist. While he denies that patriarchal authority is divinely mandated, he nevertheless believes that "there is . . . a foundation in nature for it" (p.37). His insistence that by natural law the husband has no more right to rule his wife than she has to rule him must, however, be seen as courageous. For seventeenth-century English law granted the husband total control of his wife's person and property, including the right to imprison her and beat her all but to death. Furthermore his doctrine that all men are naturally free and equal could naturally and consistently be interpreted to apply equally to women, and was so interpreted, by such early feminist philosophers as Mary Wollstonecraft and John Stuart Mill. Without Locke's influence neither liberal nor radical feminist theory would have taken the form which they have.

1.   In *Patriarcha: Or the Natural Power of Kings*, published 1680.

LORENZ, Konrad. *On Aggression* (translated by Marjorie Kerr Wilson; Harcourt, Brace and World, New York, 1963)

This is the ground-breaking study of the functions of aggression—which Lorenz defines as "the fighting instinct directed against members of the same species"—in animal behavior. Lorenz studied certain species of coral fish, on the reefs and in the laboratory, and found that each defends its home territory only against others of the same species. In this way intraspecific aggression has the function of preventing the population of any one species becoming too dense in any one area, thus depleting the food supply. It also serves in a wide range of species, including birds and mammals, to promote the selection of the strongest individuals—especially the strongest males—through competition for territory and for females.

Aggression also facilitates the forming of male-female bonds in those species in which male and female jointly care for their young. The bond may be formed and strengthened through the joint defense of a territory against other pairs or individuals, or ritualizations of the direction of aggression against one another. Thus, for example, greylag geese bond for life through a "triumph ceremony," which Lorenz interprets as a ritualized modification of aggressive behavior. Love and hate, he suggests, are inseparable, for such personal, individual bonds form only in species with highly developed instincts for intraspecific aggression, never in herd animals which lack such instincts.

Lorenz does not doubt that human beings have inherited a powerful drive toward intraspecific aggression. "It is more than probable," he says, "that the destructive intensity of the aggression drive, still a hereditary evil of mankind, is the consequence of a process of intraspecific selection which worked on our forefathers [sic] . . . throughout the early Stone Age." (p.42) He rejects, however, the popular notion (defended, for example by Robert Ardrey) that the bloodthirstiness of (some) human beings is due to the "carnivorous mentality" of our Australopithecine ancestors. On the contrary, carnivorous creatures do not normally kill one another in their disputes over territory or sex, because they have developed intinctive ritualized behaviors, e.g. certain submissive gestures, which lead to the inhibition of the attack before it becomes lethal. Our own ancestors failed to develop such instinctive aggression-inhibiting rituals precisely because they were not natural carnivores, were not equipped with lethal natural weapons, and so were not obliged to develop ways of preventing the escalation of aggression to the lethal level.

Lorenz's observations lead him to believe that the aggression drive, in humans as in animals, cannot be suppressed or eliminated; denied one outlet it will always find another. The human drive can, however, be directed into nondestructive forms, such as active sports, political struggle in worthwhile causes, or creative work. Lacking phylogenetic ways of redirecting aggression away from other people, we must value and make the fullest use of the many cultural ritualizations which perform this function. Lorenz does not specifically claim that human males have a stronger aggression drive than human females, nor does he address the mystery of male domination. His work, nevertheless, has been used to support the claim that male domination and female submission are indelible parts of human nature (see Julius Fast, *The Incompatiblity of Men and Women*). The work does not in fact support any such interpretation, since there is no reason to presume that the aggression drive (if there is such a thing) cannot be provided ample room for expression through institutions which do not promote the domination of one sex by the other.

LOVE, Barbara: See Abbott, Sidney.

LUNDBERG, Ferdinand, and **FARNHAM**, Marynia, *Modern Woman: The Lost Sex* (Grosset and Dunlap, New York, 1947)

This once-popular best seller launches an exceptionally virulent attack on feminist goals and theories, largely on the basis of Freudian theory. The thesis is that most of the unhappiness and neuroticism of our age is due to the warping of children's psychic development by insufficiently feminine and loving mothers. Feminism—along with socialism, anarchism, atheism, anti-Semitism and racism—is an expression of the prevailing neurosis, a childish temper tantrum which represents a refusal to accept authority and established principles. It is not the original cause of women's disastrous loss of femininity, however. Women's current problems spring from the destruction of the home and their traditional role within it.

Prior to the Industrial Revolution, they argue, women's role in the home gave them ample sources of self-importance, and they were not socially or legally inferior to men in any significant respect. Most work was done in and around the home, and education and recreation were also centered there. But the home and women's role there have lost most of their former economic and social importance. Having children has also been devalued, now that children are an economic liability rather than an economic asset. Since motherhood is women's deepest psychic need and the only thing which can give their lives meaning, its devaluation has left them lost and bewildered.

Feminism is a response to that bewilderment, but a perverse one, since what it advocates would only exacerbate the problem. Feminists want to restore women's sense of self-importance by making them more and more masculine, i.e. independent, aggressive and eager to compete in the outside world. But masculine women are neurotic and unhappy; they cannot enjoy sex and they make terrible mothers. They either reject their children or dominate and overprotect them. Only feminine women can love their children without tyrannizing them. And women who work outside the home cannot remain feminine (i.e. avoid masculinization) unless the work they do is of an essentially feminine sort, e.g. teaching children.

What is needed to save the lost sex and humanity as a whole, Lundberg and Farnham argue, is not equality with men (which they take to mean identity of role), but a rehabilitation of women's traditional domestic role. They suggest that towards this end subsidies should be paid to families with children and successful mothers should be given honorary degrees. Government-run information campaigns should be used to discourage women from entering "masculine" fields and educate them about their psychological need for marriage and motherhood. Unmarried women should be forbidden to teach children, thus protecting children from their influence and providing suitable work for married women. A medicare-like program should be instituted to enable more people to be psychoanalyzed, and the government should subsidize the training of more psychoanalysts. As for the population problem which might result from all this encouragement of motherhood, the authors argue that it is at least a generation or two in the future, and that if overpopulation does become a problem it can be solved by eugenic programs which determine which people are permitted to reproduce. (One may surmise that those extra psychiatrists will be sorely needed.)

M

MACCOBY, Eleanor Emmons, and **JACKLIN**, Carol Nagy. *The Psychology of Sex Differences* (Stanford University Press, 1974)

This is a thorough and definitive analysis of the results of research done between 1966 and 1973 on the psychological differences between the sexes; it includes an exhaustive 233-page annotated bibliography of this research (1). The authors' procedure is to list all of the studies done during this period, and their results, and to evaluate their implications. The results are naturally complex and often inconclusive, but are of great interest to the feminist theoretician. Of course, it is one question what the observable (and not necessarily innate) psychological differences are between boys and girls and men and women and another question why these differences occur and what ought to be done about them. While feminists have generally been more preoccupied with the second question, any answer to the second question must presuppose some answer to the first.

Maccoby and Jacklin show that a great many of the hypotheses about sex differences which have been taken for granted by (some) theorists or which have been thought to have been supported by the results of earlier research, are not supported by recent findings. Among these are the following: that girls are more socially oriented; that girls are more suggestible; that girls excel at rote learning and at simple repetitive tasks, while boys excel at tasks requiring higher level cognitive processing; that boys are more "analytic"; that girls' mental traits are more affected by heredity and boys' by environment; that girls have less achievement motivation; and that infant girls are more auditory and infant boys more visual in their perceptual orientation (pp.349–351).

The list of well-established differences is considerably shorter; there is ample evidence that girls tend to have greater verbal ability, especially from adolescence onward, and probably earlier as well; that boys are more apt to excel in visual-spatial ability and mathematics, also especially from adolescence on; and that males are more aggressive at all ages. (pp.351–352) Still unanswered are the questions whether infant girls have greater tactile sensitivity; whether boys are generally more active, competitive and dominance-seeking; whether girls tend to be more fearful, timid or anxious; whether girls are more compliant in general (they do tend to be more compliant towards *adults*); and whether girls are more nurturant and "maternal" towards younger children and animals.

As for the causal explanation of the well-established differences, the authors argue that the evidence suggests that both the differences in intellectual functioning (i.e. females' greater verbal ability and males' greater visual-spatial and mathematical ability) and the differences in behavior (i.e. males' greater aggressiveness) may be largely inherent or innate. They find no evidence of differences in the socialization of the two sexes which could produce characteristically different patterns of intellectual ability or aggressiveness. (p.362) Thus,

> We must recognize the possibility that boys are more "masculine" than girls (in some sense of this term) *despite* what their parents are doing, not because of it. (p.304)

The conclusion that male aggressiveness is to some degree innate is especially controversial, and the arguments for it are well presented here. There is, for instance, the fact that the pattern of more aggressive behavior in males is universal for virtually all known human societies; that it appears prior to any known differential conditioning of boys and girls at least with respect to aggression; that it parallels the differences which have been observed in other primate species; and that aggressive behavior in other species is known to be correlated with levels of testosterone, the primary male hormone (pp.242–247).

The usual argument of those who deny that human males have a greater inherent tendency towards aggressive behavior than do most females is that from an early age girls and boys *are* subjected to differential social conditioning with respect to aggression, boys being encouraged and girls discouraged from behaving aggressively. In fact, there is no evidence (at least none based on recent psychological research findings) that parents and other adults respond to the aggressive behavior of boys any more indulgently than to that of girls (p.323). True, mothers seem to tolerate more aggressive behavior towards *themselves* on the part of sons than daughters, but the reverse is true for fathers, who tolerate much less aggression from sons, and so there would seem to be no overall greater leniency towards boys. Indeed, many studies show that boys are reprimanded more often and more severely for aggressive behavior than girls, and that such behavior is more apt to go unnoticed in girls. (p.323) It is certainly true that aggressive behavior has to be learned, but boys seem to learn and practice it more readily, to be "more biologically prepared to learn it." (p.361)

This line of argument ignores the possibility that even though boys are not deliberately "conditioned" towards aggrssion, they may still receive greater rewards for it, e.g. in terms of self-image. For so long as aggression is part of the social definition of masculinity, it will tend to enhance a male's sense of his own sexual identity. For a female, of course, the reverse will be true, since aggression is socially defined as incompatible with femininity. In other words, males and females may behave differently because, in the given social context there are good reasons for doing so, rather than because of any instinctive compulsion.

As for the social and political implications of this apparent natural difference in aggression levels, the authors point out that in adult human society, at least, there is no necessary connection between aggression and power or status. There is "no direct evidence that dominance among adult human groups is linked either to sex hormones or to aggressiveness" (p.361), and "aggression is certainly not the method most usually employed for leadership among mature human beings." (p.369) Thus, there is probably "nothing inevitable about male achievement of all available leadership positions." (p.370) Nor, for that matter, is it inevitable that human males should continue to be more aggressive than females, since "societies have the option of minimizing, rather than maximizing, sex differences through their socialization practices." (p.374)

1.   Maccoby's earlier anthology, *The Development of Sex Differences* (Stanford, 1966), includes an almost equally extensive annotated bibliography of research done up to 1966.

MAILER, Norman. *The Prisoner of Sex* (New American Library, New York, 1971)

Mailer's works have all had a boundless capacity to anger feminists but this one is particularly noteworthy in that respect.

The Prisoner of Sex is an introspective account of Mailer's meditations on the function of sex and sex roles, prompted, as he tells us, by his fourth divorce and by accusations by feminists like Kate Millet and Mary Ellman that his novels represent the epitome of male chauvinism. The central idea of the essay is an admittedly mystical and empirically unsupported one, largely derived from the renegade Freudian, Wilhelm Reich, i.e., that sexual orgasm is the most important and transcendent experience of life, for both men and women. Unfortunately, not just any orgasm will do, but only one experienced during heterosexual intercourse and with the intention of procreation. Furthermore, Mailer thinks that this perfect orgasm will never occur unless all of one's orgasms during a given period are experienced in the process of procreative heterosexual intercourse. Hence masturbation, homosexuality, contraception, abortion, and abstinence are all to be deplored, as interferences with the all-important process of orgasmic procreation.

Even more distressing from a feminist point of view is Mailer's conviction that the perfect orgasm cannot occur unless the male dominates the female. Men and women, he insists, are fundamentally different sorts of being; women are close to nature, and indeed masculinity is in its essence a conscious struggle to transcend nature, conquer it, rise above it. (He even suggests, seemingly seriously, that a fetus can only become male by means of a mental decision to rise above nature!) Consequently, it is built into the nature of men that they must dominate women, or else lose their masculinity and sexual potency. Yet this does not mean that men are, or think of themselves as, *superior* to women. Mailer credits Henry Miller with the discovery that, on the contrary, "it was man's sense of awe before woman, his dread of her position one step closer to eternity . . . which made man detest women, revile them, humiliate them, defecate symbolically upon them, do everything to reduce them so one might dare to enter them and take pleasure of them." (p. 86)

Mailer defends the right of men to do all of this, for the greater pleasure of both sexes. But he also objects to Miller's failure to realize what Ibsen's Nora expressed so well, that women too have a right to be human beings. Women, he says, do need liberation; but the only form of liberation he offers is the right to pick their own sexual partners. Women need such freedom if they are to perform their primary mission in life, which is to find a man with whom to conceive children which will improve the species. But as for the feminist demand that women be liberated from domestic work in order to pursue careers, Mailer says he would never be willing to live with a woman who expected him to do half of the housework—not unless her work were as important as his, which it could not possibly be, given the very nature of masculinity and femininity.

MAINE, Sir Henry (1822–1888). *Ancient Law* (J. Murray, London, 1873; first published 1861)

Ancient Law is a study primarily of Roman law, the changes it underwent during Rome's history, and its continuing influences within the English and Continental legal systems. Maine considered the comparative study of ancient law to be the best way to discover the nature of prehistoric society, and his investigations led him to conclude that all primitive society was based on the patriarchal family, as illustrated by the Scriptural history of the Hebrew patriarchs. "All known societies," he claims, "were originally organized on this model. The eldest male parent is absolutely supreme in his household. His domain extends to life and death, and is as unqualified over his children as over his slaves." (page xxxii) Men were emancipated from their fathers' power only upon the latter's death, which made them (potential) heads of their own households. Women never were freed of the control of their fathers' families, remaining subject after the father's death to the nearest remaining male relatives on the paternal side. (Modern English, American and European law, he notes, tends to reverse the ancient form of women's subordination; husbands are given paternalistic power over wives, leaving unmarried or widowed women comparatively free.)

The patriarchal family, Maine thought, long antedated the institution of private property. The patriarch had absolute control over the family's property, but "in a representative rather than a proprietary way." (p. 119) At first, each patriarchal family was an independent social unit. There was no law but the word of each family head, at whose death the family holdings were generally divided between his sons. "Communities began to exist wherever a family held together instead of separating at the death of its patriarchal chieftan." (p. 123) Thus the paternal bond was the basis of civil society, rather than a social contract as Locke, Hobbes and Rousseau had argued; it could not have been such a contract, for contracts come into being much later in the history of law, after patriarchal authority has been greatly eroded. Non-related persons might be accepted into the community, but the fiction of common descent was maintained, e.g. through adoption.

Maine's was among the first scientifically argued presentations of the patriarchal theory of human social evolution, and it largely inspired the development of the early matriarchy theories of McLennan, Bachofen and Morgan. The matriarchy theorists have for the most part accepted Maine's evidence that early Roman law, and also Hebrew, Hindu and certain other ancient legal codes, were strongly patriarchal in nature, but have denied that this demonstrates that the earliest human societies were patriarchal from the beginning. Instead they have seen, in other features of ancient law and myth and in the evidence of anthropology, evidence that patriarchy was itself a reaction against an earlier state of society which was matriarchal, that is, matrilinear, matrilocal, and perhaps actually ruled or dominated by women. The evidence can be read to support either theory. However, both the matriarchal and the patriarchal theories of social evolution have long been out of favor with most anthropologists, primarily because what is now known of the numerous family systems and other forms of social organization seems to confound the hypothesis that there is any single evolutionary pattern which has been followed by all human societies.

MALINOWSKI, Bronislaw (1884–1942). *Sex and Repression in Savage Society* (Routledge and Kegan Paul, London, 1953; first published 1927)
The Sexual Life of Savages in North-Western Melanesia (Routledge and Kegan Paul, London, 1929)
Sex, Culture and Myth (Harcourt, Brace and World, New York, 1962; selections written between 1922 and 1941)

One of the leading British anthropologists of the twentieth century, and a founder of the "functionalist" school of social analysis, Malinowski produced some of the finest existing studies of primitive matrilineal cultures. He spent several years living with and observing the Trobriand Islanders, who inhabit a group of coral islands off the northeast coast of New Guinea. In the social system of the Trobrianders, kinship is reckoned through the maternal line only; a man leaves his property to his sister's children rather than those of his wife. A father is not regarded as having any blood relationship to his own children, although his personal relationship to them is generally close, and he takes an active part in caring for them in infancy. He has no authority over them based on kinship, only over his sister's children, whom he teaches and disciplines. A man grows food (largely yams) for his wife and children, but also retains a lifelong responsibility to grow food for his sisters and their children. Marriage is exogamous and patrilocal, yet egalitarian; a woman must defer to her brother, but not to her husband, who has no authority over her.

Such contemporary matrilineal societies are enormously important as potential clues to the etiology of our own patrilineal and male dominated system. They have been interpreted by

Morgan in the nineteenth century, Briffault in the twentieth, and by many others as survivals of a universal stage of human cultural evolution, which was supposedly characterized by mother right (matriliny), "group marriage" (or unregulated promiscuity), and the political supremacy (or at least equality) of women. Malinowski, however, debunks all such efforts to demonstrate a universal pattern whereby an original state of mother right yields to father right. He sees matriliny, like patriliny, as a form of social organization which has various important functions. Unilineality makes it easier for families—persons of common descent—to retain their identity and property through the generations, and it makes struggles over inheritance rights less frequent.

Thus, Malinowski argues, mother right is not a "stage" through which cultures must pass on the way to father right, but rather, "one of two alternatives of counting kinship, both of which shows certain advantages." Indeed, he suggests, the advantages of mother right "are perhaps on the whole greater than those of father-right." (*Sex and Repression*, p.273) For, in what is only an *apparent* paradox, the Trobriand father's relationship to his children is actually closer than that of a patriarch, since he is their friend and helper, but has no authority over them except what he can achieve by winning their affection and respect. Father right, on the other hand,

> is to a great extent a source of family conflict, in that it grants to the father prerogatives not commensurate with his biological propensities, nor with the personal affection which he can feel for and arouse in his children. (p.32)

But whichever lineage system prevails, Malinowski maintains, marriage and the male-dominated family remain necessary for human survival. For,

> The human family is in need of a male, as definitely as the animal family, and in all human societies this biological need is expressed in the principle of legitimacy which demands a male as the guardian, protector and regent of the family. (p.254)

Malinowski points out that the other features besides matriliny which are supposed to characterize "matriarchal" cultures—promiscuity or "group marriage" and the supremacy of women in the family, are not found in the Trobriand culture. The Trobrianders do allow almost unlimited sexual freedom (within the bounds of their incest and endogamy taboos) to children and unmarried men and women, even providing special houses for unmarried adolescents to live in with their lovers. Yet married persons, especially women, are expected to be sexually loyal to their spouses. Only chiefs have more than one wife, and marriage is fairly egalitarian; yet women must crouch down in the presence of their brothers all their lives, and all children must obey their maternal uncles. Hence the family is in no sense female-dominated.

Neither, on the other hand, is it as harshly male dominated, or as sexually repressive, as the patriarchal/patrilineal family. Trobriand men (1) experience no Oedipus Complex (i.e. desire to marry the mother and kill the father), since this is merely "the system of attitudes typical of our own patriarchal society." (p.75) There is no suppression of childhood sexuality, no latency period, and, in practice, ample sexual satisfaction for all but the least physically attractive persons. On the other hand, because the maternal uncle is the authority figure, and because sexual contact with the sister is strictly taboo, Trobriand men tend to (subconsciously) long for such contact. This is the matrilineal analogue of the patriarchal Oedipus Complex, though on the whole it is less repressive and productive of neurosis than the latter.

Malinowski thus offers some comfort to the advocates of egalitarian marriage and sexual freedom. He criticizes feminists, however, for failing to understand the necessity of the biological family and of male power within it. His analyses of the Trobriand Islanders, and of other matrilineal cultures, constitute the most powerful argument against those (e.g. Bachofen, Morgan, and Briffault) who believe that the matrilineal, mother-goddess worshiping cultures of the preclassical Near East must have also been matriarchal in the fullest sense, that is, ruled by women. Supporters of the ancient matriarchy theory have yet to come to grips with the evidence that in existing matrilineal cultures power is generally divided between the father and the maternal uncle, rather than appropriated by the mother. Of course the matrilinies of the ancient world may have been quite different from those which exist today among more or less primitive peoples; but it is no longer plausible to interpret these (recently) existing matrilineal cultures as evidence of the widespread existence in the past of true matriarchies.

1. Freud had not yet developed his theory of the distinctive development of the Oedipus Complex in females, and Malinowski does not give much attention to the psychologocial development of Trobriand, as opposed to "civilized" Western, women.

MARINE, Gene. *A Male Guide to Women's Liberation* (Avon, New York, 1972)

A cogently reasoned introduction to contemporary feminism, aimed at the unreconstructed (male) masculinist. It is valuable for its patient refutations of standard antifeminist arguments and for its extensive annotated bibliography. Men, Marine says, are "victimized into the role of the oppressor." Both sexes suffer from sex-role stereotyping (John Wayne presented an image of tragic repression), but it is still the case that ultimately it is men who dominate and oppress women rather than vice versa. He defends the much-ridiculed analogy between sexism and racism, pointing out that if there are enlightening similarities between the two forms of oppression then it is unreasonable to object to the analogy on the grounds that the phenomena are not *identical* (women being, for example, less often lynched or confined to city ghettos). Masculinists, that is defenders of male supremacy and traditional Western sexual roles, mistake women's natural reproductive *capacity* for their natural *function*. From the fact that (most) women have the *capacity* to become mothers it does not follow that motherhood is their function or destiny, any more than it follows from the fact that men are capable of swinging from trees that this is *their* natural function.

MARRIAGE   Marriage may be defined as a relatively long-term and legally sanctioned relationship between a man and a woman—or, sometimes, more than one man and/or more than one woman—involving sexual intercourse and shared responsibility for the rearing of at least some of the resulting children, if any. Occasionally, both parties to a "marriage" may be of the same sex; but in no society has this been typical. Every known society has, on the other hand, had some form of heterosexual marriage.

There are three perennially debated questions about marriage, all of which are relevant to the issues dividing feminists and antifeminists. First, when and why did the present system of monogamous, and patriarchal (i.e. patrilineal and male dominated) marriage originate? Was it the original form of marriage, or was it preceded by some other type of family, e.g. a matrifocal (and perhaps even matriarchal) one? Second, why has marriage almost always, at least since the beginning of recorded history, been such an unequal contract, with authority placed in the hands of the male, and subordination and obedience expected of the female? Is there any moral justification for this inequality? And, third, if there is not, then what needs to be done to eliminate the injustice of patriarchal marriage?

Biblical mythology holds that the first two humans were also the first married couple; and that Adam was given supremacy over Eve both because he was created first, while she was created second and as a helpmate for him, and because of Eve's misbehavior with the apple. The rule of the husband over the wife was part of God's curse against Eve; and wherever Christianity, Judaism, or Islam has prevailed, Church and state have conspired to insure that the curse is fulfilled. (See the Bible, St. Paul, Augustine, Aquinas, Kierkegaard; also Ruether, and Clark and Richardson, in Anthologies XIV.)

The presumption of male supremacy in marriage is equally clear in the Greek philosophical tradition. In Plato's *Republic* the members of the ruling class will not take individual spouses; but in spite of the apparent equality of male and female guardians, Plato describes the arrangement as one in which wives and children (not men) are held in common. Aristotle argues that women's intellectual inferiority and lack of self-control makes it natural and necessary for them to submit to male authority in marriage (1).

The earliest feminist critics of patriarchal marriage did not dispute the Biblical account of its origin. (See Astell, Wollstonecraft, Grimke.) They questioned, however, the use of Scripture to justify depriving women of the education, legal rights, and economic opportunities which, so they held, are necessary not only to their human dignity, but to the proper performance of their duties as wives and mothers. They pointed out that the inequality of rights between spouses makes it impossible for them to love and respect one another, since these sentiments are possible only between those who are at least able to think of themselves as equals. (See also W. Thompson, J.S. Mill, H. Taylor, and Bertrand Russell.) Patriarchal monogamy was assumed to be the primordial form of marriage, but it was held that reason and the material advantages of civilization would enable it to evolve towards a more egalitarian form.

In the latter part of the nineteenth century, however, the assumption that marriage has always been patriarchal was challenged by a group of scholars who found in ancient mythology and the data of anthropology what they took to be evidence of an earlier, matriarchal (i.e. matrilocal, matrilineal, and perhaps even female dominated) form of marriage. (See Matriarchy Theory.) Other theorists insisted that marriage and the family have always been patriarchal. (See Maine, Spencer, Westermarck.) Marx and Engels adopted the hypothesis of the ancient matriarchal family, arguing that it fell because private property, appropriated by men, gave them for the first time the preponderance of social power.

In the twentieth century, most Western anthropologists lost interest in the matriarchy/patriarchy debate, in part because they came to reject the assumption that all human societies must follow a single pattern of evolution, and in part because the evolutionary theories were associated with both Marxism and feminism. Recently, however, the issue of the "original" form of marriage and the family has again been raised. Arguments for the primacy and inevitability of patriarchy, based on evidence from endocrinology and ethology, have become popular. (See Ardrey, Fox, Morris, Tiger, Storr; also Biological Determinism.) In response, feminist scholars have argued that even if there has never been a truly matriarchal, or female-dominated form of marriage, the data of anthropology suggests that, during the long preagricultural, gathering and hunting phase of human existence, a relatively egalitarian form of marriage and family, often not always matrilineal, was more common that the patriarchal form. (See Davis, Reed, Stone; also Martin and Voorhies, Schneider, Reiter, and Lamphere, in Anthologies I.)

But how are such inevitably rather obscure questions about the marital relationships of prehistoric humans relevant to the justice or injustice of patriarchal marriage in our own time, or to the feasibility of eliminating it? Some feminists impatiently deny that there is any such relevance (e.g. Greer, Millett). But it seems a plausible enough (though by no means self-evident) assumption, that if the marital relationship was once, and for a very long time, (very nearly) egalitarian, then it can become so again, if the incentive and context exist to make it so. If, on the other hand, marriage has always been male dominated (even when not patrilineal or patrilocal), then it is somewhat more probable that male dominance is either genetically determined, or maintained by social forces which are apt to prove highly resistant to change. In spite of the arguments of misogynists like Vilar and Wylie, who claim that America is a matriarchy, marriage has not *yet* become a typically egalitarian institution, as is clear from contemporary sociological research. (See Bernard, Komarovsky; also Dahlstrom, Huber, and Theodore, in Anthologies XIV.)

Today, the liberal and radical wings of the women's movement disagree on the question whether monogamous heterosexual marriage can ever become truly egalitarian. Liberal, and for that matter socialist feminists hold that with legal equality between spouses, equality of economic opportunity, improved child-care facilities, and other social reforms, the essential kind of equality in marriage will become possible. Even when the sexes are fully equal, they predict, heterosexual marriage will remain at least one popular option. Radical feminists, on the other hand, hold that monogamous heterosexual marriage cannot but be male dominated; they argue that real equality between the sexes requires freer sexual and other living arrangements. (See de Beauvoir, Greer, Firestone, Millett, Mitchell.) Regardless of the utopian predictions of some radical feminists, however, marriage does not seem to be on the verge of disappearing, and thus the struggle to make it more equally conducive to the interests of both parties will continue.

1. See F. A. Wright, however, for evidence of feminist sentiment in Plato and other Athenian writers of the period.

MARTINEAU, Harriet (1802–1876). *Society in America*, Volumes I & II (Saunders and Otley, London, 1837)

Harriet Martineau was thirty-two and already well known as a political writer on the English left when she began her two-year-long tour of America. Her account of those travels stands, with de Tocqueville's *Deomcracy in America*, as one of the most valuable sources of insight into early American society. Her emphasis is on the fundamental moral and legal principles of the young nation and the way that these influenced, or failed to influence, its institutions—politics, the apparatus of government, the press, the economy, agriculture, religion, slavery, marriage, childrearing practices and the position of women. While highly impressed with American democratic and egalitarian ideals, Martineau found that the practice fell far short of the theory. Citizens were politically apathetic and afraid to voice—or even to hold—views contradictory to those of the majority. She attributed this condition to the lack of inherited status, which forced people to depend for their social standing on the opinions of others. Mob violence and lynching were frequent, especially in the South, but usually went unmentioned in the corrupt and intimidated press.

Of the evils she observed, Martineau was most distressed by slavery and by the condition of women; and she drew the analogy between these two evils, pointing out their irreconcilable opposition to the fundamental principle announced in the Declaration of Independence—that governments derive their just powers from the consent of the governed. The political nonexistence of women flouts this principle. She rejects as absurd Thomas Jefferson's argument that it would destroy "public morality" if women were to "mingle promiscuously" with men at political gatherings. Nor can women's duties as wives and mothers justify their political disenfranchisement, since they, like men, are themselves the best judges of whether and which political activities would infringe upon their other obligations.

Martineau notes that the condition of women is one of the best tests of the civilization of a society, and that "Tried by this test, the American civilization appears to be of a lower order than might have been expected . . . While women's intellect is confined, her morals crushed, her health ruined, her weakness encouraged, and her strength punished, she is told that her lot is cast in the paradise of women . . . " (Volume II, p.226) American men displayed an exaggerated chivalry towards women in superficial matters, e.g. when it came to giving a woman the best seat on the stagecoach, but this shows only that they are given "indulgence . . . as a substitute for justice." (p.227) In reality, the condition of woman in America

> differs from that of the slave, as to the principle, just so far as this: that the indulgence is large and universal, instead of petty and capricious. In both cases, justice is denied on no better plea than the right of the strongest. (*Loc. cit.*)

Women's intellect was crushed by the inadequacy of their education; for as in Europe women were educated for the single end of marriage, and intellectual activity was considered unfit for them. One symptom of this mental constraint is what Martineau called female pedantry, the narrow-minded application of petty moral principles; but this pedantry is also a hopeful sign, an indication of "the first struggle of the intellect with its restraints." (*Loc. cit.*) Not only women's but also men's morals were crushed by the prevailing notion that some virtues are masculine and others feminine (the notion against which Mary Wollstonecraft had launched a powerful attack). Since "all virtues nourish each other, and can in no otherwise be nurtured," the consequence of this pernicious notion is "that men are, after all, not nearly so brave as they ought to be, nor women so gentle." (p.234) "Men are ungentle, tyrannical [while] . . . Women are . . . weak, ignorant and subservient." (p.235)

Martineau concludes that, paradoxically perhaps, the great material wealth of America, which has made possible a state of relative equality between (white) men, is highly unfavorable to women's chances for achievement. In Europe a great many women, of whom Martineau herself was one, had been forced by economic necessity to fend for themselves and had as a result significantly improved their social condtion. In America, however, "It will be long before they are put to the test as to what they are capable of thinking and doing." (*Loc. cit.*)

MARX, Karl (1818–1883). *Economic and Philosophic Manuscripts of 1844* (translated by Martin Milligan, International Publishers, New York, 1964)
(with **ENGELS**, Friedrich) *The German Ideology* (International Publishers, New York, 1947; written 1845–46; first published 1932)
(with **ENGELS**, Friedrich) *Manifesto of the Communist Party: Basic Writings on Politics and Philosophy*, edited by Lewis S. Feuer, Anchor Books, Garden City, New York, 1959, pp. 1–41; written 1848)
Capital: A Critique of Political Economy (translated by Samuel Moore and Edward Aveling, The Modern Library, New York, 1906; first published 1867)

Marx's final theory of the oppression of women—its history and the means by which it is to be overcome—is presented not in his own published work, but rather in Friedrich Engels' *The Origin of the Family, Private Property and the State.* Engels had been Marx's friend, supporter and intellectual collaborator for almost forty years; he wrote *The Origin* on the basis of notes made by Marx not long before his death. Marx had read Louis Henry Morgan's *Ancient Society* (1877) and found confirmation of his own theory of history in Morgan's view that primitive societies were communistic and sexually egalitarian, or even matriarchal.

In Marx's own earlier work, there is no mention of the matriarchy theory. Nor is there any very extensive consideration of the oppression of women as women, as opposed to their oppression as members of the working class. Like Engels, however, Marx showed a deep and lasting concern for the suffering of women and children whose labor was exploited in the factories and sweatshops of industrial capitalism.

Marx's theory of the oppression of women is derived from his dialectical materialist philosophy of history. The concept of a historical dialectic—a progressive movement of the whole of human history, through contradictory stages, towards a final ideal state—is Hegelian. But Hegel's historical dialectic was idealist; he held that it is consciousness, the realm of spirit and ideas, which motivates the progress of history and the evolution of social and political institutions. Marx held, on the contrary, that it is material and in particular economic reality which shapes human relationships, institutions, and ideas.

Human social evolution, Marx held, is the result of human labor, the activity involved in earning a subsistence. Economic classes and the division of society into oppressed and oppressor groups developed out of divisions of labor. Once it became possible for a worker to produce a surplus product, i.e. more than he or she requires to survive and reproduce, slavery and other forms of exploitation of human labor for the purposes of those other than the laborers became inevitable. Surplus wealth leads to private property, i.e. the ownership of the means of production by individuals. Private property in turn leads to both social-class distinctions and sexual inequalities within certain social classes.

Marx is usually interpreted as viewing the oppression of women as secondary to class oppression, and as something to be explained in economic rather than biological or ideological terms. This is largely correct. Yet Marx also held that the oppression of women within the family developed in part from the natural division of labor between the sexes in the bearing and rearing of children. In *The German Ideology*, Marx and Engels wrote that the first division of labor was

> nothing but the division of labor in the sexual act, then that division of labor which develops spontaneously or "naturally" by virtue of natural predispositions (e.g., physical strength) . . . (p.21)

Consequently, all of the complex divisions of labor which eventually develop are, Marx says, originally based upon this natural division of labor in the family. Socially instituted divisions of labor imply

> the distribution, and indeed the unequal distribution, (both qualitative and quantitative), of labor and its products, hence property: the nucleus, the first form of [private property] lies in the family, where wife and children are the slaves of the husband. (p.21)

Thus, Marx's theory is not that private property and economic exploitation *preceded* the oppression of woman within the family, but rather that these two forms of oppression developed simultaneously, and that both were to some extent conditioned by the original division of labor in sex and reproduction. This original division of labor was not in itself oppressive or exploitative; for exploitation requires a surplus product and the institutions of private property. So-called monogamous marriage is such an institution; within it woman becomes the property of her husband, the means whereby he obtains a (male) heir.

Although they located the oppression of women within the

family, Marx and Engels disagreed vehemently with those anti-capitalist theorists, like Fourier, who held that the coming of socialism will entail the end of monogamous marriage and a "community of women" (*The Communist Manifesto,* p. 25). They saw this demand for the end of marriage and the family as based on the bourgeois equation between women and property, which is the very thing which the coming of socialism will destroy once and for all.

> The bourgeois sees in his wife a mere instrument of production. He hears that the instruments of production are to be exploited in common and, naturally, can come to no other conclusion than that the lot of being common to all will likewise fall to the women.(*Loc. cit.*)

Such an attitude toward women, Marx held, is a reflection of the distorted, alienated nature of all interpersonal relationships under capitalism. (See *Economic and Philosophic Manuscripts of 1844,* pp. 133–134.)

In Marx's view, the bourgeois family is essentially a continuation of the patriarchal family which has existed ever since the rise of private property, thousands of years ago. In the proletarian (i.e. working) class, however, the family had, Marx thought, been virtually shattered by industrial capitalism. He blamed the demise of the proletarian family on the introduction of machinery into the mills and factories. Machinery, Marx argued in *Capital,* made it profitable for industry to exploit the labor of women and children. The large-scale employment of women and children, he held, was responsible for the high death rate among the neglected children of female workers. It also drives down the wages of male workers, making it impossible for them to support their families, unless their wives and children also work. (*Capital*, p. 440)

This dissolution of the proletarian family is a part of the historical dialectic. As such, it prepares the way for a new and less oppresive form of the family. In Marx's words,

> However terrible and disgusting the dissolution, under the capitalist system, of the old family this may apear, nevertheless . . . [it] creates a new economical foundation for a higher form of the family and of the relations between the sexes . . . it is obvious that the fact of the collective working group being composed of individuals of both sexes and all ages, must necessarily, under suitable conditions, become a source of humane development . . . (*Op. cit.,* p.536)

These changes in the family and in the relation between the

sexes, which will come about with the end of capitalism, are further explored by Engels. (See Engels, and Socialism and Feminism.)

MARXISM: See *Socialism and Feminism*, Engels; also see Eisenstein, Jennes, Lenin, and Trotsky, in Anthologies X.

MASCULINITY   In the past, relatively little attention has been paid to the concept of masculinity, the nature of man as a sex, or the causes of male behavior. This is because—as Simone de Beauvoir has pointed out—the masculine was identified with the generically human, while the feminine was seen as a deviation and hence as that which was in need of explanation. Aristotle's theory that the female is a misbegotten male is a striking instance of this tendency; but even philosophers like Rousseau and Kant, who have flattered women for their special feminine virtues, have assumed that it is nevertheless men who represent the human norm. Some of the earliest feminists rejected both the pejorative and the romanticized conceptions of feminine nature, and claimed for women the same human capacities which men appeal to in defining themselves. (See Astell, Wollstonecraft, Fuller, W. Thompson, J.S. Mill, and Harriet Taylor.)

In the past decade, many feminist thinkers have gone beyond the necessary rejection of the myth(s) of femininity, to a critical analysis of what masculinity has meant in our culture. Feminists and advocates of psychological androgyny, many of them men, have shown that the cultural ideal of the competent, aggressive, competitive and emotionally uncommunicative male is a psychological straightjacket which limits men both in their capacity for personal fulfillment and in their moral sensitivity. (See Nichols, Steinmann and Fox, Heilbrun, Stern; also R. Firestone, Brenton, Komarovsky, Farrells, Fasteau, David, Barker-Benfield, Pleck, and Petras, in Anthologies XI.)

At the same time, there has arisen a new group of defenders of patriarchy, who claim that masculinity, the inherent psychological nature of the male, is such that he must be assured of superior social status and power over others if he is to function adequately as a social being. (See Bednarik, Gilder, Goldberg.) Aggressive and dominance or status-seeking behavior is identified as masculine, and the tendency of males to behave in such ways is said to be a result of the operation of the male hormone testosterone.

(See Goldberg, Holliday, Hutt.) Popularizers of ethology and sociobiology point to analogies between the behavior of human males and that of other male primates to suggest that male aggression and hence male supremacy is psychobiologically inevitable. (See Ardrey, Fox, Morris, Tiger.)

In opposition to such deterministic theories of male nature, there are a variety of contemporary scientific approaches which emphasize the social learning of sex roles, individual cognitive development, and the influence of cultural models, not sexual hormones or other purely physiological factors, as the determinants of what is considered masculine. (See Mead, Maccoby, Stoller, Money and Ehrhardt; and Cox, Beach, Lips and Colwill, and Bardwick, Anthologies XIII. For recent feminist critiques of the biological-determinist theory of masculinity, see Lips and Colwill (*loc. cit.*), E. Morgan, and Weisstein.)

MASTERS, William H. and **JOHNSON**, Virginia. *Human Sexual Response* (Little, Brown and Company, Boston, 1966)
Human Sexual Inadequacy (Little, Brown and Company, Boston, 1966)
The Pleasure Bond: A New Look at Sexuality and Commitment (Little, Brown and Company, Boston, 1974)

Masters and Johnson, during the late 1950s and early 1960s, conducted what—amazingly enough—were apparently the first extensive laboratory studies of human sexual behavior and its physical concomitants. The research aimed at "defining and describing the gross physical changes which develop during the human male's and female's sexual response cycles," primarily by means of "direct observation and physical measurement." (*Human Sexual Response*, p.4) Most of the physiological research was conducted at the Washington University School of Medicine, and since 1964 Masters and Johnson have operated a private clinic in St. Louis for the treatment of problems of sexual functioning in both men and women. The research results are presented in *Human Sexual Response*, and the theory and practice of the treatment program in *Human Sexual Inadequacy*. *The Pleasure Bond* presents in nonscientific language their philosophy of sexuality, which is humanistic and egalitarian.

The basic findings of Masters and Johnson have become extremely well known, both in this country and elsewhere, and they have done much to dispel a wide range of myths about human sexuality. Among these are the myth that most (or even a high proprotion of) older people become incapable of adequate sexual response; that the "missionary" (male superior) position in intercourse is usually the most satisfactory; that a man with a big penis can generally satisfy a woman better than a man with a small penis; that (female) prostitutes are either "frigid" or homosexual; and that many women are constitutionally incapable of sexual response.

While these results are important in their own right, the Masters and Johnson findings which have had the most significance for feminists concern the then-surprising magnitude of the female capacity for sexual response. Although the Judeo-Christian tradition stigmatizes women as *more* sexually driven, in the nineteenth and much of the twentieth century it has often been assumed that women tend to have a *weaker* sex drive than men, and/or a lesser capacity to respond to sexual stimulation. Even Kinsey was originally attracted to this hypothesis, though he later rejected it.

Masters and Johnson found that men and women are on the whole remarkably similar in their physiological responses to effective sexual stimulation, and that the differences which *are* observed by no means favor the hypothesis of the greater sexual capacity of the male. Aside from the obvious differences in genital anatomy, there are only two major differences between the male and female orgasm:

> First, the female is capable of rapid return to orgasm immediately following an orgasmic experience . . . Second, the female is capable of maintaining an orgasmic experience for a relatively long period of time. (**Human Sexual Response**, p.131)

The female's capacity for multiple orgasm had been previously reported by Kinsey, but it was the Masters and Johnson research which brought the significance of this fact to public awareness. While males have the ability to ejaculate only once during a time span which gradually lengthens with age, women are capable of an indefinite number of successive orgasms. Masters and Johnson report that the actual number of orgasms enjoyed by female subjects during periods of masturbation was in many cases limited only by general physical fatigue. Nor is this capacity confined to unusual women; it is, the researchers hold, a normal feature of (unrepressed) female sexuality. If women are more often "orgasmically dysfunctional" (1) than men, it is not because of any known inferiority in their physiological capacity for orgasm, but rather because of society's rejection of female sexuality. (**Human Sexual Inadequacy**, p.218) Indeed, a "woman's conscious denial of biophysical capacity rarely is a completely successful venture, for her physiological capacity for sexual response infinitely surpasses that of man." (p.219)

This finding does not in fact—as has sometimes been assumed—settle the issue of whether females tend to have a greater or lesser sex drive than males, since the *capacity* for orgasms (single or multiple) is one thing, and the drive to exercise that capacity is another. It does, however, effectively demolish the Freudian thesis that the smaller size of the female clitoris in comparison to the male penis makes the former inadequate for the expression of the female sex drive or libido. Freud held that this supposed inadequacy of the clitoris as an organ for sexual outlet forces the female to repress her active sexual impulses and leads to feminine passivity and masochism, and some of his followers, e.g. Helene Deutsch, have made this claim the cornerstone of the Freudian theory of feminine psychology.

The Masters and Johnson findings have also (let us hope) driven the final nail into the coffin of the Freudian myth that there are two distinct kinds of female orgasm, vaginal and clitoral. Freud held that while young girls generally masturbate by stimulating the clitoris, the normal mature woman transfers the locus of her sexual responsiveness from the clitoris to the vagina. But this hypothetical transfer (as Kinsey and his colleagues previously observed and as the work of Masters and Johnson clearly demonstrates) is physiologically improbable, if not impossible, because the preponderance of sensory receptors is in the clitoris, and the interior of the vagina is very poorly supplied with the relevant sorts of nerve endings. Thus they conclude that all female orgasms are primarily clitoral, regardless of whether the clitoris is stimulated directly—as often happens during masturbation—or indirectly—as is usually the case in intercourse. (Also see Seaman, Sherfey.)

MATRIARCHY THEORY "Matriarchy" means a society in which men are ruled by women. Whether or not there has ever been a genuinely matriarchal society is a question which is still open to debate. Some contemporary misogynists such as Philip Wylie have claimed that America is already a matriarchy. Most Western (male) writers, from the authors of Genesis to the Freudians, functionalists and sociobiologists of the present, have assumed, however, that all human societies always have been and always will be patriarchal. Beginning in the mid-nineteenth century, however, many researchers have found evidence of a number of early Mediterranean and Near Eastern cultures which were not only matrilineal, goddess worshiping and peace loving but—so they concluded—matriarchal (1).

The Swiss scholar J.J. Bachofen was the first of these matriarchy theorists," followed by John McLennan and Lewis Henry Morgan, the American anthropologist, who found matriarchal traditions among the Iroquois and other native American peoples. Morgan's findings influenced Karl Marx and Friedrich Engels, who theorized that all human societies were matriarchal, until the development of herding and/or large-scale agriculture enabled men to accumulate private property and with it bring about the subjugation of women. Robert Briffault presented a massive collection of anthropological data which he took to support the thesis that matriarchy is a stage through which all societies have passed. Nevertheless, most anthropologists of the twentieth century have rejected the matriarchy theory along with all other attempts to demonstrate a single universal pattern of cultural evolution.

The first matriarchy theorists (Bachofen, Morgan, McLennan) were not feminists; they saw the fall of the early matriarchies as an inevitable and by no means undesirable part of the rise of civilization. Many feminists, however, have seen in the matriarchy theory a proof of the natural equality—if not superiority—of women, as well as a basis for hope that the patriarchal system will one day be overthrown. Mathilda and Mathias Vaerting went so far as to hold that periods of matriarchy have repeatedly alternated with periods of patriarchy, with each swing of the pendulum resulting in a complete reversal of sexual roles. Feminists like Helen Diner, Elizabeth Gould Davis, and Evelyn Reed have argued that women were responsible for the most important elements of human culture, from horticulture, architecture, cooking, weaving, and pottery to religion, morality, and social cooperation.

Some feminists, such as Merlin Stone, emphasize the widespread worship of the Great Goddess in ancient times as evidence of the authority and respect enjoyed by women in the prepatriarchal era. Other writers, notably Jung and his followers (e.g. Neumann), interpret goddess worship not as evidence of matriarchy but as an expression of the archetype of the feminine, which, Jung held, resides eternally in the collective unconscious of the human race. Simone de Beauvoir sees the Great Goddess as only a phase of the male objectification of woman, an image in which woman already appears as the Other. (See *The Second Sex*, pp.70–71.)

The problem for the modern feminist, seeking her roots in the remote reaches of history and prehistory, is to separate fact from myth and wishful thinking. Matrilineal and matrilocal cultures are not necessarily matriachal or gynocratic, as Malinowski demonstrated in his study of the Trobriand Islanders. Nor is goddess worship necessarily a sign of female supremacy—though it is difficult not to believe that it must have contributed to a relatively high level of respect for women. Today anthropologists are beginning to analyze patriarchal vs. sexually egalitarian social systems not as stages in a universal pattern of social evolution, but in terms of their distinct adaptive functions in different economic, environmental and demographic contexts. (See Martin and Voorhies, Schneider and Gough, Anthologies I; and Rosaldo and Lamphere, Anthologies XIV.)

MATRILINY AND MATRILOCALITY   A matrilineal culture is one in which ancestry is traced through the female side rather than the male side as in our own patrilinear system. Matrilineal societies are often, but not always, also matrilocal; that is, married women remain in the family group of the mother and men live with the family of the wife. Both matriliny and matrilocality have sometimes been taken as signs of matriarchy, though this is by no means always the case, at least not in extant cultures. (See Matriarchy Theory; also Schlegel, and Schneider and Gough, in Anthologies I.)

McLENNAN, John Ferguson (1827–1881). *Primitive Marriage: An Inquiry into the Origin of the Form of Capture in Marriage Ceremonies* (University of Chicago Press, Chicago and London, 1970; edited by Raul Riviere. First published in 1865, by Adam and Charles Black, Edinburgh.)

John McLennan was a Scottish lawyer and one of the first systematic anthropologists, credited by some with the founding of the subject. *Primitive Marriage* is one of the earliest statements of one version of the matriarchy theory, i.e., "that the path to civilization lies through a stage of matriliny." (1) He argued, that is, not that there is a stage of cultural evolution in which women are politically dominant (true matriarchy), but that the first blood relationships recognized by all human cultures were relationships through the female line only. McLennan was preceded in this hypothesis by the Swiss classicist J.J. Bachofen (2), but apparently was unfamiliar with the latter's work at the time he

wrote **Primitive Marriage**. He seems to have been largely reacting to the work of Henry Maine. Maine argued that primitive
society was universally patriarchal, i.e. composed of family units
ruled by the eldest male parent, who held the power of life and
death over his children and grandchildren. Consequently, Maine
held, only agnatic family relationships, i.e., those between persons descended from a single male through an all-male line, were
recognized in the earliest human societies.

McLennan argues, on the contrary, that it is extremely unlikely
that agnatic relationships would be the first to be recognized and
made the basis of a social system, since this requires knowledge
of paternity, which in turn requires monogamy, at least on the
part of women; and it is doubtful that monogamy was the general
practice among the earliest humans. "As among other gregarious
animals, the unions of the sexes were probably in the earliest
times, loose, transitory, and in some degree promiscuous."
(p.67) Hence blood relationships through males would have been
difficult to determine. Blood ties through females, on the other
hand, were obvious and indisputable, and for this reason "the
idea of blood-relationship, as soon as it was formed, must have
begun to develop . . . into a system embracing them." (p.64)

McLennan speculates, therefore, that the first human families
were matrilineal and matrilocal; only relationships through
females were recognized, women remained with their mother's
family and men at least retained their allegiance to the maternal
clan, whether or not they married outside it. The brother-sister
relationship was stronger than the husband-wife relationship,
and males supported, defended and when they died passed their
property on to their sisters' children rather than to those of their
wives.

As McLennan showed, such matrilineal, matrilocal systems
are not uncommon among existing primitive peoples, and it is
unreasonable to suggest that they may "rank among the normal
(if not universal) phenomena of human development" (p.90). For
whether or not monogamy existed prior to the recognition of
blood relationships, it seems probable at least that the maternal
relationship would be recognized first, simply because it is, of
biological necessity, closer and more intimate than the paternal
relationship. McLennan's theory as to the stages of development
whereby matriliny generally gave way to patriliny is considerably
less plausible. The process, he argues, begins with the practice of
female infanticide, which must have been very comon among
primitive societies, because females "would be less capable of

self-support, and contributing, by their exertions, to the common good." (p.68)

This shortage of females had, according to McLennan, three general consequences: polyandry, exogamy and marriage by capture. In the "ruder" form of polyandry, one woman is married to a set of men who are not brothers. Once kinship through females is recognized, it becomes the basis of the "higher" form of polyandry, in which a woman is married to a set of brothers. Meanwhile exogamy and marriage by capture arose together, a necessary correlation since wives from other groups could only be obtained, at first, by violence. (McLennan invented the terms "exogamy"—marriage *outside* the family, clan or tribe—and "endogamy"—marriage *within* the group—and started a still unsettled dispute as to how and why these distinct marital customs came about.) These three consequences of female infanticide together pave the way for the rise of the patrilineal system. Captured women are married to a group of brothers, and in time their offspring come to be considered that of the eldest brother only. In this way, the concept of kinship through males was established, and with the growth of private property and "the practice of sons succeeding, as heirs direct, to the estates of fathers" (p.98) agnatic kinship gradually replaced kinship through females as the basis of the family system.

This theory of the stages of social evolution is vulnerable at nearly every point, and has long been thoroughly discredited. Nevertheless, McLennan's challenge to the millenia-old presumption that the patriarchal family is the natural and original form of human life was extremely important. His claim that matrilineal family systems generally precede patrilineal ones is unproven and perhaps unprovable; but it is not inconsistent with existing evidence. Furthermore, the very existence of matrilineal/matrilocal cultures—which generally, though not always, afford women a more equal social status than our own culture does—poses a challenge to the sort of simple-minded biological determinism with respect to sex roles which prevailed in McLennan's day and is by no means extinct in our own.

1. Editor's introduction, p. xxi.
2. Bachofen, *Das Mutterrecht* (Stuttgart, 1861).

MEAD, Margaret (1901–1978). *Sex and Temperament in Three Primitive Societies* (William Morrow and Company, New York,

1963; first published 1935)
Male and Female: A Study of the Sexes in a Changing World (Dell
Publishing Company, New York, 1971; first published 1949)

Sex and Temperament is an important landmark in the study of
sex roles; it has done more than any other single work to undermine the presumption that our own cultural stereotypes of masculinity and femininity are universal and biologically inevitable.
Mead set out to study the social conditioning of the personalities
of males and females in order, by contrast and comparison between different cultures, to shed light on the extent to which our
concepts of masculinity and femininity are merely "social constructs, originally irrelevant to the biological facts of sex-gender."
(p. ix) To this end she studied and lived among three primitive
peoples of the Sepik region of New Guinea, "the gentle moun-
tain-dwelling Arapesh, the fierce cannibalistic Mundugumor,
and the graceful head-hunters of Tchambuli." (*Loc. cit.*) Her
findings led her to the conclusion that most, though not necessarily all, of the temperamental characteristics which we associate
with one sex or the other are thus linked only through culture.

Mead describes the mountain Arapesh as a culture in which
both sexes are conditioned from birth towards traits which we
regard as feminine; both Arapesh men and Arapesh women are
"placid, contented, unaggressive and noninitiatory, non-com-
petitive and responsive, warm, docile and trusting." (p.40) The
land they inhabit is poor and game scarce, with hunger a frequent
reality. Both sexes are absorbed in the task of growing food and
children. Neither is highly sexed or sexually aggressive. They do
not hunt heads or wage war, and their mountainous territory
protects them from incursions by their fiercer neighbors. Marriage is patrilocal and patrilineal; young girls are married to older
boys well before the age of puberty. The husband and his family
are responsible for feeding the young wife, and are therefore said
to "grow" her. This debt, plus the husband's greater maturity,
accounts for the wife's obligation and tendency to defer to her
husband, in spite of the absence of temperamental differences
between them. Deviant Arapesh, those who are aggressive, competitive or highly sexed, are not punished in any official way, but
are treated as outcasts.

The Mundugumor, on the other hand, are a caricature of our
culture's traditional concept of masculinity. Both men and wom-
en are aggressive, argumentative, jealous and highly sexed. Children are regarded as nuisances and potential rivals by women
and men alike. There is a minimum of cooperation between
households, a situation made possible by the richness of the

marshy riverside they inhabit. The men are head hunters (or were until just three years before Mead began her study) and prey upon surrounding tribes; the women fish, and grow tobacco, their primary trade item. Marriage is polygamous and men become wealthy through the economic productivity of their wives; inheritance is not, however, patrilineal, as in the case of the Arapesh. Inheritance passes through a "rope" structure, in which sex alternates with each generation: property passes from a man to his daughter, his daughers' sons, his daughters' sons' daughters, and so on (or from a woman to her sons, her sons' daughters, etc.). Theoretically, marriage occurs through the process of sister-exchange, but men often coopt the rights of their sons by exchanging their daughters for additional wives. The mothers side with their sons in this struggle, preferring to add a daughter-in-law to the household rather than a rival wife.

The lake-dwelling Tchambuli are a "mirror-image" culture; there women exhibit many of the traits which we consider masculine, men many of those we consider feminine. The women are the economic providers; they provide the major food supply, fish, as well as producing the mosquito baskets (much in demand throughout the region) which are the tribe's main barter item. Tchambuli women are practical, efficient and unadorned, and they cooperate cheerfully with one another in all their work. Tchambuli men are economic dependents. They spend most of their time preparing for the presentation of religious spectacles, which are staged with the women and children as audience. They curl their hair and decorate themselves to attract the sexual attention of the women, who take the initiative in sexual interactions. Mead maintains that the women dominate the men, in spite of the fact that marriage is patrilineal and patrilocal, and outwardly patriarchal; the husband buys his wife from her father and she is theoretically his property. Despite this outward form, women's social influence is greater. Men are jealous and suspicious of one another, dependent upon women not just for economic but for emotional support.

The Tchambuli men were formerly head hunters, and the tradition remains that a boy must kill an "enemy" before his initiation; but they no longer kill an enemy in battle, and are instead provided with a helpless captive purchased from a neighboring tribe. This tradition too seemed to be dying out even before the government's intervention, and Mead does not consider it to be evidence that the men were more aggressive or socially powerful than the women. She does point out, however, that "the men are, after all stronger, and a man can beat his wife, and this serves to confuse the whole issue of female dominance." (p.264)

Mead concludes from these findings that "many, if not all of the personality traits which we have called masculine or feminine are as lightly linked to sex as are the clothing, the manners, and the form of head-dress that a society at a given period assigns to either sex." (p.280) Each culture picks out certain character traits which are found in some individuals of either sex, to emphasize in one or both sexes. Where personality is thus stereotyped, either in the uniform, sex-neutral fashion of the Arapesh and the Mundugumor or in the sexually dichotomized manner of the Tchambuli, and of our own culture, it is inevitable that certain individuals whose personal propensities do not fit the prescribed pattern will be condemned to the status of cultural deviants, their lives rendered difficult and their potential contributions to society lost. In our own culture, where aggressiveness is labeled masculine and submissiveness feminine, men who are not particularly aggressive and women who are not particularly submissive are condsidered deviant and led to doubt their masculinity or femininity. Indeed, American subcultures are so diverse with respect to sexual attitudes and expectations that no one can perfectly conform to all of the various standards of masculinity and femininity. Under such conditions there is room for virtually everyone to doubt their membership in their own sex, and everyone suffers as a result.

Mead advocates the elimination of the sexual stereotyping of personality; not through the adoption of a single, sex-neutral stereotype, as in the case of the Arapesh or the Mundugumor, but through the recognition and acceptance of a much wider range of temperamental endowments in individuals of both sexes. She maintains that to eliminate the divergent social attitudes towards women and men, differences in their legal status, and so on, would be a step backwards if it meant a reduction in human diversity. What is needed is a greater respect for human individuality, such that "no skill, no special aptitude, no vividness of imagination or precision of thinking would go unrecognized because the child who possessed it was of one sex rather than the other." (p.321)

In *Male and Female*, Mead seeks to go further than *Sex and Temperament*, to reveal not just the cross-cultural variations in masculine and femine roles, but "positive findings about similarities, about the essentials in maleness and femaleness with which every society must reckon." (p.59) She draws her data from comparisons of the sex-role customs of seven South Seas peoples, the three New Guinea tribes dealt with in *Sex and Temperament*, the Samoans, the Manus of the Admiralty Islands, the Balinese, and the Iatmul, another group of New Guinea head hunters. Whatever their culture or personality type, she argues, human males and females face certain basic regularities in their development. Girls are naturally less apt to be outgoing, aggressive and achievement oriented, because "the female child's earliest experience is one of closeness to her own nature," (p.158) i.e. to her mother, a person of the same sex, and also because a girl learns very early that she will in time experience the supreme fulfillment of motherhood, not by effort and striving but simply because she *is* a female. The male, on the other hand, faces an early need to differentiate himself from the mother by his own activity and initiative.

This male assertiveness, Mead notes, is reduced where males take an active role in childrearing, as among the Arapesh; but it has other roots as well. In every culture men tend to envy women's procreative power, and to seek compensatory modes of achievement. "The recurrent problem of civilization is to define the male role satisfactorily enough . . . so that the male may in the course of his life reach a solid sense of irreversible achievement, of which his childhood knowledge of the satisfactions of childbearing has given him only a glimpse." (p.168) To achieve a comparable sense of achievement, women need only to be permitted to fulfill their biological role. Consequently, every culture assists men's need for a sense of achievement by attaching higher status to men's activities, whatever they may be, than to women's. If women are to be as ambitious as men, they must be made so by education, and very few cultures have found, or even sought, ways to give women "a divine discontent that will demand other satisfactions than those of child-bearing." (p.169)

A successful culture, Mead holds, must provide for the needs of both sexes; if one sex suffers from artificial restrictions or inadequate outlets for its drives the other sex suffers too. Judged by this criterion, the American culture is not particularly successful. Women in America are not an abused minority, but neither are they given true equality. America presents "the contradictory picture of a society that appears to throw its doors wide open to women, but translates her [sic] every step towards success as having been damaging—to her own chances of marriage and to the men whom she passes on the road." (p.301) Men are driven to constantly prove their masculinity by achievement, by beating others—especially women—at every game, while women are taught that achievement will be bought at the cost of their own femininity and the masculinity of men. As a result each sex tends to envy the other, and the disadvantages for each are great.

What we must strive to do, then, is to eliminate the artificial stereotyping of personality traits which are in fact found in both sexes, and of roles and activities in which both sexes could usefully participate, without at the same time minimizing or denying the real differences between the sexes, "the differential vulnerability of either sex, the learnings that are harder for boys, the learnings that are harder for girls, the periods of greater physical vulnerability for one sex than the other." (p.346) It is evident that the passage between the Scylla of false sexual stereotyping and the Charybdis of denying genuine differences is narrow and perilous.

MEDICINE AND WOMEN Of all the male-dominated professions, none has resisted female participation or competition more rigorously than that of medicine. Most medical schools, here and in Europe, excluded women entirely until the latter part of the nineteenth century or later. Female midwives and other informally trained women practitioners of the healing arts were harassed for hundreds of years, first by the Church and state, on the suspicion of witchcraft, and then by organized medicine and licensing requirements for which the male medical profession campaigned (1). Women still constitute only about 7 percent of American physicians, although in some countries the figure is much higher (about 70 percent in the Soviet Union).

The result of this male monopolization of the practice of medicine has been not only a limitation of women's professional opportunities, and not only much higher medical costs than were the rule earlier when most medical and obstetric care was provided by midwives and folk healers (many of them women); but also a distressing history of medical malpractice directed largely against women. The history of obstetrics and gynecology is replete with horror stories, from the surgical mutilations (ovaridectomy and clitoridectomy) practiced on women who were thought to have psychological problems, to the excessive and unsafe use of drugs, instruments and Caesarian sections to intervene in the birth process—abuses which have by no means entirely ended. (See Arms, Barker-Benfield, Dreifus, and Frankfort, in Anthologies III.) The American Medical Association has campaigned for laws prohibiting abortion, (2) and has never lent its full support to the struggle to make safe and effective methods of contraception available to all women.

Furthermore, leading members of the medical profession have always—as contemporary feminist critics have shown—supported the most derogatory and reactionary views about the nature of women. That women are inherently masochistic; that they *need* to experience pain; that they lack intellect and emotional control; that they are prone to invent or exaggerate symptoms; these are ideas which one can still find promulgated in at least some medical and psychiatric texts (3). In short, the history of modern medicine provides many case studies in the formation and reinforcement of patriarchal ideology, and the subversion of science to the political ends of the dominant class.

1. See *Witches, Midwives, and Nurses: A History of Women Healers*, by Barbara Ehrenreich and Deirdre English (The Feminist Press, Old Westbury, New York, 1973).
2. See James G. Mohr, *Abortion in America* (Oxford University Press, 1979).
3. See Kay Weiss, "What Medical Students Learn About Women," in *Seizing Our Bodies*, edited by Claudia Dreifus, Anthologies III.

MENCKEN, H.L. (1880–1956). *In Defense of Women* (Time Incorporated, New York, 1963; first published 1922)

A raucous satirical essay, in which Mencken reveals his admiration for the ideas of Friedrich Nietzsche and Herbert Spencer, and his contempt for both women and the "common herd." Women, he argues, are too intelligent to want to be liberated. They are far more practical and cagey than men, not because their brains are different, but because they have to be more clever than men in order to maneuver them into marriage. Their mental superiority is a compensation for their physical inferiority, which includes a natural lack of beauty. Because marriage is a much better bargain for women than for men, women usually marry men who are their intellectual inferiors, while the most intelligent men tend to avoid marriage or to postpone it until late in life when it becomes more of a necessity and less of a burden. Mencken's fear that the best genes are thus lost to the species leads him to suggest the legalization of polygamy and a return to the harsh marriage laws that gave men control over their wives' property and the right to "discipline" them, in order to make marriage more attractive to "superior" men.

As for the feminists, whom he calls the "ex-suffragettes" (the vote having recently been won), Mencken advises women to ignore them, claiming that they are all ugly and frustrated spinsters who have been unable to get a man of their own and want other women to also be deprived of the advantages of marriage. Advocates of equality between the sexes fail to understand the age-old wisdom of women, which is none other than what Nietzsche called the slave morality. The supposed selflessness and devotion of the feminine woman are a bold deception, a mask concealing her wholly self-interested motives. Women would be wise to preserve that mask and not to challenge the superficial privileges of men; for if they insist on equality and on competing with men in the worldly professions, then men will cease to treat them with special consideration, and regard them as simply competitors in a harsh contest. Since women cannot hope to prevail in such a competition they will soon wish they had left well alone. (See Gilder, Vilar for contemporary versions of the same thesis.)

MENSTRUATION   As Simone de Beauvoir points out, menstruation is one of the uniquely female biological functions which, because they have been culturally interpreted as proofs of female weakness and inferiority, have served to conceal from women their own freedom and possibilities. Aristotle thought that women menstruate because, being colder than men, they cannot "concoct" semen; menstrual blood is incompletely concocted semen. But menstruation has not only been interpreted as a sign of female weakness, but also as a powerful, dangerous and polluting phenomenon. Primitive peoples throughout the world have been reported to believe in the evil influence of menstrual blood and menstruating women. (See for instance Malinowski, Mead, and Strathern on menstrual taboos among various cultures in New Guinea.) Delaney, Lupton, and Toth, in their popular study of cultural attitudes towards menstruation, argue that in primitive and civilized cultures alike, menstrual taboos have been a part of sexual politics, an excuse used to exclude women from whatever high-status roles men wished to reserve for themselves.

Superstitious beliefs about menstruation and its psychological side effects persist in our own day. There are still those who believe that women's "raging hormonal imbalances" disqualify them for high public office. (See Hormones.) In reality, the inherent psychological effects of the menstrual cycle, to the extent they do exist, are virtually impossible to distinguish from those which are induced (or imagined) because of the general *belief* that women tend to be irritable and emotionally unstable during the days just prior to menstruation (1). Nevertheless, the belief persists that the (pre) menstrual period is necessarily a difficult time for women, and that its implications are entirely negative. The psychoanalyst Erik Erikson illustrates the lengths to which this is taken; he holds that women are prone to a certain kind of despair, a despair of "emptiness," which

> can be re-experienced in each menstruation, it is a crying to heaven in the mourning over a child; and it becomes a permanent scar in the menopause (2).

Feminists have responded with indignation to such pseudo-scientific claims, which tend to vastly exaggerate the difficulties associated with what, for most women, is little more than a "friendly monthly nuisance." (Delaney, p. 2) Some feminist medical self-help groups have experimented with menstrual extraction, as a way of taking control of this process which has been thought to exercise so much control over us. (See Frankfort in Anthologies III.) Delaney, Lupton and Toth suggest that medical science should concentrate more resources on finding ways to eliminate menstruation, or at least its more undesirable side effects. But increased medical intervention in the process may also be counterproductive, a reinforcement of the idea that menstruation is inherently pathological. A more promising approach is to provide better public education on the subject and to try to improve our understanding of it, without focusing unduly on its deleterious effects and without falling prey to ancient or modern superstitions about it.

Scriven (1979, personal communication) has this comment on the moral aspect of "menstrual discrimination":

> The essential ethical point here is that no conclusions about the unfitness of a particular woman for e.g. a position of responsibility, can be drawn from the fact of female menstruation without (a) violating the right of each individual to be judged on their own merits (since the effects are often negligible); (b) assuming that men lack equally severe mood alternations of a (possibly) less regular kind; (c) assuming that a society which may have created whatever psychological effects there are can then use them to discriminate against them. Our posture and procedures with respect to minorities show that we have clearly rejected each of these fallacies in that case of discrimination; we are not yet so clear in this case.

1. See Hammer, and Lips and Colwill, in Anthologies III and XIII respectively.

2.   Erik Erikson, "Womanhood and the Inner Space," in *Women and Analysis*, edited by Jean Strouse (Anthologies XIII), pp. 305–306.

MERRIAM, Eve. *After Nora Slammed the Door* (World Publishing Company, New York, 1958)
   A voice from a period in which feminism seemed wholly eclipsed, protesting women's retreat back into the doll's house of wife and motherhood. Merriam uses a mixture of poetry, humor and sarcasm to debunk the myth of the American matriarchy, and the notion that housewifery is fulfillment for a woman. Capitalism, the shortage of jobs and the isolation of the nuclear family have made it nearly impossible for women to have both homes and useful well-paid work outside them. The Venus of Willendorf, and other prehistoric representations of the mother goddess, provide a glimpse into an era in which women's reproductive capacity was a source of worldly influence rather than a liability that resulted in their being excluded from the affairs of the world. We need to lighten the burden of motherhood, e.g. by child-care centers and programs to help women enter or reenter the job market. The book includes an ahead-of-its-time critique of sexist linguistic practices such as calling mature women "girls," the woman's loss of her name upon marriage, and the so-called generic "man."

MILL, Harriet Taylor: see Taylor, Harriet

MILL, John Stuart (1806–1873). *Early Essays on Marriage and Divorce*, in *Essays on Sex Equality*, edited by Alice Rossi (University of Chicago Press, Chicago and London, 1979; written 1832)
The Subjection of Women (M.I.T. Press, Cambridge, Massachusetts, 1970; first published London, 1869, by Longman's, Green, Reader and Dyer)
   John Stuart Mill is a giant figure in nineteenth-century British philosophy, a brilliant and passionate defender of libertarian and utilitarian principles, and one of the very few male philosophers in history to recognize that a much greater degree of equality between the sexes is necessitated by both moral and pragmatic considerations. Mill is famous as a child prodigy; his philosopher father, James Mill, believed that all human beings have the capac-

ity for genius if properly educated, and therefore exposed his son to a staggering dose of early training in the sciences and humanities, and in the utilitarian moral philosophy developed by Jeremy Bentham and himself.

Utilitarianism is central to Mill's moral and political thought; it is, essentially, the doctrine that what is morally right, and what social institutions ought to be designed to promote, is the greatest good for the greatest number of people, with the good of each person counting for no more and no less than that of any other. Utilitarians differ as to just how this intrinsic moral good is to be defined. Mill defined it as happiness, or pleasure and the absence of pain—that is the greatest possible surplus of pleasure over pain—a formulation which is consistent with his psychological thesis that all human action is ultimately motivated by the desire for pleasure or the avoidance of pain (1). Fortunately, although all of the moral arguments in *The Subjection of Women* proceed logically from this utilitarian foundation, none of them depend upon the validity of Mill's particular formulation of the utilitarian principle; they are independently persuasive and capable of being couched in terms of any humanistic, libertarian and egalitarian ethical theory. Nevertheless, it was Mill's utilitarianism—the principles of liberty and equality which he derived from it—which he applied to the relationship between the sexes, as few previous utilitarians had thought to do (2), and which shaped his feminism.

Another influence on Mill's feminist philosophy was Harriet Taylor, his friend and companion for twenty-eight years (and his wife for the last seven). Theirs was a unique love story as well as a fruitful intellectual collaboration (3). Mill credits Taylor with having originated or helped in the development of many of the ideas in his *Principles of Political Economy*, *On Liberty*, and in *The Subjection of Women*, although the *Subjection* was not written until 1861, two years after her death (4). Taylor's influence on Mill's thought is not clear; it *is* clear from what little she herself wrote that on several key points she was a much more radical feminist than Mill. Whatever its sources, the *Subjection* is a triumph of lucid argumentation, and one of the milestones of liberal feminist thought.

Mill begins by anticipating the extreme difficulty of ever persuading people, by rational argument, of the wrongfulness of men's domination of women. Their prejudice is a predictable result of the fact that male supremacy is the universal social custom. But the existence of such a custom can serve as an argument for its continuation only if the custom cannot be shown to have originated from causes other than its practical and moral soundness. Male domination was not instituted because it was found to be the best system, other systems having been tried and found wanting. "It arose," Mill says,

> simply from the fact that from the very earliest twilight of human society, every woman (owing to the value attached to her by man, combined with her inferiority in muscular strength), was found in a state of bondage to some man. (p.7)

Thus, Mill claims, woman was a slave from the beginning (5), and her present secondary and dependent status is merely "the primitive state of slavery lasting on" (p.7), into an historical age in which most other forms of slavery are being mitigated or abolished. It is understandable, he says, "that this branch of the system of right founded on might . . . would be the very last to disappear" (p.8); for not only do men inevitably retain the advantage of superior physical strength, but they are able, through all the forces of law, custom, education and social conditioning, to keep women "in a chronic state of bribery and intimidation combined." (p.12) Because men want not only women's obedience but their *willing* obedience,

> They have . . . put everything in practice to enslave their minds. . . . All women are brought up from the very earliest years in the belief that their ideal of character is the very opposite to that of man; not self-will, and government by self-control, but submission, and yielding to the control of others. (p. 16)

Custom, therefore, "affords . . . no presumption . . . in favor of the arrangements which place women in social and political subjection to men." (p.17) On the contrary, male domination is a "relic of the past [which] is discordant with the future, and must necessarily disappear." (p.17) For the whole trend of modern history, Mill optimistically maintains, is towards greater individual freedom and equality of opportunity, towards the ideal state of affairs in which all individuals will choose or earn their place in life according to their own interests and abilities, unrestricted by any accident of birth. If this is indeed a desirable goal, then

> we ought to act as if we believed it, and not to ordain that to be born a girl instead of a boy, any more than to be born black instead of white, or a commoner instead of a nobleman, shall decide a person's position through all life. (p.19)

Mill concludes, therefore, that women are entitled to exactly the same moral and legal rights as men: to complete control of their property and persons, after as well as before marriage; to vote and serve in governmental and other capacities; and to practice any profession for which they can become qualified, on exactly the same terms as men. The primary line of argument against these conclusions is that women are in some way intellectually inferior, incapable of this or that crucial intellectual performance. Previous ages, Mill notes, have been content to justify the subjection of women by its expediency (for men); but the present age feels compelled to claim that it is actually done for women's own good, because of the natural difference between women and men. To this he replies that nothing whatever can be known about the natures of the two sexes, "as long as they have only been seen in their present relation to one another."

Mill's argument here is simple and powerful: there is no justification for supposing that any of the observable differences between the characters and capacities of men and women are "natural," unless these differences cannot in any way be explained as a result of the differences in their education or their objective situation. And in fact, the distorted education which women receive, the "hot house and stove cultivation [that] has always been carried on of some of the capabilities of their nature, for the benefit and pleasure of their masters" (p.22), is fully sufficient to explain any observable differences in women's mental traits. Besides, Mill notes, we do not even really know what women's *actual* mental traits are, since men's observations of women are apt to be very incomplete and inaccurate. Most men never even understand the women they live with, in part because woman's inferior position is "unpropitious to complete sincerity and openness" (p.25) with men. Thus, he concludes,

> it is at present impossible that any man, or all men taken together, should have the knowledge which can qualify them to lay down the law to women as to what is, or is not, their vocation. (p.27)

Where Mill speaks of marriage he at times sounds almost like a modern radical feminist; for he not only equates marriage (under the harsh laws which existed in his time) with slavery, but blames the unjust power of men over their wives for a profound and socially disastrous corruption in the moral character of men. "The family at present," he says, "is a school of despotism"; for

> the almost unlimited power which present social institutions give to the man over at least one human being, the one with whom he resides . . . seeks out and evokes the latent germs of selfishness in the remotest corners of his nature . . . [and] offers him a licence for the indulgence of those points of his original character which in all other relations he would have found it necessary to repress and conceal." (p.37)

It is true, he says, that a wife has the power to make her husband miserable in turn, by scolding and nagging; but this is at best a countertyranny, and one which is effective only against men who are not wholly corrupt. It is also true that not all men take advantage of their legal power to treat their wives as slaves; but "laws and institutions require to be adapted, not to good men, but to bad." (p.35) For the happiness and personal growth of both parties, marriage must be a partnership between social, legal and intellectual equals; there would be no need for one to command and the other to obey, but rather particular responsibilities and authority would be divided on the basis of comparative qualifications.

Nevertheless, Mill stops short of advocating any basic change in the traditional division of labor within marriage; for he does not see in this division anything inconsistent with true equality. While he insists that the *power* to provide her own means of support in a respectable profession is necessary if a woman is to be independent and self-respecting, he denies that it is necessary or, as a rule, desirable that she *actually* do so, after she is married. Instead, he says that

> the common arrangement, by which the man earns the income and the wife superintends the domestic expenditure, seems to me in general the most suitable division of labour between the two persons. (p.48)

If, Mill thinks, the law treated both parties to the marriage contract equally, if the professions were open to women should they choose to enter them, and if honorable legal separation (if not divorce) were available in the case of an unworkable marriage, then there would be no need for a married woman to work outside the home in order to be the man's equal, and it would generally be impractical for her to do so.

Mill's argument for this latter claim reveals a curious blind spot. He quite correctly points out that

> If, in addition to the physical suffering of bearing children, and the whole responsibility of their care and education in early years, the wife undertakes the careful and economical application of the husband's earnings to the general comfort of the family; she takes not only her fair share, but usually the larger share, of the bodily and mental exertion required by their joint existence. (p.48)

But he does not ask just why it ought to be taken for granted that the entire responsibility for the care and education of children and the supervision of the household should automatically be the woman's. By his own arguments, there is no justification for assuming either that women are naturally better suited for such work than men, or that all of the domestic responsibilities must be borne by one partner alone rather than by both. Nor does he consider the difficulty of maintaining a relationship of equality when the work of one partner is paid but that of the other is not.

It is interesting that Mill and Taylor differed on this particular point. In her article on the "Enfranchisement of Women," (6) Taylor holds that to be independent and self-respecting a woman must not only be *able* to earn her own living, but must actually do so. Mill's more conservative position is a symptom of his tendency to mingle two ideas; on the one hand, his vision of complete equality between the sexes, presupposing no innate mental differences between them, and on the other a somewhat contradictory and romantic vision of woman as the loyal helpmate and inspiring complement of man. In his early essay on marriage and divorce, Mill supports his claim that it will be for the happiness of both partners that the wife not support herself economically by the following revealing remarks:

> her occupation should rather be to adorn and beautify [life] . . . Except in the actual class of day-labourers, that be her natural task, if task it can be called, which will in so great a measure be accomplished by *being* rather than doing . . . If she loves, her natural impulse will be to share *his* occupations . . . (7)

To be sure, Mill expresses no such blatantly androcentric opinions about woman's role in the *Subjection*. Nevertheless, a slight weakness for the notion of woman as the natural complement of man still surfaces occasionally, as when he claims that women tend to have a clearer perception of immediate fact than men, as a result of which

> Hardly anything can be of greater value to a man of theory and speculation . . . than to carry on his speculations in the companionship, and under the criticism, of a really superior woman. (p.59)

He does not hesitate, furthermore, to speculate that since women's brains are smaller than men's they tire more quickly, and that therefore women excel at sudden insights (intuitions) and tasks that can be performed quickly, while men excel at intellectual tasks which require "long hammering at a single thought." (p.66)

In these respects, Mill was clearly a product of his age rather than a prophet. So too, he was prototypically Victorian in his attitude towards the physical act of sex, which he views as a base animal impulse needing to be kept under the strict control of reason.

Nevertheless, his systematic grounding of feminist conclusions on utilitarian moral principles remains valuable, and is indeed one of the very few serious explorations (Simone de Beauvoir's **The Second Sex** is another) of the relationship between feminism and more general ethical theories. Bridging the theoretical gap between feminist conclusions and other normative philosophical systems is necessary not only to assure the firmest foundations and clearest demonstration of the truth of those conclusions, but also to help purge the abstract science of ethics of whatever masculine biases it may otherwise retain. It is regretable that Mill's efforts have, at least until recently, inspired very few serious philosophers to work along similar lines (8).

1. See Mill's **Utilitarianism** (Bobb-Merrrill Co., Inc., New York, 1971; first published 1861). There are many philosophical problems with the greatest happiness principles as a criterion of moral rightness, for instance that it appears to conflict with justice or the moral rights of the individual in some cases, namely those in which the greatest happiness of the majority would be promoted by a sacrifice of the rights of an individual. Revisons of utilitarianism have been proposed that supposedly handle this classic difficulty.
2. William Thompson is one earlier utilitarian thinker who did consider the consequences of the theory for the relation between the sexes. Thompson attacked James Mill for accepting the legal doctrine that because a woman's interests are "included" in those of her husband or father, she need not have independent legal or political rights. (See Thompson, William)
3. The story is well told by Alice Rossi, in her introduction to **Essays on Sex Equality**, which is a collection of all the known writings of both Mill and Taylor on that subject. (See Taylor, Harriet)
4. Mill delayed publishing the essay until 1869, when he thought that the public was more ready for it.
5. Mill presumably had not been exposed to (or impressed by) the notion, popular later in the nineteenth century and still defended today, that the earliest human societies were in some sense matriarchal, and that it was private property and other aspects of civilized culture that brought about the downfall of woman.
6. In Rossi, p.105; originally published in the **Westminster Review**, July 1851.
7. Rossi, pp.76–77.

8.   See Julia Annas, "Mill and the Subjection of Women" (*Philosophy*, Vol. 52, No. 200, April 1977, pp.179–194) for an excellent critical analysis of *The Subjection of Women*.

MILLER, Casey and **SWIFT**, Kate. *Words and Women: New Language in New Times* (Anchor, Garden City, New York, 1977)
   A good summary of the issues surrounding sexist linguistic usages and recent efforts to alter them. It contains a critical discussion of practices such as calling a woman by her husband's last (or even first *and* last, as in "Mrs. John Doe") name, giving girls names which are diminutives or frivolous sounding, calling women by their first names under circumstances in which men are called by their last, adding -ess or -ette to a neutral noun to signify that the referent is female, and using masculine singular pronouns when the sex of the referent is undetermined. The so-called generic use of 'man,' to refer to the human species or a typical person (as in "A man must pay his taxes.") is a myth; for it is usually impossible to tell from the context whether or not the "generic" sense is intended, and even where it is, the word clearly retains masculine connotations which distort the allegedly neutral meaning.
   Such practices express and perpetuate the cultural assumption that the male is the norm, the female a deviation. The authors carefully state and reply to the many common arguments against eliminating sexist usages, arguing that if left to change at its own rate or held artificially stable, language becomes a reactionary force. A number of realistic specific suggestions are made, e.g. using "they" instead of "he" where the sex is unspecified, a practice which they show has actually been accepted in the best literary circles for centuries. (See Marie Ritchie Key and Robin Lakoff for further discussions of sexism in language.)

MILLER, Jean Baker. *Toward a New Psychology of Women* (Beacon Press, Boston, 1976)
   This is a brief and simply written book which presents some basic feminist observations in an unusually clear and persuasive form. Miller does not address the question of innate psychological differences between the sexes, but focuses instead on their different psychological histories in a male-dominated society. As a subordinated class, women share many stereotypical psychological traits with other subordinate groups. But women have also had a special role in the family which is not shared by other

oppressed groups. This special role has developed certain strengths in women, strengths which have been much less well developed in men; these include women's so-called "intuition" (a fine attunement to the emotions of those around them); the ability to participate in the development of others; cooperation; and the capacity to create new visions of what it is to be a person. These are the elements of human experience which our patriarchal society projects onto women and not onto other subordinate groups; for though men reject these traits in themselves, they need them close at hand to service basic human needs.

Miller points out that because these virtues are socially devalued at the same time that they are projected onto women, women in our culture are constantly made to feel inadequate. The myth of feminine evil persists, since

> even in their traditional roles, women, *by their very existence*, confront and challenge men because they have been made *the embodiment of the dominant culture's unsolved problems.* (p.56)

As a result, women are often left with a global sense of being in the wrong, precisely because of their most socially valuable traits. The dominant culture defines them as passive and wholly oriented towards service to others, and women have usually accepted this definition of themselves. When women accept this definition, they do not engage in open conflict with men; instead conflict becomes constant but covert, waged around unreal issues rather than the true source of their discomfort.

Miller argues that because of the social definition of women as passive, women do not have egos in the classical Freudian sense. Because women lack the right to judge their actions with respect to direct benefit to themselves, they are forced to organize their lives, not around a direct relation to reality, but through an attempt "to transform their drives into the service of another's drives." (p.72) Thus, they tend to value affiliation above all other achievements, as the source of their sense of self. This is both a fundamental strength of women and the source of many of their current problems; for up to now the only affiliations available to women have been subservient ones.

The challenge to women now, Miller concludes, is to put their special psychological strengths to use in the service of their own ends. They must take collective action, thereby initiating open and productive conflict in place of the covert and destructive conflict which has previously characterized the war between the sexes. Till now, their strengths have not been a source of power in the world; but they will be, as they move out of their powerless position. The emergence of women will force society to change, by confronting men "with the need to reintegrate many of the essentials of human development—the essentials that women have been carrying for the total society." (p.120)

MILLETT, Kate. *Sexual Politics* (Avon Books, New York, 1971; first published 1969)
   This is the book which more than any other—with the possible exception of Betty Friedan's *The Feminine Mystique*—signaled the onset of the second great wave of feminist activism in this century. But while Friedan is a liberal feminist who has fought for reform, Millett is a radical who speaks of revolution. She sees in sexual domination the psychological and ideological core of racism, classism, imperialism, and virtually all other forms of bigotry and exploitation. Under patriarchy, sex is a status category which overrides even race and class as a determinant of power and status.
   Millet declines to speculate on the historical origins or biological basis of patriarchy, considering all such speculations inconclusive at best. She rejects the Marxist theory of the origin of patriarchy through the institution of monogamous marriage as question-begging, but accepts Engels' analysis of the oppressive financial nature and basis of the family. She concludes that if the sexual revolution is to progress beyond superficial reforms of the political system then the family must go, at least as an economic and childrearing unit. So must sexual taboos of all sorts, the double standard, prostitution, and above all the misogynist patriarchal psychology. Most of the work is devoted to the analysis of this psychology and its contempory literature.
   It was, Millett says, primarily the Marxists' ignorance of the power of patriarchal attitudes which led to the failure of the Soviet experiment in sexual revolution. In the West, patriarchal attitudes have received a powerful new pseudo-scientific underpinning in the psychoanalytic theories of Freud and his followers. Freud insidiously slides from empirical observation and description, e.g. of the symptoms of his neurotic female patients, to barely concealed prescription, maintaining that passivity, narcissism, masochism and envy of the male are the defining traits not merely of women as an oppressed, low-status group, but of woman's eternal and therefore proper nature. Contemporary psychologists like Erik Erikson continue to mistake obviously learned behavior—like that of the boys and girls in Erikson's famous block-building experiment, who preferred to depict ad-

venturous external and domestic internal spaces, respectively—
for biological givens.

But it is above all in literature, particularly the works of D.H.
Lawrence, Henry Miller and Norman Mailer, that Millett finds
the essence of the patriarchal ideology. Lawrence transforms
male ascendency into a mystical religion; without entirely deper-
sonalizing woman or abandoning the romantic ideal of sexual
love, he depicts her salvation through the passive worship of the
wonderful male phallus, her ultimate fulfillment through total
and self-annihilating submission. Miller, on the other hand, is as
unromantic and nonmystical in his treatment of sex as it is possible to be. For him the ideal woman is a mindless whore, the ideal
sexual interaction a quick rape-like act which achieves a maximum humiliation and depersonalization of the woman. "The
unconscious logic appears to be that, since sex defiles the female,
females who consent to sexuality deserve to be defiled as completely as possible." (p.309) This pernicious notion is the fundamental Judeo-Christian core of contemporary patriarchal ideology. Miller's openly sadistic attitudes constitute important cultural data, previously hidden under polite fictions, like the seductive myth that women are "separate but equal" under patriarchy. In reality women are deeply despised in the "men's
houses" of our culture, where violence resulting from repressed
homosexuality is turned outward against women, in a process
which is taken to be the very essence of masculinity.

Norman Mailer is well aware of this process whereby repressed
homosexual urges are converted into misogynous violence, but
incredibly enough he considers it both natural and good. He
quite consciously identifies sex with murder, a crime he considers
far less noxious than the homosexuality for which it is a substitute. If Mailer is right about the link between male violence and
repressed homosexuality, then by seeking to reduce the irrational
fear of homosexuality the new sexual revolution is challenging
patriarchy's most basic categories of masculinity (violence, aggression, sadism) and femininity (passivity, victimization, masochism). Unlike Lawrence, Miller and Mailer, the French homosexual playwright Jean Genet recognized women (of both sexes)
as an oppressed group. Genet reveals, through his depictions of
the lives and interactions of male homosexuals, in prison and on
the street, that "masculinity" and "femininity" are assumed social roles of a most ridiculous and tragic sort. Like Millett, he "has
fastened upon the most fundamental of society's arbitrary follies,
its view of sex as a caste structure ratified by nature." (p.19)

MISOGYNY Misogyny is the hatred of women, or sometimes, more specifically and extremely, the belief that women are not only morally and intellectually inferior to men, but dangerous, and the source of much of the evil in the world. It is interesting that there is no parallel term for the hatred of men; "misanthropy" is hostility towards "mankind" in general, not towards males in particular. There is likewise relatively little hostility or derogation directed towards males as such by Western thinkers and writers, no doubt in large part because, until recently, the large majority of them have been men. Misogyny, on the other hand, has roots in the oldest Western traditions, from the Greek myth of Pandora and the Genesis tale of Eve's temptation and sin, to Aristotle's dictum that a woman is a misbegotten man. The greatest philosophers and theologians of the Christian tradition have been guilty of misogyny. (See St. Paul, Augustine, Aquinas; also Christianity.)

Of course, not all antifeminists are also misogynists. There have been many who praise women for their special virtues and consider them the moral superiors of men, even while consigning them to a very restricted role. (See Hume, Rousseau, Kant, Jung, Deutsch, Andelin, Gilder.) On the other hand, some of the greatest philosophers of the nineteenth century were blatant misogynists (see Schopenhauer, Kierkegaard, Nietzsche), and misogynist thought found perhaps its purest expression at the beginning of this century, in the work of Otto Weininger.

In our own time, there are still some striking examples of misogynist thought. (See Reyburn, Wylie, Mailer, Vilar.) But misogyny itself has also become a subject of study and analysis. Horney, Lederer, and Mead have suggested that misogyny is fundamentally a result of men's envy of the female's capacity to give birth, and their fear of the power which this capacity seems to imply. Histories of misogyny have been written. (See Bullough, Hayes, Porter, and O'Faolain, in Anthologies VII.) Feminists have analyzed the intensely misogynous attitudes of certain contemporary writers. (See de Beauvoir, Ellman, Millett.)

Some theorists who have sought to explain misogyny in terms of the psychoanalytic tradition have held that the only solution to men's hatred and fear of women is for the latter to remain strictly within the traditional feminine role, and not to arouse men's apprehensions or hostility by competing with them in any other area. (See Lederer, Stern.) But radical feminists, many of whom have also learned a great deal from Freud, have argued that it is precisely women's traditional role in the biological family which generates male misogyny. (See Dinnerstein, Firestone, Mitchell.)

The Jungian analyst Neumann explained the archetype of the Great Goddess and Earth Mother as a representation of the original, egoless state of consciousness, which the male must struggle to rise above. Dinnerstein points out that such an association is inevitable in any society in which children are raised almost exclusively by women; for in this situation the male will always regard the female as a retarding force from which he will seek to escape into an all-male environment. On this analysis, misogyny springs from the male's fear of being dragged back into a state of dependency, and his inability to treat females as equals is a reaction to the time when he himself first learned to submit to the authority of another, who happened to be a woman.

MITCHELL, Juliet. *Woman's Estate* (Random House, New York, 1971; first published 1963)
Psychoanalysis and Feminism: Freud, Reich, Laing and Women (Random House, New York, 1975)
   Woman's Estate is a study of the contemporary international women's movement, its ideological background and divisions, its origins in the 60s, and its relationship to and treatment within socialist theory. The two main splits Mitchell describes are between liberationists, who see women's struggle as an inseparable part of a larger struggle against all forms of oppression; radical feminists, who see the feminist revolution as a primary and somewhat independent goal; and liberal feminists, who think that sexual equality or at least significant movement towards it is possible without economic, social or political upheaval. Mitchell concentrates on the ideological division between the radical feminists and the (socialist) liberationists, and is critical of those on both sides.
   Marxists and the other socialists, she holds, are right to point out that the denigration of women, as sex objects and as unpaid or underpaid labor, is essential to capitalism as it is not to socialism. But socialists have been too ready to subsume women's oppression under some theory that fits earlier socialists' analyses. Marx and Engels, like most socialist theorists since them, blame women's second-class status under capitalism on their exclusion from productive labor, and hold that sexual equality will be impossible without socialism. They do not adequately explain how male domination comes about, either originally or in this day. Women's supposedly lesser capacity for labor has rarely resulted in their exclusion from labor; rather they have usually been the primary slaves of labor. We have seen that the entry of

massive numbers of women into the public labor process (e.g. in wartime) cannot in itself produce significant changes.

But while Marxists and socialist feminists fail to come to grips with women's particular situation, radical feminists, in their adherence to their feminist instincts, have failed to make adequate use of "scientific socialism" and other available tools for the analysis of women's condition. Millett's perspective is socialist but she provides no overall analysis, no explication of the relationship between the various mechanisms of oppression. Firestone's attempt to enlarge dialectical materialism to incorporate the effects of the biological division of the sexes is materialist but neither dialectical nor historical; it is in fact a retreat to the dualistic notions that preceded dialectical materialism.

Mitchell's own analysis stresses the differentiation of women's condition into four structures—production, reproduction, sexuality and the socialization of children. Modern capitalism binds the latter three structures together, under the embrace of the first, within the patriarchal family. Production is the husband's sphere, sexuality, reproduction and socialization the wife's. The patriarchal family is preserved under capitalism, even though technology has progressively eliminated the need for such a sexual division of labor, and even though women's position becomes as a result highly contradictory. To understand women's oppression within the family and its continuation, Mitchell suggests, we will have to make use of Freudian psychoanalytic theory, which she says is the only scientific method available for investigating this "biosocial universal."

In *Psychoanalysis and Feminism* Mitchell develops this last line of argument, and defends Freud's theory against the usual feminist charge that notions like penis envy merely express patriarchal prejudices against women. Freud depicted the psychic processes whereby patriarchal values are reestablished within each individual, in the context of the biological family. The theory, she says, is descriptive, not prescriptive, and its pessimism is a result of the condition of women, not of sexism on Freud's part. Mitchell gives a careful exposition of the theory of the Oedipus complex, which results in the development of femininity (passivity, masochism and narcissism) in girls—who, like boys are inherently bisexual, i.e. possessed of masculine as well as feminine capacities. She also examines the work of Wilhelm Reich and R.D. Laing, two psychoanalysts who have departed radically from Freud; she argues that neither has properly understood or made use of the notion of the unconscious, and that their theories are the poorer for this failure.

Feminists, because they have misunderstood Freud, have also failed to make use of his discoveries. From de Beauvoir to Friedan, Millett, Firestone and Greer, they accuse him of being unaware of social realities, unable in his preoccupation with infantile sexuality to see the importance of cultural conditioning in the production of femininity. They fail to see that what he was doing was *explaining* the society by showing how the patriarchal culture is recreated in each individual.

As there appears to be a somewhat uneasy tension between the emphasis of the first book and that of the second, Mitchell points out that Marx and Freud are closer in their theoretical explanations of the genesis of patriarchy than is generally realized. Engels thinks the rise of male domination is coincident with that of private property and monogamous marriage, whereas Freud saw patriarchy as a condition of all human society; they agree that all *civilization* is patriarchal. Mitchell thinks that contemporary anthropology, especially the work of Levi-Strauss, shows that Freud was closer to the truth. Levi-Strauss argues that human society began with the incest taboo and the demand for exogamy, which in practice means the exchange of women between family groups (men are never exchanged). This exchange is the first social contact between family groups, and it is what makes human culture possible; it also results in male domination.

Freud's Oedipus complex, Mitchell suggests, can be viewed, indeed was viewed by Freud, as a recapitulation of phylogyny, i.e. of the very process whereby man entered into human culture. In contemporary industrial society, however, the incest taboo and the family, which both preserves it and contradicts it, have outlived their usefulness. Humans are adequately bonded to one another by social institutions other than the incest-prohibiting biological family. The family has become redundant and contradiction-riddled and must therefore evolve. In its evolution lies the solution of the Oedipus complex and the end of the repressed condition which is femininity.

MONEY, John and **EHRHARDT**, Anke. *Man and Woman, Boy and Girl: The Differentiation and Dimorphism of Gender Identity from Conception to Maturity* (Mentor Books, New York, 1974; first published 1972)

An important scientific study of the development of sexual dimorphism (differences) in human physiology and behavior. Evidence is presented that physiological factors, particularly the presence or absence of male hormones (androgens) at crucial periods before and after birth, are a powerful influence not only on physical development but on the formation of gender identity—but not an influence which operates independently of environmental factors.

The authors find, for instance, that genetic females who are exposed *in utero* to excessive amounts of androgen tend to grow up as "tomboys," preferring vigorous physical activity to sedentary pursuits, and functional to "feminine" attire. They tend to compete with boys for peer-group status, but not to be especially aggressive in the sense of starting or engaging in fights or quarrels. This may show either that—contrary to popular opinion and the arguments of writers like Steven Goldberg—aggressiveness in the negative sense is *not* an innate part of the androgenic behavior pattern; or that if there is such a behavioral tendency associated with fetal androgenization it is one which can readily be overridden by environmental factors. Either way the finding can be of little comfort to those who maintain that males, because of their hormones, are naturally and inalterably more aggressive than females.

The authors also emphasize that in spite of the tomboyish behavior of fetally androgenized girls, which is paralleled by the lower than average level of physical activity observable in boys who have been feminized by a deficit of fetal androgens, the key variable in the determination of both gender identity and gender role (that is, the private experience of gender and its public expressions) is not hormones, but the sex of rearing. Even the most tomboyish of the androgenized girls, including those whose bodies were visibly masculinized by high postnatal androgen levels, had gender identities which were well within the normal feminine range. So long as they were consistently treated as girls from the period of infancy onwards, they had no doubts about their sex and no desire to become boys.

Indeed, not even chromosomal sex has as strong an influence on gender identity as the sex of rearing. Genetic females have been reared as males, and vice versa; and always the sex which their parents *believe* them to be has a more powerful influence than either chromosomal sex or bodily morphology. Money and Ehrhardt studied pairs of hermaphroditic children which were matched for medical diagnosis but discordant for sex of rearing. In most such cases, whatever the biological situation, the child reared as a girl developed a normal female identity, and the reverse for the child reared as a boy: the only exceptions were those cases in which the parents themselves were uncertain about the child's sex and communicated that uncertainty to the child.

Money and Ehrhardt draw an analogy between sex-role learning and the learning of language in a bilingual environment. The child is exposed to both sexual roles and can learn either or both quite readily, especially if the one role is exhibited by one person or set of people and the other by another; if the same people exhibit portions of both roles the child will have difficulty differentiating between them. Every child, then, has a capacity for bisexuality or androgyny of character (though this not a term the authors use); but if, as is usually the case, the environment strongly encourages expressions of one gender identity and discourages expressions of the other, then the precluded range of behaviors will be "negatively coded" and strictly avoided. Gender learning is also analogous to imprinting in young birds, in that there is a crucial period in infancy and early childhood in which a more or lest permanent mental set with respect to gender is formed. After the age of eighteen months it is increasingly difficult to impose a change of gender on the child without producing mental damage. After the age of three or four, it is as difficult for a hermaphroditic child as for a normal child to change its sexual identity, even where the sex of rearing contradicts chromosomal sex, hormonal sex, genital appearance, or all three, so powerful is the force of early social conditioning.

If these findings hold up they would seem to provide considerable support for the feminist contention that sexual roles and stereotypes are social impositions rather than the inevitable results of our biology or of our innate psychological make-up. On the other hand there would also seem to be some support for the claim, defended most notably by Havelock Ellis, that human males are naturally more physically active (catabolic, energy expending) than females. The tomboyish androgenized females whom the authors examined tended to describe themselves as wanting careers more than marriage and motherhood (though many wanted both), and it is implied that this too is part of the androgenization syndrome. While this is perhaps the least well-supported of their conclusions it should not, even if true, prove threatening to the feminist point of view. If males, on the average, need and prefer a somewhat higher level of energy expenditure, then they—and the more catabolic of the females, too—can surely be provided with outlets for that need which do not imply domination, exploitation or denegration of the more anabolic (energy conserving) members of society. If females with high energy levels shun the career of housewife (not exactly a coma-tose condition in most cases) that is a perfectly good reason why they should be encouraged and respected in their explorations of alternatives to it.

MONTAGU, Ashley. *The Natural Superiority of Women* (Mac-millan Publishers, New York, 1974; first published in 1952, and revised in 1968 and 1973)

This is a popular book, in which Montagu pays homage to the greater constitutional (as opposed to muscular) strength, emo-tional stability, and human sensitivity of women. Far from being the weaker sex, women have a crucial biological advantage in that they have two X chromosomes while men have only one. The X chromosome is the larger and genetically more important one, the Y chormosome being relatively small and genetically impov-erished. Because females have two Xs, they suffer from far fewer physical and mental abnormalities; for a defective gene on one X will be apt to be corrected by the corresponding gene on the other. They are also generally healthier, better at enduring stress and deprivation, and longer-lived. This makes good evolution-ary sense since, as the bearers and rearers of the young, women are more important to the survival of the species; males are a relatively dispensable variant on the basic human form, which is feminine. Furthermore, females are evolutionarily more ad-vanced, in that they are more infantile and less ape-like in their adult form than males. (See Ellis.)

In the light of these facts, Montagu argues that men's misogyn-ism, the traditional patriarchal depreciation of the intelligence, morality and competence of women, and the relegation of wom-en to secondary status, must be seen as a reaction formation due to men's envy of women's biological superiority—in particular their capacity to give birth. In Stone Age cultures this capacity imposes little or no social handicap on women; but as the roving, hunting and fighting men gained in knowledge of the world and technological skills relative to the home-bound women, they invariably used these advantages to turn women's natural bio-logical advantages into cultural disadvantages, surrounding women with restrictions and taboos from which they themselves were exempt.

Montagu places great emphasis on what he considers the greater "maternal" capacities of women, and this, from a con-temporary feminist standpoint, is the most controversial part of his analysis. He argues that, while women should of course have the same job opportunities as men, they ought to be full-time mothers for as long as their children are preschool age. Later, he suggests, one or both parents might work parttime to give them more time with the children, but in the early years the mother's, not the father's, care and attention is all-important. He deplores those feminists who attack motherhood as a limitation of freedom, insisting that it is the most important career of all. For not only are women far better nurturers of children, they are generally more loving, understanding and morally responsible in their behavior than men. Their mission must be, as it has always been, to civilize men and teach them to be more human.

The reader is left to wonder whether such well-meant tributes to women's superior qualities might not be somewhat double-edged. There are many women who would prefer that men have more confidence in their *own* childrearing abilities, and who suspect that their protests of congenital incompetence are little more than a screen for their refusal to do their fair share of this imporant but often (in current terms) rather unglamorous work. Being labeled a superior human with the task of civilizing males and being mother to the race is certainly better than being regarded as the source of all corruption and barely human at all. Yet Montagu's conception of women might still be regarded as an alienated one. In his world, for all his emphasis on cooperation and reciprocity between the sexes, woman is still the Other, fundamentally different from men in respects far deeper than the obvious physiological ones. Many women would prefer to be accepted rather as men have accepted men, i.e, as fellow human beings, whose essential human similarity outweighs their hormonally induced differences. For some reason (perhaps for the reasons Montagu himself mentions), the gulf between male and female "nature" has always seemed much wider and deeper from the male side of the chasm than it has from the female side. Feminists are rightly wary of efforts that keep it open by stereotyping any "female role"; despite Montagu's powerful arguments against some aspects of the traditional stereotype, he ultimately falls into the same trap.

MORGAN, Elaine. *The Descent of Woman* (Bantam, New York, 1973; first published 1972, by Stein and Day)

This is an irreverent and often humorous attack on what Morgan calls the Tarzan, or Mighty Hunter theory of human evolution, as typified by the work of Desmond Morris, Lionel Tiger and Robert Ardrey. The Tarzan theory holds that it was man's (i.e. the male's) development into a hunter, protecting and providing for his mate and offspring, which brought about humanity's evolutionary upsurge. It is, she says, a politically motivated theory, which exalts male aggression and dominance, and male bonding as it occurs in the hunting or war party, as the key to human progress, and it is used to argue that it is "unnatural" for women to play any part in public or economic life.

Morgan's highly original alternative hypothesis is that, contrary to this androcentric theory, our forebears had already embarked on most of the key changes in the evolution towards *Homo sapiens* before they became hunters on the African plains. These changes resulted from a semiaquatic stage which occurred during the ten million year-long Pliocene drought, when the disappearance of the African forests drove the arboreal apes out of the heart of the continent. To survive, they became shore dwellers, living in caves and venturing into the ocean for food and safety. The upright stance developed to facilitate wading in deep water, while body hair became a hindrance and was shed in favor of a subcutaneous layer of fat; long hair on the scalp, on the other hand, was valuable, especially for females, since it gave their infants something to cling to in the water. Language developed because it was the only effective means of communication in the water, the old visual signals being useless.

During all this time, females lived and reared their young in complete independence of males, whom they sought out only when they were in estrus. But the anatomized adaptations to the aquatic habitat had an unfortunate effect on human sexuality. The upright stance and the migration of the female genitalia toward the front made the old rear-entry position unworkable, and the front-to-front necessary. The females found the new position both threatening and unsatisfying, since the clitoris had not yet developed its present sensitivity, and the sensitive part of the vagina was the ventral side, where it could only be stimulated in the old position. Consequently, males were required to take females by force; the genetic value of male aggression was thus enhanced, and the link forged between sex, violence and domination.

Morgan thus agrees with the "Tarzan theorists" that male hormones give males a greater propensity for aggression; but she denies that aggression is the sole means of attaining status and leadership (as Goldberg, for instance, claims). Male baboons, on whom the ethologists tend to dwell most fondly, do attain status and domination by pure aggression; but among the apes whom we resemble more closely, e.g. chimpanzees, status is more often gained by "display" behavior, that is by attracting attention via some novel action, object or game. The aggression mode and the display mode are both human options; neither is a biological imperative.

Morgan agrees with the radical feminists that male domination coincided with the appearance of the nuclear family, and that motherhood is an onerous burden for modern women because of its lack of status and economic reward. But she doubts that the family will vanish, or that women will soon be able to free themselves from the responsibilities of motherhood, either by the artificial womb or by communal child care. She does, however, see hope in the prospect that with economic independence and the Pill women will soon have their fingers on the "genetic trigger," and that they may so select the fathers of their children as to reduce the evolutionary value of dominance and aggression.

MORGAN, Lewis Henry (1818–1881). *Ancient Society* (edited by Leslie A. White, Harvard University Press, Cambridge, Massachusetts, 1964; first published 1877)

Lewis Henry Morgan, an American anthropologist, was one of the first to challenge the universal presumption that the patriarchal family has always been the basic unit of human society. On the basis of his study of American Indian tribes, especially those of the Iroquois nation, Morgan developed a theory of the evolution of the human family, from a primordial condition of indiscriminate intercourse, through several stages of group marriage within the matrilinear clan or gens, through patriarchal polygamy, and finally to monogamy, an ideal which has not yet been fully realized. Karl Marx was extremely impressed by Morgan's work, and adopted his conclusions almost *in toto*. He saw in *Ancient Society* confirmation of his own theory that changes in the material modes of production act as the driving force in human progress, as well as his view that humanity once enjoyed and will again achieve a condition of communist egalitarianism. Marx's extensive notes on Morgan became, after the former's death, the basis for Friedrich Engels' *The Origin of the Family, Private Property and the State*, in which the Marxist doctrine that women will achieve complete equality with men when and only when the capitalist system of private ownership is overthrown, receives its classic statement.

Morgan himself placed much less emphasis on the political— socialist and feminist—implications of his theory. His purpose, remarkably ambitious in itself, was to reveal for the first time the necessary and universal sequence of stages through which human societies naturally evolve, from savagery and barbarism to the civilized state. That such a single sequence of stages must exist Morgan never doubted; all human inventions and institutions, he maintained, spring from a small number of "original germs of thought"; and since each innovation depends on previous developments the sequence cannot be significantly varied except, perhaps, as a result of outside intervention.

Morgan's stages of cultural development, very briefly, are as follows. The two major prehistoric stages, savagery and barbarism, are each subdivided into a lower, middle and upper phase. The lowest stage of savagery precedes the use of fire but saw the development of language; humanity subsisted on fruit and nuts, meat being difficult to procure without effective weapons. The middle stage begins with the use of fire and the eating of fish, and the upper stage begins with the discovery of the bow and arrow, the first effective hunting weapon. The discovery of pottery marks the end of the savage state; the lower stage of barbarism begins there and ends, in the Western hemisphere, with the cultivation of plants and the use of adobe brick, and in the Eastern with the domestication of animals. The middle phase of barbarism ends with the invention of iron smelting, the upper phase with the invention of the phonetic alphabet, with which civilization begins.

Morgan postulates that the earliest type of human family, corresponding with the lowest phase of savagery (and the only family type of which there are no surviving representatives) was what he called the Consanguine family, i.e. the intermarriage of a group of brothers and sisters, the offspring of the same mother. This was first succeeded by the Punaluan family, a type observed in parts of Polynesia, in which a group of brothers, or sometimes of sisters, share their wives or husbands in common; and then, in the upper phase of savagery, by the Syndyasmian family, in which a single male and female are paired (for some extended period of time), but without the expectation of exclusive cohabitation. Throughout the stage of savagery, ancestry and family relationships are traced only matrilineally, the paternity of a child being unknown. The primary social organization is the maternal clan, an extended family group tracing their descent to a single female ancestor. The gentes (clans) contain the seeds of the institution of government; as barbarism progresses they are gradually organized into phratries, phratries into tribes, and tribes into nations or confederacies.

The switch to patrilineal descent and the patriarchal family began within the gens, after the beginnings of monogamy in the Syndyasmian family made it possible to determine paternity for the first time. The switch was accomplished without disrupting the structure of the clans; at some point descent simply began to be traced through the male rather than the female line. Women lose their family name and allegiance upon marriage and with their descendants are transferred to their husband's family. In the beginning, the patrilineal family tends to be patriarchal and polygamous; men insist on fidelity from their wives but refuse to practice it themselves. Morgan explains the use of patriarchy and patriliny as the result of men's desire to pass their name and property to their own children. This desire naturally appeared once property began to accumulate, particularly in the form of land and livestock. (This explanation leaves unanswered the question why a similar desire did not arise in women, or if it did why women were unable to preserve the maternal clan.) Whatever the reason for the conversion, Morgan finds evidence that it occurred in the Greek and Roman clans as well as among the Iroquois and other American tribes.

Morgan is not, strictly speaking, a matriarchy theorist, for he does not maintain that the matrilineal clans were generally gynocratic, i.e., dominated by women. On the contrary, he holds that the fact that descent was traced through the female line, for example in Lycia, Etruscia and Crete, was by no means an "homage offered to the female sex." (p.296) It was simply the inevitable result of the lack of monogamy. Nevertheless, Morgan points out that the change to descent from the male line inevitably resulted in a loss of rights and status for women. The wife and mother was isolated from her own kindred, thus weakening the maternal bond and the authority of the mother. Morgan deplores the selfishness of Greek men in imposing an inferior status upon Greek women, while at the same time suggesting that it was a necessary part of historical progress, "one of the sacrifices required of womankind to bring this portion of the human race out of the Syndyasmian into the Monogamian family." (p.401) The implication is that monogamy originally required the suppression of women. He thinks, however, that women in his own day, at least in the United States, are much closer to a position of equality. He predicts that this progress will continue until the equality of the sexes is complete; for complete equality is necessary for true monogamy.

Morgan's theory is open to a great many objections, some of them fatal to at least certain portions of it. The presumption that there must be a single evolutionary pattern which is followed by all human cultures is no longer given much credence. Nor have subsequent anthropological investigations confirmed the claim that monogamy, patriliny, and patriarchy appear only with the use of private property. Primitive people who share or lack property are quite often monogamous in tendency, and sometimes trace their descent patrilineally. Furhtermore monogamy and matriliny are not incompatible, as Morgan believed them to be. There is no evidence that Morgan's Consanguine family, the intermarriage of a group of brothers and sisters, has ever existed, let alone been the universal form of the family (1).

Such objections can be multiplied. Yet from a feminist point of view there is one enormously important claim which emerges from *Ancient Society* unrefuted—that is, as highly probable if not clearly proven. This is the claim that prior to the appearance of the patrilineal family the basic human social unit must have been, for at least many thousands of years, the matrilineal clan. It is extremely difficult to say just what the relative rights and status of women may have been within the matrilineal clan (and no doubt there was a great deal of variation), but it is quite clear that the switch to a patrilineal system entailed a loss of rights, an enforced inequality for women, from which women have not yet fully recovered. If this claim is true then it constitutes powerful evidence that the inferior social status of women is an historically contingent phenomenon, a passing phase of human evolution, rather than something which is necessitated for all time by human psychology, the male hormone system, or any other natural, let alone inalterable, state of affairs.

1. Morgan deduced its existence from his extensive study of the kinship terminology of various cultures. In the Malayan system of consanguinity, for instance, the only family relationships recognized are those of parent, child, grandparent, grandchild, brother and sister; all uncles and aunts are addressed as father and mother, all cousins as sister or brother, and so on. Morgan interpreted this as proof of the prior existence of the Consanguine family, overlooking what is now the generally accepted explanation of the Malayan terminology—that its terms denote attitudes and obligations rather than lines of descent.

MORGAN, Robin. *Going Too Far: The Personal Chronicles of a Feminist* (Vintage Books, New York, 1978)

Morgan is a radical feminist and a past member of the New York Radical Women and of WITCH (the Women's International Conspiracy from Hell). *Going Too Far* is a collection of papers, poems, letters and journal entries, written between 1968 and 1977. The earlier material records Morgan's personal development, from a feminist radical in the 1960s to a radical feminist in the 1970s. Like many radical women, she was forced to break from the male-dominated peace movement by the realization that it was the *politics* of the Left and not merely the personal leanings of some of its leaders which were male supremacist. Her "Goodbye to All That" is a now classic farewell to the "men's movement," which attacks the presumption on the part of many radicals that the liberation of women must wait until after the fall of capitalism.

On the radical feminist analysis, sexism, racism and class oppression are older than capitalism and can survive its demise. Morgan notes that the word "radical" is derived from a word meaning "root." A radical feminist, thus, is one who holds that,

> sexism is the root oppression, the one which, until and unless we *up*root it, will continue to put forth the branches of racism, class hatred, competition, ecological disaster, and economic exploitation.

Morgan holds that women are (analogous to) a colonized and exploited people. For,

> Our history, values and *cross-cultural culture* have been taken from us—a gynocidal attempt manifest most arrestingly in the patriarchy's seizure of our basic and precious "land": our own bodies.
> (p.161)

Under patriarchy, women's bodies are expropriated and "mined" for their resources, with little or no concern for the rights or even the survival of the victims. Hence the importance of the women's health movement, which is helping women to declare their independence from the patriarchal and oppressive institutions of gynecology and male-dominated medicine in general. "The speculum," she notes, "may well be mightier than the sword." (p.162)

Unlike, for instance, de Beauvoir and Firestone (to whose theories Morgan's is otherwise closely related), Morgan does not believe that male supremacy and the oppression of women has existed since the beginning of human society. Like Engels and the (other) matriarchy theorists, she views the patriarchal revolution as an historical event. Patriarchy overthrew the Goddess-centered religions of the earliest civilizations, and replaced those life-affirming creeds with the death-oriented religions which have prevailed throughout most of the world during the past four or five thousand years. (See Daly, Stone.)

As for why this event occurred, Morgan's tentative explanation is neither economic nor biological, but existential. Men, she suggests, came to experience existential despair—that is, to doubt and deny the value of life—because of their envy of women's reproductive and other creative powers. In Morgan's words,

> . . . male anguish expressed this despair as misogyny. What else to feel when faced with this female endless birthing . . . as if each woman were somehow somewhere in herself singing "I never met a universe I didn't like"? (p.309)

Man's conquest of woman's body, his appropriation of "her gods, her whole cosmos," is the result of this male anguish, "the merciless, negative, bleak, terror-filled void in which he is trapped." (*Loc. cit.*) Fearing woman's creative power, he claims it as his own; he *insists* that she bear, but for his purposes rather than her own. This is the origin of rape, and of such other patriarchal institutions as marriage, (patriarchal) motherhood, and misogynist religion.

Morgan points out that rape is "the perfected act of male sexuality in a patriarchal culture—it is the ultimate metaphor for domination, violence, subjugation, and possession." (pp.163–164) Pornography—i.e., the sadistic, gynocidal (woman-murdering) kind which is common today—is an expression of the male rape fantasy. "Pornography is the theory, and rape the practice." (p.169) Nevertheless, unlike some feminists who have reached this conclusion about pornography (See Brownmiller), Morgan explicitly rejects any form of censorship as a greater evil, and a weapon which in practice is much more apt to be used against feminist educational material than against misogynist propaganda. Rather than censorship, she advocates training women in the use of firearms and other weapons in order that we may fight against the physical violence which is increasingly directed against us.

Morgan describes her own approach to feminist theory as "metaphysical." The latter term is not used in the usual philosophical sense, but in the sense in which it is used of such poets as Dante and Blake. Metaphysical feminism, she says, is "this insistence on "going too far," the refusal to simplify or polarize." (p.16) It implies an eclectic approach to the various ways of struggling for liberation, a respect for *both* the civil rights wing of the women's movement (e.g. the National Organization for Women and the Women's Equity Action League), and the "radical fringe" groups like WITCH.

Metaphysical feminism, Morgan argues, also requires respect for the personal decisions of (feminist) women, whether they pursue a radical lesbian life style, or whether they choose to marry and even have children—as she herself has done. The point is not that the radical feminist analysis of patriarchal love, marriage and motherhood are incorrect. It is rather that none of these issues on which feminists have been divided is simple or one-sided. There is nothing intrinsically wrong with wanting both love and motherhood *and* freedom. Hence the woman who struggles for liberation within the context of a heterosexual relationship deserves respect, "and an end to psychological torture which claims we have made our choice only *because* of psychological torture." (p.14; also see Atkinson, Johnston, and Lesbian Feminism.)

Beyond this refusal to polarize or oversimplify, metaphysical feminism implies a global, ecological, spiritual (i.e. life-affirming) point of view. It demands nothing less than

> an unpolluted planet, the end of all wars and the elimination of money; reverence for the very young and very old; indifference to pigmentation, height or weight; no more poverty, ignorance, starvation and despair . . . (p.290)

In other words, the liberation of women is inseparably linked to the liberation of all human beings, and to a respect for all life. Morgan finds in the ancient philosophy of Wicce, the religion of "witchcraft," a moral and spiritual attitude which is close to the essence of metaphysical feminism.

MORRIS, Desmond. *The Naked Ape* (Dell Publishing Company, New York, 1969; first published 1967)

This is one of the more simple-minded popularizations of the ethological findings of Konrad Lorenz and others. The thesis is that human behavior is and will continue to be fundamentally controlled by the instincts which came into being when our fruit-eating ape ancestors descended to the ground and became hunters—the males, that is. Carnivorousness is the key to human evolution; it was the hunt which stimulated the development of tools and of a larger brain to improve them, which necessitated pair bonding (to keep the females loyal while the males hunted, and to reduce hostility among the males), which brought about the appearance of the female organism and generally increased human sexiness (to enable a single female to keep a male's interest longer), and which led to the development of language (useful on the hunt).

In other words, all of the important evolutionary developments that brought about the rise of the "naked ape" grew out of the all-male hunt, while the females did little besides remain at home and raise children. ("The females were too busy rearing the young to be able to play a major role in chasing and catching prey" (p.20). " . . . the females found themselves almost perpetually confined to the home base" (p.33).) Because of the hunt, men have not only the hierarchical/dominance drive which they inherited from our vegetarian ape ancestors, but also both an individual and a group territorial drive. That is, men instinctively fight to achieve status in the male hierarchy, to defend the group's territory, and to defend their individual homes and families. The extent to which these aggressive urges are supposedly confined to the male of the species is never made clear, but there is little reason to suppose that females would have developed instincts which they were never called upon to display. And although Morris does not explicitly celebrate male domination and the traditional sexual stereotypes as necessitated by these male instincts, the reader can hardly avoid the impression that he does consider them to be so necessitated, and that any society not based on the patriarchal family will "clash with or suppress our basic animal demands." (p.34) Certainly this would seem to be the logical conclusion of such a Tarzan-and-Jane theory of human evolution. (See Elaine Morgan.)

MOTHERHOOD "Motherhood" typically refers to both the female reproductive processes of gestation, giving birth, and lactation, and the social institution whereby mothers bear the primary responsibility for the care of their own children, even when the latter are well past their infancy. (See Rich.) Motherhood, in both of these senses, is one of the primary factors which contemporary radical feminists hold to be responsible for the origin and preservation of male supremacy.

The earliest feminists were by no means critics of the institution of motherhood. Instead, they believed that motherhood is a woman's highest duty (though fatherhood is *not* the highest duty for a man), but held that the equality of education and legal rights which they demanded for women were necessary in order to make them better mothers. (See Astell, Wollstonecraft, Mill.) Ellen Key, a Swedish feminist active in the early part of this century, continued to hold that a woman's place is in the home, at least if and when she has children there. Myrdal and Klein's well-known three-phase model of the life cycle of the new woman (the three phases are education and some years of paid employment, motherhood, and finally a return to paid employment) presupposes that most mothers of young children will not concurrently wish to work outside the home, although most fathers will.

For most contemporary feminists, however, the arrangement whereby mothers do most of the child care, whether or not they do other work as well, and fathers act as "breadwinners" is no longer acceptable. It requires, in the first place, much too great a sacrifice of freedom and personal and economic independence on the part of the woman. Harriet Taylor and John Stuart Mill disagreed on this issue, Mill believing that genuine equality in marriage is possible even when the woman earns no money, and Taylor insisting that it is not. Taylor held that in the ideal world women would support their own children, and thus be free from the need to depend upon a man for subsistence. How they could do this while at the same time caring for their children with little or no assistance, Taylor does not say.

Simone de Beauvoir is much more aware of this intensely practical problem. She holds that to remain free a woman must avoid not only marriage but motherhood itself, which is "one feminine function which it is actually almost impossible to perform in complete liberty." (1952, p.655) For most women, she notes, motherhood involves responsibilities and burdens which are hardly compatible with the pursuit of any other career. Parenthood can be burdensome for men too; but for women, far more than for men, it stands against whatever other goals they may have in life. (Also see Peck and Senderowitz, in Anthologies VIII.) This is true to almost the same extent in the socialist as in the capitalist systems. Where women are generally expected to work even if they happen to be mothers the double work burden still limits their ambitions and their chances for advancement. (See Hilda Scott; also Curtin, Iglitzin, Mandel, Randall, and Warshofsky, in Anthologies XV.)

The radical feminists of today, however, object to the institution of motherhood not only because it unfairly limits the freedom of mothers, but because it perpetuates, in children of both sexes, the psychological structures which the entire system of male supremacy makes so difficult to alter or overcome. Freud described some of the processes by which the personalities of male and female children are shaped within the patriarchal family. These processes, the radical feminists argue, occur as they do precisely because the family has been and remains patriarchal, with child care in the hands of the mother, but most of the social and economic power in those of the father. (See Dinnerstein, Firestone, Mitchell, Rich.)

Firestone holds that if women are to be free then we must eliminate not only the patriarchal *institution* of motherhood, but the biological process itself—i.e., the gestation of fetuses must be achieved by artificial means, outside of the human womb (1). For, she argues, it was not only private property and male supremacist ideology which originally made women and children dependent upon men for support and protection, but biology itself, and in particular the childbearing function of women. Hence, only when fetuses can be gestated artificially, and when children are cared for communally instead of by their individual parents, will it be possible for the joys and burdens of reproduction to be shared equitably by both sexes.

Dinnerstein, on the other hand, argues that what is most important is for men to become just as involved in the rearing of infants and children as women are now. She holds that if from the beginning children were cared for by persons of both sexes, then they would not form the stereotyped notions of gender role which prove so resistant to later change. Friday and Hammer have examined the mother/daughter relationship in our culture, and argued that the fact that females are cared for in infancy by a person of the same sex, while for boys the caretaker is a person of the opposite sex, makes it much more difficult for the former to develop a secure sense of their own individuality and separateness.

Another aspect of motherhood which has drawn feminist fire in recent years is the way in which childbirth and pre- and postnatal care are handled by the American medical establishment. (See Arms, Dreifus, and Frankfort, in Anthologies III; also Barker-Benfield, in Anthologies XI.)

1. See Francoeur for a survey of some of the current research on human reproduction, which makes such a suggestion appear much more feasible than might at first be supposed.

MYRDAL, Alva, and **KLEIN**, Viola. *Women's Two Roles: Home and Work* (Routledge and Kegan Paul, London, 1966; first published 1956)

A highly influential study of the contemporary movement of

women, especially married women, into the paid work force of the industrialized Western nations, in particular Sweden, England, France and the United States. (Myrdal is a Swedish sociologist, Klein is English.) The authors view the increasing employment of women outside the home as the inevitable if delayed result of the Industrial Revolution, which moved economically productive work from the home, forcing women to follow it, as men have already done, if they are to regain the productive role and rewards which they previously enjoyed. They predict that the trend towards the increasing employment of women will and indeed must continue. For as the proportion of older, retired people increases, the ratio of nonproductive to productive individuals will also increase, with an inevitable loss of prosperity, unless the reserve labor supply represented by unemployed women is tapped.

The movement of middle-class women into paid work has taken place in two stages. First, women who were free of family ties (single and childless) began to be admitted, in small numbers, to previously all-male employments; now, increasing numbers of women are struggling to combine the family role with outside employment. Poor women, of course, have long been forced to work to survive, but now married women are increasingly working out of preference rather than necessity, to *improve* the family's financial status rather than to avoid starvation, and to escape the boredom and lack of status of the unpaid housewife. Nevertheless, women are still largely confined to the less skilled, less responsible and less well-paid jobs, not just because they're of irrational prejudice aganst them, but because the strain and uncertainty of having to combine two roles prevents most women from competing effectively with men for desirable jobs. Women, even without children, tend to be absent from work somewhat more often than men; if they do have children they are absent much more often. The job turnover rate is also higher among women, at least those under 40 or 45, in part because of their unequal job status, which prevents them from taking their work as seriously as men, in part because of the demands of their family role, and in part because of the low value placed on their job role.

The best solution to the conflicting demands of work and home, Myrdal and Klein argue, is for women to work before and after, but generally not *during* the years when their children are small. Although they approve of child care facilities and cooperative arrangements for doing housework, to make it easier for women to combine motherhood with work, they think that it is "neither practicable nor desirable that mothers of very young children should go out to work." (p.187) Women, therefore, "should visualize their life span as a succession of three phases, each dominated mainly by one function: a period of training and education, followed, if possible, by years devoted to raising a family . . . succeeded by a period during which past training and experience are put to wider social use." (p.153) They admit that this will mean that women will have to restrict themselves to occupations which can be resumed after a break of ten years or more."Professions such as that of a surgeon or a diplomat might be very difficult to reconcile with family responsibilities." (p.157) They reject the option of part-time work for both parents, enabling them to share childcare duties equally, as requiring overly drastic changes in the organization of work, and they consider it much more important for the mother to be with a child during its early formative years than for the father to be with the child.

According to Myrdal and Klein, the three-phase life plan for women does not mean abandoning the feminist goal of equality, but is simply a matter of facing facts. However, as long as it remains a fact that most mothers of young children find it difficult to also work outside the home, there are few feminists who would consider the social circumstances responsible for this fact permanently acceptable. As long as mothers but not fathers are generally forced to spend some ten to twenty years—the most important years for the establishment of a professional career of almost any type—at home with their children there will be no real equality of opportunity between the sexes. Women will still have to choose between purchasing a relative degree of freedom and job opportunity at the cost of motherhood, or purchasing motherhood at the cost of what they could otherwise achieve in the larger world. It is difficult to avoid the conclusion that there is an intolerable injustice—not a natural injustice but a man-made one—in the fact that women but not men must juggle two conflicting social roles.

N

NEUMANN, Eric (1905–1960). *The Great Mother: An Analysis of an Archetype* (translated from the German by Ralph Manheim, Princeton University Press, 1955)

Neumann is an orthodox Jungian who holds that the archetype of the Feminine (like all archetypes) is an inborn psychic structure, common to all human beings and symbolized in the art of all human cultures. The book includes 185 pages of photographic illustrations of artistic, especially ancient, representations of women and goddesses, all of which Neumann considers illustrative of this inborn archetype. The archetype is a developmental one, whose two temporal stages, the elementary and the transformative, represent both the (pre) historic human passage from the primordial, holistic, magical "matriarchal" form of consciousness to the rationalistic, individualistic, "patriarchal" form of consciousness, and the potential development of each individual woman. The elementary character of the Feminine expresses the original, egoless condition of the human psyche; this aspect of the Great Mother is represented as the Great Round, a vessel which contains the world and is the world. In her subsequent transformative character the Great Mother represents the emergence of spirit and ego, of human uniqueness and the desire and promise of personal immortality. In both characters, the Great Mother possesses both a good, life-giving aspect and a terrible, death-dealing aspect.

Although he draws a good deal of inspiration from such matriarchy theorists as Bachofen and Briffault, Neumann interprets the passage from matriarchy as primarily a psychological development rather than a political one. "Masculine" consciousness, the rational, individual ego, emerges during the matriarchal phase and is first seen as an attribute of the great goddess and not sharply distinct from matter and materiality. The patriarchal consciousness appears when spirit, soul or mind (conceived as masculine) is seen as not only distinct from matter (conceived as feminine) but prior to it and dominant over it. When this happens women's consciousness tends to remain matriarchal (as it does to this day, Neumann thinks (p.79)) and the patriarchal consciousness of men becomes dominant in the culture.

Neumann does not address the issue of biological determinism and so it is difficult to say whether or not he views the supposedly inborn archetypes of the masculine and the feminine as inimical to the eventual elimination of sexual stereotyping and/or an egalitarian distribution of powers and rights between the sexes. What is clear is that the theory that the archetypes or behavior patterns characteristic of masculinity and femininity are *both* radically different *and* in some way built into our brains from birth is unpromising in the light of more recent empirical demonstrations that gender identity (i.e. whether one considers oneself a male or a female and behaves as society considers appropriate to that sex) is overridingly determined by postnatal events, in particular the way that one is treated by one's parent(s). (See Money and Ehrhardt, Stoller.)

Nor do we need to posit archetypes to explain the ubiquity of the mother goddess and her association with matter, mortality, and the preindividualist stage of human consciousness. For, as Dinnerstein has pointed out, children in virtually all cultures are nurtured in their infancy primarily by women. This makes it natural enough that women should be associated with the holistic, prerational and egoless mental state of infancy, and also that the process of intellectual growth and maturation should be conceived as an escape from femininity and therefore masculine. There is thus reason to predict that if and when childrearing ceases to be a feminine monopoly, our concepts of masculinity and femininity will be fundamentally altered and much of the artificial contrast removed.

NIETZSCHE, Friedrich (1844–1900). *The Gay Science* (translated by Walter Kaufman, Random House, New York, 1974; first published 1882)
Thus Spoke Zarathustra (translated by R.J. Hollingdale; Penguin Books, Baltimore, 1967; first published 1883–1885)
Beyond Good and Evil (translated by Marianne Cowan; Henry Regnery Company, Chicago, 1955; first published 1885)
On the Geneology of Morals, and *Ecce Homo* (translated by Walter Kaufman and R.J. Hollingdale; Vintage, New York, 1967; first published 1887, and 1908, respectively. *Ecce Homo* was written in 1888.)

Nietzsche is one of the founders of the existentialist movement in philosophy. A severe critic of Christianity and Judeo-Christian morality, he advocated a "transvaluation of all values," the over-throw of all the old moral systems, through which there would emerge the Superman, the self-determining individual who is the author of his own values.

Nietzsche is infamous for his rude remarks about women, which are second in intensity only to those of his fellow country-man and philosophical predecessor Arthur Schopenhauer. He is, in fact, an unusually ׀virilent׀ misogynist, who insists that females are good only for childbearing and amusing men, and should not be allowed to forget it. Those who would like to absolve Nietzsche of the responsibility for his statements on the subject often point to a passage in *Beyond Good and Evil*, in which he explains that his views about women are only a reflec-tion of his own inner nature, thus implying (it would seem) that he made no claim to their objective validity. On this topic he says,

> a thinker cannot relearn anything but only learn to the end what is "in him" . . . Considering this . . . I shall perhaps be permit-ted to speak aloud several truths about woman "as such." I assume that everyone understands how much these truths are only—*my* truths. (p.161)

This passage, however, makes it clear that Nietzsche did not consider his views on the subject to be any *more* subjective than those of other thinkers, or any less objective than his views on other topics. Certainly they are not stated as mere personal opinions, but boldly and without qualification. Nor is Nietzsche always so modest about his ability to speak the truth, *simpliciter*, about women, as opposed to merely his "own" truths. For in-stance, in *Ecce Homo*—one of his last and least modest books—he asks, "May I venture the surmise that I *know* woman . . . Per-haps I am the first psychologist of the eternally feminine." (p.266) There seems, therefore, little reason not to hold him fully res-ponsible for the views which he expresses.

Nietzsche's psychology of women is perhaps best presented through the words of his Biblical-style prophet, Zarathustra. Just as he anticipated Freud's discovery of the unconscious, so too he preceded Freud in depicting women as naturally passive, subor-dinate, intellectually inferior and morally backwards beings, whose only proper role in life is to love men, to submit to them, and to bear children—especially sons. (*Thus Spoke Zarathustra*, p.92)

Zarathustra's (i.e. Nietzsche's) views on women are delivered reluctantly, not to all his disciples but to one old woman whom he meets "at the hour when the sun sets." "Everything about woman is a riddle," he tells her, "and everything about woman has one solution: it is called pregnancy." (p.91) Pregnancy, Nietzsche says in *The Gay Science*, "has made women kinder, more patient, more timid, [and] more pleased to submit." (p.128)

Women, therefore—that is "real" women and not "the 'emancipated' who lack the stuff for children" (*Ecce Homo*, p.266)—want strong and dominant men who can make them obey. In Zarathustra's words,

> The man's happiness is: I will. The woman's happiness is: He will.

> "Behold, now the world has become perfect!"—thus thinks every woman when she obeys with all her love.

> And woman has to obey and find a depth for her surface. Woman's nature is surface, a changeable, stormy film upon shallow waters.

> But a man's nature is deep . . . woman senses its power but does not comprehend it. (p.92)

Zarathustra's wisdom on the subject is summarized in the admittedly epigrammatic but nevertheless chilling saying: "Man should be trained for war and women for the recreation of the warrior; all else is folly." (p.91) The same notion is given even clearer expression in the well-known line with which this section of *Zarathustra* closes, a line which Nietzsche places in the mouth of the old woman: "Are you visiting woman? Do not forget your whip!" (p.93) (1)

This tinge of sadism in Nietzsche's philosophy of male-female relations is by no means an isolated idiosyncracy, to be explained away—as it often is—in terms of his unhappy personal experiences with the opposite sex. It is a natural consequence of his entire moral and existential philosophy, which is based on admiration for the strong, dominant and uncompassionate individual, and contempt for the weak, the oppressed and the subordinate "masses." He consistently uses the term "feminine" to contemptuously dismiss all who advocate justice, equality, and other values which he associated with the "slave morality."

Nietzsche especially abhorred the notion of equality of moral rights. He insisted that the difference in power and creative ability between man—and between the sexes—makes vicious nonsense of this notion. This is a *non sequitur*, since the concept of equal rights in no way presupposes identity of strength, talent, or any other quantitative factor. All men and women, it can be argued, have the right to (for instance) life, liberty and the pursuit of happiness—not because they are all equally wise or strong, but because they are all *persons*, that is, conscious, rational, self-aware beings with interests which demand respect. In Kantian terms, they are all ends in themselves, even the most dull-witted of them.

Nietzsche, however, could only see the ideal of equality of moral rights as a plot on the part of the weak and resentful to destroy the strong and noble individuals, those who follow their own laws and create their own values. The Categorical Imperative represents a leveling of all to the level of the most mediocre. (See *The Gay Science*, p.265) Certainly the Superman will be bound by no moral laws other than those he chooses for himself; and if his self-chosen values result in the destruction or exploitation of "inferior" persons, that is simply the way it is. Nietzsche, in fact, admired men like Napoleon, who do not hesitate to inflict suffering and death on a wide scale for what they percieved as a great goal.

With such a moral philosophy, it is hardly surprising that Nietzsche advocates what he calls an "oriental" attitude towards women. Just how central this view was to the core of his world view is clear from this passage from *Beyond Good and Evil*:

> To be wrong on the fundamental problem man-woman . . . to dream of equal rights, equal education, equal claims and obligations—is a *typical* sign of short-sightedness . . . A man who has depth, on the other hand . . . can only think *orientally* about women. He *must* comprehend woman as a possession . . . as something predestined for service and thereby fulfilling its nature. (p.166)

Yet in spite of the evident chauvinism and insensitivity of this position, Nietzsche is not a *pure* misogynist. Unlike, for instance, Norman Mailer or Henry Miller, he does not appear to be motivated by *hostility* towards women so much as by an uneasy combination of fear and compassion—which he says are "the feelings that man has always had for woman." (p.166) "And," he says,

> what makes us compassionate toward this dangerous and beautiful great cat called Woman, even if we fear her, is that she is more capable of suffering, more vulnerable, more in need of love and doomed to disappointments than any other animal. (*Loc. cit.*)

One might suppose that of these two emotions, fear must have predominated in Nietzsche; why else is the whip either necessary or tolerable? But it is out of both fear and compassion that he follows Rousseau, Kant and countless other apologists for patriarchy, in holding that it is for women's own good that they be kept in ignorance and subjection. Like them, Nietzsche supports this implausible hypothesis with the further claims that, on the one hand women really *like* to be dominated, and on the other hand they gain more indirect influence when they are apparently more subordinate (2).

It does not occur to Nietzsche to wonder why, if women are unlike men in having no need or desire for freedom, they nevertheless react to the loss of freedom just as men or nations do, i.e. by seeking subtle means—from hypochondria to religion and art—to turn the tables on the oppressor. If it had, he might have glimpsed the possibility that the ideal of the Superman—the self-determined, value-generating individual, cannot consistently be recommended to one sex only. For his own insights about the covert and corrupting power of the weak point clearly enough to the conclusion that self-determination can be achieved only by both sexes or by neither.

1. Bertrand Russell's comment on this line is that Nietzsche knew that "nine out of ten [women] would get the whip away from him . . . so he kept away from women, and soothed his wounded vanity with unkind remarks." (*A History of Western Philosophy*, p.795).
2. See, for instance, *The Gay Science*, p.319, and *Beyond Good and Evil*, p.167.

O

OAKLEY, Ann. *Sex, Gender, and Society* (Harper and Row, New York, 1972)
Woman's Work: The Housewife, Past and Present (Vintage Books, New York, 1976; first published in London, 1974, as *Housewife*, by Allen Lane, Penguin Books Ltd.)
The Sociology of Housework (Pantheon Books, New York, 1974; first published in London by Martin Robinson Ltd.)

Oakley is a contemporary British sociologist who has broken new ground in the study of housework as an occupation. She is a feminist who sees in the sexual division of labor, particularly the assignment of domestic work to women, the root cause of the phenomenon of gender—i.e. the sex-typing of roles and personality—as it exists with industrial capitalist society. In *Sex, Gender and Society* she surveys the evidence from biology, sociology, psychology and anthropology, and argues that none of it supports the contention that there is any natural or inevitable connection between gender and biological sex.

Oakley points out that the only biological advantages known to be produced by the male's Y chromosome are greater average size, weight and strength. The evidence does not support the claim that women's menstrual cycles exercise a high degree of control over their emotional states, or that their biological role in reproduction handicaps them in doing heavy labor. Anthropological studies show that virtually every culture dictates which tasks are to be performed by which sex, and thereby imposes a concept of gender identity on its members; but that there are no tasks which are *invariably* assigned to men or to women. The patterning of the sexual division of labor is thus determined not by biology *per se*, but by the beliefs about masculinity and femininity, paternity and maternity, which prevail in a particular culture. Biological differences may influence the *direction* of gender differentiation, but not its extent, for there are societies, like the Mbuti pygmies and the Arapesh of New Guinea (1), which have very little gender differentiation and no sharp sexual division of labor. Furthermore, not all societies which do have a sharp division of labor confine women to domestic and men to non-domestic work; often, especially in Africa, women do most of the farming, trading, and marketing.

As for the intellectual differences which psychologists have observed, e.g. females' general superiority in verbal ability, but greater field dependence (2), and males' superiority in mathematical and spatial ability, Oakley suggests that, while more research is still needed, it is likely that these differences can be explained in terms of the different *personality* traits which society encourages in the two sexes, especially aggressiveness in males and dependence in females. Stoller and others have shown that gender identity can develop in direct conflict to chromosomal and/or genital sex; a biologically normal male may adopt a feminine gender identity, or vice versa. Such "intersexual" persons exhibit both intellectual and personality traits which are in accord with their gender identity rather than their biological sex. This would seem to imply that gender is a cultural variable, relatively independent of biological sex.

Nevertheless, Oakley is not optimistic about the chances of eliminating gender distinctions in the near future, since the power of gender-role concepts, their social inertia, is so great as to make their relative independence of biological causes pragmatically irrelevant. The aspect of gender role which seems most resistant to change is women's domestic role, the presumption that women alone are responsible for doing housework and caring for their children. In **Women's Work**, Oakley explores the history and nature of the housewife role, which, she points out, exists only within industrial society, in which economically productive work has been removed from the home. The removal of paid work from the home creates the unpaid, economically dependent, hence "nonworking" housewife.

As a result, under industrial capitalism housewifery has become the central part of the feminine gender role; a "housewife and a woman are one and the same." (p.5) Oakley defines a housewife as anyone who is in charge of running a home, and on this definition a large majority of women today, even those who also have paid jobs, are housewives. Women's identification with housewifery is a basic impediment to occupational equality between the sexes, not only because of the demands on a woman's time and strength which housework makes, but because women's paid work also tends to be subsumed under the housewife role: most women who work for pay are employed in underpaid service jobs (e.g. teaching, nursing, or clerical work), which are in one way or another analogous to the housewife role. Furthermore, however much some women may identify with the housewife role, few of them actually enjoy doing housework. This is Oakley's conclusion from the series of interviews which she conducted in 1971, with forty London housewives from both middle-and working-class backgrounds. Even those women who *say* they enjoy housework tend to reveal their dissatisfaction with it.

Women's liberation, Oakley argues, will require the abolition not only of the housewife role, but of the (nuclear, biological) family as well, and ultimately of gender itself. Housewifery must go because housework is not a fit vocation for a human being; it is "work directly opposed to the possibility of self-actualization." (p.223) And the family must go because, as it is presently constituted, it acts to preserve housewifery as the core of female gender identity:

> The family as an institution is a prescription for gender-role normalcy . . . Within the gender-role structure of the family, women are reduced to a common social type: the housewife-wife-mother. (p.70)

The Sociology of Housework is primarily a report and interpretation of Oakley's study of the forty London housewives. She points out that because of the sexist presumptions of sociologists, housewifery has been little studied as a work role; it has generally been hidden behind woman's role in marriage and in motherhood. Her study, therefore, focuses on housework as work. She finds that the women in the study value the autonomy of housework, but dislike most of the actual tasks it involves; ironing, washing dishes, cleaning and laundry, in that order, are the least popular tasks. A majority (twenty-eight of the forty) are predominantly dissatisfied with housework, and, contrary to the myth that it is only middle-class women who are discontent, social class seems to make little difference to the likelihood or degree of dissatisfaction.

Oakley does find that working-class women are more apt to *say* that they are satisfied with housewifery as a vocation, at least when first asked. She attributes this tendency to a difference between the speech habits of working-and middle-class women; working-class women's speech habits stress conformity to the social norm, while middle-class women are more apt to describe their own individual feelings. Yet women of both classes find their work monotonous, lonely and interminable; their average workweek is over seventy hours. Most receive relatively little help from their husbands, either with housework or with the mundane aspects of child care, and all consider that it is unquestionably *their* duty to do the domestic work, not that of both spouses.

This is because, in spite of their dissatisfaction with their work, housewives tend to identify personally with their role and with the feminine gender stereotypes that go with it; hence they generally disapprove of feminism. This is understandable since it is only by identifying with the role, and developing even more elaborate work routines that they can find much satisfaction as housewives. Thus, the "houseproud" woman, while she may appear neurotic, is actually using a rational strategy to cope with a dreary form of labor which brings her little social reward or recognition. If the women's movement is to help housewives to free themselves, it must help them to understand and overcome "the personal need to *be* a housewife which is at the heart of the female predicament." (p.196)

1. See Margaret Mead, 1935.
2. Field dependence is defined by psychologists as the inability to "break set," to conceptually restructure a problem in order to solve it. See Eleanor Maccoby.

OSSOLI, Margaret Fuller; See Fuller, Margaret.

P

PARSONS, Talcott. *Essays in Sociological Theory* (The Free Press, New York, Collier-Macmillan, London, 1954)
with Bales, Robert F., and Zelditch, Jr., Morris, *Family, Socialization and Interaction Process* (The Free Press, Glencoe, Illinois, 1955)

Parsons is an American sociologist of the functionalist school. He is best known among feminists for his analysis of the roles of husband and wife in the modern American family, which is couched in terms of the instrumental-expressive dichotomy. His sociology is politically conservative; he sees social roles, class and status distinctions (sexual and otherwise), as analogous to the various parts of a biological organism, in that each has an essential function in maintaining the system in working order. As a functionalist, he rejects what he calls "the ill-advised attempts of Morgan, Marx *et al.* to establish universal historical generalizations" about human social evolution. (*Essays in Sociological Theory*, p.220) Functionalists attempt, instead, to understand *existing* social systems, and the ways in which they maintain themselves through the differentiation of social roles.

Parsons argues that the sexual division of labor in the American nuclear family—whereby the husband is the (primary) breadwinner—serves to ensure the equal social status of husband and wife. This is because

> If both were equally in competition for occupational status, there might indeed be a very serious strain on the solidarity of the family unit, for there is no general reason why they would be likely to come out very nearly equally, while, in their capacity of husband and wife, it is very important that they should be treated as equals. (*Op. cit.*, p.79)

In our culture, Parsons points out, a family's social status is primarily determined by the husband's occupational role, and thus confusion and disharmony would be apt to result if the wife also had a status-determining job outside the home.

But the male's assumption of the primary breadwinning role in the American family is only one aspect or illustration of the basic

363

sex-role differentiation in the family. Parsons and Bales argue that in all human families, even those in matrilineal cultures, the husband plays a predominantly "instrumental" and the wife a predominantly "expressive" role. Indeed, they hold that this type of role differentiation is essential for all goal-oriented small groups: one person must generally be the "instrumental" or "task leader," the one who determines the relationship between the group and the outside world, while another person acts as the "emotional leader," coordinating the emotional needs of the members of the group and their relationships to one another. Thus,

> The area of instrumental function concerns relations of the system to its situation outside the system, to meeting the adaptive conditions of its equilibrium, and "instrumentally" establishing the desired relations to *external* goal-objects. The expressive area concerns the "internal" affairs of the system, and the maintenance of integrative relations between the members, and regulation of the patterns and tension levels of its component units. (*Family, Socialization and Interaction Process*, p.47)

The reason, they suggest, why it is virtually always the wife who plays the expressive role is simply the biological role of women in reproduction; for "the bearing and early nursing of children establishes a strong presumptive primacy of the relationship of mother to the small child and this in turn establishes a presumption that the man, who is exempted from these biological functions, should specialize in the alternative instrumental direction." (*Op. cit.*, p.23) Without such a role division, they claim, the family could not perform what is today its primary social function, i.e. the structuring of individual human personalities along lines suitable for the functioning of the social system as a whole.

Indeed, Parsons and Bales maintain that this sexual role division is necessary for the very existence of the family as the basic social unit. They regard the shared-role type of marriage, in which both parents work outside the home and share childrearing duties between them, as a psychological and sociological impossibility:

> Why, after all, are *two* parents necessary? For one thing, to be a stable focus of integration, the integrative-expressive "leader" can't be off on adaptive-instrumental errands all the time. For another, a stable, secure attitude of members depends . . . on a *clear* structure being given to the situation . . . (1)

Mothers, it is argued, *cannot* play a predominantly instrumental role in the family so long as their attention is primarily concentrated on the care of small infants (though of course they always perform *some* instrumental tasks). Hence it is necessary for the social maturation of children that the father play an instrumental role, since "*some* significant member of the nuclear family must "pry the child loose" from the mother-dependency so that it may "grow up" and accept its responsibilities as an "adult."" (*Op. cit.*, p.314)

Feminists will recognize most of these lines of argument as updated versions of what are in fact very ancient arguments against any attempt to change the patriarchal family, or to improve the social status of women. (See, for instance, Aristotle's objections to Plato's suggestion that male and female "guardians" within the Republic be educated for identical social roles.) The thesis of the necessity of the instrumental-expressive division of labor between the sexes is essentially a version of the age-old notion that certain virtues (rationality, courage, etc.) are masculine and others (sensitivity, ability to express emotion, etc.) feminine, and that it is best for each sex to cultivate its own virtues and not those of the other. (See, e.g., Rousseau.) Ever since the beginning of the eighteenth century, if not earlier, feminists have repeatedly demonstrated the a priori and ill-substantiated status of this traditional notion; yet its attraction is shown by its tendency to constantly resurface in new and supposedly scientific guises.

Yet Parsons is not an *overt* male supremacist, and neither is he unaware that the prevailing sex-role dichotomy has unfortunate side effects. He is able to observe, for instance, that both sexes may be rendered more hostile towards one another by the need to conform to their respective sex roles. The need to dissociate themselves from their original identification with the mother causes males to develop a cult of "compulsive masculinity." Forced to compete for success, men are vulnerable to feelings of inadequacy, for which they may try to compensate by violent or sadistic behavior. And women, excluded from the occupational world outside the family—or at least from the high-status, instrumentally-oriented portions of it—are thus

> denied a sense of participation with their men in a common enterprise . . . This drastic exclusion must serve to increase the inferiority feelings of women and hence their resentment at their condemnation by the accident of sex to an inferior role. (*Essays*, p.313)

Nevertheless, it does not occur to Parsons to ask whether women and men might not learn, or already be learning, to transcend the expressive-instrumental dichotomy, or whether such a change might not benefit not only individuals of both sexes but the family as well. Nor does he indicate that such a change, *were* it possible, would be morally desirable. This omission is probably due in large part to the fact that Parsons obscures the real power differential inherent in the traditional sex-role dichotomy by making the equal social status, and the equal power, of husband and wife within the family a matter of postulation or definition (2). To do this is to define the reality of male supremacy out of existence and hence to preclude recognition of its morally objectionable qualities.

An equally important objection is that the functionalists fail to take their basic biological metaphor seriously enough. Social systems, like biological organisms, are not eternally the same. They are not only *self-maintaining* systems, but *evolving and changing* systems, with the capacity to adapt themselves (or to give rise to other systems which are better adapted) to changing circumstances. Why then should it be assumed that the family *cannot* adapt to such changing circumstances as the diminution of the childrearing role and the just demands of women for an equal share in public life? The "functional necessities" of the past are not necessarily those of the present, much less those of the future. And of course even the past is liberally sprinkled with famous exceptions like the Curies and queens—are these to be regarded as "impossible facts"?

1. Morris Zelditch, Jr., "Role Differentiation in the Nuclear Family: A Comparative Study," *Family, Socialization and Interaction Process*, p.312.
2. See *Family, Socialization and Interaction Process*, pp.45-46.

PATRIARCHY THEORY A patriarchal social system is one whose most basic units are male dominated, patrilineal and usually patrilocal, families. Patriarchy is older than written history, and the question of when and why it began is one to which there are no definitive answers. The male-dominated family may be an inheritance from our prehuman ancestors (as some biological determinists and radical feminists, e.g. Firestone, maintain), or it may be a much more recent development, a result in part of the institution of private property (as is maintained by Marxists and socialist feminists).

The theory that the patriarchal family was the earliest human social grouping is a very old one. Plato held that patriarchal authority was the only sort of authority which preceded the state and could survive its downfall. Indeed, prior to the latter part of the nineteenth century, most Western thinkers have assumed that the first human societies were modeled more or less along the line of the patriarchal Hebrews of the Old Testament. In 1861 Sir Henry Maine argued, on the basis of early Roman law, that the patriarchal family was the original form of all known societies. His theory was soon challenged, however, by scholars who held that the patriarchal family arose only after the demise of the original human family, which was matrilineal, matrilocal, and matriarchal. (See Bachofen, McLennan, Morgan, Engels, Briffault; also Matriarchy Theory.) Westermarck responded with a defense of the patriarchy theory based on comparative anthropology. Darwin and Spencer argued that the rule of the male is natural both because he is the stronger, and because the male has been subject to a more intense selection for intelligence.

For a long time during the twentieth century the debate between patriarchy and matriarchy theorists was largely suspended, since both theories, and indeed the entire project of producing general theories of human social evolution, were in disrepute among Western social scientists and philosophers. In recent years, however, patriarchy theory has reemerged in an updated form, based on evidence gathered by ethologists, sociobiologists, and endocrinologists. (See Ardrey, Fox, Morris, Tiger, Storr; also Biological Determinism.) These new patriarchists hold that during the ages in which the survival of the species depended upon the hunting skills of the males, the latter were selected for aggression, dominance, and a tendency to form peer-group bonds (only) with other males. As a result, male supremacy is a built-in feature of human behavior, and not subject to basic alteration.

On the other side of the debate, feminists have argued for a more informed view of human prehistory, one which recognizes the importance of women's portion of the original division of labor, and does not presume that the hunting activities of the males were always the mainstay of the subsistence system. (See Elaine Morgan, Reed; also Martin and Voorhies, and Reiter, in Anthologies I.) There are few who still seriously contend that all (or even any) early societies were truly matriarchal, i.e. ruled by women; but on the other hand it is equally unlikely that they were all strictly patriarchal. It is probable that the distribution of power between the sexes has always varied quite widely from culture to culture, influenced by a variety of factors, but in particular by the relative economic importance of women's work, and by the degree to which women controlled the distribution of the products of their work. (See Friedl.) At the same time, it may well be the case that during the (extremely long) gathering and hunting phase of human existence, men rarely had the kind of absolute power over women which they acquired in barbaric and civilized cultures, and that the earliest cultures were often very nearly egalitarian. Patriarchy is not, therefore, *the* primordial form of human social organization—though it may be an option which has always been taken by at least some portion of the species.

SAINT PAUL (First Century, A.D.). *The Letters of Paul,* in the Bible (probably written between about 50 and 65 A.D.)

Paul of Tarsus is credited by historians with transforming Christianity from a local sect to a world religion. He was born of parents who were Jewish but enjoyed Roman citizenship, and he was trained in Jerusalem as a Pharisee. After his conversion to Christianity he rose to leadership in the embryonic Church, traveled throughout the Eastern Mediterranean to preach the new faith, and was eventually martyred in Rome, at least according to the tradition. His utterances on women are relatively brief and cryptic, but clearly patriarchal in tone. They have had an enormous influence for the worse upon women's position in marriage and the Church, though in fairness it must be pointed out that some of the most misogynous remarks occur in letters which are no longer generally attributed to Paul (especially Timothy I).

Paul was a self-proclaimed celibate who viewed indulgence in sexual intercourse as a moral failing, though not a sin if strictly confined within marriage. Virginity is best, but marriage is permissible insofar as it is the only alternative to extramarital sex.

> . . . is good for a man not to touch a woman. Nevertheless, to avoid fornication, let every man have his own wife and let every woman have her own husband. (1) (Corinthians I, 7: 1–3)

Paul preached the supremacy of the man in marriage, and admonished wives to obey their husbands, just as servants should obey their masters and children their parents. (Colossians, 3: 18–23) Nor did he consider women's subordination to be a merely earthly or political affair, like that of slaves. For he compares man's rule over women to Christ's rule over man, and God's over Chirst. The divine chain of command extends from the male Deity to the Son, to the human male and finally to woman; for

> . . . the head of every man is Christ; and the head of the woman is the man, and the head of Christ is God. (Corinthians I, 11: 3–4)

This, he continues, is the reason why women should pray with their heads covered but men should not cover theirs. The man, he says,

> is the image of God and reflects his glory; while woman is the reflection of man's glory. For man was not made from woman, but woman from man, and man was not created for woman, but woman was for man. That is why she ought to wear upon her head something to symbolize her subjection . . . (2) (Corinthians I, 11: 7–10)

One could hardly wish for a more explicit endorsement of male supremacy than this. Yet there are also passages from the *Letters* which seem to imply that in some other, more obscure sense, men and women are equal. Thus, for example, the passage from which the above quotation is taken continues with the remark that,

> in union with the Lord, woman is not independent of man nor man of woman. For just as woman was made from man, man is born of woman, and it all really comes from God. (3) (Corinthians I, 11: 11–13)

The same theme appears in the Letter to the Galatians, where Paul chides those who expected the Gentile Christians to follow all the laws of the Jews, especially as regards circumcision. Man, he holds, is "justified" by faith in Christ, not obedience to human law. Thus, he says,

> as many of you as have been baptized unto Christ have put on Christ. There is neither "Jew" nor "Greek," there is neither "bond" nor "free," there is neither "male" nor "female": for ye are all one in Christ Jesus. And if ye be Christ's then are ye Abraham's seed, and heirs according to the promise. (4) (Galatians, 3: 26–29)

It is probably a futile task to seek to resolve the paradoxes or perhaps contradictions, in Paul's attitude towards women. It seems that Paul saw no inconsistency between the egalitarian docrine of the Letter to the Galatians and the endorsement of male supremacy on earth—perhaps because he saw the earthly existence as a relatively unimportant prelude to the afterlife. There is, in Mary Daly's words, "an unresolved tension between the personalist Christian message and the restrictions and compromises imposed by the historical situation." (5) What is tragic is that almost without exception, for nearly two thousand years, the various Christian churches have chosen to be guided not by Paul's specifically Christian message, but by his historically contingent political conservatism with respect to the position of women. (See also the Bible.)

1. This is from the King James translation, as is the next quotation.
2. Translation from *The Complete Bible: An American Translation* (University of Chicago Press, 1923).
3. *Ibid*.
4. King James translation.
5. Daly, *The Church and the Second Sex*, p.84.

PHILOSOPHY OF WOMAN   The philosophy of man is an area of philosophy which deals with the nature of "man," usually in the so-called generic sense of that term (1). It deals with such questions as the essential properties of man; the difference between man and animal, man and the angels (see Aquinas), man and God; the duties of man to man, of man to God, and so on. One might logically suppose that the philosophy of woman would be a subarea of the philosophy of man, and that there would also be a subarea dealing with man as a sex. In fact, however, a great many philosophers who have presented theories of the nature of man which are seemingly intended to apply to all (normal, adult) human beings, turn out on closer reading to view these theories as much less applicable to women than to men. Thus, Aristotle defines man as the rational animal; but he also holds that women's rational capacity is defective, and that they are therefore naturally subject to men. The philosophy of woman is what this encyclopedia is about, even though most of the authors included are not philosophers in the academic sense.

Not all of the great philosophers of the western tradition have expressed views on the nature of woman; but of those who have, few have failed to find it in some way defective in comparison to that of the male sex. Plato and Aristotle disagreed on the question of whether women's nature, and hence their duty, is essentially different from that of men (Aristotle's view), or whether women could do all of the things that men do, but usually not as well (Plato's view). Christian philosophers have generally sided with Aristotle; there is also, in much Judeo-Christian philosophy and theology, a strong element of misogyny, which depicts women as not only different and inferior, but sinful, lustful and dangerous as well. (See the Bible, Paul, Augustine, Aquinas; also Daly and Ruether, for critiques of Christian conceptions of women.)

During the Enlightenment period, moral and political philosophers of the stature of Rousseau, Locke, Hume, and Kant defended the rights and the equality of all men, but, at the same time, the subordination of women. There was more gallantry and less overt misogyny in their appraisals of women's nature, but they clearly supported the sexual status quo. The feminist cause, on the other hand, was defended by able thinkers like Astell and Wollstonecraft, who, though not generally included among the philosophers at all, certainly deserve such recognition.

In the nineteenth century, the preponderance of philosophical opinion became, if anything, even more antifeminist. Hegel, Schopenhauer, Nietzsche, Spencer and Kierkegaard all maintained that women are mentally and morally inferior to men and must remain in subjection to them. Among the (male) philosophers of the first rank, only John Stuart Mill and later Bertrand Russell argued for the natural equality of women, and held that moral and legal equality between the sexes was an intrinsically necessary goal. Both were so-called "liberal feminists," who continued to defend the traditional division of labor in marriage, which makes the woman economically dependent upon the man. Fourier, W. Thompson, Marx, Engels, Bebel and other socialist philosophers argued for sexual equality and the end of women's complete commitment to the private domestic role; but, like Plato, they considered this goal primarily as a necessary condition for the achievement of socialism rather than as an end in itself.

Most philosophers of the Anglo-American analytic tradition—which still constitutes the mainstream of academic philosophy in this country—have, until recently, shown little or no interest in the moral and conceptual issues surrounding the sexual dichotomy and the relationship between the sexes. In the decade of the seventies, however, feminist and women's issues have become part of the philosophical agenda to a greater extent than ever before. Philosophical journals now contain articles on the concept of self-respect, oppression and repression, equality of opportunity, reverse discrimination, sexism in language, virtue, sex roles, abortion and population policy. Many but by no means all of the new feminist philosophers are women.

Other contemporary philosophers, not necessarily feminists, have produced conceptual analyses of sexuality and sexual intercourse, some of them based on the interesting analogy between erotic interaction and linguistic communication (2). Moral philosophers have reevaluated the arguments for considering homosexuality and adultery morally objectionable (3). All of these developments are part of the current and long overdue widening of philosophical concern to include issues of applied ethics and social policy. The best summary accounts of these recent philosophical treatments of feminist issues may be found in the review articles published periodically in *Signs*, the leading journal of women's studies (4). See also Abortion, Affirmative Action, Language and Women; and Vetterling-Braggin, English, Jaggar, Mahowald, Bishop, Gould, Osborne, In Anthologies XII.

1. See Janice Moulton, "The Myth of the Neutral "Man," " in *Feminism and Philosophy*, edited by Mary Vetterling-Braggin, Frederick Elliston, and Jane English, Anthologies XII.
2. See Robert Solomon, "Sex and Perversion," and Thomas Nagel, "Sexual Perversion," in *Philosophy and Sex*, edited by Robert Baker and Frederick Elliston, Anthologies XII.
3. See Richard Wasserstrom, "Is Adultery Immoral?" and Ronald Atkinson, "The Morality of Homosexual Behavior," in *Today's Moral Problems*, edited by Richard Wasserstrom, Anthologies XII.
4. See *Signs* 1:2 (Winter, 1975), 2:2 (Winter, 1976) and 3:4 (Summer, 1978), for reviews of recent philosophical research on sexism and feminism by Christine Pierce, Janice Moulton, and Jane English, respectively.

PLATO (427 B.C.–347 B.C.). *The Republic* (with an English translation by R. J. Bury; Harvard University Press, Cambridge, Massachusetts, and William Heinmann Ltd., London, 1970, in two volumes; this translation first published 1935. Written circa 380 B.C.)

Laws (with an English translation by R. G. Bury; Harvard University Press, Cambridge, Massachusetts, and William Heinmann Ltd., London, 1961, in two volumes; this translation first published 1926. Written circa 357–347 B.C.)

Plato's *Republic* is often cited as the earliest (known) work of feminist philosophy, since in this dialogue Socrates proposes the abolition of the nuclear family, as well as complete equality of education and of all social and political roles between women and men of the ruling class. Others have denied, however, that Plato was in any way motivated by a desire to improve the status of women as such. The *Republic* is above all an exposition of the concept of justice, which Socrates claims can best be understood if "writ large," in the laws and institutions of an imaginary ideally just state. This ideal state will have a semihereditary class system, with the Guardian class performing both the military and governmental functions (1). Besides the Guardians there will be farmers, merchants, sailors and manual laborers, as well, of course, as slaves; most of the dialogue, however, deals with the arrangements to be made for the Guardian class. The role of the women Guardians is discussed primarily in Book V.

The members of the Guardian class—and only of this class—will be forbidden to own property, other than a few personal items, or to so much as touch money or anything made of gold or silver. They will live and eat communally, following the principle, "all things in common between friends" (2) (Book IV, 423E–424A; see note 2), a principle which Plato makes applicable to wives and children as well as land and houses. For, as F. A. Wright points out, "Plato at first hardly escapes from the fallacy that a man's wife is as much a piece of property as a dog or a table." (3) Guardians are to have their wives in common, yet the latter will not be merely communal wives; they will be Guardians in their own right, and will perform all the same functions as the men, apart from the bearing of offspring.

Socrates begins his argument for educating and treating women Guardians as nearly like the men as possible by returning to an analogy which he has made earlier, between the Guardians and trained watchdogs guarding and protecting a flock. He asks,

> Do we expect the females of watch-dogs to join in guarding what the males guard and to hunt with them and share all their pursuits or do we expect the females stay indoors as being incapacitated by the bearing and breeding of the whelps while the males toil and have all the care of the flock?"
>
> "They have all things in common," he [Glaucon] replied, "except that we treat the females as weaker and the males as stronger."
>
> "Is it possible, then," said I, "to employ any creature for the same ends as another if you do not assign it the same nurture and education?"
>
> "It is not possible."
>
> "If, then, we are to use the women for the same things as the men, we must also teach them the same things."
>
> "Yes." (4) (Book V, 451D–452A; see note A.)

This means, Socrates continues, that women must be trained both intellectually and physically, that they must take part in war along with the men and also exercise naked in the gymnasium, just as the men do. He admits that this idea will occasion a great deal of ridicule, but insists that this should be of no concern, since anyone "who tries to raise a laugh at the sight of anything but what is foolish and wrong" (Book V, 452D) is insincere in his pursuit of the good. But there is, he notes, a more serious objection to giving the same roles to women as to men, i.e. that there is a natural difference between women and men, and therefore their roles must also differ.

To this, Socrates replies that not all differences between people are relevant to their occupations; for instance, the differences between a bald man and a man with hair is no reason to conclude that if one is a cobbler the other should be forbidden to be a cobbler. The fact that "the female bears and the male begets" is equally irrelevant to their participation in the running of a state. For there are no pursuits or capacities which are peculiar to men as men or to women as women; the only difference is that in general men are *better* than women at all of these pursuits, except those which are traditionally regarded as women's work and which a man would be ridiculed for performing well. Thus,

> the natural capacities are distributed alike among both creatures, and women naturally share in all pursuits and men in all—yet for all the woman is weaker than the man. (Book V, 455D–E)

The premise that women are generally inferior to men, at everything other than what men choose not to do, would normally be taken to support a *difference* in the social roles of the sexes. But Plato argues instead that since women do not naturally excel men in any particular activity, they have no natural pursuits, other than their biological role in reproduction. Furthermore, some women are better than some men in some activities. Hence women, like men, must be judged on their individual merits. Like men, they have no natural social role and no proper sphere other than that for which their individual capacities suit them.

As Christine Pierce points out, Plato's argument here "may be construed as an attempt to grant as much as any misogynist could desire, and still show the logical implication to be equal opportunity for both sexes." (5) On the other hand, Plato's assumption of the general inferiority of women does not appear to be one which he grants only for the sake of argument. For the same assumption appears elsewhere in Plato, and is never questioned or refuted. In the *Timaeus*, for instance, a creation myth is related, according to which human beings were created in two sexes, and, "the better of the two was that which in future would be called man." (6) According to the myth, the first generation of human beings were all male,

> And anyone who lived well for an appointed time would return home to his native star . . . but anyone who failed to do so would be changed into a woman at his second birth. And if he still did not refrain from wrong, he would be changed into some animal. (7)

If, as this passage seems to imply, Plato viewed women as a form of life intermediate between men and animals, then in spite of his belief in a sex-blind meritocracy his position is not what one would normally describe as feminist. Furthermore, it is probably more difficult than Plato supposes to reconcile the belief in the general or average inferiority of women with the assignment of identical social roles to the two sexes.

Be that as it may, once we agree that women and men are to play essentially the same social and political roles, it follows—so Plato argues—that the nuclear family must be abolished; male and female Guardians will be forbidden to live together in separate households, and children will be reared collectively, in order to free the women Guardians from as many of their domestic duties as possible; no parent is to know which children are his or hers. This collective childrearing will also make it possible for the Guardians to be bred according to a eugenic program, the best men being bred to the best and the largest number of women.

The *Laws* is Plato's last work, and is generally said to present a more conservative set of views on women. In fact, this is not obviously the case, since the imaginary state depicted in this dialogue is explicitly said to be not the best or ideal state, which Plato continues to identify with that of the *Republic*, but rather the second best, or Magnesian state, which Plato has evidently come to see as more workable in practice or more feasible to actually establish. While the *Republic* depicts an aristocracy of philosophers, the *Laws* describes a state which is a cross between democracy and oligarchy, and in which all power is in the hands of the older citizens. There are to be several thousand more or less equal portions of land, each held by a single male citizen and his male heirs—one in each generation, that is, since these parcels can be neither sold nor divided. Male citizens will be required to marry between the ages of 30 and 35, women between 16 and 20. All citizens will eat communally, whether married or not. Plato suspects that the women will not enjoy eating in public but says that they must be required to do so, since, "in as far as females are inferior in goodness to males," it is even more important that their behavior be regulated (Book VI, 781B 1–2). Married women of childbearing age will not hold public office, though they may do so thereafter. Women may not choose their own husbands, but will be betrothed by their fathers or nearest male relative; they will inherit property only when there is no male heir, and then in name only, the real control being vested in their husbands.

The Magnesian state, then, has many patriarchal features. And it is interesting that Plato endorses what in the nineteenth century became known as the patriarchal theory of cultural evolution—or something rather like it. He suggests that whenever civilization is destroyed, e.g. in the wake of a major natural catastrophe, the only authority is patriarchal authority, i.e. the rule of the father of a family over its other members. Indeed, he speaks of this rule as "of all kingships the most just." (Book III, 680C 3) He has not, however, given up the idea of educating females along much the same lines as men; after the age of six the sexes are to be taught separately, but girls are to learn much the same lessons as boys, including "riding, archery, javelin-throwing and slinging, and . . . the use of arms." (Book VII, 794, C-D) Yet there will also be differences, e.g. in the games, music and dance taught to girls and boys, "as defined by the natural difference of the two sexes." (Book VII, 802E) As to the nature of these natural differences, he says

> that what is noble and of a manly tendency is masculine, while that which inclines rather to decorum and sedateness is to be regarded as feminine . . . " (BookVII, 802E–803A)

With this qualification, Plato still holds that, "the female sex must share with the male, to the greatest extent possible, both in education and in all else." (Book VII, 805C) The major argument for this is the same as for requiring women to eat communally, with the men, namely that it is the only way to assure that their lives will be as temperate and orderly as those of the men. "The law giver," he says,

> ought to be whole-hearted, not half-hearted—letting the female sex indulge in luxury and expense and disorderly ways of life, while supervising the male sex. (Book VII, 806B)

Like the arguments of the *Republic*, this is a long way from a feminist stance—though it does recall the argument presented by Wollstonecraft and other modern feminists, that women's exclusion from the affairs of the world leads to their moral corruption. On the other hand, Plato's views are probably more sexually egalitarian than those of any major Western philosopher for the next two thousand years. It is unfortunate that Aristotle's reaction against the philosophical doctrines of Plato included a vigorous endorsement of women's absolute (essential as well as statistical) inferiority, and of the importance of confining them to a strictly domestic role. (Also see Bisexuality.)

1. Semihereditary in that children of the Guardian class who are found to be inferior in the traits required of Guardians will be demoted to the laboring class, and vice versa; superior children of the lower class will be promoted into the Guardian class.

PLATO

2. *The Republic*, translation by H. D. P. Lee (Penguin Books, Baltimore, Maryland, 1967, first published 1955). This translation is couched in more ordinary or colloquial English and is sometimes easier to follow.

3. F. A. Wright, *Feminism in Greek Literature* (Kennikat Press, Port Washington, New York; first published 1923), p.169.

4. Aristotle, in the *Politics*, objects to this analogy on the grounds that women, unlike female watchdogs, have households to manage—a question-begging response since Plato's point is precisely that this kind of role division should be eliminated in the Guardian class. (*Politics*, 1264b 15–18)

5. Christine Pierce, "Equality: Republic V," *The Monist*, 57:1 (January 1973), p. 3.

6. Plato, *Timaeus and Critias* (translated by H. D. P. Lee, Penguin Books, Middlesex, England, 1971), p. 57.

PRIVATE PROPERTY AND THE STATUS OF WOMEN: See Socialism and Feminism.

PSYCHOLOGY OF WOMEN   Beliefs or presumptions about the psychology of women lie at the heart of almost every defense of feminism or of patriarchy. Consequently, most of the thinkers dealt with in this book either propound or presuppose some theory about the psychological nature of women. The fact that it is virtually always female and not male psychology which is discussed in connection with the difference between the sexes is a reflection of male domination, in the conceptual as in the social order. There is no special subject area called the "psychology of men," simply because psychology has almost always meant the psychology of males, while it was female psychology that was assumed to be different, and the reason for women's inferior social status.

The philosophy of Plato is very nearly, but not quite, an exception to this rule. Plato held that there are no universal qualitative differences between the virtues or abilities of women and those of men, and that for the good of all, social roles and duties ought to be assigned on the basis of individual ability rather than sex. He also thought, however, that most men are better than most women at everything other than those things which are "women's work" and which a man would be embarrassed to be

377

seen doing.

Aristotle, on the other hand, held that the different biological nature of women coincides with a distinct female psychology. In women, he says, the rational and deliberative capacity which enables a man to relate his own actions, is deficient; hence it is natural for a wife to be subordinate to her husband and to be ruled by him. Augustine and the other Church fathers emphasized women's sinfulness and sexuality as justification of their subordinate status, rather than their lack of intellect. Aquinas, however, reasserted the Aristotelian doctrine of the inferior rational powers of women, as have modern philosophers of the stature of Rousseau, Kant, Schopenhauer and Nietzsche. Darwin and Spencer speculated that the superior intellectual powers of the male were the result of differential evolutionary pressures.

These self-serving presumptions of female intellectual inferiority have been repeatedly challenged and refuted by feminist writers at least as early as the seventeenth century. (See, e.g., Astell, Wollstonecraft, John Stuart Mill, Harriet Taylor.) Yet this myth has been perpetuated in our own century by, for instance, both the Freudian and Jungian schools of psychoanalysis. Freud did not claim that the female intellect is inferior, although he did stress the absence in females of a strong superego or a sense of justice. Some of his most orthodox disciples, however, drew from Freudian premises the conclusion that not only is the female intellect inferior, but its development is inconsistent with that of women's (much more important) emotional capacities. (See Deutsch, and Lundberg and Farnham.) Erik Erikson, a contemporary Freudian psychoanalyst, argues that the basic psychological orientation of males and females is analogous to the physical structure of their genitals; males are active and outgoing, females passive and receptive. This, again is a cruder theory than Freud's, yet hardly less implausible than the latter's suggestion that female psychology is based upon the envy of the male penis.

There have also been some important rebels among the (one–time) followers of Freud. Karen Horney, for instance, countered the notion of penis envy with that of womb envy, i.e. male jealousy of women's capacity to give birth. Clara Thompson argues that what women envy is not men's genitals but their superior status and freedom. Adler argued that both sexes are originally (equally) motivated by a desire for power over others, but that in women this desire is much more suppressed by the male–dominated society. Reich argued that the oppression of women and the repression of sexuality go hand in hand in the patriarchal family, and that human liberation requires the elimination of all three—male dominance, the patriarchal family, and patriarchal sexual taboos. (Also see Radical Feminism.) In spite of these exceptions, however, the major thrust of Freudian psychoanalysis and psychotherapy has been to recommend the passive, subordinate, domestic role as the only normal one for women, and to stigmatize the woman who rebels against it as psychologically abnormal, and unfeminine.

The association between femininity and the absence of intellect is even stronger in the Jungian tradition of psychoanalysis. Jung identified masculinity with Logos, i.e., reason, judgment, objectivity; femininity he defined as Eros, the principle of subjective interpersonal relationship. And, although he held that it is essential for a person of either sex to be aware of, and in communication with, the contrasexual element of his or her own psyche, he also thought that it was unnatural and undesirable for a women's intellectual capacities to be highly developed. This notion is echoed by the majority of Jungian theorists; see, e.g., Neumann, Harding, Scott-Maxwell, Stern, de Castillejo, and Singer. (For feminist critiques of psychoanalytic, particularly Freudian, views on the psychology of women, see Chesler, Figes, Millett, and Ellman; also see Mitchell, Firestone, and Dinnerstein, radical feminists who attempt to reconcile certain elements of Freudian and feminist theory.)

In the past decade there has been an enormous amount of research on sex and gender roles and male and female traits and abilities. Although some differences appear fairly regularly, none of these supports the notion of the general intellectual superiority of males. Bardwick, for instance, argues that the primary innate behavioral difference between the sexes is a greater muscular activity on the part of males. This small original difference interacts with social and cultural factors in such a way as to produce a much greater psychological difference, e.g. in aggressiveness and orientation, than could have resulted from the innate difference alone.

In their important review of the research in this area, Maccoby and Jacklin find evidence of statistical differences between the intellectual talents of males and females, but not such as to justify any attribution of overall mental superiority to either. Thus, females consistently excel in a range of skills labeled "verbal," while males excel in visual-spatial perception and analysis. They also give some credence to the evidence that males may be not only more active, but more aggressive, and inherently so. So does Juanita Williams; but neither she nor they consider that such a male propensity for aggression precludes fundamental changes in sex roles or a greater degree of social equality between the sexes.

Corinne Hutt, on the other hand, considers male aggressiveness to be not only the basic cause of male dominance, but sufficient to render the latter almost impervious to change. She also argues that women's lack of exceptional achievement in the sciences and arts is the result, not of a lesser average intelligence among women, but of the lesser variability of women's mental endowments, which means that there are not only fewer females with subnormal intelligence, but fewer female "geniuses." (See Darwin, and Ellis, for earlier defenses of this latter argument; also see Biological Determinism.)

Such theories, however, are less promising and less popular at present than those which stress social learning, cognitive development, role modeling, or some combination of these, as the explanation of observable psychological differences between the sexes. Matina Horner's research on the so-called fear of success in women suggests that if women often fail to rival men in competitive intellectual fields it is largely because they have learned that they will be punished for doing so.

Other feminists have criticized the entire project of doing "psychology of women", i.e. of focusing research efforts on the discovery of statistical differences between the various intellectual capacities, behavioral dispositions, etc., as though sex were obviously the relevant factor in explaining all such differences. We do not, after all, (still) concentrate a comparable amount of attention on the discovery of psychological differences between various races and ethnic groups; such comparative studies, when they are done, are often attacked as racist, although in fact they may not always be so. Naomi Weisstein argues, in her influential article, "Psychology Constructs the Female," that all of the supposed evidence for inherent, and even most of that for learned psychological differences between the sexes is vitiated by the methodolgical errors and sexist biases of the investigators.

Jean Baker Miller, in *Toward a New Psychology of Women*, seeks to explain the observable psychological differences between men and women in terms of women's subordinate social status on the one hand, and their special role within the family as caretaker and emotional arbiter, on the other. Another feminist psychologist, Sandra Bem, has produced evidence that the sexual stereotyping of personality interferes with the capacity of persons whose character traits are either predominantly "masculine" or predominantly "feminine," to function effectively in a wide range of contexts. Since there are feminine males and masculine women, as well as "androgynes" of both sexes, the sexual stereotyping of personality is clearly not a function of biological sex alone.

Another area of research which seems to point to the social environment as the most powerful agent in the production of whatever observable psychological differences there may be between the sexes is the study of hermaphroditic and pseudo-hermaphroditic individuals. Such persons are sometimes assigned at birth and reared as a member of the sex opposite to that indicated by their chromosomes, or even to their external genitalia and/or hormonal environment. Yet they almost always develop secure gender identities consonant with the sex of assignment, and have personalities well within the range traditionally considered normal for that sex. (See Money and Ehrhardt, Stoller.)

It should be clear even from these few references that the psychology of women (or, more accurately, of sex and gender differences) is currently in an exciting phase. Rapid theoretical development is occurring, which, perhaps for the first time, is not uniformly biased by the presumption of female intellectual inferiority. For more thorough surveys of recent research, see the review articles by Mary Brown Parlee and Reesa M. Vaughter, in *Signs*, 1:1 (pp.119–128 and 2:1 (pp.120–246); also see Lips and Colwill's *The Psychology of Sex Differences*, in Anthologies XIII. For collections of recent theoretical and research studies, see Maccoby, Beach, Cox, Miller, Bardwick, and Strouse, in the same section.

R

RADICAL FEMINISM   The major distinction within the women's movement today is that between liberal and radical feminists. The distinction is by no means a sharp one, since even
liberal feminists may be said to be radical in some respects, while
radical feminists usually also support the sorts of reforms sought
by liberals. Nevertheless, it can be said that liberal feminists, by
definition, are those who concentrate efforts on achieving legal,
educational, and sometimes economic equality for women—
goals of the same general sort as those proposed by Wollstonecraft, Mill, Harriet Taylor, and other great feminist liberals of the
past. (See Friedan.) Radical feminists, on the other hand, agree
on the need for legal and educational equality, but deny that such
reforms alone can suffice to bring about real equality between the
sexes. They argue that the basic sources of women's oppression
are the patriarchal family, the capitalist economic system, and the
ideology of hierarchy and competition, which defends patriarchy
and capitalism as both "natural" and progressive.

Radical feminists also hold that socialism (not necessarily of a
Marxist variety) is a necessary, but not a sufficient condition for
women's liberation. (See Green, Firestone, Millett, Mitchell, and
Hilda Scott.) They argue that in the socialist states women participate almost equally in the public production process, but fail to
achieve equal political and economic power because of the persistence of male supremacist ideas, and because they continue to
be burdened with the major part of the child care and other
domestic work. The elimination of this persistent inequality will
require such fundamental changes as (1) the end of the institution
of motherhood, which makes individual mothers personally responsible for most of the care which their children require, and the
rearing of children communally, and/or with equal paternal involvement (see Dinnerstein, Firestone, Millett, Rich); (2) the end,
not necessarily of heterosexuality, but of monogamous heterosexual marriage as a binding norm; (3) the end of taboos against
lesbianism and (male) homosexuality, and other nonstandard
but morally innocuous forms of sexual expression (see Abbot,

Firestone, Dworkin, Gearhardt in Anthologies XII; also Johnston, and Millett); (4) the end of the patriarchal ideology which denigrates both women and the values with which they have been associated (see Firestone, Millett, J.B. Miller, Giele, Holliday); and finally, (5) a wiser and less exploitative attitude towards and relationship with the rest of nature (See works listed above.).

Although radical (and indeed all) feminists reject the biological determinism of Freud (see de Beauvoir, Figes, Millett), many of them consider his account of the psychosexual development of children within the patriarchal family to be an invaluable tool of feminist analysis. (See Dinnerstein, Firestone, Mitchell.) However, like the renegade Freudian Wilhelm Reich, they reject the claim that the process of sexual repression represented by the Oedipus complex is necessary for civilized life (1). Sexual repression may indeed help to create people who are willing to devote themselves to dull, alienating jobs; but socialism, it is optimistically predicted, will eliminate the need for most such unfulfilling labor (see Firestone).

The socialist utopias described by some radical feminist resemble much earlier socialist utopian visions. (See Fourier, W. Thompson, and Gilman.) But radical feminism seeks to incorporate not only such utopian elements, but also the insights and analytic tools of dialectical materialism, psychoanalysis, and, increasingly, of the sciences of endocrinology, ethology and sociobiology—sciences whose findings have often been used to support antifeminist conclusions. (See Biological Determinism.) Some radical feminists view male supremacy as rooted not only in culture and social institutions, but in biological conditions which we inherit from our prehuman ancestors.

Firestone, for example, stresses the effects of pregnancy and the helplessness of infants, in making both women and children dependent to some degree upon men for support; she considers the development of an artifical womb a precondition for equality. Holliday is persuaded by the evidence that human males, if not inherently more aggressive, are more inclined to learn aggressive ways; thus she emphasizes the need to stop teaching males to be aggressive or violent. And Borgese even goes so far as to suggest that the very fact that the species is divided into lifelong sexual categories preclude equality, and to suggest that in the ideal society everyone will be female for the first half of their lives and male for the second half. (Also see Ursula Le Guin.) Although this is a minority position, even among radical feminists, such suggestions cannot be dismissed out of hand. It will in the near future become increasingly possible to alter the sexual composition of society, as well as the sex of individuals. The moral problems in doing so have barely begun to be explored. (See also Liberal Feminism, Lesbian Separatism, Spiritual Feminism, and Socialism and Feminism.)

1. See Freud, *Civilization and Its Discontents*.

RAPE   Until recent years, the subject of rape and its effect upon women's lives and social status, was subject to remarkably little discussion, research, or analysis. Rape was generally considered to be a pathological act on the part of men who are unable to control their powerful sexual urges; at the same time it was often assumed to be the fault of the female victims themselves, who "ask for it" by dressing or behaving "provocatively." In the 1960s, however, radical feminists began to perceive rape as a social institution which functons to maintain male supremacy. Susan Brownmiller documented the prevalence of rape, throughout all periods of history, and analyzed the practice as "a conscious form of intimidation by which *all men* keep *all women* in a state of fear." (*Against Our Will*, p.5) A number of other books on rape have appeared, exposing the sexist biases which have distorted the way in which the legal system has treated rapists and rape victims, and advising women as to how best to resist rape, and how to deal with the representatives of the law if they do happen to be raped (1).

Feminist philosophers have also written on the role of rape in maintaining male domination, and on the special features of rape which make it particularly apt for this role. Susan Griffin calls it "The All-American Crime." (See *Feminism and Philosophy*, edited by Vetterling-Braggin, in Anthologies XII.) Susan Rae Peterson points out that rape is a type of protection racket, in which women are forced to depend upon men to protect them against other men. (*Op. cit.*) Carolyn Shafer and Marilyn Frye analyze rape as the ultimate act of disrespect, through which women are forefullly reminded that in this society they are not accorded the status of persons. (*Op.cit.*) Pamela Foa argues, on the other hand, that it is the way in which rape reflects the society's model of heterosexual intercourse in general which makes it such a uniquely humiliating experience. (*Op. cit.*)

The significance of such issues—about the causes and culturally insitutionalized aspects of rape—to other feminist issues, such as the eventual eliminability of patriarchy, is as yet relatively unexplored. It does seem clear that if rape is a social institution rather than a male biological imperative, then the frequency of its occurrence can be reduced by changes in social attitudes towards it. If not, then the picture is bleaker; women's freedom of action will continue to be limited by the threat of rape, unless they learn and are prepared to employ violent means of self-defense. This, indeed, is what many women have chosen to do, though the choice is not an easy one to make or to carry through.

1. See, for instance **Against Rape**, by Andra Medea and Kathleen Thompson, Farrar, Straus and Giroux, New York, 1974; *How to Say No to a Rapist and Survive*, by Frederick Storaska, Random House, New York, 1975; *The Politics of Rape*, by Diana E.H. Russell, Stein and Day, New York, 1975; *Rape*, by Carol V. Horos, Toby Publishing Company, New Canaan, Connecticut, 1974; *Sexual Assault: Confronting Rape in America*, by Nancy Gager and Cathleen Schurr, Grosset and Dunlap, New York, 1976; *Rape: The Power of Consciousness*, by Susan Griffin, Harper and Row, New York, 1979; and *Rape: The First Sourcebook for Women*, by the New York Radical Feminists, edited by Noreen Connell and Cassandra Wilson, New American Library, New York, 1974 (in Anthologies IV). Recent sociological and psychological investigations of rape include *Patterns in Forcible Rape*, by Menachem Amir (University of Chicago Press, Chicago and London, 1971) and *Rape: Offenders and Their Victims*, by John M. MacDonald (Charles C. Thomas, Springfield, Illinois, 1971).

REED, Evelyn. *Problems of Women's Liberation: A Marxist Approach* (Pathfinder Press, New York, 1970; first published 1969)
Woman's Evolution: From Matriarchal Clan to Patriarchal Family (Pathfinder Press, New York, 1975)
Sexism and Science (Pathfinder Press, New York and Toronto, 1978)

Reed is a Marxist feminist who has been active for many years in the Socialist Workers' Party. *Problems of Women's Liberation* is a small but influential collection of speeches and essays presenting the Marxist view of the origins and cure for male domination. Like Engels, Reed holds that it was the rise of private property and class society which led to patriarchy and the oppression of women, and that only under socialism will the sexes be restored to their primordial state of complete equality.

In **Women's Evolution**, Reed draws upon the work of Bach-ofen, Morgan, Engels, Briffault and other anthropologists to support the theory that the earliest human societies were matriarchal. By "matriarchy," Reed means a social system characterized by matrilineal, matrilocal clams with exogamous marriage customs. Men marry women from other clans, but remain outsiders to their wife's clan, owing to their primary loyalty to the mother's clan (matrilclan), and especially to their sisters and their sister's offspring.

This matriarchal system Reed sees as both the creation of women, and as the beginning of cooperative human society. In the dawn of the race, she thinks, social cooperation among men was rendered almost nonexistent by the instinctive combativeness of males. Cannibalism was common, especially on the part of men; women retained the vegetarian diet of our prehuman ancestors much longer than men. Women's maternal instincts gave them a greater capacity for cooperation; they banded together in family groups, and sought to ameliorate the war of all men against all men by inculcating in their children beliefs in totemism and taboo. Members of the totem group, or the matriclan, were off limits to one another. Thus cannibalism was avoided, at least within the clan, and males were also prevented from fighting one another for the possession of women in the clan.

Under the matriclan system, women enjoyed a position of honor, and their social status was at least equal to that of men. They worked together and did most of the important work of society, producing such technological advances as the use of fire, the making of pottery and baskets, weaving, leather working, the building of houses, the domestication of animals, and even agriculture. Women are at the peak of their influence during the first stages of barbarism. Thereafter, their freedom and independence are increasingly eroded by the institution of marriage, via a series of changes that are both complex and obscure; private property, however, is a key factor.

Marriage was a relatively weak and transitory bond during the matriarchal era; not the husband but the brother of a woman was responsible for avenging her death and protecting and providing for her children. But with the appearance of privately owned surplus wealth—particularly in the form of cattle—the institution of marriage changes, and the husband's rights and powers increasingly erode and replace those of the wife's brother and her clan. A major index of this change is the gradual transition from the matriarchal practice of voluntary marriage gifts provided by the groom to the bride's family, to a system of bride purchase in which the woman, or rather her children, become the property of the husband and members of his clan rather than their mother's.

With the advent of purchase marriage, the husband and biological father assumes the rights and responsibilities formerly reserved to the mother's brother. For reasons that are not entirely clear, the influence of the husband proves far more detrimental to women's independence than that of the brother and the maternal clan. For the first time women are deprived of the right to decide whom to marry and when, and they are increasingly isolated into nuclear-family units, where their social role is limited to the production of male heirs. Since patriarchy is originally the result of private property, and since male surpremacy remains a cornerstone of the capitalist econmic system, Reed concludes that sexual equality is possible only under socialism.

Sexism and Science is a collection of articles, written and published between 1957 and 1977, in which Reed criticizes the theories of contemporary biological determinists, who reject the historical materialist account of the rise of patriarchy and argue that the latter is an unalterable part of our animal heritage. (See, e.g., Ardrey, Fox, Lorenz, Tiger, and Wilson.) She argues that these writers ignore the vital distinction between biological evolution and human social evolution. Male domination is a product of the latter, not the former. Only through distortions of the evidence from ethology (i.e. the study of the behavior of animals) and anthropology can it be made to appear that (anything like) patriarchy exists among nonhuman primates or in primitve (pre-private-property) human societies. Thus, there is no reason to suppose that there is anything "instinctual" about male supremacy.

> What man needs to throw off today is not animal nature, which he shed a million years ago; rather, he must throw off capitalist nature, which has been imprinted into man's conduct and psychology by this society. (p.63)

Although the martriarchy theory of human evolution receives little support from most contemporary anthropologists, it remains, in its essential outline, at least as plausible as the contrary thesis, i.e., that human society was dominated by males from the beginning. Little is known about prehistoric social structures, and therefore any such theory is necessarily highly speculative. This fact no doubt accounts in part for the loss of academic respectability which such theories of human social evolution have suffered. For the feminist, however, speculation in this area is almost unavoidable. If we are to explain why women's position throughout recorded history has been a subordinate one, we must form some reasoned hypothesis as to what it was through-out the far longer period of prehistory.

Thus, it is not the speculativeness of Reed's approach which is its major weakness. It is, rather, her failure to deal seriously with the *noneconomic* factors which must have been involved in the rise of patriarchy. Private wealth may well have been the triggering mechanism for the patriarchal revolution; but it could not have led to such a result were it not for certain biological differences between the sexes. (e.g. size and reproductive role), and perhaps also certain psychological differences which are not yet fully understood. The neglect of these genetic factors leads to the expectation that patriarchy will inevitably fade away after the demise of capitalism. This expectation is one for which the his-tory of women's role in modern socialist states provides relatively little evidence. (See Hilda Scott.)

REEVES, Nancy. *Womankind Beyond the Stereotypes* (Aldine Atherton, Chicago, 1971)

An exploration of the concept of woman, focusing on stereo-types of the feminine role, which Reeves describes as preformed patterns of behavior and thought. She argues that traditional presumptions about woman's nature and necessary nurturant role fail every test of logic, historical accuracy and cross-cultural validity, and yet continue to be the norm and to be sustained by our inherited legal, economic and family structures. Such pat-terns have a self-sustaining grip on society; they persist because they are assumed to be both natural and proper, and because they persist they continue to be seen in this light.

Reeves criticizes contemporary feminists for failing to take adequate account of economic realities. She takes their primary goal and demand to be better job opportunities for women, and argues that jobs have not been and will not be the route to women's liberation. In the past women's entry into the labor force has been peripheral to the traditional patterns. The first industrial revolution deprived upper-class women of any eco-nomic function, and made working-class women marginal work-ers, whose labor brought neither economic or social equality nor relief from the double burden of domestic responsibilities. Nor should women expect more extensive job opportunities in the future, since, Reeves predicts, the coming "cybernetic revolu-tion" will mean that most human workers are replaced by machines. Hence the new feminists are wrong to demand work as a source of identity; to do so is to reason within an already outmoded framework. A more progressive demand is that as available work diminishes it should be shared and divided by the progressive shortening of the work day.

The book includes an anthology of feminist and antifeminist readings arranged so as to supplement each of the chapters. These include passages from Xenophon, Sigmund Freud, Erik Erikson, John Stuart Mill and Olive Schreiner.

REICH, Wilhelm (1897–1957). *The Function of the Orgasm: Sex-Economic Problems of Biological Energy* (translated by Theodore P. Wolfe, Noonday Press, New York, 1961; first published by Internationalen Psychoanalytischer Verlag, Wien, 1927)
The Sexual Revolution: Toward a Self-Governing Character Structure (translated by Theodore P. Wolfe, Orgone Institute Press, New York, 1945; first published by Munster Verlag, Vienna, 1930)
The Invasion of Compulsory Sex-Morality Farrar, Straus and Giroux, New York, 1971; first published by Sexpol Verlag, Oslo, 1935)

A Freudian analyst who was also a Marxist, Reich attempted to unify the two theories through his own theory of the role of sexual repression in the maintenance of the patriarchal capitalist social order. Although he considered himself a loyal follower of Freud, he was expelled from the Vienna Psychoanalytic Society for his Marxist and other unorthodox views. He then set up practice in Berlin and was active in the Communist Party until the Nazi rise to power forced him to flee the country in 1933. In 1939 he immigrated to the United States, where he established a research center in New York for the study of his (by then extremely bizarre) "science of Orgonomy," the so-called "energy of life." He was undoubtedly guilty of the medical quackery for which he was prosecuted and convicted; this was, however, no justification for the court's order that *all* of his writings be withdrawn from the market and destroyed. Reich died after serving only a few months in prison.

Reich's post-1933 work is largely dominated by delusion, although the list of professional people who once accepted it as valid is striking. His earlier work, however, has had a powerful influence on such radical feminists as Firestone, Millett and Mitchell. Unfortunately, the English translations of the early works are sprinkled with comments about his later "discoveries," which Reich added at the time they were translated. These, however, can be fairly easily detected, and must be disregarded in evaluating Reich's contributions to psychoanalytic, Marxist, and feminist thought.

Reich's thesis is that not only all neuroses and other mental illnesses, but all forms of antisocial behavior e.g. of oppression and authoritarianism, are the result of the repression of natural sexual desires within the patriarchal family, especially during infancy and adolescence. This repression is not, as Freud held, a necessary condition for all human society and civilization. It occurs only after the rise of patriarchy and the division of society into oppressed and oppressing classes, and contributes only to the preservation of these oppressive social institutions.

In *The Invasion of Compulsory Sex-Morality*, Reich argues that Malinowski's studies of the sexual life of the Trobriand Islanders—contrary to Malinowski's own interpretations—support the Marxist theory of human social evolution. Marx and Engels held (after Bachofen and Morgan) that the primordial form of human society is not the patriarchal family, but the matriarchal clan, in which lineage is traced through the maternal side only and women enjoy complete social equality with men. In the matrilineal Trobriand society (at least prior to the arrival of the Christian missionaries), children and adolescents are free to engage in sexual activity, and they become happy, nonneurotic adults. They are not promiscuous, but settle into (serially) monogamous relationships, a pattern which Reich also considers natural in the absence of sexual repression.

Yet Reich notes that the Trobriand economic system is no longer entirely that of primitive communism. Men are required to make large annual contributions to the support of their sisters and their sisters' families, a custom which enables the chiefs, who are permitted to have a number of wives, to amass considerable private wealth. This wealth would automatically revert to the maternal clan, were it not for the custom of cross-cousin marriage. Chiefs are able to secure the inheritance for their own sons by marrying them to the daughters of their sisters; this practice is the first step in the dissolution of the matriarchy. Furthermore, the girls who are destined for cross-cousin marriage, unlike other Trobriand children, are deprived of sexual freedom from the earliest age, thus heralding the fate of all women under patriarchy.

The Trobriand culture, therefore, confirms the Marxist claim that it is private property and surplus wealth which bring about the downfall of primitive communism and the maternal clan.

Wealth provides men with both the incentive and the power to make their own sons their heirs, thus destroying the matrilineal system. Since patriliny requires a sure knowledge of paternity, it leads to monogamous marriage and the subjection of women. Monogamy, in turn, requires the suppression of childhood and adolescent sexuality, since individuals with natural "orgastic potency" will not and cannot submit to the constraints of monogamous marriage.

Thus, the patriarchal family perpetuates itself through repressing the sexual needs of its members. Sexually frustrated people, Reich claims, are submissive to authority and capable of doing alienated, uninteresting labor; hence they are well adapted to existence under an oppressive class system. They are also neurotic, unhappy, and sadistic and/or masochistic; for the desire for sexual pleasure is as powerful as the desire for food, and can be thwarted only at the expense of the health of the organism. Indeed, Reich identifies the libido, or sexual energy, with the "life force" itself—a mystical entity which he later claimed to have observed directly in the form of "bions," or "orgones." Those whose sexual energies find suitable outlet are happy and socially adjusted, devoid of aggressive, sadistic or self-destructive impulses. Where orgastic potency is lacking, however, the sexual energies cannot flow freely throughout the organism, but are held in stasis; "biological energy is dammed up, thus becoming the source of all kinds of irrational behavior." (*The Function of the Orgasm*, p. xix)

Reich concludes, therefore, that sexual happiness and hence mental health wil be impossible for most people so long as either capitalism or patriarchy endures; for these complementary structures require the repression of sexuality, as well as the domination of women by men.

> Genital sexuality, in our culture, is, in fact, debased, degraded. To the average man, the sexual act is an act of evacuation or a proof of mastery. Against this, the woman rebels instinctively, and rightly so. (*Op. cit.*, p.162)

Although Reich invariably describes the sexual act from a male rather than a female point of view, he holds that female sexuality is no different in principle from male sexuality. The Freudian notion that feminine sexuality is naturally masochistic, while masculine sexuality is naturally sadistic, is therefore wrong in his view, as is "the concept that phantasies of rape are part of normal sexuality." (*Op. cit.*, p.134) For,

> orgastic potency and strong destructive or sadistic impulses are

incompatible . . . If psychoanalysts make such assumptions, they simply fail to think in terms beyond the prevalent human sexual structure. (*Loc. cit.*)

Under communism or "work-democracy" (a term Reich later came to prefer), sexual repression will no longer be necessary. Women and children will no longer be economically dependent on men, and hence will no longer be under their sexual control. The government (if it is rational) will ensure that the work place, living units, educational system, and cultural media are all designed to maximize the sexual gratification available to each person. Children will be allowed to masturbate and to engage in sex play with one another; all of their questions about sex will be freely answered. Adolescents will be allowed to form sexual liasons, and places will be provided for them to make love in private. Marriage as a lifelong monogamous relationship will disappear, but serial monogamy, that is, relatively stable but not necessarily permanent sexual attachments, will be the rule.

Reich maintains that in such a "sex-positve" society there will be no need for moral strictures of any kind, since all antisocial impulses are the result of sexual frustration, and no one will be sexually frustrated there. Morality will be replaced by "sex-economic self-regulation." (Unfortunately, Reich uses "morality" as a synonym for "restrictive patriarchal sexual morality," a confusion which rapidly leads to absurdity.) Homosexuality—which he considers a perversion—will disappear, as will all other forms of nonnormal sexuality, rape, and pornography, since all of these result only from the blocking of normal heterosexual impulses. The abortion problem will be solved by the ready availability of contraceptives, and of childrearing facilities which will enable women to experience motherhood as a natural organic pleasure rather than a physical and economic burden.

Although Reich was at first enthusiastic about the progress of the sexual revolution in the Soviet Union, his observations of Stalinism led to disillusion. In *The Sexual Revolution* he gives an excellent analysis of the stillbirth of that revolution in Marxist Russia. After the revolution of 1917 extremely liberal laws were passed, making men and women equals in marriage, legalizing abortion and homosexuality, and making divorce accessible. But the breaking of the economic ties which had previously held families together led to a breakdown of the Soviet family and a period of apparent chaos. Instead of realizing that this chaos was only a transition period on the way to the emergence of responsible, self-regulated freedom, the authorities reacted moralistically, reverting to a negative and repressive view of sexuality.

Abstinence was treated as the socialist ideal, and sexual indulgence was regarded as degenerate and bourgeois. Restrictions on abortion were reimposed and homosexuality again became a crime. Youth communes made no provision for the sexual needs of their members. Children were not permitted to masturbate and sex education was minimal. All of this could have been avoided had there been a theory of sexual revolution, and a realization that the establishment of a socialist economy—while *necessary* for a free self-governing society—does not *guarantee* that such a society will emerge. It did not, because the necessary ideological changes were presumed to result directly from material changes, and thus were never undertaken.

Reich's work is important and in some ways remarkably contemporary. Many of us have internalized a number of his ideas without suspecting their origin. But Reich's central idea, that the gratification of the libido is *the* human need, all others being derivative from it, is one which feminists need to approach with caution, not just because it eventually led Reich to his extremely dubious work at the Orgone Institute, but because, as the class which has for millennia been defined wholly in terms of sexuality, women have a special interest in resisting the extension of that dehumanizing definition to the species as a whole. Human beings do *not* need to be *told* that what they need is X (e.g. sex) and that society is going to see to it that they get it; rather they need the freedom to discover and pursue their own individual goals, so long as these are consistent with the rights of others. Morality will never become unnecessary, insofar as it is the rational study of the sorts of goals and actions which are and are not consistent with other people's rights.

It must also be pointed out that Reich's claim that sexual potency is both necessary and suffcient for mental health fails to account for the existence of healthy celibates (which is empirically undeniable) and of nonsex-related causes of mental illness. Furthermore, Reich's confident assertions about the absence of aggressive impulses among sexually satisfied humans are less than fully convincing in the light of evidence that, at least among many animal species, aggressiveness is associated with territoriality and with (male) sexuality. (See, for instance, Lorenz, Ardrey, Tiger and Fox.) One need not conclude from this evidence that male domination and sadistic sexuality are biologically inevitable in the human species; but neither can it be assumed that they are *merely* the results of sexual repression.

REIK, Theodore. *The Creation of Woman: A Psychoanalytic Inquiry into the Myth of Eve* (McGraw-Hill, 1973; first published in 1960)

This is the third of three volumes in which Reik applies psychoanalytic theory to Biblical interpretation in an attempt to shed light on early Hebrew culture and history. Reik was a student and lifelong follower of Freud and shares Freud's fascination with the "mystery of woman." Though he draws no explicitly feminist conclusions (and indeed never mentions either male domination or women's status), his interpretation of the myth of Eve's creation from Adam's rib is in agreement with the protests of feminists who have long argued that the meaning of the Genesis story has been grotesquely distorted in the service of patriarchal and misogynous attitudes.

Reik's claim is that the rib story was not originally about the creation of woman at all. It is rather a veiled or deliberately mystified account of ancestral initiation ceremonies, in which the young men are symbolically killed or put to sleep and reborn as if to the men of the tribe. The Eve story, like the initiation ceremonies, involves an absurd reversal, and denial, of the fact that it is women who give birth, and that indeed Adam was originally descended from a mother goddess. It resembles a dream in which the situation against which the dreamer reacts is grotesquely reversed and ridiculed. Reik calls it "the hoax of the millennia" and considers it to have been, in its inception and its interpretation through the ages, a deliberate expression of misogyny.

REYBURN, Wallace. *The Inferior Sex* (Prentice Hall, Englewood Cliffs, New Jersey, 1972)

A piece of modern misogyny, remarkable for its virulence. Wallace is a journalist who has also written about the invention of the flush toilet and the bra. He claims that women are subjective beings, incapable of rational or objective thought and lacking inventiveness, and hence virtually incapable of excelling in art, architecture, musical composition, philosophy, technological innovation or any other creative intellectual enterprise (with the sole exception of the novel, which deals with emotions, women's forte.) He considers menstruation a total block to the thought process and one which disqualifies women from most sorts of professional work. "Would *you* want a woman on the floor of the Stock Exchange handling your money when there's a run on the market?" he asks (p.170). Even equal pay for equal work would be unfair to men, who work harder and longer at their jobs and do not have to take time off to menstruate. The arguments of contemporary feminists are dismissed with brief *ad hominem* remarks: Kate Millett uses too many footnotes; Shulamith Firestone tends to be obscure. Women, he insists, should forget about equality, which is impossible, and "find the contentment and the reflected happiness of being secondary to men." (p.235)

RICH, Adrienne. *Of Woman Born: Motherhood as Experience and Institution* (W.W. Norton and Company, New York, 1976)

Adrienne Rich is a poet and a mother of three sons who here writes, beautifully, of the oppressive institution which patriarchy has made of motherhood. There are few original theoretical insights, but there is an eclectic awareness of the vastness of the problem and of its urgency. "If rape has been terrorism," Rich says, "motherhood has been penal servitude." (p.14) Patriarchy requires—as prepatriarchal motherhood did not—the subordination of women to their own reproductive function. Woman's biology, which was a source of power and respect during the era of the Great Goddess, becomes the means of her subjection.

Rich pictures the patriarchal takeover as occurring not so much as a result of changes in the mode of production or the rise of androcentric religions—which can only be explained as a *result* of patriarchy—as because of men's discovery of the fact of paternity. Once man realizes that it is he who impregnates woman and not some natural force, he begins to see her children as "his," and a means of ensuring his own immortality; hence he begins to strive for such power over woman as he considers necessary to assure him of children, especially sons, of his own begetting. Thus,

> Patriarchal man created—out of a mixture of sexual and affective frustration, blind need, physical force, ignorance, and intelligence split from its emotional grounding, a system which turned against woman her own organic nature, the source of her awe and her original powers. (p.126)

Rich sees in modern male-dominated obstetrics an especially instructive illustration of the male drive to seize control of the female reproductive process. Male physicians began to replace female midwives in the latter seventeenth century, when the practice began to be a lucrative one. Throughout this process innumerable facts—such as the misuse and overuse of the forceps and similar instruments; the plague of puerperal fever spread throughout the eighteenth and nineteenth century by the unwashed hands of male physicians; their self-serving opposition to the practice of the midwives, whose methods were in fact much safer; their insistence on the lithotomy position (prone on the back) which makes giving birth much more difficult; and the interventionist habit which makes routine use of powerful drugs, episiotomies (1) and the like—all demonstrate the male physician's underlying drive: not so much to make childbirth safer and more rewarding for women, as to bring the process under complete male control regardless of the cost to women. There are well-meaning obstetricians, but few who can understand that giving birth is an action which each woman must perform in her own way and under conditions of her own choosing. For,

> So long as birth . . . remains an experience of passively handing over our minds and our bodies to male authority and technology, other kinds of social change can only minimally change our relationship to ourselves, to power, and to the world outside our bodies. (p.185)

Women must, therefore, take back the control of their own reproductive functions, and destroy the institution of motherhood—that is, not the experience itself, but the patriarchal distortion of it. This will require not just a more communal mode of childrearing, but the essential involvement of men in the process, something which has not yet come about even in the Marxist states. It will require better means of birth control, with legal abortion as a back-up measure, and complete sexual self-determination for women i.e. the unquestioned right to refuse unwanted sex. The liberation of motherhood will produce stronger, freer mothers, better able to love their children and to let them go. This in turn will bring about psychic changes in both sons and daughters—a humanizing of the former and a strengthening of the latter—which may enable society to finally free itself from the prison of gender roles.

1. Episiotomy is a surgical procedure whereby a long, deep cut is made in the inner wall of the vagina, just prior to parturition, in order to enlarge the birth canal and make the delivery easier. The procedure is often painful, and can lead to infection, and/or permanent damage to nerve and muscle tissue. Though it may sometimes be necessary, the seriousness of these side effects make its *routine* use at best morally and pragmatically dubious.

ROMANTICISM: See Rousseau, Kant, Fuller.

ROUSSEAU, Jean Jacques (1712–1778). *Emile* (translated by Barbara Foxley; J.M. Dent and Sons, London, 1963; first published 1762)

Emile is one of the most influential works of all time in the philosophy of education. It is a fictional narrative in which Rousseau tutors a single child from infancy to manhood. Emile is to be a natural man, free and independent from the start, never taught to submit to the will of another but only to the necessities of nature. His freedom begins with the elimination of the swaddling clothes with which infants were customarily restrained; he will also be nursed by his own mother. (Rousseau's praises of the benefits of breast feeding one's own baby started a massive shift in that direction among bourgeois and upper-class French women.) Emile will be allowed to run and play as much as he likes, to occupy his time exactly as he sees fit. He will be permitted neither to command others nor to receive commands from them. Rather than telling him what to do, his tutor will arrange matters such that the things he wishes Emile to learn and do will (appear to) be necessitated by the circumstances or the laws of nature. This process sometimes involves deliberate deception on the tutor's part, as when Emile is taught the importance of knowing his way about by landmarks and other navigational clues by the tutor's pretending to be lost and forcing Emile to find his own way home if he wants his lunch.

Emile is never subjected to formal schooling. As a child he learns only those practical skills whose usefulness he can readily appreciate. He will not even learn to read or write before the age of twelve, and possibly much later. He will learn no history, no philosophy and no religion until he has reached the age of reason—which Rousseau places at twelve years—and can begin to draw his own conclusions about their significance. Even in the area of religion Emile will be taught to believe nothing the truth of which is not evident to his own reason. This means that his religious creed will be a minimal one; he will see the necessity for belief in a supreme creator, a God who is good and who makes all things good, and he will respect the basic principles of morality, but he will realize that his own reason and experience are inadequate to determine which, if any, of the world's religions presents a true picture of the exact nature of God. He will not, however, flaunt his skepticism about unprovable theological dogmas, the supposed results of revelation, but will, out of respect for his neighbors and the need to live in peace, outwardly conform to whatever religion they accept. (Rousseau's own failure to keep his skepticism to himself led to his being forced to flee from France, for the religious opinions expressed in *Emile*.)

So intense is Rousseau's insistence on total freedom and autonomy for the young male that it comes as a rather depressing surprise to learn, in the final chapters of *Emile*, that he recommends no such liberty for female children. The education of Sophie, Emile's future bride, is to be entirely different from his. Since a woman's lot is to be a dependent and obedient wife and a devoted mother, she must learn from the first to please others rather than herself.

> A woman's education must . . . be planned in relation to man. To be pleasing in his sight, to win his respect and love, to train him in childhood, tend him in manhood, to counsel and console, to make his life pleasant and happy, these are the duties of woman for all time, and this is what she should be taught when young. (p.328)

Thus Sophie will have none of the freedom so carefully provided for Emile. She will be kept busy at useful household tasks, "early accustomed to restraint," (p.332) for girls "must be trained to bear the yoke from the first, so that they may not feel it, to master their own caprices and to submit themselves to the will of others." (*Loc. cit.*) Indeed, should Sophie come to *like* the work she does, she should sometimes be forced to remain idle, for on no account must she develop a will of her own. She should even be deliberately subjected to injustice, since "formed to obey a creature so imperfect as man, a creature often vicious and always faulty, she should early learn to submit to injustice and to suffer the wrongs inflicted on her by her husband without complaint." (p.333) Unlike Emile, she will be taught her parents' religion at an early age, and taught to accept it on faith. This is because (1) women are incapable of abstract reason at any age, so there is no question of waiting until they reach the age of reason and can arrive at their own conclusions; (2) women need to learn modesty and shame at as early an age as possible, in order to control their boundless sexuality (which, unlike the natural instincts of men, is *not* naturally good); and (3) they will have to accept their husband's religion on faith later, so they should learn early to believe on the basis of authority.

Also unlike Emile, Sophie will learn to care much more about what other people think of her than about what she thinks of herself; for "a woman's conduct is controlled by public opinion." (p.340) Apart from religion, she is to learn only practical home-making skills and a few minor arts such as needlework and informal singing. Her physical education should be directed toward the development of grace, not strength. She will read nothing, not even musical notation. This will enable her future husband to teach her as much or as little as he wishes her to know of history, science, geology, philosophy, politics, and so on.

It is interesting that Rousseau combines this boundless contempt for women's intellect and for their right to autonomy with a gallant acceptance of the power over men which women may gain by clever manipulation or exploitation of their sexual attraction. A clever woman contrives to get her husband to order her to do what she wants to do anyway, and in this way she rules while seeming to obey (p.335). The catch, of course, is that their erotic and manipulative power requires that women never seek or seem to act autonomously, that is, like men. "The more women act like men, the less influence they will have over men, and then men will be masters indeed." (p.327) In other words, women must be content with the limited and indirect power men permit them, or else they will lose that too.

This is a classic antifeminist argument, hardly different from the line of thought found in contemporary glorifications of the traditional feminine role, such as Helen Andelin's *Fascinating Womanhood*. Contemporary antifeminists tend to soft pedal the overt power of males in the patriarchal system and to emphasize the covert power of women, overlooking, like Rousseau, the fact that male domination and female manipulation are the two, equally corrupt, sides of the same coin. It is ironic that Rousseau, who saw more clearly than any other philosopher the debasing effects of the power of men over other men should have been blind to the parallel consequences of the power of one sex over the other. There is, however, some justice in the fact that the philosophical inconsistency of Emile so angered the British feminist Mary Wollstonecraft that it inspired her to write the *Vindication of the Rights of Woman*—the first systematic philosophical defense of the moral and legal equality of the sexes, and the work which helped to launch the first waves of feminist protest during the following century.

ROWBOTHAM, Sheila. *Woman's Consciousness, Man's World* (Penguin Books, 1974)
Women, Resistance and Revolution (Vintage Books, New York, 1974)
Hidden from History: Rediscovering Women in History from the 17th Century to the Present (Random House, New York, 1976)

Rowbotham is an Oxford-trained social historian who looks to working-class women to provide the inspiration and leadership for an effective feminist-socialist movement. She sees, however, no historical necessity in the appearance of such a movement, crucial though it is for human liberation. Not only are we a long way from it now, but there is less understanding now, in feminist and socialist camps, of the interconnectedness of the two movements than there has been at various times in the last two centuries.

Woman's Consciousness, Man's World analyzes some of the contradictions surrounding women's current role in capitalist society. Women are not yet entirely free of the older feudalist form of bondage, in which the oppressors own not just the labor power of the workers but their persons as well; nor are they even free to be exploited equally in the capitalist labor market. Working women, carrying the double burden of housework and job, straddle the two realms of production under capitalism, private and public. Their unpaid domestic labor is not considered real work, yet it is used as an excuse for confining them to the low-paid jobs outside the home. The painful inconsistencies in this situation ought to lead them to envision and struggle for radical alternatives. "The contradictory encounter between the public sphere of labor and industry and the private family production of self and of goods and services for immediate use have made a new female consciousness possible." (p.102)

Women, Resistance and Revolution is a useful history of the relationship between the socialist and feminist movements and of the two major currents of feminism, the older liberal, equal-rights feminism and the revolutionary socialist feminism. Rowbotham criticizes Marx and Engels' analysis of the oppression of women as merely a form of class oppression, and their consequent failure to perceive women's movements as distinct and crucial agents in the struggle for socialism. Such revolutionary women's movements as have occurred, for instance during the French Revolution and the Paris Commune of 1871, have grown out of poor women's relation to consumption, in particular the price of bread. Working women have occasionally glimpsed the need for a change more radical even than that proposed by (male) socialist thinkers, "the possibility of changing society so that people not only had more to eat but encountered one another in completely new ways and developed a radically different consciousness of each other." (p.116) This is the dream implied by the union women's slogan, "Bread and roses." None of the socialist revolutions, the Soviet, Chinese, Vietnamese, Cuban or (least of all) the Algerian, have yet achieved this dream, or fully liberated women; "the revolution within the revolution remains unresolved."

Hidden from History deals with women rebels and women's movements in England, from the Puritan and other prophetesses of the seventeenth century to the socialist and feminist groups of the nineteenth and early twentieth century—Chartists, Fourierians, Saint-Simonians, Owenites, social workers, legal reformers, trade unionists, Marxists, birth-control advocates, and suffragists. In spite of the richness of their shared history, the socialist and feminists movements in England were wrenched apart after the First World War, and "as the currents of liberal feminism, sexual liberation, gradual socialism and communism became increasingly divergent, the possibility of making a revolutionary feminist movement faded." (p.166) Conversely, the success of the reborn feminist movement of our own time "will depend on our capacity to relate to the working class and the action of working class women in transforming women's liberation according to their needs." (p.169) Still badly needed (and perhaps eventually forthcoming from the same author) is a much better theoretical understanding of the relationship between socialist and feminist goals.

RUETHER, Rosemary Radford. *New Woman, New Earth: Sexist Ideologies and Human Liberation* (Seabury Press, New York, 1975)

Ruether is a contemporary American historian of theology and a radical feminist, who has also written on anti-Semitism. *New Woman* is a study of the metaphysical underpinnings of Western racists and sexist ideologies, particularly within the Christian tradition. Sexism and racism both presuppose a dualistic and hierarchical ontology, in which mind and body, man and woman, humanity and nature, and God and creation are all seen as distinct and opposite to one another, and as united only by a relation of dominance and submission. Thus, mind is supposed to rule over body, man over women, humanity over nature and God over everything else. The male ruling class identifies itself with the "higher" half of each of these dualisms, but sees women and conquered races in terms of the "lower" half. "The characteristics of repressed bodiliness are attributed to them: passivity, sensuality, irrationality, and dependency." (p.4)

Ruether rejects the hypothesis that there was once a golden age of matriarchy, and argues that the symbolic view of woman as "Mother Nature," e.g. in the ancient and prehistoric mother-goddess religions of the Near East, which so many thinkers have taken as evidence of a matriarchal culture, is really the first step in the process that leads to women's total subjugation. Already woman is identified with material nature, man with consciousness and transcendence, although man's dependence on nature is still clearly recognized. This step could be taken within tribal societies, in which women could be denied political power, though they continued to have a great deal of economic power. The next step occurred through urban civilization; urban technology increased the power and wealth of men, while women, excluded from access to the new technology, were trapped in an increasingly circumscribed role. Civilization could have made men's physical advantages over women obsolete.

> But instead the priestly and scribal classes projected artificial ideologies of male intellectual superiority and female inferiority in the realm of the spirit and culture to justify the monopolization of . . . power in the hands of the male ruling class. (p.10)

During the first millennium B.C. religious ideologies appeared in the Greek and Hebrew cultures which represented men's efforts to declare their independence from nature, to master nature, not "by exalting it as an independent divine power, but by subordinating it and linking their essential selves with a transcendent principle beyond nature which is pictured as intellectual and male." (p.13) The deification of the male was also the debasement of the female, who came to be seen as mindless and corrupt. "Consciousness arose in a one-sided antagonistic way by making one half of humanity, not the partner in the struggle, but the symbol of the sphere to be transcended and dominated." (p.25)

This is the tradition, then, which Christianity inherits and perpetuates—although Ruether suggests that Jesus himself was a feminist of sorts, in that he not only behaved towards women as if he considered them his equals, but tried to model his ministry on the role of service rather than that of domination. "Jesus was trying to reinterpret the image of the fatherhood of God, so that it could no longer be used to establish a ruling class of 'fathers.'" (p.74) But the old hierarchical tradition quickly resumed control and has prevailed in most Christian churches to this day. Unlike Mary Daly, who sees in the cult of the Virgin Mary a survival of the mother-goddess religion, Ruether holds that the Virgin Mary has never been a potent divinity in her own right, but has rather been a symbol of feminine resignation to male rule.

Because of its sexual repressiveness, the Christian mentality exhibits a paranoid pattern, in which nonconformists—heretics, "witches," Jews, and even communists—are pictured as devil worshippers and sexual orgiasts, and as a menace to be stamped out. American racism is a part of this pattern, and Ruether points out that it is crucial for feminists to realize this, and also to understand why the black-liberation movement, reacting against the historical humiliation of the black male, tends to be male supremacist rather than feminist in perspective. Properly understood, the feminist movement encompasses all other liberation movements, since the dualistic ideology it opposes is also the basis of all other forms of oppression. Women's liberation ultimately requires a global democratic socialism, a reorganization of the distribution of the earth's resources, and an ecologically responsible life style. The relation between home and work must be restructured, bringing productive work back into the community and socializing domestic work, thus ending the sexual division of labor. The end of sexual stereotyping will enhance human individuality, but human consciousness must no longer be elevated to supernatural status; the idea of personal immortality probably must go. Ruether does not predict that any of this will actually occur, however, since unlike Marx, she sees no *historically inevitable* social mechanisms leading towards liberation, and she fully recognized the continuing power of the dualistic ideology.

RUSSELL, Bertrand (1872–1970). *Marriage and Morals* (George Allen and Unwin, London, 1929)

In his usual lucid and gently sarcastic manner Russell argues against restrictive sexual morality—the patriarchal Judeo-Christian creed that sex is sinful if it occurs before or outside of marriage, or for any purpose other than procreation. He would like to see parents and educators provide children with all the information about sex they want, as early as they can understand it, and to be tolerant and relaxed about nudity, masturbation and sex play. There was once a rational argument for the restriction of sexual intercourse between unmarried men or women, or adultery on the part of married women, in that it led to unwanted pregnancies and fatherless children, or to children of uncertain parentage. But with the invention of completely reliable contraception (which Russell is confident, is imminent) it is no longer reasonable or humane to suppose that sex should occur only between married persons.

Of course patriarchal society has never *really* supposed this, since in practice it has only been women who have been expected to be chaste before marriage and faithful thereafter. The *old* feminists, Russell says—not Mary Wollstonecraft, but most of the nineteenth-century reformists—wanted to eliminate this double standard by restricting the "vices" of men as well as those of women. This in fact is impossible without extremely severe repression; in practice the demand for fidelity and chastity always falls hardest on women, while men enjoy adultery, fornication and access to prostitutes with relative freedom. Consequently the new feminists, he says, are beginning to demand the same sexual freedom for themselves as has been available to men. Russell sees this sexual liberation of women, made possible by contraception, as the key to the overthrow of patriarchy. He thinks that patriarchy arose as a direct result of men's discovery of the fact of paternity. Before this families were matrilineal; children belonged only to their mothers and owed no obedience to their fathers, and chastity was not demanded of unmarried women, nor fidelity of wives. (Malinowski's Trobriand Islanders follow this pattern.) The discovery of fatherhood led men to dominate women in order to secure their virtue and hence children of known paternity. Presumably now that sex can be divorced from conception, men can afford to allow women their sexual freedom without losing the advantage of knowing which children are theirs.

Male domination, Russell argues, makes romantic love between men and women impossible, since romantic love requires that the lovers at least *feel* themselves to be completely equal. It is also, he believes, "the source of the most intense delights that life has to offer." (p.62) Furthermore, it is usually found outside of marriage. The social function of marriage—which he endorses— is not to promote romantic love, but to provide a stable environment for the rearing of children. It would be better for children if sexual incompatibility or boredom between parents were not treated as a reason for divorce, bur rather as grounds for the toleration of some adultery on both sides.

In spite of his defense of women's sexual freedom (their freedom to choose their sexual partners and to use contraceptives, though not necessarily to obtain abortions), Russell is somewhat less enthusiastic about their demands for job equality. He says that married women with children could achieve economic independence in either of two ways; by continuing to work and turning their children over to the care of creches or nurseries, or by being given a wage by the state to remain at home and care for them while they are small. He much prefers the second way, since he fears that communal child-care centers would instill in children a group morality, e.g. a rabid patriotism which would cause the children of different nations to grow up and exterminate one another in war. He fears, however, that this method would also have undesirable effects, such as reducing the role of the father in the family by depriving him of the role of providing support. Unfortunately, Russell does not think of the obvious third option, i.e. that women and men could *share* the child care and financial responsibilities. It does not occur to him, either, that fathers as well as mothers might be given state subsidies to enable them to take care of their children. Nor does he consider that women have reasons for working other than the desire to avoid financial dependence on one man; that they may want to be more in the world than mothers and lovers.

Another pervasive problem, which one might have hoped that a philosophical analyst like Russell would be able to avoid, is the continuous and confusing alteration between the use of "men" to mean *male* adult humans, and the use of "man" or "men" in contexts where it is unclear whether what is intended is this sex-specific sense or the so-called generic sense (in which women are "included"). For example, he makes an interesting point about two ways in which a "man" can reject the old morality without escaping its hold on his conscious or subconscious mind (p.245). We are given no clue as to whether these observations, expressed with masculine nouns and pronouns, are intended to be equally applicable to women or not; and this very ambiguity suggests the conclusion that they are not—since if they were, why wouldn't Russell have used sex-neutral language, as he does in many other contexts? And if they are not included then why are they not dealt with separately? As happens so frequently in philosophical discourse, they have been dropped from the universe of discourse by an apparently innocent slide of meaning.

RUSSELL, Letty M. *Human Liberation in a Feminist Perspective* (Westminster Press, Philadelphia, 1974)

A plea for—and an instance of—"liberation theology," which interprets the Gospel as calling for freedom for all oppressed peoples, on earth and not just in heaven. Salvation is seen as a social event, and its pursuit today must involve Christians in the struggle against sexism, racism, and the oppression of the Third World by the wealthier nations. Russell argues that the many sexist or patriarchal passages in the Bible, e.g. Paul's injunction against women speaking in church, are extraneous to the meaningful core of Christian belief, or, in her words, part of the useless past rather than the usable past. She advocates the use of nonsexist language (the Deity, for instance, should be referred to by both feminine and masculine names, pronouns, and metaphors), the ordination of women, and above all the thorough reform of all Christian churches, in an ecclesiastical spirit, to enable them to serve the cause of earthly freedom.

S

SAFILIOS-ROTHSCHILD, Constantina. *Love, Sex, and Sex Roles* (Prentice Hall, Englewood Cliffs, New Jersey, 1977)

Safilios-Rothschild is a native of Greece (now a professor of sociology at Wayne State University) and writes with considerable insight about the strategies used by women and men in waging the war between the sexes, in Greece, Italy and the United States.

In particular, she analyzes some of the ways in which sexual roles and stereotypes have interfered with the capacity of women and men to integrate love and sexuality. Both the masculine and the feminine stereotypes tend to produce a separation; men tend to want sex more than love, women to want love more than sex. The "masculine" man tends to treat the sex act as one of conquest or possession in which the woman is degraded to the status of an object. Thus they have difficulty loving or respecting women with whom they have sexual relations, or having satisfactory sexual relations with women they love or respect.

Ironically, the price men pay for treating women as sex objects is that they become vulnerable to sexual manipulation by women, and to reciprocal objectification in terms of money, status, and power. Sexual "teasing," and the manipulation of men by the (threatened) withholding of sex, are necessary adaptations on the part of women who lack other means of attaining money or status; their prevalence varies directly with the degree of women's oppression. But the use of this manipulative technique tends to require women to be alienated from their own sexuality, since they can effectively manipulate men by withholding sex only if they are not just as eager for sex themselves. Hence the Victorian denial of women's capacity for sexual enjoyment may actually have functioned to give socially and economically oppressed women a compensatory manipulative power over men.

SANGER, Margaret (1883-1966). *Woman and the New Race* (Maxwell Reprint Company, Elmsford, New York, 1969; first

published 1922)
The Pivot of Civilization (Maxwell Reprint Company, 1969; first published 1922)
Motherhood in Bondage (Maxwell Reprint Company, 1956; first published 1928)
My Fight for Birth Control (Farrar and Rinehart, New York, 1931)

Margaret Sanger, in the years before, during and after the First World War, fought a remarkable and almost single-handed battle to provide American women, especially lower-class women, with access to birth control—a term she herself invented. The Federal Obscenity Act of 1873, passed as a result of the activities of fundamentalists, had made it a crime for any person, even a physician, to provide another with information about the prevention of conception. The American medical profession, far from rebelling against this cruel law, complied with it willingly. As a registered nurse in New York, Sanger discovered at first hand the horrors that resulted from uncontrolled fertility among the poor; the wealthy, of course, generally had access to contraceptives in spite of the law. The story of her struggle to change these conditions—through the publication of *The Woman Rebel*, a monthly magazine which was refused access to the mails, through researching in Europe the birth control methods in use in more enlightened countries, through speaking tours and the sponsoring of national and international conferences on birth control—is told in *My Fight for Birth Control.* The philosophy behind the struggle is presented in *Women and the New Race,* and *The Pivot of Civilization. Motherhood in Bondage* is a collection of tragic letters from wives (and a few husbands) requesting information on birth control, and detailing the miseries they have suffered for lack of it.

Sanger's basic argument is simple and overwhelmingly persuasive. It is an unmitigated evil that poor women should be forced to bear one child after another, and thereby made slaves to motherhood, their health ruined, their families driven into deeper poverty. Children born into large impoverished families have a shockingly high chance of dying in infancy or childhood, and of inheriting or developing syphilis, tuberculosis, "feeble mindedness," and other psychological and physical handicaps. Criminals and prostitutes are largely recruited from large families, as Sanger had the opportunity to discover first hand when she was imprisoned for operating the first birth control clinic in New York City (and in the country). She takes the Marxists to task for their rejection of birth control as a capitalist plot against the working class. On the contrary, she argues, excessive and involuntary reproduction among the working class plays into the hands of the capitalists, by glutting the market with cheap and easily exploited labor, including that of women and children who are driven to work for pittance wages in order to avoid starvation. "Uncontrolled sex (i.e. reproduction) has rendered the proletariat prostrate, the capitalist powerful." (*The Pivot of Civilization*, p. 165)

Poverty, then, will be alleviated only when motherhood becomes at least as voluntary among the poor as among the privileged classes. Sanger rejects as cruel and wholly unrealistic the attitudes of physicians and society towards poor women who wish to avoid further conception, i.e. that they must simply avoid sexual intercourse. Long-term enforced abstinence, she maintained, destroys marital relationships, places an unbearable strain on the partners, and anyway is impossible for most women, whose husbands coerce them, or threaten them with desertion if they attempt to practice contraception by abstinence. Because she saw abortion as a crime hardly less abominable than infanticide or murder, she considered it a powerful argument for contraception that it would prevent, so she believed, most of the million or more abortions performed in the United States each year (1).

Sanger came to see birth control as the single most important issue facing not only this country but the world as a whole, in the twentieth century. She foresaw that the progress of medicine in saving infant and maternal lives would swell the populations of all but the few enlightened nations, driving some nations into hopeless poverty and creating totalitarian and expansionist regimes in others. All war, she argued, is ultimately the result of population pressures, and only those nations that maintain a modest birth rate can hope to avoid war or achieve economic advancement.

In spite of her insistence on freedom for women as a primary rationale for birth control, Sanger had little sympathy with the feminist organizations and ideas of her day. Women, she held, must indeed be free, and they must exercise far more power in society; this power, however, "will not be found in any futile seeking for economic independence or in the aping of men in industrial and business pursuits, not by joining battle for the so-called 'single-standard.' " (*The Pivot of Civilization*, p. 210) It requires, rather, that women take control of motherhood, deciding when and under what conditions they will bear childen. Liberated mothers will be able to take a larger role in the affairs of society, to "create a (more) human world by the infusion of the feminine element into all of its activities." (***Woman and the New Race***, p. 99) Their primary responsibility, however, will continue to be motherhood. Like Havelock Ellis, whom she knew and greatly admired, Sanger did not doubt that motherhood was women's primary mission in life—whereas fatherhood plays and should play a much smaller part in the life of men. She does not consider that this radically one-sided view of the obligation of parenthood is itself oppressive to women.

1.   This prediction was overoptimistic, for the increased avail-ability of (imperfect) contraceptives has not greatly reduced the demand for abortion as a backup or even substitute method of birth control. Fortunately, with the passage of time Americans have begun to realize that abortion is some-thing entirely different from murder, in that the "victim" is not yet a person and not yet possessed of a right to life.

SARTRE, Jean-Paul.   ***Being and Nothingness: An Essay on Phe-nomenological Ontology*** (translated by Hazel E. Barnes, Wash-ington Square Press, New York, 1966; first published 1953)

Jean-Paul Sartre is the best known living existentialist philos-opher. In both his fictional and his theoretical works he has emphasized the inescapable reality of human freedom and re-sponsibility. Although he makes use of many Hegelian concepts, he rejects Hegel's project of discovering objective and universal meanings in human existence. Sartre considers human life "ab-surd," in that it has no purpose or meaning other than those assigned to it by free individuals; and even these are finally extinguished by death. It is this very lack of any objective mean-ing of life which ensures human freedom and moral responsibil-ity. There is no "human nature"; in Sartre's terms, existence precedes essence, and thus we are only what we make ourselves by our own free actions. Any appeal to divine will or natural law to deny our responsibility for what we are and what we do is "bad faith," or self-deception.

In spite of his long association with Simone de Beauvoir, Sartre has never written extensively on feminist issues or on the nature of woman. Because he tends to use masculine nouns and pro-nouns in referring to the human individual, it is unclear whether or not he regards women as equally free and self-determining. On the one hand, the claim that there is no predetermined hu-man nature would seem to imply that there are no inherently masculine or feminine traits or behaviors, none, that is, which are rendered inevitable simply by a person's biological sex. Sartre certainly views women as capable of bad faith; he gives as his first example of bad faith the passive behavior of a woman who pretends (even to herself) to be unaware of her male companion's incipient sexual advances (pp.66–67). Consistency would seem to require him to hold, as de Beauvoir does, that to adopt either the traditionally feminine or the traditionally masculine role is to be in bad faith—in the one case the bad faith of denying one's own freedom, in the other that of denying the freedom of others. (See de Beauvoir.)

On the other hand, however, there are aspects of Sartre's analysis which not only seem inconsistent with this antiessentialist viewpoint, but which verge on misogyny. His discussion of the psychoanalytic significance of slime and holes is particularly susceptible to such an interpretation (1).   Sartre views sliminess as a singularly unattractive, indeed a horrible quality. Its horror consists in the fact that when it is grasped it at first seems to yield, but then turns the tables on the one who sought to possess it, by clinging to him and threatening to dissolve his very substance. It is, furthermore, described as *feminine*:

> It is a soft, yielding action, a moist and feminine sucking . . . The slime seems to lend itself to me, it invites me . . . But it is a trap . . . Slime is the revenge of The In-itself [2]. A sickly-sweet, feminine revenge . . .(pp. 746–767)

Sartre also views holes as having a stereotypically feminine quality—passive, inviting, entrapping. A hole, he says, "is originally presented as a nothingness "to be filled" with my own flesh." (p. 751) This is why children put their fingers in holes, crawl into holes, and so on. It is this original meaning of the hole, Sartre holds, which determines the meaning of the female sex (i.e., women and women's genitals). The point is not—as Freudian psychoanalysis would have it—that holes have the symbolic meaning they do because they resemble the female vagina; rather the vagina derives its meaning from the fact that it is a hole. The female, he says, is inherently obscene, not just in the eyes of (chauvinist) males, but as a fundamental, inalterable, existential fact.

> The obscenity of the feminine sex is that of everything which "gapes open." It is an *appeal to being* as all holes are. In herself woman appeals to a strange flesh which is to transform her into a fullness of being by penetration and dissolution. Conversely woman senses her condition as an appeal precisely because she is "in the form of a hole." This is the true origin of Adler's complex [i.e.,

the inferiority complex]. Beyond any doubt her sex is a mouth and a voracious mouth which devours the penis . . . The amorous act is the castration of the man; but this is above all because [the feminine] sex is a hole. (p. 252)

It is difficult if not impossible to reconcile these pronouncements with Sartre's insistence that there is no predetermined human nature—unless, of course, one supposes that Sartre does not consider women to be fully human. Sartre does not address the apparent inconsistency here. Nor does it seem to occur to him that *male* genitals are also commonly viewed as obscene and threatening. It is unclear why this fact ought to be ignored while the corresponding fact about female genitals is given such prominence.

Sartre's analysis of sexual love and desire is also of interest. The picture he paints is a profoundly pessimistic one, in which the attitudes of the lovers alternate between sadism and masochism; no stable resolution, in which each respects the freedom of the other, is ever possible (p. 501). This is because, in Sartre's view as in Hegel's, the original relationship between human individuals is one of conflict. We exist as self-aware beings only by virtue of (our awareness of) other conscious beings. Yet the encounter with the other is always problematic and fearful. To be seen by another is to experience oneself as an object in that person's world. This is distressing in itself, and it poses the danger that one may be used as an instrument toward ends that are not one's own: "being-seen constitutes me as a defenseless being for a freedom which is not my freedom." (p. 328)

Sartre holds that there are two primary ways of responding to this threat posed by the "look" of the other. One is to turn back upon the other, so as to make of him an object, and in an attempt to eradicate his freedom. (This is the attitude of sadism.) The other is to identify with the other's view of oneself as object, in an attempt to eradicate one's own freedom. (This is the attitude of masochism.) Both attitudes are futile, since it is possible to eradicate neither one's own freedom nor that of the other.

In Sartre's view, both of these fundamental attitudes are involved in love and sexuality. Love is an attempt to exist entirely within the subjectivity of the other (the loved one); the lover wants to be an object in the loved one's world, but a supremely important object, a value transcending all other values. Sexual desire, on the other hand, is an attempt to capture and incorporate within oneself the subjectivity of the other, by reducing both oneself and the other to pure carnality. Desire, like love, is doomed; the attempt to overcome the otherness of the other always degenerates into sadism and/or masochism. Sartre holds that these processes which are observed in love and desire are typical of all human interactions:

> the sexual attitude is a primary behavior toward the Other . . .the For-itself is sexual in its very upsurge in the face of the Other and . . . through it sexuality comes into the world. (p. 497)

Sartre leaves unexplored, however, the relationship, if any, between the two fundamental and sexual ways of encountering the Other and the traditional conceptions of masculinity and femininity. Apart from the discussion of the symbolic significance of holes and slime, there is little indication that he considers the sexual and other interpersonal modes of experience of the one sex to be much different from that of the other. It is de Beauvoir who has made use of the Sartrean concepts of freedom, responsibility, bad faith, and the basic hostility of conscious beings toward one another to explain the historical dominance of the male.

1. See Margery L. Collins and Christine Pierce, "Holes and Slime: Sexism in Sartre's Psychoanalysis," in *Women and Philosophy*, eds. Gould and Wartofsky, Anthologies XII.
2. The "In-itself" is the world of objects as opposed to subjects, who are free and self-determined (the "For-itself"). See also de Beauvoir.

SCHEINFELD, Amran. *Women and Men* (Harcourt, Brace and Company, New York, 1944)

A wartime book, written largely in reaction against the influx of women into formerly all-male jobs which the war necessitated. Scheinfeld aspires to provide a successor to Havelock Ellis's *Man and Woman*, but unlike Ellis, and in spite of his all-too-frequent protests to the contrary, he has a heavy antifeminist ax to grind. He is a straightforward biological determinist, who emphasizes the superior size, aggressiveness, muscular strength and abstract conceptualizing ability of the male. He admits that males are biologically weaker, more apt to die before or soon after birth, more vulnerable to death from almost every type of disease, and slower to mature throughout the childhood years. But he argues that the slower maturation rate of boys only means that to get a fair comparison they should be matched not against girls of the same chronological age, but against somewhat younger girls; when this is done it is seen that boys lead girls in physical development at every biological age.

Furthermore, he maintains, boys and girls enter the world with sharply contrasting "personality potentials." From the earliest stages of infancy, boys are more active, aggressive and rebellious, girls more shy, nervous and more prone to jealousy. Scheinfeld rejects Margaret Mead's contention that most of the personality traits which we consider masculine or feminine are in fact culturally conditioned, on the grounds that the three New Guinea tribes which Mead studied are rare exceptions which only prove the rule. (He misses Mead's point, of course, since if there were only *one* cultural exception to the purported natural law that male biology produces "masculine" personality traits and female biology "feminine" personality traits, then nothing more would be needed to show that this is not in fact a natural law at all.)

Scheinfeld maintains that the sexual double standard is justified by the biological and psychological differences between the sexes. The results of women's "running around," he says, are far more serious for them and for society than in the case of men. (He does not explain how men are to "run around" without some women doing so too.) He notes with approval the Soviet Union's wartime move towards the elimination of coeducation in elementary and secondary schools. Coeducation harms both sexes, he thinks, for it disadvantages boys by pitting them against biologically older girls, and instills in girls unrealistic hopes about their capacity to compete successfully against males in later life. Women, he holds, cannot expect to do all of the kinds of work that men do, since they are weaker and have a different sort of intelligence. In heavy labor they can keep up with men only up to a point, after which they break down or endanger their reproductive organs. And while it is impossible to use I.Q. tests to determine which sex is intellectually superior, it is apparent that they are intellectually *different*: girls excel in linguistic and clerical skills, boys at tasks involving abstract reasoning, e.g. mathematics and mechanics.

He concludes, therefore, that women are best suited for clerical work, not for manual labor or for professional or administrative positions. He appeals to the usual rationalizations for the reluctance to admit women to the better-paying professions: that they are absent from work too much, that if unmarried they will marry and quit, that if married they will devote most of their time and attention to their families rather than their work. He says that freedom of the sort the feminists demand is at best a mixed blessing for women; "it is creating a harmful illusion to instill in women the thought that they can compete with men on an equal basis in any and every kind of work, or that the situation during the war emergency can be made permanent." (p. 386) What women need, he thinks, is not careers but the opportunity to fulfill themselves through marriage and motherhood. The greatest problem for women in the future will not be inequality, but the shortage of eligible men, forcing some women to be spinsters.

SCHOPENHAUER, Arthur (1788–1860). "On Women," in **Studies in Pessimism: A Series of Essays** (selected and translated by T. Bailey Saunders, Swan Sonneschein and Co., London, 1893; republished by Scholarly Press, St. Clair Shores, Michigan, 1970; this essay first published 1851, in **Parerga and Paralipomena**)

This little jewel of misogynism has the direct and graceful style typical of the great German pessimist. Schopenhauer's philosophy combines a more or less Kantian epistemology and metaphysics with rational atheism and a partly Eastern-inspired conviction that life is essentially evil, and that the only release is the total denial of individual will and desire. But his thoughts on women seem to have relatively little to do with the rest of his philosophy. Many have explained or excused his hostility towards women by reference to his unfriendly relationship with his mother, who not only inherited more from his father than the philosopher thought was appropriate, but was a popular light novelist who attracted much more public attention than her son did, until the last decade of his life (1).

But psychological explanation seems unnecessary in view of the fact that "On Women" merely expresses a set of moral and empirical views which have probably been shared, in essence, by most of the (male) thinkers who have written on the subject, in every period prior to our own. A man's belief in the standard tenets of male supremacism need not result from a bad relationship with his mother, and in Schopenhauer's case the causal sequence may well have been the reverse.

The essay begins with some quoted words of praise for women as a source of comfort and pleasure; as such, women can be appreciated. They are, however, inferior from every other point of view:

> You need only to look at the way in which she is formed, to see that woman is not meant to undergo great labor, whether of the mind or of the body. She pays the debt of life not by what she does, but by what she suffers; by the pain of childbearing and care for the child, and by submission to her husband . . . (p.106)

Even women's apparent areas of superiority are in reality marks of inferiority and weakness. If they are better at caring for and teaching children, it is because

> they are themselves childish, frivolous and short sighted; in a word, they are all big children all their life long—a kind of intermediate stage between the child and the grown man . . . (p.106)

If they mature sooner than men, this is because all inferior things mature sooner (2). If they show more sympathy for the unfortunate, this is evidence of "the weakness of their reasoning faculty," and of their lack of a sense of justice (p.109). Women invariably lie a great deal, since "the position which nature has assigned them as the weaker sex" makes them "dependent, not upon strength, but upon craft." (p.110) Their lack of intellect makes them "incapable of taking a *purely objective* interest in anything," even art, or of producing any work of genius. They are, in short

> the *sexus sequior*—the second sex, inferior in every respect to the first . . . (p.115)

Even their physical beauty is an illusion due to men's sexual desire.

> It is only the man whose intellect is clouded by his sexual impulses that could give the name of *the fair sex* to that undersized, narrow-shouldered, broad-hipped, and short-legged race . . . (p.113)

For all of these reasons, Schopenhauer concludes, women shold be strictly kept in their natural place, as housewives (or girls who hope to become housewives), and not "unnaturally" elevated by being treated as "ladies," or by being allowed to share their husband's status and inherit his property. "Ladies" remind Schopenhauer of

> the holy apes of Benares, who in the consciousness of their sanctity and inviolable position, think they can do exactly as they please. (p.116)

The European law of monogamous marriage, he holds, not only creates the "lady nuisance," but by raising some women above their proper status it forces others to fall below it; prostitutes are "human sacrifices offered up on the altar of monogamy." Polygamy is a much better system, because all women are adequately provided for, and none are raised above their "natural station."

1. See, for instance, Frederick Copleston, **Arthur Schopenhauer, Philosopher of Pessimism** (Harper and Row, New York, 1975; first published London, 1946) pp.39–40.
2. See Aristotle's **Generation of Animals** (Book IV, Chapter VI, 775a, 13–15) for what is perhaps the earliest expression on record of this argument (in the Western literature).

SCHREINER, Olive (1855–1920). *Woman and Labour* (T. Fisher Unwin, London, 1911)

Woman and Labour is a partial reconstruction by the author, a South African woman of English descent, of a remarkably feminist work which had been nearly completed by 1888, but which was destroyed during the Boer Rebellion. Schreiner argues that women must have productive labor, a share in all the useful and honored work of government, business, industry and the professions. Modern civilization has progressively robbed women of most of their former functions in providing food, clothing, shelter and other necessities of life, leaving only their childbearing and nurturing role, and their sexual function. Women, at least those in the privileged classes, have become sexual parasites, wholly dependent on men. This is a predictable result of increasing affluence; women of the upper and middle classes are much more apt to become idle than men, since their traditional domestic work is more easily taken over by servants than are men's tasks of government, commerce and war.

If women do not win back their share of important work, Schreiner maintains, our civilization will inevitably decline, just as the Roman civilization did when its women became parasites. For parasitism weakens women's minds and bodies and distorts their character; and weakened women produce weakened offspring. The sexes are like oxen yoked together: neither can advance significantly ahead of the other. To limit the development of women is to limit the development of the species. Thus it is not only for their own sake but for the sake of humanity as a whole that women must claim as their own every field of human activity, not excluding politics and war.

Against the claim that women are naturally suited only to be wives and mothers, Schreiner argues that women have always been more, except in affluent and decadent cultures or classes. She insists that we have no data adequate to establish any conclusions whatever as to which occupations are or are not suited to the female intellect. She does, however, think that women's sexual and maternal experiences tend to give them a different point of view on certain political and social issues, such as prostitution, divorce and child-custody laws. Thus the entry of women into political life, while it probably will not alter the balance of power between liberal and conservative parties, can be expected to make a difference with respect to such sex-related issues; and this makes it all the more imperative that women be represented in decision-making councils. She also suggests that with women in government wars would be less frequent, if not entirely elimi-

419

nated, since womens' experience of bearing and nurturing children teaches them the value of life.

SCOTT, Hilda. *Does Socialism Liberate Women? Experiences from Eastern Europe* (Beacon Press, Boston, 1974)

This is an excellent study of women's social progress—or lack of it—in Eastern Europe, expecially Czechoslovakia, under Marxism. Scott argues that the failure of the socialist states to provide real equality for women is an indication both of certain weaknesses and omissions in the work of Marx, Engels and Lenin, and of the failure by socialists to go beyond these founding fathers in their analysis of the situation of women. Marx and Engels argued that since women's subordination to men came about only with the rise of private property it would vanish with the end of capitalism and and the coming of socialism. On their view, three conditions are necessary for the complete equality of women: legal equality, the integration of women into the public production process, and the socialization of domestic labor—housework and child care. This analysis, Scott argues, overlooks the power of custom and ideology, which continue to function to the detriment of women even after the coming of socialism.

The economic situation of East European women remains far inferior to that of men. They make on the average only two-thirds as much, and they are concentrated in menial jobs which men usually do not want. There is little room for women in even minor positions of authority, and overt discrimination against them persists in many professional fields. This inferiority is both the cause and the result of the fact that women are still expected to do most of the housework and to care for their children when they are ill, and whenever child-care facilities are not available. Women's dual responsibility prevents them from actively seeking advancement in their jobs and gives employers an excuse for refusing to hire them for responsible positions. Their inferior earning power, in turn, makes it difficult for them to induce their husbands to undertake their share of the domestic work.

One of the more striking results of this double burden placed on women is that the birthrate in the Eastern European states has dropped dramatically, especially since the socialist states legalized elective abortion in 1957. Unfortunately, the socialist governments reacted to this "population crisis," not by efforts to make motherhood less of a personal and financial strain for working women, but by reimposing limits on the availability of abortion and encouraging more women to remain at home, e.g.

by child allowances for nonworking mothers. There has been extensive debate over the desirability of placing small children in child care-centers while their mothers work, with some psychologists arguing that all children should remain with their mothers at least until the age of two or three. Only one-third of Czech children under six are in child-care centers. Cooking, washing and other domestic work have not been significantly socialized.

It seems then, that contrary to Marx's and Engels' expectations, domestic work under socialism will remain just that, and the family will remain a basic economic unit in which its members' fundamental needs are provided for. Hence it is impossible for women to be free to take up their rightful place in the larger economic world unless men are persuaded to undertake their half of the domestic work. So far, however, most socialist women have failed to see the need or have been unwilling to press this issue. What is needed is an enormous ideological bootstrapping operation; both men and women need to be convinced, first, that children need attention from their fathers just as much as from their mothers, and second, that women's talents are as badly needed in the worlds of industry, science, culture and politics as men's.

SCOTT-MAXWELL, Florida. *Women and Sometimes Men* (Alfred A. Knopf, New York, 1957)

Scott-Maxwell is a Jungian psychoanalyst, and her views on women, like those of Jung himself, are a mixture of biological determinism and patriarchal conservatism on the one hand, and on the other hand a seemingly progressive version of the ideal of androgyny. Femininity is seen as not only an archetype of the human mind, but as a natural and proper consequence of female biology, particularly of the fact that women bear and nurse children. Femininity cannot be clearly defined—indeed lack of definition is one of its properties—but it involves the usual elements of the feminine stereotype—feeling, passiveness, compassion, intuitiveness, self-sacrifice, and so on. Masculinity is thought, action, reason, independence and the like.

The two sexes—but especially women—are admonished to remain "true to their sexual natures"; yet both men and women are said to be both masculine and feminine to some degree. Women need to be aware of their masculine part, but not to be ruled by it. Scott-Maxwell thinks that far too many modern women, including almost all of those who have careers or interests outside the home, are ruled by their masculine sides, which is hardly an improvement over being ruled by men. It is apparently much less important for men to be wary of being taken over by their feminine sides; indeed men cannot even become aware of their feminine sides except through the mediation of a feminine woman. This crucial service which women perform for men is a key reason why they have to remain basically feminine.

This theory takes for granted, with little or no effort to prove or even render plausible, (1) that masculinity and femininity are distinct and diametrically opposed traits which are found in nature in just the form that the patriarchal tradition conceives of them; (2) that male and female biology alone will make most men predominantly masculine and most women predominantly feminine; and (3) that since relationships between predominantly masculine men and predominantly feminine women (who are nevertheless "in touch with" their opposite sides) are of the most desirable kind for both, and the best context in which to rear children, we should make no effort to become *more* androgynous, that is neither stereotypically "masculine" or "feminine," in our psychology but human beings with a full range of capacities. These, of course, are some of the assumptions which feminists since Wollstonecraft have been most concerned to dispute.

SEAMAN, Barbara. *Free and Female: The Sex Life of the Contemporary Female* (Coward, McCann and Geoghigan, New York, 1972)

A feminist exploration of some of the physiological dimensions of sexual freedom. Women's sexuality is said to be different from that of men, "both less and more: less in that it is easily suppressed and more in that the limits of our potential almost defy measurement." (p.15) Far from being an underdeveloped penis, as Freud and his followers have insisted, the clitoris is part of a system of sensitive and erectile tissues which is actually larger than the male sexual apparatus, a fact which may help explain why women tend to require more stimulation to reach orgasm, but are (probably) capable of more intense as well as more frequent orgasms. As Mary Jane Sherfey has pointed out, the so-called nymphomaniac may actually be the most natural and normal of women. Yet it must also have been a survival-conducive adaptation for women to be able to curb their own sexual appetites in order to form a bond with a single male, on whom they could rely for protection; hence the seeming paradox of greater capacity conjoined with greater control—so great indeed that many cultures have been able to suppress all knowledge of the female orgasm.

Seaman's discussion of the controversy over vaginal vs. clitoral orgasms is especially useful. Some feminists have mistaken the import of the Masters and Johnson claim that all orgasms involve and require clitoral stimulation. This does not mean that all orgasms are *felt* in the clitoris, or that vaginal stimulation, as in coitus, is not also necessary for some women. Many women prefer vaginal to direct clitoral stimulation; not only does the clitoris generally receive indirect (if not direct) stimulation during intercourse, but the vagina itself, even the upper portion which Masters and Johnson report to be devoid of sensitivity, possesses receptor cells under the skin which may not respond to a light touch but which do register a vigorous thrust.

Also useful is the chapter on "How to Liberate Yourself from Your Gynecologist." Seaman protests the authoritarian attitudes of gynecologists, which deprive women of autonomy over their own sexual functions—from their failure to provide adequate information about—originally the availability and later—the dangers of birth control pills and other prescribed drugs, to their unconscionable custom of forcing women to be "shaved, humiliated, drugged, painted and stuck up in stirrups to deliver their babies." (p.142) Exploitative malpractices such as the performance of unnecessary hysterectomies and Caesareans are rife in the field of gynecology. Seaman thinks that women can stand up to their gynecologists and demand that their rights to information and autonomy be respected; but the abuses she documents are serious enough to raise the question of whether more severe action against that profession is not called for.

SEX   A sex, in the first instance, is one of the two reproductive types—female and male—into which most of the more complex plant and animal species are divided (though many plants are hermaphroditic, both sexes being found in a single individual). In the second instance, sex is the sum total of the morphological, physiological and psychological or behavioral differences between these two types, either in general or within a particular species. And, finally, "sex" can mean genital intercourse (not necessarily between members of opposite sexes), and some of the activities leading up to, accompanying, or substituting for it.

It is primarily sex in the second sense, that is, the nature of the human sexual dichotomy—or rather the multitude of theories and opinions about it—which is the subject of this book. Biologically, sex serves the purpose of reproduction and, perhaps more importantly, it makes possible the recombination of genetic elements in each generation which is thought to underlie most evolutionary change. (See Wilson.) But no known human culture has treated sex as merely a physiological difference relevant to reproduction. All have used sex as a means of sorting people into different social roles, both within the family and in other social, economic and political institutions. (See Mead.) All of the writers dealt with here have been in some way concerned with the physical or psychological differences between women and men; with how and why distinct social roles based on sex have developed; with the moral justification, or lack of it, of existing sex roles; or with the ways in which sex roles may be rendered less oppressive. (Also see Biological Differences between the Sexes, and Sexuality.)

SEXISM The term *sexism* was coined during the feminist renaissance of the Sixties, probably by analogy with the term *racism*. Both terms reflect a rising social awareness of the oppression suffered in our culture by those who are not white males. *Sexism* and *racism* are evaluative terms, denoting a type of discrimination between persons which is morally wrong; sexism is wrongful discrimination on the basis of sex, racism wrongful discrimination on the basis of race. The wrongness of such discrimination lies in the fact that it defines individuals as inferior, limits their options, and subjects them to exploitative and demeaning treatment, on the basis of their membership in some general class (e.g. women or blacks)—which membership cannot in fact justify such treatment.

Sexism has a great many aspects. There are sexist beliefs, sexist attitudes, actions, laws, customs, cultural stereotypes, and so on. Nearly all of these function to maintain male domination and female subordination. Occasionally, sexist stereotypes like the supposed moral superiority of women, are used to argue for sexual equality or even female supremacy (see e.g. Montagu and Solanas); but these are clearly reversals of the dominant pattern. Entire cultures, including our own, may be said to be sexist. Indeed most if not all known human cultures are sexist to some degree; that is, they limit the freedom of one sex, (usually) women more than that of the other (men) and often in ways which are morally unjustifiable. Within a particular culture, of course, some individuals (of both sexes) may be said to be more sexist in their attitudes and behavior than others.

It is also useful to distinguish between practices that are more or less *directly* sexist. Sexism in the primary sense involves wrongful discrimination (overtly or covertly) based on sex itself. More subtle forms of sex discrimination may not be instances of primary sexism, but they nevertheless do place individuals of one sex at a disadvantage. For instance, a great many practices on the part of employers tend to have a discriminatory impact upon women, in present social circumstances, even though sex itself is not the basis for the discrimination. These include antinepotism rules (which forbid the employment of spouses of present employees); retention-by-seniority systems (which require that the last persons hired be the first fired when cutbacks occur); failure to provide child-care facilities; and discrimination against older workers, part-time workers, and workers who have been out of the labor market for a period of time. All of these practices discriminate de facto against women, and thus are examples of what may be called secondary sexism (1). Like primary sexism, secondary sexism functions to maintain male domination in all the major institutions of society.

From a feminist perspective, sexism is the underlying theme of the debate over the nature of woman. Theories of woman's nature are either sexist (i.e. male or, rarely, female supremacist) or sexually egalitarian in their content and implications. The rejection of sexism does not imply the rejection of *all* general theories about the differences between the sexes. Sexist theories are those which either assert empirically false claims about the difference between the sexes (e.g. that women are incapable of reasoning) which would, if true, appear to justify male domination; or they use empirical facts (e.g. that women are on the average smaller and less physically powerful than men) to argue for male supremacist conclusions which these facts do not support. Consequently, which theories one considers sexist depends both on what one believes the actual (both natural and socially conditioned) difference between the sexes to be, and on what moral consequences, if any, one believes can be derived from these empirical differences. Feminists disagree about the actual differences between the sexes, but agree that these are certainly not such as to justify male domination.

1. See Mary Anne Warren, "Secondary Sexism and Quota Hiring," *Philosophy and Public Affairs*, 6:3 (Spring, 1977), pp.240–261.

SEXTON, Patricia Cayo. *The Feminized Male: Classrooms, White Collars and the Decline of Manliness* (Random House, New York, 1969)

Sexton argues that because most elementary and secondary schoolteachers in the United States are women (or "feminized" men), most boys are either feminized by the schools or alienated from them. Women, she thinks, cannot teach boys about the things which interest them, such as sports, mechanics and technology. They emphasize nonpractical, academic subjects, learning by rote, and docile conformist behavior, all of which boys, and Sexton, consider feminine. Hence the boys who cooperate with the system become feminized, while those who resist being feminized rebel against school and become underachievers. Schools therefore need to be "defeminized" by increasing the number of (masculine) male teachers, especially in the primary grades, where they are most scarce.

At the same time, the other institutions of the society—e.g. government, industry, the universities—need to be feminized by the admission of more women to positions of power and influence. School administrations, unlike the classroom, are male dominated, and more women should be promoted from teaching to administrative positions. This will be beneficial to society as a whole, since women bring to positions of power a humanity and concern for people which is sadly lacking in American institutions. The two goals—defeminizing the schools and feminizing the power structure—are complementary, since opening more and better jobs for women in government, business and so on will reduce their concentration and influence in the classroom. The major problem with the book is, clearly, the uncritical use of the terms "masculine" and "feminine" and the lack of empirical evidence for the "results" of the disproportions on which she comments. (See Androgyny.)

SEXUALITY Sexuality means the propensity to desire sexual stimulation and sexual activity, whether heterosexual, homosexual, or autosexual (i.e. masturbatory). Some argue that women's entire reproductive role is an intrinsic part of their sexuality (see Deutsch); but this is a confusion, particularly since women who enjoy sexual activity may have no desire for motherhood, and vice versa. This confusion may help to explain the fact that, although the best evidence indicates that the sexuality of the two sexes is very similar (see Masters and Johnson), it is women who have always been associated with sexuality. Women are the sex whose sexual desires, if not stronger than men's, are thought to be harder to control and therefore dangerous to men and to the social order. It is always women and not men who are said to represent the "lower" parts of human nature—matter, passivity, and passion, sexual or otherwise. (See e.g., Aristotle, the Bible, Paul, Augustine, Aquinas, Rousseau, Hume, Schopenhauer, Weininger, Freud, Jung and Mailer; also see Bullough, and G.R. Taylor, for historical studies of the association between women and sexuality.)

The first systematic scientific collection of data about human sexuality was carried out by Havelock Ellis, in the latter nineteenth and early twentieth century. The comparative anthropologist Westermarck had argued that, contrary to the matriarchy theorists' claim that the original condition of humanity was one of complete promiscuity, that in fact "marriage" (that is, long-term heterosexual monogamy) has been the prevailing norm in all known human cultures. But Westermarck's arguments were questionable, and Ellis' work revealed the enormous variety of forms which human sexuality has taken, even in Victorian England. It is only in our own time, however, that large-scale statistical studies of the sexual behavior, and laboratory observations of the sexual physiology of women and men have become possible. Kinsey's studies revealed that very few men and a minority of women (though a somewhat larger minority) actually confine their sexual activities to the socially approved type, i.e. heterosexual marital intercourse. Masters and Johnson found that, whatever the differences in the sexual *behavior* of women and men, the physiology of their sexual response is remarkably similar—with the exception that women tend to have a greater capacity for multiple orgasms.

Sherfy and others have seized upon this last finding as evidence that women's sexual capacities, and perhaps their natural sexual appetites, are greater than those of men. Sherfey argues that prehistoric women must have been extremely promiscuous, and that controlling this rampant female sexuality was a precondition for civilized life. While it is probably foolhardy to draw any of these conclusions from the Masters and Johnson data, the latter do refute (as Sherfey also points out) a large part of the Freudian theory of the nature and development of female sexuality. Freud held that clitorally oriented sexuality—and indeed all sexuality—is masculine, and that the mature feminine woman must transfer the locus of her sexual response from the clitoris to the vagina, which can only be stimulated by the male organ. These claims are disproven by the fact that, as Masters and

427

Johnson demonstrated, the clitoris is and remains the primary organ of female sexual response; the fact that it is the direct biological analogue of the penis does not make it a "masculine" organ, any more than it makes the penis a "feminine" one. (Also see Seaman.)

There is little doubt that the increased availability of contraception and abortion has done much to change women's attitudes towards their own sexuality. For the first time in history, women's sexuality can be pragmatically as well as conceptually separated from their procreative functions. In the past, most feminists agreed completely—at least in public—with the traditional emphasis on the virtues of chastity and marital fidelity, particularly for women. (See Wollstonecraft, Fuller, J.S. Mill, Harriet Taylor; William Godwin, Charles Fourier, and Emma Goldman are noteworthy exceptions.) The radical feminists of today, however, perceive the institution of heterosexual monogamy as one of the cornerstones of the oppression of women. Whether they believe that the road to sexual liberation passes through lesbianism (see Abbot, Dworkin, Johnson), bisexuality (see Friedan, Millett), polymorphous sexuality (Firestone), solitary masturbation, voluntary chastity, or through more egalitarian heterosexual intercourse, they agree that heterosexual monogamy as a binding norm must go. Many follow Reich in holding that freedom of sexual expression is a basic human right, and a necessity for psychological health.

Whether or not it is a psychological necessity, it is difficult to dispute the claim that such freedom is an intrinsic good, and one to which all persons have an equal moral right, other things being equal. It is not any particular way of exercising that freedom which is universally intrinsically good, but that the choice be uncoerced, and left in the hands of those most intimately involved. The willingness of patriarchal systems to sacrifice the sexual freedom of women, and to a lesser extent that of men, is one of the strongest moral indictments of patriarchy—especially now that heterosexual intercourse and procreation are no longer inevitably linked. (See Hume; also see Morrison, Johnson and Hammer, in Anthologies III, and Baker and Elliston, Anthologies XII.)

SHERFEY, Mary Jane. *The Nature and Evolution of Female Sexuality* (Random House, New York, 1966)
Sherfey draws on the work of Masters and Johnson and on

428

recent discoveries about embryological development and the physiology of female genitalia to refute the Freudian "transfer" theory of female sexuality. Freud viewed the clitoris as an underdeveloped penis, and held that since the vagina remains undiscovered in childhood, childhood sexuality is essentially phallic and masculine in both boys and girls. To achieve true femininity, however, a woman must forego clitoral orgasms, such as can be achieved by masturbation, and switch to vaginal orgasms, which can be attained only through intercourse with a man. Freud in fact saw women themselves, not just their genitals, as inferior and underdeveloped deviations from the male norm.

Sherfey points out that we now know that the human male, like all mammalian males, is biologically derived from the female. A fetus of either chromosomal sex develops as a female for the first five weeks, and will continue to develop as a female in the absence of male hormones, which will induce masculine development in either sex if present during the crucial stages of fetal life. (This arrangement is necessary in viviparous animals, since if it were the female hormone which induced differential development then all fetuses would be feminized by the mother's hormones.) This biological primacy of the female form does not show that women are superior or that men are a biological mistake (as some have claimed) but it does demonstrate that the clitoris is originally a female structure, and that it is a travesty of the facts to think of it as an innately masculine organ, or to suppose that the original libido or sex drive is masculine in nature. Furthermore, Masters and Johnson argue, the clitoris is the key female sexual organ, the one which triggers all of women's orgasms, regardless of whether they are achieved through masturbation or heterosexual intercourse. The mechanism of female orgasm, which Sherfey describes in detail, involves the stimulation of the glans of the clitoris by friction against the hood or prepuce, which in effect functions as a miniature vagina. In heterosexual intercourse, the thrusting of the penis stimulates the clitoris indirectly (but effectively), and it is this and not the contact with the vagina as such which produces the woman's orgasm. Hence all female orgasms are clitoral, and there can be no shift of the kind which Freud postulated as necessary to mature femininity.

Another crucial Masters and Johnson discovery is that women, unlike men, are capable of having an indefinite number of successive orgasms; there is no limit to the number possible other than physical fatigue. For this reason, and on the basis of the behavior of various other primate females, Sherfey speculates that prehistoric women must have been exceedingly promiscuous, especially during the second half of the menstrual cycle when sexual tension is high. Not until the rise of urban life, she thinks, was women's sexual freedom curtailed; indeed this curtailment was a precondition of civilized life since without it stable family and social relations would be impossible.

SINGER, June. *Androgyny: Toward a New Theory of Sexuality* (Anchor Press, Garden City, New York, 1976)

Singer is a psychoanalyst in the tradition of Carl Jung, whose account of the *anima* and *animus* she follows in most respects. She views Masculinity and Femininity (spelled with initial capitals) as primordial archetypes inherent in the human psyche. Androgyny is an archetype too, as evidence of which status Singer describes images of androgyny in various mystical traditions, e.g. Gnosticism, alchemy, Taoism and Astrology, and in Plato's myth of the orginally hermaphroditic people who were split into male and female halves as a punishment for arrogance. (See Bisexuality.) By "androgyny" she means a dynamic interrelation between the Masculine and Feminine energies within an individual. Masculinity and Femininity, she thinks are not just archetypes, but natural forces. As such they are polar opposites and like all such opposing pairs (life/death, hot/cold, etc.) they exist only in relation to one another and therefore form a unity, a Two in One (also spelled with initial capitals). Masculinity is outward-directed energy, Femininity is energy directed inwards, absorbed, preserved. In the androgyne, these two poles are unified, in the sense of being related (energy flows between them, she says), but not in the sene of losing their distinctness. Singer has only contempt for the "psychological hermaphrodite," in whom Masculinity and Femininity are not clearly distinguished.

Men and women, she thinks, are naturally very different psychologically: "men are born with a penis which simply and naturally is used for penetration, while women need to develop their phallic potential in order to penetrate the world." (p.199) Men are essentially Masculine, even though they must be aware of their *anima*, or Feminine side, and women are essentially Feminine, even while aware of their Masculine *animus*. A woman's *animus* is her inner opposite, which gives her the strength to stand alone; yet she must remain predominantly Feminine to remain true to herself as a woman. Remaining predominantly Masculine is less important for a man; he can steer a more central course between Masculinity and Femininity. The reasons for this asymmetry are not entirely clear, though Singer does reject Jung's own sexist reasons for wanting woman's *animus* to play second fiddle to man's *anima*. Jung thought that the role of the former was primarily to provide inspiration for the latter, in order that the *man* may be creative; Singer allows women to be creative too, but without ceasing to be primarily Feminine. Just what this may mean is left to the reader's imagination. Certainly this is not an attack on sex stereotyping as such; indeed Singer says that the error of the Judeo-Christian tradition has not been in its insistence on sexual stereotypes, but in its granting of undue prominence to the Masculine principle. Masculinity and Femininity must be separate but equal.

Such a position is discomfiting to those feminists who believe that the inequality of men and women is (almost logically) guaranteed by such a postulation of Masculinity and Femininity as opposing traits which "naturally and properly" predominate in men and women respectively. But the position is anyway weak because of a lack of evidence for the asymmetry, or for the alleged inner/outer-directedness differences between the sexes.

SOCIALISM AND FEMINISM There has long been a close association between socialist and feminist ideas. Plato may have been neither a true feminist nor a socialist, in the modern sense, but it is no coincidence that in the ruling class of his *Republic, both* private property and the traditional differentiations between the roles of women and men have been abolished. Utopian socialists have often been advocates of equal rights for women. (See Fourier, W. Thompson.) Marx and Engels held that the achievement of complete moral, legal and economic equality between the sexes is both a necessary condition for true communism, and something which can only be brought about through the destruction of the capitalist system.

Marxists have typically held that the oppression of women within the patriarchal family is primarily a result of the operation of class society in general, and industrial capitalism in particular. (See Engels, Bebel, Trotsky, Lenin, Guettel, Jennes, Reed.) Other socialist feminists, while agreeing that patriarchy and capitalism are mutually reinforcing institutions, deny that an analysis wholly based on economic factors is sufficient to explain, or to provide the means of eliminating, male domination. (See Borgese, Foreman, Mitchell, Firestone, H. Scott, Zaretsky.)

SOCIOBIOLOGY: See E.O. Wilson; also see Biological Determinism and Ethology.

SOCIOLOGY OF WOMEN   If sociology is defined as the study of the structure and development of society and social relationships, then it is scarcely possible to write on the nature of women or on the relationship between the sexes without touching on the subject matter of sociology. Sociological conditions, in particular patriarchy and the domination by males of all major social institutions in almost all societies, form the data base which both feminists and antifeminists seek to describe, explain, and evaluate. As a methodologically sophisticated science, however, sociology is largely a twentieth-century phenomenon; and only in the most recent decades have feminist issues become the focus of a great deal of sociological research. Before, women tended to appear in sociology primarily in male-related roles, e.g. in studies of marriage, family life, divorce, prostitution, and the like; there were, however, some noteworthy exceptions.

Harriet Martineau wrote what is probably the best early account of the social condition of women in the United States. Unlike that other great observer of early American society, Alexis de Tocqueville, she did not romanticize women's "lofty" position in America, but argued that the state of domestic servitude combined with the legal and political status of women made up a sign that the level of American culture was far lower than it at first appeared to be. Herbert Spencer, one of the pioneers of scientific sociology, also considered that the "higher" stages of social and cultural evolution coincided with an improvement in the status of women (although he held that *complete* equality between the sexes could not be achieved in any society).

The matriarchy theorists of the latter nineteenth century held, on the contrary, that the status of women was much more nearly equal (or even superior) to that of men in the earliest and least developed societies. (See Bachofen, Morgan, McLennan, Engels.) W.I. Thomas is one of the few major sociologists of this century (or rather of the first half of it) who took this theory seriously, and explained the degraded social status of women as due at least in large part to such "civilized" institutions as law, government, private property, and patriarchal religion. (The biological differences between the sexes, he thought, were also relevant, but insufficient in themselves to explain male domination.)

Much more typical, however, has been the type of functionalist approach exemplified by Talcott Parsons. Parsons argues that a strict division of roles within the family, with the husband playing the instrumental and the wife the expressive role, is necessary for the very existence of the family, which in turn is the basic unit of society. Pitrim Sorokin, the distinguished Russian-born sociologist, took a negative view of the liberation of women, which he felt would destroy the sexual continence (that is, of women) which is necessary for civilized life. And sociobiologists, who look to ethology (i.e. the study of the behavior of animals) for clues as to the laws of human social interaction, generally argue that aggressiveness, dominance, and status seeking are inherent male traits, for which men have been selected for millions of years, and which make the prospect of real sexual equality extremely slight. (See Ardrey, Morris, Storr, Tiger, Wilson, Lorenz.)

Today, on the other hand, there are also a significant number of sociologists whose outlook is explicitly feminist, and who do not assume that the way that sex roles in fact function—whether "naturally" or by social convention—is the way that they must or ought to function. Jessie Bernard's research on marriage, motherhood, and women in the academy demonstrates the high price that women pay for conforming to the cultural stereotype of femininity and the feminine role. Ann Oakley argues that the sexual division of labor is, in every society, the root cause of the phenomenon of gender discrimination; in contemporary western culture, femininity is defined in terms of the housewife role, which, she shows, is a particularly debilitating and unfullfilling one. Constantina Safilios-Rothschild maintains that in Europe and America alike, the prevailing sexual stereotypes have required an unfortunate divorce between love and sexuality, from which both sexes suffer.

Other feminist sociologists, including Evelyn Sullerot, Ester Boserup, and Elise Boulding, have studied the economic and social roles of women in the underdeveloped or developing nations, and have argued that greater sexual equality is a necessity if those nations are to solve their economic and demographic problems. Alice Rossi, Carolyn Bird, Cynthia Fuchs Epstein and others have analyzed the continuing phenomenon of sexual segregation in the occupational world; their work reveals relatively little evidence that job segregation has been decreasing.

Mirra Komarovsky argues that the major problems women face today are the results of the radically inconsistent demands made upon them by their two social roles, as wives and mothers and as workers. Alva Myrdal and Viola Klein examine this conflict in

433

Women's Two Roles, and suggest a three-stage pattern for women's lives (education and work, childrearing, return to work). In another work, Kelin uses the perspective of the sociology of knowledge to explore the ways in which women have been conceptualized in the various scientific disciplines. **Language and Sex**, Barrie Thorne and Nancy Henley's anthology of sociolinguistic studies of the relationship between language and male dominance, illustrates another promising line of research.

These are only a few examples of recent sociological research on woman and women's social roles. For more comprehensive surveys see the review articles by Joan Huber and Helena Znaniecki Lopata, in **Signs**, 1:3 (Spring, 1976), and 2:1 (Autumn, l976) respectively. For recent collections of theoretical and research articles in the field, see Millman, Epstein, Theodore, Kreps, Safilios-Rothschild, Freeman, and Glazer-Malbin, in Anthologies XIV. Also in that section see **Gender and Sex in Society**, by Lucille Duberman, Helen Mayer Hacker and Warren Farrell, for good summaries and analyses of research in the sociology of sex-role differentiation.

SOLANAS, Valerie. *SCUM Manifesto* (Olympia Press, New York, 1968)

Valerie Solanas is known as the most radical of the radical feminists of the late 60s. Her (nonfatal) shooting of Andy Warhol dramatized her conviction that the elimination of male domination requires the elimination of males. The *SCUM Manifesto* presents the case for this conclusion: "SCUM" stands for "Society for Cutting Up Men." It is important not only as an influence upon other radical feminists, but as an especially vivid expression of what Vivian Gornick (in her Introduction) calls "the true feelings of the quintessential feminist heart . . . [which are] feelings of black rage." (p.xxiv)

Solanas maintains that male nature is inherently defective; "the male is an incomplete female, a walking abortion, aborted at the gene stage." (p.3) The defect is an emotional one.

> Completely egocentric, unable to relate, empathize or identify . . . the male is psychically passive. He hates his passivity, so he projects it onto women, defines the male as active, then sets out to prove that he is . . . (p.5)

This, she says, is the explanation for the male's obsession with sex. "Screwing" is a primary way of asserting dominance. Because they suffer from "pussy envy," men seek to reverse the truth about the sexes. They claim all desirable feminine qualities (intelligence, creativity, individuality, morality) for themselves, and label their own failings (stupidity, lack of individuality, amorality) "feminine." Their deepest desire (which most are unable to admit) is to be female; while their

> secret, most hideous fear is the fear of being discovered to be not a female, but a male, subhuman animal. (p.32)

This self-hatred of the male, Solanas claims, is the cause of all alienating, inhuman institutions of modern society, such as compulsory heterosexuality, marriage, the "money-work" system, oppressive law and government, racism, war, disease, and even death itself. If a concerted effort were made, it might be possible to solve the problems of disease, aging and death within our lifetimes. But men will never make such an effort, since

> The male likes death—it excites him sexually and, already dead inside, he wants to die. (p.36)

The only solution, therefore, is a feminist/anarchist revolution, which will culminate in the physical elimination of the male sex. The revolution, she says, will begin with a campaign by SCUM women (and male allies of SCUM) of systematic "fucking up" of the entire capitalist/patriarchal system, and the murder of selected men within it. Once women withdraw their complicity, the system will collapse within a year. Free of male control, women will refuse to endure the torture of pregnancy and childbirth. Thus, artificial reproduction will become a necessity—at least until immortality is achieved, making futher reproduction unnecessary. And, Solanas says, it will be seen that "only whole, complete beings" should be produced, "not physical defects or deficiencies . . . such as maleness." (p.38) Meanwhile, the money-work system will have been replaced by a completely automated society, in which machines will do all the boring and routine work. In the absence of men, laws and governments will no longer be needed (p.21).

It is unfortunate that Solanas does not explain her reasons for supposing that the character structure of the contemporary chauvinist male—which she describes aptly, if uncharitably—is an inevitable consequence of male physiology. Margaret Mead has shown that there are cultures (notably the Arapesh) in which males are as empathic, nurturant and noncompetitive as females. Unless there was some reason to believe that all Arapesh men possess some rare genetic anomaly which shapes their character—which there is not—we must conclude that the genetic defects of the male as such are insufficient to explain the objectionable attitudes and behavior of men in the patriarchal/capitalist context. Nor, of course—as Solanas herself makes clear—does the supposedly innately aggressive nature of males *excuse* their objectionable behavior.

SOROKIN, Pitirim A. (1889–1968). *The American Sex Revolution* (Porter Sargent, Boston, 1956)

Sorokin is a Russian-born Harvard sociologist who attacks the trend toward "sexual freedom," that is, permissiveness towards and the increased practice of extra- and premarital intercourse, as a specter which is threatening American civilization. Sexual indulgence outside of marriage, he maintains, undermines mental and physical health, destroys moral sensitivity and responsibility, diminishes creative energy, lessens respect for law, generates political turmoil, and generally brings about a society's decline and fall. Reason, creativity and social order rest on the successful sublimation of the sex drive. Rome, Greece and other great civilizations of the past fell because of the social and political anarchy associated with increased licentiousness. The Russian Revolution was preceded by such a trend in the upper class, and its leaders he says at first encouraged sexual promiscuity. In order to restore social order, however, they were forced to reverse their position, to glorify the family, premarital chastity and marital fidelity, and to prohibit abortion.

While he does not directly address the question of the relationship between sexual freedom and the freedom of women, Sorokin accepts J.D. Unwin's thesis that a high level of civilization requires not only a strict sexual code, but a strictly patriarchal family structure. He seems, indeed, to *identify* the possession of a strict moral code with the strict subordination of women. "In the whole of human history," he says, "not a single case is found in which a society advanced to the Rationalistic culture without its women being born and reared in a rigidly enforced pattern of faithfulness to one man." (p.110) A similar pattern of faithfulness on the part of men is apparently unnecessary, and has rarely been enforced. This should cause one to wonder—though Sorokin does not—why, if sexual suppression leads to superior creativity, morality, mental and physical health, and so on, women are not and have not been vastly more creative, moral, sane and rational than men. (Or are they?) Nor does he explain why, if sexual repression is such a great good, for the individual as well as the society, men have so rarely been inclined to impose the same restrictions upon themselves as upon women.

SPENCER, Herbert (1820–1903). *Social Statics* (D. Appleton and Company, New York and London, 1913; first published 1850)
The Principles of Ethics, Volumes I & II (D. Appleton and Company, New York and London, 1910; first published 1893)
The Principles of Sociology, Volume 1:2 (D. Appleton and Company, New York, 1897)
Essays, Scientific, Political and Speculative, Volume III (D. Appleton and Company, New York and London, 1910; first published 1874)

Herbert Spencer is the chief exponent of the philosophy which became known as Social Darwinism—although Spencer himself denied that Darwin had had any influence on him. Social Darwinism holds that societies, like biological species, survive and gain strength through competition, both with other societies and between individuals within the society. For this reason, Spencer thought, it is a mistake to provide welfare or relief for the poor, elderly, or ailing, since this will only increase the number of "unfit" persons who will survive and pass on their weaknesses to future generations. (See *Social Statics*, pp.149–151.) Spencer's ideas provided a made-to-order rationalization for *laissez faire* capitalism. They were enormously popular and influential in late nineteenth-century England and America, though his works are rarely read today. He wrote voluminously, not only on social ethics, but on psychology, biology, political science and sociology.

Spencer views the status of women in a given culture as an index of social progress in that culture. He holds that "among low savages the relations of the sexes are substantially like those common among inferior creatures." (*Principles of Sociology*, Vol. 1:2, p.613) That is, there is no established institution of monogamous marriage; the males fight for the females, and there is polygamy, incest, adultery and little concern for the chastity or virginity of females. Since he considers strict monogamy both the moral ideal and essential for the highest forms of social life, he sees its absence among uncivilized peoples as evidence that there is a "general association between the rudest forms of social existence and the most degraded relations of the sexes." (*Op. cit.*, p.619) Civilization, on the other hand, gradually improves the lot of women, through the establishment of monogamous—and patriarchal—marriage and the growth of the idea of justice.

That women have a much lower status in primitive than in civilized societies was often taken for granted, before the work of the matriarchy theorists, anthropologists, and archaeologists of the late nineteenth and twentieth century demonstrated that the status of women is sometimes quite high in supposedly primitive cultures. Spencer was aware of a few apparent exceptions of this kind to what he considered the general rule, e.g. ancient Egypt, which was matrilineal and relatively sexually egalitarian. He explains such cases in terms of another—and possibly more plausible—sociological principle of his own invention, namely that the position of women is improved "in proportion as warlike activities are replaced by industrial activities." (*Op. cit.* p.734) Thus, Egypt was a highly industrial, i.e. cooperative, nonmilitaristic culture; the militaristic Aryans, on the other hand, were strictly patriarchal.

There are, Spencer argues, several reasons why the status of women tends to be low in militaristic societies. First, by reducing the number of marriageable men, militarism and warfare necessitate polygyny. Polygyny, in turn, "necessarily implies a low *status* of women . . . (while) monogamy, if it does not necessarily imply a high *status*, is an essential condition to a high *status*." (*Op. cit.*, p.743) Second, militarism requires a dictatorial mode of government, and, since family life mirrors that of the state, it also produces tyranny in the home. Third and perhaps most important, militarism reduces the level of sympathetic fellow-feeling, thus lowering the level of moral awareness:

> Habitual antagonism with, and destruction of, foes, sears the sympathies; while daily exchange of products and services among citizens, puts no obstacle to increase of fellow-feeling. And the altruism which grows with peaceful co-operation, ameliorates at once the life without the household and the life within the household. (*Op. cit.*, p.744)

Spencer's claim that the status of women tends to improve both with advances in civilization and with decreases in militarism implies that civilizations tend to evolve towards greater industrialism and lesser militarism; and this, indeed, is what Spencer believes. This optimistic theory is based upon his belief in the inheritance of the psychological traits acquired in social life, especially the capacities for fellow-feeling and altruism. These traits, Spencer holds, were absent in our earliest ancestors, because the latter had almost no social existence. Family groups were small and impermanent, and outside the family there was little social cooperation. As isolated family groups conglomerate into larger units, a higher level of cooperation is required and at first, Spencer thinks, it can usually be best achieved by force. Thus cultures on the way to becoming civilized tend to be militaristic. Gradually, however, the involuntary increase in cooperation brings about a mental evolution which makes possible a more voluntary cooperation, and hence leads to a more peaceful and industrial society:

> the higher mental faculties, made possible only by an environment such as social life furnishes, evolve as this environment evolves— each increment of advance in the one being followed by an increment of advance in the other. (*Op. cit.*, p.760)

The capitalistic nations, Spencer thinks, are moving towards the ideal social state, one in which militarism and coercion will have been wholly replaced by voluntary industry, cooperation, and exchange. In this ideal state, government will function only to protect the equal liberty of all. All other functions, such as delivering mail, protecting the public against disease, fraud or pollution, and giving charity to the poor, will be more efficiently performed by private enterprise. Monogamy will become the universal standard, and the status of women will be as nearly equal as possible; there will be

> a diminution of the political and domestic disabilities of women, until there remain only such as differences of constitution entail. (*Op. cit.*, p.767)

The inequality of rights which Spencer considers to be an inevitable result of woman's "constitution" is, however, considerable. Although he holds that unmarried women should have the right to enter any profession for which they can qualify, he does not advocate complete equality between the sexes in either political or domestic rights. The husband, he argues, must have the ownership of all family property, including what would otherwise belong to the wife, because he is responsible for the family's economic support and she is not. The wife *cannot* be held responsible for support, because she bears biological burdens "which largely incapacitate for active life." (**Principles of Ethics**, Vol. II, p.161)

Spencer holds that women's childbearing function not only weakens them physically, but tends to lower their mental capacity.

> In women the intellectual capacity is frequently diminished; for the antagonism between individuation and reproduction, which is in

them most pronounced, tells more especially on the brain. (***Principles of Ethics***, Vol. I, p.536)

For this reason, man must continue to have the greater legal authority in marriage; "the law . . . will . . . continue to give, in cases of need, supremacy to the husband, as being the more judicially-minded." (***Principles of Sociology***, 1:2, p.768) Single women should have the legal right to work for pay, but only because they are excluded "from those natural careers in which they are dependent on men for subsistence." (*Loc. cit.*) Married women should be content with their dependent position, because their domestic role is a vastly important one:

> If women comprehended all that is contained in the domestic sphere, they would ask no other. (*Op. cit.*, p.769)

Not surprisingly, Spencer was an adamant foe of the women's suffrage movement. His primary antisuffrage argument was that it would be unfair to men to give women political equality so long as there is any threat of war, since women are not subject to the draft, nor could they be. Furthermore, even if a permanent peace could be achieved, women's lack of a sense of justice would ensure that they would exert only a bad influence on politics. Women tend,

> as a concomitant of their maternal functions, to yield benefits not in proportion to deserts but in proportion to the absence of deserts . . . (***Principles of Ethics*** II, p.196)

Thus, if women had the vote they might demand that the government interfere, unwisely, in the essential social process by which the strong thrive and the unfit are eliminated. (See ***Essays*** III, p.151.) Conversely, they might tend to support militaristic and authoritarian movements, because the worship of power is a "trait of nature by which women are distinguished." (***Principles of Ethics*** II, p.196) That men might also have character flaws which arise from their role in the family and make them less than ideal political participants is a possibility that Spencer does not, of course, consider.

The evaporation in the present century of Spencer's once-huge academic and popular following is not due to the shallowness of his antifeminist arguments, but to the rejection in the West of the Spencerean doctrine that societies evolve through the inheritance of acquired psychological traits. The antifeminist content of Spencer's evolutionary social ethics survives in the work of popular writers like Robert Ardrey, Lionel Tiger, and others, who argue that the hunting-ape aggressiveness of the human male makes sexual equality impossible in any culture.

It is interesting, however, that those contemporary antifeminists who appeal to Darwinian principles to demonstrate the inevitability of male supremacy conceive of human nature as in some ways more constrained by biology than Spencer did. Spencer saw cooperation and reason, not male aggressiveness, as the mainspring of human social progress. He abhorred militarism and the aggressive, insensitive mentality that goes with it, and would probably have viewed the contemporary apologists for male aggression as advocates not of what is "natural," but of a social regression towards savagery.

SPIRITUAL FEMINISM   The term "spiritual feminism" refers to that segment of the women's movement which is concerned with the development of an explicitly feminist religious awareness. Spiritual feminism is not an entirely new phenomenon; some of the earliest defenders of women's rights were religious women who interpreted the spirit (if not the letter) of the Gospels as requiring, not prohibiting, a greater degree of equality between the sexes. (See Astell, Wollstonecraft.) *The Woman's Bible*, Elizabeth Cady Stanton's 1895 commentary on Old and New Testament passages dealing with women, is one of the best examples of this approach (1).

In our own time, however, there have been much more radical feminist challenges to patriarchal religious traditions. Since the publication in 1971 of Elizabeth Gould Davis' *The First Sex*, there has been a sharp increase in feminist interest in the evidence for the existence of early goddess-worshiping, matrilineal, and woman-centered societies. Merlin Stone's *When God Was a Woman* is perhaps the best piece of recent scholarship in this area. Some spiritual feminists hope to discover in the ancient worship of the Great Goddess not only an empirical refutation of the misogynist assumptions fostered by patriarchal religion but a source of authentic religious vision, a woman-centered world view free of the patriarchal taint. Some feminists have investigated (and even revived the rituals of) ancient and medieval mystery religions and witchcraft traditions. (See Witches.) Those who draw religious inspiration from such nonstandard sources constitute what might be called the revolutionary or heretical portion of the spiritual feminist movement (2).

The majority of spiritual feminists, however, are not revolutionaries. Instead, they seek to work within the various Christian,

Jewish, and (in a few instances) Islamic churches, to increase the participation of women, to gain entry for women to the priesthood or clergy and other church offices, to alter the antifemale elements of the churches' teachings, and so on. Some even hope eventually to eliminate the presumption that the deity itself is male, or exclusively male. (See Daly, Ruether, L. Russell.) This in itself would almost of necessity change the way in which women are conceptualized; they would be no longer the second sex, an afterthought, merely the "helpmates" of men, but equal and independent reflections of the divinity.

Inasmuch as such proposed changes challenge what religious conservatives view, perhaps rightly, as the very core of the Judeo-Christian religious tradition—which is based on a (very masculine) male deity, and, in the Christian case, his male offspring—they may well prove futile. It is, however, too early to predict that this will be the case. Furthermore, so long as the patriarchal aspects of these major religious traditions persist, reformist efforts by spiritual feminists will be important as a way of making feminist ideas accessible to women whose religious convictions might otherwise preclude their sympathizing with, or even understanding, feminist demands. (See also Christianity, and the Bible.)

1. Arno Press, New York, 1972; first published 1895–98.
2. Marcia Keller (Department of Philosophy, San Francisco State), "Political-Philosophical Analysis of the U.S. Women's Liberation Movement" (unpublished manuscript).

STANNARD, Una. *Mrs. Man* (Germainbooks, San Francisco, 1977)

This is a history of the English and American practice of calling married women by their husband's surnames—and sometimes by their first names as well, as in "Mrs. John Jones." The practice is more recent than is generally assumed, being only a few centuries old. It was never mandated by English common law, which clearly permitted any adult to determine what his or her own name should be. Neither was it required by American statute law prior to the present century, when the backlash against the refusal of many married women to surrender their names led certain judges, employers and government agencies to rule that the customary name change was also legally mandatory. Some state legislatures also passed laws requiring the name change, during the 1920s and 1930s, and the struggle to overturn these laws is not yet entirely won. Indeed, so strangely twisted is masculine legal reasoning on this point that even the passage of the Equal Rights Amendment might not entirely guarantee married women the right to choose to retain their names.

After tracing in considerable detail the history of the name-change phenomenon, Stannard proposes a basically psychoanalytic explanation of the subordination of women to the wife and mother role, of which the name change is a symptom. Her thesis is that men's jealousy of women's procreative powers (Karen Horney's "womb envy"), and their desire to have children of their own, led them to claim that the male is the only true parent. (See Aristotle for an early and enormously influential statement of this theory.) The female, it was claimed, merely nourished the seed of the male, while the life, the divine substance and the genetic inheritance, came solely from the male.

This androcentric notion served as both a reason and a rationalization for men's subordination of women, whom they came to see as mere wombs which belonged to men. The changing of a married woman's name to that of her husband marks her as his property, or as a part of him, and the giving of only the male surname to children marks them as belonging solely to the male. The male-dominated legal institutions of this country continue, even in the 1970s, to resist changes in these archaic customs; for men, Stannard says, have still not fully faced the fact that they are not the sole progenitors of children.

Nor have men fully faced the fact that women have heads as well as wombs. Stannard explains the male refusal to believe in female intellect as due to the ancient identification between semen and brain matter. In fact, she holds that the glorification of male procreation is the primary source of the belief that females are inferior to males:

> Once men discovered that the Spirits of Life were not in a star or a bird or in the food a woman ate but resided in their own semen, they set themselves up as the One God of life, the sole procreators and looked upon woman, not as a mysterious Mother Goddess, but as the mere receptacle of man's seeds of life. (p.295)

The belief that the man is the sole progenitor led to the father's legal ownership of offspring; to his power to kill newborn infants (especially girls); to the denial of women's right to contraception and abortion; to the demand for female virginity before marriage and sexual fidelity after marriage; to the denial of legal rights to wives, who became submerged in the identity of the husband; in short, to the reduction of woman to the degraded role of "Mrs. Man." Now that the truth is known about women's contribution to the child's characteristics (it was discovered only a century ago), these repressive patriarchal practices can be expected to gradually give way. "Eventually . . . the new knowledge of woman's equal role in the creation of life will destroy the long reign of the Lords of Creation." (p.329)

The most obvious problem with this theory of the origins of male domination is that the denial of woman's procreative role seems at least as apt to be a *result* of their subordinate social status as a *cause* of their subordination, let alone the primary cause. That it is a significant contributing factor to the maintenance of male domination cannot, however, be doubted. Nor has adequate attention ever been given to this factor. Nineteenth-century evolutionary anthropologists like Bachofen and Morgan have held that the discovery of paternity was one of the causes and a necessary condition for the defeat of mother right; but they have ignored the role of the further "discovery" that *only* men can procreate. Thus Stannard's emphasis of this point is valuable, however implausible it may be as a universal explanation of male hegemony.

STEINMANN, Anne, and **FOX**, David J. *The Male Dilemma: How to Survive the Sexual Revolution* (Jason Aronson, New York, 1974)

Steinmann, (a psychologist) and Fox (an educator) strive to give a balanced view of the current conflict between the sexes; they are sympathetic to feminist goals but also to the problems of men who, like women, are torn between old and new ideas about how a "real" member of their sex should behave. To investigate the attitudes of contemporary men and women towards themselves and one another, they developed and administered to several thousand persons in the U.S. and seventeen other countries a number of questionnaires designed to reveal (1) how masculine and/or feminine the person feels her/himself to be; (2) how masculine and/or feminine she/he would *like* to be; (3) how masculine and/or feminine she/he thinks members of the other sex would like members of her/his sex to be.

The most interesting result of these surveys is that while both sexes wished to achieve and saw themselves as achieving some kind of balance between what the authors call masculinity (aggressiveness and self-orientation) and femininity (non-aggressiveness and home-and-family orientation), members of each sex felt that members of the other preferred them to be less "masculine" and more "feminine." The discrepancy between each sex's ideal for itself and what it thinks the other sex wants it to be leads to internal ambivalence in virtually all of us, and a lack of honest communication between the sexes. In marriage, for instance, each spouse is apt to suspect the other of being secretly hostile to his/her personal aspirations even while expressing strong support for them; and indeed each is apt to express stronger support than she/he actually feels. There is a lack of understanding and candor on both sides, though the authors' data and observations suggest that there is somewhat more of both on the male side. While women seem to be telling the simple truth when they deny any desire to "feminize" men or render them less achievement-oriented, men's professions of support for women's desire for independence and equality are underlain by the suspicion that in practice as women gain new rights, men will be deprived of rights which they previously enjoyed, and have no desire to relinquish now.

This finding is suggestive and not implausible. But the research is fatally marred by the absence of any critical analysis of the concepts of masculinity and femininity. The authors speak as though each were a single human quality, more or less indifferently described as aggressiveness, creativity, self- or achievement-orientation on the one hand; and passivity, subordinance or home-and-family orientation on the other. The two traits are presumed to be opposite ends of a single scale, and the individual's task a matter simply of picking some particular point on the scale which suits her or him. A man's choice is whether to be a "Marlboro Man," a "Milquetoast Man," or something in between. The truth is much more complicated; the stereotypes of "masculinity" and "femininity" are highly complex concatenations of virtues and vices, each of which is at least in theory somewhat separable from the rest; thus courage and rationality are masculine virtues, while excessive belligerence and the desire to dominate others are masculine vices. Since some "masculine" traits are desirable and others objectionable the rational course for a person of either sex is not to aim for some particular *degree* of "masculinity," but to develop to the fullest extent some "masculine" traits while strictly suppressing others. The same point holds, *mutatis mutandis*, for "femininity," which also has both desirable and undesirable aspects.

The authors' unreflective treatment of masculinity and femininity as unitary properties and polar opposites springs in part from their acceptance of Erik Erikson's thesis that the spatial configurations of male and female genitalia (the former external and outer directed, the latter folding inward) form a model of the basic and innate psychological differences between the sexes. Society, they hold, does not invent this basic difference, but only recognizes and reinforces it:

> We believe that women are biologically endowed, and later trained, to express the characteristics of *internal diffusion* both sexually and socially, while men are similarly endowed and trained to express the characteristics of *external concentration*." (pp.212–213; my emphasis)

It is clear that, starting with such a presumption (which is presented without supporting arguments), one cannot begin to comprehend the actual complexity either of the concepts of masculinity and femininity or of the causal factors behind these concepts. While there may indeed be biological facotrs such as hormones which influence the behavior of the sexes in different ways, we are not apt to gain much insight into these factors by drawing *ad hoc* analogies, of a sort clearly influenced by the assumption of male superiority, between the shape of people's genitals and the operation of their minds. This is about as plausible as appealing to the projecting shape of women's breasts as opposed to the flatness of men's chests to show that it is really women who are naturally outer directed and men who are not.

STERN, Karl. *The Flight from Woman* (Farrar, Straus and Giroux, New York, 1965)

A psychoanalyst with Jungian leanings, Stern maintains that our age suffers from a deficit of femininity, observable in both women and men. In men the flight from femininity takes the form of an excessive competitiveness, a fear of dependence and an inability to love. In women it means the rejection of the so-called "feminine role," i.e. that of serving as helpmate and muse to a man, of nurturing and inspiring his creative impulses. Stern maintains both that creativity in men requires feminine inspiration, and that women themselves are incapable of the highest forms of creativity, apart from motherhood. "If there had been female Bachs or Newtons, no power on earth could have kept them from producing." (p.29) (1)

Like Jung, Stern identifies masculinity and femininity with the universal cosmic forces yang and ying, and also with contrasting "modes of knowledge." Masculinity involves the objective or rational mode of thought and knowledge, the observation and analysis of objects and persons from the outside—in other words, the investigatory mode of the sciences and of analytic and positivist philosophy. Femininity on the other hand is a *subjective* or nonrational mode of knowledge, the intuitive, empathic interpersonal understanding of which the mother-child relationship is the paradigm. Stern not only holds that the objective mode of thought comes naturally to men but not to women, and the subjective to women but not men; but also that if this were *not* the case then human individuality would be nonexistent.

The case for this conclusion rests on Stern's convicton that men can develop as human individuals, fully creative and able to enjoy close personal relationships, only if they have in infancy and childhood a satisfactory relationship with their mothers, which in turn is possible only if the latter accept their feminine role. He finds evidence of a flight from femininity in Descartes' dualistic metaphysics; in Schopenhauer's glorification of the will as against bodily desires; in Sartre's reacting with nausea to the encounter with material existence; in Kierkegaard's abandonment of Regina and in Goethe's betrayal of *two* worthy fiancees; in the destructive character of Ibsen's Hedda Gabler; and in Tolstoy's supposedly Christian conversion, which led him to reject his wife and to denigrate sexuality and marriage. All of these men of genius, he argues, suffered real or imagined rejection by their (insufficiently feminine) mothers, and consequently not only had troubled relationships with women throughout their lives, but were unable at the intellectual level to reconcile the cosmic forces of masculinity and femininity, mind and body, spirit and flesh.

Thus, it seems, women's only proper contribution to civilization is to provide the ideal interpersonal environment for the flowering of male genius. They must shun their own "masculinity" in order that men may best develop both their masculine and their feminine capacities. Such a position is hardly egalitarian in its implications, although Stern denies any androcentrism on his own part and accuses feminists like Simone de Beauvoir of themselves being androcentric in their supposition that there is something inferior or degrading about the traditional feminine role. For women to object to women's being denied the androgynous wholeness which he recommends for men is, he thinks, for them to "ape" the male role. Stern's work leads one inevitably to reflect that the most remarkable feature of Jung's views is not the evidence for them but the support they receive. (See also Androgyny, and Jung.)

STETSON, Charlotte Perkins. See Gilman, Charlotte Perkins.

STOLLER, Robert J. *Sex and Gender, Volume 1: The Development of Masculinity and Femininity* (Jason Aronson, New York, 1974; first published 1968)
Sex and Gender, Volume 2: The Transsexual Experiment (Jason Aronson, New York, 1975)

Stoller is a Freudian psychoanalyst whose studies of persons with abnormalities of gender identity or of physiological sexual development have led him to some quite anti-Freudian conclusions. By "gender identity" is meant a person's own subjective conviction of his or her sexual identity, of masculinity or femininity, and the behaviors associated with it. Stoller's work seems to show that the most powerful influence upon gender identity is not biology but social environment, particularly the way the child is treated by its parents during its first few years of life. Stoller thinks that there is also a "biological force" which can affect gender identity, but that this biological force—which may involve brain changes produced by male hormones—is rarely strong enough to counteract the effects of the child's early environment (Vol. II, p.17).

Volume I concentrates on studies of intersexual patients, those whose sexual anatomy and hormonal environments are neither clearly male nor clearly female. The evidence is that except in a few very rare cases, "regardless of the biological determinants of sex present, one becomes a member of that sex to which one is assigned." (Vol. I., p.14) The assigned sex may be different from the chromosomal sex, the genital development and even the hormonal mix, and yet the child will rarely doubt its membership in the sex to which it is assigned. Most of the cases in which gender identity differs from the assigned sex are those in which the parents were unsure of the child's sexual identity and communicated that uncertainty to the child. Stoller finds that the "core gender identity" is generally formed before the age of two and one half, and that later attempts to reverse it rarely succeed without producing severe psychological damage.

So powerful is this original and socially induced sense of sexual identity, Stoller holds, that it is generally preferable, in cases where the assigned sex is found to be discordant with the chromosomal sex, to use hormone treatments to alter the patient's body in the direction of the originally assigned sex, rather than to attempt to change the gender identity in order to accord with chromosomal and/or gonadal sex. Yet gender identity is not wholly socially induced, Stoller thinks, because there are some rare individuals whose gender identity develops in defiance of the sex of assignment, and in conformity to their chromosomal sex. Such persons can successfully be reassigned to the other sex (the sex consistent with their chromosomes but inconsistent with their rearing) at much later ages, but only because their core gender identity never originally conformed to the assigned sex.

In Volume II Stoller presents further evidence of the (generally) overriding importance—in spite of this biological force—of early social environment in the formation of core gender identity. It is primarily a study of transsexual boys, those who are physiologically entirely normal, yet who are from their earliest childhood fully convinced that, in spite of their anatomy, they are really girls. Stoller distinguishes between true transsexualism and transvestitism, a condition in which the core identity is male but women's clothes are worn because this produces sexual excitement. He finds that in all the genuine cases of (male) childhood transsexualism, the boy was raised by a mother who was somewhat "bisexual," that is not enitirely feminine in her own gender identity, and who kept the child too close to her too much of the time to permit the distancing necessary for the development of a masculine identiy. The father, meanwhile, is either absent or uninvolved, and therefore fails to encourage his son's masculinity.

Stoller also describes a few cases of transsexualism in girls, though the phenomenon is much rarer in females. This may be because children of both sexes identify first with the mother, making the development of a male identity more difficult. Girl transsexuals tend to be unfeminine in appearance from birth, and/or unusually active, resulting in their parents failing to perceive or to treat them as females. Often too, Stoller says, the mother is weak and depressed and the father unsympathetic and unsupportive towards the mother, thus forcing the girl to play a protective role towards the mother. This results in the development of a masculine identity structure.

The existence of child transsexuals, Stoller holds, demonstrates that, "whatever attributes the infant brings into the world that can contribute to masculinity and femininity, these can usually be overturned, indicating that they do not play the major role in even the earliest stage of gender identity formation; parental effects do." (Vol. II, p.290) He rejects the suggestion that transsexualism is due not (only) to social environment but to undetected hormonal or other biological abnormalities; for if this were the case then the genitals of transsexuals would tend to be abnormal (as they do not), and there would be more cases in which transsexualism shows up in more than one child in a family, or in several generations.

His conclusions would seem to be grist for the feminist mill, evidence that the basic concepts of maleness and femaleness, masculinity and femininity, are not biological givens but cultural constructs, which are imposed upon originally highly malleable human individuals. Yet Stoller never explicitly questions the validity or desirability of these cultural constructs. As a result, he sees only two alternative ways of "treating" transsexuals and others whose gender identity does not "match" their biology: either alter the identity to fit the body or alter the body to fit the identity. There is, of course, a third possibility, namely helping such persons to understand that there is nothing shameful about the fact that their psychological make-up is not the one prescribed for their sex by the patriarchal culture. Given that they must still live in a sex-stereotype-ruled world this alternative may seem impractical; but it is no more so than either of Stoller's two options. For, as he points out, sex-change surgery is a dubious form of treatment, the long-term benefits of which are doubtful, while attempts to alter basic gender identity e.g. by psychotherapy, are traumatic to the patient and rarely successful. If androgyny, psychological and perhaps even biological, is recognized as a normal or at least nonpathological condition, then the best "cure" for transsexuals—as for homosexuals and others with so-called identity problems—may be no cure at all.

STONE, Merlin. *When God Was a Woman* (Dial Press, New York, 1976)

This is one of the most recent and best documented defenses of the ancient matriarchy theory, which was first put forward by J.J. Bachofen in 1861. Stone presents archeological and mythologic evidence that the predominant religion throughout the Near East (Egypt, Canaan, Mesopotamia, Asia Minor, Greece and Crete), for thousands of years prior to the arrival of the Indo-European invaders with their patriarchal deity, was the religion of the Great Goddess. The Goddess may have been worshiped as early as 25,000 B.C. , when the "Venus" figurines (small carvings of matronly shaped women) begin to appear. Her religion was well established throughout the area by 7000 B.C., and it prevailed until the light-skinned invaders from the north established the dominance of their own religion in the late third and the second millennia B.C., and survived for many centuries thereafter.

Stone maintains that the worship of the Goddess was coexistent with a matrilineal family system, in which ancestry was traced through the female line only and paternity was generally unknown or of little significance. Women were the priests and prophets, and worshiped the Goddess through sexual rites, a fact which has led male scholars of the patriarchal era to call them "temple prostitutes," or even less flattering names. They also insisted on calling the Goddess religion a "fertility cult," and the Goddess an "earth mother." In fact, She was conceived as the Queen of Heaven, the creator of the universe and the giver of life and death, as well as the deity of sexuality and childbirth. She had innumerable names in different times and places, but her essential attributes and the symbols associated with her remain fairly constant. She was generally associated with snakes, and with a certain kind of fig tree, the fruit of which was ritually eaten as the flesh of the Goddess. (This may be the origin of the Christian practice of communion.) Also part of the worship of the Goddess in many places was the ritual killing of the queen's or head priestess' consort, a young man who represented the son and lover of the Goddess. The Greek myth of Venus and Adonis, the Egyptian myth of Isis and Osiris, and probably the death-of-Christ story as well, are reflections of this practice.

Stone argues that the matrilineal descent system must have been a precondition and its continuation a consequence of the Goddess religion, since the sexual forms of worship meant that paternity could not be reliably determined. Unlike the matriarchy theorists of the nineteenth century, Stone does not see matriliny or matriarchy as a universal though relatively primitive stage in human cultural evolution, but rather a local condition which was highly conducive to cultural progress. The matrilineal, Goddess-worshiping cultures developed agriculture, architecture, written language, metallurgy, law, and some remarkably advanced civilizations, e.g. Egypt and Crete. The patriarchal invaders were barbarians in comparison to the Mediterranean peoples whom they conquered. Throughout the Near East the invaders established themselves as a ruling caste, a priestly aristocracy, which exploited the indigenous peoples and did everything in its power to eradicate the ancient religion and to reduce women's status to that of chattels.

This general pattern, Stone suggests, was probably followed by the Hebrew people, as in Egypt, Greece, Asia Minor and Mesopotamia. The Levites, the aristocratic priestly caste to which Abraham belonged, may have been related to or descended from a group of Indo-Europeans who invaded Asia Minor and the regions to the south around 2300 B.C., bringing with them a firece male deity associated with mountains and with fire. This symbolism is conspicuous in the Old Testament. The priestly class also invented new mythologies, designed to serve their political interests. The *Genesis* story of Adam and Eve gives every sign of having been a deliberate invention intended to discredit those who worshiped the Goddess, and to "justify" the strict subordination of women. The seductive snake and the forbidden tree of knowledge are symbols taken from the ancient religion, but with their original significance reversed. The Levites' insistence on absolute chastity for unmarried women and absolute fidelity for married women was clearly directed against the sexual customs of the old religion, she claims; to discredit the Goddess it was necessary to depict (female) sexuality itself as sinful, and to make sexual activity outside of marriage a crime for women, punishable by death.

While any final judgments as to the accuracy of this story will have to await a good deal of further research, the outline at least seems plausible and well substantiated. To some, the matriarchy theories seem like mere ancient history, of dubious relevance to the present debate over sex roles and women's rights. But, as Stone points out, the reactionary mythology of the Levites exerts a powerful influence to this very day, and not just on those who are traditionally religious. Women are still branded by the curse which God laid upon Eve: "in pain you shall bring forth children, yet your desire shall be for your husband and he shall rule over you. " (p.222) To understand the historical origin and the political motivations behind the misogyny of the Bible is a step towards freeing ourselves of it. If Stone is right, then patriarchy and male domination are neither biological imperatives nor intrinsic to the higher stages of cultural evolution, but historical contingencies which the further course of history may serve to reverse.

STORR, Anthony. *Human Aggression* (Atheneum, New York, 1968)

Anthony Storr is a British psychoanalyst who follows Konrad Lorenz, Robert Ardrey and others, in arguing that men have a powerful instinct for aggression. Male aggression is spontaneous, while "aggression in the female is only fully aroused in response to threat, especially if the young are involved." (p.60) In the male, aggression serves the functions of competition with other males, territoriality and display before the females; in the female it is not needed for any of these functions, at least not to a comparable degree.

Storr claims that this masculine instinct for aggression accounts not only for male domination in the family and in society at large, but also for "the undoubted superiority of the male sex in intellectual and creative achievement." (p.62) Indeed, he sees male aggression as an intrinsically desirable phenomenon, one which "underlies man's urge to independence and achievement." (p.54) Aggression becomes destructive only when its expression is inhibited, an inhibition which, in men, may result in depression, schizophrenia, paranoia, or even psychopathy. Men become mentally ill when they do not behave aggressively enough. Women, on the other hand, become mentally ill when they behave *too* aggressively (p.68).

Thus, on Storr's view, patriarchy is necessary for the mental health of both sexes:

> . . . for the male to be relatively more dominant and the female relatively less so makes both for stability of the family and also for sexual happiness of the couple. (p.61)
>
> However emancipated a woman may be, she will still, at one level, want the man to be the dominant partner. (p.65)

Some excellent criticisms of the logical and empirical weaknesses of this aggression-based theory of the sexual dichotomy may be found in *Man and Aggresion*, edited by Ashley Montagu. (Anthologies, VIII.) The problems are too many to enter into here; suffice it to say that even if Storr's account of male psychology were true it is extremely unlikely and certainly unsubstantiated that most women enjoy being dominated by men. To be dominated is a curse, not a blessing, and it is so defined in *Genesis*. From a moral point of view, it follows that however great the "natural" *desire* of men to dominate women, they lack the moral *right* to do so. To appeal to the trauma supposedly suffered by the male who is not permitted to impose his will on others is only to make poor excuses for inexcusable behavior.

SULLEROT, Evelyn. *Woman, Society and Change* (translated by Margaret Scotford Archer; McGraw-Hill, New York, 1971)

A well-known French sociologist, Sullerot provides a useful summary and comparison of the current economic, educational and political condition of women throughout Europe and the rest of the world. The picture is a depressing one; everywhere women lag far behind men in achieving the benefits of social change. They may work, and indeed many *must* work. But they make much less than men for comparable work, and then are blamed for male unemployment, divorce, and the problems of their children. Mothers, whether they work continuously (thus doing two jobs) or drop out of the labor force and reenter it later, are thereby severely handicapped in the competition for desirable jobs and promotions. In the underdeveloped nations, women constitute a large majority of the illiterate population, and in many places they are still not educated on a par with men. Sullerot draws an analogy between the condition of women and that of colonized underdeveloped countries, but points out that in the case of women violent revolution is unthinkable and change is therefore more difficult. For this, women's "unwitting revenge" is that without their assistance the world's greatest problems—overpopulation, starvation, underdevelopment and illiteracy—cannot be solved.

SUPERIOR FEMINISM: See Montagu, Davis, Solanas; also see Marlow and Davis, in Anthologies VI.

T

TAYLOR, G. Rattray *Sex in History* (Harper and Row, New York, 1973; first published 1954)

This is a psychoanalytic study of Western attitudes towards sex and sensuality in the Christian era. Starting with the Middle Ages and ending with the Victorian period, Taylor relates a series of more or less radical shifts between a guilt-ridden authoritarian and repressive climate of opinion, which he calls *patrist*, and a more positive and permissive attitude, which he calls *matrist*. Patrists are defined as men who in childhood identify primarily with their fathers and so form masculine superegos; matrists are men who identify more with their mothers and so adopt more feminine values. The story, as Taylor admits, is told from an unabashedly all-male point of view; apparently women do not become either patrists or matrists, or if they do it makes no difference to the course of history.

Taylor maintains that a restrictive patrist attitude towards sex is usually accompanied by the view that women are inferior and morally corrupt beings who must be kept under strict control. Patrists lean towards political conservatism and authoritarianism; they tend to have an exaggerated fear of homosexuality, a distrust of empirical inquiry, and a readiness to abandon reasoned belief in favor of nonrational dogmas; and finally they tend to stress the worship of male deities and to suppress the worship of female deities. Matrists, on the other hand, tend to favor greater freedom and higher status for women; to value human welfare more than chastity; to be politically democratic; to be less fearful of ecstatic and spontaneous experience in general; to fear incest more than homosexuality; to worship mother goddesses and fertility symbols; and to minimize sexual differences in dress and appearance, which patrists on the contrary insist on maximizing.

From these definitions it is clear that matrists have rarely, if ever, dominated the Western world during the Christian era. Indeed, Taylor doubts that matrists have *ever* dominated the military or political institutions of society, simply because the

455

desire for such dominance is foreign to their value system. There have, however, been a number of "outbreaks," of matrism, such as the troubadour movement in twelfth-century France with its chivalrous idealization of the beloved lady, whom Taylor claims was really a mother substitute. The witch persecutions, he thinks, were largely an attempt to suppress various psychiatric phenomena, such as hysteria and delusions, which themselves resulted from the sexual repression imposed by the Church. But they were also in part directed against an undergound matrist religion in which a horned deity was worshiped with ecstatic sexual rituals. Taylor also interprets the Italian and French Renaissance and the Elizabethan age in England as periods of matrist revolt.

Taylor argues that extreme swings towards either matrism or patrism are undesirable. Too much repression of sexuality leads to violence and sexual perversion, since the blocked sexual energies must find other outlets. Yet excessively matrist periods tend to degenerate into anarchy and amorality, as men cease to identify with either parent and so fail to develop superegos entirely. The most creative and progressive periods are those in which there is a balance between patrism and matrism, i.e. in which men tend not to identify exclusively with either parent. That this is far from being a feminist stance is apparent from the fact that Talylor believes that our own age is not only strongly matrist already but in serious danger of becoming too much so. What is immoral about this position is that it treats women's rights, and equality between the sexes, not as intrinsically desirable ends but as things which must not be taken to "extremes" for fear of upsetting men's psychic balance. (See also Vern Bullough's *The Subordinate Sex*.)

TAYLOR, Harriet (1807–1858). "Enfranchisement of Women," in *Essays on Equality*, by John Stuart Mill and Harriet Taylor Mill, edited by Alice S. Rossi. (The University of Chicago Press, Chicago and London, 1970, pp.89–122. The "Enfranchisement" was first published July 1851, in the *Westminster Review*.)

Harriet Taylor was for twenty-one years the friend and intellectual companion of John Stuart Mill, and for seven years his wife. She had married, at the age of eighteen, a man who was, in Mill's words, "upright, brave and honourable . . . but without the intellectual or artistic tastes which could have made him a companion for her"; (1) and although she remained John Taylor's wife until his death in 1849, the relationship with Mill was the center of her life, as of his. Mill gives her credit for many of the ideas and arguments, and in some cases much of the actual writing, of some of his finest works, including the *Principles of Political Economy*, *On Liberty*, and *The Subjection of Women*. She did very little serious independent writing, however, and has remained a shadowy and controversial figure, in part because the extravagance of Mill's praise of her genius has generally led to the conclusion that his affection for her caused him to vastly overestimate her intellectual gifts.

If the "Enfranchisement" essay was indeed written by Harriet Taylor, it is ample evidence of her intellectual power. Its authorship is controversial, since it was originally published under Mill's name; but Mill later republished it as hers, noting that his share in it was "little more than that of an editor." (3) As Alice Rossi points out (4), it seems probable that the essay is indeed at least primarily Taylor's, since the position taken clashes at several key points with that of Mill, both in his 1832 essay on marriage and divorce (5) and in *The Subjugation of Women*, thirty years later, but agrees with Taylor's position in her 1832 essay (6). Taylor's line of argument shows the influence of Mary Wollstonecraft and William Thompson, and above all of Mill, but at the same time she is consistently more radical than Mill.

The "Enfranchisement" begins with references to the two 1850 women's rights conferences in the United States, and the observation that Americans cannot consistently deny women the rights to vote, serve on juries and take part in politics, since "Their democratic institutions rest avowedly on the inherent right of everyone to a voice in the government." (p.95) English law is also based on doctrines which are inconsistent with the legal disabilities of women, e.g. that taxation should be based on representation, and that all persons should be tried by their peers. It is "an acknowledged dictate of justice to make no degrading distinctions without necessity" (p.97); and the disenfranchisement of women—their legal, economic and educational disadvantages—is not only unnecessary but "an unqualified mischief; a source of perversion and demoralization, both to the favored class and to those at whose expense they are favored." (p.98)

Taylor deals concisely and elegantly with the major objections to women's enfranchisement, which she broadly defines as their admission to all the legal, educational and professional rights and opportunities which are open to men. One objection is that women's subjection is customary and universal; but since this custom is originally due to mere physical force, rather than reason or justice, its existence is no argument for its continuation. In response to the claim that women's place is in the home, she says,

> We deny the right of any portion of the species to decide for another portion . . . what is and what is not their "proper sphere." The proper sphere for all human beings is the largest and highest which they are able to obtain to. (p.100)

And as for the argument that for women to play an active part in politics or business is inconsistent with the maternal role, she proclaims that

> It is neither necessary nor just to make imperative on women that they shall be either mothers or nothing . . . To say that women must be excluded from active life because maternity disqualifies them from it, is in fact to say, that every other career should be forbidden them in order that maternity should be their only resource. (pp.103–104)

Thus far Taylor's position coincides with Mill's; but where Mill had written in 1832 that although women need the *right* to earn a living, there is no need for married women to actually do so, Taylor argued that it is better for both spouses to work. Even if, as Mill had feared, the increased number of workers were to drive wages down, still it is

> infinitely preferable . . . that part of the income should be of the woman's earning . . . rather than that she should be compelled to stand aside in order that men may be the sole earners, and the sole dispensers of what is earned . . . [For,] a woman who contributes materially to the support of the family, cannot be treated in the same contemptuously tyrannical manner as one who, however she may toil as a domestic drudge, is a dependent on the man for subsistence. (p.105)

Taylor also goes farther, and is more consistent than Mill, in rejecting the notion that women's role is to be of service to men. While Mill was capable of saying that a wife's occupation ought to be to "adorn and beautify life" (7)—her husband's life, presumably—Taylor insists that women must live and be educated "for themselves and for the world, and not one sex for the other." (p.113) There is no argument for making "the existence of one-half the species . . . merely ancillary to that of the other" (p.107), except that men prefer it so. Like Wollstonecraft, she argues that women's dependent status corrupts the character of both sexes, in converse ways: "in the one it produces the vices of power, in the other those of artifice." (p.114) She ends by objecting to the demand by one of the American women's rights conventions, for a "social and spiritual union" between the sexes.

She warns against "those who would weakly attempt to combine nominal equality between men and women, with enforced distinctions in their privileges and functions." For,

> What is wanted for women is equal rights, equal admission to all social privileges; not a position apart, a sort of sentimental priesthood. (p.120)

1. *The Early Draft of John Stuart Mill's Autobiography* (edited by Jack Stillinger, University of Illinois Press, Urbana, Illinois, 1961), p.152.
2. See, for instance, *The Early Draft*, pp.152–153.
3. *Essays in Sex Equality*, p.91.
4. *Op. cit.*, p.42.
5. *Op. cit.*, pp.67–84.
6. *Op. cit.*, pp.84–87.
7. Mill's 1832 essay, in Rossi, p.75.

TESTOSTERONE: See Hormones.

THOMAS, William I. (1863–1947). *Sex and Society: Studies in the Social Psychology of Sex* (Fishr Unwin, London, 1907)

This is a collection of sociological essays, in which Thomas seeks to explain male domination and the observable differences between the sexes by separating the innate biological differences from those that are shaped by habit and custom. Many of his biological claims are outdated, but his approach is valuable in that he recognizes the need to take both sorts of cases—nature and nurture—into acccount, as well as the relationship between them. Thomas believes that the basic organic difference between the sexes is that men are catabolic, or energy consuming, and women more anabolic, or energy conserving. Men have longer limbs and more haemoglobin in their blood, which makes them fitted for sudden bursts of speed and energy, while women have more stability and endurance and are therefore inclined towards steady but less strenuous activity.

This greater stability of women and restlessness of men, he argues, brought about the original division of labor between the sexes which was not imposed upon women by men but which rather developed as a necessity for survival. Because women were both metabolically more sedentary, and of necessity more committed to the care of children, they naturally did work of a sort which could be done in or near the home base. Men engaged in hunting and warfare and were more loosely attached to the family unit, which was matrilineal and matrilocal. They married outside their mother's clan but continued to owe allegiance to it; women remained with the clan, into which their husbands were not entirely accepted. Women, he thinks, had the advantage of being less desirous of sex than men—though more involved in the reproductive process—which meant that men were at least as dependent on women as women were dependent on them (1). He does not, however, believe that early societies were ever truly matriarchal—actually ruled by women—since even in the maternal clan the greater strength of men (which he presumes existed then as now) must have given them as least equal authority.

Furthermore, he points out, the original division of labor gave men the advantage of more exciting and interesting work, while women's work was more apt to consist in dull, repetitive drudgery. Consequently, men attracted more attention and respect for their work. They also learned the value of organization, and became specialists in the use of a few tools and weapons, while women generally worked alone, and were technological generalists. Women invented the beginnings of most of the industries, yet it was men who developed large-scale argiculture, herding, manufacture and trade, after game animals became scarce and the hunters were forced to apply their skills in other directions. Thus it was men who began to accumulate private property; and it was this which enabled them to subordinate women and destroy the maternal clan. Property enabled men to purchase women from their families and remove them to their own, male-headed families, in which they were relatively powerless.

Thomas emphasizes that from the beginning human attitudes are a primary regulating and stabilizing factor in society. Habits solidify into customs which are rigidly enforced by public approval and disapproval. With the rise of father right there developed moral codes, laws and systems of government which were basically contractual agreements between men. Limitations were thus placed upon male catabolic activity which also dictated the proper behavior for women—from an exclusively male standpoint. Women themselves have accepted this standpoint, this patriarchal "definition of the situation," and modeled themselves on standards of what they take to be pleasing to men. This is the origin of narcissism in woman, i.e. excessive concern with appearance and dress, and of most other supposedly innately feminine psychological traits.

There are, Thomas argues, no significant or detectable differences between the brains, the mental capacities or the intelligence of men and women. Individuals differ greatly in these respects, but the sexes do not. Women, like the "lower" races, are accused of lacking the capacity for abstract thought, when in fact what they lack is merely the *habit*. Having been excluded from the white-man's world of technological and scientific endeavor, women naturally do not exhibit the particular skills which that world develops.

It is interesting to consider whether or not this defense of women's innate intellectual equality is consistent with the notion that they are organically more anabolic, or, as Thomas says at one point, more plant-like than men. While there may be no overt contradiction here, one would certainly expect this supposed difference in male and female nature to have persistent effects on mentality and behavior, under *any* social system. When all is said and done, the anabolic/catabolic distinction looks suspiciously like a version of the patriarchal notion that masculinity is equivalent to activity, femininity to passivity. So long as we can only study men and women who have lived and developed within a patriarchal context there would seem to be little hope of obtaining valid empirical confirmation of such a hypothesis.

1. A dubious conclusion from a dubious premise. The argument overlooks both women's sexual capacities and their economic importance in early society; the latter factor provides a better explanation for men's reciprocal dependence than does one-way sexual desire.

THOMPSON, Clara (1885–1958). *On Women*, edited by Maurice R. Green (New American Library, New York, 1971; first published 1964)

This is a selection of excerpts from Thompson's papers and from her unfinished book on female psychology, which Green has edited to form a condensed and continuous manuscript. Thompson was for thirty years one of the best known psychoanalysts in America and a rebel against the Freudian school. She was a friend and colleague of Karen Horney and resigned from the New York Psychoanalytic Institute when Horney was expelled from the Institute.

Like Horney, she follows Freud in supposing that the differences between male and female physiology must make for *some* basic differences between male and female psychology, but she rejects the particular differences which Freud posits. She points out that the very fact that the sexes are psychologically different means that a member of one sex cannot really know what a member of the other experiences (e.g. in the sex act), and hence each should be very cautious in drawing conclusions about the psychology of the other sex.

For instance, Freud held that for female children all genital sensation is clitoral in origin; the vagina, he held, remains unknown until puberty, at which time it entirely replaces the clitoris as a source of gratification, at least in "normal" women; continued clitoral sensitivity is a sign of immaturity or "masculine protest," the refusal to accept one's femininity. Thompson, on the contrary—in partial anticipation of the Masters and Johnson findings—reports that many apparently normal women remain clitorally oriented throughout their lives. It is simply part of a normal range of individual preferences. She also holds, as does Horney, that vaginal sensation is quite often present from a very early age. This is important because, if true, it undermines Freud's presumption that it is natural and inevitable that a girl will envy a boy his "superior" genital equipment since she can only compare her tiny clitoris to his much larger penis. If a girl is aware of her vagina, then she will not perceive her state as a simple *lack* of something, but as "a positive state of difference, i.e. "You have a penis and I have a vagina." "(p.34) Furthermore, the knowledge that she will one day be capable of giving birth is a natural source of pride that makes it most implausible to suppose that she must inevitably consider herself sexually inferior.

The conclusion Thompson draws is not that there is no such phenomenon as penis envy in females, but that its basis is cultural rather than biological. Women have ample objective reasons for envying men, who are allowed much more freedom and more opportunity for the expression of aggression, and who in general enjoy a much higher social status. If women become passive, masochistic and narcissistic it is not because this is a natural part of the feminine maturation process, as Freud thought, but because a complex set of social forces acts to curtail their development as independent, active and self-respecting people.

Although Thompson rejects as ridiculous Freud's assertion that women desire motherhood only as a compensation for the lack of a penis, she does believe that all normal women want to be mothers. Having herself rejected marriage and motherhood in favor of her medical career, she sees modern women's most severe problem is to be the difficulty of combining marriage and motherhood with other useful work. Now that families are smaller, childrearing takes up relatively few years of a woman's life and is in no way a satisfactory lifetime career; yet it is extremely difficult to combine the raising of even a few children with the pursuit of a professional career. There is almost no winning strategy for the middle-class woman under today's social conditions. Either she chooses a career instead of motherhood, or vice versa, in each case depriving herself of a basic need; or she tries to combine them, thus suffering social disapproval and almost inevitably neglecting one or both. This contradictory situation in which women exist is in no sense natural, but socially inflicted, and must be relieved by social accommodations (1).

1.　For an excellent exposition of Thompson's views, see Juanita Williams' *Psychology of Women: Behavior in a Biosocial Context* (W.W. Norton & Company, Inc., New York, 1977) pp.71–76.

THOMPSON, William (1775–1833). *Appeal of One Half the Human Race, Women, Against the Pretensions of the Other Half, Men, to Retain Them in Civil and Thence Domestic Slavery* (Burt Franklin, New York, 1970; first published 1825)

William Thompson is an early anticapitalist thinker, a utopian socialist, and a precursor of contemporary socialist-feminist thought. As a landowner who advocated land reform and a man who considered women more apt at government that men, he was a remarkable defender of classes whose interests were not— on the surface at least—his own (1). The *Appeal* is written in response to an *Encyclopedia Britannica* article by James Mill, the great utilitarian philosopher and father of John Stuart Mill. Mill defends the English Common Law doctrine that women's interests are "included" or "involved" in those of their fathers or husbands, and that women may therefore "be struck off from political rights without inconvenience." (2) Like Mill, Thompson is a utilitarian, but he rightly considers the legal disenfranchisement of women and in particular the gross inequality of the marriage laws of the time to be wholly irreconcilable with the principle of the greatest happiness for the greatest number.

Thompson follows Mary Wollstonecraft, whom he praises in his dedication (3), in considering male domination to be originally due to women's physical handicaps, *viz.* "permanent inferiority of strength, and occasional loss of time in gestation and rearing of infants." (p.x) Because of these handicaps, he holds, women will always have a lesser chance for happiness than men, *so long as the social system is based on individual competition for wealth*. Even complete legal equality would not make women truly equal, since "unequal powers under free competition must produce unequal results." (p.xiv) But, not satisfied with the superiority which inevitably results from these natural sources under this form of social organization, man adds legal, social and moral barriers, excludes women from education, politics, and the lucrative professions; he "paralyzes to impotence even those means which Nature has given his feebler competitor, nor ceases his oppression till he has made her his slave." (p.x) Far from justifying such oppression, women's physical weakness makes it *less* excusable: "Were he generous, were he just, knew he how to promote his own happiness, he would be anxious to afford *compensations* for these physical inconveniences, instead of aggravating them." (p.xii)

James Mill had argued, in the ***Britannica*** article, that all *men* must have equal political rights, because those who have power over others naturally seek to profit at their expense. Mill regards this as a "grand governing law of human nature," which if ignored, "would reduce each and . . . all at least to the condition of negroes in the West Indies." (p.7) Yet Mill maintains, with blatant inconsistency, that when it comes to men's relations with women this grand governing law ceases to apply, and men naturally seek the happiness of women—which conveniently happens to coincide with their own. Mill rejects the doctrine that one group, a ruling elite, can decide what is best for the rest of society. "But," Thompson notes, "increase the number of the governing party to one-fourth [4] . . . and let that one-fourth be the division to which the philosopher himself happens to belong, and he finds the philosophy admirable." (p.11)

In reality, Thompson maintains, there is no such tendency for men to know and respect the interests of women, wives or adult daughters, who are in their control. On the contrary, "the very possession of power without restraint, is in almost every instance sufficient to confound knowledge and eradicate sympathy where they previously existed, or to prevent their formation." (p.13) The doctrine of identity of interests is a hypocritical fiction, disproven by the very fact that men have used their power to deny equal rights and freedom to women. Even if true it could hardly justify depriving adult women *without husbands or fathers* of political rights; but it is in fact false, even with respect to children— though there are of course independent reasons why children cannot be given political rights. The *general* interest of all members of a family, and ultimately of all members of the species, are the same, but because of the problem of distribution their individual interests are found to differ.

Indeed, Thompson argues, even if the doctrine of the identity of the interests of wives and daughters with their husbands or fathers *were* true, it would not justify depriving the former of political rights. On the utilitarian theory, "each individual has an equal claim to the exercise of all the means of happiness in its power, not encroaching on similar claims in others." (p.74) Even if men were wholly benevolent towards women, political disenfranchisement would still reduce women's chances for happiness, because it deprives them of activities and avenues of improvement which are themselves a vital part of human happiness. It also inculcates a contempt for women's mental powers which damages the happiness of men as well as women. Man "surrenders the delights of equality, namely those of esteem, of friendship, of intellectual and sympathetic intercourse, for the vulgar pleasures of command." (p.70) As a result,

> *the whole moral structure of the mind of man* is perverted. His pride and selfishness are habitually raised to their highest standard. The monarch of the domestic circle, he would be the monarch of every circle he meets . . . In his intercourse with the world at large he carries forth that rule of force and notion of the superior importance of his own happiness to that of all around, which . . . is one of the most fruitful and perennial causes of personal annoyance, mutual depredation, and misery. (p.71)

Furthermore, if it *were* just or necessary for one sex to be given political rights to the exclusion of the other, a better case could probably be made for making women the favored sex. For women's lesser physical strength would make it impossible for them to rule by force, and thus they would have to rely much more on reason and persuasion. Thompson denies that there is proof of the intellectual superiority of men, though admitting that it is *possible* that fewer women have genius or talent for invention. If true, he says, this would be no argument for excluding women from the legislative role, since good legislation requires broad general knowledge rather than the intensive particular knowledge of the creative artist or scientist.

Be that as it may, if women are to have an equal opportunity for happiness they must have complete civil, legal, political and moral equality, including an end to the sexual double standard, which cruelly punishes women for the enjoyments which men claim as their inalienable right. They must have "every facility of access to every art, occupation, profession, from the highest to the lowest . . . the removal of *all* restraints and exclusions not applicable to men of equal capacities . . . [and] an equal system of morals, founded on utility instead of caprice and unreasoning despotism." (p.159)

But Thompson felt that equality of rights is not enough. It is also necessary to eliminate the present social system, which we in the post-Marxian era have come to call "capitalism." His utopian vision, derived in part from Charles Fourier and Robert Owen, is of a society based on "voluntary association" or "the mutual co-operation of industry and talents in large numbers." (p.151) Such an association would call upon the "equal contributions of all the various faculties of all, mental or bodily, for the equal enjoyment of all" (p.151)—a notion which foreshadows the Marxist slogan, "From each according to his abilities, to each according to his needs."

Socialism, Thompson predicts, would compensate for women's natural competitive disadvantages, as well as eliminating the artificial ones that result from the male-dominated family structure. "The whole Association would educate and provide for the children of all," (p.200) thus minimizing the time lost from other work because of motherhood; and making it no longer necessary for women to marry or remain married out of fear of economic deprivation. Prostitution would also vanish.

> Wherever the principle of Association prevailed, justice would prevail, and . . . mutual compensations—as nurturing infants against strength—would be fully admitted; no person cheerfully exercising his or her means, whatever they might be, for the common benefit, would be punished for the scantiness of these means . . . " (p.206)

In all of this Thompson was remarkably ahead of his time. He was also ahead of his time in his attack on the concept of femininity which, he points out, man defines solely in terms of those qualities which are useful and pleasing to *him* (e.g. temperance, modesty, thriftiness, devotion to the interests of men), while ridiculing as unfeminine all those qualities which are more useful to women themselves than to the men around them. "Unfeminine" is a "word, in its ordinary moral application, of supreme folly, which merely means that he does not wish that you should possess these qualities—but attempts not to show that they are not of extreme utility to the possessor." (p.193) He was aware, too, that the prevalence of such prejudicial notions means that perhaps even socialism itself will not alone suffice to secure full equality of happiness for women; for that, "we must look forward to that time when the process of knowledge and new institutions shall have obliterated a prejudice coeval with the race of man." (p.186)

1. See Shelia Rowbotham, **Hidden from History** (New York, 1976), p.39.
2. James Mill, **Encyclopedia Britannica: Supplement**, article on "Government," p.500; quoted by Thompson in the frontispiece of the *Appeal*.
3. The *Appeal* is dedicated to a woman named Anna Wheeler who, like Thompson, was an Irish Protestant, and who, having read Wollstonecroft and the French rationalists, deserted her alcoholic husband and want to live in Guernsey, where she became a force in the radical philosophical movements of her time. Thompson credits her with the origin of "those bolder and more comprehensive views" which he presents.
4. I.e. all and only adult males.

TIGER, Lionel. *Men in Groups* (Random House, New York, 1969) *The Imperial Animal*; with Robin Fox, see Fox, Robin)

Tiger, as a sociobiologist, argues that male domination of most public social institutions is a result of human male's innate predisposition to form bonds with other males. Male bonding, the close and hierarchical association of males in all-male groups, evolved, he suggests, during the millions of years when our (male) ancestors were hunters on the African plains. The hunting groups had to be all-male because the participation of women would have endangered their offspring; males who allowed females to hunt with them would have endangered their own genetic survival.

Tiger credits the male bonding phenomenon, and the need to develop social institutions to inhibit aggression between groups of bonded males, with stimulating the growth of the brain. War, politics, sports and secret societies are all male inventions and expressions of male bonding, which is by nature an aggressive force. Groups of males are inevitably aggressive, whether the aggression is directed against animals, other humans, or inanimate objects. Males who are deprived of the opportunity to form bonds and be aggressive are deprived of the essential masculine experience, just as women who have no children are deprived, he thinks, of the essential feminine experience.

For these reasons, Tiger is pessimistic about the feasibility of integrating very many more women into politics and other positions of social power. When women gain power in an institution, real power simply moves elsewhere. It may be possible to increase women's representation in government to some degree, and moral considerations make this desirable, but fundamental changes in sex roles or the distribution of power between the sexes are probably beyond the limits of the plasticity of human behavior.

This contemporary version of biological determinism is supported by two main bodies of evidence: observations of the behavior of a few other primate species (especially the Hamadryas baboons and the macaques) and evidence of male domination of most public institutions in virtually all known cultures. It can be argued that neither body of evidence is adequate to support the contention that male domination is an ineradicable species characteristic of *Homo sapiens*. For even if we assume that it makes sense to speak of human *instincts*, and even if it were plausible to suppose that males do and females do not have a bonding instinct, it remains an open question how much effect this instinct will continue to have in the face of such countervailing factors as women's increasing freedom from the burdens of reproduction, and a rising public awareness of the problems generated by traditional sex roles and sex stereotyping.

U

UNWIN, Joseph David (1895–1936). *Sex and Culture* (Oxford University Press, London, 1934)

This is an obscure but interesting work, copies of which have unfortunately become quite difficult to find. Unwin presents anthropological and historical data in support of the Freudian hypothesis that the creative energy required for cultural progress, i.e. for advance in or towards civilization, can only come from the sublimation of repressed sexual desires—especially, Unwin's view, the repressed sexual desires of women. Some eighty precivilized cultures, from Polynesia, Africa, North America and Assam, and a handful of civilizations (Sumerian, Babylonian, Athenian, Roman, Anglo-Saxon and contemporary English) are discussed. Each society's cultural level is determined according to its conception of "the powers [that] manifest themselves in the universe," and "the steps . . . taken to maintain a right relation with them." (p.13) Four basic cultural levels are posited.

The lowest level is the *zoistic*, which is characterized by what Unwin calls the "dead level of conception": anything strange or incomprehensible is described by a single word, a word connoting an awesome power which can, however, sometimes be possessed by individual men or women. This word may also be applied to the dead, especially those who possessed this power in life, but individuals among the dead are not long remembered, nor are they given any significant postfuneral attention, such as offerings or propitiatory rites. The second cultural level is the *manistic*, in which great individuals among the dead are remembered longer, and propitiated in various ways, but as yet no temples, no regular places of public worship, are built. In the *deistic* stage temples are built to the gods (gods being defined as beings to whom temples are built), and a class of priests or temple tenders emerges. Finally the *rationalist* level, though not as clearly defined as the preceding ones, appears to be marked by the emergence of an empirical or scientific approach to the solution of problems, if not instead of the magical approach, then alongside it.

Unwin's claim is that there is an absolutely invariable correlation between a society's place on this cultural scale and the extent to which it limits the sexual freedom of women. The higher the cultural level, the greater the human energy required to attain and preserve it, and the stricter the restriction of sexual behavior needed to achieve that level of energy. Zoistic societies always allow great sexual freedom to unmarried girls, though often requiring marital fidelity of them later. Manistic societies impose irregular or occasional continence, e.g. by reserving betrothed girls to their future husbands, or punishing the mothers and/or fathers of children born out of wedlock. Deistic societies are still stricter, requiring proof of virginity and imposing penalties up to and including death for its absence. Neither men nor women, however, are generally confined to a single sexual partner throughout their lives; polygyny, polyandry, divorce and remarriage may be permitted. To rise to a rationalistic condition, a society must have women born and raised into an "absolutely monogamous" tradition, i.e. one demanding both premarital chastity and postmarital fidelity for women. Supposedly, it takes three generations for a change in sexual regulation to be followed by a change in cultural condition, but any rise or fall in the degree of sexual stricture will invariably produce, three generations later, a corresponding rise or fall in cultural level.

While he refrains from claiming that the data establishes beyond doubt that it is the sexual restriction which brings about the cultural progress, Unwin theorizes that it does. This is because the frustration of the sexual desires of women results in their raising a new generation which is more active and energetic, especially mentally. The daughters of such women, in turn, raise still more energetic (and sexually frustrated) children, and the culture continues to advance until a loosening of the sexual restrictions leads to a cultural regression. Women's sexual continence matters more than men's simply because it is they who rear children, thereby shaping their characters for life.

Nevertheless, Unwin does not defend the sexual double standard. Indeed, he blames the onesidedness of the restrictions imposed upon women in all civilized societies for the periodic declines of all great civilizations; rationalistic people inevitably come to see that the inequality between the sexes is wrong, a demand for women's liberation arises, and as a result the restrictions on women are reduced (rather than those on men being raised), and the culture declines.

Unwin's evidence for a very frequent if not absolutely universal correlation between cultural progress and the progressive restriction of women's sexual opportunities is impressive, though he fails to consider some apparent counterexamples, such as Minoan Crete and ancient Egypt. He is right, however, to be modest about the case for a causal connection. There are a number of causal hypotheses which must be considered, for instance the Marxist position that cultural progress—as defined in economic terms, rather than in terms of religious conceptions—leads to the increasing subjection of women because surplus wealth accumulates in the hands of men, eventually enabling them to buy and sell women and to reduce them to the status of property. Other institutions besides private property certainly contribute in some cultures to the sexual curtailment of women, e.g. androcentric religions and the patriarchal family, and such institutions may themselves be instrumental in bringing about the kind of cultural progress which Unwin credits to the sexual restriction. Then of course there is the question of what should be regarded as a "higher" culture; and the question whether we can transcend old historical patterns (see Vaerting).

V

VAERTING, Mathilde and Mathias. *The Dominant Sex: A Study in the Sociology of Sex Differentiation* (translated from the German by Eden and Cedar Paul: George H. Doran Company, New York, 1923)

The Vaertings present the bold and rather compelling—though virtually unconfirmable—theory that humanity has periodically *alternated* between patriarchy and matriarchy. The present period of male domination, they argue, began in the Mediterranean region within historical memory, with a number of Women's States—e.g. Egypt, Sparta, Lydia and Lycia—continuing to exist well into the historical period. Most earlier records, documenting the ages in which matriarchy was predominant throughout the region, have been lost, largely because of the deliberate efforts of male historians and patriarchal rulers to suppress knowledge of the matriarchal age. There may have been many such swings of the pendulum, from one form of monosexual dominance to the other, each leading to the destruction and falsification of historical knowledge.

Monosexual dominance, the Vaertings hold, is the key force which in any given culture shapes the psychological traits of the two sexes. The qualities which we who have grown up in the Men's State call "feminine" are merely those which have always characterized the subordinate sex, while "masculine" qualities are simply those of the dominant sex. Where women ruled it was they who were more aggressive, courageous and intellectual, while men were (expected to be) modest, timid, obedient to their wives and dependent upon them. In the Women's State women were the warriors, politicians, property owners, merchants and artists, while men tended to remain at home and attend to domestic work and child care. Moral and aesthetic standards are reversed: it is men who are expected to be chaste before marriage and faithful after, who are more severely punished for adultery, and who resort to elaborate personal decoration to make themselves attractive to women. Women, on the other hand, enjoy greater sexual freedom and tend to adopt simpler and more practical modes of dress, just as men do in the Men's State. The authors even maintain that in the Women's State women are generally larger and stronger than men; their present inferior size is due to a selection process which would be reversed if women were dominant.

Monosexual dominance is a virtually universal phenomenon—the only exceptions being certain periods of equality which have occurred during a transition from one form of dominance to the other—yet it is in every respect a destructive one. It makes monogamy impossible since it entails a double moral standard. In its extreme forms it leads to militarism, despotism and other abuses of power, which eventually provoke resistance, revolt, and a swing of the pendulum in the opposite direction. Both sexes are happiest in those rare periods when neither is dominant. In such periods, work is not sharply divided along sexual lines, and the sexes become remarkably similar in size, dress and general appearance. Equality is in one sense the most natural relationship between the sexes, for it accords with the natural range of human traits of both sexes. Monosexual dominance violates the freedom of both sexes, forcing each to conform to a wholly artificial stereotype of character and behavior. After two millennia of male domination, most of the world is now approaching a period of sexual equality; what we must somehow do is to hold the pendulum at this equilibrium point and stabilize it there.

Whatever its plausibility as a literal description of human history, the Vaertings' theory is valuable as an abstract model of sexual stereotypes. They demonstrate that what we have learned to call "masculine" and "feminine" traits are little more than logical consequences of the single fact of male domination. Regardless of whether humanity has ever been female dominated to the degree that it is now male dominated, it is surely true that if such a power reversal *were* to take place then our notions of manliness and womanliness would be likely to reverse also.

But what of the empirical claim that prior to the patriarchal/historical era human societies were generally matriarchal, i.e. dominated by women, in a way closely parallel to the way in which they have since been dominated by men? It has certainly been demonstrated by Bachofen, Briffault, Davis and others, that a number of ancient Mediterranean and Near Eastern civilizations exhibited features which can be seen as symptomatic of the rule of women: the predominance of female deities, descent and inheritance through the maternal line, and the prevalence of women warriors, priests and sometimes monarchs. The Vaertings provide a number of important arguments for considering these features as proof of female supremacy rather than as male supremacy in a different form, or as factors which might have been offset by others tending to give power to males; but they overlook some arguments in the opposite direction.

They themselves admit that there must be *some* asymmetries between the status of men in the Women's State and of women in the Men's State. For instance, men's relative lack of sexual capacity makes it unlikely that they were ever kept in brothels for the use of women. This difference may not seem crucial, but it is related to another which is more serious; even in a Women's State it would presumably be men who were capable of raping women and not vice versa. Given the primitive division of labor, in which men hunted and waged war, it seems unlikely that women could at any later stage have monopolized the use of violence to the extent that men have since done.

Of course, if women in the Women's State really were considerably larger and stronger than men then they might have been unrapable, and they might have been superior fighters; but there is as yet no proof that this was the case. If it was not, then it seems unlikely that women could have succeeded in reducing men to wholly docile, timid house servants, or that the pendulum could ever swing as far in the direction of female domination as it has in the direction of male domination (1).

1. Except, perhaps, in an Amazon society in which males are killed, castrated or crippled at birth. Many ancient writers spoke of such societies, and they may have existed; but their existence does not support the symmetry hypothesis, since, while absolute male domnation has *sometimes* resulted in the gross mutilation of women (e.g. Chinese footbinding), it has generally been possible without such extreme measures.

VILAR, Esther. *The Manipulated Man* (Bantam Books, New York, 1972)

Vilar is a contemporary misogynist in the tradition of Nietzsche and Schopenhauer. She turns the standard feminist position on its head by claiming that it is women who dominate and oppress the opposite sex by "manipulating" men into marrying them and providing financial security for them and their children. Women are said to be extremely stupid, emotionally inert and naturally lazy, yet clever enough to indoctrinate men (while they are children) with a value system which gives women all the material advantages, while *appearing*, from the point of view of the indoctrinated male, to give men the upper hand. Women, by definition (Vilar says), are people who do not work. (Housework doesn't count, since it is easy and pleasant, actually a self-indulgence; neither do the jobs of working women, since women work only to amuse themselves or to look for a man to ensnare.) The women's liberation movement underestimates women by picturing them as hapless victims. Worse, it endangers women's control over men by demanding an equality which can only be bought at the sacrifice of women's manipulative power. Although this expose sold widely, men are so *thoroughly* indoctrinated that few are reported to have rushed in to take over housework in exchange for a profession or career when they discovered how they had been cheated of the easier role.

W

WARE, Cellestine. *Woman Power: The Movement for Women's Liberation* (Tower Publications, New York, 1970)

This is a survey of the major elements of the American feminist movement as it existed at the end of the sixties. As a New York based radical feminist, Ware speaks from personal knowledge of the internal struggles of such pioneering groups as NOW, the Feminists (who broke from NOW under the leadership of Ti-Grace Atkinson), the NYRW (New York Radical Women), the Redstockings, and WITCH (Women's International Terrorist Conspiracy from Hell). (She excludes NOW from the "women's liberation movement," on the grounds that it seeks to gain power in the system for women, rather than to destroy the system and abolish power.)

Ware sees radical feminism as the only genuinely radical social movement in this country. The leaders of the New Left and the black radicals never went far enough in rejecting the male ideological superstructures. The core of male ideology is the insistence on hierarchical power structures. Women are oppressed not primarily because of economics, but because of "man's psychological need for dominance." (p.81) The enemy, therefore, is not capitalism as such, but any and every social institution which gives some people power over others. For this reason, "Radical feminists advocate only those systems in which everyone has equal rights." (p.108)

Unfortunately, Ware, like many of the feminist groups she identifies with, interprets the rejection of masculine-style hierarchies to mean that every form of *leadership* is to be avoided. The movement must have no "stars," no individual members whose influence is greater than that of others, lest it fail its egalitarian principles. It is a mistake to suppose that the existence of leaders or spokespersons for the movement automatically means an inequality of rights within the movement. There is a confusion here between the coercive power to dominate others and the freely delegated authority to act in their name. The fact that the former kind of power is invariably disguised as the latter—for instance in the family—does not in any way eliminate the distinction. (Also see Ti-Grace Atkinson.)

WATTS, Alan W. (1915–1973). *Nature, Man and Woman* (Random House, New York, 1970; first published 1958)

Watts draws on Confucian, Buddhist and Taoist ideas to urge a greater awareness of man's oneness with nature. The problem of man's relation to nature raises, he says (clearly *not* using "man" in the generic sense) the problem of man's relation to woman and to sex. This is because women are always associated with nature and with sex, especially where spirit and nature are thought of as separate, opposing, higher and lower realms. Sexual yoga is an example of the proper or enlightened approach to all three (sex, women and nature), i.e. a relaxed, accepting, nongrasping approach that appreciates each moment as it comes; it is a way of healing the breach between spirit and nature by making sex a sacred act. Watts' ideal of sexual equality is mutual sexual fulfillment via a limited androgyny, with "the woman realizing her masculinity through man, and the man realizing his femininity through woman." (p.179) Economic and social barriers to equality are not addressed.

WEININGER, Otto (1880–1903). *Sex and Character* (William Heinemann, London and G.P. Putnam Sons, New York, 1906; translated from the German; first published Vienna, 1903)

Written by a precocious young philosopher who died by his own hand at the age of twenty-three, this work was popular with several generations of German youth. It is still often cited, although, in this country at least, copies have become somewhat difficult to obtain. Weininger sets himself the task of elucidating the pure concepts, the ideal types, of man and woman, which he refers to as M and F. These he defines as Platonic ideas which do not exist in pure form in nature. No individual is entirely M or entirely F, and there are indefinitely many intermediate types.

Maleness and femaleness, Weininger begins, are originally physiological differentiations. Every part of an M body is different from the corresponding part in an F body, and the difference extends all the way down to the cellular level, although the prevalence of intermediate types means that it is never possible to say with certainty that a particular body part is that of a (person classified as a) man or a woman. The M'ness or F'ness of a person's character, he maintains, is primarily determined by physical constitution. Sexual orientation, for example, is a direct function of the relative proportion of M'ness or F'ness; a person will always be sexually attracted to another person whose degree of M'ness and F'ness is the exact complement of his own. A very masculine man will be attracted to very feminine women, while intermediate types will be attracted to other intermediate types. This, he believes, is the explanation of homosexuality, which he considers an entirely natural phenomenon and not something which can or should be "cured."

Weininger's analysis of the characterological dimensions of masculinity and femininity is straightforward: women (insofar as they are F) are purely sexual beings, "completely occupied and content with sexual matters" (p.87), while men (insofar as they are M) are sexual but also rational and creative beings, capable of genius. By "genius" he means the highest forms of artistic and/or philosophical creativity. Genius is utterly beyond the capacity of women; and here Weininger ceases to speak of F in the abstract and generalizes at length about women as if they were, after all, pure instantiations of F. Women are incapable of conceptual thought; their mental processes are compose of mere "henids," incompletely developed impressions which are pervaded with emotional tones and conceptually incoherent. Women's mental condition does not even constitute a form of consciousness: "The male lives consciously, the female lives unconsciously." (p.102) Genius is the highest development of consciousness, and is therefore "a kind of higher masculinity." (p.111)

In Weininger's view, women are not only nonrational but nonmoral. All women lie, quite naturally and inevitably, both because they have very bad memories and because they lack any comprehension of the notion of truth or of acting from principle. Women have no transcendental egos; they are not Leibnizian nomads, reflecting the universe and comprehending it. In short, "the female is soulless and possesses neither ego nor individuality, personality nor freedom, character nor will." (p.206) Weininger even denies, in the tradition of Schopenhauer, that women can be beautiful, at least in the nude; he considers their genitalia aesthetically offensive.

It is interesting that, in spite of this display of extreme misogyny, Weininger skates perilously close to a feminist analysis when, in apparent contradiction to his biological determinism, he argues that it is man who *creates* woman, by treating her as a mere means of sexual gratification rather than as an end in herself, as a person. "Woman is the sin of man," he says (p.299). Womanliness is the result of male oppression, and once men begin to treat women as human beings they will be able to overcome their femininity.

Weininger's equation of womanliness with sexuality leads him to conclude that womanliness cannot be overcome without abandoning sexual intercourse altogether, and this is just what he advocates. He insists that the sex act is intrinsically humiliating to women, and that the only way that men can treat women as people is to remain (heterosexually) chaste. He does not consider the alternative possibility, i.e., that whatever degradation woman may suffer in the act of sex is the *result*, not an independent cause of men's failure to treat them as human beings and ends in themselves.

WEISSTEIN, Naomi. "Psychology Constructs the Female," (in *Sex Equality*, edited by Jane English; Prentice-Hall, Englewood Cliffs, New Jersey, 1977)

This is a brief but enormously influential article, which was first published in 1969 and has since been reprinted many times. Weisstein, who holds a Harvard Ph.D. in psychology, concludes that,

> Psychology has nothing to say about what women are really like, what they need and what they want, essentially because psychology does not know. (p.208)

Psychoanalysts like Bruno Bettelheim, Erik Erikson, and Joseph Rheingold have not hesitated to claim that what women desire above all else is motherhood, and a slavish dependence upon a man. Such theories, Weisstein notes, are not supported by "the tiniest shred of evidence." The "years of clinical experience" upon which they are based may suffice as an inspiration for theory *formation*, but are no substitute for scientific evidence that the theory is *true*.

Such theories ignore the social context in which people act; the fact is that "what a person does and who he believes himself to be will in general be a function of what people around him expect him to be, and what the overall situation in which he is acting implies that he is." (*Loc. cit.*) Experimental studies of human behavior often run afoul of this principle, for (as other experimental studies have shown), the results obtained may be largely determined by the expectations of the experimenters.

The biologically based theories of female psychology are no better supported than the psychoanalytic and experimental ones.

Those who argue that sex-role behavior is determined by the effects of sex hormones on the brain fail to show that such physiological differences necessarily produce behavioral differences. As for the popular theories of human psychology which are based on studies of the behavior of nonhuman primates there are several serious problems. One is that it cannot be assumed that what other primates do is natural, necessary, or desirable for humans; another is that it is not known whether the observed animal behavior is due to physiological or environmental conditions; and, finally, there is such a wide variety of sex-role patterns among primates that it is possible to support almost any thesis about what is "natural" for humans, simply by choosing the right examples. (See Ardrey, Morris, Tiger.)

In short, Weisstein concludes, psychologists of all schools have approached the study of women through myth and personal bias, and with utter disrespect for the evidence. This is why psychology has had nothing of substance to offer towards the discovery of human potential. (The fact that now, ten years later, it is no longer possible to support such a blanket statement is surely evidence of remarkable progress.)

WESTERMARCK, Edward (1862–1939). *The History of Human Marriage*, in three volumes (Fifth edition, Macmillan and Company, London, 1925; first published 1891)
A Short History of Marriage (The Macmillan Company, New York, 1930; first published 1926)
Ethical Relativity (Harcourt, Brace and Company, New York, 1932)
The Future of Marriage in Western Civilization (The Macmillan Company, New York, 1936)

A Finnish anthropologist (though he wrote primarily in English), Westermarck is best known among philosophers for his defense of moral relativism (1). In the works on marriage, he attacked the views of the matriarchy theorists such as Bachofen, McLennan and Morgan, who held that monogamous marriage is a relatively recent development, and that the primordial condition of humanity was one of promiscuity, or group marriage, in which descent was traced through the maternal line only, and paternity was unimportant or even unknown.

Westermarck held that marriage—which he defined somewhat idiosyncratically as the cohabitation of a man and one or more women until after the birth of their offspring—is not an artificial social institution but a primitive and instinctive habit, probably inherited from our prehuman ancestors. "It was," he claims, "even in primitive times, the habit for a man and a woman (or occasionally several women) to live together, to have sexual relations with each other, and to rear their children in common, the man being the protector and supporter of his family and the woman being his helpmate and the nurse of their children." (*The History of Human Marriage*, Vol. I, p.28)

Furthermore, Westermarck clearly viewed this primordial nuclear family as patriarchal, i.e. male dominated, though not necessarily patrilineal.

Part of Westermarck's argument for the primordial and instinctive nature of marriage is Darwinian. The habit of (usually monogamous) marriage must have been conducive to and indeed necessary for the survival of the earliest humans, just as it is for many species of birds and some of the great apes. For human offspring, like those of other species which form monogamous "marriages," are few in number and extremely helpless, and thus need the care and protection of both parents. Larger social groupings, e.g. the horde or extended family, could have provided care for the young, but such larger groupings would have been impractical and impermanent, since our ancestors were fairly large and primarily vegetarian, and thus large groups of them would have rapidly exhausted the food supply of an area. Nor could women have raised their young alone, since in primitive times, so Westermarck assumed, "a woman is a helpless being who depends on the support of a man." (2) (*The History of Human Marriage*, Vol. I, p.393) Hence, he concludes, the male-headed nuclear family unit must have been necessary for successful reproduction: "the more or less durable union between man and woman and the care which the man takes of the woman and their common offspring are due to instincts which were once necessary for the preservation of the human race." (*The History of Human Marriage*, Vol. I, p.53)

The rest of Westermarck's argument for marriage as a primitive habit (and most of the bulk of *The History of Human Marriage*, which by the fifth edition had reached some sixteen hundred pages in length) consists of anthropological data collected from around the world, which, Westermarck claims, supports this theory. The method is that of what he called comparative anthropology, which means that seemingly endless lists of facts about a huge number of cultures are presented as evidence for various general claims. Most contemporary anthropologists reject this method, on the grounds that individual customs and facts cannot be isolated from their cultural context and compared as though their meaning were apparent apart from the entire way of life of which they form a part (3).

Most of the first volume of the *History* is devoted to discrediting the hypothesis of primitive promiscuity. Westermarck maintains that there are no undisputed human cultures which practice promiscuity in place of predominantly monogamous marriage. Premarital intercouse is often permitted, but usually only as a way of proving the woman's fertility, and hence as a prelude to marriage. Polygyny, too, is often permitted, but it is almost always the perogative of relatively few men, with monogamy remaining the normal pattern. Polyandry is much rarer and generally occurs only where there is an extreme shortage of women, or where many men are unable to undertake the entire support of a wife. The only existing custom resembling group marriage is the occasional combination of polygyny and polyandry, which is still rarer. Group marriage could not have been the primordial state of humanity, since male jealousy, which occurs in every society, insures that except under special circumstances women at least will generally be forced to remain monogamous, usually under threat of severe penalty.

As for matrilineal descent systems, these undoubtedly exist but are not evidence for the earlier existence of matriarchy or group marriage. Matriliny is consistent with the patriarchal family, and all matrilineal cultures regard the father as having some rights and powers over "his" wife and children. Furthermore, matriliny, polygyny and polyandry are not any more frequent among primitive than among civilized peoples, as ought to be the case if group marriage and woman-headed families were the primordial custom. It is, indeed, economic progress, particularly the accumulation of wealth and power, in the hands of some men and not others which promotes polygyny and polyandry. If monogamy is becoming less common in our own time and culture it is because modern civilization creates, for the first time, the means whereby a woman can survive and earn a living without support or protection from a man.

Though he does not explicitly say so, Westermarck gives the distinct impression of disapproving of this trend, and of anything which might undermine the patriarchal family. Like Darwin, he believes that sexual selection has made men naturally belligerent, and women naturally submissive, if not masochistic. "Woman," he says, "enjoys the display of manly force even when it turns against herself." (Vol. II, p.3) Freud also believed in the naturalness of female masochism; but Westermarck rejected Freud's theories, especially his view that children wish to have sexual intercourse with their opposite-sex parent. He held that humans have an instinctive repugnance toward incest (that is, toward sexual relationships with persons with whom they have grown up in the same household), an instinct which developed along with the family, because of the need to avoid the ill effects of inbreeding. In this as in other respects, he held, the institution of patriarchal marriage is the basis of innate patterns of human behavior which seem unlikely to change. (Also see Levi-Strauss.)

1.　He argued, in *Ethical Relativity*, that since moral judgments originally developed out of instinctive emotional reactions, sentiments of approval or disapproval, gratitude or desire for revenge, they cannot have objective truth value of the kind presupposed by both teleological and deontological theories of morality. Fortunately for those of us who consider feminism, as a moral stance, to be objectively true, this by no means follows. Emotional reactions may be triggered by external events and so may point to objective realities, though not of course in as reliable a manner as could be desired (hence the importance of moral analysis and theory to improve our judgment). See also Westermarck's *The Origin and Development of the Moral Ideas* (Macmillan and Company, London, 1924)

2.　Contemporary matriarchy theorists such as Evelyn Reed have attacked this assumption, arguing that women's labor may well have been more important than men's in producing the basic necessities of life. See her *Woman's Evolution*.

3.　Westermarck is aware of this objection; he points out that Darwin used a similar comparative method in seeking the evolutionary causes of biological phenomena. This reply misses the point, since the biological features of nonhuman animals are not as a rule artifacts which take their meaning from a particular cultural context. (See Vol. I, p.24)

WILLIAMS, Juanita H. *Psychology of Woman: Behavior in a Biosocial Context* (W.W. Norton and Company, New York, 1977; first published 1974)

　This is an introductory text on the psychology of women, written from a feminist perspective. It includes good summary expositions of the ideas of the psychoanalytic school (e.g. Freud, Deutsch, Erikson) and the major rebels within it (e.g. Horney, Clara Thompson, Adler). Williams shows that there is as yet no valid evidence that female biology has any direct or universal influence on women's psychology; what observable differences there are result rather from the *meanings* which societies give to the various biological events which are unique to women. She does, however, give credence to the evidence that (human as well as other) males are generally more aggressive than females, and not wholly because of their social conditioning. She says,

> The suggestion from the data on sex differences in aggression is that a biological substratum exists which predisposes males to be more aggressive in situations which elicit that behavior. (p.154)

Nevertheless, the evidence also indicates that aggressive behavior is learned, not inborn, and that it can be minimized in either sex by the right training; hence no pessimistic conclusions about the inevitability of patriarchy follow from the male propensity for aggression. (See Goldberg.)

Williams rightly attacks the stereotyped notions of masculinity and femininity prevalent in the literature of psychology. She endorses the concept of androgyny, i.e. of sex-neutral standards of human development and fulfillment. She concludes that the entire project of looking for general psychological differences between the sexes is counterproductive; not only has it been unfruitful thus far, but it has seriously impeded scientific understanding of the individual person in all her complexity and uniqueness.

WILSON, Edward O. *Sociobiology: The New Synthesis* (Harvard University Press, 1975)
On Human Nature (Harvard University Press, 1978)

Sociobiology is a compendious work which surveys and partly creates that entire field of study. Sociobiologists deal with the social behavior of organisms, from amoebas to human beings. The subject is synthetic in that it draws upon the findings of biology, ethology, genetics, biochemistry, population theory, and in the case of primates, anthropology and sociology. Its ultimate goal is the complete causal explanation of all social behavior, including human social behavior, in terms of the environmental cues which elicit it, the physical mechanisms which effectuate it, and the evolutionary pressures and environmental constraints which determine its emergence. Although over 90 percent of the book deals with nonhuman societies, with insect societies getting perhaps half the overall coverage, most of the interest and controversy it has provoked stem from the final chapter on "man." This, like the chapter on sex and on aggression, contains arguments and conclusions which feminists and antifeminists alike have to take into account.

Sexual reproduction, it is said, is genetically advantageous: it increases genetic diversity and the mixing of different genetic strains, diversifies the offspring of individual parents. Hence it is virtually essential for all complex animal species. But it is *not* socially advantageous, i.e. conducive to orderly and efficient social organization, because it leads to conflicts of interest—especially between males and other males, but also between males and females, between females and offspring, and, least often, between females and other females. Darwin had the essential insight about why the sexes tend to differ from each other much more than is necessary simply for the process of sexual reproduction. He argued that sexual dimorphism is the result of competition for mates among one sex or the other, which leads to the evolution of traits peculiar to that sex. Since it is usually males who compete for access to females, it is usually they who develop special sexual traits, e.g. brighter display plumage or greater size, strength and aggressiveness.

To this, modern sociobiologists have added the insight that it is males' smaller investment of time and energy in each offspring which accounts for the more intense sexual selection to which they are subject; for the smaller the per-offspring investment by a sex, the greater its potential reproductive success, and thus the more its members will compete for access to the other sex. (In the few species where it is males who care for the young after their birth, it is females who compete for males, rather than vice versa.) There is always a strong tendency for the mate with the smaller necessary investment to desert the other and seek additional mates. Animals are therefore fundamentally polygamous, with polygyny (one male mating with a number of females) being far more common than polyandry (one female mating with a number of males), simply because the females' per-offspring investment is generally greater. Monogamy is a special condition which evolves only when the reproductive advantage to both mates of rearing the young cooperatively outweighs the advantage to either partner of seeking other mates. While birds are often monogamous, mammals are generally polygynous—a condition which promotes a marked sexual dichotomy, and male dominance over females.

Wilson is relatively cautious in applying such general insights as these to human social behavior. He criticizes the "advocacy" approach of popular writers (e.g. Lorenz, Ardrey, Morris, Tiger and Fox) who apply the insights of sociobiology to human behavior only in order to support certain predetermined conclusions about human nature. Human cultural variation, he notes, demonstrates that the human "biogram" is extremely flexible; even apparently highly maladaptive cultures can often survive for rather long periods. He does argue, however, that certain general features of the behavior of nonhuman primates may also prove useful in explaining human behavior. The most "conservative" behavioral traits of other primates, those least likely to shift from species to species, are also those "most likely to have persisted in relatively unaltered form into the evolution of *Homo*." (p.551) "These conservative traits," he continues, "include aggressive dominance systems, with males generally dominant over females; scaling in the intensity of responses, especially during aggressive interactions; intensive and prolonged maternal care, with a pronounced degree of socialization in the young; and matrilineal social organization." (1)

Like the popularizers of sociobiology, Wilson sees the conversion of our vegetarian, tree-dwelling African ancestors, some twelve million years ago, to a savanna-roaming life style and an increasing dependence on the hunting of large animals, as a key factor leading to the emergence of *Homo sapiens*. He adds, however, that the shift to the savannas may also have led to the eating of grass seeds, which would have placed a premium on manual dexterity. Since gathering plant foods was probably a predominantly female activity, one might infer that it was not only the hunting activities of the males which led to the emergence of human intelligence; besides, as Wilson points out, we do not know that it was only the males who hunted. But the evolutionary pressures exerted upon hunting and gathering activities cannot explain the later social evolution of humanity, and Wilson suggests that sexual selection, i.e. the competition between males for females, may have been "the auxiliary motor that drove human evolution all the way to the *Homo* grade." (p.569)

In *On Human Nature*, Wilson continues to explore the application of evolutionary theory to the explanation of human behavior. He views all human social behavior, even the most complex institutions of modern civilization, as essentially composed of hypertrophies, that is, further developments and exaggerations of simple behavioral patterns which became genetically encoded during the hunting and gathering phase of human existence. Heterosexual pair bonding, some sexual division of labor, some degree of male dominance, and the existence of all-male group activities from which women are excluded, are all universal human traits, and are probably genetically conditioned. Advanced cultures, however, exhibit these traits to a much more marked degree than do the few surviving hunting and gathering societies.

In Wilson's view, male domination provides an example of this process of hypertrophy. There are certain innate but initially fairly small differences in the behavioral tendencies of the sexes, e.g. the greater aggressiveness of the male and the female's greater aptitude for close personal relationships. These differences are evident even in the most primitive human societies; but with economic and cultural progress these initially small differences are greatly magnified, and give rise to increasingly severe male rule and female subordination.

Wilson realizes, however, that the partly biological basis of male domination does not make it permanent or inevitable. Since the innate differences are small, it should be possible for future societies, should they choose to do so, to so train and educate their members as to eliminate all sexual diferences in behavior. The other two choices are to continue to exaggerate sexual differences and male privilege, or to provide legal equality of opportunity but take no further action. Each alternative has disadvantages, and Wilson does not opt for any particular one of them. He does, however, argue that human sociobiology favors the recognition of human moral equality. This is because mammalian, and hence human, altruism is "soft" rather than "hard," that is, ultimately directed towards the benefit of the self rather than the other. This is why slavery and unjust class systems are unworkable in the long run. Thus,

> We will accede to universal human rights because power is too fluid in advanced technological societies to circumvent this mammalian imperative; the long-term consequences of inequity will always be visibly dangerous to its temporary beneficiaries. (p.199)

The application of sociobiological theory to the explanation of human behavior is still extremely speculative. It does not follow—as Wilson tends to assume—that if a particular behavior has proved adaptive in a wide range of human cultures, then it must be genetically encoded. It might be, but it might also be the result of rational (or irrational) calculations of individual and group interest, under relevantly similar circumstances. Thus, on the one hand, the evidence is fairly persuasive that human males have a biologically conditioned tendency towards aggressive behavior greater than that of females. But on the other hand, when Wilson suggests that such cultural traits as the use of calendars, cooking, dream interpretation, medicine, ethics and religion might also be in some way genetically encoded, one may begin to suspect the soundness of his methodology (2). (See pp.21–22.)

1. By a matrilineal social organization Wilson means one in which the most important cross-generational bonds are those between mothers and their offspring. It is interesting to note that matriliny in this sense is quite compatible with both polygyny and male dominance.
2. Wilson's treatment of homosexuality provides a particularly striking example of this tendency to classify behaviors as genetically determined simply because a Darwinian explanation of their occurrence is *possible*. Wilson suggests that the tendency towards (exclusive) homosexuality in some individuals may have adaptive value, in that the homosexual members of the tribe could have acted as assistant parents to their siblings' children.

> If the relatives . . . were benefitted by higher survival and reproduction rates, the genes these individuals shared with the homosexual specialist would have increased at the expense of alternative genes . . . A minority of the population would consequently always have the potential for developing homophilic preferences. (p.145)

Like many of Wilson's hypotheses, this is a fascinating conjecture, but little more, since the evidence that the tendency towards homosexuality is inheritied (only) by certain individuals is slight.

WITCHES We are exposed at an early age to the fairy-tale image of the witch, who is usually depicted as a singularly unattractive old woman. In Western superstitious lore, a witch is a person who has made a compact with the devil, which is typically sealed through obscene sexual rites of various kinds. In recent years, feminists have repeatedly raised the question of why witches have been conceived as being nearly all women, and what this fact demonstrates about the psychology of Western man.

The belief in witchcraft is considerably older than Christianity, and prior to the thirteenth century it was opposed by the Church as a heresy. Yet between the twelfth and seventeenth centuries perhaps as many as nine million persons, most of them women, were tortured and killed as witches, with the approval of the Catholic and later the Protestant Churches. The causes of this enormous bloodbath are not well understood. Some historians have argued that the witchcraft hysteria was initiated by the Church in order to eliminate the last remaining vestiges of pagan religion (1). Some hold that many or most of the women who were persecuted as witches were actually midwives and folk healers, whose supposedly magical powers aroused the fear of the Church (2). Others have argued that there never were any such secret societies of women practicing ancient rites or possessing special knowledge, and that witchcraft was never more than a fantasy of paranoid and perhaps sexually repressed men, in the Church and other positions of authority (3). G.R. Taylor finds the source of this paranoia in men's fear of women as sexual beings, while Bullough points out that at the time of the witch hunts, changing economic conditions were permitting some women to step outside of their assigned place, a tendency which the fear of being accused of witchcraft must have done much to suppress.

The suggestion that the witchcraft craze was in large part a result of male paranoia about female sexuality gains considerable support from the words of the *Malleus Maleficarum* (i.e. *Hammer Against Witches*). This document was published in 1486 by two Dominican inquisitors, with the authorization of Pope Innocent VIII, and it became the witch hunters' Bible during the height of the Inquisition. The *Malleus* ascribes the preponderance of female witches to women's excessive sexuality:

> All witchcraft comes from carnal lust, which is in women insatiable. See Proverb 30; There are three things that are never satisfied, yea, a fourth thing which says not, It is enough; that is, the mouth of the womb. Wherefore for the sake of fulfilling their lusts they consort even with devils. (4)

It can be argued, therefore, that the very concept of witchcraft represents the epitome of misogynism, and must be understood in these terms. Some recent feminist writers have looked upon the legends and rituals of witchcraft as a part of women's spiritual heritage, and have found in the witch an inspiring image of female strength (5).

1. See Maragaret A. Murray, *The Witch-Cult in Western Europe* (Oxford University Press, 1971; first published 1921), and *The God of the Witches* (Oxford University Press, New York, 1970; first published 1931; also Daly, 1973, pp.146–149.)
2. See Barbara Ehrenreich and Deirdre English, *Witches, Midwives, and Nurses: A History of Women Healers* (in Anthologies VII); also Jules Michelet, *Satanism and Witchcraft: A Study in Medieval Superstition* (Arco Publications, London, 1958).

3. See Norm Cohn, *Europe's Inner Demons: An Enquiry Inspired by the Great Witch-Hunt* (Basic Books, New York, 1975); also G.R. Taylor, 1954, pp.125–131; Janeway, 1971, pp.126–128, and Bullough, 1973, pp.223–225.
4. Excerpted in *Women and Religion*, edited by Elizabeth Clark and Herbert Richardson (in Anthologies XII), p.125.
5. See Daly, and Robin Morgan; also see Nancy Garden, *Witches* (J.B. Lippincott, Philadelphia and New York, 1975) for a concise account of the contemporary practice of witchcraft.

WOLFF, Charlotte. *Love Between Women* (Harper and Row, New York, 1972)

Wolff is a British psychiatrist who draws upon both the Freudian and the existentialist traditions in an attempt to explain the nature and etiology of lesbian love. In this book she reports on a study of 108 homosexual women who were otherwise normal (i.e. not mental patients).

Like Freud, Wolff considers female homosexuality to have both physiological and environmental causes. Freud held that women are more bisexual than men in their genital structure, in that they have a sexually functional biological analogue of the penis (the clitoris), while men have no functional analogue of the vagina (he ignored the anus). Women are thus capable of two fundamentally different kinds of response—masculine/clitoral and feminine/vaginal (1). The lesbian woman is the one who clings to the former.

Wolff theorizes that if the inherently bisexual potential of the girl child is to develop into homosexuality, there must be either a physiological bias towards masculinity, or a family situation which prevents her from transferring to her father her original love and sexual attraction towards her mother. The "normal" female (at least in patriarchal society) makes this shift quite early, out of disillusion with the mother's lack of power (symbolized by the penis), and in order to win the father's protection and perhaps share his power. To win the affection of the father, however, she must adopt the "feminine" attitude—that of submission and passivity. This the (future) homosexual female refuses to do. Instead she struggles to prove herself as good as the male in every way:

> The lesbian girl is the one who . . . will try to find a place of safety inside and outside the family, through her fight for equality with the male. (p.69)

Wolff differs from Freud insofar as she does not hold that such a stance on the part of a female is necessarily pathological. She applauds Simone de Beauvoir's defense of lesbianism as at least sometimes an authentic mode of existence. She doubts, however, de Beauvoir's further implication that it is something which can be freely chosen. Lesbians do not experience their sexual orientation as a choice, but as something which they would be unable to change even if they wanted to (and most do not).

But although they do not *choose* to be homosexual, lesbian women are "unquestionably in the avant-garde of the fight for the equality of the sexes, and for the psychological liberation of women." (p.79) For, Wolff holds, the lesbian woman's love of independence is more intense, closer to the core of her being, than is ever the case with heterosexual women.

> The lesbian's refusal to be an inferior to man is absolute, while with "normal" women the rejection of man's superiority remains relative. (pp.82–83)

This is because the heterosexual woman is always vulnerable to being "put back into the place of an object." (p.89) It is not her sexual activity as such which makes her thus vulnerable, but rather her emotional relationship with men—who in the final analysis are unable to perceive her as a fellow human being. In contrast, the lesbian, in her "virility and freedom from the fetters of being an object of the male" (p.102) resembles the stronger, freer (image of) woman of the ancient matriarchy.

Nevertheless, lesbians pay a high price for their relative independence from the male. They rightly perceive the world as hostile, and thus tend to develop paranoid traits. If they choose to pass as "straight" they must lead a double life, concealing their true identity from most of their acquaintances. Because of their incurable mother-fixation, they have a virtually insatiable longing for love. Since no real relationship can live up to their ideal, and because no children can be conceived of their love, lesbian relationships have a necessarily tragic cast.

Lesbianism, therefore, is not true liberation. But exclusive heterosexuality is even worse, since it isolates a woman from other women and forces her into the humiliated role of a sex object. Wolff concludes that the answer must be bisexuality, "the expression of the whole bisexual nature of every man and woman." (p.81) This means not only sexual interaction with partners of both sexes, but rejecting traditional gender roles. Bisexuality would eliminate the patriarchal nuclear family, and with it the asymmetrical Oedipal situation which gives rise to contrasting masculine and feminine gender identities.

A major problem with this theory is the apparent confusion between what Wolff calls gender identity—i.e. conformity to traditional notions of masculinity or femininity—and erotic orientation. Are all lesbians "masculine"? Must a psychological androgyne (one who is both rational and intuitive, strong and gentle, independent and nurturant, etc.) also be erotically bisexual? Common sense would suggest that the answer to these questions is "no," and that there are as many kinds of lesbians as of hetero- or bisexual women. Further scientific research in this area would be extremely valuable. Another problem is Wolff's assumption that all girls originally love only their mothers. This too is an empirical claim which requires further investigation.

1.   The work of Masters and Johnson has discredited this distinction between vaginal and clitoral responsiveness in women. This would seem to be a fatal objection to the Freudian approach to the explanation of female homosexuality.

WOLLSTONECRAFT, Mary (1759–1797). *A Vindication of the Rights of Woman* (W.W. Norton and Company, New York, 1967; first published 1792, by Joseph Johnson, London)

Mary Wollstonecraft is probably the first feminist philosopher worthy of the name. Though there were a number of French and English thinkers in the latter part of the eighteenth century who were also asking why the human rights proclaimed by the French Revolution, and by English utilitarians like Jeremy Bentham, should not be extended to both sexes, few of them put their thoughts in writing and none produced so powerful and comprehensive a work as Wollstonecraft's *Vindication of the Rights of Woman*. The *Vindication* was the first effective challenge to the entire system of male supremacy, to the traditional concepts of masculinity and femininity, and the presumption of female inferiority. It created an international sensation, made Wollstonecraft the most infamous woman in Europe, and inspired Horace Walpole to refer to her as a "hyena in petticoats."

There have been a number of fine biographies of Mary Wollstonecraft (1), and her character and personality have been subjected to analysis by Freudians anxious to prove that feminism is merely the manifestation of penis envy and the masculinity complex (2). It is, perhaps, understandable that her flamboyant personality and her short, tempestuous life should have attracted more public attention than the actual conceptual content of her work, especially since the latter is somewhat obscured by her rather baroque style. There is, however, little excuse for the way in which most commentators continue to dismiss her work as an illogical emotional outburst (3). It is true that her novels, **Mary** and **Maria or the Wrongs of Woman** (which was left unfinished at her death) are, as works of literary fiction, rather amateurish, and that the **Vindication** itself is no model of organizational clarity. Yet all of her work exhibits a remarkably clear perception of the oppressed status of women, of its social origin, its corrupting effect upon all human relations, and its inconsistency with the Enlightenment ideals of liberty and equality for all. Whatever its literary flaws, the **Vindication**'s major lines of thought are coherent and powerfully argued. From it emerge, fully formed, most of the tenets of what today is called liberal—as opposed to radical or socialist—feminism.

Wollstonecraft's primary theme is that the age-old presumption that the virtues proper for men—rationality, independence, strength of character and so on—are unnecessary or even improper in women, is wholly false and pernicious. She was incensed by Rousseau's contention that women should be taught nothing except how to please men and be useful to them. Virtue, she argues, can have no sex; for it can only come through the exercise of Reason, which God gave to both sexes, that they might not only perform their earthly duties but merit and prepare for their future immortality. Education ought to

> enable the individual to attain such habit of virtue as will render it independent. In fact, it is a farce to call any being virtuous whose virtues do not result from the exercise of its own reason. (p.52)

Instead, women are corrupted by "false education, gathered from books . . . written by men who, considering females rather as women than human creatures, have been more anxious to make them alluring mistresses than affectionate wives and mothers." (p.32) It has been argued by libertarian philosophers, including Rousseau himself, that any form of unearned power, such as hereditary rank and property, corrupts the possessor by making it unnecessary for him to develop virtue or self-control; so too, Wollstonecraft points out, women are corrupted by the fact that they are valued for their beauty and refinement, rather than their rationality and attention to duty. Rousseau claims that women would have less power over men if they were educated in the same way as men, rather than to be pleasing to men and to at least seem to obey them. "This," Wollstonecraft replied, "is exactly the point I am at. I do not wish them to have power over men; but over themselves." (p.107)

In women's education, she points out, "strength of body and mind are sacrificed to libertine notions of beauty, to the desire of establishing themselves—the only way women can rise in the world—by marriage." (p.35) Deprived of autonomy, women naturally seek (and often gain) power over others; their "artificial weakness produces a propensity to tyrannize, and gives birth to cunning." (p.36) Yet, "the illegitimate power, which they obtain by degrading themselves, is a curse." (p.52) For,

> Women, as well as despots, have now, perhaps, more power than they would have if the world, divided and subdivided into kingdoms and families, were governed by laws deduced from the exercise of reason; but in obtaining it, to carry on the comparison, their character is degraded, and licentiousness spread through the whole aggregate of society. (p.77)

It was argued then as now that women do not need equality, since they are happier as they are, and since their primary duty and satisfaction is to be wives and mothers. Wollstonecraft (all too readily) concedes that for most women the duties of marriage and motherhood are paramount and always will be. But she insists that given equality before the law, equal education and the means for economic independence, women would not only be happier and more rational, but, for these very reasons, they would be better wives and mothers. She agrees with the traditionalists that "whatever tends to incapacitate the maternal character takes woman out of her sphere" (p.263), but says that it is not the attempt to gain masculine virtues, but rather the cultivation of so-called feminine traits which makes women inadequate mothers. For women who have charm rather than virtue are certain to lack the "character necessary to manage a family or educate children." (p.69) Furthermore, if such women are widowed or abandoned by their husbands they are unable to support themselves or their children.

Thus, like the liberal (or perhaps conservative) feminists of today, Wollstonecraft has no objection to the traditional division of labor in marriage, whereby the man earns the money and the woman manages the household and cares for the children. Indeed, she deplores the artificial delicacy of upper-class women, which prevents them from nursing and caring for their own children. She stresses, however, that there are some gifted women who can contribute more to society by careers other than marriage, and that there are others who, while they wish to marry never do, or who must contribute to or take the full responsibility for the economic support of their families. Hence she objects to the fact that most respectable and remunerative occupations have been closed to women. Women should be able to practice medicine—"and be physicians as well as nurses" (p.221)—midwifery, and the business professions, and to take part in politics. For, like men, "women ought to have representatives, instead of being arbitrarily governed without having any direct share allowed to them in the direction of government." (p.220)

As for women's much-maligned mental capacities, Wollstonecraft carefully refrains from claiming that they are identical to those of men. Like John Stuart Mill after her, she holds that we can know nothing of women's natural abilities when we have been able to observe women only as they have been shaped by a highly artificial system of education.

> Let their faculties have room to unfold, and their virtues to gain strength, and then determine where the sex must stand in the intellectual scale. (p.70)

Even supposing that women were in some way mentally inferior to men, this would not in any way justify confining them to the so-called feminine virtues of "gentleness, docility, and a spaniel-like affection." (p.68)

> If women are by nature inferior to men, their virtues must be the same in quality, if not in degree, or virtue is a relative idea . . . (p.58)

If women are naturally inferior, then "men have increased that inferiority till women are almost sunk below the level of rational creatures." (p.70) So too, woman is evidently physically weaker than man; but Wollstonecraft asks, "whence does it follow that it is natural for her to labor to become still weaker than nature intended her to be?"

Having herself run a boarding school for girls, and having written her first book on the subject of female education (*Thoughts on the Education of Daughters*, 1786), Wollstonecraft concentrates on educational reforms as the best way to ameliorate the condition of women. (She does promise to deal at length with the subject of legal reform in a second volume; but this was never written.) Her experience convinced her that boarding schools tend to corrupt children's character and to deprive them of the good influence of the home, but that educating children entirely at home was worse since it deprived them of the company of their peers. Hence she advocated a system of state-run day schools, which would be entirely coeducational and would teach the same subjects to both sexes, though it would also segregate children into vocational or academic channels at the age of nine. (Apart from this latter point, she might, in fact, have been describing the school system that did come into existence, and that still exists e.g. in England and the United States.)

Education, she stresses, must strengthen both mind and body. Girls require the same physical freedom and activity as boys, and the sedentary existence enforced on girls impairs their health and character. Rousseau had claimed that little girls naturally care more about dress and dolls than anything else; to this, she replies,

> I have, probably, had an opportunity of observing more girls in their infancy than J.J. Rousseau . . . [and] I will venture to affirm, that a girl whose spirits have not been damped by inactivity, or innocence tainted by false shame, will always be a romp, and the doll will never excite attention unless confinement allows her no alternatives. (p.81)

Wollstonecraft is also bold enough to attack the double standard of sexual morality, which forgives every vice but one in women, while winking at that same vice in men. She advocates, however, not more sexual freedom for women, but more "modesty and chastity" for men. In fact, she holds male lustfulness largely responsible for the faults men find in women:

> all the causes of female weakness, as well as depravity . . .
> branch out of one grand cause—want of chastity in men. (p.208)

For, she reasons, it is the sexual lustfulness of men which makes them want women who are docile and subordinate, trained only to be pleasing; and it is to make them more attractive to men that women's education and intellect are stunted and their attention fixed on dress and manners.

Wollstonecraft's distaste for the way that women are subordinated to male lust carries over to her attitude towards the sex act itself; sexual passion, she thinks, should be avoided as much as possible, even within marriage. "Love, considered as an animal appetite, cannot long feed on itself without expiring." Hence it is better that marriage be based on friendship and mutual esteem, rather than love or sexual attraction. She speaks with contempt of men who are carried to such lengths by "an intemperate love of pleasure . . . that they seduce their own wives." (p.121) She views sexual passion as existing only that it might be controlled by the force of reason, and considers the sex act undesirable not just because of its possibles consequences—in the absence of birth control and penicillin—but because it means yielding to a base animal instinct.

It is ironic, therefore, that Wollstonecraft has been remembered as a sexual libertine. (One nineteenth century dictionary listed her name as a synonym for "prostitute.") It was only after the publication of the *Vindication* that she fell in love with the American, Gilbert Imlay (who abandoned her after fathering her first child), carried on a scandalous though Platonic affair with the artist, Henry Fuseli, and finally enjoyed a brief but happy marriage to the philosopher William Godwin. Had she survived the birth of her second child, she might have written of love and sexuality from a less artificial perspective.

In the end, what is important about Wollstonecraft is her reasoned and radical attack on the traditional notions of "masculinity" and "femininity," or in her words, the giving of a sex to virtue. These notions, and the patriarchal system they uphold, *are* inconsistent with the central moral injunctions of Christianity, and with the Enlightenment ideals of liberty and equality of opportunity. Wollstonecraft was the first to make these points, loudly and clearly, and the first to reveal the ideal of the pretty, helpless, irrational, and emotional woman as a self-serving creation of men.

1. See, for instance, Eleanor Flexner's *Mary Wollstonecraft* (Coward, McCann & Geoghegan, New York, 1972), Clair Tomalin's *The Life and Death of Mary Wollstonecraft* (Harcourt, Brace, Jovanovich, New York, 1974), and Ralph Wardle's *Mary Wollstonecraft, A Critical Biography* (University of Nebraska Press, Lincoln, Nebraska, 1951).
2. This is essentially the position of Ferdinand Lundberg and Marynia Farnham, in their once popular book, *Modern Woman: The Lost Sex*.
3. For instance, Clair Tomalin says that the *Vindication* "is a book without any logical structure: it is more in the nature of an extravaganza." (*Op. cit.*, p.103) And Charles Hagelman, in his introduction to the 1967 edition, says that what is important about Wollstonecraft's work is "not primarily the originality or the profundity of her ideas (for they have neither) . . . but her devotion to her fellow men [sic] and her concern for their well being." (p.19)

WOMEN'S MOVEMENT The women's movement (or women's liberation movement) is the organized political struggle for the implementation of feminist goals—from legal equality between the sexes and equality of occupational opportunities for women to—for some groups within the movement—such more radical goals as the end of patriarchal marriage and the nuclear family. Although there were feminist writers and thinkers in the eighteenth century and even earlier, the women's movement began to gain in size and strength only in the second half of the nineteenth century. There have been two major waves of feminist activity in this country, paralleled by similar developments in England, France and elsewhere. The first major American feminist movement grew out of the abolitionist activities of the mid-nineteenth century, and continued until after 1920, when the primary goal of women's suffrage was finally obtained. For historical accounts of the long struggle for the vote, the tactical and ideological divisions within the suffrage movement, and the decline of the movement in the twenties, see Chafe; and Flexnor, Kraditor, and O'Neill, in Anthologies VI.

The second great wave of feminist activity began in the sixties and has continued through the seventies. It arose in part from the civil rights struggle and the anti-Vietnam War protests, in part from the realization by a new generation of women that the victory of suffragists had been at best a very partial one. For accounts of the contemporary women's movement—written from varying theoretical and political perspectives within it—see Atkinson, Brown, Friedan, Mitchell, Robin Morgan, Ware, and Yates. Also see Deckard, Fritz, Hole and Levine, Freeman, and Gornick, in Anthologies IV.

WOOLF, Virginia (1882–1941). *A Room of One's Own* (Harcourt, Brace and Company, New York, 1929)
Three Guineas (Harcourt, Brace and Company, New York, 1938)

Though primarily a novelist and critic, Virginia Woolf is remembered almost as often for her feminist utterances, especially *A Room of One's Own*, which has become almost a feminist Bible. For although she urges women to write without conscious awareness of their sex and without stressing any grievance, she nevertheless ignores her own advice and speaks as a woman who is intensely aware of her membership in an oppressed class. At the same time she displays a whimsical humor, which sometimes almost belies the seriousness of her complaints. The book began as a series of lectures on the topic "Women and Fiction," but expanded into a general discussion of woman's situation, interwoven throughout with autobiographical reflections.

Woolf's contention is that to write fiction—or by implication to produce anything of intellectual or artistic value, a woman must have an independent income and a room of her own. In her own case, she says, it was possible to write, in freedom and without bitterness, only because of a legacy of five hundred pounds per year, left her by an aunt. If women have produced little of artistic value it is because they have been poor, financially dependent upon men and excluded from the male realms of higher education and the professions. If Shakespeare had had a sister, equally talented, ambitious and energetic, she would almost certainly have had no education, no income and no way to earn a living while learning to write; she would probably have died young and been forgotten. Even had she managed to somehow write poetry, she would have been so harassed and reviled for her efforts that she could never have retained the calm and luminous state of mind necessary for writing well, i.e. "without hate, without bitterness, without fear, without protest, without preaching." (p.117)

A room of one's own and an income are blessings Woolf considers far more important than the vote, which women can put to little use so long as they are dependent upon men for their subsistence and so, necessarily, for their political opinions. But this is *not* to say that women should become like men; they need, rather, to transcend the sexual dichotomy, to achieve an androgynous unity of mind. Like Jung, she thinks that there is within each human being a masculine force and a feminine force; in a man, the former force prevails, in a woman the latter. The trick is to achieve cooperation between these two sexes in one's mind—though not necessarily *equality*, for Woolf thinks that the sexes will probably continue to be fundamentally different, ruled by different principles.

It is from this limited ideal of androgyny that Woolf derives the conclusion that a woman writer must never "speak consciously as a woman." "It is," she says, "fatal for a woman to lay the least stress on any grievance, to plead even with justice any cause . . . " (p.181) This is obviously a *non sequitur*, and it is well that she disregarded her own advice. For it is surely possible (if unusual) for a person of either sex to plead rationally for a just cause without losing that clarity of mind, that necessary degree of detachment, which Woolf so prized. There is, after all, a difference between bias and commitment, and some moral claims are objectively true. Her philosophical confusion about this point mars the work. At the same time, however, one can sympathize with Woolf's impatience with the unconcealed sexual chauvinism which may be perceived on both sides of the debate over feminism:

> All this pitting of sex against sex, of quality against quality; all this claiming of superiority and imputing of inferiority, belong to the private-school stage of human existence where there are "sides," and it is necessary for one side to beat another side, and of the utmost importance to walk up to a platform and receive from the hands of the Headmaster himself a highly ornamental pot. (p.184)

Three Guineas is a less well-known work, although Woolf here develops her feminist position a good deal more fully. Writing in the intense awareness of the approach of war, she asks what a woman can do to help prevent future wars. There is, she argues, an enormous gap in the understanding and attitudes of men and women with respect to war. To men it is a glamorous expression of their masculinity, of their drive to fight; this drive is innate to men and utterly incomprehensible to women. What can middle-class women do, when they are the weakest of all social classes? They have little power except their supposed power to influence the men in their lives; and experience shows that such influence is "very low in power, very slow in action, and very painful to use." (p.20)

Woolf's reply is that, before she can give a metaphorical guinea to support the society to prevent war, she must first give a guinea for the rebuilding of a women's college, and one to the society to open the professions to women. Women, that is, must have education and income before they can hope to alter the institutions which create war. Yet this raises a paradox: it would seem that in pursuing degrees and professional careers women risk becoming more like men, and less capable of challenging male-created institutions. Woolf emphasizes the dangers of cooptation, but argues that they can be avoided and are in any case the lesser evil. There is no real alternative, for women must have "paid-for" education if they are to earn their livings, and they must earn their livings if they are to exert any pressure against war. Women who do not, who are confined to the private home, are generally in favor of war, both consciously and unconsciously—consciously in order to support and flatter men, and unconsciously as an escape from boredom.

Woolf holds that women who enter the previously masculine professions can escape corruption by masculine values if and only if they cling to the "four great teachers of the daughters of educated men—poverty, chastity, derision and freedom from unreal loyalties." (p.121) By "poverty" she means enough to live on comfortably, but no more; by "chastity" she means not sexual abstinence but the refusal to prostitute one's brain in order to make more than the necessary minimum; by "derision" she means steadfastly refusing to seek or accept honors or distinctions (a refusal she herself practiced); and by "unreal loyalties" she means patriotism, sex chauvinism and the like. A woman can function in a man's world without being destroyed or contaminated by it only if she remains an Outsider, taking from that world only what is necessary to *preserve* her independence and never enough to destroy it.

An Outsider has no country; she owes her allegiance to humankind as a whole. She will contribute a guinea to the society to prevent war, but she will not join it. She will neither participate in patriotic activities nor denounce them, but merely hold herself aloof from them:

> The small boy struts and trumpets outside the window: implore him to stop; he goes on; say nothing; he stops . . . the daughters of educated men should give their brothers neither the white feathers of cowardice nor the red feather of courage, but no feather at all; . . . they should shut the bright eyes that rain influence, or let those eyes look elsewhere when war is discussed. (p.167)

This is clearly a feminist (1) stance in which there is more heroic resignation than revolutionary optimism. It is not an escapist position, however, for Woolf maintains that domestic patriarchy is the source of the militaristic mentality, and that by securing their own independence women are taking the most effective course open to them in combatting that mentality.

1. Woolf repudiates "feminism" as a label which is outdated and meaningless now that women have won the vote, good for nothing except childish name-calling. But her dislike for the term does not alter the fact that her philosophical position is a feminist one, in the sense of the term that survived after suffragism.

WRIGHT, Frederick Adam (1869–1946). *Feminism in Greek Literature: From Homer to Aristotle* (Kennikat Press, New York and London, 1969; first published 1923)

Wright is a classical scholar who attacks the Greeks of the Classical era—Greek men that is, and particularly those of Athens—for their ill treatment of women. "The Greek world," he says, "perished from one main cause, a low ideal of womanhood and a degradation of woman which found expression both in literature and in social life." (p.1) Athenian wives were kept in "Oriental" seclusion in small, dark and unsanitary houses. They had fewer rights than slaves, with whom they were constantly compared. Female infanticide was common, and real love between the sexes was considered impossible, though the hetaerae (high-class prostitutes, usually foreign born) made amusing companions.

Though he does not mention the early matriarchy theory, Wright does suggest that this situation represented a regression from the higher degree of respect which women appear to have enjoyed during the era depicted in the Homeric epics, half a millennium earlier: "the entire framework of *The Odyssey* presupposes a condition of society in which women are regarded as not in the least, *qua* women, inferior to men." (p.13) Not until the Archaic period, specifically the 7th century B.C., do we find Greek literature being used to degrade women. Simonides of Amorgos, who compares women to pigs, dogs, asses, polecats and monkeys, is a prime example of this.

However, as Sarah Pomeroy notes, Wright's book now in part "appears quaint in its blatant polemicism"(1); in particular, his evident loathing for male homosexuality, which he blames, along with infanticide and "the harem system," for "the slow process of race suicide" (p.49) which began in the sixth century. But on his main theme he is steadfast. "At Athens the restriction of women to one function [i.e. childbearing] meant that even that one function was badly performed, and all through the great period the Athenian race was slowly declining in numbers." (p.60) Wright believes that homosexuality, infanticide and the seclusion of women were all transplanted to Athens from the cities of Ionia (on the Aegian coast of Asia Minor), whence came the "Milesian tales," pornographic stories with a viciously misogynous intent. Milesia suffered from a particularly intense enmity between the sexes, since the Greek invaders had killed all the Milesian men and taken their wives and daughters for slaves and wives; for this, generations of Milesian women took symbolic revenge by refusing to eat with their husbands.

As an explanation of Athenian misogyny this "Ionian influence" theory seems simplistic and perhaps circular. But whatever its causes, the degradation of women was not wholly unprotested in Classical Athens. Wright argues that Euripides, Aeschylus, Aristophanes, Socrates, Plato and Xenophon were all feminists, to varying degrees. The most profound critic of women's inequality is Euripides, who "championed the cause of woman's freedom against the decadents of Ionia," (p.89) albeit subtly, and in a way which allowed Athenians to either take the message or ignore it. In the *Alcestis*, for example, Admentis, who asks his young wife Alcestis to die in his place, is clearly shown as a coward unworthy of such devotion; yet most Athenians probably saw nothing reprehensible in his behavior, since they themselves "treated women much as the baser sort still treat animals." (p.132)

The great comic playwright Aristophanes, though he made fun of Euripides and called him (with deliberate irony) a woman hater, was also a feminist, Wright argues. In the *Lysistrata* and other less well-known plays on the same theme, he suggests, not entirely in jest, "that women are as capable, intellectually and morally, as men . . . and [that] a feminist administration might solve many problems that have proved too hard for men." (p.152) In *The Republic*, Plato argued for the communality, rather than private ownership, of women, as of (other) property, and although he "at first hardly escapes from the fallacy that a man's wife is as much a piece of property as a dog or a table" (p.169), he ends by advocating complete equality of education and social function for women. Unfortunately, it was Aristotle, with his supposedly scientific defense of slavery and male supremacy as natural and proper, who has had the most influence on subsequent thought.

Though one may fault Wright for his bias against homosexuality (he does not even refer to it by name, but speaks merely of "perversion"), he is surely right to hold that for all its intellectual and artistic brilliance and (proto-) democratic political life, Classical Athens represented in some ways a relatively low point for women's rights. There is a paradox here which would repay further exploration. But it should not be forgotten that the misogynous climate of Athens produced the first feminist works known to history (Sappho was a lyric poet, not a feminist philosopher), and the first serious reflections on women's role in society. As the topic was rarely addressed with such vigor during the next two thousand years, this is no small credit to the Greeks.

1.   Pomeroy, *Goddesses, Whores, Wives and Slaves*, p. 58.

WYLIE, Philip. *Generation of Vipers* (Rinehart and Company, New York and Toronto, 1955; first published 1942)

A contemporary misogynist, in this best seller Wylie expresses outrage against the American cult of "Momism." Wylie claims that American has become a matriarchy, in which 80 percent of the material wealth is controlled by idle women, while most men slave to produce things for women to purchase. (No such figure has ever been substantiated.) Men, he says, are emotionally smothered by their mothers and economically exploited by their wives, while organizations of middle-aged women have taken over the schools, churches and industries, and are exercising a baleful influence upon the government. Wylie blames the "moms" for most of the evils of our age, including "a new all-time low in political scurviness, hoodlumism, gangsterism, labor strife, monopolistic thuggery, moral degeneration, civic corruption, smuggling, bribery, theft, murder, homosexuality, drunkenness, financial depression, chaos and war." (p.201) The only solution he suggests is for men to "overthrow the matriarchy" by taking their pocketbooks away from their wives and untying the maternal apron strings.

In all of this there is little trace of awareness of the point so often reiterated by feminists, namely that the undoubted tendency of some women to dominate their husbands and children is the natural result of their confinement to a role which allows them too *little* autonomy, and too little participation in social institutions outside the family, not too *much*. (See John Stuart Mill.) Insofar as "Momism" is a real (though often exaggerated) phenomenon, then, it is an argument for expanding women's sphere of direct involvement and responsibility, not for contracting it still further. The latter, reactionary course can only intensify women's drive to compensate for their own lack of autonomy by exercising control over others.

Y

YATES, Gayle Graham. *What Women Want: The Ideas of the Movement* (Harvard University Press, Cambridge, Massachusetts and London, 1975)

A useful analysis of some of the ideological strands of the women's liberation movement. Yates identifies three distinct feminist paradigms which have prevailed at successive historical stages of the movement and which are still competing with one another in contemporary feminism: the masculine-egalitarian paradigm, the women's liberationist paradigm and the androgynous paradigm. Most of the early feminists, from colonial times to the winning of the vote in 1920, were masculine egalitarians, primarily concerned to make women equal to men by winning for women the rights, privileges and opportunities already available to men. Their approach was nonrevolutionary, in that they did not challenge basic social institutions—e.g. the nuclear family, heterosexuality, capitalism, and the public school system—in themselves, but only sought to make them operate in a more sex-neutral manner.

The ideological descendants of these early feminists are the "womens's rights" branch of contemporary feminism. Betty Friedan and Carolyn Bird, for instance, have demanded more equal job opportunities for women and urged women to follow the "male model," by working away from home, and by treating work as the primary defining value in human life. The National Organization for Women (NOW), the National Women's Political Caucus (NWPC), and the Women's Equity Action League (WEAL) are masculine-egalitarian organizations; the Equal Rights Amendment is a masculine-egalitarian goal. Religious feminists like Rosemary Ruether and Mary Daly (in her earlier work, *The Church and the Second Sex*) follow a masculine-egalitarian model, seeking a larger role for women within the existing patriarchal structures of the church.

What Yates calls the women's liberationist perspective, on the other hand, is a product of the late 1960s and the 1970s. It is radically prowoman, antimasculinist, and revolutionary. Women's liberationists like Kate Millett and Shulamith Firestone analyze women's status in terms of class or caste, and identify men as the dominant class, the oppressor and the enemy. Values that are perceived as masculine are rejected and women's own values are discovered and affirmed through the concept of sisterhood and the method of consciousness raising. The model is one of conflict and confrontation; women are to unite *against* men and to establish their own social structures apart from men. Radical feminists have challenged patriarchal notions about sexuality on many fronts; they have argued for a women's right to abortion as part of her right to control her own body, have affirmed the clitoris (rather than the vagina) as the locus of the female orgasm, and acclaimed lesbianism and the avoidance of sexual and even social relationships with men as a revolutionary political action.

Finally, the third or androgynous perspective—which may be coming to the fore in the later seventies—operates on the principle not that women must be equal to men but that women and men must be equal to each other. Rather than blaming men for the oppression of women, androgynists blame attitudes and institutions which have placed arbitrary limitations on the personal development of both men and women. The androgynous ideal is in a sense a synthesis of the old feminism and the radical liberationist perspective, in that it seeks to combine "masculine" and "feminine" values into a social order in which women and men can cooperate as equals. Central to the androgynous perspective is the abandonment of the myth of motherhood, and the development of living patterns which will not only free mothers to work but make men their equal partners in childrearing. Gloria Steinem and Germaine Greer are androgynists, stressing cooperation and equality between the sexes.

Androgyny requires the end of the sexual double standard in all its manifestations, and the sanctioning of a variety of marital and family group arrangements. Communal childrearing will be one option, but both the nuclear family and the decision to remain single and/or childless will be respectable choices, carrying no social stigma. The androgynous marriage may involve a fifty-fifty sharing of housework, child care and breadwinning, or it may not. "In an atmosphere of mutual trust and support, wife and husband can decide to work and stay home in stages, each being primarily responsible in one sphere at one time, in another sphere at another time." (p.181) Democratic socialism, while perhaps not necessary for androgynous living patterns, would—Yates thinks— make their development easier. (See Zaretsky.)

Z

ZARETSKY, Eli. *Capitalism, the Family, and Personal Life* (Harper and Row, New York, 1976; first published in Great Britain by Pluto Press, 1976)

This is an attempt to heal the theoretical breach between radical feminism and socialism, by revealing this break as a consequence of the artificial division between the family and the economy, a division which is characteristic of capitalism. Both the radical feminists (e.g., Firestone, Atkinson, Millett, Mitchell) and the socialists (from Marx and Engels on), Zaretsky argues, have been guilty of treating the family and the economy as separate and independent realms. Prior to capitalism, material production and family life were unseparated. Capitalism, and the Industrial Revolution, removed "work," i.e. wage labor, from the home, and the ideology of capitalism placed no economic importance on the equally necessary residue of labor which remained within the family (i.e. housework and childrearing). This process led to a dichotomy between the "personal" and the "political," between the family—supposed to be "natural," and the refuge of the personal, the subjective and the feminine—and the public, objective practical, competitive masculine world.

The cure for this artificial dichotomy in our conceptualization of the world, Zaretsky holds, is the realization that the family is "a historically formed part of the mode of production." (p.31) Accordingly much of the essay is devoted to describing the progressive isolation of the family, over the past two centuries, from what was deemed economically productive labor. We must realize, Zaretsky says, that it was through this process that

> The split in society between "personal feelings" and "economic production" was integrated with the sexual division of labour. Women were identified with emotional life, men with the struggle for existence. (1) (p.64)

To overcome this dichotomy within the social system itself will require socialism, but a socialism which takes account of and thoroughly restructures *all* forms of socially necessary labor, including housework and child care. Marxism alone cannot provide adequate guidelines for such a restructuring, since it over-looks the economic importance of women's domestic work under capitalism. Engels "reinforces the bourgeois equation of produc-tion with the production of surplus value, and of work with wage labour, and therefore portrays women's labor within the family as marginal to society." (p.94) The family can be transformed only through the transformation of the capitalist economy, which in turn will succeed only insofar as the sexual division of labor within the family can be overcome.

Although Zaretsky's position is intended to be a reconciliation of socialism and radical feminism, combining the best insights of each, it would seem to share many of the weaknesses of the former. Granted that the particular form of the human family has always been shaped in large part by the conditions of material production, and that the particular forms of sexual inequality from which we suffer at present are undoubtedly conditioned in important ways by the capitalist economic system, it by no means follows that even the most thorough reorganization of the condi-tions of production would suffice to bring about equality in the family, or elsewhere. Radical feminists such as Shulamith Fire-stone have argued that there are certain physiological factors (e.g. women's biological role in reproduction) which may make genuine equality between the sexes within the biological family virtually impossible, whatever the economic system. If this is true then these noneconomic factors will have to be addressed direct-ly, and the struggle for sexual equality will include but also necessarily transcend the struggle for economic justice.

1. See Talcott Parsons for an analysis which treats this particu-lar aspect of the sexual division of labor as a universal feature of the human family, and independent of any particular economic system.

CURRENT ANTHOLOGIES AND OTHER SOURCEBOOKS

In the past decade or so, there have appeared a great many collections of writings relating to the nature and social status of women. Some of these are useful as a convenient way of sampling the work of well-known thinkers of the past and present, some provide examples of popularized material from the public medial and some contain important original work not readily available elsewhere. Because of the nature of the subject, most of these anthologies are to some extent inter- or cross-disciplinary. Nevertheless, they have for convenience been classified according to the *general* nature of the material and the approach taken towards it.

ANTHOLOGIES &
SOURCEBOOKS I.
ANTHROPOLOGY AND
ARCHEOLOGY

Catal Huyuk: A Neolithic Town in Anatolia, by James Mellaart (McGraw Hill, New York, 1967)

This is an illustrated account of the first excavations of the site of an early agricultural town (sixth and seventh millennia B.C.), in what is now southern Turkey. The discoveries at Catal Huyuk appear to provide some support for the hypothesis of a "matriarchal era" in this part of the ancient world. The religious shrines, images and objects all indicate that the primary deity was a goddess, who is mistress of wild animals—especially leopards— and mother of a male deity who remains her subordinate.

While the images of the goddess emphasize her fertility it is probably a mistake to assume, as Mellard does, that the goddess-centered religion was merely a "fertility cult." As Merlin Stone and others have argued, it was apparently a religion of cosmic import; it was also widespread and long lived, enduring for an as yet unknown number of millennia.

There is, of course, a (frequently ignored) difference between proving the occurrence of goddess worship and proving that the society of Catal Huyuk was gynocratic or woman-dominated. The extent to which the latter was the case may never be known. However, the larger number of female burials in the shrines and private houses, and the assignment of the largest and highest platform in each house to the woman, would seem to confirm that the status of women was one of great respect, if not supremacy.

Female of the Species, by M. Kay Martin and Barbara Voorhies (Columbia University Press, New York and London, 1975)

This is an excellent survey, feminist in spirit, of past and current anthropological approaches to the exploration of sex-role dichotomies. The authors examine data on the behavior of non-human primates and surviving human societies of the hunting and gathering type, and argue that for our earliest human ancestors the foraging activities of the women must have been at least as important a food source as the hunting activities of the men.

Next, they examine the typical roles of women in the various economic types of society: from gathering to horticultural, agricultural or pastoral, and finally the socialist and capitalist forms of industrialized society. Their thesis is that egalitarian and patriarchal gender roles serve distinct adaptive functions. Matrilocal, matrilineal societies tend toward equality between the sexes, and promote stability and cooperation between social units by dispersing the men outside their (maternal) family of origin. Patrilocal, patrilineal and patriarchal family structures, on the other hand, are survival conducive where there is less stability and more competitive and warlike relations with neighboring cultures. This, and not the rise of surplus wealth in itself, explains why patriarchal institutions tend to prevail in the economically more "advanced"—i.e. pastoral, agricultural and industrial—societies. Nevertheless, they predict that dichotomous gender roles will fade away in the future, as the social functions they once served are taken over by other and more adaptive social institutions.

Male Dominance and Female Autonomy: Domestic Authority in Matrilineal Societies, by Alice Schlegel (Hraf Press, 1972)

This is an interesting study of patterns of domestic authority in 73 existing matrilineal cultures. The 73 cultures were chosen to represent as wide a variety as possible. Schlegel divides them into five types, according to whether a married woman is primarily under the authority of her husband or her brother, whether both have some authority over her but one has more, or whether their authority is more or less evenly balanced. Her statistical studies show that women are most free, are least often victimized by male aggression, and have the most control over property and the highest social status in matrilineal societies of the last type. Husband-dominant and brother-dominant matrilineal societies are equally male supremacist; but where neither is dominant, male authority over women is dispersed and thereby weakened. Schlegel notes that this finding suggests that the critical factor determining the degree of women's subjection is "not the descent system *per se* but rather the organization of the domestic group."

Matrilineal Kinship, edited by David M. Schneider and Kathleen Gough (University of California Press, Berkeley, 1961)

This book is an outgrowth of a series of seminars held at Harvard in 1954. It is a gold mine of information on surviving matrilineal societies in all parts of the world. These include the Plateau Tonga of Rhodesia; the Navaho; the people of Truk (in the Caroline Islands); the Trobrianders (studied by Malinowski earlier in this century); the Ashanti (Ghana); and the Nayor, Tiyyar, and Mappilla of India, each of which groups receives a chapter in Part I. Parts II and III, by Kathleen Gough and David Aberle, respectively, are cross-cultural explorations of the possible general significance of economic and other social variables upon matrilineal descent systems.

The general conclusions which emerge from the book are (1) that matriliny is not a stage in general cultural evolution, but a result of convergent specific evolution; (2) that it is associated with "horticulture" (gathering-based agriculture) as the primary means of subsistence, and the absence of large scale, organized, economically important male activities, such as herding or plough agriculture; and (3) that it is rapidly disappearing in most parts of the world with the approach of modern industrial development.

Toward An Anthropology of Women, edited by Rayna R. Reiter (Monthly Review Press, New York and London, 1975)

This is an excellent collection of contemporary articles by women anthropologists concerned with the status of women in non-Western and prestate societies. Leila Leibowitz surveys the widely differing sex roles of nonhuman primates and argues that they do not support the theory that human sex roles are biologically determined. Sally Slocum criticizes the androcentrism of (mostly male) anthropologists who systematically ignore or underestimate the importance of the food-gathering activities of women in hunting-gathering societies. Kathleen Gough argues that pair bonding and a subsequent degree of male dominance were probably a result of the organized hunting activities of men, and the full-fledged sexual division of labor which these entailed.

The authors agree, however, that the status of women is generally higher in so-called primitive cultures, prior to the institution of private property and the state. Patricia Draper describes the contemprary !Kung woman's loss of status as a result of that tribe's recent abandonment of the traditional nomadic life of the bush for a settled existence. Ruby Rohrlich-Leavitt, Barbara

Sykes, and Elizabeth Weatherford argue for male bias in the accounts, by male anthropologists, of the supposedly dismal status of the native Australian woman. Elizabeth Faithorn shows that male anthropologists have misinterpreted Papuan concepts of pollution as applying only to women. Paula Webster reviews the matriarchy theory and concludes that it is still unproven, yet valuable as a feminist vision.

Particularly interesting is Gayle Rubin's essay on "The Traffic in Women." Rubin argues that the practice of exchanging women to establish ties between groups of men, which Levi-Strauss sees as the foundation of all kinship systems, was probably also the basis of male domination and the sex/gender system. Also included: Karen Sacks on Engels; Judith Brown on Iroquois women; Susan Harding on the function of women's "gossip" in a Spanish village; Anna Rubbo on the Colombian peasant woman; Dorothy Remy on Nigerian women; Norma Diamond on women in post-revolutionary China.

Woman, Culture and Society, edited by Michelle Zimbalist Rosaldo and Louise Lamphere (Stanford University Press, Stanford, California, 1974)

Sixteen articles by American women anthropologists, most of which were written especially for this anthology. Michelle Rosaldo argues—and indeed all of the articles illustrate—that women in all societies invariably have less socially sanctioned authority than men, and that this is especially true the more they are confined to the domestic role. Nancy Chodorow explains male dominance from a psychoanalytic perspective, as due to the fact that women raise children and are therefore more defined than men in terms of motherhood and other interpersonal relations. Sherry B. Ortner suggests that the key to the subordination of women is men's association of women with nature rather than culture. Other articles include Jane Fishburne Collier on women as political agents; Louise Lamphere on the relation between family structure and women's power strategies in domestic groups; Carol Stack on the survival strategies of urban black women; Nancy Tanner on matrifocal societies in Africa, Indonesia and among black Americans; Margery Wolf on Chinese women before the revolution; Peggy Sanday on economic determinants of female status; Karen Sacks on Engels' thesis that the superior power of the male in class society is a result of private property; Nancy Leis on women's political associations in Western Africa; Joan Bamberger on "The Myth of Matriarchy"; and others.

516

Women in Between: Female Roles in a Male World: Mount Hagen, New Guinea, by Marilyn Strathern (Seminar Press, London and New York, 1972)

The Hageners are a group of seventy related tribes, inhabitants of the highlands of eastern New Guinea. They are predominantly patrilinear and patrilocal, with land being communally owned by the men. They practice marriage by exchange; that is, women are exchanged as wives between groups of men. The social and economic bonds thus formed constitute the primary means of social organization above the village level. Women are "in between" groups of men, both as exchange brides and as mediators.

Strathern's description of Hagen life is one of the best available illustrations of the typically less-than-equal, yet not entirely subordinant position of women in many existing prestate societies. As such, it provides an interesting test case for many of the theories of the origin of male domination. For instance, Engels' theory, that it is through the *private* property of males that women are first subordinated, would seem to be unable to explain the degree of male dominance which exists among the Hageners. On the other hand, any theory which assumes that a very high degree of male supremacy has been a universal social trait (See, e.g., de Beauvior, Firestone, Goldberg.) will have difficulty accounting for the relatively high degree of independence and social influence enjoyed by Hagen women.

ANTHOLOGIES & SOURCEBOOKS II. ART AND LITERATURE

About Women: An Anthology of Contemporary Fiction, Poetry and Essays, edited by Stephen Berg and S.J. Marks (Fawcett Publications, Greenwich, Connecticut, 1973)

Includes poetry by Erica Jong, Sylvia Plath, Adrienne Rich, Muriel Rukeyser and Anne Sexton, and fiction by Joyce Carol Oates, Edna O'Brian and others. The essays include Bruno Bettelheim's "Growing Up Female," Eldridge Cleaver's "To All Black Women, From All Black Men," Erik Erikson's "Inner and

Outer Space," and pieces by Germaine Greer, Lillian Hellman, and Gloria Steinem.

Art and Sexual Politics: Women's Liberation, Women Artists, and Art History, edited by Thomas B. Hess and Elizabeth C. Baker (Collier Macmillan Publishers, London, and Collier Books, New York, 1973)

A collection of reactions to the question, "Why have there been no great women artists?" Linda Nochlin attacks the "golden nugget" theory of genius (i.e., that it is an inborn gift, rather than something which is developed in a context), and argues that it has been *"institutionally* impossible for women to achieve excellence or success on the same footing as men, *no matter what* their talent, or genius." (p.37) Lee Hall (an art professor at Drew University) speaks of the continuing bias in the academic world against both women and artists. Thomas Hess argues that gifted women had more opportunities in the Middle Ages than since the Renaissance; and Elizabeth Baker discusses prejudice against women artists in galleries, museums and art schools.

by a Woman writt: Literature from Six Centuries by and About Women, edited by Joan Goulianos (Penguin Books, Baltimore, 1973)

This is an excellent collection of writings by, for the most part, little-known women, many of whom are passionate feminists. The earliest piece is from the autobiography of Margery Kempe, a fourteenth-century Christian mystic who was torn between the obligations of a wife and mother and her religious calling. A very early and virtually unknown sixteenth-century feminist names Jane Auger (possibly a pseudonym) defends her sex against misogynist attacks. Margaret Cavendish, Dutchess of Newcastle (1623–1673), turns her considerable wit to observing the follies and "inferiorities" of her own sex. Also included: excerpts from the feminist poetry of Anne Finch (1661–1720); from the letters of Alphra Benn (1640–1689), who is known as the first woman to earn her living by the pen; from Mary Wollstonecrafts' ***Vindication of the Rights of Woman***; from the journal of Mary Shelley, Wollstonecraft's daughter; from the travelogues of Harriet Martineau; and, in the twentieth century, Olive Schriener, Dorothy Richardson, Anais Nin, Muriel Rukeyser and others.

The Experience of the American Woman: 30 Stories, edited by Barbara H. Solomon (Mentor, New York, 1978)

Stories about the lives of ordinary American women by nineteenth- and twentieth-century writers, half of them men. The authors include Mary Wilkins Freeman; Charlotte Perkins Gilman; Kate Chopin; Edith Wharton; Theodore Dreiser; Sherwood Anderson; Ernest Hemingway; William Faulkner; Katherine Ann Porter; John Steinbeck; William Carlos Williams; Dorothy Canfield; Jessamyn West; John Updike; Shirley Schoonover; Joyce Carol Oates; and others.

The Female Imagination, by Patricia Meyer Spacks (Avon Books, New York, 1972)

This is an examination of the work of selected women writers from the seventeenth to the twentieth century, aimed at uncovering common elements of the "female imagination," i.e., feminine modes of thought, feeling, representation and creation. The book parallels the progress of the course on women writers which Spacks teaches at Wellesley, and includes students' comments. Spacks and her students find that in all the women whose works they study there is a more or less controlled, yet inescapable anger at the limits which society imposes on them because they are women. At the same time there is always an insidious self-doubt, an insecurity about their own individual worth, which is also a result of their socially imposed limits. Women writers and their female protagonists deal with these feelings of anger and inadequacy in numerous and imaginative ways, some self-destructive, some leading to self-transcendence. But the anger and rebellion are always present as an undercurrent, reflecting the extent to which society has failed to speak to women's needs—needs which, "one feels after reading many of their books, are identical with men's."

A House of Good Proportion: Images of Women in Literature, edited by Michele Murray (Simon and Schuster, New York, 1973)

Portraits of women in the various stages of life, drawn from American, English, French and Russian fiction and poetry of the past two centuries. Includes pieces by Dorthea Rutherford, Louisa May Alcott, Samuel Richardson, Adrienne Rich, Emily Dickinson, Sarah Orne Jewett, Kate Chopin, Charlotte Bronte, Henry James, Leo Tolstoy, Anton Chekov, Tillie Olsen, Colette, Sylvia Plath, George Eliot, Charles Dickens, and others.

Images of Women in Literature, edited by Mary Anne Ferguson (Houghton Mifflin Company, Boston, 1977)

A good collection of stories, poems, and plays, mostly English and American. The pieces are selected to illustrate the classic stereotypes of woman: as the submissive or domineering wife, as a good or evil mother, as the inspirer of men, as sex object, as "old maid" and finally as the overt or covert rebel.

Literary Women: The Great Writers, by Ellen Moers (Anchor Press, Garden City, New York, 1977)

A compendium of information about women poets, novelists and other literary figures, especially those of the late eighteenth and nineteenth centuries. Moers approaches women writers with the question, What difference did it make to their work that they were women? She argues that there has never been a single feminine style in literature, in spite of the fact that there has always been *thought* to be such a style. There are, however, shared themes and concerns, and women writers have drawn inspiration from one another's work, resulting in shared metaphors and images running through the work of women writers. For instance there is a strong strain of practical realism in the work of women like Jane Austen, whose young women are continuously and intensely aware that their status and material security depend upon making a good marriage. On the other hand, women have been prominent in the Gothic genre and have produced works that deal symbolically with feminine experience; Mary Shelley's *Frankenstein*, for instance, she sees as a parable about birth.

Moers explains women's domination of the novel in the nineteenth century, especially in England, as the result of their having few other avenues for public expression, politics being entirely closed to them. The novel was a new genre, not yet solidified into male-defined patterns, and therefore women were able to adapt it to their needs. Women like Mary Wollstonecraft, George Sand, Madame de Stael, and Charlotte and Emily Bronte used fiction to protest women's condition and other social wrongs. On the other hand, not all women writers have been feminists; George Eliot clearly was not, and Virginia Woolf thought it fatal for a woman to write from an explicitly female point of view, a pronouncement which Moers considers incompatible with feminism. (And, one might add, with some of Woolf's practice.)

The New Women, edited by Joanne Cooke, Charlotte Bunch-Weeks, and Robin Morgan (Fawcett Publications, Greenwich, Connecticut, 1970)

A collection of contemporary feminist articles and poetry, originally published in the March-April 1969 issue of **Motive**. (**Motive** is published in Nashville by the Board of Education of the United Methodist Church.) Includes Francis Beal on being black and female; Del Martin and Phyllis Lyon on Lesbianism; and, most notably, Naomi Weisstein's "Kinder, Kuche, Kirche as Scientific Law: Psychology Constructs the Female," which is discussed under her name in the main part of this volume.

The Oven Birds: American Women on Womanhood 1820–1920, edited by Gail Parker (Anchor Books, Garden City, New York 1972)

Letters, stories and essays about American women by nine American women writers. The editor argues that the century from 1820 to 1920 was one in which women suffered from a diminished self-image, in part because of the demise of the Romantic and Sentimental literature in which (some) women had been depicted as heroines. The nine authors: Lydia Huntley Sigourney; Lydia Maria Child; Angelina Grimke; Catharine Beecher; Harriet Beecher Stowe; Sarah Orne Jewett; Elizabeth Cady Stanton; Jane Addams; and Charlotte Perkins Gilman.

Psyche: The Feminine Poetic Consciousness, An Anthology of Modern American Women Poets, edited by Barbara Segrity and Carol Rainey (Dell Publishing Company, New York, 1973)

Includes poetry by Emily Dickinson, Elinor Wylie, Marianne Moore, Anne Sexton, Adrienne Rich, Sylvia Plath, Margaret Atwood, Erica Jong, and others.

Revelations: Diaries of Women, edited by Mary Jane Moffat and Charlotte Painter (Vintage Books, New York, 1975)

Well-selected excerpts from the personal journals of nineteenth- and twentieth-century women, arranged around the themes of love, work, and power. The diarists include Sophie Tolstoy, George Sand, George Eliot, Virginia Woolf, Anais Nin, Florida Scott-Maxwell, Anne Frank, Gertrude Stein, and many others.

521

Rising Tides: 20th Century American Women Poets, edited by Laura Chester and Sharon Barba (Pocket Books, New York, 1973)

An extensive collection, including poetry by Gertrude Stein, Amy Lowell, Elinor Wylie, Marianne Moore, Edna St. Vincent Millay, Muriel Rukeyser, Anne Sexton, Adrienne Rich, Sylvia Plath, Erica Jong, and a great many others.

Through the Flower: My Struggle as a Woman Artist, by Judy Chicago, with an introduction by Anais Nin (Doubleday and Company, Garden City, New York 1975)

This is an autobiography by a contemporary woman artist who is known for her radiant abstracts, often with vaginal motifs. The history of women's struggles, past and present, to gain a place in the male world of art is sensitively discussed. Chicago dreams of a "truly feminine" style of art, which will enable us to "reach across the great gulf between masculine and feminine and gently, tenderly, but firmly close it." (p.206)

The Troublesome Helpmate: A History of Misogyny in Literature, by Katherine M. Rogers (University of Washington Press, Seattle and London, 1966)

A good overview of Western misogynist writings, from Genesis to the present century with its literary and psychoanalytic attacks on "Mom." Rogers suggests that the misogynist tenor of much of Western literature is explicable in part by the Oedipus Complex; the boy's first erotic object, his mother, rejects him in favor of his father, leaving him permanently resentful of all women. It is also, of course, a way of rationalizing patriarchy, the real motive for which—that it gratifies man's desire for power—is too selfish to be admitted by most male authors.

We Become New: Poems by Contemporary American Women, edited by Lucille Iverson and Kathryn Ruby (Bantam Books, New York, 1975)

Includes the work of 43 contemporary woman poets, e.g., Adrienne Rich, Rita Mae Brown, and Erica Jong; feminist radicals like Robin Morgan, Third World or black women; and many less well-known women, most of whose work is feminist in tone.

Women and Creativity, by Jocelynn Snyder Ott (Les Femmes Publishing, Millbrae, California, 1978)

Drawings and meditations by an artist who, like Judy Chicago, asserts the existence of a special kind of feminine imagery in the work of women artists. Ott suggests that Stonehenge is an example of such female imagery, and presents a series of exquisite graphite drawings based on this perception. She notes that, "the belittlement of women's contributions to the arts can no longer be tolerated." (p.11) The great women artists of the past (e.g. Angelica Kaufman, Elizabeth Vigee-Lebrun, Rosa Bonheur, Berthe Morisot) must be rediscovered, and their work must be rescued from the back rooms of museums and exhibited.

Women Artists: Recognition and Reappraisal, From the Early Middle Ages to the Twentieth Century, by Karen Peterson and J.J. Wilson (Harper Colophon, New York, 1976)

This is an excellent history of women's art—massively researched, richly illustrated (though unfortunately not in color) and beautifully printed.

A World of Her Own: Writers and the Feminist Controversy, edited by John N. Miller (Charles E. Merrill Publishing Company, Columbus, Ohio, 1971)

A selection of fiction, poetry and essays written in reaction to the feminist movement by nineteenth- and twentieth-century writers, both pro- and antifeminist. These include Nathaniel Hawthorne; John Stuart Mill; Henrik Ibsen; Karl Stern; Friedrich Engels; August Strindberg; Henry James; Leo Tolstoy; D.H. Lawrence; Virginia Woolf; Philip Wylie; Simone de Beauvoir; Alice Rossi; and Kate Millett.

ANTHOLOGIES & SOURCEBOOKS III. BIOLOGY AND MEDICAL/ SEXUAL ETHICS

Abortion and the Sanctity of Human Life, by Baruch Brody (MIT Press, Cambridge, Massachusetts, 1975)

Brody argues for a conservative position with respect to the moral and legal status of abortion. He holds that a human being begins to exist at the time when the fetal brain first begins to show signs of activity (at about six weeks after conception), and that to permit abortion for any reason at all after this time is morally wrong, except in the very rare circumstance in which *both* the woman and the fetus would otherwise certainly die. Brody does a good job of showing that *if* abortion is morally wrong (in some cases) then it ought to be prohibited by law (in those cases), but his argument for its wrongness not only exaggerates the rights of the (very small) fetus, but ignores those of the woman entirely.

Abortion: Law, Choice and Morality, by Daniel Callahan (The Macmillan Company, New York, 1970)

This book provides a clear and balanced coverage of the central medical, legal, social, moral, religious and philosophical aspects of the abortion issue. The material on the observable effects of, on the one hand, highly restrictive abortion laws (e.g. Mexico), and relatively "permissive" laws on the other (e.g. Japan, Eastern Europe and Scandanavia) is particularly valuable. Callahan defends essentially the same sort of compromise position on the legal status of abortion as was later—in 1973—taken by the United States Supreme Court, i.e. a compromise between the Roman Catholic position—which would make almost all abortion illegal—and what he calls the "abortion-on-demand" position. He would permit abortion on demand up to the twelfth week of pregnancy, but restrict it to special cases thereafter.

Contemporary Issues in Bioethics, edited by Tom L. Beauchamp and LeRoy Walters (Dickenson Publishing Company, Encino and

Belmont, California, 1978)

An excellent collection of contemporary articles on a broad range of topics in medical and bioethics. The section on abortion contains articles by both pro- and antiabortionist philosophers, who focus either on the humanity-personhood—or lack of it—of the fetus (e.g. John Noonan, Mary Anne Warren, and Baruch Brody) or on the case which can be made for abortion even on the assumption that a fetus *is* a human being with a right to life (Judith Jarvis Thomson and Jane English). Many of the issues dealt with in other sections, such as the rights of the patient to informed consent and to access to medical care regardless of economic status, and the rights of human subjects of medical experimentation, are also relevant to feminist concerns about the present American health-care system.

The Frontiers of Sex Research, edited by Vern Bullough (Prometheus Books, Buffalo, New York, 1979)

Recent articles by leading sex researchers on the physiology of sexual function, sex therapy, transsexual surgery, legal and psychiatric attitudes towards homosexuality, the development of sexual identity, and related topics.

Human Sexuality: Contemporary Perspectives, edited by Eleanor S. Morrison and Vera Borosage (National Press Books, Palo Alto, California, 1973)

A collection of contemporary writings on psychosexual development; the changing concepts of masculinity and femininity; heterosexual intercourse, inside and outside of marriage; homosexuality and lesbianism; abortion; and the regulation of pornography. Includes selections by Desmond Morris, Jo Freeman, Myron Brenton, Gloria Steinem, Simone de Beauvoir, Eldridge Cleaver, Rollo May, Albert Ellis, S.I. Hayakawa, and others.

Immaculate Deception: A New Look at Women and Childbirth in America, by Suzanne Arms (Houghton Mifflin Company, Boston, 1975)

This is probably the best of the many recent defenses of home birth; Arms makes a careful and quite devastating case against hospital birth in normal cases. The impersonality and coerciveness of hospitals; the overly interventionist tendencies of physicians; the overuse of drugs and instruments like the forceps; the separation of the mother and infant after birth; the mandatory supine position and routine episiotomy—all increase rather than decrease the danger of childbirth and argue for giving birth at home, with a midwife (unless of course there are special complications requiring hospitalization). Beautifully illustrated.

Mandatory Motherhood: The True Meaning of "Right to Life," by Garrett Hardin (Beacon Press, Boston, 1974)

This is a book which defends the right conclusion for incomplete reasons. Hardin gives several reasons for resisting the reinstitution of legal prohibition of abortion: overpopulation, the social unfitness of many unwanted children, the cost of supporting them on welfare, and the virtual impossibility of preventing illegal abortions. Such considerations carry decisive weight only when it has *already* been established that fetuses are not persons, are not human in the sense which implies having a full-fledged right to life. Hardin does claim that fetuses are not human in this sense, but he does not deal adequately with the various arguments to the contrary.

The Morality of Abortion: Legal and Historical Perspectives, edited by John T. Noonan, Jr. (Harvard University Press, Cambridge, Massachusetts, 1970)

This is a collection of papers by leading theorists of the anti-abortion position, all of whom are inspired by the Judeo-Christian tradition. John Noonan traces the history of opposition to abortion within the Catholic Church, from St. Augustine and Tertullian to the pronouncements of the second Vatican Council under Pope Paul VI (1965). Paul Ramsey argues against intervention in either the beginning or the end of human life; respect for life, he holds, not only rules out abortion and euthanasia, but also precludes the use of extraordinary measures to prolong the lives of severely defective fetuses or neonates or of the terminally ill.

Representing the Protestant viewpoint, James M. Gustafson suggests that a fuller consideration of the entire abortion situation—not just the doctor-patient relation—suggests at least a slightly wider range of permissible exceptions to the general prohibition of abortion than the Catholic position permits; for instance, he would allow a divorced woman with no visible means of support who was pregnant due to a vicious rape to have an abortion—though he might try to persuade her not to.

From a theological perspective, Bernard Haring questions various details of the official Catholic position, e.g. the doctrine that ensoulment occurs at the time of conception. George Huntston Williams argues for the concept of the "sacred condominium," i.e. a joint sovereignty between the state and the two parents over the life of the fetus; abortion would be permitted only in such special circumstances as rape, incest, adultery or a very badly deformed fetus. Legal theorist John M. Finnis argues that the strict legal prohibition of abortion in all cases where the woman's life is not endangered is the most efficient way to protect fetal life and to prevent the loss of respect for all human life which he fears would result if abortion were legally sanctioned in any way. David W. Louisell and John Noonan argue that English common law and the United States Constitution not only allow but require that fetuses be legally classified as persons and their lives protected.

Our Bodies, Ourselves; A Book By and For Women, by the Boston Women's Health Book Collective (Simon and Schuster, New York, 1971)

This is a groundbreaking feminist handbook of female physiology and self-care (though now outdated in a few respects). The book is a collective effort which grew out of a small discussion group in Boston in 1969, and it is one of the classic expressions of the feminist critique of the male-dominated American medical establishment. Contains basic medical, legal and other practical information about female sexual anatomy; sexual intercourse; homosexuality; nutrition; exercise; rape and self-defense; birth control; abortion; childbirth, at home and in the hospital; menopause; and women's treatment by and relationship to the American health-care establishment.

The Problem of Abortion, edited by Joel Feinberg (Wadsworth Publishing Company, Belmont, California 1973)

This collection includes some of the most important philosophical treatments of the problem of abortion, all of them recent, as well as excerpts from the United States Supreme Court decision in the case of *Roe* v.*Wade* and of a suit for wrongful death (*Williams* v. *State of New York*). On the antiabortion side, John Noonan claims that a human conceptus is a human being from the time of conception, while Baruch Brody considers that it becomes human as soon as it possesses an active brain—at about six weeks. Both consider abortion after that point to be a form of murder, and think it should be prohibited by law.

On the prochoice side, Judith Thomson argues that abortion is morally permissible regardless of whether or not a fetus is a human being, since its mother is under no obligation to perform the act of (extremely) good Samaritanship necessary to sustain its life. Michael Tooley, on the other hand, argues that it is demonstrably false that a fetus is human in the sense of having a full-fledged right to life. Marvin Kohl uses linguistic analysis to support the same conclusion. Roger Wertheimer argues that either positon—that a fetus is human or that it is not—is ultimately subjective, that is, unverifiable and perhaps meaningless. Daniel Callahan argues that whatever its moral status, abortion does not fall within the proper sphere of government regulation, and should be left to private conscience. And, finally, S.I. Benn suggests some pragmatic reasons for prohibiting infanticide, though not abortion.

The Right to Abortion: A Psychiatric View, by the Group for the Advancement of Psychiatry's Committee on Psychiatry and Law (Charles Scribner's Sons, New York, 1970)

This is a brief statement of the pragmatic grounds for allowing women freedom of choice with respect to abortion. Overpopulation, the unhappiness of unwanted children, the dangers of illegal abortions, and the destruction of women's lives by compulsory motherhood are given as the main reasons for the reform or elimination of restrictive abortion statutes. (This, of course, was before the 1973 Supreme Court decision in *Roe* v. *Wade*.) The moral issues are said to be a matter of religion and private conscience and hence not a fit subject for social policy. The problem with this approach, clearly enough, is that if abortion is or were murder then it ought to be prohibited *regardless* of overpopulation and the other ill effects of such prohibition. Hence the legal argument cannot be divorced from the moral one in this case.

The Rights and Wrongs of Abortion: A Philosophy and Public Affairs Reader, edited by Marshall Cohen, Thomas Nagel, and Thomas Scanlon (Princeton University Press, Princeton, New Jersey, 1974)

This is a set of articles on the moral status of abortion which originally appeared in *Philosophy and Public Affairs* between

1971 and 1973. Of these, the most important is Judith Thomson's "A Defense of Abortion," in which she argues that even if we assume that a fetus is a human being with a full-fledged right to life, it does not necessarily follow that abortion is wrong, at least in all cases. For the fetus' right to life does not give it an automatic right to whatever may be required to keep it alive, e.g. the continued use of its mother's body. She draws a now-famous analogy between an unwanted pregnancy and the situation of someone who is kidnapped and hooked up through a kidney-connector to an ailing violinist, who will die if he is not permitted the use of the other person's kidneys for nine months. No one would call the kidnap victim a murderer if he or she refused to spend nine bedridden months linked to the violinist in order to save the latter's life; similarly, abortion should be viewed not as murder but as the refusal to be a Very Good Samaritan towards the fetus. Completing an unwanted pregnancy, then, may be morally praiseworthy, but it is not morally mandatory (1).

The remaining articles are by Roger Wertheimer, Michael Tooley and John Finnis. Wertheimer argues that the issue between the pro- and antiabortion forces cannot be resolved by rational means, since it turns not on any disagreement over *facts*, but on a difference in the *attitude* taken towards the fetus. Tooley argues that, on the contrary, the issue can be settled by an analysis of the concept of personhood. He defines a person as a being which has a concept of itself as an ongoing subject of conscious experiences. Neither fetuses nor newly born infants fit this definition; hence they are not persons, and killing them cannot be an act of murder—though in the case of neonates there are independent reasons why they should not be killed. And, finally, Finnis criticizes Thomson's argument on the grounds that abortion is unlike refusing to be a Good Samaritan because abortion involves direct killing while the other is only indirect. Thomson replies that this begs the question, and that the distinction between direct and indirect killing will not bear this much weight.

1. For a critique of this argument see Mary Anne Warren, "On the Moral and Legal Status of Abortion" (1973), reprinted in e.g. **Today's Moral Problems**, edited by Richard Wasserstrom, and **Social Ethics**, edited by Thomas A. Mappes and Jane S. Zembaty.

ANTHOLOGIES & SOURCEBOOKS III.

Seizing Our Bodies: The Politics of Women's Health, edited by Claudia Dreifus (Vintage Books, New York, 1978)
A collection of articles by contemporary "health feminists" on the male-dominated history and present practice of modern gynecology, and the problems for women that arise from male control of the health-care system in general. (A successor to *Our Bodies, Ourselves*.) Some noteworthy inclusions: G.J. Barker-Benfield on the horrendous story of gynecological surgery (e.g. clitoridectomy and female castration) in the nineteenth century; Barbara Seaman on the dangers of the oral contraceptive, of estrogen replacement therapy for menopausal women, and of other medical uses of sex hormones; Mark Dowie and Tracy Johnson on the scandal of the Dalkon Shield (an intrauterine contraceptive device which killed an unknown number of women); Claudia Dreifus on the involuntary sterilization of poor women; Rita Arditti on why there is no male pill, and little research on contraceptives for men; Deborah Larned on the "epidemic" of unnecessary hysterectomies in the United States; Kay Weiss on sexism in gynecology texts; and Ellen Frankfort's doubts about the safety of some of the medical self-help methods (e.g. menstrual extraction) developed by the women's health movement.

Sex and Human Relationships, edited by Cecil E. Johnson (Charles E. Merrill Publishing Company, Columbus, Ohio, 1970)
Popular essays on sex and sexual relationships as they currently exist. Includes Maragret Mead on the permanence of marriage; Albert Ellis on the game of romantic love; Lawrence Lipton on sex on campus; Garrett Hardin in defense of the right to abortion; William Masters and Virginia Johnson on the function of the clitoris; Frank Caprio on male impotence; Marie Robinson on the joys of "sexual surrender"; Milton Sapirstein's attack on the mechanical approach to sex taken by marriage manuals; James McCary on "Sexual Attitudes and Sexual Behavior"; and Allan Fromm's "Towards a Better Sexual Orientation."

Social Ethics: Morality and Social Policy, edited by Thomas A. Mappes and Jane S. Zembaty (McGraw-Hill, New York, 1977)
This is a good collection of articles, mostly by contemporary philosophers, on the topics of abortion, euthanasia, capital punishment, sexual equality, (so-called) reverse discrimination, sex-

ual behavior (homo- and heterosexuality), pornography and censorship, violence, economic justice, ecology and population control. The section on abortion contains the majority and dissenting opinions in *Roe* v. *Wade* (the 1973 Supreme Court decision which legalized abortion in the first trimester), and articles by John Noonan, Mary Anne Warren and Daniel Callahan. On sexual equality, there is an excerpt from John Stuart Mill's *The Subjection of Women* and Steven Goldberg's *The Inevitability of Patriarchy*, and articles by Kate Millett, Joyce Treblicot, J.R. Lucas, and Susan Haack. Sidney Hook and Lisa Newton argue against "reverse discrimination" (less pejoratively known as "affirmative action"), and Tom L. Beauchamp argues in favor of it.

Under sexual integrity, there are Richard Taylor and Peter Bertocci on love and sex; Albert Ellis on sex without love; and John Wilson and Burton M. Leiser on homosexuality. And, finally, on the issue of pornography there are articles by John Stuart Mill, Burton M. Leiser, G.L. Simons, Edward J. Mishan, and Joel Feinberg.

Today's Moral Problems, edited by Richard Wasserstrom (Macmillan Publishing Company, New York, 1975)

This is a collection of articles by contemporary philosophers on such current moral issues as privacy, abortion, racism and sexism, sexual morality, civil disobedience, war, and pacifism. The abortion section includes Germain Grisez (arguing that abortion is wrong because a fetus is a human being), Judith Jarvis Thomson (defending abortion as at least sometimes permissible regardless of the fetus' humanity), and Mary Anne Warren (arguing that the fetus is not *morally* human). Other articles of relevance to the women's movement: Thomas E. Hill, Jr., "Servility and Self-Respect"; Robert Baker, ""Pricks" and "Chicks": A Plea for "Persons"" (an analysis of sexist language which is both funny and enlightening); Sharon Hill, "Self-Determination and Autonomy"; Lisa Newton, "Reverse Discrimination as Unjustified"; Bernard Boxill, "The Morality of Reparation"; Richard Wasserstrom, "Is Adultery Immoral?" and Ronald Atkinson, "The Morality of Homosexual Behavior."

Vaginal Politics, by Ellen Frankfort, (Bantam Books, New York, 1972)

This is an indictment of the American medical profession's

insensitivity towards and exploitation of women patients. The inflated price and grotesque profiteering from abortion (especially in New York during the late 60s and early 70s); the over-pricing of drugs and the continued use of drugs (such as DES) known to be dangerous; the failure to push for the development of a male contraceptive, or even a safe and effective contraceptive for women; the paternalistic attitude that leads physicians to deny patients the information they need to make rational decisions; the eagerness of some surgeons to perform unnecessary hysterectomies and their continued preference for radical mastectomy in the face of considerable evidence that it is little or no more effective than e.g. simple mastectomy; the inferior care available to poor patients and their exploitation as guinea pigs; and the general mystification, depersonalization and commercialization of American medicine all come under fire.

To counteract these abuses, Frankfort endorses self-help groups in which women can educate one another about health-care techniques, self-examination, the treatment of various ailments, the names of doctors who do or do not appear reasonably competent and humane, and about what to expect from a doctor and how to deal with doctors. If women are to have control over their own bodies they must do all they can to assume the responsibility for their own health care. (Frankfort does, however, express a healthy skepticism about do-it-yourself menstrual extraction, a current interest of some New York women's groups at the time the book was written.)

Witches, Midwives and Nurses: A History of Women Healers, by Barbara Ehrenreich and Deirdre English (The Feminist Press, Old Westbury, New York, 1973)

This is a small but important pamphlet which uncovers some of the long-suppressed history of women lay healers, from the Middle Ages to the present. The authors argue that many of the women who were tortured and killed in Europe during the witch-hunting era (fourteenth to seventeenth centuries) were actually medical practitioners; midwives were particularly abhorred by the Catholic Church and by the witch hunters. The organized (male) medical profession joined with the Church and the state in denigrating and eventually eliminating most female healers. It was in this context that the nursing profession arose, to fill a strictly subordinate role of helper to the male physician.

Women, Body and Culture: Essays on the Sexuality of Women in a Changing Society, edited by Signe Hammer (Harper and Row, New York, 1975)

This is a collection of essays from a range of disciplines—but especially psychoanalysis—that bear on such issues as mechanisms of psychosexual differentiation in the female child; female homosexuality; clitoral eroticism; the causes of "frigidity" in women; and the psychological effect of menstruation, pregnancy, childbirth, menopause, and various childrearing practices. Includes work by Karen Horney, John Money, Masters and Johnson, Ruth Moulton, Clara Thompson, Helene Deutsch, Margaret Mead, and others.

Woman's Body: An Owner's Manual, by the Diagram Group (Bantam Books, New York, 1977)

A lavishly diagrammed primer containing basic information, medical, sexual and anatomical, about the female body. No overt political slant.

ANTHOLOGIES & SOURCEBOOKS IV. CONTEMPORARY FEMINISM

The Black Woman: An Anthology, by Toni Cade (New American Library, New York, 1970)

Writings by contemporary American black women, focusing on their oppression as blacks and as women, both by the WASP capitalist society and by supposedly revolutionary black men who believe that a women's place should be "ten steps behind" her man. Many of the authors attack the myth of the black matriarch, e.g., as presented by Danial Patrick Moynihan. Others (see especially the two articles by Pat Robinson) link the black woman's so-called matriarchal role in the American black family with the egalitarian traditions of the agrarian villiages of Africa. All agree that black women must walk beside black men, not behind them, if real revolution is to occur.

Class and Feminism, edited by Charlotte Bunch and Nancy Myron (Diana Press, Baltimore, 1974)

Six essays from the Furies, a radical feminist collective, on the ways in which middle-class women oppress and offend working-class women with their classist attitudes and behavior.

Dreamers and Dealers: An Intimate Appraisal of the Women's Movement, by Leah Fritz (Beacon Press, Boston 1979)

Personal observations about the politics and personalities of the women's movement, particularly in New York, over the past decade. Fritz points to the danger of media- or government-appointed women "leaders," to the sabotage of feminist goals by (mostly) male leftists, and to the divisiveness of lesbian separatists who make lesbianism a necessary condition for true feminism (see e.g. Atkinson). She also presents an analysis of the impact of the movement upon women in different economic categories. All women, she says, belong to the class of slaves, though within that class their economic status varies widely. The destitute poor long for the family security which feminists reject; the "respectable poor" also need that economic security and thus are targets for right-wing puppet women like Mirable Morgan and Phyllis Schafley; educated poor women are the ones most apt to become feminists. Middle-class women function as overseers of other slaves (children, household workers, and lower-level employees). Rich women, of whom there are very few, often become Marxists or liberals without becoming aware of their own oppression as women.

Essays in Feminism, by Vivian Gornick (Harper and Row, New York, 1978)

Essays on women and the women's movement, written between 1969 and 1978. Includes reviews and criticism of women novelists and of the treatment of women by male writers; biographical sketches of women like Margaret Fuller, Dorothy Thompson (the great journalist, who was married to Sinclair Lewis), Alice Paul, and Matina Horner; and political analysis and commentary. Gornick has consistently warned women against adopting rigid "party lines," e.g. that only lesbians are true feminists or that liberals and reformers are the enemy of the movement rather than (sometimes) its allies.

CONTEMPORARY FEMINISM

The First Ms. Reader, edited by Francine Klagsbrun (Warner Paperback Library, New York, 1973)

This is a set of pieces from the first year of **Ms.** magazine's publication. Includes, among other, Gloria Steinem on sisterhood; Judy Syfers' "I want a Wife"; Vivian Gornick on "Why Women Fear Success"; Cellestine Ware on "The Black Family and Feminism"; Daniel Ellsberg on "Women and War"; Erica Jong on "The Artist as a Housewife"; Del Martin and Phyllis Lyon on lesbian love; and Angela Davis on "The Myth of the Black Matriarch."

Liberation Now! Writings from the Women's Liberation Movement, edited by Deborah Babcox and Madeline Belkin (Dell Publishing Company, New York, 1971)

This collection includes many now-classic pieces, most of them from the contemporary women's movement, but with a few earlier writers as well. Among the authors are Marlene Dixon; Vivian Gornick; Sally Kempton; Gloria Steinem; the Redstockings (a New York radical feminist group); Deborah Babcox on child liberation; Charlotte Perkins Gilman; Rose Gladstone on the "planned obsolescence" of the middle-aged woman; Jane Harriman on being "In Trouble"; Francis Beal's "Double Jeopardy"; Elizabeth Sutherland on "The Chicana"; Margaret Mead; Simone de Beauvior; Eve Merriam on "Sex and Semantics"; Virginia Woolf; Juliet Mitchell; Naomi Weisstein's "Psychology Constructs the Female"; the Radicalesbians on "The Woman-Identified Woman"; Florence Howe on women's education; Anne Koedt's "The Myth of the Vaginal Orgasm"; Alice Wolfson's critique of the male-dominated health-care system; and Sonya Okoth, Charlotte Bunch-Weeks, and Chris Camarano, on African, Asian and Cuban women, respectively.

Mother Was Not a Person, edited by Margret Andersen (Black Rose Books, Montreal, Canada, 1972)

Feminist poems and essays by Canadian women. Includes Marlene Dixon's critique of the feminist movement as middle class and reactionary; Christine Garside's "Women and Persons," and some forty other pieces.

New Feminist Scholarship: A Guide to Bibliographies, by Jane Williamson (The Feminist Press, Old Westbury, New York,

1979)

An annotated biblio-bibliography which lists recent bibliographies on every aspect of women's lives, women's history, and other areas of women's studies.

On Being Female, edited by Barbara Stanford, (Pocket Books, New York, 1974)

An illustrated collection of short popular pieces (for the most part), some fictional, dealing with women's condition today and their efforts to change it. Includes Vivian Gornick on "Why Women Fear Success" (an interview with Matina Horner, who made this thesis so well known as to be come a cliche); Sharon Smith on "The Image of Women in Film"; Jeannie Sakol on "The Case for Spinsterhood"; excerpts from (then) Congresswoman Bella Abzug's diary; Joan Baez on going to jail for peace; Carolyn Bird on successful women (who require supportive husbands); Ellen Peck on the pragmatic case against motherhood; and many others. Also includes a large number of brief vignettes by the editor on women who are succeeding in stereotypically male-dominated professions.

The Politics of Women's Liberation, by Jo Freeman (David McKay Company, New York, 1975)

An excellent analysis of the underlying causes and political evolution of the contemporary women's movement. Freeman argues that the reason that middle-class women have been the leaders of this movement is that they are the ones who have suffered most from "relative deprivation," i.e. from the fact that society has provided them fewer opportunities and rewards than they had learned to expect, and fewer than it has provided middle-class men, the group with which middle-class women tend to compare themselves. This condition of frustration, she says, has existed at least since the end of the Second World War, when women were largely pushed out of their new wartime jobs to make room for the returning men.

What was needed in addition to this felt frustration, Freeman says, was a national communications network linking women of like mind. In the sixties, this was provided on the one hand by the organizations of the radical left and on the other by "reformist" women's groups like NOW (the National Organization of Women), WEAL (Women's Equity Action League), FEW (Federally Employed Women), the NWPC (National Women's Political

Caucus), and the federal and state Commissions on the Status of Women. Together, these groups provided dissatisfied women with a degree of political effectiveness which had been lacking since the passage of the Nineteenth Amendment, and which Freeman credits with bringing about important anti-sex-discrimination legislation of the sixties and seventies.

Radical Feminism, edited by Anne Koedt, Ellen Levine, and Anita Rapone (Quadrangle/The New York Times Book Company, New York, 1973)

Writings from the radical wing of the contemporary women's movement. Noteworthy entries include: Judith Hole and Ellen Levine on nineteenth-century American feminism; "The Bitch Manifesto", by Joreen; Judy Syfers' "Why I want a Wife"; Susan Brownmiller on prostitution; Cellestine Ware on "Black Feminism"; Dana Densmore on exploitative aspects of the "sexual revolution"; Lucinda Cisler on the subversion of abortion law reforms; Pauli Murray and Mary Eastwood on the significance of Title VII of the Civil Rights Act of 1964 (the sex discrimination prohibition); Naomi Weisstein's "Psychology Constructs the Female"; Anne Koedt's "The Myth of the Vaginal Orgasm"; Barbara Mehrhof and Pamela Kearon's "Rape: An Act of Terror"; the Radicalesbians on "The Woman-Identified Woman"; Mary Daly on "The Spiritual Dimension of Feminism"; Kate Millett's "Manifesto for Revolution"; Barbara Burris' "Fourth World Manifesto"; and Elaine Showalter on "Women Writers and the Female Experience."

Rape: The First Sourcebook for Women, by the New York Radical Feminists, edited by Noreen Connell and Cassandra Wilson (New American Library, New York, 1974)

Articles and interviews dealing with the feminist analysis of rape, the formation of consciousness-raising and anti-rape groups, and the necessary legal reforms, modes of self-defense, and other aspects of rape. The contributors include Florence Rush, on "The Sexual Abuse of Children"; Phyllis Chandler on the rape of women patients by psychotherapists; Lynne Farrow, on the depiction of rape in popular films and fiction; and many others.

Rebirth of Feminism, by Judith Hole and Ellen Levine (Quadrangle Books, New York, 1973)

This is a study of the resurgence of American Feminism during the 1960s and early 70s. Levine and Hole review the rise and fall of radical feminism in the nineteenth century; the legal foundations for equality established in the past two decades (e.g. Congressional passage of the ERA, the 1964 Civil Rights Act, and Executive Orders 11375 and 11246, the origin of "affirmative action" as a government policy); the national women's organizations that have led the struggle for legal reform (e.g. NOW, WEAL and FEW—Federally Employed Women); and the emergence of more radical feminist groups (e.g. WITCH—The Women's International Conspiracy from Hell, the Redstockings, the New York Radical Women, the Feminists). They discuss the ideology of biological determinism (the notion that traditional sex roles are necessitated by the biological differences between the sexes), and the feminist critique of it; the (still) current backlash against the women's movement; and the key areas of society that need reform: the media, abortion laws, child care, education, the professions, and the churches.

Roles Women Play: Readings Toward Women's Liberation, edited by Michelle Hoffnung Garskof (Brooks/Cole Publishing Company, Belmont, California, 1971)

Articles by contemporary American feminists. Includes Caroline Bird on sex discrimination in the work place; Susan Tydon on "The Politics of Orgasm"; Naomi Weisstein's "Psychology Constructs the Female"; Matina S. Horner on the fear of success, Sandra and Daryl Bem on sexist ideology; Alice Rossi's "Equality Between the Sexes"; and others.

Sex and Caste in America, by Carol Andreas (Prentice Hall, Englewood Cliffs, New Jersey, 1971)

A sociologically oriented introduction to feminist thought. Andreas summarizes the evidence that sex roles are culturally determined and describes the roles of the education system, religions, the family and the capitalist economic structure in enforcing sex roles in the United States. In the economic world as elsewhere, a caste-like system operates, wtih women providing a supply of inexpensive and expendable labor. The sexual caste system dehumanizes both sexes, and must be replaced by an "androgynous or non-sexist" society. The last chapter provides an excellent capsule history of the feminist struggle in the United States, beginning with the American Revolution.

Sisterhood is Powerful: An Anthology of Writings from the Women's Liberation Movement, edited by Robin Morgan (Vintage Books, New York, 1970)

This is an important early anthology of writings—mostly popular but some academic—from the current American feminist movement. A few noteworthy entries: Joreen (a pseudonym of Jo Freeman) on "The 51 Percent Minority Group"; Mary Daly on "Women and the Catholic Church"; Naomi Weisstein's "Psychology Constructs the Female"; Mary Jane Sherfey on female sexuality; Martha Shelley on radical lesbianism; Kate Millett on sexism in the work of Henry Miller and Norman Mailer; Frances Beal on being black and female; Florence Kennedy on "Institutionalized Oppression"; and Roxanne Dunbar on "Female Liberation as the Basis for Social Revolution."

Up Against the Wall, Mother, edited by Elsie Adams and Mary Louise Briscoe (Glencoe Press, Beverly Hills, California, 1971)

Introductory readings, organized around different stereotypical images of women—e.g. the Judeo-Christian image, the psychoanalytic image, the paranoid misogynist image, the image of the eternal feminine—and feminist responses to these stereotypes. Includes Greek, Elizabethan and modern poetry; fiction by Sinclair Lewis, Henrik Ibsen, Bernard Shaw, Doris Lessing and others; excerpts from John Stuart Mill and Friedrich Engels; and pieces by contemporary feminists such as Betty Friedan, Carolyn Bird, Valerie Solanas, Dana Densmore, Naomi Weisstein, and Matina Horner.

Voices from Women's Liberation, edited by Leslie B. Tanner (New American Library, New York, 1971)

A good collection of historical and contemporary feminist statements. The voices from the past include Abigail Adams, Frances Wright, Mary Wollstonecraft, Sarah and Angelina Grimke, Elizabeth Cady Stanton, Susan B. Anthony, Elizabeth Blackwell and Lucretia Mott. The contemporary material includes the Redstockings Manifesto; Anne Koedt's "The Myth of the Vaginal Orgasm"; Evelyn Reed on "The Myth of Women's Inferiority"; Carol Driscoll's "The Abortion Problem"; Betsy

Warrior on "Sex Roles and Their Consequences"; Dana Densmore "On Celibacy"; Robin Morgan's "Goodbye to All That"; Margaret Benston on "The Political Economy of Women's Liberation"; Naomi Weisstein's "Woman as Nigger"; and a great many others.

Voices of the New Feminism, edited by Mary Lou Thompson (Beacon Press, Boston, 1971)

Articles from the contemporary women's movement. Includes Joyce Cowley on the "Pioneers of Women's Liberation"; Betty Freidan on the feminist revolution, Roxanne Dunbar on "Female Liberation as the Basis for Social Revolution"; Alice S. Rossi on the concept of sexual equality; Elizabeth Koontz on "Woman as a Minority Group"; Pauli Murray on "The Liberation of Black Women"; Mary Daly on women and the Catholic Church; Caroline Bird on androgyny; Shirley Chisolm's "Women must Rebel"; Lucinda Cioleu's "Women: A Bibliography"; and others.

Women: A Feminist Perspective, edited by Jo Freeman (Mayfield Publishing Company, Palo Alto, California, 1975)

A wide range of recent articles by sociologists, psychologists, anthropologists and others, on various aspects of the oppression of women. A few noteworthy examples: Linda Phelps' "Female Sexual Alienation"; Susan Griffin on rape; Kathleen Gough on "The Origin of the Family"; Dair Gillespie, on the relative power of the sexes in marriage; Inge Bell on the double standard of age; Pamela Roby's "Structural and Internal Barriers to Women in Higher Education"; Martha White on obstacles to women in science; Shirley Bernard's attack on the myth that women control most of the wealth of the United States (see Philip Wylie); Mary Nelson's "Why Witches Were Women"; Phyllis Chesler's comparison between "Marriage and Psychotherapy"; and Helen Hacker on "Women as a Minority Group."

Woman in Sexist Society: Studies in Power and Powerlessness, edited by Vivian Gornick and Barbara K. Moran (New American Library, New York, 1971)

This is an especially good collection of feminist writings, most of them from the late 1960s, and including scientific, literary, historical and popular essays. Contributions include two feminist plays by Myrna Lamb; Kate Millet's interviews with four prostitutes; Vivian Gornick on "Woman as Outsider"; Jessie Bernard on why housewives claim to be happy when, typically they are not; Pauline Bart on the causes of depression in middle-aged women; Una Stannard on stereotypes of female beauty; Naomi Weisstein's "Psychology Constructs the Female"; Judith Bardwick and Elizabeth Douvan on "The Socialization of Woman"; Christine Pierce on the logic of natural law language as applied to women; Nancy Chodorow on the cross-cultural variations in sex roles; Alix Shulman on myths surrounding the female orgasm; Ethel Strainchams on sexism in the American English language; Phyllis Chesler on the role of psychotherapy in defusing feminine dissatisfaction; Cynthia Ozick on "Women and Creativity"; Elaine Showalter on "Women Writers and the Double Standard"; Linda Nochlin on women artists; Sidney Abbott and Barbara Love on the relation between lesbianism and feminism; Catherine Stimpson on the rift between the women's liberation and black civil rights movements; and Shulamith Firestone on the political evolution of American feminism (a chapter from *The Dialectic of Sex*).

Women in a Changing World, edited by Uta West (McGraw-Hill, New York, 1975)

Essays, fiction and poetry by prominent contemporary writers who are taking stock of feminism, now that the first exhilaration of its reemergence in the 1960s has passed. Includes pieces by Elizabeth Janeway; Doris Lessing; Barbara Harrison; Michael Weiss' "Diary of a Mad Househusband"; Jane Lazarre on "What Feminists and Freudians Can learn From Each Other"; Anais Nin's, "In Favor of the Sensitive Man"; Louis Gould on "Pornography for Women"; Caryl Rivers on "The New Anxiety of Motherhood"; Mary Daly's "God is a Verb"; and others.

The Women's Movement: Political, Socioeconomic and Psychological Issues, by Barbard Deckard (Harper and Row, New York, 1975)

This is a good overall summary of the social, historical, and ideological background of the feminist movement, and its present issues, methods, goals and the political divisions within it, not only in this country but around the world.

Women's Liberation edited by Michael E. Adelstein and Jean G. Pival (St. Martin's Press, New York, 1972)

Mostly articles by contemporary popular writers, both feminist and antifeminist. Includes pieces by Betty Friedan, Caroline Bird, Germaine Greer, Ashley Montagu, Betty Rollin, Gloria Steinem, Margaret Mead, Lionel Tiger, and others.

ANTHOLOGIES & SOURCEBOOKS V. EDUCATION AND THE MEDIA

Academic Women on the Move, edited by Alice S. Rossi and Ann Calderwood (Russell Sage Foundation, New York, 1973)

An excellent set of commissioned articles on all aspects of women's role and status in the academy, and current efforts to improve them. Includes Jo Freeman, on the historical background of the women's movement; Pamela Roby, on "Institutional Barriers to Women Students in Higher Education"; Pepper Schwartz and Janet Lever on the problems faced by women students during the first year that Yale admitted women undergraduates (1969–70); Michelle Patterson and Lucy Sells, on "Women Dropouts from Higher Education"; Jean W. Campbell on new programs for returning women students; Helen S. Astin, on "Career Profiles of Women Doctorates"; Patricia A. Graham on the problems of status transition which women face in becoming graduate students; Constance M. Carroll, on the neglect of black women in higher education; Myrna M. Weisman *et al* on "The Faculty Wife"; Lora H. Robinson on "Institutional Variation in the Status of Academic Women"; Laura Morlock on the varying rates of underutilization of women in different academic disciplines; an important study by Helen Astin and Alan E. Bayer which shows that sex is a better predictor of academic rank and salary than the Ph.D., number of years of experience, or number of publications; Kay Klotzburger on (then-) recently formed academic women's political action groups; Florence Howe and Carol Ahlun on women's studies programs; Berenice Sandler on "WEAL and Contract Compliance"; Lenore J. Weitzman on "Affirmative Action Plans for Eliminating Sex Discrimination in Academe"; and others.

And Jill Came Tumbling After: Sexism in American Education, edited by Judith Stacey, Susan Bereaud, and Joan Daniels (Dell Publishing Company, New York, 1974)

Over forty articles—mostly contemporary, both popular and academic—on the ways in which sex-role stereotyping is reinforced by the American school system, from nursery to graduate school. Some noteworthy contributions: Anna Garlin Spencer on why there are no women geniuses; Philip Goldberg's research on women's bias against women; Matina S. Horner on women's fear of success; Ruth Hartley on "Sex Role Pressures and the Socialization of the Male Child"; Richard Rothstein on how tracking works to reinforce both racial and sexual hierarchy; Ann Sutherland Harris on "The Second Sex in Academe"; Mary Ellman and Alice Rossi (separately) on discrimination against women in the academic world; and Marilyn Webb on feminist studies.

From Reverence to Rape: The Treatment of Women in the Movies, by Molly Haskell (Penguin Books, Baltimore, Maryland, 1974)

Haskell examines the images and roles of women in the Hollywood and European film industries, from the silent era to the early 1970s. She argues that although women's roles have always been limited and stereotyped relative to those of male actors, they have become more so during the decade before she wrote. This shift, she thinks, is part of the male backlash against women's liberation; "The closer women come to claiming their rights and achieving independence in real life, the more loudly and stridently films tell us it's a man's world." (p.363)

Hearth and Home: Images of Women in the Mass Media, edited by Gaye Ruckman, Arlene Kaplan Daniels, and James Benet (Oxford University Press, New York, 1978)

Fourteen papers dealing with various aspects of the treatment of women in television programming, women's magazines, and women's sections of newspapers. The contributors include sociologists, psychologists and educators.

Sexism and Language, by Aileen Pace Nilsen, Haig Bosmajian, H. Lee Gershuny, and Julia P. Stanley (National Council of Teachers of English, Urbana, Illinois, 1977)

This book demonstrates, with abundant and well-selected examples, the linguistic sexism which is evident in the very grammar and semantics of English. Separate chapters deal with sexist usages in the journalistic media, in school textbooks, dictionaries, the language of the law, and the language of literature, and a counterattack is made against those who defend sexist language in the name of linguistic purity. It also includes the "NCTE Guidelines for Nonsexist Use of Language," in which the suggested changes are neither cumbersome or ungrammatical, nor so radical as to call undue attention to themselves.

Unlearning the Lie: Sexism in School, by Barbara Grizzuti Harrison (William Morrow and Company, New York, 1974)

An account of how some of the mothers of girls enrolled in Woodward School (a private, nonsectarian elementary school in Brooklyn organized a "Sex-Roles Committee" to attack sex-role stereotyping in the school's curriculum and the teachers' behavior.

Women and the Power to Change, edited by Florence Howe (McGraw-Hill Book Company, New York, 1975; volume sponsored by the Carnegie Commission on Higher Education)

Here, four academic women describe their struggle with a system of higher education whose rules were designed not for them, but for "the traditional man and his traditional wife." Each suggests ways of making the university more "women-centered." Adrienne Rich foresees a feminist renaissance which will revolutionize both curriculum and teaching styles. Arlie Russell Hochschild points out that the established academic career pattern, and the use of age-based criteria of academic merit, discriminate against women—especially if they marry or have children; she envisions a less fiercely competitive academic world in which both men and women could successfully combine parenting and careers. Aleta Wallace writes of the continuing androcentrism of law schools and the legal profession, and argues that equal educational opportunity for women requires all-woman or woman-controlled professional schools. Florence Howe emphasizes the need for women to develop firm bases of power, and suggests that at least during this period in which universities are no longer expanding rapidly (if at all), it would be better for women to concentrate their efforts in the female-typed fields where there are already many women than to be spread thin among the heavily male-dominated fields.

Women in Higher Education, edited by W. Todd Furniss and Patricia A. Graham (American Council on Education, Washington, D.C., 1974)

A collection of papers prepared for the American Council on Education's 1972 Annual Meeting, which, the editors suggest, illustrate the current transition from the ideology of social change to the practical technology for bringing it about. Contributors include Patricia Robert Harris, on institutionalized sexism in the universities; Patricia Cross on the social barriers faced by the woman student; Joan I. Roberts on the sexism of male academics; Juanita M. Kreps on "The Woman Professional in Higher Education"; Heather Sigworth on the discriminatory consequences of nepotism rules; Jacquelyn A. Mattfeld on the scarcity of women administrators; Sheila Tobias and Maragaret L. Rumbarger on the need to improve the status of part-time faculty; McGeorge Bundy, who uses John Rawls' concept of justice as fairness to support women's demand for equality; Catharine R. Stimpson, on the conflict between feminism and the black movement; Leo Kanowitz on "Some Legal Aspects of Affirmative Action Programs"; Berenice Sandler, answering some common objections to the concept of affirmative action; and many others.

Women's Movement Media: A Source Guide, by Cynthia Ellen Harrison (R.R. Bowker Company, New York and London, 1975)

Contains listings and descriptions of 550 current feminist organizations in the United States and Canada. These include publishing houses; periodicals; book stores; libraries and research centers; governmental and quasi-governmental agencies; women's studies programs; abortion-counseling groups and clinics; self-defense and anti-rape organizations; lesbian groups; and women's professional organizations.

ANTHOLOGIES & SOURCEBOOKS VI. HISTORY OF FEMINISM

The American Search for Woman, by H. Carleton Marlow and Harrison M. Davis (Clio Books, Santa Barbara, California, 1976)

This is a useful history of American attitudes—popular, religious, medical and "scientific"—towards woman's nature and place. Marlow and Davis interpret this history, in terms of four basic attitudes; *innatism*, which holds that women are mentally and biologically inferior and thus must be kept in total subjugation; *environmental feminism*, which interprets the observable mental (and to some extent physical) differences between the sexes as due to cultural factors rather than biology; *superior feminism*, which views women as in some respects superior to men and thus longs for the return of ancient matriarchal patterns; and *differential egalitarianism*, which holds that the sexes are fundamentally and inalterably different in both psychology and physiology, but that the difference does not justify the conclusion that either is or should be superior.

The authors themselves strongly endorse the fourth view of woman's nature, and use it to argue against adoption of the Equal Rights Amendment. The ERA, they claim, would eliminate legislation protective of women workers, as well as alimony and child support laws, which discriminate against men. Nor would extending such benefits to both sexes solve the problem, since men don't need the same sorts of protection and would only be handicapped by it. (They overlook the alternative of basing protective legislation on directly relevant features of the situation, e.g. the strength, size, skills, age and health of the worker.)

The American Sisterhood: Writings of the Feminist Movement from Colonial Times to the Present, edited by Wendy Martin (Harper and Row, New York, 1972)

A collection of American feminist writings and speeches, from the early colonial period to the present. Includes pieces by Anne Hutchinson; Sarah Grimke; the 1948 Seneca Falls Convention; Lucy Stone; Lucretia Mott; Amelia Bloomer; Elizabeth Cady Stanton; Susan B. Anthony; Sojourner Truth; Alice Stone Black-

well; Francis Wright; Margaret Fuller; Jane Addams; Charlotte
Perkins Gilman; Emma Goldman; Margaret Sanger; and Isadora
Duncan. Contemporary work includes articles by Marlene Dixon;
Alice Rossi; Shirley Chisolm; Natalie Shainess on abortion;
Maxine Williams on liberation and black women; Gloria
Steinem's "What it Would be Like if Women Win"; Barbara
Walter on "The Cult of True Womanhood"; Wendy Martin on the
"fallen" woman in American fiction; Florence Howe on women's
education; Matina Horner on women's fear of success; Naomi
Weisstein's "Woman as Nigger"; Clara Thompson on derogatory
attitudes toward female sexuality; Susan Lydon on "Understanding Orgasm"; Dana Densmore on sex roles; the Radicalesbians; Sally Kempton; Robin Morgan; and others.

*Century of Struggle: The Woman's Rights Movement in the United
States*, by Eleanor Flexner (Atheneum, New York, 1973; first
published 1959)
This is still perhaps the best account of the struggle of nine-
teenth- and early twentieth-century American women to obtain
higher education, legal rights and political suffrage.

Everyone Was Brave: The Rise and Fall of Feminism in America,
by William O'Neill (Quadrangel Books, Chicago, 1969)
A good critical history of the women's suffrage movement in
this country. O'Neill considers the movement a failure because it
failed to maintain its momentum after the vote was won in 1920.
He attributes this failure to the failure of suffragists to develop a
realistic analysis of what the vote could and could not be expected
to do for women and for society. Because they expected too much
from the vote, he argues, they often compromised too much to
obtain it, e.g. when some suffragists used racist arguments or
exploited the Victorian idea of female purity to win support for
their cause.

Female Liberation: History and Current Politics, edited by
Roberta Salper (Alfred A. Knopf, New York, 1972)
Historical and contemporary writings from the women's liber-
ation movement. The earlier writers include Mary Wollstone-
craft; Harriet Taylor Mill; Elizabeth Cady Stanton; Frederick
Douglas; Sojourner Truth; Charlotte Perkins Gilman, and Emma
Goldman. Contemporary contributions include Kathy McAfee

and Myrna Wood's "Bread and Roses"; "The Fourth World Manifesto," by Barbara Burns *et al*; Roberta Salper on "The Development of the American Women's Liberation Movement, 1967–1971"; Kate Ellis on day care; and pieces by Marlene Dixon, Roxanne Dunbar, Dana Densmore, Frances Beal, and Meredith Tax.

Feminism: The Essential Historical Writings, edited by Miriam Schneir (Vintage Books, New York, 1972)

A collection of eighteenth- to early twentieth-century feminist writings. Includes pieces by Mary Wollstonecraft; Abigail Adams; Francis Wright; George Sand; Sarah Grimke; Thomas Hood; Margaret Fuller; the Seneca Falls Convention; Frederick Douglas; William Lloyd Garrison; Sojourner Truth; Lucretia Mott; Lucy Stone; Elizabeth Cady Stanton; Susan B. Anthony; Victoria Woodhull; John Stuart Mill; Henrik Ibsen; Friedrich Engels; August Bebel; Thorstein Veblen; Charlotte Perkins Gilman; Anna Garlin Spencer; Carrie Chapman Catt; Emmeline Pankhurst; Emma Goldman; Margaret Sanger; Clara Zetkin; Virginia Woolf; and others.

The Feminist Papers: From Adams to de Beauvoir, edited by Alice S. Rossi (Bantam Books, New York, 1976)

This is an especially fine anthology, not just because of the selection of feminist writings but because of the excellent biographical and analytic introductions provided for each writer. The authors include: Abigail Adams; Judith Sargent Murray; Mary Wollstonecraft; John Stuart Mill; Angelina and Sarah Grimke; Elizabeth Cady Stanton; Friedrich Engels; August Bebel; Emma Goldman; Margaret Sanger; Suzanne La Follette; Charlotte Perkins Gilman; Jane Addams; Virginia Woolf; Margaret Mead; and Simone de Beauvoir.

Herstory: A Woman's View of American History, by June Sochen (Alfred Publishing Company, New York, 1974)

This text provides a good "feminist-humanist" commentary on American history. Sochen concentrates on the perpetual gap between American ideals and American reality, between the egalitarian pronouncements of the Declaration of Independence and the Constitution and the actual practice and attitudes of American WASMs (white Anglo-Saxon males) towards all human beings different from themselves. Particularly valuable are the many fine illustrations and capsule biographies of noteworthy American women of all kinds—from writers, religious and political leaders, and revolutionaries, to movie queens and presidents' wives.

The Ideas of the Woman Suffrage Movement 1890–1920, by Aileen S. Kraditor (Doubleday and Company, Garden City, New York, 1971)

A study of the ideological permutations which took place within the suffrage movement in the decades prior to its final success in 1920. Kraditor shows that the earlier prosuffrage agruments, which were based on justice and the essential *similarity* between women and men, gradually gave way to arguments based on expediency, and emphasizing women's supposed special qualities. Many suffragists employed racist and nativist—i.e. anti-immigrant arguments.

Movers and Shakers: American Women Thinkers and Activists 1900–1970, by June Sochen (Quadrangle Books, New York, 1973)

A good historical study; biographical sketches of twentieth-century American women writers, political activists, social reformers, union organizers, educators, and others who have fought for social change. These include such once prominent but now almost forgotten women as Rita Childe Dorr, Henrietta Rodman, and Elizabeth Gurley Flynn, as well as such major figures as Emma Goldman, Margaret Sanger, Charlotte Perkins Gilman, and Margaret Mead.

The New Feminism in Twentieth Century America, edited by June Sochen (D.C. Heath and Company, Lexington, Massachusetts, 1971)

Writings of American feminists of the 1900s and 1910s, and of the 1960s. The representatives of the first wave of twentieth-century feminism include Charlotte Perkins Gilman, Margaret Sanger, Henrietta Rodman, Florence Seabury and Susan B. Anthony. The feminists of the sixties include Brigid Brophy, Paula Stern, Alice Rossi, Pat Mainardi, Naomi Weisstein, Anne Koedt, Jo Freeman and Roxanne Dunbar.

The Right to be People, by Mildred Adams (J.B. Lippincott Company, Philadelphia and New York, 1967)

A basic history of the women's rights movement in the United States, especially the campaign for the vote and the somewhat disappointing decades after it was won. Adams concentrates on the personalities and political tactics of the major leaders and the differences and disputes between them on their philosophical stances. She asks why it took so long to win the vote—seventy-two years from the Seneca Falls Conference where the struggle was officially launched—and why women seem (in 1967) to have made so little real progress since that victory. The reason it took so long, she argues, is that on the one hand the movement was always divided and unclear about its goals, and on the other hand it was always faced by powerful opposition, from conservative politicians, the clergy, the liquor lobby, and big business in general. It is harder to explain the movement's loss of momentum after 1920, but she suggests that some of the factors were the age of the remaining suffragist leaders and their refusal to remain in public life after the vote was won; their Victorian moralism which women of the younger generation rejected and which made feminism seem old fashioned; and of course continuing male resistance to equality.

The Rise of the Modern Woman, edited by Peter N. Stearns (Forum Press, St. Louis, Missouri, 1978)

Analyses by contemporary scholars of the changing roles of women in the nineteenth century. Includes pieces by Simone de Beauvior, Evelyn Sullerot, William H. Chafe, Nancy Cott, Linda Gordon, William O'Neill, Peter Gabriel Filene, and others.

This Great Argument: The Rights of Woman, edited by Hamida Bosmajian and Haig Bosmajian (Addison-Wesley Publishing Company, Reading, Massachussetts, 1972)

A very diverse collection of both historical and contemporary contributions to the debate over women's rights. The historical section includes excerpts from Genesis, Hesiod, and Plato; poetical statements by Petrarch, William Shakespeare, John Donne, Anne Finch, Jonathan Swift and John Milton; philosophical arguments by Jean Jacques Rousseau, Mary Wollstonecraft, and John Stuart Mill; and a passage from Ibsen's **A Doll's House**. Contemporary contributors include Bruno Bettelheim; Gunnar Myrdal; Helen Hacker; and Shirley Chisolm. Also included are Senate testimony and debate from the 1970 hearings on the Equal Rights Amendment, and statements by President Kennedy's Commission on the Status of Women and President Nixon's Presidential Task Force on Women's Rights and Responsibilities.

Unsung Champions of Women, edited by Mary Cohart (University of New Mexico Press, Albuquerque, 1975)

An excellent collection of now little-known feminist writings, mostly from the nineteenth and early twentieth centuries. Includes excerpts from Elizabeth Burt Gamble and Lester Frank Ward, American evolutionists who argued for the natural priority of the female in both physical and cultural evolution; Johan Jacob Bachofen on the goddess-centered religions of the ancient world; Mathilde and Mathias Vaerting, who argued that sexual dominance is the sole factor determining which traits are considered masculine or feminine within a given society; Plato's argument for a meritocratic rather than sex-based division of labor; views of women's role in history by Lydia Maria Child, Lady Sydney Morgan, Otis Tufton Mason, and Eugene A. Heckler; and a remarkable early feminist essay by the Marquis de Condorcet, a philosopher who was a victim of the terrorism of the French Revolution.

Up From the Pedestal: Selected Writings in the History of American Feminism, edited by Aileen S. Kraditor (Quadrangle Books, Chicago, 1968)

Feminist and antifeminist essays, letters and speeches, from the seventeenth century to the present. The pieces are well classified, according to the line of argument or position taken. The authors include Anne Bradstreet; John Winthrop; Sarah and Angelina Grimke; Margaret Fuller; Lucy Stone; Catherine Beecher; Anna Garlin Spencer; Elizabeth Cady Stanton; Thorstein Veblen; Susan B. Anthony; Charlotte Perkins Gilman; Carrie Chapman Catt; President Grover Cleveland; Jane Addams; and a great many others.

The Woman Movement: Feminism in the United States and England, edited by William L. O'Neill (Quadrangle Books, Chicago, 1969)

A brief comparative history of the women's suffrage movement in England and the United States, plus twenty-two articles, speeches and other documents from the suffrage movement; these include pieces by Sarah Grimke, Lucy Stone, Elizabeth Cady Stanton, Charlotte Perkins Gilman, Grover Cleveland, Vida Scudder, Anna Howard Shaw, Carrie Chapman Catt, and others.

ANTHOLOGIES &. SOURCEBOOKS VII. HISTORY OF WOMEN

The American Woman: Who Was She? edited by Anne Firor Scott (Prentice-Hall, Englewood Cliffs, New Jersey, 1971)

This is a well-orchestrated collection of short pieces descriptive of various aspects of women's situation in this country, from colonial times to the present. Includes excerpts from the writings of Charlotte Perkins Gilman, Carrie Chapman Catt, Edna St. Vincent Millay, Lucy Stone, Jane Addams, Anna Garlin Spencer, Mary Beard, Eleanor Roosevelt, W.I. Thomas, Bruno Bettelheim, Margaret Sanger, Walter Lipman, Betty Friedan, Marya Mannes, Carolyn Bird, and many others. (Also see Ann Firor Scott's *The Southern Lady*, later in this section.)

Black Women in White America: A Documentary History, edited by Gerda Lerner (Vintage Books, New York, 1973)

Writings, speeches and stories by and about black women, their situation and their struggles both under slavery and thereafter. Includes pieces by Harriet Tubman, Sarah Douglas, Charlotte Grimke, Sojourner Truth, Mahalia Jackson, Mary McLeod Bethune, Ella Baker, Shirley Chisolm, and many others.

Clio's Consciousness Raised: New Perspectives on the History of Women, edited by Mary Hartman and Lois W. Banner (Harper and Row, New York, 1974)

This is a collection of fourteen papers representing recent research in women's history. Includes Ann Douglas Wood, Carroll Smith-Rosenberg, and Regina Morantz on nineteenth-century

American medicine's treatment of women; Linda Gordon on the early voluntary motherhood movement; Catherine Bodard Silver on women in the professions in France; Elizabeth Fee on the ancient matriarchy vs. patriarchy theories of Victorian social anthropologists; JoAnn McNamara and Suzanne Wemple on medieval women; Daniel Scott Smith on domestic feminism in Victorian America; Barbara Welter on women's religious activism in the nineteenth century; Dee Garrison on the feminization of public librarianship; Patricia Branca on the Victorian woman; Judith and Daniel Walkowitz on the effects of the Contagious Diseases Acts in Southampton and Plymouth; Laura Owen on women in English working-class families; and Ruth Schwartz Cowan on "The Washing Machine and the Working Wife."

The Emancipation of the American Woman, by Andrew Sinclair (Harper and Row, New York, 1965)
    This is an offensively condescending history of the American feminist movement in the nineteenth century and until the winning of the vote. Sinclair professes sympathy with feminist goals, yet has little but contempt for individual feminist leaders: Elizabeth Stanton is described as "lazy and corpulent" (p.75), Lucy Stone as a manhater (p.256). He thinks that women have already won, or been given, all the legal and social reforms necessary for complete equality, but have mysteriously failed to take advantage of their opportunities.

The Feminization of American Culture, by Ann Douglas (Avon Books, New York, 1977)
    This is an enlightening study of the ideological alliance, during the period between 1820 and 1875, between the northwestern Protestant clergy and certain middle-class literary women. Both groups had suffered a loss of social power, the clergy as the result of the disestablishment (i.e. termination of state support) of their churches, the women because of the diminution of their productive economic role, as paid labor moved out of the family setting. Both groups sought to regain their influence through the sentimental glorification of the "feminine" virtues. Both defended the exclusion of women from the economic and political realm by depicting their role as one of privilege, of exemption from corruption, which qualifies them to serve as arbiters of morality and of the softer emotions. This sentimental falsification of women's social role became an ubiquitous part of American mass culture,

where—as the tenor of the current opposition to the Equal Rights Amendment demonstrates—it retains a great deal of power.

For Her Own Good: 150 Years of Experts' Advice to Women, by Barbara Ehrenreich and Deirdre English (Anchor Press/Doubleday, Garden City, New York, 1978)

This is an interesting study of the so-called scientific answers to the "Woman Question," as developed in this country and "elaborated over the last hundred years by a new class of experts— physicians, psychologists, domestic scentists, child-raising experts." (p.3) Throughout this period, the (male-dominated) medical profession in particular played a distinctly political role. The "experts" nearly all supported the romanticist solution to the Woman Question: that woman's place was in the home, and that she was by nature unsuited to participate in the larger world of the male. The history of the medical profession's persecution of women lay healers, from the European witch-burning craze (1) to the continuing suppression of women midwives in this country, is particularly instructive.

1. See **Witches, Midwives and Nurses**, by the same authors, also in Anthologies VII.

Goddesses, Whores, Wives and Slaves: Women in Classical Antiquity, by Sarah B. Pomeroy (Schocken Books, New York, 1975)

A careful and balanced social history of women in the Classical Greek and Roman worlds. On the whole the picture is a rather grim one, though during the Empire Roman women gained considerable *de facto* freedom, while still under the absolute *de jure* control of their fathers or other male relatives. At no time did they enjoy any political power beyond what they could gain indirectly, through personal influence over men. Spartan women were a good deal freer than Athenian women, largely because of the socialist system which existed in Sparta, and the greater separation between the sexes due to the men's frequent and long-term absence during war. Pomeroy considers the evidence for the existence of Amazon societies, and earlier matriarchies and mother-goddess worshiping cultures in the area inconclusive, though not to be entirely discounted. After all, she notes, "it is as foolish to postulate masculine dominance in prehistory as to postulate feminine dominance." (p.15) One interesting note is that throughout antiquity women appear—largely on the evidence of the proportion of female names on grave markers and tombs—to have been greatly outnumbered by men, often more than two to one. This was the result of female infanticide, and also of the very early age of marriage for women coupled with the very high rate of death in childbirth.

Liberating Women's History: Theoretical and Critical Essays, edited by Berenice A. Carroll (University of Illinois Press, Urbana, Illinois, 1976)

A collection of papers representing contemporary research and theory in the field of women's history. Noteworthy articles include: Anne J. Lane's critique of Friedrich Engels; Berenice A. Carroll's reappraisal of Mary Beard's *Woman As Force In History*; Ann M. Pescatello on "Latina Liberation"; Joyce A. Ladner on "Black Womanhood in Historical Perspective"; Sarah B. Pomeroy's reflections on the hypothesis of Bronze Age matriarchies in the eastern Mediterranean region (she considers it improbable); Gerda Lerner arguing that feminism and the study of women as a group are useless as tools for historical research; Hilda Smith disputing this claim and defending feminism as a guiding principle in the study of women's history; and Juliet Mitchell's "Four Structures in a Complex Unity."

Not in God's Image: Women in History from the Greeks to the Victorians, edited by Julia O'Faolain and Laura Martenes (Harper and Row, New York, 1973)

An excellent collage of short pieces on the nature of women and their social and legal status—e.g. excerpts from legal codes, letters, poems, scientific, medical, philosophical and religious tracts, histories, diaries, and autobiographies. Includes passages from Homer, Hesiod, Hippocrates, Aristotle, Xenophon, Demosthenes, Euripides, Cicero, Juvenal, the Bible, the Koran, St. Augustine, Tertullian, St. Thomas Aquinas, Albertus Magnus, Christine de Pisan, Martin Luther, John Calvin, Jean Jacques Rousseau, John Knox, Immanuel Kant, and many others. Needless to say, most of the views expressed are antifeminist, if not overtly misogynist.

"Remember the Ladies": New Perspectives on Women in American History, edited by Carol V.R. George (Syracuse University Press, Syracuse, New York, 1975)

Ten contemporary articles on women's history in America. Includes: Carol V.R. George on Ann Hutchinson; Marguerite Fisher on "Eighteenth-Century Theorists of Women's Liberation"; Ralph Ketcham on Abigail Adams and Thomas Jefferson; David Bennett on the collaboration between the suffragist and nativist movements; Jane Donegan on "Man-Midwifery and the Delicacy of the Sexes"; Atey Scruggs on Harriet Tubman; William O'Neill on the struggle over divorce laws; Gerald Critoph on the flapper; James Johnson on the founding of the United States Children's Bureau; and four Japanese women on "Echoes of American Cultural Feminism in Japan."

Root of Bitterness: Documents of the Social History of American Women, edited by Nancy B. Cott (E.P. Dutton, New York, 1972)

An assorted collection of materials—articles, letters, speeches, court records, etc.—illustrative of the general condition of American women, from the colonial period to the end of the nineteenth century. Includes pieces by Alexis de Tocqueville; Catharine Beecher; Angelina Grimke, Francis Wright; Victoria Woodhull; Dr. Elizabeth Blackwell; Jane Addams; Charlotte Perkins Gilman; and many others.

The Southern Lady: From Pedestal to Politics 1830–1930, by Anne Firor Scott (The University of Chicago Press, Chicago, 1970)

This is a study of the circumstances and activities of middle- and upper-class (white) Southern women, from the antebellum period to the Great Depression. Scott focuses on the ideal of the Southern belle—pious, chaste, charming and submissive; on the women (such as the Grimke sisters) who rebelled against this restrictive standard of femininity; and on the forces and events (e.g. slavery, the Civil War, the reconstruction, industrialization, and the suffrage movement) which gradually brought about its near but still not total demise.

Woman as Revolutionary, edited by Frederick C. Griffin (Mentor, New York, 1973)

Biographical comments and excerpts from the writings of or about twenty-two revolutionary women. Some of these women: Christine de Pisan (a fourteenth-century French protofeminist and defender of women's rights); Joan of Arc; St. Teresa; Olympe de Gouges (beheaded during the French Revolution for demanding political recognition for women); Mary Wollstonecraft; Mercy Otis Warren (patriot and historian of the American Revolution); Susan B. Anthony; Sofia Perovskaya (executed in 1881 for conspiring in the assassination of Czar Alexander II); Jane Addams; Helen Keller; Emma Goldman; Rosa Luxemburg; Isodora Duncan; Margaret Sanger; Maria Montessori; and Joan Baez.

Woman: From the Greeks to the French Revolution, edited by Susan G. Bell (Wadsworth Publishing Company, Belmont, California, 1973)

A collection of both historical and contemporary materials, designed to serve as an introduction to women's history, and men's attitudes towards women, in Western civilization. Includes excerpts from Plato, Aristotle, the Bible, St. Augustine, Tertullian, St. Thomas, Chaucer, Erasmus, Jean Jacques Rousseau and other historical figures; as well as nineteenth- and twentieth-century articles on the situation of women in Greece, Rome, early Christianity, medieval Europe, the Renaissance and the Enlightenment periods.

Woman in Science, by H.J. Mozans, pseudonym of John Augustine Zahm. (MIT Press, Cambridge, Massachusetts, 1974. First published 1913, by D. Appleton and Company, New York)

Although it is sentimental and quaintly written, this book is a good source of basic information about dozens of women philosophers, mathematicians, astronomers, physicists, chemists, archeologists and inventors, from Aspasia and Hypatia to Madame Curie. Unfortunately, the author takes a patronizing attitude towards these women, insisting that although they have "masculine" minds, they retained their "feminine" virtues and did not neglect their "domestic duties." Like John Stuart Mill, he believes in an intellectual division of labor; men's minds, he claims, are suited to the study of particular facts and the making of inductive inferences, while women are better at deductive reasoning from abstract general ideas. A very large proportion of the examples he gives do not, however, support such an interpretation.

Women and Womanhood in America, edited by Ronald W. Hogeland, foreword by Aileen S. Kraditor (D.C. Heath and Company, Lexington, Massachusetts, 1973)

This anthology combines contemporary essays on women's

history in the United States with historical material. The latter includes pieces by Cotton Mather, Thomas Jefferson, Alexis de Tocqueville, Harriet Martineau, Catherine Beecher, Harriet Beecher Stowe, and Charlotte Perkins Gilman. The contemporary authors include Aileen Kraditor and Gerda Lerner (separately) on approaches to the study of women in American history; Ann Stanford on the poet Ann Bradstreet; Winthrop Jordan on interracial sex in American history; Barbara Welter on "The Cult of True Womanhood 1820–1860"; Benjamin Spock on the (supposedly innate) motherhood instinct in women; Francis Beal on "Double Jeopardy: To be Black and Female"; David Kennedy on feminism and the family in the nineteenth century; James McGovern on the pre-World War I "flapper"; and Alice Rossi on "Equality Between the Sexes."

ANTHOLOGIES & SOURCEBOOKS VIII. INTERDISCIPLINARY

The American Woman: Who Will She Be? edited by Mary Louise McBee and Kathryn A. Blake (Glencoe Press, Beverly Hills, California, 1974)

In this book, ten distinguished American women comment on the question posed in the title. They are: the psychologist Judith Bardwick; the sociologist Jessie Bernard; Juanita Kreps, an economist (later to become a member of the Carter administration); Patsy Mink, U.S. Representative from Hawaii; Carol Nadelson, professor of psychiatry at Harvard; historian Anne Firor Scott; and Judith Miller and Leah Margolis, media researchers. As Margaret Mead remarks in the foreword, their comments are balanced and thought provoking.

Beyond Intellectual Sexism: A New Woman, a New Reality, edited by Joan I. Roberts (David McKay Company, New York, 1976)

Twenty women academics analyze and document, each in her own field of study, the distortions and omissions which foster an 'intellectual' rationalization of female inferiority and sex discrimination." (p. x) The contributors include Ruth Bleier, on sex differences in the brain and presumptions about their behavior effects; G. Kass-Simon on ethology (the study of animal behavior); Hania Ris on birth control; Julia Sherman on psychological "facts" about women; Jane Allyn Piliavin "On Feminine Self-Presentation in Groups"; Diane Kravetz on women social workers and their women clients; Auvis V. Pratt on the new feminist literary criticism; Germaine Bree on French women writers and their belittlement by male critics; Victoria Junco Meyer on "The Images of Women in Contemporary Mexican Literature"; Katherine Clarenbach on women and the law; Bonnie Freeman on women in politics; Anne Seidman on women wage earners; Ingrid Camerini on women in Sweden; Kay Ann Johnson on women in China; Rae Blumberg on women in the kibbutz; Elizabeth Fenna on "Women and Girls in the Public Schools"; Karen Merritt on women in higher education; Julia Brown on women and physical education; and Elizabeth Monk and Laura Burger on "The Status of Home Economics and the Status of Women."

Exploring Sex Differences, edited by Barbara Lloyd and John Archer (Academic Press, London, New York and San Francisco, 1974)

Eleven English and American scholars—sociologists, psychologists, physiologists, and others—comment on what is and is not known about the differences between the sexes, each from the point of view of their own particular field. The contributors include Dorothy Ullian, who presents a cognitive-developmental model of children's conceptions of masculinity and femininity; anthropologist Marilyn Strathern, who uses her observations of the Hagan of New Guinea to illustrate her thesis that gender is a culturally-determined set of ideas, which reflect such other cultural values as the need for a system of rules governing communication between the sexes; Paul Rosenblatt and Michael Cunningham, who examine cross-cultural evidence indicating the influence of the division of labor on the relative status of the sexes, and of the enormous plasticity of sex roles; Diane McGuinness, who explores early differences in the perceptual organization of male and female infants, and the possible effects of these initial differences on later perceptual and cognitive development; Lesley Rogers on the effects of male hormones on animal and human behavior; Peter Messent on the effects of female hormones; and Peter Mayo on possible explanations of the different sorts of psychopathology typical of men and women, respectively, in our culture.

Humanness: An Exploration into the Mythologies about Women and Men, edited by Ella Lasky (MSS Information Corporation, New York, 1975)

This is an extensive collection of, for the most part, academic pieces by American sociologists, psychologists and educators, dealing with contemporary sex-role stereotyping and its psychological effects upon women and men. The articles are photocopies from the original published (or typed) version, which results in variable legibility; the work, however, is generally of high quality. Contributors include Jo Freeman on the origins of the contemporary women's movement; Joanna Russ on "The Image of Women in Science Fiction"; Dean Knudsen on the declining economic and occupational status of women; Matina Horner on women's (supposed) fear of success; Robert Gould on homosexuality; Abraham Maslow on the direct relation between women's "dominance-feeling" and their sexuality; Jessie Bernard on marriage; Mirra Komarovsky on stresses induced by the masculine sex role; Susan Sontag on "The Double Standard of Aging"; Ruth Hartley on "Sex-Role Pressures and the Socialization of the Male Child"; and many others.

Woman in the Year 2000, edited by Maggie Tripp (Dell Publishing Company, New York, 1974)

Twenty-eight contemporary writers—including journalists, novelists, politicians, teachers, futurists and others—comment on life-style changes for women (and men) which they expect to occur by the end of this century. Worth noting: Jane Trakey, who looks at the image of woman in contemporary electronic media and sees little hope for fundamental change; futurist Alvin Toffler, who looks forward to dramatic changes in the form of the family, from group marriage and homosexual parents raising their own or adopted children, to "test tube" babies (not just conceived but fully gestated outside the human body); Carolyn Bird on the system-wide effects of equal pay for women workers; Rona Cherry on overcoming of the male monopoly in medicine; Robert and Anna Francoeur on sexual behavior in the age of the single standard; Lois Gould's "X: A Fabulous Child's Story"; and F.M. Esfandiary's implausible but inspiring predictions about the total disappearance of gender, childbearing (in the old-fashioned manner) and death.

Women and the Scientific Professions: The M.I.T. Symposium on American Women in Science and Engineering, edited by Jacquelyn A. Mattfeld and Carol G. Van Aken (The M.I.T. Press, Cambridge, Massachusetts, and London, 1965)

This is the text of a much publicized symposium held at M.I.T. in 1964. The speakers included sociologists (e.g. Alice Rossi and Jessie Bernard), Freudian psychoanalysts (Bruno Bettelheim, Erik Erikson), and practicing scientists and engineers. Rossi addresses the "Barriers to the Career Choice of Engineering, Medicine, or Science Among American Women," and Jessie Bernard describes the situation of women engineers in the academic world. Some of the speakers exhibit attitudes of the sort feminists have rightly labeled sexist; most notably, Bruno Bettelheim insists that a woman's commitment to a career is essentially different from a man's, since, he claims,

> as much as women want to be good scientists or engineers, they want first and foremost to be womanly companions of men and to be mothers. (p.15)

Another conference participant, Chien-Shiung Wu, argues with some justification that the latter claim is unobjectionable insofar as it is also realized that "this noble human desire to be devoted companions and good parents must, ideally, be equally shared by men." (p.41)

Women's Role in Contemporary Society: The Report of the New York City Commission on Human Rights, foreword by John V. Lindsay and introduction by Eleanor Holmes Norton (Avon Books, New York, 1972)

This is the complete text of the Commission's public hearings, with testimony from experts of all kinds—sociologists, psychologists, public officials, political activists, lawyers, educators and politicians. The witnesses include Mirra Komarovsky, Betty Friedan, Florynce Kennedy, Jo-Ann Gardner, Margaret Mead, Bess Meyerson, Kate Millett, Bella Abzug, Gloria Steinem and many others. As (then) Mayor John Lindsay says in the foreword, "The hearings richly document (that) women are victims of discrimination in employment at all levels, in housing, in mortgage lending and credit practices, in health care and social services, in higher education, in civil and criminal statutes of many kinds, in literature and the mass media, and, not least of all, in politics." (p.18) The Commission recommended passage of the Equal Rights Amendment, and other legal correctives.

Women's Studies: The Social Realities, edited by Barbara Bellow Watson (Harper and Row, New York, 1976)

A good introductory text, with sections on the philosophical, sociological, psychological, anthropological, and activist feminist approaches to the understanding of women and of sex roles. Each section has a different author/editor, and contains excerpts from important works in the areas, together with biographical material on the authors and critical commentary. For instance, the section on the philosophical arguments for sexual equality, edited by Barbara Watson, contains subsections on Mary Wollstonecraft, John Stuart Mill, George Bernard Shaw, Virginia Woolf, and Simone de Beauvoir.

ANTHOLOGIES & SOURCEBOOKS IX. LAW

The Law for a Woman: Real Cases and What Happened, by Ellen Switzer (Charles Scribner's Sons, New York, 1975)

This is a basic introduction to those areas of American law which are of special concern to women. These include the Constitutional rights of citizens; rights related to education, employment, marriage, and medical treatment; divorce law; the law of wills, estates and trusts; the legal rights of children; the predictable legal consequences if the ERA passes; and the status of women in the legal profession. Each chapter begins with a set of brief case studies and discusses the legal issues raised by each case, and the way it was legally resolved.

Reverse Discrimination, edited by Barry R. Gross (Prometheus Books, New York, 1977)

A good collection of articles dealing with the issues raised by "affirmative action," in particular the issue of whether the practice of giving some degree of preference to women and members of racial minority groups, in hiring and university admission, in order to increase the numbers of women and minorities hired or admitted, is just, or legal. Some of the contributors oppose this practice as a form of reverse discrimination, which is immoral or illegal; these include Lee Nisbet, F.K. Baruch, Sidney Hook, Paul Seabury, Thomas Sowell, Virginia Black, and Lisa Newton. Those who argue that such a practice is *not* necessarily unfair or illegal include J. Stanley Pottinger, Bernard Boxhill, James W. Nickel, Michael D. Bayles, and Hardy E. Jones.

The Rights of Women: The Basic ACLU Guide to a Woman's Rights, by Susan Deller Ross (Avon Books, New York, 1973)

A good practical handbook which explains women's legal rights in this country and ways in which they may be implemented. Includes chapters on Constitutional rights (i.e. the Equal Protection Clause of the Fourteenth Amendment and the Equal Rights Amendment); employment discrimination; educational opportunities; the portrayal of women by the mass media; the criminal justice system; reproductive rights (abortion, contraception and sterilization); divorce; names and name changes; and miscellaneous legal issues. Ross advocates legally mandated wages, vacations and other benefits for housewives (or househusbands), and suggests strategies for pursuing that goal. Appendices list relevant state and federal statutes, women's legal self-help groups, and national women's organizations and publications which provide news and information about legal developments affecting women.

Sex Discrimination and the Law: Causes and Reasons, by Barbara Allen Babcock, Ann E. Freedman, Eleanor Holmes Norton, and Susan C. Ross (Little, Brown and Company, Boston and Toronto, 1975).

This is a large volume of case-study material, designed for use as a text in courses on women and the law. It deals with hundreds of important cases and problematic areas of the law, providing case materials, historical background, commentaries and related testimony from various sources, analyses of the practical impact of each decision, and proposals for further legal reform in each area. Among the legal areas dealt with are: Constitutional law and women (e.g. protective labor legislation, the Nineteenth Amendment, modern equal protection theory, and the Equal Rights Amendment); discrimination in employment, and efforts to overcome it through Title VII of the Civil Rights Act, the Equal Pay Act, and affirmative action programs; family law (e.g. marital property law, marriage contracts, divorce law, social security, inheritance law); women and criminal law (rape law, prostitution, the treatment of female prisoners, differential sentencing of men and women); and law relating to women's rights to abortion, equal educational opportunities, and equal access to public accommodations (housing, restaurants, etc.).

Sexism and the Law, by Abbie Sachs and Joan Hoff Wilson (The Free Press, New York, 1978)

A survey of the major judicial decisions affecting women's rights in nineteenth- and twentieth-century Britain and the United States. The authors show that virtually all nineteenth- (and most twentieth-) century bids to extend the legal and political rights of women, or to open the professions to them, were met with a judicial hostility and gender bias "so striking and so explicit as to contradict totally the idea of judicial impartiality." (p.7) These include the British "persons" cases (1867–1922), in which women were denied various rights—e.g. to enroll in law school, practice law, vote, or hold public office—on the grounds that they are not "persons" in the meaning of the law.

American judges also tended to deny women these rights, but on different grounds: on the one hand, Blackstone's strictly patriarchal interpretation of English Common Law, and on the other a seemingly chivalrous notion that women's legal disabilities are really privileges which they are granted because of their greater virtue and delicacy. In both countries, the legal profession has been and continues to be structured so as to maintain male domination and female subordination. The intransigence of the law seems to be a direct result of the material interest which men have in maintainting their monopoly. Both the law and the profession will have to be restructured to remove the remaining institutional barriers to women, and to incorporate the humanistic values with which women have been associated.

Sexist Justice, by Karen DeCrow (Random House, New York, 1975)

A good feminist analysis of ongoing sexist discrimination in American law, by a past president of the National Organization of Women who has been active in contemporary struggles for legal reform. DeCrow argues that the equal protection clause of the Fourteenth Amendment—though finally ruled applicable to women in 1971—has not and will not serve as an adequate means for achieving legal equality between the sexes, and that the Equal Rights Amendment would be a much more powerful weapon. Even if the ERA were to have little specific legal impact, its psychological value would be enormous. The major argument against it has been that it would lead to the loss of legislation designed to protect or even seemingly to favor women, e.g. laws setting minimum wages and maximum hours for women in certain industries, limiting the amount of weight women workers can be required to lift, and providing for alimony and child support. DeCrow argues that if the ERA were to pass, most worker protection laws need not and almost certainly would not be dropped by the legislature, but rather extended to cover men as well. Alimony and support laws can and should be rewritten to provide equal protection for both sexes. The ERA would probably require that women be drafted—that is if men are—but DeCrow presents a strong case that this is exactly as it should be.

Women and the Law: The Unfinished Revolution, by Leo Kanowitz (University of New Mexico Press, Albuquerque, 1969)

An excellent and not overly technical study of women's legal status and sex-discriminatory laws in the United States, up to and including the Civil Rights Act of 1964. Kanowitz argues that all legal distinctions based on sex alone should be eliminated. Voting, driving, and drinking ages, the age of majority and the age at which marriage is permitted should be the same for both sexes. "Protective" laws that limit women's working hours or working conditions or set minimum wages for women only should be either eliminated or rewritten in sex-neutral terms. For instance, the absolute requirements that women not lift more than a certain number of pounds should be relativized and extended to men by requiring that no worker be required to lift more weight than she or he can do without undue physical strain. There are a number of limitations on married women's property rights, vestiges of the English Common Law doctrine of coverture which held that the legal existence of a woman is suspended during marriage, which need to be rooted out. If prostitution remains a crime it should be a crime for the male customer as well as for the female prostitute. Rape, statutory rape and seduction laws should extend the same protections to males as to females, rather than being defined in terms of a necessarily female victim. Alimony, spousal and child-support laws should be retained in some form, but stated in terms of circumstances rather than sex.

In spite of his consistent opposition to any legal discrimination on the basis of sex, Kanowitz argues against the adoption of the Equal Rights Amendment. He thinks that the ERA is a diversion from more important issues, and a shotgun approach to legal equality which would add little or nothing to the Constitutional protections already beginning to be recognized by the courts as implicit in the Fifth and Fourteenth Amendments. One must ask whether this line of argument underestimates the pragmatic as well as philosophical superiority of an explicit over an implicit Constitutional guarantee against sex discrimination in the law.

Women's Rights and the Law: The Impact of the ERA on State Laws, by Barbara A. Brown, Ann E. Freedman, Harriet N. Katz, and Alice M. Price (Praeger Books, New York, 1977)

An in-depth study of the effects which the Equal Rights Amendment—if and when it is ratified—can be expected to have upon various portions of state law. These include laws on rape, prostitution, and sentencing; laws affecting domestic relations, e.g. domicile, wive's and children's names, consortium, spousal support, grounds for divorce, property division and alimony, child custody, child support, and the legal status of children of unmarried women; laws regulating conditions of employment such as worker protection, unemployment compensation, and disability insurance; and antidiscrimination laws in the areas of credit, housing, insurance and education. The discussions of protective labor laws and school athletic programs are particularly important, as these are areas in which ERA opponents have predicted consequences harmful to women's interests. Each section includes policy recommendations and charts of recent court cases in the area, and their outcomes.

ANTHOLOGIES &
SOURCEBOOKS X.
MARXISM

Capitalist Patriarchy and the Case for Socialist Feminism, edited
by Zillah R. Eisenstein (Monthly Review Press, New York and
London, 1979)

An excellent group of papers by contemporary socialist feminists, women who seek to unify and synthesize the Marxist and
radical feminist analyses. Some noteworthy articles: Zilla Eisenstein on "Developing a Theory of Capitalist Patriarchy"; Nancy
Chodorow on "Mothering, Male Dominance, and Capitalism";
Linda Gordon on three phases of the (late nineteenth- and twentieth-century) birth control movement; Ellen DuBois on "The
Nineteenth-Century Woman Suffrage Movement and the Analysis of Women's Oppression"; Mary P. Ryan on "Femininity and
Capitalism in Antebellum America"; Jean Gardiner on domestic
labor; Heidi Hartman on job segregation by sex; Margery Davies
on "The Feminization of the Clerical Labor Force"; Carollee Ben-
gelsdorf and Alice Hageman on women in Cuba; Judith Stacey on
the Chinese family revolution; and the black feminist statement
by the Combahee River Collective.

The Emancipation of Women, from the writings of V.I. Lenin;
with an appendix, "Lenin on the Woman Question," by Clara
Zetkin (International Publishers, New York, 1966)

Speeches, letters and articles by Lenin, on the topic of women.
Lenin's analysis is that of Engels. Perhaps most interesting is the
interview between Lenin and Clara Zetkin (recalled by the latter),
in which Lenin objects to Rosa Luxemburg's interest in organizing prostitutes into a political force, and to Zetkin's own efforts to
organize women around their own oppression in sex and marriage. (He considered an excessive interest in such topics to be
essentially bourgeois.)

Feminism and Marxism: A Place to Begin, A Way to Go, by
Dorothy E. Smith (New Star Books, Vancouver, Canada, 1977)

A small but useful essay in which Smith explains the Marxist-feminist analysis of the oppression of woman, and examines the reasons for the rejection of feminism by most Marxists. Marxist leaders, most of them men, tend to regard the demand for equality between the sexes as a threat to working-class solidarity. Their call for unity presupposes the continuation of male dominance; it is, in fact, "a built-in complicity within Marxist thinking and within the working class itself with the institutions by which the ruling class dominates the society." (p.51) Working-class men and their labor unions, Smith argues, have cooperated with the capitalists to maintain the oppression of women, which is itself part of the capitalist system. A true revolutionary must therefore be *both* a Marxist and a feminist.

Feminism and Socialism, edited by Linda Jennes (Pathfinder Press, New York, 1972)

Writings by women members of the Socialist Workers Party who hold that the primary basis for the oppression of women is economic and that the liberation of women will require the abolition of capitalism. The articles include Maxine Williams on "Why Women's Liberation Is Important to Black Women"; Mirta Vidal on the women of La Raza; Betsy Stone, who attacks the argument that feminists should oppose the ERA because it would eliminate protective labor legislation which favors woman; Dianne Feely, on the Marxist analysis of the family; Kipp Dawson, Evelyn Reed and Diane Feeley (separately) on Kate Millett; Linda Jennes on Norman Mailer; and "Towards a Mass Feminist Movement," a resolution of the 1971 Socialist Workers Party national convention.

The Woman Question: Selections from the Writings of Karl Marx, Friedrich Engels, V.I. Lenin and Joseph Stalin (International Publishers, New York, 1971)

Excerpts from the speeches and writings of the four Marxist leaders. The basic position shared by all four of them is that women's oppression is to be understood as a result of and through analogy with class oppression; and that the means to women's liberation is through active participation in the public production process.

Women and the Family, by Leon Trotsky (Pathfinder Press, New York, 1970)

This is a short collection of speeches and articles written by Trotsky between 1923 and 1936, expressing his support for the Marxist revolutionary goal of complete equality for women. His views are strictly in line with those of Engels; he argues that equality requires not only economic and legal parity, but the socialization of housework and child care. He explains the early failure of Soviet society to achieve this third goal as the inevitable result of the scarcity of material resources, but he does not surrender the hope that with increasing prosperity in the Soviet Union the early progress towards equality, interrupted by the Stalinist counterrevolution, will be resumed.

ANTHOLOGIES & SOURCEBOOKS XI. THE OTHER SEX (MEN)

The American Male, by Myron Brenton (Coward-McCann, New York, 1966)

A popular study of the problems of contemporary American men in adjusting to their changing roles *vis a vis* work and women. Men who suffer from a "patriarchal hangover"—that is most men of our time—have difficulty in reconciling the increasing participation of women in formerly all-male activities with their own masculine self-image, which is based on the contrast between themselves and all things feminine. Such men feel deeply threatened by women's increasing independence and assertiveness; but the answer is not to take a reactionary stance against the "feminization" of America (1). The answer is to outgrow the archaic mode of thought by which men place themselves in a mental and emotional straightjacket by labeling such essential human capacities as sensitivity and an intuitive understanding of other people as feminine, and therefore taboo.

Rigid stereotypes of masculinity and femininity, Brenton argues, not only ride roughshod over individual needs and preferences, but have long since ceased to perform any desirable social function. Marital happiness demands equality, which does not mean identity of role or behavior, but rather an interpenetration of roles, and a flexibility that permits the more active or responsible role to shift freely from one spouse to the other depending on the demands of the situation. The man who insists on being the boss at home becomes vulnerable to manipulation by his supposed subordinates and soon comes to feel that it is they who are exploiting him. Since woman's progress towards equality is inexorable, men must change along with it or remain "a sex at bay."

1. See, for instance, Philip Wylie, "The Womanization of America," *Playboy*, September, 1958.

A Book of Men: Visions of the Male Experience, edited by Ross Firestone (Stonehill Publishing Company, New York, 1975)

Excerpts from the writings of poets, novelists, playwrights, artists, actors and philosophers, describing their own experiences as sons, lovers, husbands and/or fathers. Some of the (over sixty) authors: C.G. Jung; Alan Watts; George Bernard Shaw; Hermann Hesse; Henry Miller; James Baldwin; Soren Kierkegaard; Andre Gide; Jack Kerouac; Edmund Wilson; Eugene Ionesco; John Updike; Havelock Ellis; Salvador Dali; Bertrand Russell; Theodore Dreiser; Henry de Montherlant; Huey Newton; D.H. Lawrence; Paul Goodman; Aldous Huxley; Vladimir Nabokov; and F. Scott Fitzgerald. (The book is beautifully illustrated with collage engravings by Jim Herder.)

Dilemmas of Masculinity: A Study of College Youth, by Mirra Komarovsky (W.W. Norton and Company, New York, 1976)

This book reports on a study of 62 college men, seniors at an Eastern ivy league school. These men tend to suffer from role conflict, particularly the difficulty of living up to social expectations of masculine superiority and sexual knowhow. They tend to (say that they) accept women's career aspirations and their demand for equality in the public sphere, yet also to insist that women must bear the primary responsibility for raising children. At the same time, ironically, they tend to blame their fathers for not giving enough of themselves to their children, and their mothers for giving too much. They also tend to cling to the sexual double standard, even while admitting that they *ought* not to feel this way.

The Forty-Nine Percent Majority: The Male Sex Role, edited by Deborah S. David and Robert Brannon (Addison-Wesley Publishing Company, Reading, Massachusetts, 1976)

This is the best of the recent collections of writings on the personal problems associated with the masculine stereotype. The editors identify four themes, constitutive of that stereotype—the taboo on openness or vulnerability, the need for status and success, for toughness and confidence at all times, and an excessive admiration for aggression and violence—and the selections are arranged under these headings. Includes pieces by Warren Farrell, Marc Feigen-Fasteau, Myron Brenton, Thorstein Veblen, Michael Korda, Rudyard Kipling, James Thurber, Ruth Hartley, Joseph Pleck, Jack Sawyer, and others.

The Horrors of the Half-Known Life: Male Attitudes Toward Women and Sexuality in Nineteenth-Century America, by G.J. Barker-Benfield (Harper and Row, New York, 1976)

Barker-Benfield argues that nineteenth-century American men reacted to the pressures of competitive democratic society by suppressing both their emotions and their sexuality, on the theory that only in this way could they succeed in the rat race. At the same time, they sought to tighten their control over women, whom they saw as the "objective correlative" of their own sexual and emotional nature. The author takes as a prime example of this tendency the rise of male-dominated American obstetrics and gynecology, with their inherent misogyny and their readiness to cut into women's sexual parts and to remove ovaries and clitorises. He claims—though without adequate argument—that this masculine pathology is a result not of capitalism or patriarchy, but of democracy. From a feminist point of view, on the contrary, it is a sign of too *little* democracy, not too much.

The Liberated Man: Freeing Men and Their Relationships with Women, by Warren Farrell (Bantam, New York, 1975)

A popular guide to men's consciousness raising, designed to help men internalize the insights of the women's liberation movement. Farrell notes that men are not apt to cooperate in the changes necessary to bring about equality between the sexes unless the liberation movement is broadened so as to include both sexes, and unless the movement can offer them advantages over their present situation which are sufficient to make the changes worthwhile. Towards this end, he argues that the dominant masculine role, as it exists in the contemporary U.S.A., is wholly self-defeating; the very men who succeed in appearing most masculine seem to suffer most from insecurity. Sexual equality requires that the role and character differences between the sexes be minimized, and, above all, that men and women share equally in the responsibility for childrearing. In the two-wage-earner family, this will be facilitated by part-time jobs, child-care centers, staggered working days or hours, paternity leaves, and the like. And should some men or women choose to be full-time homemakers while their attaches (1) work for pay, he suggests that their dignity, and equal status with the wage-earner, be assured by the legal requirement that half the earner's salary be paid to the homemaker.

The second half of the book consists mainly of dialogues taken from men's, and mixed, consciousness-raising groups, together with suggestions for running a C-R group and avoiding some of the problems that arise in such groups. The emphasis is on personal (supposed) revelation rather than "intellectualizing": "John made a few references to William Reich and Marcuse; in disgust we consciously ignored him." (p.241)

1. Farrell introduces "attache" as a term for one's lover, or the person to whom one is emotionally attached. He also proposes a set of sex-neutral pronouns: *te* (he or she), *tis* (his or her), and *ter* (him or her).

The Male Machine, by Marc Feigen-Fasteau (McGraw-Hill, New York, 1972)

A critique of the masculine mystique in contemporary America, which describes the damage done to men themselves by male supremacist traditions. The story is a familiar one: men must continually demonstrate their maleness by competing with other men, preferably within groups or contexts from which women are excluded. In order to appear tough and competent they must suppress and deny their "feminine" emotions and attitudes, e.g. fear, self-doubt, sympathy for others and the desire for intimacy. As a result they become unable to understand their own needs and desires and incompetent in personal relationships. Unable to be close to other men, they depend upon women for emotional and ego support, which support they usually do not reciprocate.

This stereotyped ideal of masculinity leads not only to personal unhappiness for men (who either fail to measure up to the standard or find their success hollow), but to untold social damage, ranging from street violence and military adventures like the Vietnam War to the Watergate mentality in government and business. The cure, it is argued, is a more androgynous view of personality, which acknowledges that each human individual has the capacity to develop both "masculine" and "feminine" strengths, and that the happiest and most effective people of both sexes are apt to be those who develop both sides of themselves. Also necessary is a more androgynous division of labor within the family, since the traditional male-as-breadwinner model perpetuates the old stereotypes. A more careful analysis of the concept of androgyny would have been extremely useful here. Also left unexplored is the key question of whether the fact of an individual's maleness or femaleness ought to play any role at all in the formation of her or his self-concept. We must decide whether men's and women's liberation ultimately commits us to ceasing to think of ourselves as men and women in any but a biological sense.

Men and Masculinity, edited by Joseph H. Pleck and Jack Sawyer (Prentice-Hall, Englewood Cliffs, New Jersey, 1974)

Contemporary articles, mostly but not all popular, on the ways in which men are oppressed in a patriarchal society. Includes Ruth E. Hartley's "Sex-Role Pressures and the Socialization of the Male Child"; Sidney M. Jourard on "Lethal Aspects of the Male Role"; I.F. Stone on "Machismo in Washington"; Gloria Steinem's "The Myth of the Masculine Mystique"; John Gagnon on "Physical Strength, Once of Significance"; Jack Sawyer "On Male Liberation"; and others.

Men's Liberation: A New Definition of Masculinity, by Jack Nichols (Penguin Books, New York, 1975)

A critique of contemporary "masculinist values," such as toughness, aggressiveness, competition for its own sake, and (unfortunately) rationality. Nichols argues that these values, which pervade our culture and are absorbed largely unconsciously by its males, are outmoded, destructive of men's happiness, and dangerous to society. Men need to question, for instance, the value of rationality as an exclusive alternative to intuition, and the cultivation and expression of "feelings." (Like too many people, he considers reason antithetical to intuition and emotion, not suspecting that it may in fact be the height of rationality to pay attention to one's intuitions and emotions; this confusion mars much of the argumentation.) Most men's lives are stunted and impoverished by their constant striving for control and domination. He praises passivity, openness, spontaneity and playfulness as far more rewarding than the pursuit of power, which turns out to be mostly illusory anyway. If men would stop competing so hard they could form deeper friendships, enjoy sex more, and free themselves from the rat race enough to begin to enjoy life.

Nichols argues that it makes little sense to claim that men have oppressed women any more than women have oppressed men. Indeed he gives considerable credence to Esther Vilar's claim that it is women who oppress men, by manipulating them into providing financial support. But, he argues, this manipulation is only a defensive response to men's domineering treatment of women, and one that will become unnecessary as men abandon masculinist values. Men can help to liberate women as well as themselves by refusing to enter into relationships with women which involve the provision of economic support. Children too should be economically independent, supported and educated at public expense and as independent of their parents as possible. Yet, in spite of the socialist cast of such a proposal, he denies that the capitalist economic system is to blame for our current social problems; the destructive features of capitalism, technology and the like, are primarily the result of masculinist values (not vice versa) and can be changed only by changing the latter.

Nichols does not describe his proposed alternatives to masculinist values as either feminine or femininist. Instead, he associates them with the ancient Chinese philosopher Lao-tzu, with Zen Buddhism, Vedantic mysticism and the poetry of Walt Whitman. In spite of these sources of inspiration, he seems to be only groping towards a specifically ethical stance. His arguments persistently remain on the level of individual pragmatism, on the apparent assumption that men will do what is in their own enlightened best interest, if only they can be made to see, or to feel, that it is so; and that in the process they will naturally make the world a better place. This helps, perhaps, to account for the impression that, while criticizing the traditional value system of the American male, Nichols yet manages to remain substantially within that system.

The Myth of American Manhood, edited by Leonard Kriegal (Dell Publishing Company, New York, 1978)

This is a collection of fiction and essays by American male writers, each of whom either presents or bemoans the passage of the ideal of the American man as macho super-stud. The editor seems more nostalgic than critical with respect to this masculine mystique, and chooses stories that tend to glamorize (or at least forgive) the man who embodies the myth. The authors include Cotton Mather, James Fenimore Cooper, Herman Melville, Ulysses S. Grant, Mark Twain, Henry James, Stephen Crane, Ernest Hemingway, Ring Lardner, Edmund Wilson, James Baldwin, and Norman Mailer.

Psychoanalysis and Male Sexuality, edited by Hendrik M. Reitenbeck (College and University Press, New Haven, Connecticut, 1966)

Papers by noted psychoanalysts, dealing with various aspects of male sexual behavior, and male psychosexual development and pathology. Includes Clifford Kirkpatrick and Eugene Kamin on male sexual aggression; Melanie Klein on the Oedipus conflict; Karen Horney on "The Dread of Women"; Ralph Greenson, "On Homosexuality and Gender Identity"; Heinz Lichtenstein on narcissism; Felix Bechem on "The Femininity Complex in Men"; Sandor Ferenczi on the psychoanalytic treatment of impotence; Franz Alexander on the castration complex; Rudolph Loewenstein on phallic passivity; Otto Fenichal on transvestism; Robert C. Bak on fetishism; and others.

Sex:Male/Gender:Masculine, edited by John W. Petras (Alfred Publishing Company, Port Washington, New York, 1975)

Includes both popular and academic articles on male (and sometimes female) gender roles in this country. For instance: Lionel Tiger on male aggression; John Money and Anke Ehrhardt on the "Rearing of a Sex-Reassigned Normal Male Infant After Traumatic Loss of the Penis"; humorous pieces by Julius Lester and Bill Cosby; Mirra Komarovsky on cultural contradictions in the male sex role; Carole Joffe on "Sex Role Socialization and the Nursery School"; an excerpt from Norman Mailer's **Prisoner of Sex**; Michael Korda on domestic chauvinism; Myron Brenton on the American father; Margaret Polatnick on "Why Men Don't Rear Children"; and others.

ANTHOLOGIES & SOURCEBOOKS XII. PHILOSOPHY & RELIGION

Feminism and Philosophy, edited by Mary Vetterling-Braggin, Frederick A. Elliston and Jane English (Littlefield, Adams and Company, Totowa, New Jersey, 1977)

This is an excellent collection of articles by contemporary philosophers on topics related to women's liberation. Includes Alison Jaggar's "Political Philosophies of Women's Liberation"; Ann Ferguson and Joyce Treblicot on the ideal of androgyny; Patrick Grim, Elizabeth Beardsley, Janice Moulton, Carolyn Korsmeyer and Virginia Valican on various aspects of sexism in language; Onora O'Neill on the concept of equality of opportunity; Lawrence Crocker, Robert Fullinwider, and Alan Goldman on preferential hiring or so-called reverse discrimination; Lyla O'Driscoll, Sara Ann Ketchum, Joseph and Mary Ann Barnhart and Joseph and Clorinda Margolis on marriage; Susan Griffin, Carolyn Shafer, Marilyn Frye, Pamela Foa and Susan Roe Peterson on rape; Susan Nicholson, Elizabeth Rapaport, Paul Segal, Jane English and Howard Cohen on abortion; and articles by Sandra Bartley and Anne Dickason.

Feminist Frameworks: Alternative Theoretical Accounts of the Relations Between Men and Women, edited by Alison M. Jaggar and Paula Rothenberg Struhl (McGraw-Hill Book Company, New York, 1978)

A good collection of (mostly but not all contemporary) articles by philosophers, psychologists, ethologists, educators, political leaders and others. The selections are organized under five basic philosophical perspectives: conservatism, liberalism, traditional Marxism, radical feminism, and socialist feminism. A few of the authors: Sigmund Freud; Steven Goldberg; John Stuart Mill; Friedrich Engels; Evelyn Reed; Shulamith Firestone; Charlotte Perkins Gilman; Juliet Mitchell; Lionel Tiger and Robin Fox; Patricia Cayo Sexton; V.I. Lenin; Bruno Bettelheim; Alix Kates Schulman; Rita Mae Brown; Eli Zaretsky; Albert Ellis; Clara Zetkin; Ti-Grace Atkinson; and Sheila Rowbotham.

Having Children: Philosophical and Legal Reflections on Parenthood, edited by Onora O'Neill and William Ruddick (Oxford University Press, New York, 1979)

This is an anthology produced under the auspices of the Society for Philosophy and Public Affairs. It includes some historical selections (e.g. from Rousseau, Locke and Mill), and a number of relevant recent court decisions. The focus is on the right of persons to become parents, of parents to control their (minor or dependent) childrens' lives, and of children to free themselves of parental control. Most relevant to the rights of women as such are the discussions of abortion by Martha Brandt Bolton and Raymond Herbenick, and Virginia Held's "The Equal Obligations of Mothers and Fathers."

Bolton argues that fetuses logically cannot have the same right to life as humans who are undisputedly persons, because they cannot be granted that right without also being granted the continued nurturance and support of the pregnant women—which the latter may not, in all cases, be reasonably required to provide. Herbenick, on the other hand, assumes that the fetus's right to life is the overriding moral consideration, and makes the (rather horrifying) suggestion that the state should take custody of fetuses which would otherwise be aborted, forcing the woman to complete the pregnancy and to put the infant up for adoption. Held's article emphasizes that equality of opportunity for women will require that we abandon the presumption that parenting is primarily the responsibility of mothers rather than of both parents, and the realignment of social arrangements (e.g. the working hours of parents) to make the equal sharing of parental responsibilities more feasible.

History of Ideas on Woman: A Source Book, edited by Rosemary Agonisto (G.P. Putnam's Sons, New York, 1977)

Important historical writings about woman, from the most misogynist to the most adulatory. The authors included are: Plato; Aristotle; (the unknown writers of) Genesis; Plutarch; Saint Paul; Saint Augustine; Saint Thomas Aquinas; Francis Bacon; Thomas Hobbes; John Locke; Jean Jacques Rousseau; David Hume; Immanuel Kant; Mary Wollstonecraft; Georg Hegel; Soren Kierkegaard; Arthur Schopenhauer; Ralph Waldo Emerson; John Stuart Mill; Charles Darwin; Friedrich Nietzsche; Friedrich Engels; Bertrand Russell; Sigmund Freud; Karen Horney; Ashley Montagu; Betty Friedan and Herbert Marcuse. The introductory remarks on each thinker are especially helpful.

Loving Women/Loving Men: Gay Liberation and the Church, edited/authored by Sally Gearhart and William R. Johnson (Glide Publications, San Francisco, 1974)

Essays on the connection between gay liberation and the Christian churches. Articles by Donald Kuhn and the editors relate the recent history of efforts by gay people within the churches to organize and to force the churches to alter their hostile and ignorant condemnation of homosexuality and homosexuals. Robert Trees argues that the Bible does not condemn homosexuality as such, but rather as a manifestation of paganism, and that there is every reason to believe that "the homosexual is accepted by God." (p.52) Bill Johnson maintains that gay men within the churches must lead the fight for the acceptance of homosexuality, the rejection of the sexual stereotypes that underlie Christian homophobia, and the reconceptualization of God as androgynous (or gyandrous). Gearhart, on the other hand, argues that the necessary changes cannot occur within the churches, for the latter cannot afford to recognize the past and present misogyny of the Judeo-Christian tradition and so cannot accommodate the demands of feminists and women-identified women. The battle will have to be waged outside of and against the churches; for "the Christian church is a great and splendid drama, but it plays the boards in the service of falsehood and woman-hatred." (p.150)

Man and Aggression, edited by M.F. Ashley Montagu (Oxford University Press, London, Oxford and New York, 1968)

This is a collection of much-needed rebuttals to the theories of Konrad Lorenz and Robert Ardrey concerning the human "instincts" for aggression and territoriality. These theories, Ardrey's in particular, are clearly and repeatedly shown to be based on distortions, oversimplifications and insupportable inferences from scientific data. They are contemporary reincarnations of Social Darwinism, used as rationalizations of capitalism, imperialism and male supremacy—though this last point is one which none of the contributors stress. The contributors include Ashley Montagu, Sally Carrighar, Kenneth Boulding, Edmund Leach, and a dozen others.

Male and Female: Christian Approaches to Sexuality, edited by Ruth Tiffany Barnhouse and Urban T. Holmes, III (Seabury

Press, New York, 1976)

Christian writers, most of them fairly conservative, examine the concepts of masculinity and femininity; the treatment of women in the Bible and in the various Christian churches; the institution of marriage; the ordination of women; the moral and legal status of homosexuality; the sexuality of God; and related issues.

Masculine/Feminine: Readings in Sexual Mythology and the Liberation of Women, edited by Betty Roszak and Theodore Roszak (Harper and Row, New York, 1969)

An assorted collection of writings, some historical, mostly contemporary, on the man-woman problem. Male writers include both male supremacists (Friedrich Nietzsche, August Strindberg, Sigmund Freud, Robert Graves, and Lionel Tiger) and male sympathizers (George Bernard Shaw, Havelock Ellis, Gunnar Myrdal, and Theodore Roszak). The rest are feminist women, including Karen Horney; Dorothy Sayers; Ruth Herschberger; Helen Hacker; Simone de Beauvoir; Juliet Mitchell; Alice Rossi; Marlene Dixon; Robin Morgan, and others. Also includes the radical feminist manifestos of WITCH (The Women's International Conspiracy from Hell), SCUM (Valerie Solanis' Society for Cutting Up Men), the Redstockings and other activist groups.

The Monist, January, 1973, Volume 57, Number 1.

A special issue on the topic of women's liberation. Includes Christine Pierce on Plato's treatment of women in *The Republic*; Virginia Held on "Reasonable Progress and Self-Respect"; Abigail Rosenthal on "Feminism Without Contradictions"; Mary Anne Warren on the morality of abortion; Jan Narveson on "The Moral Problems of Population"; Thomas E. Hill, Jr. on "Servility and Self-Respect"; and Mary Mothersill's "Notes on Feminism."

Philosophy and Sex, edited by Robert Baker and Frederick Elliston (Prometheus Books, Buffalo, New York, 1975)

An important collection of recent articles by American (and some British) philosophers, on topics ranging from the moral status of abortion to the sexist connotation of four-letter words. The editors point out that most western philosophers have had little or nothing to say about sexual issues, and that this was particularly true of twentieth-century philosophers prior to 1969. At that time, however, the reawakening of the feminist movement seemed to reach into philosophy, and articles on sex and sexual relations began to appear regularly in the philosophical journals. Among those included here are papers by Barbara Lawrence, Janice Moulton and Robert Baker on sexism in sexual language; Marilyn Frye's "Male Chauvinism: A Conceptual Analysis"; Sara Ruddick on the concept of "Better Sex"; John McMurty's "Critique of Monogamy"; responses to McMurty by David Palmer and Michael D. Bayles; Richard Wasserstrom on the morality of adultery; Frederick Elliston's defense of promiscuity; Thomas Nagel on "Sexual Perversion"; Michael Slate arguing that sexual perversion is an inapplicable concept; Robert Solomon, who compares sexual interaction to a language; Joseph Margolis' examination of the classification of homosexuality by the psychiatric profession; Judith Jarvis Thomson's "Defense of Abortion"; Alison Jaggar's "Abortion and a Woman's Right to Decide"; Baruch Brody on "Fetal Humanity and the Theory of Essentialism"; and Richard Hare's "Abortion and the Golden Rule."

Philosophy and Women edited by Sharon Bishop and Marjorie Weinzweig (Wadsworth Publishing Company, Belmont, California, 1979)

A good collection of philosophical essays on sexism and sexual equality, some historical but most contemporary. The noncontemporary pieces include excerpts from Plato, Aristotle, St. Thomas Aquinas, John Stuart Mill, Sigmund Freud and Margaret Mead. Articles by current American philosophers include Richard Wasserstrom's "Racism and Sexism;" Robert Baker's "Pricks and Chicks" (an analysis of sexist slang); Marilyn Frye on "Male Chauvinism"; Sandra Lee Bartley "On Psychological Oppression"; Sharon Bishop Hill on "Self-Determination and Autonomy"; Janice Moulton's "Sex and Reference"; Wasserstrom on the morality of adultery; Ann Garry on feminist objections to pornography; Pamela Foa on "What's Wrong with Rape"; Shulamith Firestone's critique of heterosexual love and Virginia Held's defense of it; Judith Jarvis Thomson and Mary Anne Warren (separately) on the morality of abortion; Thomson, Warren and Wasserstrom on preferential hiring; and others.

Philosophy of Woman: Classical to Current Concepts, edited by Mary Briody Mahowald (Hackett Publishing Company, Indianapolis, 1978)

An excellent collection of philosophical views, ancient to modern, on women and the relation between the sexes. Includes selections from Plato; Aristotle; Aquinas; Augustine; David Hume; Jean Jacques Rousseau; Immanuel Kant; Mary Wollstonecraft; Arthur Schopenhauer; John Stuart Mill; Soren Kierkegaard; Friedrich Nietzsche; Simone de Beauvoir; Friedrich Engels; V.I. Lenin; and Bertrand Russell. Also contemporary pieces by feminists (Germaine Greer, Betty Friedan and Ti-Grace Atkinson), antifeminists (Esther Vilar and Midge Decter), and philosophers (Hilde Hein, Christine Allen, Christine Pierce, Joyce Treblicot, Joseph Lucas, Trudy Govien, and Carol Gould).

The Potential of Woman, edited by Seymour M. Farber and Roger H.L. Wilson (McGraw-Hill, New York, 1963)

This is a set of papers and panel discussions by a group of distinguished academicians from many fields, which were presented as one of a series of colloquia at the University of California San Francisco Medical Center in January of 1963. The overall tone is clearly pre-women's-liberation-movement, and a few of the papers are unabashedly sexist (a term which had not yet been invented). For instance, we find gynecologist Edmund Overstreet suggesting that the whole of women's post-menopausal existence may be characterized as a disease state (since nature did not intend women to outlive their childbearing capacity); art critic Thomas Howe maintaining that women's significance in the field of art is solely as collectors and patrons, not as creators; and Alan Watts suggesting that men need to develop the "feminine" in themselves, but without even considering the possibility that the converse may also be true. Other (nonsexist) contributions include: Eleanor Maccoby on "Women's Intellect"; John Money on the interaction of biological and environmental factors in the developmental differentiation of masculinity and femininity; Peter Koestenbaum on the existentialist view of woman's situation and Marya Mannes on "The Problems of Creative Women."

Pronatalism: The Myth of Mom and Apple Pie, edited by Ellen Peck and Judith Senderowitz (Thomas Y. Crowell Company, New York, 1974)

An excellent collection of (mostly recent and mostly academic) articles which challenge the traditional assumption of the universal desirability of parenthood and examine the ways in which our society pressures people towards becoming parents. Includes, among other: Leta Hollingworth (feminist psychologist of the early twentieth century), Judith Blake (sociologist), Helen Franzwa (communications scholar), Ellen Peck (popular antinatalist writer), and Nancy Cox (educator), on various aspects of pronatalism in America; Robert Chester (sociologist) on the relationship between childlessness and divorce; Edward Pohlman (psychologist) on pronatalist bias in marriage and family textbooks, and why (some) people want children; Betty Rollin (NBC news correspondent) on the myth of the motherhood instinct; sociologist E.E. LeMaster's study of "Parenthood as Crisis"; sociologist Harold Feldman's study of the (distinctly negative) effect of parenthood on marital happiness; and Paul Popenoe, J.E. Veevers, Susan O. Gustavus and James Henly (all sociologists) on the many reasons for voluntary childlessness.

Religion and Sexism: Images of Women in the Jewish and Christian Traditions, edited by Rosemary Radford Ruether (Simon and Schuster, New York, 1974)

Contemporary historians and theologians writing on women's place in Judeo-Christian theory and practice, from the Old Testament to the Reformation and the modern crises over the ordination of women. Includes essays by Patricia Martin Doyle; Phyllis Bird on women in the Old Testament; Bernard P. Prusak; Constance F. Parvey on New Testament women; Rosemary Radford Ruether on "Misogynism and Virginal Feminism in the Fathers of the Church"; Judith Hauptman on the treatment of women in the Talmud; Eleanor McLaughlin on "Woman in Medieval Theology"; Clara Henning on women and canon law; Jane Douglass on "Women and the Continental Reformation"; Joan Romero comparing Barth and Tillich on women; and Judith Goldenberg's vision of the triumphant return of Lilith.

Sex Equality, edited by Jane English (Prentice-Hall, Englewood Cliffs, New Jersey, 1977)

A good collection of basic materials in the philosophy of feminism. The historical section includes excerpts from Plato, Aristotle, John Locke, Jean Jacques Rousseau, J.G. Fichte, John Stuart

Mill, Friedrich Engels, and Simone de Beauvoir. The contemporary philosophers include Bernard Williams, on "The Idea of Equality"; Alison Jaggar, arguing against the institutionalization of sexual differences. J. Lucas, who claims that certain kinds of sexual discrimination are justified by pragmatic considerations; Joyce Treblicot, arguing that natural psychological differences between the sexes, even if they exist, do not justify the sexual segregation of social roles; Christine Pierce, on "Natural Law Language and Women"; Onora O'Neill on the concept of equality of opportunity; Lisa Newton, arguing against "reverse discrimination"; Irving Thalberg, who defends it; and Thomas Hill, Jr., who argues that servility (e.g. in a wife) is morally objectionable on Kantian grounds. There are, finally, a few nonphilosophers, including Sam Ervin, Jr., arguing against the Equal Rights Amendment; Steven Goldberg on "The Inevitability of Patriarchy"; Naomi Weisstein's "Psychology Constructs the Female"; Robin Lakoff on "Language and Woman's Place"; and others.

Sexist Religion and Women in the Church, edited by Alice L. Hageman (Association Press, New York, 1974)

A good collection of papers by feminist theologians, which were delivered in a 1972 seminar at the Harvard Divinity School. Includes Nelle Morton and Letty Russell on the impact of the ordination of women to the ministry; Theressa Hoover on black women and the church; Dorothy D. Burlage on the repression of female sexuality in the Judeo-Christian tradition; Mary Daly's "Theology after the Demise of God the Father"; Gail B. Shulman on sexist elements in Judaism; Alice Hageman on women's ambiguous role as Christian missionaries during the nineteenth and twentieth centuries; and others.

Sexuality Today and Tomorrow: Contemporary Issues in Human Sexuality, edited by Sol Gordon and Roger W. Libby (Duxbury Press, North Scituate, Massachusetts, 1976)

Articles by contemporary biologists, anthropologists, clerics, historians, physicians, educators, and sexologists on such topics as the women's liberation movement, abortion, rape, prostitution, pornography, sex education, premarital sex, homosexuality, bisexuality, and sexual inadequacy. The authors include Jessie Bernard; Helen Hacker; Joseph Pleck; Susan Griffin; Nena and George O'Neill; Margaret Mead; Albert Ellis; Susan Sontag; and many others.

The Study of Women: Enlarging Perspectives of Social Reality, edited by Eloise C. Snyder (Harper and Row, New York, 1979)

This is a good introductory text in women's studies, with individually authored chapters on the ways women have been dealt with in the past by the male-dominated fields of sociology, economics, law, psychology, literature, history, education, and religion, and on the new feminist-inspired approaches to the study of women in each of these areas. Also includes a chapter on minority women in America, with articles on black, native American, Chicana and Asian American women; and a foreword and afterword by Jessie Bernard.

Woman in Western Thought, edited by Martha Lee Osborne (Random House, New York, 1979)

This is a good selection of excerpts from Western philosophers on the subject of women, with commentaries by contemporary feminist philosophers. Includes Plato, and Julia Annes on Plato; Aristotle, critiqued by Christine Garside Allen; St. Augustine, commented on by Rosemary R. Ruether; St. Thomas Aquinas, and Eleanor C. McLaughlin on women in medieval theology; Benedictus de Spinoza, Immanuel Kant and Friedrich Hegel, criticized by Carol C. Gould; John Locke; Jean Jacques Rousseau, and Elizabeth Rapaport on Rousseau; Mary Wollstonecraft, and Carolyn Korsmeyer on Wollstonecraft; Margaret Fuller; Soren Kierkegaard; Arthur Schopenhauer; Ashley Montagu; Friedrich Nietzsche, and Kathryne Pyne Parsons on Nietzsche; Auguste Comte; John Stuart Mill, commented on by Alice Rossi; Friedrich Engels; Bertrand Russell; Emma Goldman; Jean-Paul Sartre, criticized by Margery L. Collins and Christine Pierce; Simone de Beauvoir; and Shulamith Firestone.

Women and Men: Changing Roles, Relationships and Perceptions, edited by Libby A. Cater, Anne Firor Scott and Wendy Martyna (Praeger Publishers, New York, 1977)

Discussions held and papers given at the Aspen Workshop for Women and Men, sponsored in 1975 by the Aspen Institute for Humanistic Studies. Contributors include Tamara K. Hareven, on the history of the nuclear family; Myra H. Strober, on the sex segregation of jobs; Marcia Guttentag and Susan Salasin, on why women are more often depressed than men; Joseph H. Pleck, on recent developments in the psychology of sex roles; and Catharine R. Stimpson, on "Sex, Gender, and American Culture."

Women and Philosophy: Toward a Theory of Liberation, edited by Carol C. Gould and Marx W. Wartofsky (G.P. Putnam's Sons, New York, 1976)

This is an anthology of recent philosophical work, most of it reprinted from a special issue of **The Philosophical Forum** (Volume V, numbers 1–2). The contributors are: Carol Gould, who explores the challenge to traditional philosophical methodology posed by the philosophy of feminism; Ann Dickason, writing on the apparent changes in Plato's view of female nature; Carolyn Whitbeck, arguing that the major theories about the difference between the sexes can be traced to early misconceptions that arise in the minds of boys; Diana Hall, on "Biology, Sex Hormones and Sexism in the 1920s"; Carolyn Korsmeyer on Mary Wollstonecraft; Margery Collins and Christine Pierce on "Sexism in Sartre's Psychoanalysis"; Robert Paul Wolff, on the contradictions inherent in our ways of conceptualizing persons; Mikalio Markovic on "Women's Liberation and Human Emancipation"; Virginia Held on the Marxist analysis of sexual relations; Elizabeth Rapaport, comparing the views of Rousseau and recent radical feminists about the nature of love; Judith Torney on the oppressive norm of feminine self-sacrifice; Larry Blum *et al* on the distorted altruism required by the traditional female role; Hilde Hein on the male backlash against women's liberation; Sandra Harding on whether feminist demands are reformist or revolutionary; Elizabeth Beardsly on "Referential Genderization"; Irving Thalberg, Marlene Gerber Fried, Mary Vetterling-Braggin and Michael Martin (separately) on preferential hiring or reverse discrimination; Onora O'Neill on the concept of equality of opportunity; and Alison Jaggar, on "Abortion and a Woman's Right to Decide."

Women and Religion, edited by Judith Plaskow and Joan Arnold (Scholars Press, Missoula, Montana, 1974)

An excellent collection, in which contemporary feminist scholars and theologians explore the sexism inherent in patriarchal religion, and search for alternative religious conceptions which take account of the spiritual perceptions of women as well as those of men. Includes Mary Daly's "Theology After the Demise of God the Father"; Carol Christ on Doris Lessing's vision of **The Four-Gated City**; Joan Arnold on sexism in the theology of Karl Barth; Elizabeth Farians on phallic idolatry; Nancy Falk on the decline of the status of women in the Buddhist tradition; Janice Raymond's "Beyond Male Morality"; Jean MacRae on the feminist view of abortion; Rita Gross on the methodology of the history of women in religion; Leonard Swindler on sexism as a sign of decadence in religion; and others.

Women and Religion: A Feminist Sourcebook of Christian Thought, edited by Elizabeth Clark and Herbert Richardson (Harper and Row, New York, 1977)

A good selection of excerpts from the works of Western religious thinkers, on the subject of woman and her relation to man; the editors provide useful introductions to the life and thought of each author. Includes passages from Aeschylus' *Eumenides*; comments on the Old and New Testaments; excerpts from the church fathers Clement of Alexandria, Jerome, and Augustine; from Thomas Aquinas, Dame Julian of Norwich (a fourteenth century Anchorite) and Margery Kempe (a Christian mystic and contemporary of Dame Julian, who wrote the first autobiography in the English language); from the *Malleus Maleficarium*, the fifteenth-century handbook for witch hunters; Martin Luther and John Milton on marriage from the Protestant viewpoint; accounts of Ann Lee, the Shaker who claimed to be a female Messiah; Friedrich Schleiermacher and Franz von Baader, theologians of the romantic era who praised androgyny as a symbol of both human and divine wholeness; John Humphrey Noyes, founder of the Oneida Community, who advocated group marriage and intercourse without male ejaculation as an expression of Christian love; Sarah Grimke's response to the Massachusetts ministers who attacked her public speaking against slavery and for women's rights; from Elizabeth Cady Stanton's *The Woman's Bible*; from the *Casti Connubi* of Pope Pius XI; from Karl Barth, who holds that women are equal to men yet second in the divinely ordained sequence; and, as a harbinger of the future, Mary Daly's sermon on "The Woman's Movement: An Exodus Community."

ANTHOLOGIES & SOURCEBOOKS XIII. PSYCHOLOGY

Beyond Sex-Role Stereotypes: Readings Toward a Psychology of Androgyny, edited by Alexandra G. Kaplan and Joan P. Bean (Little, Brown and Company, Boston and Toronto, 1976)

Research and review articles bearing on the topic of androgyny (i.e., freedom from sex-role stereotypes) as a model of psychological health. Includes an overview of the research on sex differences, by Jessie Bernard; Anne Constantinople's critique of the standard psychological tests designed to measure "masculinity" and "femininity"; Sandra Bem on sex-typed vs. androgynous individuals; Jeanne Humphrey Block's cross-cultural study of sex-role conceptions in northern Europe and the United States; Alice S. Rossi on "Sex Equality"; "A Model of Sex-Role Transcendence" by Meda Rebecca, Robert Hefner, and Barbara Oleshansky; Miriam Rosenberg's critique of research that purports to show that sex roles are biologically based; Mary Brown Parlee on "The Premenstrual Syndrome"; Estelle Ramey arguing that men also have monthly mood cycles; Suzannah Lessard on the emotional aspect of the decision to abort a pregnancy; Karen F. Rotkin on phallocentric distortions of human sexuality; the Radicalesbians on "The Woman-Identified Woman"; Walter Gove on "The Relationship Between Sex Roles, Marital Status, and Mental Illness"; Lois Wladis Hoffman's review of research on the effects on children of maternal employment; Virginia O'Leary on attitudes that obstruct the occupational aspirations of women; Mae C. King on the stereotyping of black women in America; Alexandra Kaplan's "Androgyny as a Model of Mental Health for Women"; Cary Cherniss' "Personological Study of Women's Liberation"; and a number of recent studies of sex-typed and androgynous behaviors in children of various ages.

The overriding theme of all of these pieces is that sex-stereotyping, in the culture and in the behavior of individuals, is less conducive to psychological well-being than is the androgynous ideal which permits persons to behave in *either* a "masculine" or a "feminine" way, depending upon the demands of the situation. (See Androgyny.)

The Development of Sex Differences, edited by Eleanor E. Maccoby (Stanford University Press, Stanford, California, 1966)

This is an important collection of papers, which grew out of a series of group discussions at Stanford. David Hamburg and Donald Lunde present a survey of (then) recent research on sex hormones and their possible effects on the development of sex differences in human behavior. Maccoby gives a summary of research findings on "Sex Differences in Intellectual Functioning," and arrives at some tentative conclusions about the relative IQs and verbal, spatial, analytic and mathematical abilities of boys and girls, some of which are modified in her more recent work. (See Maccoby, *The Psychology of Sex Differences*, 1974.) Walter Mischell defends "A Social-Learning View of Sex Differences and Behavior," which stresses social conditioning of various types as the primary cause of sex-typed behavior, and sees sex identity as a product of previously learned behavior. Lawrence Kohlberg, on the other hand, supports "A Cognitive-Developmental Analysis of Childrens' Sex-Role Concepts and Attitudes," which stresses the causal role of the child's own conceptual processes in shaping behavior into gender roles. Finally, Ray D'Andraale explains the anthropological point of view, which treats sex-role behaviors as cultural products rather than individual psychological traits.

Female Psychology: The Emerging Self, edited by Sue Cox (Science Research Associates, Chicago, 1976)

This is an illustrated anthology, intended for use as an undergraduate text. It includes feminist art and poetry, and exercises for personal consciousness raising, as well as articles by contemporary feminist scholars. The latter include Estelle Ramey, arguing against the notion that sex hormones control male and female behavior; Mary Parlee on the premenstrual syndrome; Margaret Mead's conclusion to *Sex and Temperament*; Esther Newton and Paula Webster on matriarchy; Naomi Weisstein's "Psychology Constructs the Female"; the conclusion of Eleanor Maccoby and Carol Jacklin's *Psychology of Sex Differences*; Helen Hacker on "Women as a Minority Group"; Sandra and Daryl Bem on sexism as a nonconscious but behavior-shaping ideology; Dair Gillespie arguing that the modern husband still has much more power in the family than the wife; Linda LaRue on "The Black Movement and Women's Liberation"; Anna Nieto-Gomez on Chicana Women; Irene Fugitomi and Diane Wong on Asian-American Women; Shirley Ward Hill on native American women; Mary

Jane Sherfey on female sexuality; Anne Koedt's "The Myth of the Vaginal Orgasm"; Susan Griffin on "Rape: The All-American Crime"; the Radicalesbians on women-identified women; Phyllis Chesler on women and psychotherapy; Betsy Belote on masochism and hysteria as supposedly normal feminine traits; Pauline Bart on "Depression in Middle-Aged Women"; Jack Sawyer on men's liberation; and others.

Half the Human Experience: The Psychology of Women, by Janet Shibley Hyde and B.G. Rosenberg (D.C. Heath and Company, Lexington, Massachusetts, Toronto and London, 1976)

A good introductory text, authored by a male-female team. The authors discuss the Jungian, Freudian, social learning, and cognitive developmental models of sex-role development; the supposed cognitive and motivational differences between the sexes; the possible significance of women's monthly cycles (and the possibility that men may also have monthly cycles); the alleged connection between fetal exposure to testosterone, and aggressive behavior (which they question); the suggestion that the higher level of uric acid in the blood serum of men may account in part for their supposedly higher achievement motivation (to which they give some credence); lesbianism and female sexual response; sex differences in animal behavior; cross-cultural perspectives on sex roles; the psychology of black women and of women as a "minority" group; and possible new directions for further research on the psychology of women.

Human Sexuality in Four Perspectives, edited by Frank A. Beach (Johns Hopkins University Press, Baltimore and London, 1977)

Psychologists, psychiatrists and others report and analyze recent research on human sexual differences. The four perspectives are the developmental, sociological, physiological, and evolutionary. Includes Milton Diamond on the effects of hormones on the fetal brain; John Money on hermaphroditism; Jerry Kagan on the "Psychology of Sex Differences"; William Davenport on cross-cultural differences in sexual behavior; Martin Hoffman on "Homosexuality"; Robert Stoller on "Sexual Deviations"; Richard Whalen on "Brain Mechanism Controlling Sexual Behavior"; Frederick Melges and David Hamburg on the psychological effects of the menstrual cycle in women; and Frank Beach on cross-species comparisons of sexual behavior, and on the effects of hormones on human behavior.

Psychoanalysis and Women, edited by Jean Baker Miller (Penguin Books, Baltimore, 1973)

Essays by prominent early and contemporary psychoanalysts, criticizing various aspects of the Freudian theory of female psychology. Includes pieces by Karen Horney; Alfred Adler; Clara Thompson; Frieda Fromm-Reichmann; Virginia Gunst; Gregory Zilboorg; Mary Jane Sherfey; Mabel Blake Cohen; Paul Chodoff; Leon Salzman; Judd Marmor; Ruth Moulton; Robert J. Stoller; Alexandra Symonds; Robert Seidenberg; and Lester Gelb.

The Psychology of Sex Differences, by Hilary M. Lips and Nina Lee Colwill (Prentice-Hall, Englewood Cliffs, New Jersey, 1978)

This is a good survey of contemporary psychological research and theory on the nature of the sex difference. The authors contrast the approaches of functional psychology, psychoanalysis, social learning theory, and cognitive developmental theories. They favor the social psychological approach, which emphasizes "the learning of behavior through observation, imitation, and reinforcement." (p.38) Especially valuable are their criticisms of the standard psychological tests of "masculinity" and "femininity." They also argue persuasively against the claim that existing research, e.g. on animals, human hermaphrodites, and XYY males, supports the conclusion that the hormone testosterone is a cause of aggression in human males. (See Goldberg, Hutt, and Money and Ehrhardt.)

Psychosexual Imperatives: Their Role in Identity Formation, edited by Marie Coleman Nelson and Jean Ikenberry (Human Sciences Press, New York and London, 1979)

Psychoanalytically oriented essays on psychosexual development and gender identity, some feminist and some conservative in tone. Includes Naomi Goodman on the Adam and Eve myth as an illustration of the theme of father-daughter incest; Judith H. Balfe on Mariolatry and guilt as a moral force; Jean Rhys Bram on the ancient mythology of sex reversal; Joel Fineman on the Freudian conception of bisexuality; Janine Chasseguet-Smirgel on (male) transsexuality and paranoia as due to the repression of femininity; Sallie Sears on the madness of creative women as a function of their oppression; John Munder Ross on the role of the father in shaping the gender identity of both boys and girls, Robert Seidenberg on feminism and psychoanalysis; and others.

Readings on the Psychology of Women, edited by Judith M. Bardwick (Harper and Row, New York, 1972)

An excellent collection of contemporary theory and research papers bearing on female psychology. There are forty-seven entries, of which a few of the most noteworthy are: John Money on "Sexual Dimorphism and Homosexual Gender Identity"; Eleanor E. Maccoby on "Sex Differences in Intellectual Functioning"; Judith M. Bardwick and Elizabeth Donvan on "Ambivalence: The Socialization of Women"; Mirra Komarovsky's "Cultural Contradictions and Sex Roles"; Matina Horner on "The Motive to Avoid Success"; Alice S. Rossi on "Barriers to the Career Choice of Engineering, Medicine, or Science Among American Women"; Rita James Simon *et al.* on "The Woman Ph.D."; Ruth E. Hartley on "Current Changes in Sex Role Patterns"; Pauline B. Bart on "Depression in Middle-Aged Women"; Lee Rainwater on "Some Aspects of Lowerclass Sexual Behavior"; and the important study by Inge K. Broverman *et al.* of "Sex-Role Stereotypes and Clinical Judgments of Mental Health."

Sexual Inversion: The Multiple Roots of Homosexuality, edited by Judd Marmor (Basic Books, New York and London, 1965)

Contemporary articles on the psychological and sociological aspects of homosexuality in men and women. Most of the contributors consider homosexuality to be—if not a mental illness—a "deviance," which involves "impaired gender identity." Thomas Szasz, on the other hand, argues that (the repression of) homosexuality is a moral and legal, rather than a psychiatric problem. And Gordon Rattray Taylor associates repressive attitudes towards homosexuality with "patristic" cultures (those in which young males identify primarily with their fathers), whereas he thinks that in matristic cultures (in which males identify more with their mothers) homosexuality tends to be accepted.

Women and Analysis: Dialogues on Psychoanalytic Views of Femininity, edited by Jean Strouse (Grossman Publishers, New York, 1974)

This collection combines classic papers in the mainstream Freudian theory of the psychology of women with contemporary critiques of the same ideas. Includes Freud's three major essays on femininity and critiques by Juliet Mitchell, Elizabeth Janeway, and Margaret Mead; Karl Abraham on the female castration complex, with a critique by Joel Kovel; Helene Deutsch, criticized by Marcia Cavell; Karen Horney, with a comment by Robert Coles; Emma Jung on the animus and Barbara Charlesworth Gelpi on the androgyne; Marie Bonaparte, with a critique by Ethel Person; Clara M. Thompson, with a commentary by Ruth Moulton; Erik Erikson's "Womanhood and Inner Space"; and Robert Stoller's critique of the Freudian concept of bisexuality.

ANTHOLOGIES & SOURCEBOOKS XIV. SOCIOLOGY

Another Voice: Feminist Perspectives on Social Life and Social Science, edited by Marcia Millman and Rosabeth Moss Kanter (Anchor Press/Doubleday, Garden City, New York, 1975)

Twelve feminist sociologists contributed essays to this book, each surveying the ways in which sociologists have dealt with women in a particular field of study. The authors are: Thelma McCormack, on social change; Rosabeth Kanter, on organizational structures; Judith Lorber, on medical sociology; Sara Lawrence Lightfoot, on the sociology of education; Lyn Loftland on urban sociology; Gaye Tuckman on the creation of culture; Pamela Roby on the sociology of women workers; Lena Myers on black women; Marcia Millman on the sociology of deviance; Arlie Hochschild on the sociology of emotion; David Tresemer on gender roles; and Arlene Kaplan Daniels, on "Feminist Perspectives in Sociological Research."

The Changing Roles of Men and Women, edited by Edmund Dahlstrom; translated by Gunilla and Steven Anderman; foreword by Alva Myrdal (Beacon Press, Boston, 1971)

This is a condensed English version of a collaborative work by seven Swedish and Norwegian social scientists, which was first published in 1962. Sverre Brun-Gulbrandsen shows that children are subjected to differential sex-role socialization from the beginning; Edmund Dahlstrom and Rita Liljestrom discuss the problems of working women; Per Olav Tiller presents evidence that the traditional division of parental roles which leaves the mother dominant in the home may cause damage to the personality development of male children; Annilea Baude and Per Holmberg document the inferior position of women in the labor market; Siv Thorsell explores the frequently biased attitudes of employers towards female employees; and finally Dahlstrom offers an "Analysis of the Debate on Sex Roles," which is carefully neutral as between the various points of view—moderate, radical, and liberal-radical.

Also included, as an appendix, is the 1968 Report to the United Nations on the Status of Women in Sweden. This is a remarkably progressive document, in which the position is taken that, if women are to attain their rightful place in the world outside the home, "man must assume a greater share of the responsibility for the upbringing of children and the care of the home." (p.214) Swedish legislation now incorporates special features to facilitate this.

Changing Women in a Changing Society, edited by Joan Huber (University of Chicago Press, Chicago, 1973)

This is a collection of articles by American sociologists which was originally published as a special edition of the *American Journal of Sociology* (Volume 78, Number 4, January 1973). The contributors include Helen Hughes, on faculty wives who are employed on campus; Jessie Bernard, on the four "revolutions" in sociological theory in which she has participated since the 1920s; Jo Freeman on "The Origins of the Women's Liberation Movement"; Walter Gove and Jeannette Tudor, arguing that adult sex roles contribute to mental illness, especially in the case of women; Mirra Komarovsky on cultural contradictions in the masculine sex role; Anne-Marie Henshel, who shows that it is much more often the husband who decides to involve the couple in "swinging"; Nancy Goldman on women in the armed forces; Cynthia Fuchs Epstein on explanations of the success of black professional women; Saul Feldman, who shows that marriage is an impediment to the success of female but not male graduate students; Anna Russell Hochschild, reviewing sociological research on sex roles; Carol Erlich on "The Woman Book Industry"; Diane Scully and Pauline Bart on "Women in Gynecology Textbooks"; and others.

Female and Male: Socialization, Social Roles, and Social Structure, by Clarice Stasy Stoll (Wm. C. Brown Company, Dubuque, Iowa, 1974)

This was written as an undergraduate text, and provides a good introduction to what is known about the mean differences between the sexes, biological and psychological, plus a feminist perspective on the way that sociologists have dealt with gender roles.

Gender and Sex in Society, by Lucille Duberman, with chapters by Helen Mayer Hacker and Warren T. Farrell (Praeger Publishers, New York, 1975)

This is a survey of current theory and research in sociology of sex roles. Duberman compares the biological, social-learning, cognitive-developmental, psychoanalytic and sociological explanations of gender-role differentiation, and discusses the ill effects of current gender roles on male-female relations and on the work lives of women and men. Helen Hacker summarizes the effects of class, race and culture on gender roles, and Warren Farrell speaks of the need to liberate men as well as women from the prison of gender.

Language and Sex: Difference and Dominance, edited by Barrie Thorne and Nancy Henley (Newbury House Publishers, Rowley, Massachusetts, 1975)

This is an excellent collection of sociolinguistic studies of the relationship between language and sex. The editors point out that, although ethnographers have often noted differences between the speech of men and women of different cultures (e.g. in the case of the Caribs), linguists have, until recently, paid very little attention to the speech of female speakers of English. The papers include Cheris Kramer on indications of subordination in women's speech; Alma Graham on "The Making of a Nonsexist Dictionary"; Muriel Schulz on the tendency for (virtually all) terms for women to develop disparaging connotations; Marjorie Swacker's Fresno study of the relative verbosity of male and female speakers (the former talk much longer); Ruth M. Brend on the differences between male and female intonation patterns in standard American English; Peter Trudgill on the function of linguistic differences as a male route to covert prestige, in Norwich; a study by Dom. H. Zimmerman and Candace West which shows that males use interruptions and silences (delayed responses) to control cross-sex conversations; Ann Bodine's cross-cultural survey of "Sex Differentiation in Language"; Jacqueline Sachs' study of cues used by adults in recognizing sex in children's speech; Louise Cherry on verbal interactions between teachers and male and female children; and Nancy Henley on nonverbal cues ("body language") as indices and means of maintaining superior male power and status. (See also Language and Women.)

The Other Half: Roads to Women's Equality, edited by Cynthia Fuchs Epstein and William J. Goode (Prentice Hall, Englewood Cliffs, New Jersey, 1971)

Contemporary articles on women's social roles, by sociologists and popular writers. Includes pieces by Jessie Bernard; William J. Goode; Lionel Tiger; Kate Millett; Dean Knudsen, on the failure of functionalism; Alice S. Rossi on why there are so few women in the sciences; Cynthia Fuchs Epstein on professional women; William O'Neill; Helen Dudar; the NOW Statement of Purpose; the Redstockings Manifesto; and others.

The Professional Woman, edited by Athena Theodore (Schenkman Publishing Company, Cambridge, Massachusetts, 1971)

Fifty articles—most published in the 1960s and most by sociologists—dealing with the entry (or relative lack of entry) of women into the professionalized occupations. Articles by Athena Theodore, Edward Gross, and Cynthia Epstein demonstrate the persistence of sex segregation in most professional areas. A few other contributors: Wilbur Bock on "Negro Female Professionals"; David Campbell on "The Clash Between Beautiful Women and Science"; Lorraine Rand on the relative "masculinity" and "femininity" of career-oriented versus homemaking-oriented college women; Philip Goldberg, who shows that women are themselves prejudiced against the professional work of women; William Rushing on the social-psychological function of the deferential behavior of nurses towards doctors; Norton Dodge on "Women in the Soviet Economy"; Matina Horner on women's fear of success; Elizabeth Almquist and Shirley Anguist on the influence of role models on the career choices of college women; Ruth Eckert and John Stecklein on "Academic Women"; Lotte Bailyn on "Career and Family Orientations of Husbands and Wives in Relation to Marital Happiness"; Alice Rossi on why there are so few women in science; Margaret Poloma and T. Neal

Garland on "The Myth of the Egalitarian Family"; and many others.

Sexism: Scientific Debates, edited by Clarice Stasy Stoll (Addison-Wesley Publishing Company, Reading, Massachusetts, 1973)
Eight articles by contemporary social scientists focusing on sex roles. Includes John Money on the "Developmental Differentiation of Femininity and Masculinity"; Judith Bardwick on "Infant Sex Differences"; Lionel Tiger on male bonding; Patricia Sexton on the supposed "feminization" of the American male; Clarice Stoll and Paul T. McFarlane on "Sex Differences in Game Strategy"; Marijean Suelzle on women laborers; Charles Winick, who fears that the loss of traditional sexual distinctions may lead to the extermination of the species; and Jessie Bernard's "Adjusting the Lives of Women to the Establishment."

Toward a Sociology of Woman, edited by Constantina Safilios-Rothschild (Xerox College Publishing, Lexington, Massachusetts, 1972)
This is a well-selected and well-organized collection of contemporary articles by American, and some Greek, sociologists, educators, and popular writers. Most contributors present nontechnical summaries of sociological research on various aspects of sex roles. A few of the over thirty contributors: Diana Warshay, on "Sex Differences in Language Style"; Philip Goldberg, presenting evidence that even women are prejudiced against women; Lovelle Ray on the archaic images of women in the mass media; Jane Lambiri-Dimaki on the dowry in modern Greece; Gael Greene's "A Vote Against Motherhood"; Alice Rossi on why there are so few women in science, and on different visions of sex equality; Caroline Bird, arguing that women should be subject to the military draft; Margaret Poloma on "Role Conflict and the Married Professional Woman"; Patricia Graham on "Women in Academe"; Jessie Bernard on "Women, Marriage and the Future"; and Jeanne Clare Ridley on "The Effects of Population Change on the Roles and Status of Women."

Woman in a Man-Made World: A Socioeconomic Handbook, edited by Nona Glazer-Malbin and Helen Youngelson Waehrer (Rand McNally and Company, Chicago, 1972)

Selected excerpts from the writings of (mostly) twentieth-century sociologists, psychiatrists, biologists and economists, selected for their bearing on the social and economic status of American women today. The authors include William J. Goode; Helen Hacker; Juliet Mitchell; Sigmund Freud; Mary Jane Sherfey; Karen Horney; Erving Goffman; Friedrich Engels, and a critique of Engels by Kathleen Gough; Talcott Parsons; Kate Millett; and many others.

Woman's Role in Economic Development, by Ester Boserup (St. Martin's Press, New York, 1970)

This is an important cross-cultural survey, which shows that in many of the developing nations of Asia, Africa and Latin America, economic development is occurring in ways which tend to reduce the relative economic contribution of women, and hence their economic independence and social status. In many parts of Africa, for example, women still do much of the farming and marketing of agricultural products. But where improved methods and machinery have been introduced, their use has usually been monopolized by men. Furthermore, African towns offer employment in the modern sector primarily to men.

In general, Boserup shows, women suffered a loss of status under European rule, which is further aggravated as industrialization progresses. The employment of women in business and industry is often limited to unskilled or low paid specialized work. The argument is frequently made that the employment of urban women takes jobs from men and creates unemployment. Boserup points out, however, that from the point of view of promoting economic progress, it would be preferable for more urban women to be gainfully employed. If there are too few jobs in the towns, then more jobs should be created in the villages, thus reducing the urban population and the expense to the society of providing housing and other services to town dwellers, since village dwellers can provide these services for themselves.

Women and the American Economy: A Look at the 1980s, edited by Juanita M. Kreps (Prentice Hall, Englewood Cliffs, New Jersey)

This is an excellent set of studies, by leading sociologists, economists and others, of women's (not so rapidly) changing economic role. Includes a historical retrospective by William

Chafe; Karl Taeuber and James Sweet on the evolution of women's "social life cycle"; Juanita Kreps and John Leaper on women's allocation of time between paid work, domestic work and leisure (the paid work crowds out the leisure, not the domestic work); Harris Schrank and John Riley, Jr., on the continuing sex segregation of job categories; Kristen Moore and Isabel Sawhill on the "Implications of Women's Employment for Home and Family Life"; Phyllis Wallace on the uneven enforcement of the equal employment opportunity laws; Martha Griffiths on "Requisites for Equality"; and Nancy Smith Barrett warning of the danger of further declines in women's relative economic status in the 1980s due to inflation and high rates of unemployment.

Women and the Workplace: The Implications of Occupational Segregation, edited by Martha Blaxall and Barbara Reagan (University of Chicago Press, Chicago and London, 1976)

Studies of occupational segregation by sex in America today, its causes and consequences and the legal means by which it can be fought. Includes pieces by Martha Griffiths, Jean Lipman-Blumen, Kenneth Boulding, Constantina Safilios-Rothschild, Jessie Bernard, Elise Boulding, Gail Warshofsky Lapidus, Heidi Hartman, Isabel Sawhill, and others.

Women Working: Theories and Facts in Perspective, edited by Anne H. Stromberg and Shirley Harkness (Mayfield Publishing Company, Palo Alto, California, 1978)

A volume of specially commissioned articles in which sociologists present the most current data on the paid and unpaid labor of women in this country, and present original research and analysis. Includes chapters on the androcentric biases of previous sociological studies of women's work; women's economic role in American history; minority women workers; economic explanations of the income differential between men and women workers; "protective" legislation for women workers; the socialization of girls for work; the double burden of the employed mother; middle-aged working women; women in the male-dominated professions of law, medicine, and higher education; the "female-dominated" professions (e.g., nursing, social work, and elementary school teaching); blue-collar women; domestic workers; housewives as (unpaid) workers; and ways of altering public policy to improve conditions for women workers.

ANTHOLOGIES & SOURCEBOOKS XV. WOMEN OUTSIDE THE UNITED STATES

Cuban Women Now: Interviews with Cuban Women, by Margaret Randall (Women's Press Publications, Toronto, 1974)

These interviews provide an enthusiastic account of a socialist revolution which, in its effects upon women, is in many ways impressive (e.g. most women work for pay, and enjoy access to child care, better educational opportunities and more equal pay), but is still incomplete in other respects (e.g. women are still barred from some jobs, still make less, still do most of the domestic work).

The Proper Sphere: Women's Place in Canadian Society, edited by Ramsay Cook and Wendy Mitchinson (Oxford University Press, Toronto, 1976)

Popular writings and speeches by nineteenth- and early twentieth-century Canadians, feminists and antifeminists, on the topics of women's proper sphere, their legal rights, education and future emancipation.

Sex and Class in Latin America, edited by June Nash and Helen Icken Safa (Praeger Publishers, New York, 1976)

An excellent collection of papers by Latin American and North American scholors, originally presented at a conference in Buenos Aires in 1974. The authors deal with the roles—especially the economic and political roles—of women in the Latin American nations, and with the inadequacy of the methods and assumptions with which the social sciences have approached the study of these roles. The countries spotlighted in particular articles include Brazil, Chile, the Dominican Republic, Mexico and Puerto Rico.

Soviet Women, by William M. Mandel (Anchor Press/Doubleday, Garden City, New York, 1975)

This is an excellent study of the situation and struggles of Russian women, before and since the Bolshevik Revolution. Mandel praises the (indeed striking) progress which Soviet women have made in the worlds of work, politics, art, literature, the professions, and even sports. Yet he also recognizes that full equality has not been achieved, and that further progress towards it is impeded by (among other things) men's refusal to do their share of the domestic work.

Woman to Woman: European Feminists, by Bonnie Charles Bluh (Starogubski Press, New York, 1974)

Conversations with European women on feminist topics, conducted on a journey which took the author to Ireland, England, Holland, France, Italy, and Spain.

Women and Children in China: A Firsthand Report, by Ruth Sidel (Penguin Books, Baltimore, 1974)

A rather glowing report of the post-revolutionary progress of Chinese women towards social equality, and the new child care and early educational institutions in Mao's China.

Women in China, by Katie Curtin (Pathfinder Press, New York, 1975)

This is a brief but incisive critique of the social progress of women in Mao's China. Some of the repressive practices of the past—e.g. the arranged marriage—have been eliminated, but women are still oppressed by unequal work and unequal pay, lack of political power, the double burden of public and domestic work, the Chinese Communist Party's Puritan attitude toward sexuality, and the sexual double standard.

Women in Soviet Society: Equality, Development and Social Change, by Gail Warshofsky Lapidus (University of California Press, Berkeley and Los Angeles, 1978)

An excellent in-depth study of the social roles of women in Russia and the Soviet Union, from the nineteenth century to the present. The picture, on the whole, is not very optimistic. After the 1917 revolution, women were increasingly drawn into the public production process, but the complete equality between the sexes which Marx and Engels thought would result from this change failed to materialize. The sexual segregation and stratification of most professions, and women's "double burden" of wage and domestic labor, reinforce one another and combine to keep women in an inferior economic position. Women have not gained significant political power, and (just as in the United States) their representation in the most prestigious occupations seems to be declining rather than increasing. Soviet ideology continues "to subordinate libertarian to utilitarian concerns" (p.338), and thus no radical improvements in women's status can be predicted for the near future.

Women in the New Asia: The Changing Social Roles of Men and Women in South and South-East Asia, edited by Barbara E. Ward (United Nations Educational, Scientific, and Cultural Organization, Amsterdam, Netherlands, 1963)

A collection of articles, most of which are by women native to the region dealt with, and which provide both sociological and personal observations about the past and present status of women in Burma, Ceylon, India, Indonesia, Laos, Malaya, Pakistan, the Phillipines, Singapore, Thailand, and Viet Nam.

Women in the World: A Comparative Study, edited by Lynne B. Iglitzin and Ruth Ross (Clio Books, Santa Barbara, 1976)

This is a collection of papers which grew out of a series of seminars at the University of California, Santa Barbara, and the Center for the Study of Democratic Institutions. The contributors—political scientists, sociologists and other social scientists, most but not all American—examine traditional attitudes towards and contemporary problems of women in developing, capitalist and socialist nations. Countries dealt with in individual articles include Italy, Ireland, France, West Germany, Great Britain, the United States, Ghana, Iran, Colombia, Mexico, Yugoslavia, the USSR, Israel, China and Sweden. Concluding comments by Elizabeth Mann Borgese and Alva Myrdal

Women of Vietnam, by Arlene Eisen Bergman (Peoples Press, San Francisco, 1975)

An illustrated and enthusiastic account of the suffering and heroism of Vietnamese women during the long war against French and American imperialism.

Women: Roles and Status in Eight Countries, edited by Janet Zollinger Giele and Audrey Chapman Smock (John Wiley and Sons, New York, London, Sidney and Toronto, 1977)

Studies by seven social scientists of the past and present status of women in eight countries. Janet Giele suggests that these collected data support the theory that there is "a curvilinear relationship between societal complexity and sex equality." (p.9) In other words, women's status tends to be highest in the most primitive and the most highly developed cultures, and lowest at the intermediate levels of cultural complexity. The eight nations studied are: Egypt, by Audrey Smock and Nadia Haggaz Youssef; Bangladesh, by Audrey Smock; Japan, by Susan Pharr; France, by Catherine Bodard Silver; the United States, by Janet Giele; and Poland, by Magdalena Sokolowska.

PERIODICALS

Since the resurgence of feminist activity in the sixties, a great many feminist and women's studies journals, newsletters and magazines have emerged, many of them short-lived or distributed only locally. It is almost impossible to keep up with all of them. The following are some of the more important currently available periodicals which publish feminist theory and analysis; news of the women's movement; art, fiction and poetry by and about women; and reviews of books and other publications in women's studies.

The subscription prices, where given, are those for 1979; updates on prices may be obtained by writing directly to the subscription department of the periodical, or—in some cases—from the current *Advertiser's Guide to Scholarly Periodicals*, published biannually by American University Press Services (One Park Avenue, New York, New York 10016).

PERIODICALS

APHRA

A feminist literary magazine, named for Aphra Benn (1640–1689), who is said to be the first woman to earn her living by writing. Publishes poetry, fiction, drama, visual art, criticism, and nonfiction articles. Founded 1969. Published quarterly. (Box 893, Ansonia Sta., New York, New York, 10023)

CANADIAN NEWSLETTER OF RESEARCH ON WOMEN

An excellent newsletter which publishes reviews of books, journals and articles in all areas of women's studies, commentary and discussion, and reports on conferences and other developments in the area. Includes both Canadian and international material. Published three times a year. Founded 1971. Editors Magrit Eichler *et al*. (Department of Sociology, Ontario Institute for Studies in Education, 252 Bloor Street West, Toronto, Canada M5S IV6) Annual subscriptions $12 individual, in Canada ($13 elsewhere), $25 institutional.

CHRYSALIS: A MAGAZINE OF WOMEN'S CULTURE

A quarterly feminist magazine of unusually broad scope and high quality. Includes theory, criticism, historical research, book reviews, interviews, poetry, fiction, and visual art. Emphasis is given to work which attempts to break new ground in the feminist analysis of society and the creation of feminist culture. Founded 1976. Managing Editor, Kirsten Grimstad. (The Woman's Building, 1729 N. Spring St., Los Angeles, California 90012) Annual subscriptions $10 individual, $15 insitutional and foreign.

HECATE: A WOMEN'S INTERDISCIPLINARY JOURNAL

An Australian feminist journal which publishes creative writing, visual art, articles and reviews of books, plays, films (etc.), and research in the humanities and social sciences. Published twice yearly. Founded 1975. (P.O. Box 99,St. Lucia, Queensland, Australia, 4067)

HERESIES: A FEMINIST PUBLICATION ON ART AND POLITICS

A quarterly journal, "devoted to the examination of art and politics from a theoretical perspective." Publishes fiction, poetry, visual art, analysis, research and theoretical articles. Founded 1977. (P.O. Box 766, Canal Street Station, New York, New York 10013) Annual subscription $10.

INTERNATIONAL JOURNAL OF WOMEN'S STUDIES

An interdisciplinary journal which publishes scholarship in all areas of women's studies; also abstracts of current papers on women published elsewhere. Published bimonthly. Founded 1978. Editor, Sheri Clarkson. (1538 Sherbrooke St. W. #201, Montreal, Canada H3G 1L5.) Annual subscription $22 individual, $35 institutional.

JOURNAL OF MARRIAGE AND THE FAMILY

A quarterly journal of research, theory and critical discussion on subjects related to marriage and the family, e.g. public policy issues, male and female psychology, male and female parenting, etc. Founded 1938. Editor, Felix M. Berardo. (The National Council on Family Relations, 1219 University Avenue Southeast, Minneapolis, Minnesota, 55414.) Annual subscriptions, $20 individual, $30 institutional.

MS.

Ms. is the most successful popular feminist magazine of all time, featuring news, articles and commentary on a wide range of women's issues, historical articles, book reviews, poetry, short fiction and visual art. Founded 1972; published monthly. Edited by Gloria Steinem *et al.* (**Ms. Magazine**, 370 Lexington Avenue, New York, New York 10017) Annual subscription $10 in the United States and Canada, $12 elsewhere. (123 Garden Street, Marion, Ohio 43302)

NEW DIRECTIONS FOR WOMEN

A quarterly feminist newsjournal which reports on issues and events of women to the women's movement. Founded 1971. Editor Vivian J. Schienmann. (223 Old Hook Road, Westwood, New Jersey 07675) Annual subscriptions, $4 individual, $7 institutional and foreign.

NEW LEFT REVIEW

An important international journal which presents socialist and Marxist analysis and criticism, including work by or about socialist feminists, and theoretical analyses of economic exploitation of women. Published bimonthly. Editor, Perry Anderson. (7 Carlisle Street, London W1V 6NL) Annual subscriptions, $18 for individuals, $30 for institutions.

PHILOSOPHY AND PUBLIC AFFAIRS

A highly respected journal which publishes philosophical analyses of the ethical dimensions of public policy issues; these include many of concern to feminists, e.g. abortion, affirmative action, the concept of equality, the alleged duty to reproduce, etc. Published quarterly. Founded 1971. Editor, Marshall Cohen. (Princeton University Press, P.O. Box 231, Princeton, New Jersey 08540) Annual subscription, $7.50 individual, $10 institutional.

PERIODICALS

PSYCHOLOGY OF WOMEN QUARTERLY

Publishes research and theoretical articles on the psychology of women, methods of therapy, and related topics; also book reviews. Founded 1976. Editor Georgia Babladelis. (Human Sciences Press, 72 Fifth Avenue, New York, New York 10011) Annual subscription $20 individual, $40 institutional.

SIGNS: JOURNAL OF WOMEN IN CULTURE AND SOCIETY

Signs is the most important of the interdisciplinary feminist journals. It publishes theoretical and research articles and criticism in fields including art, literature and literary criticism, anthropology, history, psychology, philosophy, law, theology, medicine and biology. Founded 1975. Editor Catharine R. Stimpson, Barnard Hall, Barnard College, New York, New York 10027. (The University of Chicago Press, 5801 Ellis Avenue, Chicago, Illinois 60637) Annual subscription $14 student, $16 individual, $24 institutional.

SPARE RIB

A monthly feminist magazine of international scope. Publishes news, reviews, criticism, poetry, and articles on a broad range of topics. Founded 1972. Editors Anny Brackx *et al.* (Spare Rib Limited, 27 Clerkenwell Close, London EC1, England) Annual subscriptions, £5 Britain and Ireland, £6.50 United States.

THE SPOKESWOMAN

An excellent monthly newsletter, which supplies news on current actions by women's organizations, and on legal and other developments in education, employment, welfare, child care, abortion reform and other areas. Also reviews books, articles, conferences and reports of interest to feminists. Founded 1970. Editor Karen Willisdi. (5464 South Shore Drive, Chicago, Illinois) Annual subscriptions $12 individual, $20 institutional.

PERIODICALS

WOMEN AND LITERATURE

A semiannual journal devoted to scholarship on women writers, and on the treatment of women and of women writers in literature; also includes book reviews. Founded 1973. Editor Janet M. Todd. (Department of English, Douglass College, Rutgers University, New Brunswick, New Jersey 08903) Annual subscription $7, $9 outside of U.S.

WOMEN'S RIGHTS LAW REPORTER

Excellent quarterly journal which publishes news, articles, commentary and reviews of current publications in all areas of the law which are of special concern to women. Founded 1974. Editor-in-chief, Susan Vercheak. (Rutgers Law School, 15 Washington Street, Newark, New Jersey 07102) Annual subscription $14 individual, $28 institutional; add $4 outside of United States.

WOMEN'S STUDIES

A scholarly journal which publishes work on women in the humanities and sciences; also publishes book reviews, poetry and short fiction. Published three times a year. Founded 1972. Editor Wendy Martin, Department of English, Queens College, CUNY, Flushing, New York 11367. (Gordon and Breach Science Publishers, Inc. One Park Avenue, New York, New York, 10016) Annual subscriptions $17 individual, $51.50 institutional.

WOMEN'S STUDIES INTERNATIONAL QUARTERLY

A scholarly journal which publishes theoretical and research articles on a wide range of feminist topics, from abortion and rape to women's studies programs. Also includes book reviews and editorial comment. Published quarterly. Founded 1978. Editor Dale Spender. (Pergamon Press, Headington Hill Hall, Oxford OX3 OBW, England) Annual subscriptions $30 individual, $50 institutional, $20 students and women's groups.

WOMEN'S STUDIES NEWSLETTER

A quarterly report on issues and events in feminist education, e.g. women's studies programs, periodicals, courses and other projects. Official newsletter of the National Women's Studies Association. Founded 1972. Editor, Florence Howe. (The Feminist Press, P.O. Box 334, Old Westbury, New York 11568) Annual subscription $7 individual, $12 institutional, foreign $3 extra.

BIBLIOGRAPHY

This listing includes all of the authors of books who are dealt with either in the alphabetical part of this book or in the Anthologies and Sourcebooks section. Persons who are mentioned only as authors of articles are listed in the Bibliography only in the rare cases when they are dealt with in separate articles in the main part of the book. To locate references to authors not listed here, consult the general index.

An asterisk (*) beside an author's name indicates that the author is discussed in a separate article in the main part of the book, under the author's last name. Where a book is reviewed in the Anthologies section that section is given in parenthesis at the end of the reference. Books in the Anthologies sections are listed alphabetically by title (not by author), under the various topic headings, because of the importance of juxtaposing different works on the same topic. The exact page references to a particular author may be found in the general index.

BIBLIOGRAPHY

*ABBOTT, Sidney, and LOVE, Barbara
Sappho Was a Right-On Woman: A Liberated View of Lesbianism, Stein and Day, New York, 1973.

ADAMS, Elsie, and BRISCOE, Mary Louise (editors)
Up Against the Wall, Mother, Glencoe Press, Beverly Hills, California, 1971 (Anthologies IV).

ADAMS, Mildred
The Right to Be People, J.B. Lippincott Company, Philadelphia and New York, 1967 (Anthologies VI).

ADELSTEIN, Michael E., and PIVAL, Jean G. (editors)
Women's Liberation, St. Martin's Press, New York, 1972 (Anthologies IV).

*ADLER, Alfred
Understanding Human Nature, translated by W. Bean Wolfe, New York, 1927.

AGONISTO, Rosemary (editor)
History of Ideas on Woman: A Source Book, G.P. Putnam's Sons, New York, 1977 (Anthologies XII).

*AMUNDSEN, Kirsten
The Silenced Majority: Women and American Democracy, Prentice Hall, Englewood Cliffs, New Jersey, 1971.

*ANDELIN, Helen
Fascinating Womanhood: A Guide to a Happy Marriage, Pacific Press, Santa Barbara, 1974.

ANDERSON, Margret (editor)
Mother Was Not a Person, Black Rose Books, Montreal, Canada, 1972 (Anthologies IV).

ANDREAS, Carol
Sex and Caste in America, Prentice Hall, Englewood Cliffs, New Jersey, 1971 (Anthologies IV).

*AQUINAS, Thomas
Summa Theologica, translated by the Fathers of the English Dominican Province, Berringer Brothers, New York, 1947.

ARCHER, John: See LLOYD, Barbara.

*ARDREY, Robert
African Genesis: A Personal Investigation into the Animal Origins and Nature of Man, Atheneum, New York, 1963.
The Territorial Imperative: A Personal Inquiry into the Animal Origins of Animals and Nations, Atheneum, New York, 1966.
The Hunting Hypothesis: A Personal Conclusion Concerning the Evolutionary Nature of Man, Bantam Books, New York, 1977.

*ARISTOTLE
The Nichomachean Ethics, with an English translation by H. Rackham, Harvard University Press, Cambridge, Massachusetts, 1947.
The Politics, with an English translation by H. Rackham, William Heinemann, London, 1932.
Generation of Animals, with an English translation by A.L. Peck, Harvard University Press, Cambridge, Massachusetts, 1943.

ARMS, Suzanne
Immaculate Deception: A New Look at Women and Childbirth in America, Houghton Mifflin Company, Boston, 1975 (Anthologies III).

ARNOLD, Joan: See PLASKOW, Judith.

*ASTELL, Mary
A Serious Proposal to the Ladies for the Advancement of their True and Greatest Interest, Source Books Press, New York, 1970; first published 1701.
Some Reflections Upon Marriage, Source Books Press, New York, 1970; first published 1730.

*ATKINSON, Ti-Grace
Amazon Odyssey, Links Books, New York, 1974.

*SAINT AUGUSTINE
The Confessions, in **A Select Library of the Niocene and Post-**

Niocene Fathers of the Christian Church, edited by Philip Schaff, Volume I; translated by J.G. Pilkington, William B. Eerdmans Publishing Company, Grand Rapids, Michigan, 1956.
The City of God, *op. cit.*, Volume II; translated by Marcus Dodds.
On the Good of Marriage, *op. cit.*, Volume III; translated by C.L. Cornish.
Of Holy Virginity, *op. cit.*
Of the Work of Monks, *op. cit.*; translated by H. Brown.
Sermons on Selected Lessons of the New Testament, *op. cit.*, Volume VI, translated by R.G. MacMullen.

BABCOCK, Barbara Allen, FREEDMAN, Ann E., NORTON, Eleanor Holmes, and ROSS, Susan C. (editors)
Sex Discrimination and the Law: Causes and Reasons, Little, Brown and Company, Boston and Toronto, 1975 (Anthologies IX).

BABCOX, Deborah, and BELKIN, Madeline (editors)
Liberation Now! Writings from the Women's Liberation Movement, Dell Publishing Company, New York, 1971 (Anthologies IV).

*BACHOFEN, Johan Jacob
Myth, Religion and Mother Right: Selected Writings of J.J. Bachofen, translated by Ralph Manheim, Princeton University Press, Princeton, New Jersey, 1967.

BAKER, Elizabeth C.: See HESS, Thomas B.

BAKER, Robert, and ELLISTON, Frederick (editors)
Philosophy and Sex, Prometheus Books, Buffalo, New York, 1975 (Anthologies XII).

BANNER, Lois W.: See HARTMAN, Mary.

BARBA, Sharon: See CHESTER, Laura.

*BARBER, Benjamin R.
Liberating Feminism, Dell Publishing Company, New York, 1975.

*BARDWICK, Judith M.
Psychology of Women: A Study of Bio-Cultural Conflicts, Harper and Row, New York, 1971.
Readings on the Psychology of Women, (editor) Harper and Row, New York, 1972 (Anthologies XIII).

BARKER-BENFIELD, G.J.
The Horrors of the Half-Known Life: Male Attitudes Toward Women and Sexuality in Nineteenth-Century America, Harper and Row, New York, 1976 (Anthologies XI).

BARNHOUSE, Ruth Tiffany, and HOLMES, Urban T. (editors)
Male and Female: Christian Approaches to Sexuality, Seabury Press, New York, 1976 (Anthologies XII).

BEACH, Frank A. (editor)
Human Sexuality in Four Perspectives, Johns Hopkins Press, Baltimore and London, 1977 (Anthologies XIII).

BEAN, Joan P.: See KAPLAN, Alexandra G.

*BEARD, Mary
On Understanding Women, Longmans, Green and Company, New York, 1931.
Woman as a Force in History: A Study in Traditions and Realities, Collier Books, New York, 1973; first published 1946.

BEAUCHAMP, Tom L., and WALTERS, Le Roy (editors)
Contemporary Issues in Bioethics, Dickenson Publishing Company, Encino and Belmont, California, 1978 (Anthologies III).

*BEBEL, August
Women Under Socialism, translated by Daniel de Leon, Schocken Books, New York, 1971; first published 1883.

*BEDNARIK, Karl
The Male in Crisis, translated by Helen Stebba, Alfred A. Knopf, New York, 1970.

BELKIN, Madeline: See BABCOX, Deborah.

BELL, Susan B. (editor)
Woman: From the Greeks to the French Revolution, Wads-

worth Publishing Company, Belmont, California, 1973 (Anthologies VII).

*BEM, Sandra L.
"Probing the Promise of Androgyny," in *Beyond Sex-Role Stereotyping*, edited by Alexandra G. Kaplan and Joan P. Bean, Little, Brown and Company, Boston, 1976: pp.48–61.

BENET, James: See RUCKMAN, Gaye.

BEREAUD, Susan: See STACEY, Judith.

BERG, Stephen, and MARKS, S.J. (editors)
About Women: An Anthology of Contemporary Fiction, Poetry and Essays, Fawcett Publications, Greenwich, Connecticut, 1975 (Anthologies II).

BERGMAN, Arlene Eisen
Women of Vietnam, People's Press, San Francisco, 1975 (Anthologies XV).

*BERNARD, Jessie S.
American Family Behavior, Harper and Brothers, New York, 1942.
Academic Women, Meridian, New York, 1974.
The Sex Game, Prentice Hall, Englewood Cliffs, New Jersey, 1968.
Women and the Public Interest: An Essay on Policy and Protest, Aldine-Atherton, Chicago and New York, 1971.
The Future of Marriage, Bantam, New York, 1973.
The Future of Motherhood, Penguin Books, New York; 1975.
Women, Wives, Mothers: Values and Options, Aldine Publishing Company, Chicago, 1975.
(Also see BRODERICK, Carlfred B.)

*THE BIBLE

*BIRD, Carolyn, and BRILLER, Sara Welles
Born Female: The High Cost of Keeping Women Down, Pocket Books, New York, 1968.

BISHOP, Sharon, and WEINZWEIG, Marjorie (editors)
Philosophy and Women, Wadsworth Publishing Company, Belmont, California, 1979 (Anthologies XII).

BLAKE, Kathryn A: See MCBEE, Mary Louise.

BLAXALL, Martha, and REAGAN, Barbara (editors)
Women and the Workplace: The Implications of Occupational Segregation, University of Chicago Press, Chicago and London, 1976 (Anthologies XIV).

BLUGH, Bonnie Charles
Woman to Woman: European Feminists, Starogubski Press, New York, 1974 (Anthologies XV).

*BONAPARTE, Marie
Female Sexuality, translated by John Rudken, International Universities Press, New York, 1953; first published 1949.

*BORGESE, Elizabeth Mann
Ascent of Woman, George Braziller, New York, 1963.

BOROSAGE, Vera: See MORRISON, Eleanor S.

BOSERUP, Ester
Woman's Role in Economic Development, St. Martin's Press, New York, 1970 (Anthologies XIV).

BOSMAJIAN, Haig: See NILSEN, Aileen Pace, and BOSMAJIAN, Hamida.

BOSMAJIAN, Hamida, and BOSMAJIAN, Haig (editors)
This Great Argument: The Rights of Women, Addison-Wesley Publishing Company, Reading, Massachusetts, 1972 (Anthologies VI).

BOSTON WOMEN'S HEALTH BOOK COLLECTIVE
Our Bodies, Ourselves: A Book By and For Women, Simon and Schuster, New York, 1971 (Anthologies III).

*BOULDING, Elise
The Underside of History: A View of Women Through Time, Westview Press, Boulder, Colorado, 1976.
Women in the Twentieth Century World, John Wiley and Sons, New York, 1977.

BRANNON, Robert: See DAVID, Deborah S.

BRENTON, Myron
The American Male, Coward-McCann, New York, 1966 (Anthologies XI).

*BRIFFAULT, Robert
The Mothers: A Study of the Origins of Sentiments and Institutions, Macmillan, New York, 1963; first published 1959.

BRILLER, Sara Welles: See BIRD, Carolyn.

BRISCOE, Mary Louise: See ADAMS, Elsie.

BRODERICK, Carlfred B., and BERNARD, Jessie (editors)
The Individual, Sex, and Society, Johns Hopkins Press, Baltimore, 1969.

BRODY, Baruch
Abortion and the Sanctity of Human Life, MIT Press, Cambridge, Massachusetts, 1975 (Anthologies III).

BROWN, Barbara A., FREEDMAN, Ann E., KATY, Harriet N., and PRICE, Alice M.
Women's Rights and the Law: The Impact of the ERA on State Laws, Praeger Books, New York, 1977 (Anthologies IX).

*BROWN, Rita Mae
A Plain Brown Rapper, Diana Press, Oakland, California, 1976.

*BROWNMILLER, Susan
Against Our Will: Men, Women, and Rape, Simon and Schuster, New York, 1975.

*BUCK, Pearl S.
Of Men and Women, John Day Company, New York, 1971.

*BULLOUGH, Vern L.
The Subordinate Sex: A History of Attitudes Toward Women, Penguin Books, Baltimore, Maryland, 1974.
The Frontiers of Sex Research (editor), Prometheus Books, Buffalo, New York, 1979 (Anthologies III).

BUNCH-WEEKS, Charlotte: See COOKE, Joanne.
Class and Feminism (editor, with Nancy Myron), Diana Press, Baltimore, 1974, (Anthologies IV).

*BUYTENDIJK, Frederick Jacobus Johannes
Woman: A Contemporary View, translated by Denis J. Barrett, Newman Press, New York, 1968.

CADE, Tony (editor)
The Black Woman: An Anthology, New American Library, New York, 1970 (Anthologies IV).

CALDERWOOD, Ann: See ROSSI, Alice S.

CALLAHAN, Daniel
Abortion: Law, Choice, and Morality, Macmillan, New York, 1970 (Anthologies III).

CARROLL, Berenice A. (editor)
Liberating Womens's History: Theoretical and Critical Essays, University of Illinois Press, Urbana, Illinois, 1976 (Anthologies VII).

CATER, Libby A., SCOTT, Anne Firor, and MARTYNA, Wendy, (editors)
Women and Men: Changing Roles, Relationships, and Perceptions, Praeger Publishers, New York, 1977 (Anthologies VIII).

*CHAFE, William H.
The American Woman: Her Changing Social, Economic, and Political Roles, 1920–1970, Oxford University Press, London, 1972.
Women and Equality: Changing Patterns in American Culture, Oxford University Press, New York, 1977.

*CHESLER, Phyllis
Women and Madness, Avon, New York, 1972.

CHESTER, Laura and BARBA, Sharon (editors)
Rising Tides: 20th Century American Women Poets, Pocket Books, New York, 1973 (Anthologies II).

CHICAGO, Judy
Through the Flower: My Struggles as a Woman Artist, Doubleday and Company, Garden City, New York, 1975 (Anthologies II).

CLARK, Elizabeth and RICHARDSON, Herbert (editors)
Women and Religion: A Feminist Sourcebook of Christian Thought, Harper and Row, New York, 1977 (Anthologies XII).

COHART, Mary (editor)
Unsung Champions of Women, University of New Mexico Press, Albuquerque, 1975 (Anthologies VI).

COHEN, Marshall, NAGEL, Thomas, and SCANLON, Thomas (editors)
The Rights and Wrongs of Abortion: A Philosophy and Public Affairs Reader, Princeton University Press, 1974 (Anthologies III).

COLWILL, Nina Lee: See LIPS, Hilary M.

CONNELL, Noreen: See NEW YORK RADICAL FEMINISTS.

COOK, Ramsay, and MITCHINSON, Wendy (editors)
The Proper Sphere: Women's Place in Canadian Society, Oxford University Press, Toronto, 1976 (Anthologies XV).

COOKE, Joanne, BUNCH-WEEKS, Charlotte, and MORGAN, Robin (editors)
The New Women, Fawcett Publications, Greenwich, Connecticut, 1970 (Anthologies III).

COTT, Nancy F. (editor)
Root of Bitterness: Documents of the Social History of American Women, E.P. Dutton, New York, 1972 (Anthologies VII).

COX, Sue (editor)
Female Psychology: The Emerging Self, Science Research Associates, Chicago, 1976 (Anthologies XIII).

CURTIN, Katie
Women in China, Pathfinder Press, New York, 1975 (Anthologies XV).

DAHLSTROM, Edmund (editor)
The Changing Roles of Men and Women (translated by Gunilla and Steven Anderman), Beacon Press, Boston, 1971 (Anthologies XIV).

*DALY, Mary
   The Church and the Second Sex, Harper and Row, New York, 1975; first published 1968.
   Beyond God the Father: Towards a Philosophy of Women's Liberation, Beacon Press, Boston, 1974.
   Gyn/Ecology: The Metaethics of Radical Feminism, Beacon Press, Boston, 1978.

DANIELS, Arlene Kaplan: See RUCKMAN, Gaye.

DANIELS, Joan: See STACEY, Judith.

*DARWIN, Charles
   The Descent of Man and Selection in Relation to Sex, D. Appleton and Company, New York, 1874; first published 1871.
   The Origin of Species, New American Library, New York, 1958; first published 1859.

DAVID, Deborah S., and BRANNON, Robert (editors)
   The Forty-Nine Percent Majority: The Male Sex Role, Addison-Wesley Publishing Company, Reading, Massachusetts, 1976 (Anthologies XI).

*DAVIS, Elizabeth Gould
   The First Sex, Penguin Books, Baltimore, 1973; first published 1971.

DAVIS, Harrison M.: See MARLOW, H. Carleton.

*DE BEAUVOIR, Simone
   The Second Sex, translated by H.M. Parshley, Bantam Books, New York, 1952; first published 1949.

*DE CASTILLEJO, Irene Claremont
   Knowing Woman: A Feminine Psychology, Harper and Row, New York, 1974; first published 1973.

DECKARD, Barbara (editor)
   The Women's Movement: Political, Socioeconomic, and Psychological Issues, Harper and Row, New York, 1975 (Anthologies IV).

DE CROW, Karen
Sexist Justice, Random House, New York, 1975 (Anthologies IX).

*DECTER, Midge
The Liberated Woman and Other Americans, Coward, Mc Cann, and Geoghegan, New York, 1971.
The New Chastity and Other Arguments Against Women's Liberation, Capricorn Books, New York, 1972.

*DELANEY, Janice, LIPTON, Mary Jane, and TOTH, Emily
The Curse: A Cultural History of Menstruation, New American Library, New York, 1977.

*DEUTSCH, Helene
The Psychology of Women, Bantam, New York, 1973; first published 1944 and 1945.

DIAGRAM GROUP
Woman's Body: An Owner's Manual, Bantam, New York, 1977 (Anthologies III).

*DINER, Helen
Mothers and Amazons: The First Feminist History of Culture, translated by John Philip Lundin, Anchor Press, Garden City, New York, 1973; first published 1930.

*DINNERSTEIN, Dorothy
The Mermaid and the Minotaur, Harper and Row, New York, 1976.

DOUGLAS, Ann
The Feminization of American Culture, Avon Books, New York, 1977 (Anthologies VII).

DREIFUS, Claudia
Seizing Our Bodies: The Politics of Women's Health (editor), Vintage Books, New York, 1978 (Anthologies III).
Woman's Fate: Raps from a Feminist Consciousness-Raising Group, Bantam, New York, 1973.

DUBERMAN, Lucille, HACKER, Helen Mayer, and FARRELL, Warren T.

Gender and Sex in Society, Praeger Publishers, New York, 1975 (Anthologies XIV).

*DWORKIN, Andrea
Woman Hating, E.P. Dutton and Company, New York, 1974.
Our Blood: Prophecies and Discourses on Sexual Politics, Harper and Row, New York, 1970.

EHRENREICH, Barbara, and ENGLISH, Deirdre
Witches, Midwives and Nurses: A History of Women Healers, The Feminist Press, Old Westbury, New York, 1973 (Anthologies III).
For Her own Good: 150 Years of Experts' Advice to Women, Anchor Press, Garden City, New York, 1978 (Anthologies VII).

EISENSTEIN, Zillah R. (editor)
Capitalist Patriarchy and the Case for Socialist Feminism, Monthly Review Press, New York and London, 1979 (Anthologies X).

*ELLIS, Havelock
Man and Woman: A Study of Human Secondary Sexual Characteristics, The Walter Scott Publishing Company, London and New York, 1904; first published 1894.
Studies in the Psychology of Sex, Random House, New York, 1942; first published 1898–1928.
Little Essays on Love and Virtue, George H. Doran Company, Garden City, New York, 1931.
Psychology of Sex, Emerson Books, New York, 1944; first published 1933.
Sex and Marriage: Eros in Contemporary Life, edited by John Gawsworth, Random House, New York, 1952.

ELLISTON, Frederick A.: See VETTERLING-BRAGGIN, Mary, and BAKER, Robert.

*ELLMAN, Mary
Thinking About Women, Harcourt Brace Jovanovich, New York, 1968.

*ENGELS, Friedrich
The Condition of the Working Class in England in 1844, George Allen and Unwin Ltd., London, 1950; first published 1845.
The Origin of the Family, Private Property and the State, Inter-

national Publishers, New York, 1970; first published 1884.
(Also see MARX, Karl.)

ENGLISH, Deirdre: See EHRENREICH, Barbara.

ENGLISH, Jane (editor)
Sex Equality, Prentice Hall, Englewood Cliffs, New Jersey, 1977 (Anthologies XII).
(Also see VETTERLING-BRAGGIN, Mary.)

*EPSTEIN, Cynthia Fuchs
Woman's Place: Options and Limits in Professional Careers, University of California Press, Berkeley, California, 1970.
The Other Half: Roads to Women's Equality (and GOODE, William J., editors), Prentice Hall, Englewood Cliffs, New Jersey, 1971 (Anthologies (XIV).

*ERIKSON, Erik H.
"Womanhood and the Inner Space," in *Women and Analysis*, edited by Jean Strouse.
"Once More the Inner Space: Letter to a Former Student," *op cit*.

FARBER, Seymour M., and WILSON, Roger H.L. (editors)
The Potential of Woman, McGraw-Hill, New York, 1963 (Anthologies VIII).

FARRELL, Warren
The Liberated Man: Freeing Men and Their Relationships with Women, Bantam, New York, 1975 (Anthologies XI).
(Also see DUBERMAN, Lucille.)

*FAST, Julius
The Incompatibility of Men and Women and How to Overcome It, Avon Books, New York, 1971.

FEIGEN-FASTEAU, Marc
The Male Machine, McGraw-Hill, New York, 1972 (Anthologies XI).

FEINBERG, Joel (editor)
The Problem of Abortion, Wadsworth Publishing Company, Belmont, California, 1973 (Anthologies III).

FERGUSON, Mary Anne (editor)
Images of Women in Literature, Houghton Mifflin Company, Boston, 1977 (Anthologies II).

*FIGES, Eva
Patriarchal Attitudes, Fawcett Publishers, Greenwich, Connecticut, 1971.

*FILENE, Peter
Him/Her Self: Sex Roles in Modern America, Harcourt Brace Jovanovich, New York, 1974.

FIRESTONE, Ross (editor)
A Book of Men: Visions of the Male Experience, Stonehill Publishing Company, New York, 1975 (Anthologies XI).

*FIRESTONE, Shulamith
The Dialectic of Sex: The Case for Feminist Revolution, Bantam, New York, 1972; first published 1970.

FLEXNOR, Eleanor
Century of Struggle: The Woman's Rights Movement in the United States, Atheneum, New York, 1973; first published 1959 (Anthologies VI).
Mary Wollstonecraft, Coward, McCann and Geoghegan, New York, 1974.

*FOURIER, Francois Marie Charles
Design for Utopia: Selected Writings of Charles Fourier, translated by Julia Franklin, Schocken Books, New York, 1971.
The Utopian Vision of Charles Fourier: Selected Texts on Work, Love, and Passionate Attraction, translated by Jonathan Brecker and Richard Bienvenu, Beacon Press, Boston, 1971.
Harmonian Man: Selected Writings of Charles Fourier, translated by Susan Hanson, Doubleday and Company, Garden City, New York, 1971.

*FOX, Robin, and TIGER, Lionel
The Imperial Animal, Holt, Rinehart and Winston, New York, 1971.

*FRANCOEUR, Robert T.
Utopian Motherhood: New Trends in Human Reproduction, A.S. Barnes and Company, New York, 1973; first published

1970.
Eve's New Rib: Twenty Faces of Sex, Marriage, and Family,
Dell Publishing Company, New York, 1972.

FRANKFORT, Ellen
Vaginal Politics, Bantam, New York, 1972 (Anthologies III).

FREEDMAN, Ann E.: See BROWN, Barbara A., and BAB-
COCK, Barbara.

FREEMAN, Jo
Women, A Feminist Perspective (editor), Mayfield Publishing
Company, Palo Alto, California, 1975 (Anthologies IV).
The Politics of Women's Liberation, David McKay Company,
New York, 1975 (Anthologies IV).

*FREUD, Sigmund
Three Essays on the Theory of Sexuality, translated by James
Strachey, The Hogarth Press, London, 1974; first published
1905.
"Some Psychical Consequences of the Anatomical Distinction
Between the Sexes," ***Women and Analysis***, edited by Jean
Strouse, Grossman Publishers, New York, 1974, pp.17–26.
"Female Sexuality," *op. cit.*, pp.39–56.
"Femininity," *op. cit.*, pp.73–94.
"Civilized Society and Modern Nervousness," ***On War, Sex
and Neurosis***, edited by Sander Katz, Arts and Science Press,
New York, 1947.

*FRIDAY, Nancy
My Secret Garden: Women's Sexual Fantasies, Pocket Books,
New York, 1976; first published 1973.
My Mother/My Self: The Daughter's Search for Identity, Dela-
court Press, New York, 1977.

*FRIEDAN, Betty
The Feminine Mystique, W.W. Norton and Company, New
York, 1963.
It Changed My Life: Writings on the Women's Movement, Ran-
dom House, New York, 1976.

*FRIEDL, Ernestine
Women and Men: An Anthropologist's View, Holt, Rinehart
and Winston, New York, 1975.

FRITZ, Leah
Dreamers and Dealers: An Intimate Appraisal of the Women's Movement, Beacon Press, Boston, 1979 (Anthologies IV).

*FULLER, Margaret
Woman in the Nineteenth Century, W.W. Norton and Company, New York, 1971; first published 1845.

FURNISS, W. Todd, and GRAHAM, Patricia Albjerg (editors)
Women in Higher Education, American Council on Higher Education, Washington, D.C. 1974 (Anthologies V).

GARSKOF, Michelle Hoffnung (editor)
Roles Women Play: Readings Toward Women's Liberation, Brooks/Cole Publishing Company, Belmont, California, 1971 (Anthologies IV).

GEARHART, Sally, and JOHNSON, William R.
Loving Women/Loving Men: Gay Liberation and the Church, Glide Publications, San Francisco, 1974 (Anthologies XII).

GEORGE, Carol V.R. (editor)
"Remember the Ladies": New Perspectives on Women in America, Syracuse University Press, Syracuse, New York, 1975 (Anthologies VII).

GERSHUNY, H. Lee: See NILSEN, Aileen Pace.

*GIELE, Janet Zollinger
Women and the Future: Changing Sex Roles in Modern America, The Pree Press, New York, 1978.
Women: Roles and Status in Eight Countries (and SMOCK, Audrey Chapman, editors), John Wiley and Sons, New York, London, Sidney and Toronto, 1977 (Anthologies XV).

*GILDER, George
Sexual Suicide, Bantam, New York, 1973.

*GILMAN, Charlotte Perkins Stetson
Women and Economics, Harper and Row, New York, 1966; first published 1898.
The Home: Its Work and Influence, University of Illinois Press, Urbana, 1972; first published 1903.
The Man-Made World, or Our Androcentric Culture, T. Fisher

Unwin, London, 1911.
His Religion and Hers: A Study of the Faith of Our Fathers and the Work of Our Mothers, Hyperion Press, Westport, Connecticut, 1976; first published 1923.

GLAZER-MALBIN, Nona, and WAEHRER, Helen Youngelson (editors)
Woman in a Man-Made World: A Socioeconomic Handbook, Rand McNally and Company, Chicago, 1972 (Anthologies XIV).

*GOLDBERG, Steven
The Inevitability of Patriarchy, William Morrow and Company, New York, 1973.

*GOLDMAN, Emma
Anarchism and Other Essays, Dover Publications, New York, 1969; first published 1917.
Red Emma Speaks: Selected Writings and Speeches by Emma Goldman, edited by Alix Kate Shulman, Random House, New York, 1972.

GOODE, William J.: See EPSTEIN, Cynthia Fuchs.

GORDON, Sol, and LIBBY, Roger W. (editors)
Sexuality Today and Tomorrow: Contemporary Issues in Human Sexuality, Duxbury Press, North Scituate, Massachusetts, 1976 (Anthologies VIII).

GORNICK, Vivian
Woman in Sexist Society: Studies in Power and Powerlessness (and MORAN, Barbara K., editors), New American Library, New York, 1971 (Anthologies IV).
Essays in Feminism, Harper and Row, New York, 1978 (Anthologies IV).

GOUGH, Kathleen: See SCHNEIDER, David M.

GOULD, Carol C., and WARTOFSKY, Marx W. (editors)
Women and Philosophy: Toward a Theory of Liberation, G.P. Putnam's Sons, New York, 1976 (Anthologies XII).

GOULIANOS, Joan (editor)
by a Woman writt: Literature from Six Centuries by and about

Women, Penguin Books, Baltimore, 1973 (Anthologies II).

GRAHAM, Patricia Albjerg: See FURNISS, W. Todd

*GREER, Germaine
The Female Eunuch, Granada Publishing, London, 1970.

GRIFFIN, Frederick C. (editor)
Woman as Revolutionary, New American Library, New York, 1973 (Anthologies VII).

*GRIFFIN, Susan
Woman and Nature: The Roaring Inside Her, Harper and Row, New York, 1978.
Rape, The Power of Consciousness, Harper and Row, New York, 1979.

*GRIMKE, Sarah
Letters on the Equality of the Sexes and the Condition of Woman, Burt Franklin, New York, 1970; first published 1838.

GROSS, Barry R. (editor)
Reverse Discrimination, Prometheus Books, New York, 1977 (Anthologies IX).

GROUP FOR THE ADVANCEMENT OF PSYCHIATRY'S COMMITTEE ON PSYCHIATRY AND LAW
The Right to Abortion: A Psychiatric View, Charles Scribner's Sons, New York, 1970 (Anthologies III).

*GUETTEL, Charnie
Marxism and Feminism, The Woman's Press, Toronto, 1974.

HACKER, Helen Mayer: See DUBERMAN, Lucille.

HAGEMAN, Alice L. (editor)
Sexist Religion and Women in the Church, Association Press, New York, 1974 (Anthologies XII).

*HAMILTON, Roberta
The Liberation of Women: A Study of Patriarchy and Capitalism, George Allen and Unwin, London, 1978.

BIBLIOGRAPHY

*HAMMER, Signe
Daughters and Mothers: Mothers and Daughters, New American Library, New York, 1976.
Women, Body and Culture: Essays on the Sexuality of Women in a Changing Society (editor), Harper and Row, New York, 1975 (Anthologies III).

HARDIN, Garrett
Mandatory Motherhood: The True Meaning of "Right to Life," Beacon Press, Boston, 1974 (Anthologies III).

*HARDING, Esther M.
The Way of All Women, Harper and Row, New York, 1970; first published 1933.
Woman's Mysteries, Ancient and Modern, Putnam, New York, 1971.

HARKNESS, Shirley: See STROMBERG, Anne H.

HARRISON, Barbara Grizzuti
Unlearning the Lie: Sexism in School, William Morrow and Company, New York, 1974 (Anthologies V).

HARRISON, Cynthia Ellen
Women's Movement Media: A Source Guide, R.R. Bowker Company, New York and London, 1975 (Anthologies V).

HARTMAN, Mary, and BANNER, Lois W. (editors)
Clio's Consciousness Raised, Harper and Row, New York, 1974 (Anthologies VII).

*HASKELL, Molly
From Reverence to Rape: The Treatment of Women in the Movies, Penguin Books, Baltimore, 1974 (Anthologies V).

*HAYS, H.R.
The Dangerous Sex: The Myth of Feminine Evil, G.P. Putnam's Sons, New York, 1964.

*HEGEL, Georg Wilhelm Friedrich
The Phenomenology of Mind, translated by J.B. Ballie, George Allen and Unwin, London, and Humanities Press, New York, 1966; first published 1807.
Philosophy of Right, translated by T.M. Knox, Oxford Univer-

sity Press, London, Oxford and New York, 1952; first published 1821.

*HEILBRUN, Carolyn G.
Toward a Recognition of Androgyny, Alfred A. Knopf, New York, 1973.

HENLEY, Nancy: See THORNE, Barrie

*HERSCHBERGER, Ruth
Adam's Rib, Harper and Row, New York, 1970; first published 1948.

HESS, Thomas B., and BAKER, Elizabeth C. (editors)
Art and Sexual Politics: Women's Liberation, Women Artists, and Art History, Collier Macmillan Publishers, London, and Collier Books, New York, 1973 (Anthologies II).

HOGELAND, Ronald W. (editor)
Women and Womanhood in America, D.C. Heath and Company, Lexington, Massachusetts, 1973 (Anthologies VII).

HOLE, Judith, and LEVINE, Ellen (editors)
Rebirth of Feminism, Quadrangle Books, New York, 1973 (Anthologies IV).

*HOLLIDAY, Laurel
The Violent Sex: Male Psychobiology and the Evolution of Consciousness, Bluestocking Books, Guerneyville, California 1978.

HOLMES, Urban T.: See BARNHOUSE, Ruth Tiffany.

*HORNER, Matina
"The Motive to Avoid Success and Changing Aspirations of College Women," *Readings on the Psychology of Women*, edited by Judith M. Bardwick, Harper and Row, New York, 1972, pp.62–67.

*HORNEY, Karen
Feminine Psychology, edited by Harold Kalman, W.W. Norton and Company, New York, 1967.

BIBLIOGRAPHY

HOWE, Florence (editor)
Women and the Power to Change, McGraw-Hill, New York, 1975 (Anthologies V).

HUBER, Joan (editor)
Changing Women in a Changing Society, University of Chicago Press, Chicago, 1973 (Anthologies XIV).

*HUME, David
A Treatise of Human Nature, edited by L.A. Selby-Bigge, Clarendon Press, Oxford, 1967; first published 1739–40.
Essays, Moral, Political, and Literary, Longman, Green, and Company, London, 1875; first published 1842 and 1848.

*HUTT, Corinne
Males and Females, Penguin Books, Baltimore, 1972.

HYDE, Janet Shibley, and ROSENBERG, B.G. (editors)
Half the Human Experience: The Psychology of Women, D.C. Heath and Company, Lexington, Massachusetts, Toronto and London, 1976 (Anthologies XIII).

IGLITZIN, Lynne B., and ROSS, Ruth (editors)
Women in the World: A Comparative Study, Clio Books, Santa Barbara, 1976 (Anthologies XV).

IKENBERRY, Jean: See NELSON, Marie Coleman.

IVERSON, Lucille, and RUBY, Kathryn (editors)
We Become New: Poems by Contemporary American Women, Bantam, New York, 1975 (Anthologies II).

JAGGAR, Alison M, and STRUHL, Paula Rothenberg (editors)
Feminist Frameworks: Alternative Theoretical Accounts of the Relations Between Men and Women, McGraw-Hill, New York, 1978 (Anthologies XII).

*JANEWAY, Elizabeth
Man's World, Woman's Place, Dell Publishing Company, New York, 1971.
Between Myth and Morning: Women Awakening, William Morrow and Company, New York, 1975; first published 1972.

JENNES, Linda (editor)
Feminism and Socialism, Pathfinder Press, New York, 1972 (Anthologies X).

*JEWITT, Paul K.
Man as Male and Female: A Study in Sexual Relationships from a Theological Point of View, William P. Eerdmans, Grand Rapids, 1975.

JOHNSON, Cecil E. (editor)
Sex and Human Relationships, Charles E. Merrill Publishing Company, Columbus, Ohio, 1970 (Anthologies III).

JOHNSON, William R.: See GEARHART, Sally.

*JOHNSTON, Jill
Lesbian Nation: The Feminist Solution, Simon and Schuster, New York, 1973.

*JUNG, Carl Gustav
"Woman in Europe," in *The Collected Works of C.G. Jung*, Volume 10, translated by R.F.C. Hull, Random House, New York, 1964, pp.131–133; first published 1927.
"Mind and Earth," *Collected Works*, Volume 10, pp.29–49; first published 1927.
The Relations between the Ego and the Unconscious, *Collected Works*, Volume 7, Princeton University Press, 1966, pp.123–244; first published 1928.
"Concerning the Archetypes, with Special Reference to the Anima Concept," *Collected Works*, Volume 9, Part I, Princeton University Press, 1959, pp.54–74; first published 1936.
Aion: Researches into the Phenomenology of the Self, *Collected Works*, Volume 9, Part II, Princeton University Press, 1968; first published 1951.

KANOWITZ, Leo
Women and the Law: The Unfinished Revolution, University of New Mexico Press, Albuquerque, 1969 (Anthologies IX).

*KANT, Immanuel
Observations on the Feeling of the Beautiful and the Sublime, translated by John T. Goldwait, University of California Press, Berkeley, 1960; first published 1764.

KANTER, Rosabeth Moss: See MILLMAN, Marcia.

KAPLAN, Alexandra G., and BEAN, Joan P. (editors)
Beyond Sex-Role Stereotypes: Readings Toward a Psychology of Androgyny, Little, Brown and Company, Boston and Toronto, 1976 (Anthologies XIII).

KATZ, Harriet N.: See BROWN, Barbara A.

*KEY, Ellen
The Century of the Child, G.P. Putnam's Sons, New York and London, 1909.
The Morality of Woman and Other Essays, translated by Mamak Bouton Borthwick, The Ralph Fletcher Seymour Company, Chicago, 1911.
Love and Marriage, translated by Arthur G. Chater, G.P. Putnam's Sons, 1911.
The Woman Movement, translated by Mamak Bouton Borthwick, G.P. Putnam's Sons, 1912.
The Renaissance of Motherhood, translated by Anna E.G. Fries, G.P. Putnam's Sons, 1914.
The Younger Generation, translated by Arthur G. Chater, G.P. Putnam's Sons, 1914.

*KEY, Mary Ritchie
Male/Female Language, Scarecrow Press, Metuchen, New Jersey, 1975.

*KIERKEGAARD, Soren
Either/Or, translated by David F. Swenson, Lillian M. Swenson, and Walter Lowrie, Princeton University Press, 1971 (Volume I) and 1974 (Volume II); first published 1843.
Stages on Life's Way, translated by Walter Lowrie, Schocken Books, New York, 1967; first published 1845.
The Concept of Dread, translated by Walter Lowrie, Princeton University Press, 1957; first published 1844.

*KINSEY, Alfred C.
Sexual Behavior in the Human Male (and POMEROY, Wardell B., and MARTIN, Clyde E.), W.B. Saunders Company, Philadelphia, 1948.
Sexual Behavior in the Human Female (and POMEROY, Wardell B., MARTIN, Clyde E., and GEBHARD, Paul H.), W.B. Saunders and Company, 1953.

KLAGSBURN, Francine (editor)
The First Ms. Reader, Warner Paperback Library, New York, 1973 (Anthologies IV).

*KLEIN, Viola
The Feminine Character: History of an Ideology, University of Illinois Press, Chicago, 1971; first published 1946.
Women's Two Roles: Home and Work (and MYRDAL, Alva), Routledge and Kegan Paul, London, 1966; first published 1956.

KOEDT, Anne, LEVINE, Ellen, and RAPONE, Anita (editors)
Radical Feminism, Quadrangle, New York, 1973 (Anthologies IV).

*KOMAROVSKY, Mirra
Women in the Modern World: Their Education and Their Dilemmas, Little, Brown and Company, Boston, 1953.
Dilemmas of Masculinity: A Study of College Youth, W.W. Norton and Company, New York, 1976 (Anthologies XI).

KRADITOR, Aileen S.
The Ideas of the Woman Suffrage Movement, Doubleday and Company, New York, 1971 (Anthologies VI).
Up From the Pedestal: Selected Writings in the History of American Feminism (editor), Quadrangle Books, Chicago, 1968 (Anthologies VI).

KREPS, Juanita M. (editor)
Women and the American Economy: A Look at the 1980's, Prentice Hall, Englewood Cliffs, New Jersey (Anthologies XIV).

KRIEGAL, Leonard (editor)
The Myth of American Manhood, Dell Publishing Company, New York, 1978 (Anthologies XI).

*LAKOFF, Robin
Language and Woman's Place, Harper and Row, New York, 1975.

LAMPHERE, Louise: See ROSALDO, Michelle Zimbalist

*LANG, Theo
The Difference between a Man and a Woman, Bantam, New

York, 1973; first published 1971.

LAPIDUS, Gail Warshofsky
Women in Soviet Society: Equality, Development and Social Change, University of California Press, Berkeley and Los Angeles, 1978 (Anthologies XV).

LASKY, Ella (editor)
Humanness: An Exploration into the Mythologies about Women and Men, MSS Information Corporation, New York, 1975 (Anthologies VIII).

*LEDERER, Wolfgang
The Fear of Women, Harcourt, Brace, Jovanovich, New York, 1968.

*LE GUIN, Ursula
The Left Hand of Darkness, Ace Books, New York, 1972, first published 1969.

LENIN, V.I.
The Emancipation of Women (with an appendix by Clara Zetkin), International Publishers, New York, 1966 (Anthologies X).
(Also see MARX, Karl.)

LERNER, Gerda (editor)
Black Women in White America: A Documentary History, Vintage Books, New York, 1973 (Anthologies VII).

*LEVI-STRAUSS, Claude
The Elementary Structures of Kinship, translated by J.H. Bell, J.R. von Sturmer, and R. Needham, Eyre and Spottiswoode, London, 1969; first published 1949.

LEVINE, Ellen: See KOEDT, Anne, and HOLE, Judith.

*LEWIS, Helen Block
Psychic War in Men and Women, New York University Press, 1976.

LIBBY, Roger W.: See GORDON, Sol.

BIBLIOGRAPHY

LIPS, Hilary M., and COLWILL, Nina Lee
The Psychology of Sex Differences, Prentice Hall, Englewood Cliffs, New Jersey, 1978 (Anthologies XIII).

LLOYD, Barbara, and ARCHER, John (editors)
Exploring Sex Differences, Academic Press, London, New York and San Francisco, 1974 (Anthologies VIII).

*LOCKE, John
Two Treatises of Government, Hafner Publishing Company, New York, 1947; first published 1690.

*LORENZ, Konrad
On Aggression, translated by Marjorie Kerr Wilson, Harcourt, Brace and World, New York, 1963.

LOVE, Barbara: See ABBOTT, Sidney.

*LUNDBERG, Ferdinand, and FARNHAM, Marynia
Modern Woman: The Lost Sex, Grosset and Dunlap, New York, 1947.

*MACCOBY, Eleanor Emmons
The Psychology of Sex Differences (and JACKLIN, Carol Nagy), Stanford University Press, 1974.
The Development of Sex Differences (editor), Stanford University Press, 1966 (Anthologies XIII).

MAHOWALD, Mary Briody (editor)
Philosophy of Woman: Classical to Current Concepts, Hackett Publishing Company, Indianapolis, 1978 (Anthologies XII).

*MAILER, Norman
The Prisoner of Sex, New American Library, New York, 1971.

*MAINE, Sir Henry
Ancient Law, J. Murray, London, 1873; first published 1861.

*MALINOWSKI, Bronislaw
Sex and Repression in Savage Society, Routledge and Kegan Paul, London, 1953; first published 1927.
The Sexual Life of Savages in North-Western Melanesia, Routledge and Kegan Paul, London, 1929.
Sex, Culture, and Myth, Harcourt, Brace and World, New York, 1962.

MANDEL, William M.
Soviet Women, Anchor Press/Doubleday, Garden City, New York, 1975 (Anthologies XV).

MAPPES, Thomas A., and ZEMBATY, Jane S. (editors)
Social Ethics: Morality and Social Policy, McGraw-Hill, New York, 1977 (Anthologies III).

*MARINE, Gene
A Male Guide to Women's Liberation, Avon, New York, 1972.

MARKS, S.J.: See BERG, Stephen

MARLOW, H. Carleton, and DAVIS, Harrison M.
The American Search for Woman, Clio Books, Santa Barbara, 1976 (Anthologies VI).

MARMOR, Judd (editor)
Sexual Inversion: The Multiple Roots of Homosexuality, Basic Books, New York and London, 1965 (Anthologies XIII).

MARTENES, Laura: See O'FAOLAIN, Julia.

MARTIN, M. Kay, and VOORHIES, Barbara
Female of the Species, Columbia University Press, New York and London, 1975 (Anthologies I).

MARTIN, Wendy (editor)
The American Sisterhood: Writings of the Feminist Movement from Colonial Times to the Present, Harper and Row, New York, 1972 (Anthologies VI).

*MARTINEAU, Harriet
Society in America, Saunders and Otley, London, 1837.

MARTYNA, Wendy: See CATER, Libby A.

*MARX, Karl
Economic and Philosophic Manuscripts of 1844, translated by Martin Milligan, International Publishers, New York, 1964.
Manifesto of the Communist Party (and ENGELS, Friedrich), in *Basic Writings on Politics and Philosophy*, edited by Lewis S. Feuer, Anchor Books, Garden City, New York, 1959, pp.1–41; written 1848.

Capital: A Critique of Political Economy, translated by Samuel Moore and Edward Aveling, the Modern Library, New York, 1906; first published 1867.
The Woman Question: Selections from the Writings of Karl Marx, Friedrich Engels, V.I. Lenin and Joseph Stalin (and ENGELS, Friedrich, LENIN, V.I. and STALIN, Joseph), International Publishers, New York, 1971 (Anthologies X).

*MASTERS, William H., and JOHNSON, Virginia
Human Sexual Response, Little, Brown and Company, Boston, 1966.
Human Sexual Inadequacy, Little, Brown and Company, Boston, 1966.
The Pleasure Bond: A New Look at Sexuality and Commitment, Little, Brown and Company, Boston, 1974.

MATTFELD, Jacquelyn A., and VAN AKEN, Carol G. (editors)
Women and the Scientific Professions: The M.I.T. Symposium on American Women in Science and Engineering, M.I.T. Press, Cambridge, Massachusetts, and London, 1965 (Anthologies VIII).

MC BEE, Mary Louise, and BLAKE, Kathyrn A. (editors)
The American Woman: Who Will She Be?, Glencoe Press, Beverly Hills, California, 1974 (Anthologies VIII).

*MC LENNAN, John Ferguson
Primitive Marriage: An Inquiry into the Origin of the Form of Capture in Marriage Ceremonies, University of Chicago Press, 1970; first published 1865.

*MEAD, Margaret
Sex and Temperament in Three Primitive Societies, William Morrow and Company, New York, 1963; first published 1935.
Male and Female: A Study of the Sexes in a Changing World, Dell Publishing Company, New York, 1971; first published 1949.

MELLAART, James
Catal Huyuk: A Neolithic Town in Anatolia, McGraw-Hill, New York, 1967 (Anthologies I).

*MENKEN, H.L.
In Defense of Women, Time Incorporated, New York, 1963; first published 1922.

*MERRIAM, Eve
After Nora Slammed the Door, World Publishing Company, New York, 1958.

*MILL, John Stuart
The Subjection of Women, M.I.T. Press, Cambridge, Massachusetts, 1970; first published 1869.
"Early Essays on Marriage and Divorce," in *Essays on Sex Equality*, edited by Alice Rossi, University of Chicago Press, Chicago and London, 1970; written 1832.

*MILLER, Casey, and SWIFT, Kate
Words and Women: New Language in New Times, Anchor, Garden City, New York, 1977.

*MILLER, Jean Baker
Toward a New Psychology of Women, Beacon Press, Boston, 1976.
Psychoanalysis and Women (editor), Penguin Books, Baltimore, 1973 (Anthologies XIII).

MILLER, John N. (editor)
A World of Her Own: Writers and the Feminist Controversy, Charles E. Merrill Publishing Company, Columbus, Ohio, 1971 (Anthologies II).

*MILLETT, Kate
Sexual Politics, Avon Books, New York, 1971; first published 1969.

MILLMAN, Marcia, and KANTER, Rosabeth Moss (editors)
Another Voice: Feminist Perspectives on Social Life and Social Science, Anchor Press, Garden City, New York, 1975 (Anthologies XIV).

*MITCHELL, Juliet
Woman's Estate, Random House, New York, 1973; first published 1971.
Psychoanalysis and Feminism: Freud, Reich, Laing and Women, Random House, New York, 1975.

MITCHINSON, Wendy: See COOK, Ramsay.

BIBLIOGRAPHY

MOERS, Ellen
Literary Women: The Great Writers, Anchor Press/Doubleday, Garden City, New York, 1977 (Anthologies II).

MOFFAT, Mary Jane, and PAINTER, Charlotte (editors)
Revelations: Diaries of Women, Vintage Books, New York, 1975 (Anthologies II).

*MONEY, John, and EHRHARDT, Anke
Man and Woman, Boy and Girl: The Differentiation and Dimorphism of Gender Identity from Conception to Maturity, Mentor Books, New York, 1974; first published 1972.

*MONTAGU, Ashley
The Natural Superiority of Women, Macmillan Publishers, New York, 1974; first published 1952.
Man and Aggression (editor), Oxford University Press, London and New York, 1968 (Anthologies VIII).

MORAN, Barbara K.: See GORNICK, Vivian.

*MORGAN, Elaine
The Descent of Woman, Bantam, New York, 1973; first published 1972.

*MORGAN, Lewis Henry
Ancient Society, Harvard University Press, Cambridge, Massachusetts, 1964; first published 1877.

*MORGAN, Robin
Going Too Far: The Personal Chronicles of a Feminist, Vintage Books, New York, 1978.
Sisterhood is Powerful: An Anthology of Writings from the Woman's Liberation Movement (editor), Vintage Books, New York, 1970 (Anthologies IV).
(Also see COOKE, Joanne.)

*MORRIS, Desmond
The Naked Ape, Dell Publishing Company, New York, 1969; first published 1967.

MORRISON, Eleanor S., and BOROSAGE, Vera (editors)
Human Sexuality: Contemporary Perspectives, National Press Books, Palo Alto, California, 1973 (Anthologies III).

MOZANS, H.J. (pseudonym of ZAHM, John Augustine)
Woman in Science, M.I.T. Press, Cambridge, Massachusetts, 1974; first published 1913 (Anthologies VII).

MURRAY, Michelle (editor)
A House of Good Proportion: Images of Women in Literature, Simon and Schuster, 1973 (Anthologies II).

*MYRDAL, Ava, and KLEIN, Viola
Women's Two Roles: Home and Work, Routledge and Kegan Paul, London, 1966; first published 1956.

NAGEL, Thomas: See COHEN, Marshall.

NASH, June, and SAFA, Helen Icken (editors)
Sex and Class in Latin America, Praeger Publishers, New York, 1976 (Anthologies XV).

NELSON, Marie Coleman, and IKENBERRY, Jean (editors)
Psychosexual Imperatives: Their Role in Identity Formation, Human Sciences Press, New York and London, 1979 (Anthologies XIII).

*NEUMANN, Eric
The Great Mother: An Analysis of an Archetype, translated by Ralph Manheim, Princeton University Press, 1955.

NEW YORK CITY COMMISSION ON HUMAN RIGHTS
Women's Role in Contemporary Society: The Report of the New York City Commission on Human Rights, Avon Books, New York, 1972 (Anthologies VIII).

NEW YORK RADICAL FEMINISTS
Rape: The First Sourcebook for Women (edited by Noreen Connell and Cassandra Wilson), New American Library, New York, 1974 (Anthologies IV).

NICHOLS, Jack
Men's Liberation: A New Definition of Masculinity, Penguin Books, New York, 1975 (Anthologies XI).

*NIETZSCHE, Friedrich
The Gay Science, translated by Walter Kaufman, Random House, New York, 1974; first published 1882.

Thus Spoke Zarathustra, translated by R.J. Hollingdale, Penguin Books, Baltimore, 1967; first published 1883–85.
Beyond Good and Evil, translated by Marianne Cowan, Henry Regnery Company, Chicago, 1955; first published 1885.
On the Geneology of Morals, and *Ecce Homo*, translated by Walter Kaufman and R.J. Hollingdale; Vintage, New York, 1967; first published 1887 and 1908.

NILSEN, Aileen Pace, BOSMAJIAN, Haig, GERSHUNG, H. Lee, and STANLEY, Julia P. (editors)
Sexism and Language, National Council of Teachers of English, Urbana, Illinois, 1977 (Anthologies V).

NOONAN, John T., Jr. (editor)
The Morality of Abortion: Legal and Historical Perspectives, Harvard University Press, Cambridge, Massachusetts, 1970 (Anthologies III).

NORTON, Eleanor Holmes: See BABCOCK, Barbara.

*OAKLEY, Ann
Sex, Gender, and Society, Harper and Row, New York, 1972.
Women's Work: The Housewife, Past and Present, Vintage Books, New York, 1976; first published 1974.
The Sociology of Housework, Pantheon Books, New York, 1974.

O'FAOLAIN, Julia, and MARTENES, Laura (editors)
Not in God's Image: Women in History from the Greeks to the Victorians, Harper and Row, New York, 1973 (Anthologies VII).

O'NEILL, Onora, and RUDDICK, William (editors)
Having Children: Philosophical and Legal Reflections on Parenthood, Oxford University Press, New York, 1979 (Anthologies XII).

O'NEILL, William
Everyone Was Brave: The Rise and Fall of Feminism in America, Quadrangle, Chicago, 1969 (Anthologies VI).
The Woman Movement: Feminism in the United States and England, Quadrangle, Chicago, 1969 (Anthologies VI).

OSBORNE, Martha Lee (editor)
Woman in Western Thought, Random House, New York, 1979
(Anthologies XII).

OTT, Jocelynn Snyder
Women and Creativity, Les Femmes Publishing, Millbrae, California, 1978 (Anthologies II).

PAINTER, Charlotte: See MOFFAT, Mary Jane.

PARKER, Gail (editor)
The Oven Birds: American Women on Womanhood, 1820–1920
Anchor Books/Doubleday, Garden City, New York, 1972 (Anthologies II).

*PARSONS, Talcott
Essays in Sociological Theory, The Free Press, New York, 1954.
Family Socialization and Interaction Process (and BALES, Robert F.), The Free Press, Glencoe, Illinois, 1955.

SAINT PAUL
The Letters of Paul, in The Bible.

PECK, Ellen, and SENDEROWITZ, Judith (editors)
Pronatalism: The Myth of Mom and Apple Pie, Thomas Y. Crowell Company, New York, 1974 (Anthologies VIII).

PETERSON, Karen, and WILSON, J.J.
Women Artists: Recognition and Reappraisal, From the Early Middle Ages to the Twentieth Century, Harper Colophon, New York, 1976 (Anthologies II).

PETRAS, John W. (editor)
Sex: Male/Gender: Masculine, Alfred Publishing Company, Port Washington, New York, 1975 (Anthologies XI).

PIVAL, Jean G.: See ADELSTEIN, Michael E.

PLASKOW, Judith, and ARNOLD, Joan (editors)
Women and Religion, Scholars Press, Missoula, Montana, 1974
(Anthologies XII).

*PLATO
The Symposium, translated by Walter Hamilton, Penguin

Books, New York, 1974.
The Republic, with an English translation by R.G. Bury, Harvard University Press, Cambridge, Massachusetts, 1970.
Laws, with an English translation by R.G. Bury, Harvard Universiy Press, Cambridge, Massachusetts, 1961.
Timaeus and Critias, translated by H.D.P. Lee, Penguin Books, Middlesex, England, 1971.

PLECK, Joseph, and SAWYER, Jack (editors)
Men and Masculinity, Prentice Hall, Englewood Cliffs, New Jersey, 1974 (Anthologies XI).

POMEROY, Sarah B.
Goddesses, Whores, Wives and Slaves: Women in Classical Antiquity, Schocken Books, New York, 1975 (Anthologies VII).

PRICE, Alice M.: See BROWN, Barbara A.

RAINEY, Carol: See SEGRITY, Barbara.

RANDALL, Margaret
Cuban Women Now: Interviews with Cuban Women, Women's Press Publications, Toronto, 1974 (Anthologies XV).

RAPONE, Anita: See KOEDT, Ann.

REAGAN, Barbara: See BLAXALL, Martha.

*REED, Evelyn
Problems of Women's Liberation: A Marxist Approach, Pathfinder Press, New York, 1970.
Women's Evolution: From Matriarchal Clan to Patriarchal Family, Pathfinder Press, New York, 1975.
Sexism and Science, Pathfinder Press, New York and Toronto, 1978.

*REEVES, Nancy
Womankind Beyond the Stereotypes, Aldine Atherton, Chicago, 1971.

*REICH, Wilhelm
The Function of the Orgasm: Sex-Economic Problems of Biological Energy, translated by Theodore P. Wolfe, Noonday Press,

New York, 1961; first published 1927.
The Sexual Revolution: Toward a Self-Governing Character Structure, translated by Theodore P. Wolfe, Orgone Institute Press, New York, 1945; first published 1930.
The Invasion of Compulsory Sex Morality, Farrar, Straus and Giroux, New York, 1971; first published 1933.

*REIK, Theodore
The Creation of Woman: A Psychoanalytic Inquiry into the Myth of Eve, McGraw-Hill, 1973.

REITENBECK, Hendrick (editor)
Psychoanalysis and Male Sexuality, College and University Press, New Haven, Connecticut, 1966 (Anthologies XI).

REITER, Rayna R. (editor)
Toward an Anthropology of Woman, Monthly Review Press, New York and London, 1975 (Anthologies I).

*RAYBURN, Wallace
The Inferior Sex, Prentice Hall, Englewood Cliffs, New Jersey, 1972.

*RICH, Adrienne
Of Woman Born: Motherhood as Experience and Institution, W.W. Norton and Company, 1976.

RICHARDSON, Herbert: See CLARK, Elizabeth.

ROBERTS, Joan I. (editor)
Beyond Intellectual Sexism: A New Woman, A New Reality, David McKay Company, New York, 1976 (Anthologies VIII).

ROGERS, Katharine M.
The Troublesome Helpmate: A History of Misogyny in Literature, University of Washington Press, Seattle and London, 1966 (Anthologies II).

ROSALDO, Michelle Zimbalist, and LAMPHERE, Louise (editors)
Woman, Culture and Society, Stanford University Press, 1974 (Anthologies I).

ROSENBERG, B.G.: See HYDE, Janet Shibley.

ROSS, Ruth: See IGLITZIN, Lynne B.

ROSS, Susan C.: See BABCOCK, Barbara.

ROSS, Susan D.
The Rights of Women: The Basic ACLU Guide to a Woman's Rights, Avon Books, New York, 1973 (Anthologies IX).

ROSSI, Alice S.
The Feminist Papers: From Adams to de Beauvoir (editor), Bantam, New York, 1976 (Anthologies VI).
Academic Women on the Move (and CALDERWOOD, Ann, editors), Russell Sage Foundation, New York, 1973 (Anthologies V).
Essays on Sex Equality (editor), by John Stuart Mill and Harriet Taylor Mill The University of Chicago Press, Chicago and London, 1970.

ROSZAK, Betty and ROSZAK, Theodore (editors)
Masculine/Feminine: Readings in Sexual Mythology and the Liberation of Women, Harper and Row, New York, 1969 (Anthologies VIII).

ROSZAK, Theodore: See ROSZAK, Betty.

*ROUSSEAU, Jean Jacques
Emile, translated by Barbara Foxley, J.M. Dent & Sons, London, 1963; first published 1762.

*ROWBOTHAM, Sheila
Woman's Consciousness, Man's World, Penguin Books, New York, 1974.
Women, Resistance, and Revolution, Vintage Books, New York, 1974.
Hidden from History: Rediscovering Women in History from the 17th Century to the Present, Random House, New York, 1976.

RUBY, Kathryn: See IVERSON, Lucille.

RUCKMAN, Gaye, DANIELS, Arlene Kaplan, and BENET, James (editors)
Hearth and Home: Images of Women in the Mass Media, Oxford University Press, New York, 1978 (Anthologies V).

RUDDICK, William: See O'NEILL, Onora.

*RUETHER, Rosemary Radford
New Woman, New Earth: Sexist Ideologies and Human Libera-tion, Seabury Press, New York, 1975.
Religion and Sexism: Images of Women in the Jewish and Chris-tian Traditions (editor), Simon and Schuster, New York, 1974 (Anthologies XII).

*RUSSELL, Bertrand
Marriage and Morals, George Allen and Unwin, London, 1929.
A History of Western Philosophy, and Its Connection with Political and Social Circumstances from the Earliest Times to the Present Day, George Allen and Unwin, London, 1946.

*RUSSELL, Letty M.
Human Liberation in a Feminist Perspective, Westminster Press, Philadelphia, 1974.

SACHS, Abbie, and WILSON, Joan Hoff
Sexism and the Law, The Free Press, New York, 1978 (Anthol-ogies IX).

SAFA, Helen Icken: See NASH, June.

*SAFILIOS-ROTHSCHILD, Constantina
Love, Sex, and Sex Roles, Prentice Hall, Englewood Cliffs, New Jersey, 1977.
Toward a Sociology of Woman (editor), Xerox College Publish-ing, Lexington, Massachusetts, 1972 (Anthologies XIV).

SALPER, Roberta (editor)
Female Liberation, History and Current Politics, Alfred A. Knopf, New York, 1972 (Anthologies VI).

*SANGER, Margaret
Woman and the New Race, Maxwell Reprint Company, Elms-ford, New York, 1969; first published 1922.
The Pivot of Civilization, Maxwell Reprint Company, 1969; first published 1922.
Motherhood in Bondage, Maxwell Reprint Company, 1956; first published 1928.
My Fight for Birth Control, Farrar and Rinehart, New York, 1931.

*SARTRE, Jean-Paul
Being and Nothingness: An Essay on Phenomenological Ontology, translated by Hazel E. Barnes, Washington Square Press, New York, 1966; first published 1943.

SAWYER, Jack: See PLECK, Joseph H.

SCANLON, Thomas: See COHEN, Marshall.

*SCHEINFELD, Amran
Women and Men, Harcourt, Brace and Company, New York, 1944.

SCHLEGEL, Alice (editor)
Male Dominance and Female Autonomy: Domestic Authority in Matrilineal Societies, Hraf Press, 1972.

SCHNEIDER, David M. and GOUGH, Kathleen (editors)
Matrilineal Kinship, University of California Press, Berkeley, 1961 (Anthologies I).

SCHNEIR, Miriam (editor)
Feminism: The Essential Historial Writings, Vintage Books, New York, 1972 (Anthologies VI).

*SCHOPENHAUER, Arthur
"On Women," in *Studies in Pessimism: A Series of Essays*, translated by Q. Bailey Saunders, Scholarly Press, St. Clair Shores, Michigan, 1970; first published 1893.

*SCHREINER, Olive
Woman and Labor, T. Fisher Unwin, London, 1911.

SCOTT, Anne Firor
The American Woman: Who Was She? (editor), Prentice Hall, Englewood Cliffs, New Jersey, 1971 (Anthologies VII).
The Southern Lady: From Pedestal to Politics 1830–1930, The University of Chicago Press, Chicago, 1970 (Anthologies VII). (See also CATER, Libby A.)

*SCOTT, Hilda
Does Socialism Liberate Women? Experiences from Eastern Europe, Beacon Press, Boston, 1974.

*SCOTT-MAXWELL, Florida
Women and Sometimes Men, Alfred A. Knopf, New York, 1957.

*SEAMAN, Barbara
Free and Female: The Sex Life of the Contemporary Female, Coward, McCann and Geoghigan, New York, 1972.

*SEGRITY, Barbara and RAINEY, Carol (editors)
Psyche: The Feminine Poetic Consciousness, An Anthology of Modern American Women Poets, Dell Publishing Company, New York, 1923 (Anthologies II).

SENDEROWITZ, Judith: See PECK, Ellen.

*SEXTON, Patricia Cayo
The Feminized Male: Classrooms, White Collars and the Decline of Manliness, Random House, New York, 1969.

*SHERFEY, Mary Jane
The Nature and Evolution of Female Sexuality, Random House, New York, 1966.

SIDEL, Ruth
Women and Children in China: A Firsthand Report, Penguin Books, Baltimore, 1974 (Anthologies XV).

SINCLAIR, Andrew
The Emancipation of the American Woman, Harper and Row, New York, 1965 (Anthologies VI).

*SINGER, June
Androgyny: Toward a New Theory of Sexuality, Anchor Press, Garden City, New York, 1976.

SMITH, Dorothy E.
Feminism and Marxism: A Place to Begin, a Way to Go, New Star Books, Vancouver, Canada, 1977 (Anthologies X).

SMITH, Florence M.
Mary Astell, Columbia University Press, New York, 1916.

SMOCK, Audrey Chapman: See GIELE, Janet Zollinger.

651

SNYDER, Eloise C. (editor)
The Study of Women: Enlarging Perspectives of Social Reality, Harper and Row, New York, 1979 (Anthologies VIII).

SOCHEN, June
The New Feminism in Twentieth Century America (editor), D.C. Heath and Company, Lexington, Massachusetts, 1971 (Anthologies VI).
Movers and Shakers: American Women Thinkers and Activists 1900–1970 Quadrangle, New York, 1973 (Anthologies VII).
Herstory: A Woman's View of American History, Alfred Publishing Company, New York, 1974 (Anthologies VII).

*SOLANAS, Valerie
SCUM Manifesto, Olympia Press, New York, 1968.

SOLOMON, Barbara H. (editor)
The Experience of the American Woman: 30 Stories, Mentor, New York, 1978 (Anthologies II).

*SOROKIN, Pitirim A.
The American Sex Revolution, Porter Sargent, Boston, 1956.

SPACKS, Patricia Meyer
The Female Imagination, Avon Books, New York, 1972 (Anthologies II).

*SPENCER, Herbert
Social Statics, D. Appleton and Company, New York, 1913; first published 1850.
The Principles of Ethics, D. Appleton and Company, 1910; first published 1893.
The Principles of Sociology, D. Appleton and Company, 1897.
Essays, Scientific, Political, and Speculative, D. Appleton and Company, 1910; first published 1874.

STACEY, Judith, BEREAUD, Susan, and DANIELS, Joan (editors)
And Jill Came Tumbling After, Dell Publishing Company, New York, 1974 (Anthologies V).

STALIN, Joseph: See MARX, Karl.

STANFORD, Barbara (editor)
On Being Female, Pocket Books, New York, 1974 (Anthologies IV).

STANLEY, Julia P.: See NILSEN, Aileen Pace.

*STANNARD, Una
Mrs. Man, Germainbooks, San Francisco, 1977.

STEARNS, Peter N. (editor)
The Rise of the Modern Woman, Forum Press, St. Louis, Missouri, 1978 (Anthologies VII).

*STEINMANN, Anne, and FOX, David J.
The Male Dilemma: How to Survive the Sexual Revolution, Jason Aronson, New York, 1974.

*STERN, Karl
The Flight from Woman, Farrar, Straus and Giroux, New York, 1965.

STOLL, Clarice Stasy
Female and Male: Socialization, Social Roles, and Social Structure, Wm. C. Brown Company, Dubuque, Iowa, 1974 (Anthologies XIV).
Sexism: Scientific Debates (editor), Addison-Wesley Publishing Company, Reading, Massachusetts, 1975 (Anthologies XIV).

*STOLLER, Robert J.
Sex and Gender, Volume 1: The Development of Masculinity and Femininity, Jason Aronson, New York, 1974; first published 1968.
Sex and Gender, Volume 2: The Transsexual Experiment, Jason Aronson, New York, 1975.

*STONE, Merlin
When God Was a Woman, Dial Press, New York, 1976.

*STORR, Anthony
Human Aggression, Atheneum, New York, 1968.

STRATHERN, Marilyn
Women in Between: Female Roles in a Male World: Mount

Hagen, New Guinea, Seminar Press, London and New York, 1972 (Anthologies I).

STROMBERG, Anne H., and HARKNESS, Shirley (editors)
Women Working: Theories and Facts in Perspective, Mayfield Publishing Company, Palo Alto, California, 1978 (Anthologies XIV).

STROUSE, Jean (editor)
Women and Analysis: Dialogues on Psychoanalytic Views of Femininity, Grossman Publishers, New York, 1974 (Anthologies XIII).

STRUHL, Paula Rothenberg: See JAGGAR, Alison.

*SULLEROT, Evelyn
Woman, Society, and Change, translated by Margaret Scotford Archer, McGraw-Hill, New York, 1971.

SWITZER, Ellen
The Law for a Woman: Real Cases and What Happened, Charles Scribner's Sons, New York, 1975 (Anthologies IX).

TANNER, Leslie B. (editor)
Voices from Women's Liberation, New American Library, New York, 1971 (Anthologies IV).

*TAYLOR, G. Rattray
Sex in History, Harper and Row, New York, 1973; first published 1954.

*TAYLOR, Harriet
"Enfranchisement of Women," in *Essays on Sex Equality*, by John Stuart Mill and Harriet Taylor, edited by Alice S. Rossi, University of Chicago Press, 1970; essay first published 1851.

THEODORE, Athena (editor)
The Professional Woman, Schenkman Publishing Company, Cambridge, Massachusetts, 1971 (Anthologies XIV).

*THOMAS, William I.
Sex and Society: Studies in the Social Psychology of Sex, Fisher Unwin, London, 1907.

BIBLIOGRAPHY

*THOMPSON, Clara
On Women, edited by Maurice R. Green, New American Library, New York, 1971; first published 1964.

THOMPSON, Mary Lou (editor)
Voices of the New Feminism, Beacon Press, Boston, 1971 (Anthologies IV).

*THOMPSON, William
Appeal of One Half of the Human Race, Women, Against the Pretensions of the Other Half, Men, to Retain Them in Civil and Thence Domestic Slavery, Burt Franklin, New York, 1970; first published 1825.

THORNE, Barrie, and HENLEY, Nancy (editors)
Language and Sex: Difference and Dominance, Newbury House Publishers, Rowley, Massachusetts, 1975 (Anthologies XIV).

*TIGER, Lionel
Men in Groups, Random House, New York, 1969.
The Imperial Animal (and FOX, Robin), Holt, Rinehart and Winston, New York, 1971.

TOMALIN, Claire
The Life and Death of Mary Wollstonecraft, Harcourt Brace Jovanovich, New York, 1974.

TRIPP, Maggie (editor)
Woman in the Year 2000, Dell Publishing Company, New York, 1974 (Anthologies VIII).

TROTSKY, Leon
Women and the Family, Pathfinder Press, New York, 1970 (Anthologies X)

*UNWIN, Joseph David
Sex and Culture, Oxford University Press, London, 1934.

*VAERTING, Mathilde and Mathias
The Dominant Sex: A Study in the Sociology of Sex Differentiation, translated by Eden and Cedar Park, George H. Doran Company, New York, 1923.

VAN AKEN, Carol G.: See MATTFELD, Jacquelyn A.

VETTERLING-BRAGGIN, Mary, ELLISTON, Frederick A., and ENGLISH, Jane (editors)
Feminism and Philosophy, Littlefield, Adams and Company, Totowa, New Jersey, 1977(Anthologies XII).

*VILAR, Esther
The Manipulated Man, Bantam Books, New York, 1972.

VOORHIES, Barbara: See MARTIN, M. Kay.

WAEHRER, Helen Youngelson: See GLAZER-MALBIN, Nona.

WALTERS, LeRoy: See BEAUCHAMP, Tom L.

WARD, Barbara E. (editor)
Women in the New Asia: The Changing Social Roles of Men and Women in South and South-East Asia, United Nations Educational, Scientific, and Cultural Organization, Amsterdam, Netherlands, 1963 (Anthologies XV).

WARDLE, Ralph
Mary Wollstonecraft: A Critical Biography, University of Nebraska Press, Lincoln, Nebraska, 1951.

*WARE, Cellestine
Woman Power: The Movement for Women's Liberation, Tower Publications, New York, 1970.

WARTOFSKY, Marx W.: See GOULD, Carol C.

WASSERSTROM, Richard (editor)
Today's Moral Problems, Macmillan Publishing Company, New York, 1975 (Anthologies III).

WATSON, Barbara Bellow (editor)
Women's Studies: The Social Realities, Harper and Row, New York, 1976 (Anthologies VIII).

*WATTS, Alan W.
Nature, Man and Woman, Random House, New York, 1970; first published 1958.

*WEININGER, Otto
Sex and Character, G.P. Putnam Sons, New York, 1906.

WEINZWEIG, Marjorie: See BISHOP, Sharon.

*WEISSTEIN, Naomi
"Psychology Constructs the Female," in *Sex Equality*, edited by Jane English, Prentice Hall, Englewood Cliffs, New Jersey, 1977.

WEST, Uta (editor)
Women in a Changing World, McGraw-Hill, New York, 1975 (Anthologies IV).

*WESTERMARCK, Edward
The History of Human Marriage, Macmillan and Company, London, 1925; first published 1891.
A Short History of Marriage, The Macmillan Company, New York, 1930; first published 1926.
Ethical Relativity, Harcourt, Brace and Company, New York, 1932.
The Future of Marriage in Western Civilization, The Macmillan Company, New York, 1936.

*WILLIAMS, Juanita H.
Psychology of Woman: Behavior in a Biosocial Context, W.W. Norton and Company, New York, 1977; first published 1974.

WILSON, Cassandra: See NEW YORK RADICAL FEMINISTS.

*WILSON, Edward O.
Sociobiology: The New Synthesis, Harvard University Press, 1975.
On Human Nature, Harvard University Press, 1978.

WILSON, J.J.: See PETERSON, Karen.

WILSON, Joan Hoff: See SACHS, Abbie.

WILSON, Roger H.L.: See FARBER, Seymour M.

*WOLFF, Charlotte
Love Between Women, Harper and Row, New York, 1972.

*WOLLSTONECRAFT, Mary
Thoughts on the Education of Daughters: With Reflections on

Female Conduct, in the More Important Duties of Life, London, 1787.
A Vindication of the Rights of Men, in a Letter to the Right Honorable Edmund Burke, London, 1790.
A Vindication of the Rights of Woman, W.W. Norton and Company, New York, 1967; first published 1792.
Maria, or The Wrongs of Woman, W.W. Norton and Company, New York, 1975; written 1797.

*WOOLF, Virginia
A Room of One's Own, Harcourt, Brace and Company, New York, 1929.
Three Guineas, Harcourt, Brace and Company, 1938.

*WRIGHT, Frederick Adam
Feminism in Greek Literature: From Homer to Aristotle, Kennikat Press, New York and London, 1969; first published 1923.

*WYLIE, Phillip
Generation of Vipers, Rinehart and Company, New York, 1955; first published 1942.

*YATES, Gayle Graham
What Women Want: The Ideas of the Movement, Harvard University Press, 1975.

*ZARETSKY, Eli
Capitalism, the Family, and Personal Life, Harper and Row, New York, 1976.

ZAHM, John Augustine: See MOZANS, H.J.

ZEMBATY, Jane S.: See MAPPES, Thomas A.

ZETKIN, Clara: See LENIN, V.I.

GLOSSARY

The following are terms which occur fairly frequently in this book and which may be unfamiliar to some readers; or which are used in this literature in a sense which is somewhat different from the most usual one.

GLOSSARY

Androcentric: male-centered; exhibiting an exclusively or predominantly or excessively male point of view.

Androgyne: an androgynous person.

Androgens: hormones associated with the biological development and sexual functioning of the male; e.g. testosterone (which is also produced by the female system, but in smaller quantities).

Androgynous: exhibiting both the (stereotypically) "masculine" and "feminine" characteristics, especially psychological ones.

Antifeminist: one who opposes feminist ideas, such as the right of women to moral and legal equality, equality of opportunity, and freedom from sex-role stereotyping.

Antimasculinist: one who is opposed to androcentric or male-supremacist ideas, actions, and institutions.

Bisexual: one whose erotic orientation is both homosexual and heterosexual.

Capitalism: an economic system based on the private ownership of most means of production (e.g. land, factories, resources); and on the production, distribution and exchange of goods for private profit, in a more or less free and competitive market.

Circumcision, female: removal of the clitoris and, usually, the labia minora.

Clitoridectomy: surgical removal of the clitoris.

Ecology: the interrelationships between organisms and their environment, or the study thereof.

Episiotomy: a surgical procedure in which a long incision is made in the inner wall of the vagina, in order to enlarge the vagina and facilitate childbirth.

ERA: the Equal Rights Amendment to the United States Constitution, which was passed by Congress and sent to the states for ratification in 1972, forty-three years after it was first proposed. Although the original deadline of March 1979 has been extended for three years, the ERA has not yet been accepted by the thirty-eight states required for it to become law.

Estrogens: certain hormones associated with female sexual development and functioning (also produced in males, but in smaller quantities).

Ethology: the scientific study of the behavior of animals.

Feminism: the thesis that male domination is morally wrong, and that women and men ought to enjoy equal moral, social, legal and political rights; organized political activity in support of this position.

Gender: (1) biological sex, i.e. maleness or femaleness; (2) the masculinity or femininity of a person's character and self-concept; thus transsexuals are said to have a gender identity in conflict with their biological sex.

Gender identity: an individual's perception or conviction of her- or himself as masculine or feminine.

Gender role: the functions and status assigned, within a particular society, to persons believed to be of a particular gender or sex.

Gynecology: the branch of medicine which deals with the diseases and other physiological (or sometimes mental) problems which are or are thought to be peculiar to women.

Gynocentric: women-centered; based on traditionally feminine values.

Gynocide: the murder of women, especially on a large scale.

Gynocracy: the political supremacy of women.

Hermaphrodite: a person whose sexual biology is neither unequivocably male nor unequivocably female, but to some extent intermediate between the two. The term is imprecise and covers a wide range of medical conditions: it should however be sharply distinguished from **transsexual** and **transvestite**.

Heterosexual: (1) relating to sexual relations between persons of opposite sexes; (2) a person whose eroticism is directed towards individuals of the opposite sex.

Homosexual: (1) relating to sexual relations between persons of the same sex; (2) a person whose erotic orientation is primarily toward persons of the same sex.

Intersexual: an individual whose sexual anatomy and other physiological traits are neither unequivocably masculine nor unequivocably feminine; see hermaphrodite.

Liberal feminist: a feminist who believes that sexual equality can be achieved through the reform of existing social institutions, especially law, education, and employment practices.

Marriage: (1) a legal or customary union between a woman (or sometimes more than one woman) and a man (or sometimes more than one man), typically (but not always) involving cohabitation, heterosexual intercourse between the married parties, and joint responsibility for the rearing of the resulting offspring, if any. (2) A relatively permanent union between (usually) two persons of the same sex, typically involving cohabitation and sexual intercourse, if not social or legal sanction.

Masculinist: a male supremacist (not a symmetrical concept with **feminist**).

Matriachate: a matriarchy.

Matriarchy: a society or condition of society in which women hold social and poltical power over men. (Such a society might or might not also be matrilineal in its family structure.)

Matriclan: an extended matrifocal family, usually matrilineal and/ or matrilocal.

Matrifocal family: any family structure in which the mother-child relationship is (considered) more important than the paternal one; usually matrilineal and/or matrilocal.

Matriliny: the practice of recording descent through the mother's line—as opposed to **patriliny**.

Matrilocality: the practice whereby married couples reside in or near the family or clan of the wife, rather than that of the husband.

Monogamy: (1) the marriage or cohabitation of one woman with one man, with at least a theoretical expectation of sexual fidelity on both sides; (2) an analogous relationship between persons of the same sex.

Morphology: the form and structure of organisms, or the scientific study thereof.

NOW: the National Organization for Women, founded in 1966 and now the largest and probably the most influential feminist organization in the United States.

Patriarchy: a society in which men exercise authority over women, in the family and other social and political institutions.

Patriliny: the practice of recording descent through the father's line.

Patrilocality: the practice in which married couples reside in the family or clan of the husband rather than that of the wife.

Polyandry: The marriage of one woman to more than one man.

Polygamy: the marriage of one man to more than one woman, or (sometimes) of one women to more than one man; nonmonogamous marriage.

Polygyny: the marriage of one man to more than one woman.

Pronatalist: one who advocates the maintenance of a high birth rate. Pronatalists frequently—though not always—oppose the practices of contraception and abortion.

Radical feminist: a feminist who holds that sexual equality can be achieved only through revolutionary changes in the structure of society, particularly in the institutions of marriage, motherhood, and heterosexuality.

GLOSSARY

Sex: (1) the physiological distinction between male and female; (2) one of the two categories of organism based on this distinction, e.g. the female sex; (3) the act of sexual intercourse, whether heterosexual, homosexual, or autoerotic.

Sexism: unfair or otherwise morally objectionable discrimination on the basis of sex, based either on false beliefs about the difference between the sexes (usually derogatory towards women) or on the inappropriate application to particular cases of (true or false) generalizations about the differences between women and men.

Sex object: a person who is sexually exploited, i.e. treated by others as solely a means toward their own sexual gratification, rather than as a fellow human being.

Socialist feminist: a feminist who holds that sexual equality cannot be achieved within a capitalist society, but only in one in which the means of production are collectively owned and operated for the benefit of all.

Spiritual feminism: the pursuit or development of religious insights or experiences which reflect feminist rather than male supremacist convictions.

Suffragette: a (sometimes derogatory) term for a woman suffragist, now often used without awareness of its originally pejorative connotations.

Suffragist: a supporter of women's right to vote, particularly during the decades prior to the passage of the Nineteenth Amendment; sometimes corrupted to "suffragette," a diminutive form which most feminists consider demeaning (and which excludes men, as "suffragist" does not).

Transsexual: a person whose gender identity (i.e. sense of maleness or femaleness) is incongruent with her or his sexual biology, which is typically entirely normal.

Transvestite: a person (usually male) who derives sexual pleasure from dressing in clothing designed for the opposite sex.

WEAL: the Women's Equity Action League, a feminist organization formed in 1968, which concentrates on legal and economic issues, especially in education and employment.

INDEX

An asterisk (*) after a page reference indicates the basic relevant article in one of the main sections, where there is one. This would normally be the place to find a term defined or the major discussion of an author, book or topic.

667

INDEX

INDEX

INDEX

INDEX

ACKNOWLEDGMENTS

Christine Pierce carefully read an early draft of the manuscript and made many very valuable suggestions.

Although the number of other colleagues, students and friends who have indirectly contributed to this work is too great to permit a listing, there is one person whom I must not fail to thank, namely my spouse, Michael Scriven. It was he who suggested this project, persuaded me of its feasibility, and provided the moral and material support which has enabled me to devote full attention to it during the past three years. The fact that he is also my publisher only increases my indebtedness, and my gratitude.

THE AUTHOR

Mary Anne Warren received her PhD in philosophy from the University of California, Berkeley, for a dissertation on the mind-body problem. She has taught in the philosophy departments at Sonoma State College and San Francisco State University. Her first published article, "On the Moral and Legal Status of Abortion," has been reprinted ten times, and subsequent articles are starting to follow this example. She is an accomplished painter as well as philosopher. Her next book is planned to be on personhood.

COLOPHON

Edited, designed & published at Edgepress by M. Scriven
Proofread by J. Stewart
Pasted up by R. Cooney
Typeset by J. Welch, J. Simmons, N. Lewis, S. Schrom,
     B. Wolohan and W. Meyers
Set at Edgepress on Mergenthaler Linoterms in Palatino 10/11;
     title and cover in Raleigh & Cartier
Printed and bound by Edwards Bros. at Ann Arbor, Michigan on
     50 lb. Bookwhite

NOTES & ADDENDA

These pages are for readers to add their own notes or clippings of book reviews, of this and other books. If you would like to be informed of the availability of inexpensive (i.e. half the cost of short-order photo-copying) update pamphlets, the first one probably covering new material published in 1980 and part or all of 1981 (plus omissions from this collection), please send a card with your name and address to Encyclopedia Update, Edgepress, Box 69, Pt. Reyes,California, 94956, U.S.A.

NOTES & ADDENDA

NOTES & ADDENDA

NOTES & ADDENDA